Luxembrg 25 IX 2008

To Adam
with great esteem &
admiration,

Trade in Food:
Regulatory and Judicial Approaches in
the EC and the WTO

A Gianfranco e Biancamaria senza il cui incondizionato sostegno e sconfinato amore questo libro mai avrebbe visto la luce.

Trade in Food:
Regulatory and Judicial Approaches in the EC and the WTO

Alberto Alemanno

CAMERON MAY

INTERNATIONAL LAW & POLICY

Published 2007 by Cameron May Ltd
Reprinted 2008

7 Cornwall Crescent, Notting Hill, London, W11 1PH
Tel: +44 (0)20 7792 0075 Fax: +44 (0)20 7792 1055
email: info@cameronmay.com
Website: www.cameronmay.com

ISBN 10: 1 905017 37 5

ISBN 13: 978 1 905017 37 9

Printed in the United Kingdom by The Good News Press Ltd

TABLE OF CONTENTS

8

ACKNOWLEDGMENTS

This book has grown out of my doctoral thesis defended at Bocconi University in Milan. The PhD adventure has been a fabulously errant experience. It began while I was studying and teaching in Bruges, it continued in Cambridge, Massachusetts, and was finally completed in Luxembourg, where I currently live and work.

During this peripatetic voyage of work and study I had the good fortune to meet a number of people who offered me their support and encouragement in pursuing this project. Of all these people too numerous to mention, some deserve a special word of appreciation. In the first place, I should like to express my gratitude to my mentor, Professor Giorgio Sacerdoti, from my PhD "Alma Mater". I would like to thank him not only for giving me the chance to embark on his unique Italy-based PhD programme in International Economic Law, but also for guiding me through the process of writing my thesis.

I am also greatly indebted to Professor Alfonso Mattera for stimulating my interest not only in the legal foundations of the Community internal market but also in the broader historical and political rationale underlying the European integration process.

In addition, I am most grateful to Professor Peter Barton Hutt who introduced me to the 'oldest arena of federal consumer protection legislation' in the world, i.e. the US Food & Drug Law, during my stay at Harvard Law School. His mastery of the Socratic teaching method, combined with his natural lawyer's acumen have made his classes amid the New England snow the most memorable law course I ever attended. A special thanks goes also to Justice Allan Rosas for inviting me to join his chambers at the ECJ while I was still in the process of drafting my thesis. Allan, it was indeed a privilege to be part of your team.

A word of gratitude should also not go amiss to my Harvard friends, particularly Leo Graffi and Matteo Trapani, for such a stimulating and yet friendly working environment during our time in Cambridge. You really made that time a memorable moment in my life.

A special thanks goes to Enrico Bonadio, Thibaut Partsch, Miguel Rato, Luigi Malferrari, John Morijn, Fabio Spitaleri, Felix Ronkes Agerbeek, Paolo Bertolino, Jacopo Torriti and Martin Bailey for being friends over and above mere colleagues. You have always been generous in advice, counsel, and giving credit whenever I turned to you.

I also would like to thank Luis Gonzalez Vaqué, of the European Commission, for having nurtured my growing passion for food law since my LLM paper at the College of Europe and for constantly keeping me abreast of *de iure condito* and *de iure condendo* novelties relating to our beloved precautionary principle.

I owe a great debt to Gary Dennis for his careful revision of the manuscript. Gary, your work has been invaluable: without your intervention many of the points I wanted to make in this book would not have been anything as sharp and cogent as they are now. In addition, I would like to thank our first *stagiaire* in the Moavero Milanesi Chambers, Vanessa Jégo, for working on the index to this book and for her omnipresent smile. None of the above friends and colleagues bears any responsibility for the views expressed in this book, which are entirely my own.

And of course I owe a great deal to my parents, Gianfranco and Biancamaria, to whom I dedicate this book. Without their unconditional support and love, this work would have never seen the light of day.

Finally, a very special thanks goes to my future wife, Mariana, for her boundless patience and understanding during the many weekends we spent at home instead of being somewhere else. ¡*Gracias de corazón!* Now, believe it or not, a *post librum* life is waiting for us …

I thank you all.

Alberto Alemanno

FOREWORD

This book deals with a crucial matter in the ongoing debate as to the relationship between the regulatory competence of states in the furtherance of domestic policies of general interest and concern, such as food safety, and the preservation of a liberal international trade framework.

The negotiators of the Uruguay Round have addressed these concerns through the WTO Sanitary and Phytosanitary Agreement (SPS) which covers new grounds hitherto not regulated internationally. The SPS Agreement provides for a regime where non-trade concerns and responsibilities of governments as to food products are fully legitimised, even if this results in restrictions to trade, provided that there is no discrimination and that a risk assessment is conducted so that food safety measures be science-based. A distinct feature of the SPS Agreement is that it is not limited to prescribing minimum standards; it sets instead detailed rules as to national SPS measures covered, the goals that may be legitimately pursued through them and requirements of the proceedings ('risk assessment') that must be carried out as a necessary underpinning of any restriction to trade in a given food product.

This global framework has been adopted at a time when more and more countries have enacted and are progressively enacting domestic risk regulations and are setting up specialised agencies to carry out the necessary investigations and controls. A prominent example of this evolution is offered by the European Union, the main focus of this book.

The starting point of the analysis of Alberto Alemanno is the evolution of food regulation in the EC and the establishment, role and activities of the European Food Safety Agency (EFSA) which is the cornerstone of the new food safety policy of the European Community. EFSA is a relative new institution, still not well known even by experts, and whose organisation and efficiency is subject to conflicting evaluations. In this context Alberto Alemanno points to its modest responsibilities compared with the pivotal role attributed to the Food & Drug Administration in the US.

I would like to stress here the original approach followed by Alberto Alemanno in his analysis throughout his book. In comparable investigations authors tend to follow one of two approaches. The first one is to highlight a certain national regulation within the domestic system concerned and thereafter examine its compatibility with relevant international regulation taking into account domestic implementation. The opposite approach is to highlight a given international regulation, including the limitations and requirements it imposes on member countries, in order to test thereafter whether a given national regime is in compliance with the applicable international obligations.

Alberto avoids both approaches. He considers the SPS Agreement not just as a set of prescriptions for WTO member states, but as a food safety regime of its own, against which a national system such as the European one may not only be tested in order to detect resulting limitations and possible conflicts, but to which it may be compared with a view to analysing divergence or convergence of the two regimes. This original approach is justified by the comprehensiveness of the SPS Agreement, which relies moreover on various international standards as an indirect tool for harmonising national regulations in certain respects.

Alberto Alemanno also approaches, in an innovative way, the issue of judicial review of food safety measures in the EC and in the WTO, focusing on the different intensity of the respective reviews and the problems that judges face when reviewing science-based measures. According to the author, the different standards of review which tend to be applied are due to the fact that the WTO Agreements do not deal with risk management, and to the different normative and institutional contexts. Of course, while the focus of the WTO is on minimising the negative impact of legitimate SPS measures on international trade and thus on restraining governmental policies, the EC aims at protecting the health of the consumer from potentially hazardous food product within the unified internal market.

The book thus offers an innovative contribution to the relationship between the WTO and EC regimes both as to substance in the area of ensuring food safety, while taking into account the role of science and precaution, and as to the implications of the respective judicial review mechanisms in a broad comparative perspective.

Thanks to his multifaceted legal background in international, US and European law and his daily experience at the European Court of Justice, the author has succeeded in mastering the various challenges, so as to offer a comprehensive piece of research which is at the same time informative and provocative. Indeed, by examining WTO law through the lenses of the experience of the major domestic regulatory systems, he injects into his evaluation an element of realism often lacking in those scholars who are more prone to detecting conflicts than engaged in trying to reconcile differences.

Giorgio Sacerdoti

Professor of International Law and
Jean Monnet Chair of European Law,
Bocconi University and
Chairman of the WTO Appellate Body.

Glossary

AB	Appellate Body
ACF	EFSA Panel on Food Additives, Flavourings, Processing Aids and Materials in Contact with Food
ADI	Acceptable Daily Intake
AFFSA	French Food Safety Authority (Agence française de sécurité sanitaire des aliments)
AGRC	EFSA's Advisory Group on Risk Communications
AHAW	EFSA Panel on Animal Health and Welfare
BIOHAZ	EFSA Panel on Biological Hazards
BIPs	Border Inspection Posts
BSE	Bovine Spongiform Encephalopathy
BST	Bovine Somatropin
CAC	Codex Alimentarius Commission
CAP	Common Agricultural Policy
CBD	Convention on Biological Diversity
CCGP	Codex Committee of General Principles
CDC	Centers for Disease and Control
CFI	European Court of First Instance
CONTAM	EFSA Panel on Contaminants in the Food Chain
CPMB	EMEA Committee for Proprietary Medicinal Products
CU	Custom Unions
DG	Directorate General
DG SANCO	Directorate General on Consumer Policy and Consumer Health Protection
DSB	Dispute Settlement Body
DSU	Dispute Settlement Understanding (Understanding on Rules and Procedures Governing the Settlement of Disputes)
EC	European Community
ECB	European Central Bank
ECJ	European Court of Justice
EEA	European Economic Area
EEA	European Environmental Agency
EFA	European Food Authority
EFPHA	European Food and Public Health Authority
EFSA	European Food Safety Authority
EFTA	European Free Trade Association
EMEA	Agency for the Evaluation of Medicinal Products
EP	European Parliament

FAO	Food and Agriculture Organization
FDA	Food and Drug Administration
FEEDAP	EFSA Panel on Additives and Products or Substances used in Animal Feed
FTA	Free Trade Agreement
FVO	Food and Veterinary Office
GATT	General Agreement on Tariffs and Trade
GI	Geographical Indication
GMO	EFSA Panel in Genetically Modified Organisms
GMOs	Genetically Modified Organisms
IGTF	Codex Ad-Hoc Intergovernmental Task Force on Food Derived from Biotechnology
IPPC	International Plant Protection Convention
ISO	International Standards Organization
JECFA	Joint FAO/WHO Expert Committee on Food Additives
JMPR	Joint FAO/WHO Meeting on Pesticides Residues
JRC	Joint Research Centre
LMOs	Living Modified Organisms
LTR	Least Trade-Restrictive
MBM	Meat and Bone meal
MEE	Measure Having Equivalent Effect
MRAs	Mutual Recognition Agreements
MRLs	Maximum Residues Levels
NAFTA	North American Free Trade Agreement
NDA	EFSA Panel on Dietetic Products, Nutrition and Allergies
NGOs	Non-Governmental Organisations
NRC	National Research Council
NTBs	Non-Tariff Barriers
OIE	International Office of Epizootics (World Organisation for Animal Health)
OMB	US Office of Management and Budget
PLH	EFSA Panel on Plant Health
PP	Precautionary Principle
PPR	EFSA Panel on Plant Health, Plant Protection Products and their Residues
PRAPeR	EFSA Pesticide Risk Assessment Peer Review Unit
QRs	Quantitative Restrictions
RA	Risk Assessment
RASFF	Rapid Alert System for Food and Feed
RBST	Recombinant Bovine Somatotropin
RM	Risk Management
SCAN	Scientific Committee for Animal Nutrition
SEAC	UK Spongiform Encephalopathy Advisory Committee

SPS	Sanitary and Phytosanitary Agreement
SRMs	Specified Risk Materials
SSC	Scientific Steering Committee
STOA	Scientific and Technical Options Assessment
SVC	Scientific Veterinary Committee
SVC	Standing Veterinary Committee
TBT	Technical Barriers to Trade
TRIPS	Trade-Related Aspects of Intellectual Property Rights
TSEs	Transmissible Spongiform Encephalopaties
UK	United Kingdom
UK SEAC	United Kingdom Spongiform Encephalopathy Advisory Committee
UN	United Nations
UNCITRAL	United Nations Commission on International Trade Law
UNCTAD	United Nations Conference on Trade And Development
UNEP	United Nations Environment Programme
USA	United States of America
WHO	World Health Organization
WTO	World Trade Organization

INTRODUCTION

The last decade has witnessed a rise in genuine concern for the quality and safety of the food we eat. While food safety has always been the focus of regulatory attention,[1] the recent food crises that have outraged Europe have shown that the regulation of the food sector by the economic instruments of the internal market may well be inadequate to address the new challenges brought about by the emerging perception of risks. As a result, the recently reformed European regulation of food aims at assuring:

> a high level of protection of human health and consumers' interests in relation to food, by taking into account in particular the diversity of supply of food including traditional products, whilst ensuring the effective functioning of the internal market.[2]

The objective of this book is to explore the evolution of the European regulation of food – from the adoption of the very first directives in the matter to the establishment of the European Food Safety Authority – within the broader framework set by the WTO Agreements. After analysing in detail the interpretation and application of the main provisions relating to food existing in the two systems, this study offers a comparison between these two emerging food safety regimes. It does so by looking not only at their substantive disciplines and regulatory philosophies but also at how these disciplines have been judicially reviewed by their respective courts. This comparison has come to be all the more decisive as the regulation of food safety has rapidly become a source of growing tension in the international trade arena.

In this introductory chapter, which defines the scope and the structure of the research (C), a justification for such an attempted comparison will be provided, together with its underlying methodology (B). But first, one may legitimately wonder why the regulation of food was chosen as the main subject for writing a book on international economic law. Several reasons may be given to justify this choice (A).

---

[1] For an overview of early food regulations, see, eg, P. Barton Hutt and R.A. Merril, *Food & Drug Law*, Cases and Materials, 2nd ed, New York, Foundation Press, 1991.

[2] Article 2 of Regulation (EC) No 178/2002 of 28 January 2002 laying down the general principles and requirements of food law, establishing the European Food Safety Authority and laying down procedures in matters of food safety, in OJ 2002 L31 (hereinafter: the 'general food law regulation' or, merely, the 'Regulation'). Also available at http://europa. eu.int/comm/food/fs/efa.

A.   Why Food Law?

First, this dynamic and emotive area of law provides not only an excellent vehicle for understanding the evolution of the European integration process, by illustrating the progressive abandonment of the original functionalist approach to integration, but also represents a mini-history of European law. As all EC law students are aware, an entire course of European law may successfully be taught by focusing exclusively on the European Court of Justice's case law developed on foods, such as pasta, feta cheese or chocolate, and drinks, such as beer, wine, liquors or energy drinks. However, no food better explains the evolution of EC food law than British beef. In short, looking into food policy enables us to trace how, why and by whom European policies have developed.

Secondly, over the last decade the food safety crises that have outraged Europe have presented the EC institutions with the challenge of developing an appropriate risk regulation model. For its effectiveness and speed, this process may be seen as a model for the conception and the development of new EC policies. In less than five years, the Community managed to develop not only an institutional reform of its food policy, symbolised by the establishment of the European Food Safety Authority (hereinafter 'EFSA'), but also to combine this innovation with a profound regulatory reform paving the way for the launch of the first EC model for risk analysis, which is addressed not solely to the EC institutions but also to its Member States. In the light of the above, food law, now an autonomous branch of EC law besides competition law and environmental law, provides a privileged perspective from which to examine the development of an emerging European risk analysis framework.

Thirdly, the production and consumption of food play a crucial role in any society. On any given day every European citizen requires food, and more than 10 million of those work in the agro-food sector[3]. The food and drink industry is a leading industrial sector in the European Union with an annual production worth almost • 800 billion[4]. This amounts to almost 15 per cent of total manufacturing output in the EU. The agricultural sector alone has an annual production of more than • 220 billion.

---

[3] While it is estimated that more than 4 million workers are employed by the Food and drink industry, around 7 million work in the agricultural sector. See Confederation of the Food and Drink Industries (CIAA) of the EU Key Figures, 15 November 2005 available at http://www.ciaa.be/pages_en/news_events/news_list.asp?news _id=168 and A. Barthelemy, *Changes in agricultural employment*, available at http://europa.eu.int/ comm/ agriculture/envir/report/en/emplo_en/ report_ en.htm, respectively.

[4] See the Confederation of the Food and Drink Industries of the EU Key Figures, 15 November 2005, available at http://www.ciaa.be/ pages_en/news_events/ news_list.asp?news_id=168.

Fourthly, this area of EC law, being subject to the WTO rules, offers the opportunity to analyse the WTO framework for food safety (as provided for by the Sanitary and Phytosanitary Agreement (SPS)) and, accordingly, to single out the main points of tension between the reformed EC food safety regime and the WTO obligations. The Uruguay Round sketched out a set of legal obligations constraining Member States' ability to regulate the food sector and paved the way for the development of a risk analysis model mandating the use of risk management science-based measures. This discipline has to be enforced through a strengthened dispute settlement mechanism to prevent countries from misusing their regulatory measures. During the first 10 years of the lifetime of the WTO, more than 30 disputes have arisen over food measures and, although most of them have not led to the adoption of a report, around 20 of them found their origin in complaints brought against the EC.[5] This share shows how an understanding of the WTO represents an inescapable dimension in order to have a full command of the EC food regime.

Fifthly, the prescribed science-based character of food safety measures in both the EC and WTO legal systems raises one of the most difficult and unexplored aspects of the controversial relationship between law and science: the judicial review of regulations based on scientific evidence. How can a judge, by definition a non-scientist, conduct an assessment of whether a measure is scientifically supported? What is the level of intensity of the scrutiny that this judge can exert over the risk regulation being reviewed? These questions are currently sources of endless controversy in the international legal arena[6] and are at the centre of some international trade disputes.[7]

---

[5] For an overview of the relative importance of food safety in complaints brought against the EC, see A.R. Young and P. Holmes, 'Protection or Protectionism? EU Food Safety Rules and the WTO', in D. Vogel and C. Ansell (eds.), *What's the Beef? The Contested Governance of European Food Safety*, MIT Press, (2006), pp 283–285 and T. Jostling, D. Roberts and D. Orden, *Food Regulation and Trade, Toward a Safe and Open Global System*, Institute for International Economics, Washington, D.C., 2004, pp 63–68.

[6] See C.D. Ehlermann, 'Six Years on the Bench of the "World Trade Court": Some Personal Experiences as Member of the Appellate Body of the World Trade Organization', in 36 *J. World Trade* (2002) 605, pp 612–13, who, when leaving the organ, has noted that 'during the last months, the question of standard of review has thus become one of the most controversial aspects of the Appellate Body's jurisprudence'.

[7] In May, 2003, the US, Canada, and Argentina filed a complaint at the World Trade Organization (WTO), alleging that European restrictions (notably, the EC general moratoria, the product specific moratoria and the national bans) on the importation of genetically modified organisms (GMOs) violate WTO rules, notably several SPS provisions. These violations can be divided into two groups: violations of procedural requirements (Article 8 and Annex B, Article 7 and Annex C) and violations of substantive obligations (Article 5.1 and Article 2.2). These alleged violations would entail a disguised restriction on international trade in accordance with Article 5.5 and Article 2.3 of the SPS Agreement. See Request for Consultations by Argentina, *European Communities — Measures Affecting the Approval and Marketing of Biotech Products*, WT/DS293/1, 2003 WL 21191302 (WTO May 21, 2003); Request for Consultations by Canada, *European Communities —*

(continued...)

Last, but not least, it is believed that, in what must be viewed as a delicate moment in the European project, with integration put somewhat on the back burner, the new European food safety regime and the establishment of the EFSA may, by effectively responding to citizens' concerns, contribute to the EU regaining popular legitimacy and thereby proving itself to be a system capable of reconciling scientific expertise, traditions and free movement.

B.   Why a Comparison between the EC and the WTO?

Rather than focusing on each specific piece of legislation relating to food, this study takes a comparative outlook, by making an attempt to identify the main points of tension existing between the EC food regime and WTO law. The decision to take such a comparative perspective reflects the conviction according to which 'one can no longer disregard the doctrinal developments of the WTO even if one's primary interest rests in the doctrinal market of the EU'[8]. This statement best illustrates Weiler's vision of the emergence of a nascent Common Law of International Trade. Without going so far as unconditionally to embrace this vision, which still sounds more a prediction than a tangible truth, this study relies on this emerging comparative method by applying it to the food sector.[9]

Measures Affecting the Approval and Marketing of Biotech Products, WT/DS292/1, 2003 WL 21180725 (WTO May 21, 2003); Request for Consultations by the United States, *European Communities—Measures Affecting the Approval and Marketing of Biotech Products*, WT/DS291/ 1, 2003 WL 21180726 (WTO May 20, 2003) [hereinafter *Biotech case*]. For a complete background report on this pending case, see *U.S. v EC Biotech Products Case – WTO Dispute Backgrounder*, The Institute for Agriculture and Trade Policy, September 2005. The panel's confidential final report has been circulated to parties in Spring 2006 and the final report has been circulated to all WTO Members on September 29, 2006. See *EC–Measures Affecting the Approval and Marketing of Biotech Products*, Panel Report, available at http:// www.wto.org/english/news_e/news06_e/ 291r_e.htm [hereinafter "EC–Biotech Report"].
[8] J.H.H. Weiler, 'Cain and Abel – Convergence and Divergence in International Trade Law', J.H.H. Weiler (ed.), *The EU, the WTO, and the NAFTA, Towards a Common Law of International Trade?*, Oxford University Press, 2000.
[9] There already exist a growing number of comparative studies which follow this innovative EC/WTO perspective. While some of them relate to the different liberalisation tools and 'constitutional dimension' of the two legal systems, others focus on some specific common substantive areas, such as environmental protection, public health, trade in services, state aids and taxation. Among the former studies, besides the above-mentioned Weiler's leading book, see also eg J. Scott, *GATT and Community Law: Rethinking the 'Regulatory Gap'*, Shaw and More (eds.), *New Legal Dynamics of EU*, 1995; N. Emiliou and D. O'Keefe (eds), *The European Union and World Trade Law: After the Uruguay Round*, London, John Wiley and Sons, 1996; G. De Burca and J. Scott (eds), *The EU and the WTO: Legal and Constitutional Aspects*, Oxford, Hart Publishing, 2003; and the more recent F. Ortino, *Basic Legal Instruments for the Liberalization of Trade* Oxford and Portland Oregon, 2004 and M. Slotboom, *A Comparison of WTO and EC Law*, London, Cameron May Ltd, 2006. In particular regard to the environmental field, see, eg, N. Notaro, *Judicial Approaches to Trade and the Environment: The EC and the WTO, alias the Comparative Disadvantage of Dolphins and Turtles*, London, Cameron May International Law Publishers, 2003; J. Wiers, *Trade and the*
(continued...)

During recent years, we have witnessed not only a 'juridification' of the GATT/WTO legal framework,[10] but we have also experienced a certain degree of convergence in the substantive law areas between EC and WTO legal systems. Thus, apart from the introduction of a compulsory and automatic decision-making process settlement disputes system,[11] based on a two-tier mechanism of panels of first instance and a permanent Appellate Body (AB), the WTO Agreements represent a departure from the traditional GATT-type framework, by moving beyond matters dealing with market access to deal with issues of national regulation. In particular, notwithstanding its less evolved normative framework, it will be shown that the WTO is going beyond its main organisational principle, ie non-discrimination,[12] by developing some

---

Environment in the EC and in the WTO: A Legal Analysis, Groningen, Europa Law Publishing, 2002; E. Neumayer, 'Greening the WTO Agreements – Can the Treaty Establishing the European Community be of Guidance?', 35 *Journal of World Trade* 145 (2001); J. Scott, 'Of Kith and Kine (and Crustaceans): Trade and Environment in the EU and WTO' in Weiler (ed.), *The EU, NAFTA and the WTO: Towards a Common Law of International Trade*, Oxford: OUP, 2000 and D. Esty and D. Geradin, 'Market Access, Competitiviness, and Harmonization: Environmental Protection in Regional Trade Agreements', 21 *Harvard Environmental Law Review* p 265 (1997). In the public health field, see N. Mc Nelis, 'The Role of the Judge in the EC and the WTO: Lessons from the BSE and Hormones Cases', 4 *Journal of International Economic Law* 1 (2001); M.M. Slotboom, 'Do Public Health Measures Receive Similar Treatment in European Community and World Trade Organization Law?', in *Journal of World Trade* 553 (2003) and C. Button, *The Power to protect*, Oxford and Portland, Oregon, 2004. With regard to the liberalisation of services, see, eg, L. Radicati di Bronzolo, *Un primo confronto tra la liberalizzazione delle telecomunicazioni nel sistema del WTO e della Comunità europea*, SIDI (Società Italiana di Diritto Internazionale), *Diritto ed organizzazione del commercio internazionale dopo la creazione della Organizzazione Mondiale del Commercio*, Milano, Editoriale Scientifica, 1998 and P. Eeckhout, *Constitutional Concepts for Free Trade in Services*, G. De Burca and J. Scott (eds.), *The EU and the WTO: Legal and Constitutional Aspects*, Oxford, Hart Publishing, 2001. In the area of state aids, see A. Biondi, P. Eeckhout and J. Flynn (eds), *The Law of State Aid in the European Union*, Oxford University Press, 2004. And, finally, with regard to the taxation field, see, for instance, P.J. Kuyper, 'Booze and Fast Cars: Tax Discrimination Under GATT and the EC', 23 *Legal Issues of European Integration* 129 (1996).

[10] See, eg, C. Joerges and J. Neyer, 'Politics, Risk Management, World Trade Organization Governance and the Limits of Legalisation', in *Science and Public Policy*, June 2003, pp 221 ss, who argue that both polities are based on the idea according to which intergovernmental bargaining should follow legal principles and that non-partisan bodies, such as the ECJ and the WTO Dispute Settlement Body, should adjudicate if the disputing parties are unable to compromise in accordance with those legal principles.

[11] The adoption of panel reports by the DSB can no longer be blocked by the losing party as was the case under the GATT system. A refusal of the report is possible only within 30 days of circulation by consensus (thus also including the highly improbable vote of the winning party). See, Articles 16.4 and 17.14 DSU.

[12] It must be observed that, although is it true that the concept of non-discrimination, in particular, that of de facto discrimination, is very broad, stretching this concept to include even the 'sound science' principle of the SPS Agreement or other positive requirements, such as those contained in the TRIPs Agreement, "runs the great risk of depriving the term discrimination of a meaningful content". See J. Bohanes, 'Risk Regulation in WTO Law: A procedure-Based Approach', 40 *Columbia Journal of Transnational Law*, pp 323 ss (2002).

tools of positive integration whose ambitions are similar to those pursued by the EC harmonisation instruments. In that sense, the food sector represents a particularly appropriate area to show the shift of the GATT/WTO from a regime designed to eliminate discrimination to a system aimed at eliminating obstacles to trade. This shift having prompted great criticism for encroaching upon national sovereignty, also the 'trade and domestic policy' debate will be examined. Moreover, the EC being a full Member of the WTO, and being thereby bound by its agreements, it may be useful to analyse the WTO food safety regime (part II) in order to determine to what extent the current EC discipline, as established by the general food law regulation, may be held to be compatible with the WTO regime (part IV). In particular, this study will highlight some points of tension currently existing between the two legal orders.

Finally, there is little choice but to take a comparative path in a regulatory area where tensions exist not only between the national and the supranational levels of governance, but also between the newly-established internal regulatory framework and the emerging multilateral discipline of the WTO.

C.   Structure of the Research

Before commencing the analysis of the EC and WTO regulation of food, it is necessary to sketch out a tentative scheme for our comparative analysis of the two systems. The focus will mainly be on their respective regulatory frameworks, risk analysis schemes and the standards of judicial review employed by the respective courts, in that order. Special attention will be given throughout this book to the role played by science within both food regimes.

This work is divided into four parts.

Part I is entirely devoted to an analysis of the evolution of European food safety regulation, from the adoption of the first directives in the matter to the establishment of the European Food Safety Authority.

Chapter I provides an account of the historical shift that has occurred in European food policy in the wake of the food scandals. It identifies four different eras in the evolution of EC food policy: the 'Genesis', starting from 1962 through to the mid-1980s; the 'New Approach', which developed between the Single European Act of 1986 and the BSE's crisis of 1997 (BSE stands for Bovine Spongiform Encephalopathy and has been commonly referred to as 'Mad Cow Disease'); the 'Emergency', lasting from 1997 to 2001; and, finally, the current phase: the 'Global approach' to food safety.

Chapter II focuses on the emerging regulatory regime stemming from Regulation 178/2002 laying down the general principles of EC Food law and establishing the EFSA (hereinafter the 'general food law regulation' or, merely, the 'Regulation').

Chapter III is entirely dedicated to the EFSA. After providing a detailed description of its origins and institutional structure, the analysis will shift to the EFSA's substantive powers, stressing, when necessary, the main differences between the US Food and Drug Administration (FDA) and its European counterpart. This chapter, by taking a rather critical stance on the EFSA's organisational independence, looks at the composition of its organs and brings to light the 'grey areas' existing in its relationship with the EC Commission. Finally, it offers some elements of comparison between EFSA and its US counterpart.

Part II deals with the broader context of the multilateral regulation of food provided by the WTO/SPS Agreements. Before introducing the reader to the main obligations imposed by the SPS Agreement, an attempt is made to illustrate the different logics governing the EC and WTO regimes for food safety.

While Chapter I provides for an historical background to the GATT/WTO provisions dealing with food safety, the following chapter illustrates the main obligations stemming from the EC full membership of the WTO, by analysing their scope as defined by the relevant WTO courts' case law.

Whereas the previous two parts provide an in-depth analysis of the food safety regulatory disciplines existing within the EC and the WTO, Part III completes that analysis by examining how these disciplines have been judicially reviewed by their respective courts.

Chapter I sums up the main food safety obligations imposed by both regimes on their respective Member States, by focusing in particular on the scientific justification requirement. Chapter II, after having introduced the reader to the issue of judicial review of food safety measures, examines the standards of review developed by the EC and the WTO courts when called upon to scrutinise the legality of food safety regulations. Having analysed the WTO expert consultation practice, it lastly formulates some proposals aimed at reorienting the role of the WTO and EC judicial bodies in order to make them less involved with science when conducting reviews of science-based measures.

Finally, Part IV, by building upon the previous parts, ventures a comparison between the EC and WTO food safety regimes in order to show the main points of tension existing between them.

In particular, Chapter I contains a comparison between the EC and WTO food disciplines, by looking at their respective goals and at their instruments. Chapter II furthers this examination by, in particular, comparing their food safety risk analysis models, thereby identifying the main points of tension existing between the two regimes, namely, the role of 'other legitimate factors' in risk analysis and the status of the 'precautionary principle'. Due to the lack of risk management policy within the WTO/SPS risk analysis model, the analysis expands, when appropriate, on the Codex principles for risk analysis. Chapter III then offers a comparison of the standards of review applied by the EC courts[13] and the WTO judicial bodies,[14] by focusing notably on the respective levels of scientific involvement required from them. It finally proposes the development of a procedural, intensity-variable standard of review of science-based measures within the WTO as a viable solution for recovering the balance originally contained in the SPS Agreement between members' regulatory autonomy and free trade. It will be shown that, varying its intensity depending on the rights and obligations of the Member States within each step of risk analysis, the proposed standard of review would tend to focus more on the risk response component of the contested measure than on its risk assessment and risk choice elements, thus accommodating the legitimate democratic preferences of a given society.

---

[13] For the purpose of this work, the term 'EC courts' means the European Court of Justice (ECJ) and the Court of First Instance (CFI), both based in Luxembourg.

[14] For the purpose of this work, the term "WTO judicial bodies" refers to both the WTO ad hoc panels and the permanent WTO Appellate Body, both based in Geneva at the WTO Secretariat.

PART I: THE EUROPEAN FOOD REGULATION

CHAPTER I

THE EVOLUTION OF EUROPEAN FOOD LAW:
ITS FOUR MAJOR ERAS OF DEVELOPMENT

For the purpose of this chapter, four main periods in the evolution of EC food policy are identified. The first phase is the 'Genesis', stretching from 1962 to the mid-1980s. During this foundational period, the Community, animated by the goal of establishing an internal market for foodstuffs, pursued a detailed harmonisation programme consisting in the adoption of directives setting up compositional standards for individual foods. The second period, the 'new approach', was developed between the Single European Act of 1986 and the BSE crisis of 1997. This phase is characterised by the introduction of an innovative approach to harmonisation based on the mutual recognition principle, combined with the use of the minimum harmonisation method. The BSE and other food emergencies triggered the development of a third phase: the 'Europeanisation of food risk', lasting from 1997 to 2001. During these years the Commission transformed the policy efforts expressed in its communications into a concrete legislative proposal laying down a new food safety regime for Europe in order to avoid the balkanisation of the internal market. The entry into force of Regulation 178/2002 and the establishment of the European Food Safety Authority symbolise the current phase: the 'global approach' to food safety.

1.   The 'Genesis': the Free Movement of Foodstuffs and the European 'Standards of Identity' (1962–1985)

Food safety regulations adopted on a sectoral basis have played a major role in European legislation since the early days of the Community. As the Treaty of Rome[1] did not contain any express legal basis for the establishment of a common food policy, the original EC food legislation has come into being as a result of both the application of the common market prohibitions and the gradual harmonisation of national rules which was necessary in order to guarantee the free movement of goods and prevent distortions of competition in the establishment of the single market.[2] The application of EC law to foodstuffs has been made possible

---

[1] Treaty establishing the European Community (hereinafter 'EC'), consolidated version published in the OJ (C-325) 24 Dec. 2002, available at http://europa.eu.int/eur-lex/en/treaties/dat/EC_consol.pdf.
[2] On the gradual widening of Community policies to non-economic sectors, see J.H.H. Weiler, 'The Transformation of Europe', 100 *Yale Law Journal*, 2403. For a reconstruction
(continued...)

by the early case law recognising them as falling within the meaning of 'goods', as enshrined in Article 23 EC. Moreover, foodstuffs may also qualify as agricultural products when they are enumerated within Annex I to the EC Treaty, regardless of whether they fall within the scope of the definition given by Article 32 EC. In any event, agricultural products also being 'goods' within the EC meaning, all foodstuffs are subject to the free movement principle stemming from the Treaty prohibitions and harmonisation rules.

Furthermore, the Founding Fathers having affirmed in the preamble of the Treaty of Rome that the 'essential objective of their efforts' was 'the constant improvements of the living and working conditions of their peoples',[3] the Community was able to develop, although gradually and by relying on a variety of different legal bases provided in the Treaty, a European policy in the food sector.

1.1 The Internal Market and the Free Movement Rules

The creation of a common market lies at the heart of the EC as the privileged instrument upon which the Community relies in order to achieve its final objectives of 'peace and prosperity', as enshrined within Article 2 EC. Article 2 says that the Community has as its task the establishment of a common market, and one of the activities of the Community listed in Article 3 is the creation of an:

> internal market characterised by the abolition, as between Member States, of obstacles to the free movement of goods, persons, services and capital.

The free movement of goods is therefore only one of the EC's main instruments for achieving the creation of the internal market[4] as:

> an area without internal frontiers in which the free movement of goods, persons, services and capital is ensured.[5]

---

of the birth and evolution of EC food policy, see P. Deboyser, *Le Droit Communautaire Relative aux Denrées Alimentaires*, Story-Scientia, Louvain-La-Neuve, 1989 and L. Azoulay, 'La Sécurité Alimentaire dans la Législation Communautaire', in J. Bourrinet and F. Snyder, *La Sécurité Alimentaire dans l'Union Européenne*, Bruxelles, Bruylant, 2003, p 32.
[3] See preamble of the EC Treaty.
[4] On the importance of the common market in goods in European constitutionalism, see J.H.H. Weiler, 'The Constitution of the Common Market Place: Text and Context in the Evolution of Free Movement of Goods', in P. Craig and G. De Burca (eds.), *The Evolution of EU Law*, OUP Oxford 1999, p 349; M. Poiares Maduro, *We the Court*, Hart Publishing, Portland, 1999.
[5] Article 14.2 EC.

While free trade agreements (FTA) and custom unions (CU) focus solely on the free movement of products, a common market allows for the free movement of production factors (workers and capital) as well as goods.[6] In order to achieve the objective of the creation of the internal market and to ensure the free movement of production factors, two sets of rules are provided within the Treaty: 'negative integration' and 'positive integration' provisions.[7] While the former consists of a set of prohibitions aimed at eliminating a number of impediments to the proper operation of an integrated area, such as the internal market, the latter consists of measures allowing for the creation of new policies (see Diagram 1).

Diagram 1: The structure and the main provisions of the internal market according to Tinbergen's dichotomial view of integration

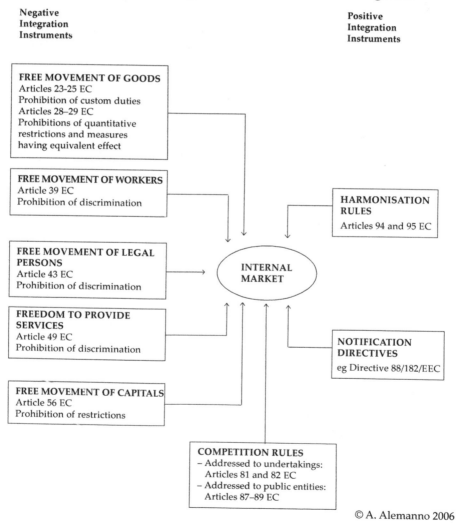

Negative
Integration
Instruments

Positive
Integration
Instruments

FREE MOVEMENT OF GOODS
Articles 23-25 EC
Prohibition of custom duties
Articles 28–29 EC
Prohibitions of quantitative
restrictions and measures
having equivalent effect

FREE MOVEMENT OF WORKERS
Article 39 EC
Prohibition of discrimination

HARMONISATION
RULES
Articles 94 and 95 EC

FREE MOVEMENT OF LEGAL
PERSONS
Article 43 EC
Prohibition of discrimination

INTERNAL
MARKET

FREEDOM TO PROVIDE
SERVICES
Article 49 EC
Prohibition of discrimination

NOTIFICATION
DIRECTIVES
eg Directive 88/182/EEC

FREE MOVEMENT OF CAPITALS
Article 56 EC
Prohibition of restrictions

COMPETITION RULES
– Addressed to undertakings:
 Articles 81 and 82 EC
– Addressed to public entities:
 Articles 87–89 EC

© A. Alemanno 2006

Foodstuffs, being goods within the meaning of the EC treaty , are subject to both the 'negative integration' provisions of Articles 28–29 prohibiting quantitative restrictions on imports and exports or measures having an equivalent effect, and to the 'positive integration' Articles 94–95 of the EC, which allow the EC institutions:

> to adopt the measures for the approximations of the provisions laid down by law, regulation or administrative action in Member States which have as their object the establishment and functioning of the internal market.

A.   Negative Integration Rules: the Scope and Application of Article 28 EC

Article 28 enjoins Member States from imposing quantitative restrictions (QRs) on imports or measures having an equivalent effect (MEE).[8] According to this general principle of Community law,[9] Member States are prohibited from hindering the entry of goods from other Member States into their territories, unless their measures can be saved by one of the grounds of derogation listed in Article 30.

Similarly, Articles 39, 43, 49 and 56 limit Member States' ability to adopt measures capable of restricting intra-Community trade in order to allow for the free movement not only of goods, but also of natural and legal persons, services and capital. As the court put it in *Gaston Schul*, the aim of the negative integration provisions is to eliminate:

> 'all obstacles to intra-community trade in order to merge the national markets into a single market bringing about conditions as close as possible to those of a genuine internal market'.[10]

While quantitative restrictions have been easily defined by the ECJ as those 'rules restricting the importation (or exportation) of one or more

---

[6] According to the levels of intensity of market integration, there exist different forms of integration: a FTA is characterised by a common internal policy (free movement of goods between participating States) but different external policies (each State retains competence to regulate trade with third countries); a CU is similar to an FTA internally, but differs from an FTA externally because its States have a common commercial policy vis-à-vis non-Members). Both forms have been originally recognized by Article XXIV GATT as an exception to the MFN principle and therefore subject to several conditions of validity.

[7] The distinction between negative and positive integration was originally formulated by J. Tinbergen, *International Economic Integration*, Amsterdam, 1954.

[8] Similarly, Article 29 EC requires that any restrictions on exports and measures having an equivalent effect should be abolished.

[9] Case 240/83 *Association de Défense des Brûleurs d'huiles Usagées* (ADBHU) [1985] ECR 531, para 584. All EC courts' judgments are available at http://www.curia.eu.int.

[10] Case 15/81 *Gaston Schul Douane Expediteur BV v Inspecteur der Invoerrechten en Accijnzen, Roosendaal* [1982] ECR 1409, para 33.

products according to quantitative norms',[11] the interpretation of 'measures having an equivalent effect' has proved more difficult. Accordingly, given the necessity to give interpretation to Article 28 EC, a vast body of ECJ case law has developed on this concept.

Before examining this case law, the following paragraph provides a short introduction to Article 30, which allows Member States, under specific severely restricted conditions, to make exceptions to the prohibition of quantitative restrictions.

1. The Exceptions: Article 30 EC

The prohibition established in Article 28 EC is subject to the exceptions laid down in Article 30, which enumerates the grounds which may justify trade barriers:

- public morality;
- public policy or public security:
- *the protection of health and life of humans*, animals or plants;
- the protection of national treasures possessing artistic, historic or archaeological value or the protection of industrial and commercial property.

Thus, Member States, by virtue of this provision, are allowed to maintain national measures aimed at protecting inter alia the health and life of humans.

The generous wording of this article clearly shows that large sectors of non-economic regulation, such as public health and food policy, are still regarded as matters which remain in the hands of the Member States. Thus, domestic trade-restrictive measures which by themselves infringe Article 28 EC may nevertheless be lawful if they are justified on grounds of public health. However, the second sentence of Article 30 EC, similar to the *chapeau* of Article XX GATT,[12] adds that those restrictive measures:

> shall not, however, constitute a means of arbitrary discrimination or a disguised restriction on trade between Member States.

---

[11] Case 2/73 *Geddo* [1973] ECR 865.

[12] Although these provisions may appear prima facie similar, by laying down an exception inspired by non-economic goals, it is worth noting from the outset that: a) in Article 30, contrary to Article XX, there is no reference to the notion of 'unjustifiable discrimination'; b) the list of Article XX GATT covers larger sets of non-economic interests; c) Article XX requires that trade restrictive measures be either 'necessary, essential or related' to one of the justifications rather that merely 'justified on grounds of ' (however, this textual difference has been overcome by the introduction of the proportionality principle). See infra Part II, Chapter I, Section 1, SPS Measures under the GATT.

The interpretation of this requirement has given rise to the 'proportionality principle', according to which a national regulation grounded on public health will only be considered lawful under Article 30 EC if it is restricted to what is actually necessary to secure this protective goal. Thus, this principle limits the availability of the public policy exceptions by imposing on a Member State that has a choice between various measures to attain the same objective to choose the measure that least restricts the free movement of goods.

2. The Case Law Developed on Article 28 EC

2.1 Dassonville

In the 1974 *Dassonville* judgment[13], the ECJ gave a broad definition of the notion of 'measure having an equivalent effect to a quantitative restriction' concept by holding that:

> all trading rules enacted by Member States which are capable of hindering, directly or indirectly, actually or potentially, intra-Community trade are to be considered as measures having an equivalent effect to quantitative restrictions.

This case concerned parallel imports of Scotch whisky into Belgium. Belgian legislation required all whisky sold within its territory to be accompanied by a certificate of origin. Mr Dassonville, who bought Scotch whisky in France for reimportation into Belgium, was accused of fraud as he could not obtain the British certificates of origin in France. The Belgian court, having been asked to find him guilty of fraud, submitted a question to the ECJ. The Belgian measure was found to fall within the scope of Article 28 and was thus prohibited. In particular, the court stated that this provision could not be applied to Scotch whisky which had been lawfully imported and put into free circulation in France and re-exported to Belgium, because it was much more difficult to obtain the certificate of origin for whisky imported into Belgium by way of a third country than for direct imports from Scotland. The ECJ ruled that the Belgian legislation was in fact a hindrance to trade and amounted in particular to a measure having an equivalent effect to a quantitative restriction.

The wide interpretation given by the court in this landmark case amounts to saying that even rules which are not designed to restrict cross-border transactions may hinder the free movement of goods. Any sovereign measure, even only likely 'indirectly or potentially',[14] to negatively affect

---

[13] Case 8/74 *Dassonville* [1974] ECR 837.

[14] Thus, the ECJ, by relying on the Dassonville formula, has held that a French rule on the composition of *foie gras* breached Article 28 EC although very little *foie gras* was produced

(continued...)

the flow of goods between States is, in principle, a prohibited measure under Article 28 EC.

As such, these measures come under the court's scrutiny, thus restraining Member States' regulatory capacity.[15] The consequence of this ruling was that overnight, thousands of national laws and regulations relating to imported products fell within the scope of the provisions contained in Articles 28–30 EC.

This basic rule has been repeated by the court in a large number of later judgments, and continues to be the ritual starting point for the court's analysis of national measures under Article 28.[16]

2.2   *Cassis de Dijon* and the Principle of Mutual Recognition

After having developed such a 'broad, catch-all criterion', the court faced a dilemma if it did not want to subject the Member States' power to regulate to the complete control of Article 28 EC. Either it could have restricted the notion of measure having an equivalent effect or it could have extended the list of justifications contained in Article 30 EC.

With the well-known judgment in the 'Cassis de Dijon' case of 1979,[17] the court did both, thereby laying the foundations for a new approach to harmonisation policy in the area of free movement of goods.[18]

This case involved a German law which prohibited the marketing of liqueurs with alcohol strength of less than 25 per cent. Rewe-Central AG sought an authorisation from the German authorities to import the Cassis de Dijon liqueur from France.[19] As Cassis contains only 15-20 per cent by volume of alcohol, the authorities informed the importer that the liqueur could not be sold in Germany. Although there were some exceptions to the German minimum alcohol content regulations, the company was told that Cassis was not one of them.

---

in other Member States (the national measure was found to be 'capable of hindering, at least potentially, inter-State trade'). Case 184/96 *Commission v France (foie gras)* [1998] ECR-I-6197, para. 17. See, for a review of this judgment, A. Mattera, 'L'arrêt "foie gras" du 22 octobre 1998 : Porteur d'une Nouvelle Impulsion pour le Perfectionnement du Marché Unique Européen', in *Revue du Marché Unique Européen*, fasc. 4, 1998, p 113.

[15] Case 178/84, *Commission v Germany* [1987] ECR 1227.

[16] Among the last judgments, see, eg, Case 20/03, *Burmanjer*, [2005] not yet reported.

[17] Case 120/78, *Rewe-Zentrale AG v Bundesmonopolverwaltung fur Brantwein*, [1979] ECR 649.

[18] See infra Section 3, The New Approach.

[19] Crème de Cassis is a blackcurrant liqueur, which is mainly consumed stirred with alcohol, under the Kir label. When it is stirred with champagne it becomes the Kir Royal.

A German national court referred a question to the ECJ as to whether the national legislation was consistent with Article 28 EC. The court found that the German legislation produced a restrictive effect, regardless of the fact that it was not discriminatory, to the extent that it amounted to a de facto prohibition of Cassis in the German market. In particular, facing for the first time a measure applicable without distinction to domestic and imported products, the court stated that:

> – first, in the absence of Community regulations in manufacturing and marketing, it is up to Member States to enact the relevant regulations for their territory; and

> – second, that barriers to community internal trade arising from these (inevitably) different national regulations must be accepted as long as these provisions are necessary in order to meet binding requirements, notably the requirements of effective tax control, public health protection, the integrity of trade and consumer protection.

In the light of the above, it concluded by stating that:

> the requirements relating to the minimum content of alcohol beverages do not serve a purpose which is in the general interest such as to take precedence over the requirements of free movement of goods, which constitutes one of the fundamental rules of the Community.

In view of an increasing number of obstacles to the free movement of goods stemming from regulatory divergence, the Commission took *Cassis* as a basis for developing the principle of mutual recognition and explained it to Member States, the European Parliament and the Council in its well-known 1980 communication.[20]

It was there established that:

> The principles deduced by the court imply that a Member State may not in principle prohibit the sale in its territory of a product lawfully produced and marketed in another Member State even if the product is produced according to technical or quality requirements which differ from those imposed on its domestic products. Where a product fulfils the legitimate objectives of a Member State's own rules (public safety, protection of the consumer or the environment, etc.), the importing country cannot justify prohibiting its sale in its territory by claiming that the way it fulfils the objectives is different from that imposed on domestic products.

---

[20] Communication on the mutual recognition principle, OJ C 256, 3 October 1980, at 2–3.

These 'legitimate objectives' are the so-called mandatory requirements.

At the same time, the court in *Cassis* also gave some clarification to the exceptions recognised by Article 30 EC. The German Government tried to justify its measure under the public health ground by arguing that a limitless authorisation for liqueurs of different alcoholic strengths would have led to an increase in consumption of alcohol as a whole and, accordingly, to an increase in the dangers of alcoholism in the population. The court held that such considerations could not be:

> [...] decisive since the consumer can obtain on the market an extremely wide range of weakly or moderately alcoholic products and furthermore a large proportion of alcoholic beverages with a high alcoholic content freely sold on the German market is generally consumed in a diluted form.[21]

In the absence of Community harmonisation with regard to a certain product, Member States are at liberty, in principle, to choose the level of protection of public health they intend to ensure within their own territory. They may, for instance, establish a procedure under which prior authorisation is required for the marketing of foodstuffs authorised in other Member States. This freedom is, however, restricted by Article 28 EC governing the free movement of goods within the EC. That means that, in our example, recourse to a system of pre-market approval is compatible with the requirements of the free movement of goods only if it is justified by the aim of protecting public health and is proportionate to the objective envisaged.[22] In other words, the Member State should invoke Article 30 EC and show that the objective of protecting health cannot be achieved by having recourse to a less trade-restrictive procedure.

As will be further demonstrated,[23] the role played by the mutual recognition principle in the food sector is particularly relevant to the extent, by neutralising the negative impact stemming from divergent regulatory food safety frameworks, that it exempts the legislator from a complex and all-encompassing effort aimed at harmonising food

---

[21] Case 120/78, *Rewe-Zentrale AG* [1979] ECR para 11.
[22] This case law has originally developed in the pesticides sector (Case 272/80, *Frans-Nederlandse Maatschappij Voor Biologische Producten* [1981] ECR 3277, para 12), but it has been extended to vitamins (Case 174/82, *Sandoz* [1983] ECR 2445, para 18) and to additives (Case 247/84 *Motte* [1985] ECR 3887, para 20). For a more recent application of this principle, see Case C-443/02, *Schreiber* [2004] not yet reported, where a national measure introducing a market authorisation procedure for the marketing of blocks of red cedar wood having natural anti-moth properties has been held to comply with EC law.
[23] See infra Section 3. The 'New Approach': mutual recognition principle and minimum harmonisation standards (1985–1997)

requirements throughout Europe.[24] In other words, the application of this principle makes it possible to reconcile the free movement imperative with national regulatory diversities.

2.3   Keck

The *Keck* judgment represents the last of the three landmark decisions defining the scope of Article 28 EC.[25] After having given a broad interpretation to this prohibition by also including within its scope indistinctly applicable measures, where they could not be explained in terms of mandatory requirements, the ECJ felt the need to limit this broad approach. As a result it held that 'certain selling arrangements', that is, measures concerning the circumstances of selling the goods, are not covered by Article 28 EC 'so long as they affect in the same manner, in law and in fact, the marketing of domestic products and of those from other Member States'.[26]

The opportunity for this historical *revirement* came in a case involving the prosecution of Mr Keck and Mr Mithouart for having resold products at a price lower than their actual purchase price. The question referred to the court was whether the French legislation prohibiting 'resale at loss' was compatible with Article 28 EC.

'[C]ontrary to what has previously been decided', the court held that:

> the application to products from other Member States of national provisions restricting or prohibiting certain selling arrangements is not such as to hinder directly or indirectly, actually or potentially, trade between Member States within the meaning of the Dassonville judgment [...], so long as those provisions apply to all relevant traders operating within the national territory and so long as they affect in the same manner, in law and in fact, the marketing of domestic products and of those from other Member States.

Moreover, the court stated that:

> [p]rovided that those conditions are fulfilled, the application of such rules to the sale of products from another Member State meeting the requirements laid down by that State is not by nature such as to prevent their access to the market or to impede access any more than it impedes the access of domestic products. Such rules therefore fall outside the scope of Article 30 of the Treaty.[27]

---

[24] Contra, see F. Capelli, 'Il Principio del Mutuo Riconoscimento Non Garantisce Buoni Risultati nel Settore dei Prodotti Alimentari', in *Jus* 1992, pp 141 ss.

[25] Joined Cases 267 and 268/91 *Keck and Mithouard* [1993] ECR 6097.

[26] Ibid, para 16.

[27] Ibid, paras 16–17.

These two paragraphs of the *Keck* judgment have indisputably been the most commented upon ever in the ECJ's case law and they remain the subject of discussion. What is sure is that this judgment represents a severe constraint on the *Dassonville* catch-all formula, by ruling out from the scope of Article 28 all indistinctly applicable selling arrangements. What is not clear is whether the market access criterion developed as an obiter dictum in paragraph 17 of the *Keck* judgment is presently the test applied by the court.[28]

B.   Positive Integration Rules: Articles 94 and 95 EC

As previously stated, to ensure the establishment of an internal market and the realisation of the free movement of goods, the Treaty also provides for positive integration rules. This is based on the assumption that Treaty prohibitions, being by definition limited to an ex-post application, do not suffice per se to attain this goal.[29] Economic operators may indeed create again those barriers which are addressed by the negative integration prohibitions.

Since the divergence existing among national food provisions appeared to be the main obstacles to achieve a single marketplace for foodstuffs, it was necessary to proceed to the harmonisation of this legislation. To take but one example, it became apparent that, in the absence of any coordination, a given food would need to meet the standards set by the different national product safety rules in order to enter their markets. More specifically, as these food safety provisions were likely to constitute justified barriers to trade under Article 30 EC, the only mechanism to remove such obstacles was by means of Community harmonised rules. One of the main avenues for Community intervention was Article 100 (current Article 94) of the original Treaty of Rome, which allows the EC institutions to adopt directives aimed at harmonising national provisions that 'directly affect the establishment or functioning of the common market' (note that this Article reads: 'The Council shall, acting *unanimously* on a proposal from the Commission and after consulting the European Parliament and the Economic and Social Committee, issue directives for the approximation of such laws, regulations or administrative provisions of the Member States as directly affect the establishment or functioning of the common market').

---

[28] For an innovative reading of the *Keck* jurisprudence see Case 20/03, *Burmanjer*, not yet reported, as commented on by A. Alemanno, 'Libre Circulation des Marchandises: Arrêt Burmanjer', in *Revue du Droit de l'Union Européenne*, 02/05, p 392. See also Opinion of A.G. Poiares Maduro in C-158/04 and C-159/04, Alfa Vita Vassilopoulos AE, formerly Trofo Super-Markets AE, delivered on 30 March 2006.
[29] This proved to be true even after the ECJ gave a broad interpretation of Article 28 of the EC Treaty, thereby limiting Member States' room of manoeuvre.

The relationship between the negative integration prohibitions and those of positive integration has been aptly defined by the ECJ which has declared that while:

> [...] the purpose of Article 28 is, save for certain specific exceptions, to abolish in the immediate future all quantitative restrictions on the imports of goods and all measures having an equivalent effect', '[...] the general purpose of Article 100 is, by approximating the laws, regulations and administrative provisions of the Member States, to enable obstacles of whatever kind arising from disparities between them to be reduced.[30]

The Community could also rely on Article 235 (current Article 308) EC which, by providing a legal basis for measures which could not show a direct link to the establishment or functioning of the internal market, allows the EC institutions to intervene when the Community's action is necessary to attain one of the objectives for which the Treaty has not provided the necessary power. Unlike Article 100, it requires a looser link with the common market and allows the adoption of 'all appropriate measures'.

Although the original EEC Treaty had envisaged the setting up of such positive integration rules, the legal bases provided (notably Articles 100 and 235) required unanimous voting in Council, thus weakening their utility. It was only in 1987 that the Single European Act incorporated, in line with the Community's 'New Approach on Technical Harmonisation and Standards', Article 100A (current Article 95) into the Treaty.[31] This new 'harmonisation provision', by requiring a qualified majority in the legislative process instead of unanimity, paved the way for a smoother harmonisation process. However, the price to be paid for the introduction of qualified majority voting in the Treaty was the insertion of an express provision (current paragraph 4 of this article) allowing Member States to derogate from a measure adopted under Article 100A (current Article 95) in specific circumstances.[32] In the words of AG Saggio, the introduction of such a safeguard clause:

---

[30] Case 193/80, *Commission v Italy*, ECR [1980] 3019.

[31] For an overview on the safeguard clauses of Article 95 EC and the related interpretative problems, see, eg, P. Oliver, *Free Movement of Goods in the European Community*, 2003, p 466 ; N. De Sadeleer, 'Les Clauses de Sauvegarde Prévues à l'article 95 du Traité CE – L'efficacité du Marché Intérieur en porte-à-faux avec les Intérets Nationaux Dignes de Protection', *Revue Trimestrielle de Droit Européen* 38, 2002, p 63; R. Verheyen, 'The Environmental Guarantee in European Law and the New Article 95 EC in practice – A Critique', *RECIEL*, 1/2000, pp 180–187; H. G. Sevenster, 'The Environmental Guarantee after Amsterdam: Does the Emperor have New Clothes?', *Yearbook of European Environmental Law*, 2000, vol. I, pp 236 ss. For an analysis of the conditions of application of Article 95, paragraph 4, see Opinion by AG Tizzano in Case C-3/00, [2003] *Denmark v Commission*. For a critical comment on this opinion and the final judgment, see A. Alemanno, Case C-3/00, [2003] *Denmark v Commission*, in *Revue du Droit de l'Union Européenne*, 02/03.

[32] While the safeguard clause contained in paragraph 4 had been introduced by the 1987
(continued...)

[...] essentially serves to offset the mechanism requiring a qualified majority, which, although it has led to a notable increase in the efficiency of the decision-making process for establishing the internal market, has on the other hand entailed a sacrifice of national interests which merit protection. Thus, Article 100a(4) permits a Member State which so desires to continue to apply, in the wake of a harmonising measure, provisions of national law which are justified in terms of the important (non-economic) needs contemplated by Article 36 or which are necessary to protect the environment or the working environment, provided that a certain procedure is followed, and subject to both administrative checks (entrusted to the Commission) and judicial review.[33]

Although initially this derogation was confined to national measures existing at the time the harmonised directive was adopted, the Amsterdam Treaty extended the possibility to derogate from harmonised measures to national regulations adopted after the enactment of the Community measure.[34] Hence, current Article 95(5) allows Member States 'to introduce national provisions based on new scientific evidence [...] on grounds of problems specific to that Member State arising after the adoption of the harmonisation measure'. Despite some alarming reactions by some commentators,[35] Article 95(4) and (5) has not often been invoked by Member States.[36]

Single European Act, the one expressed within paragraph 5 has been inserted 10 years later by the Amsterdam Treaty, which has redesigned the whole provision. Paragraph 4, on the one hand, retains the same invocability conditions (the protection of the interests mentioned in Article 30 EC and the protection of the environment or working envionrment). Paragraph 5, on the other hand, imposes, at least apparently, stricter limitations on the introduction of national measures after harmonisation. These measures must be 'based on scientific evidence relating to the protection of the environment or the working environment', on the grounds of a problem specific to that Member State which has arisen after the adoption of a Community measure.

[33] Opinion of AG Saggio in Case 319/97, *Kortas* ECR [1997] 3143, at 17.

[34] However, according to AG Tizzano, the original paragraph 4 of Article 95 'ne se limitait pas du tout à l'hypothèse du 'maintien' de règles nationales par dérogation à l'harmonisation; au contraire, il se référait plus généralement au cas où un Etat membre entendrait « appliquer » lesdits règles, de sorte que cette disposition avait déjà un caractère englobant par rapport à l'une et à l'autre hypothèses considérées : à savoir tant le maintien de règles pré-existantes que l'introduction de règles nouvelles' (Opinion in Case C-3/00, [2003] *Denmark v Commission*). For a critical comment on this opinion and the final judgment, see A. Alemanno, Case C-3/00, [2003] *Denmark v Commission*, supra note 31.

[35] See, eg, P. Pescatore, 'Some Critical Remarks on the European Single Act', in 9 *Common Market Law Review* 1987.

[36] See, on this point, Alemanno, supra note 31. For a detailed analysis of the safeguard clauses contained in Article 95, focusing on their origin, functioning and current practice, see N. de Sadeleer, 'Les Clauses de Sauvegarde Prévues à l'Article 95 du Traité CE – L'Efficacité du marché intérieur en porte-à-faux avec les intérets nationaux dignes de protection', supra note 31, and by the same author, 'Safeguard clauses under Article 95 of the EC Treaty', *Common Market Law Review*, 2003, n° 40, pp 889–915. For a more recent analysis of the Commission practice developed on Article 95(4) and (5), see J. Scott and E. Vos, 'The Juridification of Uncertainty: Observations of the Ambivalence of the Precautionary Principle within the EU and the WTO', in C. Joerges and R. Dehousse, *Good Governance in Europe's Integrated Market*, 2002, footnote 63.

In the words of the ECJ, the relationship between paragraphs 4 and 5 of Article 95 may be explained as follow:

> [t]he difference between the two situations envisaged in Article 95 EC is due to the existence, in the first, of national provisions predating the harmonisation measure. They are thus known to the Community legislature, which cannot or does not seek to be guided by them for the purpose of harmonisation. It is therefore considered acceptable for the Member State to request that its own rules remain in force. To that end, the EC Treaty requires that such national provisions must be justified on grounds of major needs referred to in Article 30 EC or relating to the protection of the environment or the working environment. By contrast, in the second situation, the adoption of new national legislation is more likely to jeopardise harmonisation. The Community institutions could not, by definition, have taken account of the national provisions when drawing up the harmonisation measure. In that case, the needs referred to in Article 30 EC are not taken into account, and only grounds relating to protection of the environment or the working environment are accepted, on condition that the Member State provides new scientific evidence and that the need to introduce new national provisions results from a problem which is specific to the Member State concerned and subsequent to the adoption of the harmonisation measure.[37]

According to settled case law, it is for the Member State which invokes Article 95(4) and (5) EC to prove that the conditions for application of that provision have been met.[38]

In particular, Article 95(6) obliges the Commission to verify that the notified national provisions are not a means of arbitrary discrimination or a disguised restriction on trade between Member States and that they do not constitute an obstacle to the functioning of the internal market. The last condition cannot be interpreted in such a way that it prohibits the approval of any national measure likely to affect the functioning of the internal market. This is because any national measure derogating from a harmonised measure aiming at the establishment and operation of the internal market inherently constitutes a measure that it is likely to affect the internal market. Accordingly, to guarantee the *effet utile* of the derogating procedure under Article 95 EC, the Commission tends to consider that, in the context of Article 95(6), the concept of obstacle to

---

[37] Joined Cases T-366/03 and T-235/04, *Land Oberösterreich and Republic of Austria v Commission*, not yet reported, at 62. See also Case C-3/00 *Denmark v Commission* [2003] ECR I-2643, paras 56–58.

[38] See opinion of Advocate General Tizzano in Case C-512/99, *Germany v Commission* [2003] ECR I-845, at 71 and, with regard to Article 95(4), Case C-3/00, *Denmark v Commission* [2003] ECR I-2643, para 84.

the functioning of the internal market must be understood as a disproportionate effect in relation to the pursued objective.[39] The proportionality assessment implies, in turn, a judgment on whether the notified measure exceeds the limits of what is appropriate and necessary to achieve the declared objective of environmental and health protection.[40]

Article 95(8) states that where a problem relating to public health is raised by a Member State in a field which has been the subject of prior harmonisation measures, it needs to bring this matter to the attention of the Commission which should immediately examine whether it is necessary to propose appropriate measures aimed at tackling the newly emerged problem. A combined reading of paragraphs 5 and 8 would seem to exclude the possibility of introducing new unilateral measures in the public health field.

C.   Other Positive Integration Rules

Although under the original Treaty of Rome the Community largely relied on Articles 100 (current Article 94) and 235 (current Article 308) EC, rules applicable to foodstuffs have developed from a variety of different legal bases provided in the Treaty, in order to serve different policy objectives.[41] Among the most common legal bases for the adoption of EC food legislation are: Article 152, for the adoption of measures in the veterinary and phytosanitary fields whose direct objective is to protect public health;[42] Article 153 relating to consumer protection measures[43] and Article 37, for the replacement of national market organisations by common organisations and the adoption of legislation when agricultural aspects predominate. In addition, Article 130R (currently Article 174), which established that Community action in the

---

[39] For one of the latest applications of this provision, see Commission Decision 2006/372/EC concerning draft national provisions notified by the Kingdom of the Netherlands under Article 95(5) of the EC Treaty laying down limits on the emissions of particulate matter by diesel powered vehicles, OJ L142/16 ss.

[40] Case C-3/00 *Denmark v Commission* [2003] ECR I-2643, para 49.

[41] The EC food legislation is also based on a complex division of responsibilities between the Commission and the Member States. It is therefore no surprise that the Community lacked, for more than 40 years, a coherent policy towards the foodstuffs sector as a whole, and approached the different aspects of food safety in an uncoordinated fashion. See, eg, M. Lugt, *Enforcing European and National Food Law in the Netherlands and England*, Koninklijke Vermande ed., 1999, p 254.

[42] These measures may derogate from the Common Agricultural Policy and fall under the co-decision procedure. Possible examples of such measures are legislation involving zoonoses, BSE or reuses of veterinary medicines or pesticides.

[43] This article, as reformulated after Amsterdam, improves the protection of consumers because it obliges the Community to contribute to protecting the health, safety and economic interests of consumers, as well as to promoting their right to information, education and to organise themselves in order to safeguard their interests.

environmental field also had to contribute to the protection of human health, has also been interpreted as justifying the adoption of measures aimed at the protection of food safety. Notably, the second sentence of Article 130r(2), pursuant to which 'environmental protection requirements shall be a component of the Community' s other policies', has led to this result. An example of such an overstretching of the EC legal basis can be found in *Greece v Commission*. Herein, following the Chernobyl nuclear accident, a regulation that subjected the free circulation of certain agricultural products originating in non-member countries to compliance with maximum permitted levels of radioactive contamination has been found to be legitimate even though it is based on the common commercial policy. Although Advocate General Darmon recognised that 'the precautions relating to the import into the Community of food products correspond to the need to protect public health more than to prevent any damage to the environment', the court concluded that '[t]he fact that maximum permitted levels of radioactive contamination are fixed in response to a concern to protect public health and that the protection of public health is also one of the objectives of Community action in environmental matters, in accordance with the Article 130r(1), likewise cannot remove Regulation No 3955/87 from the sphere of the common commercial policy'.[44]

The EC Treaty contains a separate title on agriculture, Articles 32–38, which constitutes the Common Agricultural Policy (CAP). The CAP's main objectives differ from the Community's food law objectives as they focus mainly on promoting the increase in agricultural productivity and on ensuring a fair living for the agricultural community. However, although consumer and public health protection is not mentioned explicitly as one of the CAP's objectives, the Community has enacted a great deal of legislation for common market organisations covering nearly all agricultural products, for instance, eggs, bananas and wine.[45] Delimitation between food law *stricto sensu* and the CAP can be recognised by means of the Treaty basis of legislative instruments. While food law legislation is based on Articles 100A (94) and 100 (95) EC Treaty, CAP legislation is based on Article 43 EC. Some legislation shows that the Council and the Commission choose to use Article 43 EC when the legislative measure involves agricultural products, these being agro-food and foodstuffs in a strict sense, as well as agricultural products only. However, more and more often, measures based on Article 43 do not solely involve CAP objectives, but also other objectives such as consumer protection.

[44] Case C-62/88, *Hellenic Republic v Council*, ECR 1527, at 18.
[45] Regulation 2771/75 of the Council of 29 October 1975 on the common organisation of the market for eggs, OJ L282/49; Council Regulation 822/87 of 16 March 1987 on the Common organisation of the market for wine, OJ L84/1; Council Regulation 404/93 on the Common organisation of the market in bananas, OJ L47/1.

Due to the introduction of Article 95 EC (formerly Article 100A) in the EC Treaty, there are no longer any differences in the decision procedures between Article 37 EC and Article 95 EC. The only remaining difference involves the European Parliament (EP): while Article 37 EC requires only consultation with the EP, according to Article 95 EC the cooperation of the EP is required under the codecision procedure.

D.   Conclusions on the 'Genesis'

The Community has stepped into the regulation of food safety by pursuing, primarily, the goal of eliminating the trade barriers arising from diverging national food measures and, secondly, the aim of laying down a proper food policy throughout Europe. Thus, EC food law has traditionally been conceived as a set of rules prompted mainly by the desire to eliminate trade obstacles within the European internal market[46] and having the force of law in all Member States. Like several other European policies, the legislative framework of food law has been primarily designed to answer economic rather than safety or societal concerns. In fact, apart from the health and life exceptions to the prohibition laid down in Article 30, the Treaty did not provide for a specific power of the Community in this area until the adoption of the Single European Act (1986) and the Maastricht Treaty (1992).[47]

We have seen that the Community involvement in health and consumer protection, notably in the food area, found its roots not only in the combined use of both negative and positive integration measures, but also in other sources. In light of the principle of enumerated powers contained in the Treaty, the determination of the correct legal basis for health and consumer regulation, notably for food safety legislation, is of great importance. According to this principle, every binding Community act must rely on a direct or indirect legal basis in the provisions of the Treaty itself. This requirement pursues two main functions: an instrumental and a guarantee function. EC institutions must refer to a legal basis first to show that they are performing their tasks in accordance with the Community objectives set forth in Article 2 EC, but also to demonstrate that no decisions are taken where the Community lacks competence.[48]

---

[46] The original Treaty of Rome, signed by Belgium, France, Germany, Italy, Luxembourg and the Netherlands in 1957, provided that in order to establish a common market Member States should eliminate customs duties and quantitative restrictions applied between them and approximate their legislations to the extent required for the functioning of the common market. See Article 2 EC.

[47] Following the entry into force of the Maastricht Treaty (1992), the Community has acquired new responsibilities to contribute to the attainment of a high level of human health protection (Article 129), of protection of consumers (Article 129a) and of the environment (Article 130r).

[48] See R. Barents, 'The Internal Market Unlimited: Some observations on the Legal Basis of Community Legislation' (1993) 30 *CMLRev*, pp 85–86.

We will see that for almost three decades the EC maintained this 'economic' approach to food law, by using Article 100 (current Article 94) of the EC Treaty to harmonise a few specific areas of national food legislation. Because the different national provisions on food appeared to be the main obstacles to the achievement of a single marketplace for foodstuffs, it was necessary to proceed to the harmonisation of this legislation. The task was not easy to accomplish given that national regulations of foodstuffs were not only profoundly diverse, but they also embodied different administrative traditions. Quite surprisingly, one of the very first ever directives to be adopted by the Community is the directive relating to the use of colourings in foodstuffs.[49]

E.   The Genesis of Food Law on the Other Side of the Atlantic: the First Developments in US Food Law

In the U.S., before Congress enacted the 1906 Federal Food and Drugs Act (which became the Federal Food, Drug and Cosmetic Act in 1938),[50] the governmental involvement in food regulation was based on the Commerce Clause.[51] At that time, in contrast to the situation within the EC Community, the regulator's main purpose was 'to protect against fraud in the market place'[52] rather than to pursue a free trade objective. However, through time, the economic purpose has also found its way into the US approach.

As has been stated:

> Regulators in both jurisdictions ultimately derive their legal authority to define and control food safety risks from their constitutional power over the free or inter-State movement of goods and both share some aspects of that authority with their constituent States.[53]

---

[49] See OJ 1962 L 115/2645. The directive has no number because at that time a numbering system was not yet established. O'Rourke has ironically observed that 'this was not an auspicious start for the establishment of EU Food law as a major concern of EU legislators'. See R. O'Rourke, *EC Food Law* 185 (1st edn, 1998), p 3. See also P. Gray, 'Food Law and the Internal Market. Taking Stock', *Food Policy*, 1990, p 111.

[50] For a comment on the evolution of the Federal Food and Drug Legislation, see P. Barton Hutt & R.A. Merrill, *Food and Drug Law*, Cases and Materials, II[ed], New York, Foundation Press, 1991, pp 6–15. The text of the Act is reproduced in P. Barton Hutt & R.A. Merrill, *Food and Drug Law, Cases and Materials* – 2nd ed, 1996 Statutory Supplement, pp 1–269 and it is also available at http://www.fda.gov/opacom/ laws/fdcact/fdctoc.htm.

[51] G.C. Shaffer and M.A. Pollack, 'Les Différentes Approches de la Sécurité Alimentaire', in J. Bourrinet and F. Snyder, *La Sécurité Alimentaire dans l'Union Européenne*, supra note 2.

[52] P. Barton Hutt, 'Government Regulation of the Integrity of the Food Supply', 4 *Annual Review of Nutrition* 1 (1984).

[53] M.A. Echols, 'Food Safety Regulation in the European Union and the United States: different cultures, different laws', *Columb. J. Eur. L.* 525, p 530 (1998).

2. The 'Traditional' Approach to Foodstuffs: the 'Europroducts' (1969–1985)

Recognising that there were substantial trade barriers caused by differences in legislation, in 1969 the Commission drew up the General Programme for the Elimination of the Technical Obstacles to Trade, thus launching the so-called 'traditional approach'[54] to harmonisation.

The second part of the programme notably addressed the technical obstacles to the free movement of foodstuffs stemming from the different legislative, regulatory and administrative measures existing among Member States. Thus, the Community made an attempt to speed up its harmonisation efforts by setting out 43 areas for harmonising legislation including butter, cacao, pasta, ice cream, jam, sugar, soft drinks, beer, cheese, additives etc. These areas being divided into five different phases with the programme provided different deadlines for the presentation of harmonisation proposals to the Council according to each phase.

The idea behind this harmonisation programme was that every national product in principle required a Community measure in order to ensure the free circulation of goods. All restrictions to the intra-Community trade of foodstuffs owing to different national legislation could only be resolved when a similar provision was issued at Community level so that each national provision had to be replaced by a European measure. This explains why the harmonisation took place in areas that were predominantly 'vertical', leading to the drafting of very detailed directives (so-called recipe legislation).[55] This legislation introduced obligatory designations for foodstuffs whose use was made subject to a clearly described composition of the foodstuff in question, for example, chocolate, honey and fruit juices.[56] Although the programme was due to be completed within about two years, only four measures had been agreed by 1973.

This programme was then replaced by the 1973 'Industrial Policy Programme',[57] which replaced the deadlines previously decided on by the Council for the adoption of around 35 'vertical' directives aimed at establishing compositional standards for individual food, the so-called

---

[54] As adopted by the Council in its Resolution [1969] OJ C 76/1. See, on this document, Azoulay, supra note 2.

[55] They apply only to one foodstuff or to a group of foodstuffs. Vertical legislation can be distinguished from horizontal legislation, which applies to all foodstuffs, for instance, provisions on additives or hygiene.

[56] See infra note 58.

[57] Council Resolution of 17 December 1973 on industrial policy, JO C 117, at 1–14. See notably Annex 1, timetable for the removal of technical barriers to trade in foodstuffs, setting out different deadlines for the adoption of the Commission's proposal by the Council.

'recipe laws'.[58] The first 'europroduct' conceived by the EC legislator was chocolate.[59]

The standards dictating permissible ingredients and prohibiting products which do not satisfy these requirements from using a designated trade description were highly detailed and inclusive. It is clear that the common goal pursued by these directives was to facilitate the free movement of foodstuffs within the European Common market, rather than promoting health and consumer protection goals. The latter were tackled only to the extent that it was necessary to ensure regular intra-Community trade and were mainly left to the choice of the Member States.[60]

This total harmonisation approach to food law was not limited to Europe at that time. These EC food recipe laws recall to some degree the food standards of identity promulgated by the US FDA until the 1970s[61]. However, unlike the EC standards, the US recipe laws were primarily aimed at preventing 'economic adulteration, by which less expensive ingredients were substituted so as to make the product inferior to that which the consumer expected to receive when purchasing a product with the name under which it was sold'.[62] In short, the US standards were not conceived as promoting trade but rather as a tool for consumer protection. However, while the FDA abandoned this strategy in the 70s, the Community realised the failure of its traditional approach to harmonisation at the beginning of the 1980s. Two factors contributed towards the failure of recipe laws.[63] First, Article 94 of the Treaty,

[58] Much of this food legislation was developed by the Internal Market Directorate General (former DGIII, today DG MARKT). These directives lay down detailed specifications for certain sugars intended for human consumption, 73/437/EEC, 1973 OJ L 356/71; Coca and chocolate products, 73/241/EEC, 1973 OJ L 228/23; honey, 74/409/EEC, 1974 OJ L 221/10; fruit juices and certain similar products, 75/726/EEC, codified by 93/77/EEC, 1993 OJ L 244/23; partly or wholly dehydrated preserved milk, 76/118/EEC, 1976 OJ L 24/49; coffee extracts and chicory extracts, 77/436/EEC, 1977 OJ L 172/20; fruit jams, jellies and marmalades, and chestnut puree, 79/639/EEC, 1979 OJ L 205/5.

[59] Council directive 73/241/EEC, 1973 OJ L 228/23.

[60] On this line of thought, Ellen Vos affirms that the Community involvement in health and safety regulation may be considered 'as an accidental consequence of the market integration objective (spill-over)'. See E. Vos, *Institutional Frameworks of the Community Health and Safety Regulation. Committees, Agencies and Private Bodies* (1999), p 9.

[61] The FDA has promulgated approximately 300 standards of identity, covering – at their maximum reach – about 45 per cent of the American food supply shipped in interstate commerce, excluding fresh fruits. See 44 *Fed. Reg.* 75990, as reported by Hutt, supra note 1, at 107. For an historical presentation of the introduction of these standards in the US, see R.A. Merril and E.M. Coller, '"Like Mother used to Make": an Analysis of FDA Food Standards of Identity', 74 *Columbia L. Rev.* 561 (1974).

[62] See P. Burton Hutt & R.A. Merril, *Food & Drug Law*, Cases and Materials, 2nd ed, New York, Foundation Press, 1991, p 99.

[63] For an analysis of the factors leading to the failure of the Old Approach see R.H. Lauwaars, 'The Model Directive on Technical Harmonization and Standardisation', in R. Bieber, R. Dehousse, J. Pinder, J.H.H. Weiler (eds.), *1992: One European Market? A Critical Analysis of the Commission's Internal Market Strategy*, Nomos, Baden-Baden, 1988, p 155.

requiring unanimity for the adoption of the directives, turned out to be inadequate in promoting the creation of the internal market because it enabled Member States to block any Commission action with which they did not agree and, even when consensus was reached, it contributed to slowing down considerably the adoption of directives.[64] Second, sensitive questions of culinary cultures and traditions[65] combined with the rigidity of the total harmonisation instruments[66] contributed to rendering the decision-making procedure extremely cumbersome and provided a shelter for the protection of home trade.[67] By 1985, directives had been adopted only in 14 of the 50 sectors identified by the general harmonisation programme.[68] These difficulties in harmonising food quality requirements for all foodstuffs led the Commission to rethink its traditional approach, leading to a 'new strategy' of harmonisation.

3. The 'New Approach': Mutual Recognition Principle and Minimum Harmonisation Standards (1985–1997)

In 1985, the EC Commission decided to abandon its titanic effort to introduce universally applicable 'recipe laws' for all European-made foodstuffs, and launched the 'New Approach to Harmonisation of national legislations',[69] in particular to those related to foodstuffs.[70] In

---

[64] J. Pelkmans, 'The New Approach to Technical Harmonisation and Standardization', *Journal of Common Market Studies*, 1987, p 249 ss. and L. Costato, 'Dal Mutuo Riconoscimento al Sistema Europeo di Diritto Alimentare: il Regolamento 178/2002 Come Regola e Come Programma', in *Rivista di Diritto Agrario*, 3/2003, p 290.

[65] Gray, supra note 49, p 112.

[66] According to Mattera: 'on est en présence d'une harmonization totale lorsqu'une directive impose des règles qui se substituent entièrement aux règles nationales existantes en la matière ... L'effet d'une telle méthode est de dessaisir les Etats membres de leurs competences dans les secteurs specifiquement reglementes au niveau communautaire'. See A. Mattera, *Le Marché Unique Européen* (Jupiter ed, 1990), p 180.

[67] See D. Welch, 'From "Euro Beer" to "Newcastle Brown"', 'A Review of European Community Action to Dismantle Divergent "Food Laws"' (1983-4) 22 *Journal of Common Market Studies* 57 and M. Lugt, supra note 41, p 17.

[68] COM(85)603 final, 3.

[69] Communication on the completion of the internal market 'New Approach to Technical Harmonisation and Standards', COM(85) 19 final, then adopted by the Council Resolution on a New Approach to Technical Harmonisation and Standards [1985] OJ C136/1. For a detailed description of the 'New Approach', see A. Mattera, 'L'article 30 du Traité CE, la Jurisprudence Cassis et le Principe de la Reconnaissance Mutuelle', in *Revue du Marché Unique Européen*, fasc. 4, 1992, pp 35–36. Since the beginning of the 1980s the Commission has begun using the tool of Communications, acts designed to either interpret case law (so-called 'interpretative Communications'), or to show intentions and to set up guidelines to direct operators. See A. Mattera, *Le Marché Unique Européen*, supra note 66 and R. Rossolini, *Libera Circolazione degli Alimenti e Tutela della Salute nel Diritto Comunitario*, CEDAM, 2004, p 5, footnote 4. Although all these documents tend to be qualified under the label of 'soft law' because of their lack of binding character, EC courts have recently recognised some legal effects stemming from those Communications falling within the latter category. In particular, the CFI has held that 'the Community institutions may lay down for themselves

(continued...)

doing so, the Commission relied on the mutual recognition principle formulated by the European Court of Justice in the 1979 *Cassis de Dijon* judgment.[71] According to this principle a Member State should allow the free circulation in its territory of goods produced or marketed in conformity with the rules, tests or standards found in another Member State which offer an equivalent level of protection to its own rules, tests or standards.[72] Suddenly, it appeared that there was no longer a need to

guidelines for the exercise of their discretionary powers by way of measures not provided for in Article 189 of the EC Treaty (now Article 249 EC), in particular by communications, provided that they contain directions on the approach to be followed by the Community institutions and do not depart from the Treaty rules. In such circumstances, the Community judicature ascertains, applying the principle of equal treatment, whether the disputed measure is consistent with the guidelines that the institutions have laid down for themselves by adopting and publishing such communications. See Case T-13/99 *Pfizer Animal Health v Council*, 2002 E.C.R. II-3305, para 119. See also, to that effect, Case T-7/89 *Hercules Chemicals v Commission* [1991] ECR II-1711, para 53; Case T-149/95 *Ducros v Commission* [1997] ECR II-2031, para 61; and Case T-214/95 *Vlaams Gewest v Commission* [1998] ECR II-717, paras 79 and 89).

[70] More precisely, the Commission extended the 'New Approach' to foodstuffs by publishing the communication to the Council on the completion of the internal market: Community legislation on foodstuffs, COM(85) 603 final, also called in Brussels's jargon the 'Mini White Paper' or 'White Paper-bis'.

[71] Case 120/78, *Rewe-Zentrale AG v Bundesmonopolverwaltung fur Brantwein*, 1979 ECR 649. In this case the Court stated that Member States could not refuse entry to products (in this case a French blackcurrant liqueur, the Cassis de Dijon) even if their national legislation prohibited the sale of the product.

[72] This formulation of the principle was developed for the first time by the Communication of the Commission concerning the consequences of the judgment given by the Court on 20 February 1979 in Case 120/78 *Cassis de Dijon*, OJ 1980 C 256/2, where it is stated that: 'The court's interpretation has induced the Commission to set out a number of guidelines. The principles deduced by the Court imply that a Member State may not in principle prohibit the sale in its territory of a product lawfully produced and marketed in another Member State even if the product is produced according to technical or quality requirements which differ from those imposed on its domestic products. Where a product 'suitably and satisfactorily' fulfils the legitimate objective of a Member State's own rules (public safety, protection of the consumer or the environment, etc), the importing country cannot justify prohibiting its sale in its territory by claiming that the way it fulfils the objective is different from that imposed on domestic products. In such a case, an absolute prohibition of sale could not be considered 'necessary' to satisfy a 'mandatory requirement' because it would not be an 'essential guarantee' in the sense defined in the court's judgment. The Commission will therefore have to tackle a whole body of commercial rules which lay down that products manufactured and marketed in one Member State must fulfil technical or qualitative conditions in order to be admitted to the market of another and specifically in all cases where the trade barriers occasioned by such rules are inadmissible according to the very strict criteria set out by the court. The Commission is referring in particular to rules covering the composition, designation, presentation and packaging of products as well as rules requiring compliance with certain technical standards.
The Commission's work of harmonisation will henceforth have to be directed mainly at national laws having an impact on the functioning of the common market where barriers to trade to be removed arise from national provisions, which are admissible under the criteria set by the court. The Commission will be concentrating on sectors deserving priority because of their economic relevance to the creation of a single internal market. To forestall later difficulties, the Commission will be informing Member States of potential
(continued...)

harmonise all the food legislation of Member States by agreeing on common food quality requirements for 'Euro Bread', 'Euro Chocolate', 'Euro Beer', etcc.[73] As has been said by one of the most prominent supporters of the 'New Approach':

> Il ne s'agissait plus de créer un ensemble d'europroduits – une bière européenne, un pain européen, un jouet européen ... – mais d'instaurer une plus grande liberté d'échange de « produits légalement fabriqués dans la Communauté » et d'arriver ainsi a l'acceptation, par chaque Etat membre, des diversités nationales des autres pays. [74]

The European Court of Justice endorsed this interpretation of the *Cassis* judgment by systematically holding that the protection of consumers cannot be a legitimate ground upon which a Member State may prohibit the marketing in its territory of foodstuffs that are compositionally different from those generally sold there. According to the court, the consumer protection objective could be achieved by the inclusion of additional information on the labelling of products indicating differences in compositional and production methods existing in the exporting Member. This measure allowed individuals to make informed choices.

The principle of mutual recognition, while preserving all traditions, richness and diversity existing among the different national culinary traditions, allowed the Community to realise an internal market without having to adopt hundreds of 'vertical' directives.[75] However, even amongst the relatively similar European Member States in terms of regulatory approach, national regulations cannot always ensure equivalent levels of protection. This stems from the different approaches to regulation adopted in each Member State, reflecting differences in culture, the peculiar functioning of their political institutions and also their different attitudes towards the management of risk. As a consequence of the resulting differences in regulation, the goals of free

---

objections, under the terms of Community law, to provisions they may be considering introducing which come to the attention of the Commission. It will be producing suggestions soon on the procedures to be followed in such cases'. For a review of this communication see, eg, Vos, supra note 60, p 56.

[73] See S.M. Stephenson, 'Mutual Recognition and its Role in Trade Facilitation', in *Journal of World Trade*, 1999, p 141 ss., according to whom the New Approach 'served to remove the largest stumbling block from the creation of the EU, as progress on integration had been held up for years by the impossibility of harmonising "en bloc" all of the differing national standards'.

[74] A. Mattera, 'L'article 30 du Traité CE, la Jurisprudence Cassis et le Principe de la Reconnaissance Mutuelle', supra note 69, p 35.

[75] This new approach to harmonisation was launched by the Commission in its White Paper on the Completion of the Internal Market, COM (85) 603, para. 7, published in June 1985, eventually becoming the cornerstone of the '1992 Programme'. See A. Mattera, *Le Marché Unique Européen*, supra note 66.

movement could not have been achieved without some form of 'positive integration', by agreeing common rules in order to overcome the obstacles that could not have been tackled solely by the mutual recognition principle.

In accordance with the new strategy, Community food legislation would henceforth be limited to the harmonisation of national rules justified on four grounds:

- the need to protect public health;
- the need to protect other consumer interests, notably consumers' need for information;
- the necessity to ensure fair trading; and
- to necessity to provide appropriate official controls.[76]

The idea was that the EC could lay down harmonised rules only on a horizontal basis to set forth the 'essential requirements' necessary for the free circulation of foodstuffs.[77] The mutual recognition principle combined with a reinforced labelling regime guaranteeing consumer information would realise an internal market for foodstuffs. Although the Council would always adopt the 'essential requirements' of food law, there would be delegated to the Commission the task of implementing these rules under the conditions provided by the Council.

However, it quite soon turned out that the *Cassis de Dijon* doctrine combined with a reinforced labelling regime guaranteeing consumer information would not have been a sustainable strategy. First, there was the fear that the application of the mutual recognition principle would have led to a 'race to the bottom' situation, where Member States would have given up higher quality standards in favour of adaptation to the

---

[76] The Commission in its 1985 'MiniWhite Paper' stated that '[i]n the absence of harmonised Community rules, the Member States have the power to lay down, in respect of their own production, rules governing the manufacture, composition, packaging and presentation of foodstuffs. However, in line with the mutual recognition principle, they are required to admit to their territory foodstuffs lawfully produced and marketed in another Member State unless it can be demonstrated that a restrictive measure is: a) necessary in order to satisfy mandatory requirements (public health, protection of consumers, fairness of commercial transactions, environmental protection); b) proportionate to the desired objective; and is the means of achieving that objective which least hinders trade'. See supra note 70.

[77] Under the New Strategy, the EC institutions, apart from legislating only 'essential requirements', would have also delegated the determination of more detailed standards to quasi-public European Standards organisations and then coordinated quasi-public national bodies in charge of assessing the conformity of products produced in any one Member State for sale throughout the EC market. See G. Shaffer, 'Reconciling Trade and Regulatory Goals: The Prospects and Limits of New Approaches to Transatlantic Governance Through Mutual Recognition and Safe Harbor Agreements', 9 *Columbia Journal of European Law* 33 (2002).

lowest common denominator.[78] Secondly, the functioning of the mutual recognition principle could be hindered by its operational requirement, which is the functional equivalence (or parallelism) of national legislations. In fact, as there are many products presenting genuine differences in their regulatory regimes, their nature may require a single pan-European standard, which involves harmonisation. Thirdly, the elimination of barriers to trade through the mutual recognition principle presupposes, unless Member States voluntarily refrain from asserting specific domestic standards for the imported products, an initiative by economic operators (manufacturers or importers) or the Commission and which can come about only reactively and on a case-by-case basis[79].

Only approximation of legislation could respond to these three problems. However, it would have been inconceivable to go back to the traditional approach to harmonisation, especially because Article 94 EC still required unanimity. The new intervention should have to rely on new premises. The 1986 Single European Act provided the answer by introducing a new legal basis, Article 100A (current 95), which modified voting rules for the enactment of EC internal market legislation. This article requires a qualified majority in the legislative process instead of unanimity as required under Article 100 EC. It thereby eliminated Member States' veto rights in the Council, thus speeding up the harmonisation process.[80]

[78] The original formulation of this argument can be found in the *Cassis de Dijon* case, where the Federal Republic of Germany affirmed that: 'Ultimately, the regulation binding in all Member States would be that of the country setting the lowest requirements; since this legal conclusion would be based on the directly applicable provision of Article 30, these legal changes will have to have been effected already, at latest by 1 January 1970. Because of the automatic effect of Article 30, in the future further amendments to national legal provisions could be adopted continually as soon as only one Member State adopted a new regulation with lower requirements. In the extreme case, then, one Member State could, without any cooperation or information of other Member States, determine legislation for the whole Community. The outcome would be that the minimum requirements would, without the harmonisation provided for in Article 100 EEC, requiring consensus by Member States, be reduced to the lowest level to be found in the regulations of any one of the Member States'.

[79] One should also bear in mind that the ECJ judgments can only act by abolishing without substitution the national measures. They never replace them by new requirements.

[80] Article 100A (current Article 95) EC reads '1. By way of derogation from Article 94 and save where otherwise provided in this Treaty, the following provisions shall apply for the achievement of the objectives set out in Article 14. The Council shall, acting in accordance with the procedure referred to in Article 251 (qualified majority vote) and after consulting the Economic and Social Committee, adopt the measures for the approximation of the provisions laid down by law, regulation or administrative action in Member States which have as their object the establishment and functioning of the internal market. 2. Paragraph 1 shall not apply to fiscal provisions, to those relating to the free movement of persons nor to those relating to the rights and interests of employed persons. 3. The Commission, in its proposals envisaged in paragraph 1 concerning health, safety, environmental protection and consumer protection, will take as a base a high level of protection, taking account in particular of any new development based on scientific facts.

(continued...)

As a part of this approach, the EC Community adopted a wide-ranging set of framework (horizontal) directives, the so-called 'New Approach directives',[81] dealing with 'essential requirements' in the fields of additives,[82] extraction solvents,[83] flavouring agents,[84] colours,[85] sweeteners,[86] food additives other than colours and sweeteners (ie

Within their respective powers, the European Parliament and the Council will also seek to achieve this objective. 4. If, after the adoption by the Council or by the Commission of a harmonisation measure, a Member State deems it necessary to maintain national provisions on grounds of major needs referred to in Article 30, or relating to the protection of the environment or the working environment, it shall notify the Commission of these provisions as well as the grounds for maintaining them. 5. Moreover, without prejudice to paragraph 4, if, after the adoption by the Council or by the Commission of a harmonisation measure, a Member State deems it necessary to introduce national provisions based on new scientific evidence relating to the protection of the environment or the working environment on grounds of a problem specific to that Member State arising after the adoption of the harmonisation measure, it shall notify the Commission of the envisaged provisions as well as the grounds for introducing them. 6. The Commission shall, within six months of the notifications as referred to in paragraphs 4 and 5, approve or reject the national provisions involved after having verified whether or not they are a means of arbitrary discrimination or a disguised restriction on trade between Member States and whether or not they shall constitute an obstacle to the functioning of the internal market. In the absence of a decision by the Commission within this period the national provisions referred to in paragraphs 4 and 5 shall be deemed to have been approved. When justified by the complexity of the matter and in the absence of danger for human health, the Commission may notify the Member State concerned that the period referred to in this paragraph may be extended for a further period of up to six months. 7. When, pursuant to paragraph 6, a Member State is authorised to maintain or introduce national provisions derogating from a harmonisation measure, the Commission shall immediately examine whether to propose an adaptation to that measure. 8. When a Member State raises a specific problem on public health in a field which has been the subject of prior harmonisation measures, it shall bring it to the attention of the Commission which shall immediately examine whether to propose appropriate measures to the Council. 9. By way of derogation from the procedure laid down in Articles 226 and 227, the Commission and any Member State may bring the matter directly before the Court of Justice if it considers that another Member State is making improper use of the powers provided for in this Article. 10. The harmonisation measures referred to above shall, in appropriate cases, include a safeguard clause authorising the Member States to take, for one or more of the non-economic reasons referred to in Article 30, provisional measures subject to a Community control procedure'.

[81] For an overview of the results obtained by the New Approach, see M. Egan, *Constructing a European Market: Standards, Regulation, and Governance*, Oxford: Oxford University Press, pp 166-167 (2001) and G. Majone, 'State, Market, and Regulatory Competition in the European Union: Lessons for the Integrating World Economy', in A. Moravscsik, *Centralizing or Fragmentation? Europe Facing the Challenges of Deepening, Diversity and Democracy*, 1998, 94, pp 107–8.

[82] Council Directive 89/107/EEC [1989] OJ L 40/27. After much discussion, this framework directive was agreed in December 1988 and published in early 1989. Following problems in developing the specific directives for the additives, it was necessary to amend the framework directive in 1994.

[83] Council Directive 88/344/EEC [1988] OJ L157/28.

[84] Council Directive 88/388/EEC [1988] OJ L184/61.

[85] European Parliament and Council Directive 94/36/EC [1994] OJ L 237/13.

[86] European Parliament and Council Directive 94/35/EC [1994] OJ L 237/3, then amended by 96/83/EC OJ L 48/4.

preservatives, antioxidants, emulsifiers etc),[87] labelling foods for particular nutritional needs, hygiene and official controls[88]. The 'New Approach directives' aim at laying down basic standards and guiding Member States in the development of more detailed rules.[89] These directives contained positive lists of authorised substances to be used in the food sectors but, being framework directives, they needed to be supplemented by implementing measures by the Commission, in accordance with a regulatory committee procedure.

National food regulations, constrained by the respect of the framework directives, would have been accepted within the Community by virtue of the mutual recognition principle. The existing vertical directives would have remained in place and the Community would still have been in charge of periodically updating and replacing their texts[90]. However, in principle, the Community was not to issue new vertical harmonisation legislation, not only in order to preserve the culinary richness and diversity of Member States, but also to avoid the introduction of legislative rigidity that would prevent innovation and commercial flexibility.[91] Yet, the vertical approach is still partly pursued by the Community, which regularly updates and replaces several directives concerning specific foodstuffs adopted in the 1970s.[92]

Moreover, in order to reduce the negative impact stemming from the creation of new national provisions on food, the Community extended the scope of the 'informative directives' to foodstuffs by requiring Member States to notify their draft food-related regulations to the Commission's services.[93] This initiative appears to be of great importance to the extent that the food sector is one of the regulatory areas where various new national measures continued to be adopted.

---

[87] European Parliament and Council Directive 95/2/EC [1995] OJ L61/1, then amended by 96/85/EC, OJ L 86/1.

[88] Council Directive 89/397/EEC [1989] OJ L186/23.

[89] P. Deboyser, 'Le Marché Unique des Produits Alimentaires', *Revue du Marché Unique Européen*, 1991, pp 65 ss.

[90] See supra note 15. See also L. Azoulay, supra note 2, p 36.

[91] 'Mini White paper', supra note 70, at 16-17.

[92] See Vos, supra note 60, p 135 (several examples are offered).

[93] Council Directive 88/182/EEC, 1988 O.J. L 81/75 amending Directive 83/189/EEC laying down a procedure for the provision of information in the field of technical standards and regulations (then amended by European Parliament and Council Directive 94/10/EC, 1994, OJ L100/30). Each year the services of the Commission consider some 60-80 new national measures relating to the foodstuffs sector under the procedure laid down by the 'informative directives'. This procedure enables the Commission to comment on draft legislation and to ask Member States to reshape their drafts in order to bring them into conformity with EC law thus minimising the impact on the intra-community trade. For an analysis of the 'informative directives', see Mattera, supra note 66.

Although the Community tried in these years to reorient EC food policy towards the achievement of new goals, such as the protection of public health or consumer protection, these aspects of EC food law were still neglected at the time and implemented as ancillary to the economic requirements of the internal market.[94] The only priority was the completion of the internal market widely-publicised by the 1992 single-market programme. Even though much national food legislation had already been harmonised at the Community level, European food law continued to develop in a fragmented fashion.[95] Thus, for instance, there was no unifying text that clearly defined the responsibilities of the different stakeholders concerned, such as manufacturers, producers, distributors etc.

There is therefore no doubt that, before 1992, following more than 30 years of legislative activity, Community action in the area of food policy remained largely conditioned by the Community's emphasis on the removal of barriers to trade, rather than on safety issues.[96] This was the case even though in 1992 the goal of attaining 'a high level of health protection' was given the status of a general objective of the EC Treaty.[97] Although a significant number of EC legislative texts were adopted and the same Treaty had been modified to achieve a high level of health protection, one could not properly speak of a 'common food policy'.[98]

---

[94] For instance, in the 1985 Communication it is stated that EC food legislation should be limited to provisions justified by the need to provide consumers with information not exclusively related to the health and fair trade and to provide for adequate and necessary official controls of foodstuffs. See supra note 70.

[95] E. Vos, 'EU Food Safety Regulation in the Aftermath of the BSE Crisis', 23 *Journal of Consumer Policy* 233 (2000) and F.D. Lafond, 'The Creation of the European Food Authority. Institutional Implications of Risk Regulation', 10 *European Issues* 4 (November 2001).

[96] R. Dehousse speaks of 'dual subsidiarity' of social regulation in the structure of the Treaty of Rome: 'subsidiarity with respect to the Community's main raison d'être, namely market integration, and subsidiarity with respect to national regulatory policies'. See R. Dehousse, 'Integration v Regulation? On the Dynamics of Regulation in the European Community', *Journal of Common Market Studies*, vol. XXX, n. 4, 1992, p 388.

[97] This amendment of the Treaty brought the 'scientific factor' into EC law. This is because the aim to attain a high level of protection was given the status of general objective of the Treaty, Article 100a (current Article 95) was amended so as expressly to require the Commission, 'in its proposal [...] concerning health, safety, environmental protection' to take into account 'any new development based on scientific facts'.

[98] C. Lister, in 1992, identified the following deficits in the Community food law: absence of substantive regulatory goals, tendency towards rigidity (recipe directives), tendency towards ambiguity, tendency towards new trade barriers by means of rigid rules, tendency towards double standards (for the EU and for third countries), tendency towards uncoordinated policy-making, particularly between food law and the common agricultural policy, and tendency towards non-transparent rule-making expressed by a lack of public discussion common in democratic societies. See C. Lister, *Regulation of Food Products by the European Community*, 285, Butterworths, 1992, pp 285–292.

4. The 'Emergency': Towards the 'Europeanisation' of Food Risk (1997–2002)

In the mid-1990s, in the wake of several food safety emergencies and food scares,[99] it became clear that the free movement of foodstuffs could no longer be the overriding principle of EC food law. Food safety was not only a consumer's concern, but also a condition *sine qua non* for a proper functioning of the internal market. A clear sign of this shift came from the ECJ's case law, which for the first time held that:

> [...] the protection of public health which the contested decision is intended to guarantee must take precedence over economic considerations.[100]

In the light of the above, it was therefore necessary to figure out how to reshape this European policy.

The BSE crisis contributed heavily to spreading this awareness among citizens and institutions by showing the inadequacy of the existing regulatory regime in ensuring a high level of public health and consumer protection.[101] As Chalmers notes:

> [t]he BSE crisis marked a Year Zero for the European Union food regime by forcing both Member States and the Community to acknowledge the shortcomings of the existing European approach to food safety issues.[102]

---

[99] In the long list of food safety crises and scandals of that time appear olive oil, contaminated wine, Perrier water, E.coli listeria, salmonella, polluted drinking water, BSE, dioxin sludge, animal feed, pesticides etc.

[100] C-183/95, *Affish* [1997] ECR 4315, at 43. See also the order in Case C-180/96 R *United Kingdom v Commission* [1996] ECR 3903, at 93.

[101] For further analysis of the impact of the BSE crisis on the evolution of the European Food regulatory system, see A. Alemanno, 'Food Safety and the Single European Market', in D. Vogel and C. Ansell (eds), *What's the Beef? The Contested Governance of European Food Safety*, MIT Press, 2006, pp 237–258; E. Vos, 'EU Food Safety Regulation in the Aftermath of the BSE Crisis', supra note 95, pp 227–255 (2000); Lafond, supra note 95; M. Hagenmeyer, 'Modern Food Safety Requirements – according to EC Regulation 178/2002', 4 *ZLR* 443 (2002); E. Millstone, 'Recent developments in EU food policy: institutional adjustments or fundamental reforms?', 6 *ZLR* 815 (2000); L. Buonanno et al, 'Politics Versus Science in the Making of a New Regulatory Regime for Food in Europe', 5 *EIPoP* (2001); S. Krapohl, 'Risk Regulation in the EU between interests and expertise – The case of BSE', 10 *Journal of European Public Policy* 189 (April 2003); P. Shears, F.E. Zollers and S.N. Hurd, 'The European Food Safety Authority. Towards coherence in food safety policy and practice', 106 *British Food Journal* 336–352 (2004) and K. Vincent, 'Mad Cows and Eurocrats – Community Responses to the BSE Crisis', 10 *European Law Journal* p 51, 2004.

[102] D. Chalmers, '"Food for thought": reconciling European risks and traditional ways of life', 66 *The Modern Law Review* 532, 534 (2003).

Facing a motion of censure from the European Parliament for alleged mismanagement of the BSE crisis[103], the Santer Commission promised radically to revise its internal organisation and to establish a new EC food regulatory regime and also made reference, for the first time, to the idea of establishing an independent European Food Agency (EFA).[104]

4.1   The New Approach to Food Safety after the BSE Crisis

A.   Green Paper on the 'General principles of Food Law and New Approach to Consumer Health and Safety'

The first highly symbolic step in the Santer manifesto was the adoption, on 30 April 1997, of a long-awaited Green Paper on the General Principles of Food Law in the EC (hereinafter: the Green Paper) aimed at launching a public debate on how the European Community should best regulate the area of food law.[105] The Community seriously envisaged the possibility of adopting a 'general Directive on food law',[106] containing

[103] In the European Parliament's debate on the report by the Temporary Committee of Inquiry into BSE on the 18 February 1997, the Parliament called on the Commission to bring together all the activities spread out among the various directorates-general within a single DG, to set up a framework directive on food law, to ensure the safety of the foodstuffs which circulate freely within the Community, to change the way in which scientific committees work etc. See Debate in plenary session of the EP, 18 Feb. 1997, 1-2 EU Bulletin 163–6 (1997). The Temporary Committee of Inquiry into BSE was set up by the European Parliament in July 1996, on the alleged contraventions or maladministration in the implementation of Community law in relation to BSE, without prejudice to the jurisdiction of the Community and the national courts of 7 February 1997, A4-0020/97/A, PE 220.544/fin/A.

[104] In his speech to the EC Parliament, the President of the Commission, Jacques Santer, after conceding that 'mistakes and errors have been made, some by the Commission', he appealed for 'the gradual introduction of a genuine food policy which places particular emphasis on the protection of consumer health'. See speech by President Santer, 19 February 1997, 1-2 *EU Bulletin* 163–6 (1997).

[105] The General Principles of Food Law in the European Union - Commission Green Paper. COM (97) 176, 30 April 1997 available at http://europa.eu.int/scadplus/leg/en/lvb/l21220.htm. Green Papers are texts of 'soft law' by which the Commission raises many issues relating to a certain area of regulation and ask opinions thereon of all interested parties, but without presenting its own point of view on the issues debated.

[106] This idea was not completely new. For several years there had been a call for a European regulatory framework for food. The most significant initiative was the 1993 publication, at the request of the EC Commission, of draft texts for a framework food directive by three food experts (C. Castang, A. Cleary, D. Eckert). The introduction to these proposals by the Commission for a 'first draft directive' setting out a general approach to food law explains this initiative by saying that '[...] a 'European framework law' might allow more effective systematic consistency and integration of the directives and regulations currently in force (both vertical and horizontal)'. Because the final conclusions of the three experts were too different to be summed up in a single document, they had each prepared their own draft. For a collection of these documents and to know more about this initiative, see F. Snyder, *A Regulatory Framework for Foodstuffs in the Internal Market*, Report on the Conference 6–7 May 1993, European University Institute, Department of Law, Florence, EUI Working Papers in Law No 94/4. Among the other voices pleading for the creation of
(continued...)

definitions of the fundamental terms of food law, particularly of the term 'food' itself.[107] Such an EC-wide definition was considered essential to determining the scope of the EC food laws.

In this context, although not putting into question the fundamental goals of EC Food law,[108] the Commission stressed that

> The BSE crisis has highlighted the need for a European food policy centred on the requirement that *only foodstuffs which are safe*, wholesome and fit for consumption be placed on the market. Health protection in relation with consumption of foodstuffs is to be an absolute priority at any time and not only something to be looked at in emergency situations.[109]

The protection of public health was gradually entering the EC food law policy as a goal deserving as much coverage as the other economic goals related to the CAP and free movement.[110] In order to ensure the development of a 'true food policy which attaches fundamental importance to the protection of the consumer and his health', the Commission proposed that:

> − the most recent and complete scientific evidence be considered when adopting new legislative measures;[111]

a general community framework for foodstuffs, see eg R. O'Rourke, supra note 49; M. Lugt, supra note 41, p 256; H. Mettke, 'Uber die Notwendigkeit eines Europaischen Rahmengesetzes fur das Lebensmittelrecht', *EFLR* 1/91, 5, p 19.

[107] Green Paper, supra note 105, at 3.

[108] More precisely, these are: the need to ensure a high level of protection of public health and safety, and of consumer protection; the need to ensure the free circulation of goods within the single market; the need for legislation to be based primarily on scientific evidence and risk assessment, in respect of our international obligations; the need to ensure the competitiveness of the European industry, allowing for flexible adaptation of the legislation to incorporate new technical developments as well as to enhance Community export prospects; the need to place the primary responsibility for safe food with industry, producers and suppliers, including imports from third countries, through self-checking provisions (so-called Hazard Analysis Critical Control Points systems or HACCP) backed up by official controls and appropriate enforcement; the need for legislation to be coherent, rational, consistent, simpler, user-friendly and developed in full consultation with all interested parties.

[109] Green Paper, supra note 105, at 11.

[110] This shift of objectives also clearly stems from the ECJ's judgment in the *BSE* case: Case C-180/96 R *United Kingdom v Commission* [1996] ECR 3903, pp 90–93 where the court recognised that in the application of emergency measures, such as those adopted by UK after the 1996 BSE scare, paramount importance must be accorded to the protection of public health, even at the expense of serious and possibly irreparable damage to commercial interests. See O'Rourke, supra note 49, pp 93–94 and Lugt, supra note 41, p 254.

[111] By referring to the scientific requirement ('The Community will increasingly be required to provide scientific justification for its measures at international level'), the Green Paper was the first document to underline the need for EC food law to comply with the Community's WTO obligations, thus echoing the programmatic idea of the SPS. See Green Paper, supra note 105, at 62, para 2.3.1.

- the precautionary principle approach be the rule in case of lack or incomplete scientific evidence;
- there is a clear responsibility for the safety of food at all stages of the food chain (primary production, processing, transport, handling and distribution, display at final point of sale);
- control and inspection measures are taken at all critical points throughout the food chain. The same rule applies to imported foodstuffs;
- appropriate measures are taken to inform consumers about the nature and content of the food;
- the responsibilities of the various controlling agents (producers, Member States' authorities, the Commission, etc.) are clearly established.[112]

The Green Paper also began considering a possible involvement of the Community with nutrition and health issues without, however, providing any definitive answers.

From a policy perspective, the aim of the Green Paper was to examine the extent to which current legislation was meeting the needs and expectations of consumers, producers, manufacturers, and traders; to consider whether official control and inspection systems were operating effectively; and to determine future food law developments. The ultimate objective was to provide legislation which takes a harmonised approach to control and inspection for each part of the food production chain. The Community role in the field of control was not to replace the Member States, but to verify that the necessary controls are carried out in an effective and equivalent manner throughout the internal market. Steps should be taken to reinforce administrative and scientific cooperation between Member States and with the Commission in order to ensure equivalence of enforcement throughout the Community. While recognising that it is impossible to offer a zero-risk system, the legal framework should cover all potential risks at all stages, to the greatest extent possible.

According to the Green Paper, simplification and rationalisation of the existing food legislation should not result in a reduction of the level of protection of public health or consumer protection. Rather it should strike the balance between general provisions and more detailed prescriptive legislation, between the use of binding legislation and recourse to voluntary instruments, and between horizontal approaches and specific rules applicable to particular categories of foodstuffs.

---

[112] Green Paper, supra note 105, at 11–12.

In November 1997, the European Commission and the European Parliament organised a conference to discuss the Green Paper and the 140 reactions to this document made by all parties interested, but it did not lead to a proposal for Community legislation[113].

Along the same lines, the Amsterdam Treaty, agreed by the European Union's political leaders on 17 June and signed on 2 October 1997, fully acknowledged public health protection and consumer protection as objectives of the European integration process and, accordingly, conferred on the Commission new responsibilities as to their attainment.[114]

The next step in reshaping EC food law was the Commission's publication of the 'Communication on Consumer Health and Safety' in May 1997.[115] This text, almost simultaneously with the Green Paper, laid down the foundations for a new EC food regime as announced by the Commission's president, Jacques Santer, before the European Parliament on 18 February 1997.[116] In particular, the Commission set out the action which it was taking to reinforce the manner in which it obtains and makes use of scientific advice, and operates its control and inspection services, in the interests of consumer health and food safety. The new approach, laying down a new political departure, was based on three general principles:

- separation of legislative responsibilities (risk management) and those relating to scientific advice (risk assessment);[117]
- separation of legislative responsibilities and those relating to controls and inspections;
- enhanced transparency and dissemination of information throughout the decision-making process and monitoring activities.[118]

In order better to satisfy these objectives and to enhance consumer health protection, Directorate General (DG) XXIV of the European Commission was reorganised.

---

[113] A summary of the reactions to the Green Paper are available at http://europe.eu.int/comm/dg03/publicat/ consumer/ foodcom.pdf. For a report of the conference, see G.H. Schipper, 'Herstel consumentenvertrouwen en niet de interne markt stond centraal', *VMT* 18 December 1997, No. 26–27.

[114] The Amsterdam Treaty is available at http://europa.eu.int/abc/obj/amst/en/.

[115] Communication from the Commission on consumer health and food safety, COM(97) 183 final.

[116] Speech by Jacques Santer, President of the European Commission, to Parliament on 18 February 1997 available at http://europa.eu.int/abc/doc/off/bull/en/9701/p203001.htm.

[117] Although laying down this crucial conceptual framework to be used in the analysis of risk, the Commission had not yet provided a theoretical design to realise a distinction between risk assessment and risk management.

[118] Communication on consumer health, see supra note 115, at 9–10.

The division between 'responsibility for legislation' and 'scientific consultation' was established by entrusting the latter to DG XXIV, renamed DG on Consumer Policy and Consumer Health Protection (DG SANCO),[119] which thus became responsible for the scientific assessment system. The Commission had in particular placed the management of all the Scientific Committees working in the field of foodstuffs[120] and responsibility for inspection and control under the authority of this DG and had reorganised the relevant Directorate General to have specific responsibility for consumer health.[121] Thus, the scientific committees, being subject to the exclusive control of a DG totally oriented to the consumer, were distanced from the legislative wing of the Commission services. At the same time they were removed from direct industrial pressures.[122] In particular, the committees were regrouped and coordinated by a Scientific Steering Committee (SSC) in order to achieve greater synergy and effective coordination.[123]

The proper functioning of these Committees was to be based on three main principles: excellence, independence and transparency. To satisfy the principle of excellence, scientific evaluation had to be undertaken by eminent scientists.[124] The principle of independence required scientists

[119] DG SANCO stands for *Direction Générale de la Santé et de la Protection des Consommateurs*.

[120] Since 1974, the European Commission has established several scientific committees, such as the Scientific Committee on Food, the Scientific Committee on Veterinary Medicine, the Scientific Committee on Pesticides and the Scientific Committee on Animal Nutrition. These committees were located in different Directorates General and were in charge of 'critically examining risk assessments made by scientists belonging to Member State organisations' and advising the Commission on any scientific problem related to their specific competence. After being heavily criticised for lack of coordination and for being too close to the needs of industry in the wake of the *BSE* outbreak, the European Parliament urged the Commission to revise the structures of the scientific committees. This led to two commission decisions, one establishing a Scientific Steering Committee (SSC), regrouping all the chairpersons of the Committees in the field of consumer health and food safety, and the other to establish eight Scientific Committees. See, respectively, Commission decision 97/03/EC and Commission decision 97/579/ EC.

[121] However, some areas of food law remained outside of DG Health and Consumer Policy (now DG-SANCO), falling within the competence of DG AGRI.

[122] Communication on Consumer health, see supra note 115, at 9–10

[123] Commission Decision 97/404/EC of 10 June 1997 setting up a Scientific Steering Committee (SSC), OJ 1997 L 169/85, and Commission Decision 97/579/EC setting up Scientific Committees in the Field of Consumer Health and Food Safety, OJ 1997 L 237/ 18. The SSC was set up to coordinate the work of the individual Scientific Committees and to address scientific issues that cut across two or more of the Committees and scientific issues outside all of their remits.

[124] In accordance with directive 97/404/EC, setting up a Scientific Steering Committee, the Commission has established the selection criteria for the appointment of the committee member in the 'Call for expressions of interest for the post of Member of one of the Scientific Committees' (available at http://europe.eu.int/comm/dg24/health/dc/call_en.html). In accordance with these criteria, the Commission gives preference to those scientists with: professional experience in the field of consumer health and more specifically in the areas covered by the field of competence of the committee concerned;

(continued...)

serving in the scientific committees to be free from interests which might be in conflict with the requirement of providing independent advice. Lastly, to improve openness and transparency, all documents, minutes, pre-opinions and opinions were to be available on the internet for easy access by all interested parties (individuals and associations, EC institutions and national authorities).

The Community response to the new regulatory challenge was based on the assumption that good management would have helped in solving the difficulties that had arisen from the possible ways of dealing with scientific advice.

In particular, the Communication introduced its official doctrine of 'risk analysis', made up of three distinct components: risk assessment,[125] risk management[126] and risk communication.[127] This crucial conceptual distinction would subsequently be reiterated in all Community documents and legislative texts relating to scientific expertise. This distinction aimed at enabling decision-makers to act with the best knowledge of the scientific data relating to a certain phenomenon. Only once the risk assessment is carried out by an independent body of experts, is it possible to act at the risk management stage by deciding whether to authorise a certain activity or substance on the market. Risk communication should then be entrusted with the task of exchanging information with all parties concerned in as transparent a manner as possible.

As for control and inspections, the new approach aimed at providing a harmonised system of control for all parts of the food production chain by following three main orientations. First, in view of the broad range of areas covered by the legislation, control and inspection were to follow a scheme of priorities established by risk assessment procedures and, secondly, they were to ensure that the whole of the food production chain is covered (from 'plough to plate'). Thirdly, the control activities were to be exercised through the introduction of formal audit procedures enabling the Community to assess the control systems operated by the national authorities. This new regime had to be implemented through the Food and Veterinary Office ('FVO').

experience in risk assessment; experience in delivering scientific opinion at national or international level; professional experience in a multidisciplinary and international environment; attested scientific excellence; experience in scientific management. See directive 97/404/EC, 1997 OJ L169/85.

[125] According to the definition provided by the *Codex Alimentarius*, risk assessment is a scientifically based process consisting of the identification and characterisation of hazards, the assessment of exposure and the characterisation of the risk.

[126] Risk management may be defined as the process of weighing policy alternatives in the light of the results of risk assessment and, if required, selecting and implementing appropriate control options, including regulatory measures.

[127] Risk communication consists in the exchange of information with all parties concerned.

Although food inspections are outside the scope of this book, it is important to observe that since 1997, the FVO, situated in Dublin, Ireland, assures effective control systems and evaluates compliance with EU standards within the EU and in third countries in relation to their exports to the EU. The FVO does this mainly by carrying out inspections in Member States and in third countries exporting to the EU. In particular, its 163 inspectors are in charge of monitoring the observance of food hygiene, veterinary and plant health legislation within the European Union.[128]

If the reforms introduced by the 1997 Consumer Health and Safety communication have represented a significant change in the way food law was produced within the EC, the reformed scientific system did not erase the link existing between the scientific committees and the Commission. This outcome was unsatisfactory to the extent that it could have triggered popular discontent in the wake of the BSE food scandal. However, although that communication only represented a first Community rough reaction to the new challenges of food safety, these efforts to protect consumer health by focusing on scientific advice, risk analysis and control and inspection heralded the future European Food Authority and the newly-established regulatory food safety regime.

Two years after the changes undertaken in 1997, the then Director General of DGXXIV (now termed SANCO), H. Reichenbach, mandated three scientists – Philip James, Fritz Kemper and Gerard Pascal – to assess the existing system of scientific advice and, ultimately, to conceive a better system in terms of independence (to ensure that the scientists are free from conflicting interests), transparency (easy access to information on the activities of the committees and their advice) and excellence (risk evaluation is undertaken by eminent scientists).[129]

Their report, submitted to the newly appointed Commission in December 1999, sketched out the blueprint for a European Food Authority and was immediately endorsed by the newly-appointed Commission President Prodi as one of the priorities of his mandate in his first speech before the European Parliament.[130]

---

[128] For a detailed reconstruction of the history of the FVO, see Lugt, supra note 41, pp 33–35. It must be observed that all FVO inspection reports are published on the internet so that the cases in which Member States are acting in an insufficient way are brought to attention of the public.

[129] The full text of the mandate given to them has been made public at http://europa.eu.int/comm /food/fs/sc/future _mandate _en.html.

[130] Speech of Romano Prodi to European Parliament, Plenary Session, 3 October 2000 (SPEECH 00/352).

B.   The White Paper on 'Food Safety: Towards a Comprehensive and Integrated Approach to EC Food Policy'

In the meanwhile, several events contributed to speeding up the food safety policy reform, by actively counteracting the Member States' resistance to the establishment of an independent European Food Authority. Such events included the ongoing BSE crisis, growing consumer concerns about the safety of GM foods and, lastly, the dioxin contamination outbreak in Belgium.

In the wake of these food emergencies and consumer scares, the European Commission proposed combining the envisaged radical reform of the EC food regulatory framework with an innovative institutional reform by publishing the White Paper on Food Safety on 12 January 2000.[131]

By launching a debate and involving the governments and all other parties affected by the new regime, this text expressed the need for a major structural change in the food safety regime in order to achieve the twin objectives of ensuring the highest standard of food safety and restoring consumer confidence. In order to achieve these goals, it proposed the establishment of a European Food Authority within the framework of a broader EC food safety legal reform mainly driven by the need to guarantee a high level of food safety throughout the Community.

The guiding and somewhat 'revolutionary' principle of the White Paper was that food safety policy must be based on a 'comprehensive, integrated approach' throughout the food chain; across all food sectors; between the Member States; at the EC external frontier and within the EC; in international and EC decision-making for and at all stages of the policy-making process. The assumption was that a comprehensive, integrated, approach would lead to a more coherent, effective and dynamic food policy.

More precisely, the strategic priorities of the White Paper were:

–   to create as soon as possible a 'European FDA':[132] the European Food Authority;

---

[131] White Paper on Food Safety COM (99) 719, 12 Jan. 2000 available at http://europa.eu.int/comm/dgs/health/ consumer /library/pub/pub06_en.pdf.

[132] The US Food and Drug Administration (FDA), together with the EU Medicines Evaluation Agency (EMEA), represent the two main models the EC Commission relied upon in conceiving the European Food Safety Authority (EFSA). The EFSA then inspired the creation of two other agencies, the European Maritime Safety Agency and the European Aviation Safety Agency. See Chalmers, supra note 102, p 532.

–   to propose a new legal framework laying down the general
     principles of Food law such as:
     –   responsibility of feed manufacturers, farmers and
          food operators;
     –   traceability of feed, food and its ingredients;
     –   proper risk analysis through
          –   risk assessment (scientific advice and
               information analysis),
          –   risk management (regulation and control) and
          –   risk communication, and
          –   the application of the precautionary principle
               if appropriate
–   consistently to implement a 'farm to table' approach in food
     legislation;
     –   to establish the following principles:
     –   that the information for consumers should include
          that the Commission shall test the performance of
          Member States' control capacities and capabilities
          through audits and inspections;
     –   all the instructions needed by way of an appropriate
          labelling to allow consumers to make more informed
          choices;
     –   that Member States need to ensure surveillance and
          control of the economic operators.

Following the two 1997 Communications (the Green Paper and the
Consumer Health and Safety Communication), the Commission
confirmed the central role of risk analysis as 'the foundation on which
food safety policy is based'[133] and described its three components: risk
assessment (scientific advice and information analysis), risk management
(regulation and control) and risk communication.

Relying on this conceptual framework, the White Paper proposed to
entrust the authority with particular responsibilities for both risk
assessment and communication on food safety issues, while denying it
any role in risk management activities. Thus, the scope of the mandate
to be given to the authority reflected the 'generally accepted need to
functionally separate risk assessment and risk management'[134] already
sketched out by the Commission in its Communication on Consumer
Health. The EFA was envisaged as being: 'guided by the best science';
'independent of industrial and political interests'; 'open to rigorous
public scrutiny'; 'scientifically authoritative' and closely intertwined
'with national scientific bodies'.[135] As such, the EFA was designed to

[133] See White Paper, supra note 131, at 12.
[134] Ibid, at 29.
[135] Ibid, at 38.

become the 'automatic port of call' when scientific information on food safety and nutritional issues were sought.

Moreover, the White Paper advocated the adoption of 84 distinct measures (involving around 30 directives and regulations) forming a complete and coherent corpus of legislation covering all aspects of food products from 'farm to table'. The new legal framework should have virtually covered the whole of the food chain, including animal feedstuffs, animal health and welfare, hygiene, contaminants and residues, new types of food, food additives and flavors, packaging materials and ionising radiation.

As for food safety controls, in light of the wide variations in the manner in which Community legislation is being implemented and enforced at national level,[136] the Commission proposed that, in cooperation with the Member States, a Community framework for the development and operation of national control systems would be developed. In this regard, the White Paper revamped the Rapid Alert System,[137] whereby there is a coordinated exchange of information between the Commission and Member States regarding potential threats to the health and safety of consumers, by extending obligations on economic operators to notify food safety emergencies and to ensure that appropriate information is provided to consumers and trade organisations. The EFA would be entrusted with this operation.

5.   The 'Global Approach': the New Food Safety Regime and the Establishment of EFSA (2003–Present)

It took more than two years for the Commission to transform the White Paper into a proposal for a regulation 'laying down the general principles of food law, establishing the European Food Authority, and providing for urgent measures in matters of food safety'.[138] This proposal, published

---

[136] Under the EC Treaty, the main responsibility for food control and the enforcement of EC food law lies with the national authorities of the Member States, while the EC Commission monitors how these competent authorities exercise their powers.

[137] The Rapid Alert System has been established by Directive 92/59/EEC and is a network of national authorities managed by the European Commission that exchanges information on measures taken to address potential health risks in the area of food and feed. See infra Chapter 3, Section 4.2. The Rapid Alert System for Foodstuffs (RASFF).

[138] Proposal for a Regulation of the European Parliament and of the Council laying down the general principles and requirements of food law, establishing the European Food Authority, and laying down procedures in matters of food, COM/2000/0716 final, OJ 2001 (C 96 E), at 247–268 then modified by amended Proposal for a Regulation of the European Parliament and of the Council laying down the general principles and requirements of food law, establishing the European Food Authority, and laying down procedures in matters of food safety (presented by the Commission pursuant to Article 250 (2) of the EC Treaty), COM/2001/0475 final, OJ 2001 C 304 E, at 273–326.

in March 2001, contained all the main features originally sketched out by the White Paper and was subsequently adopted, with few amendments,[139] as Regulation (EC) No 178/2002 on the 28th of January 2002 with a title only slightly modified.[140] Its legal basis can be found in Articles 37, 95, 133 and 152(4)b of the EC Treaty.

This regulation represents the first attempt to address all aspects of food safety at EC level by laying down a comprehensive EC food policy covering horizontally all stages of production, processing and distribution of food and feed (from 'farm to fork'), thus encompassing raw materials, intermediate products and finished food products as well as feedstuffs (Article 3.3).[141] Being addressed not only to the EC institutions, but also to the Member States, the scope *ratione personae* of this policy is unusually broad.[142]

The overriding principles of the new EC food regime are that food law, enacted either by the Community or by its Member States, should seek to achieve a high level of protection of human health and consumer interest, while ensuring the effective functioning of the internal market. The Regulation seeks to achieve these twin principles in two main ways:

a) It establishes a comprehensive EC-wide food policy, addressed to both the Community and its Member States, by setting forth:
    i.   general principles (Articles 5–10);
    ii. obligations and requirements of Food Law (Articles 10–21); and also
    iii. some procedures in matters of food safety (Articles 50–57).
b) It creates a new independent agency:
    the European Food Safety Authority (Articles 21–49).

These aspects will be the subject of the following two chapters. While the general food law part of the regulation will be discussed within Chapter II, the new institutional configuration of the EC food policy, the European Food Safety Authority, will be the main focus of chapter III.

[139] For a detailed analysis of the differences between the two proposals, see L. Gonzalez Vaqué, 'Objetivo: la Seguridad Alimentaria en la Union Europea', in 223 *Gaceta Juridica de la UE* 59 (2003), pp 61–71.
[140] For some comments on the new EC Food Regulatory framework, see L. Gonzalez Vaqué, 'Objetivo: la seguridad alimentaria en la Union Europea', supra note 139; M. Hagenmeyer, 'Modern food safety requirements – according to EC Regulation 178/2002', supra note 101, pp 443–459 (2002); F. Aubry-Caillaud, 'La Sécurité Alimentaire au Sein de l'Union Européenne: les Apports de l'approche Globale', in 4 *Europe* 4–7 (2003).
[141] See Articles 1.3. and 4 defining the scope *ratione materiae* of the Regulation. According to Article 1.3 this regulation does not apply to 'primary production from private domestic use or to the domestic preparation, handling or storage of food for private domestic consumption'.
[142] L. Gonzalez Vaqué, 'Objetivo: la Seguridad Alimentaria en la Union Europea', supra note 139, p 62.

CHAPTER II
THE EUROPEAN REGULATORY REGIME FOR FOOD SAFETY

### 1.	The New Regulatory Regime for Food Safety in Europe: a Brief Analysis

This chapter aims at exploring the philosophical rationale underpinning the first comprehensive EC food regime, by analysing its main principles and obligations and focusing in particular on the risk analysis scheme set forth by the new regulation.

Risk analysis, building upon the distinction between risk assessment and risk management, represents the conceptual frame within which the new food safety regime must operate. Indeed, the dichotomy between risk assessment and risk management not only dictates the procedural dimension to be followed by both the EC institutions and the Member States when adopting food safety legislation but also determines the institutional framework of the new regime by imposing a clear cut separation between the risk assessors (EFSA) and the risk managers (EC Institutions).

Before setting out the regulatory and institutional framework of the new food policy, the regulation provides, for the first time, common definitions in the food area, thus injecting legal certainty into an area which has hitherto been extremely empirical, having been left to the legislative autonomy of Member States. Although EC food law has been enacted since the beginning of the 1960s, a uniform Community definition of foodstuff has never been introduced. Only some vertical directives dealing with specific products contain a specific description of the regulated products.[1]

Therefore, to give full meaning to the new European food regime it has been necessary to formulate a clear-cut definition of food, thereby defining its scope of application.

### 1.1	Definitions

The provision that best exemplifies the 'global approach' pursued by this regulation is represented by Article 2, providing for the first time a common definition of 'food' throughout the Community:

---

[1] See, eg, for a definition of milk Directive 2001/114/CE in OJ L15 2002, at 19, for a definition of honey, Directive 2001/110/CE in OJ L10 2002, at 47 and for a definition of cacao and chocolate Directive 2000/36 in OJ L 197, at 19 ss.

> [For the purpose of this Regulation], 'food' (or 'foodstuffs') means any substance or product, whether processed, partially processed or unprocessed, intended to be, or reasonably expected to be ingested by humans.

In accordance with the notion of 'foodstuffs' contained in the *Codex Alimentarius*[2] and in the majority of Member States' legislation,[3] this definition is deliberately wide in scope, including – by virtue of paragraph 2 of Article 2 – drinks, chewing gum and any substance, 'intentionally incorporated into the food during its manufacture, preparation or treatment'. It therefore includes all of the food chain and it extends also to those substances 'reasonably expected to be ingested by humans'.

The concept of ingestion seems to suggest that it is intended to cover all products which may be consumed by mouth or nose or administered by gastric intubation. Conversely, it might also be inferred that it would not cover products administered directly into the blood stream.

However, the ingestion criterion should not be overestimated in determining whether a product should be classified as food. Having being asked whether the method of ingesting a product is significant for its classification as a medicinal product or as a foodstuff, the court has held in the case *HLH Warenvertirebs GmbH* that:

> the competent national authority must decide on a case-by-case basis, taking account of all the characteristics of the product, in particular its composition, its pharmacological properties, to the extent to which they can be established in the present state of scientific knowledge, the manner in which it is used, the extent of its distribution, its familiarity to consumers and the risks which its use may entail.[4]

---

[2] The *Codex Alimentarius* Commission is an intergovernmental body jointly sponsored – since 1962 – by the World Health Organization and the Food and Agriculture Organization (WHO/FAO, both United Nations bodies) to develop international food standards. Over 160 countries are members, including all EU Member States and, since 2003, the EC itself. The definition of foodstuffs elaborated within Codex is: 'materials which are intended to be eaten, chewed or drunk by human beings, whether in a changed or unchanged state, to satisfy their nutritive requirements or for enjoyment. Materials which when correctly used form a permanent constituent of a food may be considered as foodstuffs'. Codex functions through two types of committees: Codex Committees, which prepare the norm proposals, and the coordination committees, which intervene when groups of countries are involved and can propose norms for the geographical area involved. All member countries participate equally in Codex and have one vote each. Recognised international Non-Governmental Organisations (eg consumer, industry and academic bodies) are also free to attend as observers, and are able to speak, but not vote. For a more detailed presentation of Codex, see Part II, Section 4.1 The SPS and the Relevant International Standards Organisations, point A Codex Alimentarius Commission.

[3] See Gonzalez Vaqué, 'Objetivo: la Seguridad Alimentaria en la Union Europea', in 223 *Gaceta Juridica de la UE* 59 (2003), p 62.

[4] Cases C-211/03, C-299/03 and C-316/03 to C-318/03, *HLH Warenvertriebs GmbH* [2005]

(continued...)

However, the ingestion criterion plays a crucial role in delimiting the scope of regulation 258/97 on novel foods. To distinguish between food, within the meaning of regulation 178/2002, and novel food, as falling within the above-mentioned directive, one has to verify whether the food or the food ingredient in question has been consumed to a significant degree by humans before the reference date. As stated by the court, 'that condition refers to consumption, in the sense of ingestion by humans'.[5]

Moreover, the reference to 'partly processed' and 'unprocessed food' resolves the long-standing question as to whether EC food laws also covered primary products, which may either be for human consumption or for industrial use. Their clear inclusion within the scope of the definition means that producers are subject to all relevant obligations arising under EC food legislation for all substances used in food.

The inclusion within the notion of foodstuff of those substances 'reasonably expected to be ingested by humans' is also noteworthy. The rationale underpinning this formulation is clearly to guarantee that a substance which may enter the food chain, but which is also susceptible to be used in other industrial sectors, must be subject to the same discipline as required for foodstuffs as long as it appears that it won't be marketed within a food product.

The insertion of a definition of food must be welcomed for several reasons. As shown above, it introduces legal certainty in determining the scope of the different EC food laws, by solving several interpretative questions which had arisen through time. Lacking a common definition of food, the scope of several pieces of horizontal legislation, such as those relating to additives or hygiene, was determined on a case by case basis by the Member States concerned. Moreover, to avoid possible problems of interpretation, the last paragraph of Article 2 clearly lists those items that do not fall within the food definition: feedingstuffs, live animals (unless prepared for human consumption), plants (prior harvesting), medicinal, cosmetics, tobacco and tobacco products, narcotics, residues and contaminants. Finally, it paves the way for a broad application of the new EC food regime, covering virtually the whole 'farm to fork' distribution chain.[6]

---

not yet published, at 89–94. See L. González Vaqué, 'Novedades en la Jurisprudencia del Tribunal de Justicia de las Comunidades Europeas Relativa a las Nociones de Medicamento y Alimento?: una Primera Valoración de la Sentencia HLH Warenvertriebs', *Revista de Derecho Alimentario*, Julio 2005, p 21.

[5] Cases C-211/03, C-299/03 and C-316/03 to C-318/03, *HLH Warenvertriebs GmbH* [2005] not yet published, at 83.

[6] It must, however, be noted that in non-harmonised sectors, the notion of food provided for by the general food regulation does not prevail over national legislation.

Although the wide definition of the word 'foodstuff' provided in the regulation may seem to include medicinal products, it is apparent from point (d) of the third paragraph of that article that 'food' does not cover medicinal products within the meaning of Directive 2001/83. Likewise, Article 1(2) of Directive 2002/46 relating to food supplements[7] provides that that directive is not to apply to medicinal products as defined by Directive 2001/83.

However, what is the position when a product satisfies equally well the conditions for classification as a foodstuff and the conditions for classification as a medicinal product? In those circumstances, one may wonder which provisions of EC law may be applicable to this particular product. In *HLH Warenvertirebs GmbH* the ECJ has held that only the provisions of Community law specific to medicinal products may apply to this particular product. This interpretation is supported by Article 2, paragraph 2, of Directive 2004/27/EC amending Directive 2001/83/EC, which is worded as follows:

> [...] in case of doubt, where taking into account all its characteristics, a product may fall within the definition of a 'medicinal product' and within the definition of a product covered by other Community legislation the provisions of this Directive shall apply.[8]

The general regulation's efforts are not limited to the notion of foodstuff. Although the definition of foodstuff is the only one to which an entire Article of the regulation is devoted, Article 3 provides definitions for many other expressions such as 'food law', 'food business', 'food business operator', 'feedingstuff', 'placing on the market', 'risk analysis' and its three components, and also 'traceability', 'hazard', 'final consumer', so that they form a 'common basis for measures governing food taken in the Member States and at Community level'.[9]

Finally, the horizontal and 'global' nature of the first EC definition of foodstuffs implies that not only are national legislators bound by it, but that the EC institutions are similarly bound. Indeed, by virtue of Article 4 of the regulation, both national and EC prior food legislation has to conform to the general principles of EC food law by January 2007.

---

[7] Directive 2002/46 of 10 June 2002 on the approximation of the laws of the Member States relating to food supplements, OJ L 183/51.

[8] Directive 2004/27/EC of the European Parliament and of the Council of 31 March 2004 amending Directive 2001/83/EC on the Community code relating to medicinal products for human use, OJ L 136/34.

[9] See Recital (4) of the preamble of the regulation.

1.2 General Principles and Requirements of Food Law

Chapter II of the regulation, listing the general principles of food law, principles of transparency, general obligations of food trade and general requirements of food law, forms 'a general framework of a horizontal nature to be followed when measures are taken' by both the Community and its Member States. Finally, EC food law disposes of a central unifying text setting out the fundamental principles of Community food law.

A.   General Objectives

Article 5 provides that EC food law must pursue one or more of the general objectives as sketched out in the preamble:

-    high level of protection of human life and health;
-    protection of consumers' interests, including
     -    fair practices in food trade
     -    the protection of animal health and welfare, plant health and the environment;
-    the free movement in the Community of food and feed.

Furthermore, the same provision, demonstrating the EC's willingness to honour fully the obligations stemming from the WTO TBT and SPS Agreements,[10] establishes the duty to take into consideration, in the development of food policy, the existing international standards, unless such standards would not be an effective means to achieve fulfilment of the food policy's legitimate objectives, or where there is a scientific justification for not doing so or where such standards would result in a different level of protection from the one pursued by the Community.[11]

[10] These two agreements were concluded at the end of the Uruguay Round to prevent technical legislation which is intended for the protection of human health or safety, the protection of health or life of humans, animals or plants, and consumer protection against deceptive practices resulting in unjustified barriers to international trade. In particular, the agreements encourage WTO members to participate actively in the development of harmonised international standards in order to reduce the obstacles to trade arising from conflicting national rules. Measures adopted in conformity with these standards are presumed to comply with the provisions of the agreements. However, WTO members are free to adopt measures that provide a higher level of protection than that ensured by the relevant international standard, provided that these measures do not result in unjustifiable restrictions on international trade. The basic aim of these two agreements is to maintain the sovereign right of any member to establish the level of health protection it deems appropriate, but to make sure that this right is not misused for protectionist purposes. By imposing on members the duty to implement international standards in their legislation, these agreements introduce for the first time a form of positive integration within the WTO: not only do measures not have to discriminate, but they also have to be adapted to international standards in order to reduce their divergence. See infra Part II, Chapter I, Historical background of the GATT/WTO Regulation of Food.

[11] Article 13 lett. a) encourages the EC not only to adopt legislation in conformity with international standards but also to contribute to their development within international organisations and non-governmental organisations.

In accordance with Article 4 of the SPS Agreement, the regulation also encourages the development of bilateral agreements on recognition of equivalence (MRAs) of specific food and feed-related measures.[12]

B.   Risk Analysis: the EC 'Specificity' in Assessing Risk

1.   *The principles of Risk Analysis*

The risk analysis scheme, set forth by Article 6 of the regulation, represents the foundation (*Grundnorm*) on which the new EC food policy is based. This is the main tool upon which the regulation relies in seeking to achieve its primary two-fold objectives: a high level of protection of human health and life and the free movement of foodstuffs.[13] In the absence of an express definition within the regulation, risk analysis may be described as a process designed to control situations where an organism, system or population could be exposed to a hazard.[14]

Both the Community and national food laws should be based on a risk analysis scheme structured upon the following three different components:

–   risk assessment,
–   risk management, and
–   risk communication.

These three interconnected components of risk analysis provide a systematic methodology for the determination of effective, proportionate and targeted measures or other actions to protect health. This structured approach incorporating the three distinct but closely linked stages of risk analysis was firstly developed and popularised by the US National Research Council (NRC)[15] and today finds support in the main guidelines

---

[12] For an analysis of the Mutual Recognition Agreements (MRAs) concluded by the EC, see A. Alemanno, 'Gli Accordi di Reciproco Riconoscimento di Conformita dei Prodotti tra Regole OMC ed Esperienza Europea', 2–3 *Diritto del Commercio Internazionale* 379–406; A. Alemanno, 'Le Principe de la Reconnaissance Mutuelle au delà du Marché Intérieur. Phénomène d'Exportation Normative ou Stratégie de "Colonialisme" Règlementaire?', in *Revue du Droit de l'Union Européenne*, 2/2006, p 273 ss and O'Rourke, *EC Food Law* 185 (1st ed., 1998), pp 196–7.

[13] Article 5 (1) of the regulation.

[14] See, Descriptions of selected key generic terms used in chemical hazard/risk assessment; OECD/IPCS, October 2003, available at http://www.oecd.org.

[15] For decades the National Research Council (NRC) has been called on to consider how to improve decisions about risks to public health, safety and environmental quality. The NRC has conducted a series of studies on how society can understand and cope with those risks. In particular, the distinction between risk assessment and risk management has been originally conceived in 1983 with the publication of *Risk Assessment in the Federal Government: Managing the Process* (also called the Red Book), a study that sought 'institutional mechanisms that best foster a constructive partnership between science and
(*continued...*)

developed by national and international organisations dealing with risk analysis.[16]

Although, as will be seen below, a clear-cut distinction between risk assessment and risk management is not unproblematic, its main rationale is to provide decision-makers with scientifically-grounded data on which to base regulatory choices. According to AG Mischo, this distinction meets a dual goal: it ensures a rational technocratic dimension to the decision-making process, while enabling the political process to be independent from the results of scientific assessments.[17]

While not clearly expressed by Article 6 of the regulation ('food law shall be based on risk analysis'), the duty to conduct a risk analysis when adopting food law bears not only on the EC institutions but also on Member States. This may be inferred from the fourth and fifth recitals in the preamble of the regulation where it is stated that since there are important differences in relation to concepts, principles and procedures between the food laws of the Member States, 'it is necessary to approximate these concepts, principles and procedures so as to form *a common basis for measures governing food and feed taken in the Member States and at Community level'*.

However, the duty to conduct a risk analysis procedure before adopting a piece of legislation related to food law allows of an exception. Article 6 explicitly recognises that food law should not be based on risk analysis

government'. Subsequently, this distinction played a crucial role in the development of an organisational separation of risk assessment and risk management in many US regulatory agencies. However, as we will see further, later publications of the NRC recognised the difficulties of maintaining a sharp dividing line between the two processes and emphasised the importance of ensuring interaction and communication between risk assessors and risk managers. See P. Stern and H. Fineberg (eds), *Understanding Risk: Informing Decisions in a Democratic Society*, National Academy Press, Washington DC, 1996 and for a brief account of this development see also I. Suezenauer, M. Tamplin, B. Buchanan, S. Dennis, L. Tollefson, A. Hart, 'Briefing Paper: US Experience', European Workshop on the interface between Risk Assessment and Risk Management, 2003 available at http://www.ra-rm.com.

[16] See, within the US, *National Research Council Report on Science and Judgment, National Academy Press*, 1994 Washington, DC 1994, at 4 (prepared by a committee of the National Research Council/National Academy of Science in response to a US Environmental Protection Agency request mandated by the Clean Air Act Amendments of 1990); see, within the OECD, Descriptions of selected key generic terms used in chemical hazard/risk assessment; OECD/IPCS, October 2003, available at http://www.oecd.org; see within FAO and WHO, Joint FAO/WHO Expert Consultation, Application of Risk Analysis to Food Standards Issues (WHO/FNU/FOS/95.3, 13–17 March, 1995, Geneva 1995), p 6; Joint FAO/WHO Expert Consultation, Risk Management and Food Safety, (27–31 January, 1997), FAO Food and Nutrition Paper 65, 1997; Joint FAO/WHO Expert Consultation, The Application of Risk Communication to Food Standards and Safety Matters, Rome, 2–6 February 1998, FAO Food and Nutrition Paper 70, 1999.

[17] Opinion in Case 192/01 *Commission v Denmark* [2003] ECR 9693.

where this is not appropriate to the circumstances or the nature of the measure. There are good reasons to believe that this derogation refers to crisis or emergency situations and therefore, although apparently open-ended, such a provision is narrowly framed.

One may wonder whether this obligation to conduct a risk analysis implies a duty to consult a particular organism. As will be illustrated below, there is no general obligation to request a scientific opinion from EFSA, unless this is expressly provided for by EC secondary legislation as, for instance, in the case of a pre-market approval mechanism or a system of positive lists.[18]

Furthermore, the duty to conduct a risk analysis may seem to exist only to the extent that a particular measure aims at achieving the general objective of a high level of protection of 'human health and life'. In contrast, the precautionary principle, according to Article 7, applies in order to ensure a high level of health protection regardless of whether it is human, animal or plant health at stake. It might be presumed that the risk analysis scheme does not have to be followed when a measure to be adopted in the food sector does not put public health at risk or when it may potentially endanger only animal or plant health.

However, according to Article 152, paragraph 4(b), the duty to conduct a risk analysis within the Common Agricultural Policy may exist in relation to measures in the veterinary and phytosanitary fields which have as their direct objective the protection of public health.

Finally, this duty seems to have been given general application to all science-based measures by the Court of First Instance ('CFI'), which has stated that:

> when a scientific process is at issue, the competent public authority must, in compliance with the relevant provisions, entrust a scientific risk assessment to experts who, once the scientific process is completed, will provide it with scientific advice.[19]

---

[18] While the former mechanism regulates the introduction and marketing of GMO foods (Regulation 1829/2003 on Genetically Modified Food and Feed, OJ L 287), the latter controls the marketing of food supplements within the EC (Directive 2002/46 of 10 June 2002 on the approximation of the laws of the Member States relating to food supplements, OJ L 183/51).

[19] Case T-13/99 *Pfizer Animal Health v Council*, [2002] ECR II-3305, at 157.

Diagram 2. This diagram illustrates the relationship between the three components of risk analysis (Source: WHO/FAO 1997):

Risk Analysis Framework

1.1   The nature of Food Risks

Before examining the risk analysis framework provided by Regulation 178/2002, it may be useful to briefly look at the nature of risks addressed by this risk analysis model.

The regulation is rather ambiguous on this point to the extent that its provisions sometimes refer to both human health and life[20] risks and at other times solely to health risks.[21] To alleviate this ambiguity, one should have regard to Article 152 EC, which is one of the legal bases for the general food regulation. This provision, in defining EC action in the public health sector, refers to life-threatening diseases, thus clearly showing that all risks relating to human health may be included in the notion of health risks.[22] Therefore, one may conclude that when EC law employs the term 'health' it also includes human life.

At the same time it may reasonably be argued that food risks consist of those health risks stemming from the ingestion of foodstuffs. However, the general food regulation seems to distinguish between food risks

[20] Preamble 2, and Article 5.1.

[21] See Article 1.1. This is the result of an amendment that has taken away the original reference made to human life on the ground that the expression 'protection of life might give rise to confusion and it is already included within 'protection of health'. See A5-0416/2001, 22 November 2001.

[22] In particular, Article 152, paragraph 1, reads: ' [...] Community action, which shall complement national policies, shall be directed towards improving public health, *preventing human illness and diseases, and obviating sources of danger to human health*. Such action shall cover the fight against the major health scourges, by promoting research into their causes, their transmission and their prevention, as well as health information and education'.

which consist of the 'biological, chemical or physical agent in [...] food or feed with the potential to cause an adverse health effect'[23] and risks stemming from the existence of hazards which are 'a function of the probability of an adverse health effect and the severity of that effect, consequential to a hazard'. It remains uncertain as to why the legislator has adopted such different definitions of risks.

What is clear is that the risks covered by the regulation are those stemming from normal conditions of use of the food by the consumer and at each stage of production, processing and distribution.

The existence of risk may be expressed both in qualitative and in quantitative terms. A quantitative evaluation provides information on the probability of adverse effect occurrence, whereas a qualitative one only expresses the possibility of a causal link, without indicating its likelihood.

The case law developed thus far on the nature and main characteristics of food risk is quite advanced.

Thus, for instance, it has been held that a food risk, to be considered as such, must either threaten the health of the whole population or merely that of particular, sensitive categories of people, such as children and elders.[24] The risk may be not only immediate but also may occur gradually and, according to Article 14(4)(a) of the regulation, it may even arise in relation to subsequent generations of those who have ingested the dangerous substance. Moreover, a food risk may be genuine and real but also potential, ie a risk which, although scientifically confirmed, has to be fully demonstrated.[25] However, as has been noted in the case law, a potential risk includes neither a 'hypothetical [n]or academic consideration'[26] nor 'a mere conjecture'[27], but requires 'nevertheless to be adequately backed up by the scientific data available at the time when the measure was taken'.[28] Thus, for instance, in the *BSE* line of cases, the potential food risk that was feared by the British authorities was essentially experimental, not being fully scientifically proven but merely based on ten identified cases of a variant of Creutzfeldt-Jakob disease. Here, although there was no direct evidence of a link between this disease and ingestion of beef, 'on current data and

---

[23] Article 3 of the regulation.
[24] Case 97/83, *Melkunie*, [1984] ECR 2386 and Case C-375/90, *Commission v Greece*, 1993 ECR 2055.
[25] See, eg, Case T-13/99 *Pfizer Animal Health v Council*, [2002] ECR II 3305 para 157.
[26] Case E-3/00 *Efta Surveillance Authority v Norway* [2001] EFTA Court Report 2000/2001, 73, at 25.
[27] Pfizer, Case T-13/99 *Pfizer Animal Health v Council*, [2002] ECR II 3305, para 389.
[28] Ibid, at 144.

in the absence of any credible alternative', the most likely explanation at that moment was that these cases were linked to exposure to BSE before the introduction of the ban in 1989. It is against this backdrop that the Spongiform Encephalopathy Advisory Committee ('SEAC'), an independent scientific body which advised the United Kingdom Government, concluded that '[T]his is cause for great concern'.[29] This shows that whilst the pressure of public opinion and mass media campaigns may not be enough to justify the adoption of a precautionary measure, the collection of 'reliable scientific data' combined with 'logical reasoning' may enable the decision-makers to act in situations of scientific uncertainty.[30] However, as will be shown below, to trigger the adoption of precautionary measures one has to prove not only that the scientific data are 'reliable' but also that they are insufficient, inconclusive or imprecise in nature, making it impossible to determine with sufficient certainty the risk in question.[31] In other words, although the available scientific evidence data find their origin in reliable and reputable sources it does not allow a causal link to be established between the suspected public health threat and the factors examined.

1.2   Risk Assessment (RA)

Risk assessment is defined by Article 3 of the regulation as 'a scientifically based process' consisting of four steps:

   −   hazard identification;
   −   hazard characterisation;
   −   exposure assessment;
   −   risk characterisation.[32]

It shall be based on the available scientific evidence and undertaken in an independent, objective and transparent manner.

Risk assessment is typically seen as a method for organising and analysing scientific information. According to its best known definition it may be described as a 'systematic approach to organising and

---

[29] Case C-180/96, *United Kingdom v Commission* [1998] ECR 2265, at 9.
[30] Commission Communication on the Precautionary Principle, COM(2000) 1, 2 Febuary 2000, at 5.1.2 Scientific Evaluation.
[31] Ibid, at 5.1.3 Scientific Uncertainty.
[32] The identification of these four scientific stages in risk assessment was originally sketched out by the National Research Council (NRC) in *Risk Assessment in the Federal Government: Managing the Process* (Washington DC: National Academy Press, 1983), supra note 15. Note that although the NRC talks about dose-response assessment instead of hazard characterisation, this different wording does not seem to hide any conceptual difference for present purposes. The same steps within risk assessment may be found in Descriptions of selected key generic terms used in chemical hazard/risk assessment; OECD/IPCS, October 2003, available at http://www.oecd.org.

analysing scientific knowledge and information for potentially dangerous activities or for substances that might pose risks under specified conditions'.[33] A typical result of risk assessment may be that the intake of, or the exposure to, a certain substance may give rise to a risk probability of 1/1,000 000 of developing a disease in a given period.

The first step of RA, the so-called hazard identification, is meant to guarantee a risk analysis which focuses on the descriptive elements of the potential risks by identification of known or potential inherent health hazards. Hazard is the potential of an identified source, biological, chemical or physical agent, to cause an adverse legal effect.[34]

The next stage, the heart of RA, is generally expected to offer a more structured overview of the probabilities of certain phenomena or events. It aims at providing a qualitative and, wherever possible, quantitative description of the inherent properties of an agent or situation having the potential to cause adverse effects. Finally, there is an intermediary phase in which the exposure of an organism, system or population to an agent is evaluated, before leading the way to the final risk management stage: risk characterisation. This is the stage of risk assessment in which the balance between confidence and uncertainty in the assessment is characterised and in which the risk assessment results are expressed in a form which is useful to decision-makers and risk managers. It may be defined as the qualitative or quantitative determination, including attendant uncertainties, of the probability of occurrence of known and potential adverse effects of an agent in a given organism, system or population, under defined exposure conditions.[35] The assessment may include a range of possibilities from a risk that is unlikely to occur, but which is potentially calamitous, to a risk with a very high probability of occurring, but whose impact is minor.

The EC courts' case law has also endorsed this four-steps analysis as the main component of risk assessment.[36]

EFSA's role in relation to risk assessment is defined in recital 34 of the preamble to the regulation: 'the Authority should take on the role of an independent scientific point of reference in risk assessment'. A separation of responsibilities for risk assessment and risk management is implied later in the same paragraph where it is stated that EFSA 'may be called

---

[33] NRC Science and Judgment, supra note 16, at 4.

[34] Article 3 (14) of the regulation.

[35] See Descriptions of selected key generic terms used in chemical hazard/risk assessment; OECD/IPCS, October 2003, available at http://www.oecd.org, reflecting the most up-to-date and harmonised descriptions of risk analysis terms adopted by OECD/IPCS, October 2003.

[36] See Case T-13/99, *Pfizer Animal Health v Council* [2002] ECR II 3305, para 156.

upon to give opinions on contentious scientific issues, thereby enabling the Community institutions and Member States to take informed risk management decisions'.

The definition of risk assessment in the general food regulation as a 'scientifically based process' relies on scientific research, both in the establishment of general procedures and in the production of data for particular assessment. The regulation requires EFSA to commission scientific studies necessary for the performance of its mission and to cooperate and avoid duplication with Member States or Community research Programmes. Thus, many projects in the Commission's 5th and 6th Framework programmes are providing basic knowledge for risk assessment.

Although this risk analysis framework would seem to be presented as a harmonised model to be followed by virtually all bodies carrying out scientific activities throughout the Community, it is limited to the food sector. For this reason, a Working party is currently developing a harmonised approach to risk assessment procedures among the Scientific Committees advising the European Commission in the area of human, animal and plant health and on the environment.[37] Unfortunately, at this stage of the work, it has not been possible to consider the risk assessment activities of scientific committees in Directorates General other than DG SANCO.[38]

1.3   Risk Management (RM)

Having verified the existence and the nature of the risk at stake, the competent authorities are supposed to decide whether and how to act. Both national and EC Member States are called upon to manage the health risk by first establishing the risk threshold which may be acceptable for the whole of society. In doing so, the EC institutions, unlike the Member States, are under the Treaty obligation to pursue a 'high level of protection'[39].

---

[37] Notably, a working party has been established on 'Harmonisation of Risk Assessment Procedures' specifically to address the general principles of risk assessment and its application to broad consumer health issues, with a particular reference to measures that would enhance compatibility of approaches between the Scientific Advisory Committees. See the Updated Opinion of the Scientific Steering Committee on Harmonisation of Risk Assessment Procedures, adopted on 10–11 April 2003. A full Second Report on the Harmonisation of Risk Assessment Procedures was expected by the end of 2004.

[38] Opinion of the Scientific Steering Committee on Harmonisation of Risk Assessment Procedures, July 2005.

[39] Article 95, paragraph 3, EC. In fact, as illustrated above, in the absence of Community harmonisation with regard to a certain product, Member States are free, at least in principle, to choose the level of protection of public health they deem appropriate to ensure within their own territory. This freedom is, however, restricted by Article 28 EC governing the free movement of goods within the EC.

Competent authorities' discretion is not limited to the evaluation of the significance of a risk, which leads to a determination of the acceptable level of protection, but it also extends to the choice of the action to be taken to achieve that protection threshold.

Risk management is defined by Article 3 of the regulation as a process, distinct from risk assessment, of weighing policy alternatives in consultation with interested parties, considering risk assessment and other legitimate factors, and, if need be, selecting appropriate prevention and control options.[40] Therefore, this definition contains, without separating them, two stages of risk management. The first stage is the evaluation of the significance of a risk, which leads to determining the level of protection deemed appropriate by that society. The second is the choice of the measure intended to achieve that level of protection.

In particular, it must be noted that this definition impliedly contains a clear recognition that scientific risk assessment alone cannot, in some cases, provide all the information on which a risk management decision should be based, and that other factors relevant to the matter under consideration should legitimately be taken into account. Recital 20 of the preamble, containing a list of such factors, mentions societal, economic, traditional, ethical and environmental factors and the feasibility of controls.[41] Hence, it seems that the competent authorities must take into account the impact of their chosen measure on the collective interests rather than on those of single subjects. This is confirmed by the White Paper on Food Safety, which has paved the way for the elaboration of the general food regulation, wherein it is said that

> [i]n the decision making process in the EU, *other legitimate factors* relevant for the health protection of consumers and for the promotion of fair practices in food trade can also be taken into account. The definition of the scope of such legitimate factors is presently being studied at international level particularly in Codex Alimentarius. Examples of such other legitimate factors are environmental considerations, animal welfare, sustainable

---

[40] Similarly, risk management is defined within the OECD as a decision-making process involving considerations of political, social, economic, and technical factors with relevant risk assessment information relating to hazard so as to develop, analyse, and compare regulatory and non-regulatory options and to select and implement appropriate regulatory response to that hazard. See Descriptions of selected key generic terms used in chemical hazard/risk assessment; OECD/IPCS, October 2003, available at http://www.oecd.org. For a more cautious definition of risk management see Joint FAO/WHO Consultation Risk Management and Food Safety, at 9, where it is defined as the process of weighing policy alternatives in the light of the results of risk assessment and, if required, selecting and implementing appropriate control options, including regulatory measures.
[41] The inclusion of 'other legitimate factors' in food risk assessment is confirmed by Article 7(1) of Regulation 1829/2003 on Genetically Modified Food and Feed [2003] OJ L 287.

agriculture, consumers' expectation regarding product quality, fair information and definition of the essential characteristics of products and their process and production methods.[42]

Therefore, while risk assessment is seen as a technical or scientific phase in which experts analyze information, risk management is conceived as the political or value-laden stage in which risk managers consider scientific, political, economic and social information in order to determine what the acceptable level of risk is and how it should be attained.

As a result, the risk management of a decision does not consist solely of a selection of both the facts and the methods of assessment, but it also implies a complex decision on whether to accept the risks in question or not (risk choice). In particular, in contrast to risk assessment, risk management is 'the public process of deciding how safe is safe'.[43]

While in principle risk management deals with real and known risks, it might also be conducted *vis-à-vis* unknown risks. In the latter case, it is the precautionary principle which will inform the risk management stage.

As has been stated, in this last scenario: 'the decision is no longer to be regarded as the final point of a linear process of decision-making, but is, instead, to be regarded as a decision which is meant to bind uncertainty while, at the same time, allowing for a re-entry of uncertainty, because it uses the decision and proposed decision process for the generation of new knowledge which can, in the future, be used for the revision of the assumptions on which the decision was based'.[44]

The question whether the precautionary principle may also play a role within risk assessment is particularly controversial.[45] Unfortunately, as will be illustrated below, this question does not seem to find a clear-cut answer within the general food regulation.[46] According to some,

---

[42] White Paper on Food Safety COM (99) 719, 12 Jan. 2000 available at http://europa.eu.int/ comm/dgs/health/ consumer /library/pub/pub06_en.pdf, at 15.
[43] N. de Sadeleer, 'The Precautionary Principle in EC Health and Environmental Law', 12 *European Law Journal* 147.
[44] K.H. Ladeur, 'The Introduction of the Precautionary Principle into EU law: A Phyrric Victory for Environmental and Public Health Law? Decision-making Under Conditions of Complexity in Multi-Level Political Systems', 40 *Common Market Law Review* 1465.
[45] C.R. Sunstein, *Laws of Fear: Beyond the Precautionary Principle*, Cambridge: Cambridge University Press, 2005; J. Bohanes, 'Risk Regulation in WTO Law: A procedure-Based Approach', 40 *Columbia Journal of Transnational Law*, pp 342–343 and De Sadeleer, supra note 43, pp 179–195.
[46] See infra Chapter II, Section 1.2. General Principles and requirements of food law, C. The Precautionary Principle: from Scientific Uncertainty to Legal Certainty.

incorporating the principle into the risk assessment phase would inject an excessive dose of subjectivity into a process which is supposed to be value-free and evidence-based.[47] Some, in contrast, believe that precaution should be applied both by scientists completing the risk assessment, 'on the basis of science policy guidelines issued to them by risk managers' authorities', and by the regulatory authorities themselves, 'which have to draw the necessary implications'.[48] This position rests on the controversial assumption according to which 'risk assessors' technical precaution (when developing hypotheses, modelling and interpreting evidence and data)' would be distinguishable from 'the risk managers' regulatory precaution (when taking normative regulatory action)'.[49]

According to the risk analysis model provided by Article 6 of the regulation, while risk assessment must be based on the available scientific evidence and carried out independently, risk management must take its results into account. In other words, the scientific assessment of risk to the consumer from a product forms the basis for risk managers to develop risk reduction or containment measures. Once the risk has been identified, it is the decision-maker's responsibility to decided if it is acceptable, which may mean adopting an attitude of zero tolerance.
In particular, risk managers (EC institutions and the Member States' authorities) have to take into account:

a)   the results of risk assessment, in particular the 'opinions' of the EFSA;
b)   'other factors legitimate to the matter under consideration' (the so-called 'social factors'[50] or 'non-economic factors'), and
c)   the 'precautionary principle' within the limits laid down in Article 7

in order to achieve the general objectives of food law.

Article 5, paragraph 3, adds to this list:

d)   'international standards [...] except where such standards or relevant parts would be:
    a.   an ineffective or inappropriate means for the fulfilment of the legitimate objectives of food law, or
    b.   where there is a scientific justification, or

---

[47] D.A. Wirth, 'The Role of Science in the Uruguay Round and NAFTA Trade Disciplines', *Cornell International Law Journal*, Vol. 27, pp 817–859, 1994, p 837; Bohanes, note 45, pp 339–340.
[48] T. Christoforou, 'The Precautionary Principle and Democratizing Expertise: a European Legal Perspective', in 30 *Science and Public Policy* 3, 2003, p 210.
[49] Ibid.
[50] Echols, 'Food Safety Regulation in the European Union and the United States: Different Cultures, Different Laws', *Columb. J. Eur. L.* 525, p 530.

c.   where there would result in a different level of protection
from the one determined as appropriate in the Community'.

While the role of the precautionary principle and of EFSA's scientific
opinions will be discussed in later chapters, the next section focuses on
the 'other factors' to be considered within risk management. Finally, the
relevance of international standards will be dealt with in the next part
dedicated to the WTO food regulatory regime.

1.4   Role of Non-scientific Factors

Although science plays the major role at the risk management stage, the
regulation reserves the right of risk managers to take other factors into
consideration when reaching a final decision.[51] This is because

> it is recognized that scientific risk assessment alone cannot,
> in some cases, provide all the information on which a risk
> management decision should be based'.[52]

These relevant factors for the health protection of consumers may consist,
for instance, of societal, economic, traditional, ethical and environmental
factors.[53] This approach is in line with the Communication on the
precautionary principle, which indicates that in case of scientific
uncertainty

> [...] judging what is an 'acceptable' risk for society is an eminently
> political responsibility. Decision-makers faced with an
> unacceptable risk, scientific uncertainty and public concerns have
> a duty to find answers'.[54]

The perceived need to also consider non science-based factors within
the decision-making process characterises the European approach to
risk analysis by differentiating it greatly from the one adopted by the
US regulatory agencies and by the WTO/SPS legal frameworks.[55]

---

[51] Several provisions of the Regulation provide that risk management decisions may
consider not only risk assessment but also 'other legitimate factors'. See preamble (19),
Article 3(12) and Article 6(3). See also Article 7(1) of Regulation 1829/2003 on Genetically
Modified Food and Feed [2003] OJ L 287.

[52] See Recital (19) of the Regulation.

[53] The list of examples provided by the Preamble of the Regulation seems slightly narrower
than the one contained within the White Paper (see supra note 42), which mentions
'environmental considerations, animal welfare, sustainable agriculture, consumers'
expectation regarding product quality, fair information and definition of the essential
characteristics of products and their process and production methods'. However, both lists
containing mere examples, their differences do not carry any particular value and should not
be overemphasised.

[54] Commission Communication on the precautionary principle, supra note 30, at 5 of the
summary.

[55] See infra part IV, chapter II.

The former EC Health and Consumer Protection Commissioner, David Byrne, has recently confirmed that the Commission will take into consideration not 'only science, but also many other matters, for example, economic, societal, traditional, ethical or environmental factors, as well as the feasibility of controls'.[56]

The EC approach to risk analysis has been effectively described as a system in which 'scientific knowledge is authoritative, but not exclusively so'.[57]

What are the consequences stemming from such a European non-exclusively science-based approach to risk analysis?

The well-known *Hormones* dispute,[58] 'one of the longest running trade disputes in the modern trading system',[59] between the EC and the US exemplifies the impact which the EC analysis of risk may have, not only on its external trade relations, but also on its internal market dimension.[60] This dispute involved a complaint by the United States and Canada against an EC regulatory regime prohibiting the administration of growth hormones (such as estrogen, progesterone and testosterone) to cattle.[61] This prohibition not only addressed the use of these hormones domestically, but also banned the production and importation of meat

[56] D. Byrne, *EFSA: Excellence, Integrity and Openness*, Inaugural meeting of the Management Board of the European Food Safety Authority, Brussels, 18 December 2002, available at http://www.europa.eu.int/rapid /start/ cgi/guesten.ksh?p_action.gettxt=gt&doc=SPEECH/ 02/405/0/RAPID&lg=EN&display=.

[57] G. Skogstad, 'The WTO and Food Safety Regulatory Policy Innovation in the European Union', in 39 *Journal of Common Market Studies* 485, 490 (2001).

[58] See Appellate Body Report, *European Communities–Measures Concerning Meat and Meat Products*, WT/DS26/AB/R, WT/DS48/AB/R (Jan. 16, 1998) (adopted February 13, 1998; Panel Report, *European Communities–Measures Concerning Meat and Meat Products*, WT/DS26/R/USA (Aug. 18, 1997) (hereinafter: *EC–Hormones*). For a detailed reconstruction and insightful analysis of the dispute, see T. Christoforou, 'Science, Law and Precaution in Dispute Resolution on Health and Environmental Protection: What Role for Scientific Experts?', in J. Bourrinet and S. Maljean-Dubois (eds), *Le Commerce International des Organismes Génétiquement Modifiés* (2003), p 239 and D. Wüger, 'The Implementation Phase in the Dispute Between the EC and the United States on Hormone–Treated Beef', 33 *Law & Pol'y Int'l Bus.* 777 (2002).

[59] A.O. Sykes, 'Domestic Regulation, Sovereignty and Scientific Evidence Requirements: A Pessimistic View', G. Bermann and P.C. Mavroidis (eds), *Trade and Human Health and Safety*, Cambridge University Press, 2006, p 260.

[60] On this dispute, notably on its genesis, see, eg, T. Christoforou, 'Settlement of Science-Based Trade Disputes in the WTO: A Critical Review of the Developing Case Law in the Face of Scientific Uncertainty', (2000) 8 *N.Y.U. Environmental Law Journal*, pp 622 ss.; J. Scott, 'Of Kith and Kine (and Crustaceans): Trade and Environment in the EU and WTO' in J.H.H. Weiler (ed), *The EU, NAFTA and the WTO: Towards a Common Law of International Trade*, Oxford: OUP, 2000; S. Pardo Quintillán, 'Free Trade, Public Health Protection and Consumer Information in the European and WTO Context', 33 *Journal of World Trade* p 147 (1999) and R. Howse, 'Democracy, science and Free Trade: Risk Regulation on Trial at the WTO' (2000) 98 *Mich.L.R.* 2329.

[61] See Council Directive 81/602/EEC concerning the prohibition of certain substances having a hormonal action and of any substances having a thyrostatic action (OJ L222 32-

(continued...)

derived from animals treated with non-therapeutic growth hormones. The concern was the potential for cancer in humans resulting from the consumption of hormone-treated beef. This regulatory regime was adopted by the EC institutions notwithstanding the advice of the Scientific Working Group proving that the outlawed growth-hormones were harmless to human health. The ban triggered not only the US and Canadian reactions but also some internal resistance.[62] Member States were split over the decision: while France, Germany, Italy and the Netherlands supported the total prohibition, the UK and EIRE opposed it so strongly as to lead to the controversial legislation being brought before the European Court of Justice.[63]

The EC ban turned out to be motivated by a complex mix of political, social, economic and conflicting scientific factors that, as we have seen, may now formally enter into the EC food decision-making process directed at the adoption of safety measures. Today we would probably define such a mix of different interests under the 'collective preference' label launched by Pascal Lamy.[64]

Notwithstanding the existence of a scientific consensus concerning a certain substance, the possibility of taking 'other legitimate factors' into consideration may lead to divisions across Member States over controversial food safety measures, while at the same time bringing the EC measures into conflict with the WTO framework.

Although understandable in terms of policy *realpolitik*, this opening up to non-science-based factors may increase the existing division between Member States in the assessment of the level of protection to be provided to their citizens. But what is worse is that it puts the EC regulatory

---

33); Council Directive 88/146/EEC prohibiting the use in livestock farming of certain substances having a hormonal action (OJ L70 16–18) and Council Directive 88/299/EEC on trade in animals treated with certain substances having a hormonal action and their meat, as referred to in Article 7 of Directive 88/146/EEC (JO L128/36–38). Other measures relevant to the dispute are contained in Directives 72/462/EEC, 81/602/EEC, 81/851/EEC, 81/852/EEC, 85/358/EEC, referenced in Directive 88/146/EEC; the decisions, control programme and derogations referred to in Article 6(2), Article 6(7) and Article 7, respectively, of Directive 88/146/EEC; and any amendments or modifications, including Directives 96/22/EC and 96/23/EC.

[62] Thus, for instance, an association of pharmaceutical manufacturers sought the annulment of the Directive prohibiting the use of certain hormonal growth promoters for the purpose of fattening cattle. See Case 160/88 *Fedesa v Council* [1988] ECR 6399.

[63] Case C-180/96, *United Kingdom v Commission*, [1998] ECR 3903, at 93. See also Case C-157/96, *The Queen v Ministry of Agriculture, Fisheries and Food, ex parte National Farmers' Union et al* [1998] ECR I-2211. Contrary to the former case, the latter was not a direct action for annulment of the EC ban, but rather a preliminary ruling pursuant to a question about the validity of the EC measure from the UK High Court.

[64] See Pascal Lamy, *The Emergence of Collective Preferences in International Trade: Implications for Regulating Globalisation*, 15 September 2004, available at http://trade.ec.europa.eu/doclib/docs/2004/september/tradoc_118925.pdf.

framework in conflict with the WTO SPS Agreement. As will seen below, this agreement subjects all sanitary and phytosanitary measures to scientific evidence and risk assessment procedures by imposing on Member States the duty to demonstrate that their measures are necessary to protect human health. Under the existing SPS Agreement, scientific evidence is, at least textually, the only legitimate criterion upon which to base SPS measures. Yet, during the Uruguay Round negotiations, the EC tried hard to introduce other criteria besides scientific evidence upon which measures under the SPS Agreement could be based. It is curious to observe that, although the EC failed in its attempt, the WTO AB report in the *Hormones* case stated that:

> [...] there is nothing to indicate that the listing of factors that may be taken into account in a risk assessment of Article 5.2 was intended to be a closed list. It is essential to bear in mind that the risk that is to be evaluated in a risk assessment under Article 5.1 is not only risk ascertainable in a science laboratory operating under strictly controlled conditions, but *also risk in human societies as they actually exist,* in other words, the actual potential for adverse effects on human health in the real world where people live and work and die.[65]

The interpretation of this statement is controversial. While it might reasonably be argued that the EC approach to food safety regulatory policy would seem to find support in this reading of the SPS Agreement, the same ruling has been described as a demonstration that 'the SPS Agreement exalts the role of science far beyond the point it is appropriate, attempting to eliminate all 'non-science' factors from standard setting'.[66] Chapter II of Part IV offers a comparison of the role played by 'other legitimate factors' in the EC and the WTO, by also looking at Codex's risk management policies as well.

The next paragraph further explores the EC risk analysis model by focusing on the thorny relationship between risk assessment and risk management.

1.5   The Relationship between RA and RM

The relationship between risk assessment and risk management has been a topic of discussion since at least the early 1980s, when a report by the US National Research Council recommended that a clear conceptual

---

[65] *EC–Measures Concerning Meat Products* Appellate Body Report WT/DS26/AB/R, WT/DS48/AB/R adopted on 13 February 1998, para 187.
[66] J. Cameron, *The Precautionary Principle, in Trade, Environment and the Millenium,* G.P. Sampson and W.B. Chambers (eds) 1999, p 261.

distinction be made between them.[67] As we have seen, the EC food risk analysis model interprets and promoted this relationship in terms of clear-cut separation. This partition between the two main risk analysis components has found not only a normative dimension but also an institutional application within the general food regulation.

In particular, Article 6 of the regulation gives for the first time a normative expression to the 'functional separation' of risk assessment (RA) and risk management (RM), originally introduced by the 1997 Communication on Consumer Health and Safety and subsequently confirmed by the Green Paper on food law and the White Paper on food safety.[68]

The primary reason given for such a distinction or separation between these two components of risk analysis is a desire to ensure the independence and objectivity of the scientific process as conducted during the risk assessment stage. The idea was that only the introduction of a clear cut separation between risk assessors, who discuss facts, and managers, who discuss values, would effectively insulate scientific activity from political pressure and, accordingly, maintain an analytical distinction between the magnitude of a risk and the cost of coping with it.

As seen above, following the publication of such documents, several steps have been undertaken within the Commission institutionally to implement this approach to risk analysis by functionally separating those responsible for production, or the promotion of the market, from those responsible for the assessment of food safety. Thus, for instance, the management of the scientific committees was firstly transferred into what is now the Directorate General for Health and Consumer Protection (DG SANCO), and subsequently to the EFSA, a supposedly independent scientific body lacking any decision-making power.

Since the beginning of the 'emergency' period, a watertight separation between the risk assessment stage and risk management in the field of food has been increasingly seen as essential not only to guarantee independence and objectivity to the scientific process,[69] but also as a means of enhancing the democratic legitimacy of the decision-making

---

[67] National Research Council, 1983. *Risk Assessment in the Federal Government: Managing the Process*, supra note 15.

[68] White paper, supra note 42, para 32.

[69] Among the major drivers for this separation there was also a clear desire to remove value judgments from risk assessment and to prevent risk assessors from being unduly influenced by risk managers.

process by ensuring that decisions are ultimately taken by those who are accountable to the public.[70] The current regulatory regime, establishing a comprehensive EC food policy and the EFSA, is built upon this conceptual scheme, turning it into a regulatory and institutional reality.

The underlying rationale is self-evident: it is assumed that the separation between risk assessors and risk managers will make it clear who is responsible for what is decided. Therefore this 'functional separation' has been advocated not only for assuring the purity of scientific assessment, but also, at the time of the establishment of the EFSA, for enhancing the democratic legitimacy of the decision-making process.

However, this distinction between the purely technical assessment of risks by scientists and the management of these risks by the decision-makers needs to be questioned today.[71] As has been observed rhetorically, to what extent could we realistically conceive a risk analysis model where risk assessment is a first phase after which one would pass definitively across a certain demarcation line in order to engage in the second phase, ie risk management?[72] This division does not seem to be very credible insofar as it appears to be totally cut off from the concrete reality of scientific and political work processes. In fact, today neither science nor Politics may plausibly be perceived as constituting two definite disciplines capable of mechanically interacting in such a way that the second could only function once the first is terminated. Rather, as will be illustrated in the next paragraph, in the real world risk assessment and risk management inevitably overlap, both being characterized by a process which moves back and forth constantly. Thus, for instance, it is

---

[70] According to the Commission's White Paper, the EFSA should not be entrusted with risk management tasks because this would reduce democratic accountability within the Union, supra note 42, at 32.

[71] This distinction has been criticised for being artificial and difficult to maintain in reality. For a European perspective, see A. Alemanno, 'Le Principe de Précaution en Droit Communautaire: Stratégie de Gestion des Risques ou Risque d'atteinte au Marché Intérieur?', in *Revue du Droit de l'Union Européenne*, 4/2001, p 937; C. Noiville and N. De Sadeleer, 'La Gestion des Risques Ecologiques et Sanitaires à l'épreuve des Chiffres – Le Droit entre Enjeux Scientifique et Politiques', in *Revue du Droit de l'Union Européenne*, 2/2001, pp 406–8; and, more, recently, Ladeur, supra note 44. The US National Research Council has also questioned the wisdom and the appropriateness of the separation between risk assessment and risk management for excluding other sources of information which are necessary for good decision-making, see *NRC Understanding Risk*, 1996, supra note 15, pp 33–35. For a US perspective, see Walker, V.R., 'The Myth of Science as a 'Neutral Arbiter' for triggering Precautions', 26 *Boston College International and Comparative Law Review* 197, p 252 and Wirth, 'The Role of Science ...', supra note 47, pp 833–34.

[72] C. Noiville and N. De Sadeleer, 'La Gestion des Risques Ecologiques et Sanitaires à l'épreuve des Chiffres – Le Droit entre Enjeux Scientifique et Politiques', in *Revue du Droit de l'Union Européenne*, supra note 71, p 408.

well known that risk managers, when implementing precautionary measures, are supposed to combine risk management with new assessments which can in the end allow an adjustment of risk management to the evolution of knowledge. But, what such an artificial separation between risk assessment and risk management is especially liable to neglect is the relevant phenomenon of 'science policies' in risk analysis. As will be illustrated in the next section, these consist in decision rules about the way in which risk assessment scientists should proceed when they encounter specified types of uncertainties. These methodologies, techniques and processes, by influencing all steps of risk analysis, tend to inevitably predetermine the scope and nature of scientific assessment leading to an inherent bias towards certain unwanted outcomes.[73] As a result, science is susceptible of being perceived not only as a neutral process but as a socially constructed one. This is especially true when the underlying scientific knowledge is uncertain and calls for precautionary action.

Moreover, should these policies not be established by risk managers, such assumptions and techniques are likely to be established by the risk assessors, who would be empowered with management tasks. This outcome manifestly goes against the philosophy of 'separation' underpinning the whole EC food risk analysis model, by thus rendering it fictitious.

Therefore, although the 'functional separation' characterising the EC risk analysis model reflects the legitimate attempt to depoliticise the heavily scientific stage of risk assessment, which finds support within Codex,[74] it is guilty of overlooking the growing phenomenon of 'science policies' in risk assessment.[75] More generally, the introduction of such a straightforward distinction fails to take into due account the realities of the world in which risk assessment is conducted and risk management is performed.

Although there may well be a separation between the two processes, this separation is anything but clear-cut and, as will be demonstrated below, is a distinction which may well not even be desirable.

---

[73] Walker, 'The Myth of Science as a 'Neutral Arbiter' for Triggering Precautions', supra note 71, p 197; Wirth, supra note 47, pp 833–36; de Sadeleer, supra note 43, p 185 and J. Bohanes, 'Risk Regulation in WTO Law: A procedure-Based Approach', 40 *Columbia Journal of Transnational Law*, pp 354–359.

[74] Decision of the 24th CAC Session, 2001, *Criteria for Consideration of the Other Factors Referred to in the Second Statement of Principle*, at 32.

[75] On the role of science policies in risk analysis, see V. R. Walker, 'The Myth of Science as a 'Neutral Arbiter' for Triggering Precautions', supra note 71, pp 198 ss.

(a)   Science Policies and the Structural Limitations of
       Scientific Knowledge

If risk assessment is virtually an objective and neutral stage of risk
analysis, its purely scientific nature may be compromised by the
extensive use of methodologies and techniques which tend to
predetermine the expected outcomes of risk assessment. Although, at
least in principle, scientists provide their scientific assessment within
various scenarios and risk-mangers decide what the acceptable level of
risk is, it might happen that uncertainties are such that any scientific
method does not allow the presentation of any factual conclusion because
a proper scientific study cannot be conducted. In the presence of such a
scientific uncertainty, which is inherent in scientific judgments under
each of the four elements of risk assessment, scientists rely on a number
of assumptions and techniques to overcome such uncertainties.[76]
Scientists do so because of the pragmatic goal of risk assessment: to
provide risk managers with a faithful description of the scientific status
quo in relation to a specific substance.

These assumptions and techniques form part of a mainstream scientific
method called 'science policies'.[77] These may be defined as 'decision
rules about the way in which risk assessment scientists should proceed
when they encounter specified types of uncertainties', which are
established at political level.[78] Thus, for example, one of the most
common science policies is the presumption that a certain agent that
can cause disease in laboratory animals can equally cause disease in
humans. Other examples include the use of a linear dose-response model,
the assumption that absorption in animals and humans is approximately
the same or the use of body weight scaling for interspecies comparisons.[79]

Such polices are commonly used by US regulatory agencies in risk
assessment as a way of improving the consistency and transparency of
risk assessment undertaken in situations of scientific uncertainties.

---

[76] T. Christoforou, 'The Precautionary Principle and Democratizing Expertise: a European
Legal Perspective', supra note 48, p 207.
[77] Because these policies usually specify which assumptions must be used to bridge gaps
in scientific knowledge, they are also called 'inference guidelines' or 'default assumptions'.
See NRC 1983, at 28–37.
[78] V.R. Walker, 'The Myth of Science as a 'Neutral Arbiter' for Triggering Precautions',
supra note 71, p 214.
[79] For an illustration of the most common risk assessment policies used by the Codex
bodies in charge of conducting most of the risk assessment leading to the adoption of the
Codex standards (JECFA and JMPR), see Joint FAO/WHO Consultation Risk Management
and Food Safety, (FAO Food and Nutrition Paper 65, Rome 1997), pp 7–9. On science
policies see also S. Breyer, *Breaking the Vicious Circle*, Harvard University Press ed., 1993,
pp 43–44.

As a Joint FAO/WHO report has found, science policies are necessary since there are inevitable gaps in the science of risk assessment that need to be filled with default assumptions in order to be able to conduct a risk assessment. Each of these represent 'scientific value judgments', and, inevitably, the assumptions embodied in them can significantly influence the outcome of risk assessment. Each also represents a choice between a number of plausible alternatives. In fact, although substantially grounded in scientific data, these policies inevitably represent the outcome of a political selection. In fact, the need for science policy arises notably because of the limited scientific knowledge allowing multiple versions that are scientifically plausible. In other words, when dealing with decisions involving technical and scientific aspects, scientific expertise and political decisions become so intertwined as to become impossible to separate. In fact, the elaboration of these policies and assumptions boil down to a risk management activity.[80] As has been stated:

> [...] when normal science does not indicate definitely which data, models, or assumptions will, if used, provide a positive and verifiable risk assessment outcome, it is primarily the task of the risk managers to provide risk assessors with precise and binding guidance on the science policy to apply in such risk assessments.[81]

But *quid* when science policies have not been formulated by risk managers?

In these particular circumstances, decision-makers are confronted with situations where decisions about what is an acceptable risk are likely to have already been taken. It follows that, in the EC food context, where the question of science policies has not specifically been addressed at regulatory level, the European Food Safety Authority is never simply conveying information, but is inevitably endorsing a particular ideological model of politics.[82] Although many efforts (both normative and institutional) have been made to separate risk assessment and risk management's activities within the new regulatory regime, it would seem impossible to avoid some overlaps between the two.

In these circumstances, one may legitimately wonder whether the use of these policies and assumptions may jeopardise risk assessment as an objective and neutral basis for regulatory action. In other words, how is it possible to ensure that science retains its central role in the decision-making process, while taking appropriate account of the structural limitations of science?

---

[80] Walker, supra note 71, p 263.

[81] Christoforou, 'The Precautionary Principle and Democratizing Expertise: a European Legal Perspective', supra note 48, p 207.

[82] Along these lines of thought, see Chalmers, '"Food for thought": reconciling European risks and traditional ways of life', 66 *The Modern Law Review* 532, p 543.

And finally, *de iure condito*, what use is the separation between risk assessment and risk management?

Although a uniform and explicit use of science policies in scientific risk assessment may ensure consistency in approach,[83] it inevitably leads to the stripping of the 'functional separation' between risk assessment and risk management of its original goals: purity of scientific assessment and accountability of risk managers.

In order to avoid this, it is crucial to frame the growing use of science policies in risk analysis by the injection of some transparency. As 'science policies' pervade risk analysis and are crucial to completing most risk assessments today, awareness of the exact role they play within risk assessment is imperative. Notably, it may be important to understand the origin, methods and principles upon which underlying assumptions and techniques of science policies are developed, as well as elaborating a harmonised approach to risk assessment. The need to inject some transparency into the scope of science policies is particularly important to the extent, as seen above, that their use by risk assessors is capable of determining the outcome of risk assessment, thus dramatically blurring the separation between risk assessment and risk management. In particular, this need is strengthened by the fact that the assumptions of science policies may contain different biases. Thus, some authors, mainly from the US, have argued that existing risk-assessment methods and protocols are inherently biased in favour of avoiding overly stringent regulatory measures, which they fear may impose undue costs on innovation and technological progress and ultimately on society (progressive risk estimations).[84] On the other hand, others assert that such assumptions and policies tend to be chosen in order to arrive at the most conservative risk estimations.[85] The latter refer to the *Hormones* case, where the scientific experts advising the panel made repeated references to the way in which ADI (acceptable daily intake) figures were established using very sensitive end points from human primates, with the vulnerability of sensitive members of the population taken into account when establishing safety factors.[86]

---

[83] Walker, supra note 71, p 261; C. Button, *The Power to Protect*, Oxford and Portland, Oregon, 2004, p 99.
[84] Breyer, supra note 79; C.F. Cranor, *Regulating Toxic Substances – A Philosophy of Science and the Law*, 1993.
[85] Button, supra note 83, p 98.
[86] Button, supra note 83, p 98, refers to the *Hormones* Panel Report, Annex: Transcript of the joint meeting with experts, para 65. See also, Breyer, *Breaking the Vicious Circle*, Harvard University Press ed., 1993, p 46; Walker, 'The Myth of Science as a "Neutral Arbiter" for triggering Precautions', 26 *Boston College International and Comparative Law Review* 197, p 166.

It is argued that, notwithstanding the growing phenomenon of science policy, the distinction between risk assessment and risk management may still be maintained today, at least formally, within the EC context. This is because the former, in contrast to the latter, may rely solely on science, or on science combined with explicit science policies, while the latter may build upon 'other factors'.[87] However, to maintain the original goals pursued by this separation, it is imperative to render science policies not only explicit but also harmonised among the different scientific committees conducting food safety risk assessment.

Unless the assumptions and policies that have been employed to overcome scientific uncertainties in risk assessment are made explicit, courts may struggle in reviewing the legality of a science-based measure. In fact, lacking a transparent science policy, courts will not be able to analyse a measure and to determine to what extent it is science-based and whether 'other factors' have already been included within the risk assessment stage. As we have seen above, what it is likely and, therefore, foreseeable is that science policies tend to predetermine the scope and nature of risk assessment, leading to an inherent, either conservative or progressive, bias towards certain types of outcomes.

At the same time, it may be advisable to continue the current EC Commission's efforts aimed at harmonising risk assessment procedures within the Community. In its attempt to develop a harmonised common methodology for the Scientific Committee's activities, the Commission should improve consistency in the horizontal application of science policies and risk assessment techniques by developing some robust assessment practices.[88] The Scientific Steering Committee advised the Commission to establish a working party on 'Harmonisation of Risk Assessment Procedures' specifically to address the general principles of risk assessment and their application to broad consumer health issues, with particular reference to measures that would enhance compatibility of approaches within the Scientific Committees. Although it has been recognised that a completely common methodology for the activities of the Commission Scientific Committees may not be achievable, it is imperative to avoid the same chemical, biological or physical agent being dealt with quite differently by the EFSA Committees and the other Scientific Committees in different contexts, resulting in potential inconsistency in assessment and confusion in application.[89]

[87] Walker, supra note 71, p 166.
[88] A recent initiative has been launched by the European Consumer Safety Association (ECOSA) in the occasion of the Edinburgh Risk Assessment Conference. A working party has been established with the aim of developing a common nomenclature for risk assessors and a more standardised framework for the actual risk assessment process.
[89] Updated Opinion of the Scientific Steering Committee on Harmonisation of Risk Assessment Procedures, adopted on 10 April 2003, at 2.

It is argued that this is the only way in which, by maintaining consistency and transparency in the face of scientific uncertainty, risk assessment can remain scientifically 'objective'. At the same time, the suggested approach is also the only means of ensuring that the 'functional separation' can still have a meaning in the emerging EC food safety risk analysis scheme, by enabling, at the same time, the judiciary to accomplish its task of reviewing the legality of science-based measures. In conclusion, in light of all of the above, it is argued that the introduction of common scientific procedures, comprising explicit science policies, to inform risk assessment would be the most appropriate mechanism for achieving a transparent interface between risk assessment and risk management.

If some overlapping between risk assessment and risk management is inevitable, it is imperative that these 'overlapping areas' be rendered visible and be somehow accommodated within the EC food risk analysis model.

(b)   Links between Risk Assessors and Risk Managers

By showing some sensitivity to this growing trend of questioning the appropriateness of drawing a clear-cut distinction between the purely technical assessment of risks by scientists and the management of these risks by decision-takers, the same general food regulation expresses the need, not without some ambiguity, to strengthen the 'link between risk assessors and risk managers' in order to promote coherence and transparency between the risk assessment, risk management and risk communication functions.[90] Several other parts of the regulation emphasise the need for EFSA to combine its autonomous character with effective interaction; notably Article 40 underlines the need for close collaboration in relation to risk communication. This attempt to move towards a more fluid model of risk analysis which eschews formal conceptual distinctions and focuses on multiple inputs to the decision-making process, communication and public participation follows the trend launched by the same National Research Council in its 1996 Report on Understanding Risk.[91]

---

[90] Recital (35) of the preamble.
[91] NRC *Understanding Risk – Informing Decisions in a Democratic Society*, supra note 15. The mandate ('letter') given to the NRC called on the committee for 'guidance [...] to improve the dialogue between risk assessors and risk managers prior and during the development of a comprehensive assessment so that policy and management concerns are understood by all parties'. See preface, p xi.

As the debate on risk policies has clearly illustrated, the main reasons justifying the need for such an interaction is to ensure that risk assessment addresses the right questions and that the answers are properly interpreted in risk management. Recently, former EU Commissioner Byrne emphasised the importance of this interaction:

> [w]e must ensure productive interaction between risk assessors and risk managers. The process of objectively establishing, analyzing and scientifically interpreting the facts has to be done independently but not in a vacuum. This calls for close collaboration, interaction and exchanges between the Authority and those charged with the responsibility of managing risk'.[92]

There is therefore within the Community a growing belief that it is essential that risk assessment and risk management interact in an efficient manner, and that public perceptions and values are included in decision-making. What is needed is an interface between assessment and management that achieves an appropriate balance between these goals. In other words, there is a need to find ways for risk assessment and risk management to interact efficiently, while at the same time maintaining appropriate functional separation. In the 2003 EFSA annual report,[93] we read that Commission officials have attended all scientific panel meetings to 'ensure a seamless interface between the scientific advisor and the decision makers'. According to the Commission, the main reasons justifying the need for such an interaction is to ensure that risk assessment addresses the right questions and that the answers are properly interpreted in risk management. It will be seen below that, notwithstanding this noble intention, the attendance of Commission officials at the scientific panels raises serious doubts about scientists' independence by jeopardising the main goal pursued by the strict separation between risk assessors and risk managers.

The attendance of Commission officials at EFSA meetings is not bad per se, but it becomes so insofar as it is absolutely intransparent and takes place in a legal vacuum.

As EFSA's role is to provide 'an independent scientific point of reference in risk assessment [...] enabling the Community institutions and Member States to take informed risk management decisions', it is crucial to its proper functioning to find an appropriate interface between risk assessment and risk management in decision-making. A clear understanding of this interface is also crucial for the Scientific Committee

---

[92] Speech by David Byrne, European Commissioner for Health and Consumer Protection. Inaugural meeting of the Management Board of EFSA, Brussels, 18 September 2002.
[93] EFSA Annual Report 2003, at 17.

and panels of independent experts, which have been established to provide the EFSA's scientific opinions.

It is worth noting that even before the spread of concerns about the independence of risk assessment that were stimulated by food crises, many Community directives and regulations specified procedures for risk assessment and risk management for a wide range of issues. However, none of these pieces of legislation specify the distinction between these two instances as clearly as the general food regulation. Thus, for instance, both the procedures for the control of new and existing chemicals, as laid down in Council Directive 92/32/EEC and Council Regulation 793/93, and the procedures for biocides, as laid down in Directive 98/98, imply that both the acceptability of risk and the measures necessary to reduce risk in these sectors are decided as part of risk assessment, rather than risk management.

The issue of the relationship between risk assessment and risk management has recently been discussed thoroughly by a European workshop convened to consider ways of improving the interface between these instances, especially in the food safety area.[94] The conclusion of this workshop identified six key principles which, it is submitted, all go in the right direction:[95]

1. there is a need for functional separation of risk assessment and risk management, to ensure the independence of risk assessment;
2. efficient interaction between risk assessors and risk mangers is essential to ensuring that risk assessment is relevant to the needs of risk management and to optimising regulatory decision-making;
3. risk management should take into account all relevant factors including the social, economic and cultural consequences of alternative decisions, as well as their effects on health and the environment;
4. it is important to involve all stakeholders (interested parties) in the risk analysis process;
5. openness and effective communication are essential throughout the risk analysis process, and should facilitate increased trust between all those involved;
6. clear policies and appropriate expertise are essential for efficient risk analysis.

---

[94] RA-RM – European Workshop on the Interface between Risk Assessment and Risk Management, Brussels, September 2003.
[95] The conclusions of the RA – RM European Workshop are available at http://www.ra-rm.com/.

A number of different approaches have been developed that could be considered when implementing each principle. Thus, for instance, it has been proposed that in order to achieve a functional separation, there is no need to introduce a structural separation between the two instances, but rather that there should be a clear definition of roles, responsibilities and authorities of risk managers and risk assessors, including the responsibilities of different scientific committees or bodies.

These conclusions seem to confirm the position taken in the previous section where the imperative need to render science policies explicit and to harmonise their use within the emerging EC food risk analysis model has been stressed.

1.6 Conclusions: Flaws and Limits of the First European Risk Analysis Model

Regulation 178/2002 represents the first piece of EC legislation formally laying down a risk analysis model for Europe. This model is largely inspired by the scheme originally developed on the other side of the Atlantic by the National Research Council and, accordingly, builds upon the following three distinct aspects of risk analysis: risk assessment, risk management and risk communication. However, it also presents some particular features giving it some specificity.

The EC food risk regulation model has not solely found normative expression within the EC, but it has also largely inspired its food safety institutional framework, by providing the conceptual basis underpinning the current European food safety architecture. It relies on the assumption according to which scientific risk assessment delivers the facts to risk managers who then consider which regulatory action to undertake in light of 'other (non-scientific) factors'.

However, this vision presents some limits and flaws. First, a risk assessment cannot realistically be considered a neutral-value exercise but should rather be seen as a socially constructed exercise. This is because the assessment of whether a risk exists, its magnitude and its likelihood at occuring, tends in practice to require subjective decisions about how to ponder evidence, evaluate conflicting results and interpret uncertainties. However, the choice is not between a wholly objective or subjective assessment but between one which explicitly recognises the inherent scientific uncertainties and tries to tackle them and one which does not.

Secondly, notwithstanding the tremendous efforts aimed at maintaining a strict separation between risk assessment and risk management, the current practice of scientific risk assessment involving science policies questions its validity. In particular, lacking clearly defined 'science policies', risk assessors tend to set up assumptions and techniques for guiding themselves among the multiple versions that are scientifically plausible in situations of scientific uncertainties, thus inevitably influencing the outcomes of their scientific assessments. Against this backdrop, it is argued that the phenomenon of science policies should obtain regulatory recognition and that these guidelines should be consistently developed by risk managers and then visibly communicated to risk assessors.

While it is true that science policies may blur the existing distinction between risk assessment and risk management, it is equally true that such a phenomenon does not necessarily strip this 'functional separation' of its meaning. This is because, even if it is illusory to believe that all policy factors are confined to risk management, we know that, in contrast to risk management, risk assessment is limited to drawing inferences based on scientific evidence, science alone or on science combined with science policies. In other words, according to the suggested model of risk regulation, risk assessors may follow science policy guidelines, but they should not take on the role reserved for risk managers, by, for example, making decisions on the acceptability of a certain risk level for protecting public health or selecting procedures for reducing risks. However, to ensure that this separation will maintain its original meaning, it is crucial to render science policies more explicit. This is the only manner in which risk assessment, by maintaining consistency and transparency in the face of scientific uncertainty, could remain scientifically 'objective' while simultaneously allowing the judiciary to accomplish its task of reviewing the legality of science-based measures.

The efforts currently undertaken by EFSA, in particular by its Scientific Committee, to prepare a guidance document aimed at ensuring transparency in risk assessment carried out by EFSA seem to go in the right direction. The purpose of this document is to highlight all procedural aspects related to risk assessment that can be considered beneficial for improved transparency, including: a) selecting qualified scientists to participate in EFSA's activities and ensuring their independence; b) overall handling by EFSA of requests for scientific opinions; c) scientific opinions and other types of EFSA document; d) ensuring the availability of relevant data; d) information exchange between the Scientific Committee, the panels and the originator of the request; e) involvement of other stakeholders; f) dealing with diverging scientific opinions; g) adoption of scientific opinions; h) dissemination of documents and underlying data; i) confidentiality aspects; and l) revising and updating scientific opinions.[96]

Besides this document, most of the EFSA scientific panels are in the process of adopting guidance documents aimed at establishing their way of conducting risk assessment.[97]

C.   The Precautionary principle (PP): from Scientific Uncertainty to Legal Certainty

Another important factor risk managers have to take into account when devising new food legislation is the controversial precautionary principle,[98] allowing the adoption of protective measures in situations of scientific uncertainty.[99] In particular, this principle, by playing a role in the specific context of balancing the requirements of the free movement of goods and health protection, permits the adoption of measures aimed

[96] Transparency Document in Risk Assessment carried out by EFSA: Guidance Document on Procedural Aspects, Prepared by a working group consisting of members of the Scientific Committee and various EFSA Departments Request No EFSA-Q-2005-050. Endorsed on 11 April 2006 by the Scientific Committee. See *The EFSA Journal* (2006) 353.

[97] Thus, for instance, the Scientific Panel on Genetically Modified Organisms has adopted a Guidance document for the risk assessment of genetically modified microorganisms and their derived products intended for food and feed use (*The EFSA Journal* (2006) 374, 1–115 Summary) and also a Guidance document for the risk assessment of genetically modified plants and derived food and feed (*the EFSA Journal* (2004) 99, pp 1–94).

[98] For a wide-ranging review of this principle in Community and International law, see Alemanno, 'Le Principe de Précaution en Droit Communautaire: Stratégie de Gestion des Risques ou Risque d'Atteinte au Marché Intérieur?', supra note 71; L. Gonzalez Vaqué, L. Ehring, C. Jacquet, 'Le Principe de Précaution dans la Législation Communautaire et Nationale Relative a la Protection de la Santé', in *Revue du Marché Unique Européenne* 1, 79 (1999); T. Christoforou, 'The Origins, Content and Role of the Precautionary Principle in European Community Law', in C. Leben & J. Verhoeven, *Le Principe de Précaution : Aspects de Droit International et Communautaire* (LGDJ : Éd. Panthéon-Assas, 2002); T. Christoforou, 'The Precautionary Principle, Risk Assessment, and the Comparative Role of Science in the European Community and the US Legal Systems', in N.J. Vig and M.G. Faure, eds., *Green Giants? Environmental Policies of the United States and the European Union* (Cambridge: MIT Press, 2004), pp 17–51; T. Christoforou, 'Science, Law and Precaution in Dispute Settlement Resolution on Health and Environmental Protection : What Role for Scientific Experts ?', *Le Commerce International des Organismes Génétiquement Modifiés* (2003), pp 79–120; N. de Sadeleer, *Environmental Principles: From Political Slogans to Legal Rules* (Oxford, UK: Oxford University Press, 2002) pp 74–75; J.B; Wiener, 'Whose Precaution After All? A Comment on the Comparison and Evolution of Risk Regulatory Systems', 13 *Duke Journal of Comparative and International Law* 207 (2003) ; J. Cameron, *The Precautionary Principle, in Trade, Environment and the Millennium*, (London: Cameron May, 1998); T. O'Riordan, J. Cameron and A. Jordan, *Reinterpreting the Precautionary Principle* (London: Cameron May, 2001) and L. Marini, *Il Principio di Precauzione nel Diritto Internazionale e Comunitario, Disciplina del Commercio di Organismi Geneticamente Modificati e Profili di Sicurezza Alimentare*, Padova, 2004.

[99] In the preamble (21) of the general food regulation, the principle is defined as 'a mechanism for determining risk management measures or other actions in order to ensure the high level of health protection chosen in the Community'.

at the protection of health when uncertainties persist as to the existence or extent of the risks without having to wait until the reality and seriousness of those risks become fully apparent.

Because it focuses on situations with significant scientific uncertainty, the precautionary principle should be distinguished from the preventive principle, which restricts authorities to preventing risks only when their existence has been proven.

As has been said: 'The distinction between the preventive principle and the precautionary principle rests *on a difference of degree in the understanding of risk*. Prevention is based on certainties: it rests on cumulative experience concerning the degree of risk posed by an activity (Russian roulette, for example, involves a predictable one-in-six chance of death) [...] Preventive measures are thus intended to avert risks for which the cause-and-effect relationship is already known [...] Precaution, in contrast, comes into play when the probability of a suspected risk cannot be irrefutably demonstrated. The distinction between the two principles is thus *the degree of uncertainty surrounding the probability of risk*. The lower the margin of uncertainty, the greater the justification for intervention as a means of prevention, rather than in the name of precaution. By contrast, precaution is used when scientific research has not yet reached a stage that allows the veil of uncertainty to be lifted'.[100]

It follows, therefore, that recourse to the precautionary principle presupposes that scientific evaluation does not allow the risk to be determined with sufficient certainty. Under this principle, it is desirable not to wait for a risk to materialise before assessing and withdrawing from the market a product whose safety is uncertain. Hence the trend of summing up the precautionary philosophy under the well-know aphorisms 'stitch in time saves nine' and 'better safe than sorry'. In line with the 'other factors' philosophy' enlightening the EU decision-makers dealing with risks, it assumes that, in instances of scientific uncertainty, the results of risk assessments cannot (and should not) monopolize the policy decision.[101] This is because science can rarely provide definitive answers and therefore it should not be the only factor relied upon, for obvious reasons of democratic accountability. Seen from this perspective, the precautionary principle aims at ensuring that, in situations of scientific uncertainty, the ambiguities associated with future and unknown risks will be dealt with by democratic authorities, rather than

---

[100] N. de Sadeleer, *Environmental Principles: From Political Slogans to Legal Rules* (Oxford, UK: Oxford University Press, 2002) pp 74–75.
[101] C. Noiville, 'EU Food Safety Pattern and the WTO', in Ansell C. and Vogel D. (eds), *What's the Beef? The Contested Governance of European Food Safety*, (MIT Press, 2006).

only by scientists. Unlike the latter, the politically accountable managers are deemed to be in the best position to guarantee a high level of health protection, which is increasingly required by the public as a legitimate regulatory expectation.

Besides expressing such a preference for a democratic regulatory response, as opposed to a technocratic one, the principle also reveals a useful decision-making tool addressed to risk managers. In particular, it urges the competent authorities to err on the side of caution when assessing whether to act and how to address uncertain risks.

Therefore, its significance as a guiding principle in risk regulation, notably in food safety issues, lies not solely in the shift in the nature of valuation techniques in favour of a more participatory democracy, but also in its challenge to conventional science.[102]

As will be seen further, the conduct of a scientific study is the first prerequisite for the invocation of the principle. Moreover, to reduce the risk of abuses stemming from its invocation, several other requirements have been formulated through time by both the Community courts' jurisprudence and by the EC legislation in order to restrain its application. This set of requirements aims at turning the scientific uncertainty triggering precautionary action into legal certainty.

As will be shown, the principle may be relied upon not only by the Community institutions but also by the Member States.[103] However, different consequences flow from recourse to the principle, depending on whether it is invoked by the former or the latter. Although all precautionary-based measures, whether of national or Community origin, inevitably lead to a partitioning of the single market, and this regardless of whether or not their adoption is guided by protectionist consideration, national measures, unlike Community measures, lead to such a result without necessarily taking the view of other Member States into account. It will be illustrated further how this circumstance may explain the more stringent requirements imposed by Community courts on the Member States than on the EC institutions for the invocation of the precautionary principle.

---

[102] T. O'Riordan, J. Cameron and A. Jordan, *Reinterpreting the Precautionary Principle*, (Cameron May, 2001), p 13.

[103] After the ECJ *Artegodan* judgments, it might be argued that the precautionary principle, as a general principle of Community law, *requires* the competent authorities to take appropriate measures to prevent specific potential risks to public health, safety and the environment. See Joined Cases T-144/00, T-76/00, T-83/00, T-84/00, T-85/00, T-132/00 and T-141/00 *Artegodan a.o. v Commission* [2002] ECR 4945.

1. Origin at International and Community Level

Since public concern associated with decision-making in the face of scientific uncertainty has grown considerably in recent years, the need has been felt to develop a principle capable of restoring public confidence by requiring public authorities to take action or adopt measures to reduce risk, even in the absence of scientific evidence. In other words, the acknowledgment of the limitations of scientific understanding in providing conclusive evidence has led to the development of this principle. To the extent that this deficit in predictive capability is unacceptable to society, the precautionary principle permits actions aimed at preventing uncertain risks. Uncertain risks are those for which scientific data on the likelihood of the beginning of a hazard and the nature or the importance of the hazard are insufficient or impossible to identify.

References to the principle in domestic legal systems and international treaties have grown incessantly over the years. Increasing international consensus on the principle culminated in 1992 in its formulation into the Rio Declaration, which, continuously quoted, undoubtedly still represents the most famous definition of the principle:

> [i]n order to protect the environment, the precautionary approach shall be widely applied by States according to their capabilities. Where there are *threats of serious or irreversible damage*, lack of full scientific certainty shall not be used as a reason for postponing cost-effective measures to prevent environmental degradation'.[104]

However, notwithstanding this early recognition, the current status of the principle in international law remains controversial. Indeed, although general consensus exists on its implicit normative recognition within, for instance, the WTO legal order (see Article 5.7 of the SPS Agreement),[105] the scope, nature and impact of the precautionary principle in international law is yet to be established. The WTO AB has effectively summarised the debate over the status of the principle in international law by observing that while that principle:

> [...] is regarded by some as having crystallised into a general principle of customary international environmental law [...] whether it has been widely accepted by Members as a principle of general or customary international law appears less than clear.[106]

---

[104] Article 15 of the 1992 UN Conference on the Environment and Development (UNCED) in Rio de Janeiro (Rio Declaration).
[105] In the view of the AB, not only Article 5.7 SPS but also the preamble and Article 3.3 SPS would reflect the normative essence of the precautionary principle. See *EC–Hormones* AB Report, paras 123–125.
[106] See *EC–Hormones* AB Report, para 123.

The endorsement of this principle by the Cartagena Protocol on Biosafety does not seem to have clarified that issue.[107] The definition provided by Article 10.6 of the protocol is the following:

> Lack of scientific certainty due to insufficient relevant scientific information and knowledge regarding the extent of the potential adverse effects of a living modified organism on the conservation and sustainable use of biological diversity in the Party of import, taking also into account risks to human health, shall not prevent that Party from taking a decision, as appropriate, with regard to the import of the living modified organism in question as referred to in paragraph 3 above, in order to avoid or minimize such potential adverse effects.

As has been observed, this formulation of the principle appears to be more the fruit of a compromise between those countries which export genetically modified organisms ('GMOs') and those countries more sensitive to a precautionary approach than the fruit of a deliberate choice to adopt a consistent and viable definition of it.[108]

The question as to the status of the precautionary principle has been recently revamped by the *EC-Biotech* dispute. In its submissions, the European Community contends that the WTO Agreements, by virtue of the customary rules of treaty interpretation, as codified in the Vienna Convention on the Law of the Treaties, must be interpreted and applied by reference to relevant rules of international law arising outside the WTO context, notably as reflected in international treaties and declarations. In particular, because Article 31(3) of the Vienna Convention mandates the treaty interpreter to look not only at the context but also at 'any relevant rules of international law applicable in the relations *between* the parties', the precautionary rules such as those enshrined in the 1992 Convention on Biological Diversity and in its 2000 Cartagena Protocol on Biosafety must be taken into account as they reflect 'a general principle of international law'. The United States strongly disagrees with the notion that the precautionary principle as enshrined in the Biosafety Protocol has become 'a rule of international law' for the purposes of interpreting the WTO Agreements in accordance

---

[107] Cartagena protocol on Biosafety to the Convention on Biological Diversity, signed in Montreal on 29 January 2000 and entered into force on 11 September 2003. For an analysis of 'precautionary action' under the Cartagena Protocol, see, eg, R. Hill, S. Johnston and C. Sendashonga, 'Risk Assessment and Precaution in the Biosafety Protocol', in *RECIEL* 13 (3), 2004.

[108] E. Ni Chaoimh, 'Trading in Precaution – A Comparative Study of the Precautionary jurisprudence of the European Court and the WTO's Adjudicating Body', 33(2) *Legal Issues of Economic Integration* 139–165, p 141 (2006) and N. Salmon, 'A European Perspective on the Precautionary Principle, Food Safety and the Free Trade Imperative of the WTO', 27 *European Law Review*, p 138 (2002).

with the principles in Article 31(3) of the Vienna Convention and notes that, in any case, the protocol is not applicable to relations between the USA and the EC because the former is not party to it ('any relevant rules [...] applicable in the relations *between* the parties').

A look at the panel report reveals that it is precisely by relying on this argument that the panel dismisses the EC's position according to which WTO Agreements must be interpreted in the light of other rules of international law:

> [...] if a rule of international law is not applicable to one of the four WTO Members which are parties to the present dispute, the rule is not applicable in the relations between all WTO Members [...].[109]

However, although dismissing the EC's argument in these terms, the panel in its report has made an attempt to assess the current legal debate over the status of the precautionary principle in international law. Even though the precautionary principle has not only 'been incorporated into numerous international conventions and declarations' but has also 'been referred to and applied by States at the domestic level [...] there remain questions regarding the precise definition and content of the precautionary principle'[110]. Moreover, the panel noted *ad colorandum* that 'there has, to date, been no authoritative decision by an international court or tribunal which recognises the precautionary principle as a principle of general or customary international law'[111]. In the light of the above, the panel came to the *déjà-vu* conclusion according to which:

> [s]ince the legal status of the precautionary principle remains unsettled, like the Appellate Body before us, we consider that prudence suggests that we not attempt to resolve this complex issue, particularly if it is not necessary to do so.[112]

This proves that, although almost ten years have passed since the *Hormones* dispute, the legal debate ranging over whether the precautionary principle constitutes a recognised principle of general or customary international law is still ongoing. Notwithstanding great expectations on this particular point, the *Biotech* panel report does not seem to have contributed to shedding some light on the controversial status of the principle in international law.

---

[109] *EC–Biotech* Panel Report, para 7.71.
[110] *EC–Biotech* Panel Report, para 7.88.
[111] *EC–Biotech* Panel Report, para 7.88.
[112] *EC–Biotech* Panel Report, para 7.89.

1.1   Origin of the PP in the ECJ's Case Law

At EC level, the precautionary principle was originally introduced by the Treaty of Maastricht in Article 130r(2) (now Article 174(2)) of the EC Treaty as one of the guiding principles of EC environment policy.[113]

Yet, at the moment of its incorporation into the Treaty, the principle not only lacked a definition but its scope seemed to be limited to the environmental field. However, as anticipated by some commentators,[114] the precautionary principle could validly be invoked beyond the field of the environment because of the horizontal nature of Article 6 EC.[115] This provision states that:

> environmental protection requirements must be integrated into the definition and implementation of the Community policies and activities.[116]

On this basis, both the EC courts and the Commission widened the scope of this principle so as to apply it to other fields of EC law.

For its part, the ECJ has declared that:

> [...] although the precautionary principle is mentioned in the Treaty only in connection with environmental policy, it is broader in scope. It is intended to be applied in order to ensure a high level of protection of health, consumer safety and the environment in all the Community's spheres of activity. In particular, Article 3(p) EC includes `a contribution to the attainment of a high level of health protection' among the policies and activities of the Community. Similarly, Article 153

---

[113] Article 174 EC provides that the Community's policy on the environment 'shall be based on the precautionary principle and on the principles that preventive actions should be taken, that environmental damage should as a priority be rectified at source and that the polluter should pay'.

[114] Gonzalez Vaqué, Ehring, Jacquet, supra note 95 and Alemanno, 'Le Principe de Precaution en Droit Communautaire', supra note 71.

[115] The possibility to also invoke the principle outside of the environmental field has been first recognised by the ECJ. It follows from the EC courts' case-law that 'the precautionary principle may also apply in policy on the protection of human health which, according to Article 152 of the EC Treaty likewise aims at a high level of protection', see, to that effect, Case C-157/96 *National Farmers' Union and Others* [1998] ECR I-2211, at 63 and 64; Case C-236/01 *Monsanto Agricoltura Italia and Others* [2003] ECR I-8105, at 128 and 133. See also, Case T-13/99 *Pfizer Animal Health v Council* [2002] ECR II-3305, at 139 and 140; Case T-70/99 *Alpharma v Council* [2002] ECR II-3495, at 152 and 153; and Case T-177/02 *Malagutti-Vezinhet v Commission* [2004] ECR not yet reported, at 54.

[116] It must also be observed that Article 3(p) EC, also inserted by the Treaty of Maastricht, provides that the Community 'contributes to achieve a high consumer protection level' among the policies and activities of the Community. Similarly, Article 153 EC refers to a high level of consumer protection.

EC refers to a high level of consumer protection and Article 174(2) EC assigns a high level of protection to Community policy on the environment. Moreover, the requirements relating to that high level of protection of the environment and human health are expressly integrated into the definition and implementation of all Community policies and activities under Article 6 EC and Article 152(1) EC respectively.[117]

The Commission quoted it not solely in the general policy guidelines set out in the Green Paper on the General Principles of Food Safety, but also in the Consumer Health Communication before finally declaring, in its 2000 Communication on the precautionary principle, 'that the precautionary principle is a general one which should in particular be taken into consideration in the fields of environment protection and human, animal and plant health'. A justification for extending the principle beyond environmental protection can be found in the same Communication wherein it is stated:

> Although the precautionary principle is not explicitly mentioned in the Treaty except in the environmental field, its scope is far wider and covers those specific circumstances where scientific evidence is insufficient, inconclusive or uncertain and there are indications through preliminary objective scientific evaluation that there are reasonable grounds for concern that the potentially dangerous effects on the environment, human, animal or plant health may be inconsistent with the chosen level of protection.[118]

Further, the Council, in its resolution of 4 December 2000 on the use of the precautionary principle, also welcomed the Commission's communication by endorsing its main guidelines.[119]

(a)   The PP as an Obiter Dictum

The European Court of Justice had to deal with some issues related to a precautionary approach well before the start of the above described process of formal integration of the principle into the EC legal order.

This is because, back in the 1980s, more and more Member States began invoking public health reasons, in situations of alleged scientific uncertainty, to prohibit specified substances contained in foodstuffs. In so doing, they prevented the importation of those foodstuffs into their own territories. From an analysis of this line of cases emerges, notably

---

[117] Joined Cases T-144/00, T-76/00, T-83/00, T-84/00, T-85/00, T-132/00 and T-141/00 *Artegodan a.o. v Commission* [2002] ECR 4945, at 183.

[118] Commission Communication on the precautionary principle, supra note 30.

[119] Council Resolution of 4 December 2000 on use of the precautionary principle, (Doc. Council 14328/00).

from the judgments concerning additives and pesticides,[120] the development of an embryonic form of the precautionary principle.

Most of these cases fit into the following scenario:

1. A Member State prohibits the importing of or the placing on the market of foodstuffs containing either additives or pesticides which are not allowed by the importing state legislations.
2. The rejected foodstuff was legally produced and marketed in another Member State.
3. Criminal proceedings are instituted against the importer due to a violation of the individual state prescription.
4. Regularly, the relevant criminal court referred the case to the ECJ for a preliminary ruling aimed at determining whether the national prohibition infringed Article 28 EC or whether this infringement could be justified according to Article 30 EC.

According to the ECJ case law, Member States may successfully invoke public health under Article 30 EC to justify a prohibition on the free movement of goods only if they prove the existence of a 'serious risk to public health'.[121] But *quid* when the current state of research does not offer any clear result about the existence of a health risk?

The ECJ had to face this critical situation in *Kaasfabriek Eyssen*.[122] The court had to consider whether a Dutch prohibition on the use of an antibiotic, nisin, as a preservative in processed cheese was justified on the ground of health protection. Here the evaluation of health risks for the additive in question could not reach any clear conclusion. As the risks caused by nisin depended on variable factors, in particular on different, indeterminable eating habits in the Member States, the ECJ deemed it necessary to grant Member States, in situations of scientific uncertainty, a wide margin of manoeuvre and to consider domestic prohibitions grounded on public health justified under Article 30 EC. The ECJ came to this conclusion after having noted that the controversial doubts about nisin led several international organisations, such as FAO and WHO, to undertake scientific studies on the risk of ingestion, not only from cheese but from all other sources. Similarly, in the *Sandoz* case, the ECJ, facing the uncertainty relating to the daily intake of vitamins by the citizens,[123] held that:

---

[120] For a detailed review of this line of cases related to additives, see L. Gonzales Vaqué, 'La Législation Communautaire Relative aux Additives Alimentaires', *Revue du Droit de l'Union Européenne*, 3/1993, p 119.

[121] See, eg, case C-227/82 *Van Bennekom* [1983] ECR 3883.

[122] Case C-83/80, *Officier van Justitie/Kaasfabriek Eyssen* [1981] ECR 409.

[123] Although ingestion of vitamins, as contained in foodstuffs, is harmless and even necessary for the human body, it may produce negative effects in case of excessive consumption in addition to regular diet over a longer period of time.

> In so far as there are uncertainties in the present state of scientific research with regard to the harmfulness of a certain additive, it is for the Member States, in the absence of full harmonization, to decide what degree of protection of the health and life of humans they intend to assure, in light of the specific eating habits of their own population.[124]

Therefore, since science could neither determine the exact critical quantities of vitamins nor the specific effects stemming from their consumption, the relevant prohibition of vitamins was justified under Article 30 EC. Although expressed in a mere obiter dictum, this 1983 judgment probably represents the first (judicial) recognition, at EC level, of the idea underlying the precautionary principle: a criterion allowing for public action even in the absence of conclusive scientific evidence. Indeed, according to AG Mischo:

> [...] this judgment seems to me to constitute an application of the precautionary principle before the fact.[125]

Further recognition of this approach may be found in the *Heijn*[126] and *Mirepoix*[127]cases, where although there was no doubt as to the harmfulness of pesticide residues for the human organism, there was uncertainty with respect to the non-calculable intake quantity of such residues. This degree of uncertainty was sufficient for the court to justify the restrictive national measure on public health grounds. However, it must be noted that, notwithstanding the general trend legitimising domestic prohibitions of free movement whenever there is an uncertain level of evidence, the ECJ did take into express account in all the abovementioned cases some particular conditions of the specific situation, such as eating habits, climatic conditions, the state of health of the population and particularly sensitive consumers. Which specific criteria are referred to by the ECJ and which role is played by each of them in the court's legal reasoning depends on the pleading of the parties concerned and also on the circumstances of the individual case.

In general, it appears from this case law that Member States have been allowed a large dose of discretion when deciding to err on the side of caution when adopting food safety measures. This freedom is limited

---

[124] Case 174/82, *Sandoz BV* [1983] ECR 2445, para 16.
[125] Opinion in Case C-192/01, *Commission v Denmark*, para 50 («En ce sens, cet arrêt me parait constituer une application avant la lettre du principe de précaution ») quoting Alemanno, 'Le principe de précaution ...', supra note 71, ('[f]or the first time, the Court would seem to have recognised, although in an obiter dictum which does not explicitly mention the precautionary principle, the possibility of Member States adopting measures in a situation of scientific uncertainty').
[126] Case 94/83 *Heijn* [1984] ECR 3263.
[127] Case 54/85 *Mirepoix* [1986] ECR 1067.

by only one condition: Member States must deliver some scientific evidence by referring to the 'results of international research'.[128] However, where there is uncertainty as to the existence or extent of a risk, the threshold of risk, which must be established by a Member State in order to justify its trade restrictive measure, is not clearly defined.

(b)   The Early Judicial Shaping of the PP

Although in this set of judgments the ECJ dealt with issues that might today be described as coming under the 'precautionary principle' label,[129] it was only in the so called '*BSE* judgments' on the validity of the Commission decision prohibiting the export from the UK of beef in any form or in the form of products derived from beef that the precautionary approach began to assume the form it takes today.[130] Notwithstanding the ECJ's efforts to define the scope of a precautionary approach as stemming from Article 130R(1) and (2), it did not refer expressly to the precautionary principle in its reasoning.

It is worth analysing these cases not only because they represent the first cases in which the precautionary principle was upheld by the court, but also because they laid the ground for the development of this principle within EC law.

Following the UK Spongiform Encephalopathy Advisory Committee (SEAC) opinions concerning the existence of a possible link between BSE and a variant of Creuzfeldts-Jakob disease,[131] the Commission adopted decision 96/239/EC of 27 March 1996 ('BSE decision') imposing, on a temporary basis, a ban on exports of bovine animals, bovine meat

[128] See, eg, Case 304/84 *Ministere Public v Muller and others* [1986] ECR 1511, para 24 and Case C-42/90 *Bellon* [1990] ECR 4863, para 17.

[129] Besides the line of cases illustrated above, see also Case C-212/91 *Angelopharm v Hambourg,* [1994] ECR 17, in which the ECJ, called to assess the validity of Directive 90/121(adapting to technical progress Annexes II, III, IV, V and VI to Council Directive 76/768/EEC on the approximation of the laws of the Member States relating to cosmetic products, OJ 1990 L71/40) had to define the extent of the obligation for the Commission to consult the competent scientific committee, notably the Scientific Committee on Cosmetology; and also Case C-151/98 P, *Pharos v Commission* [1999] ECR 8157, relating to the conditions under which the Commission was entitled to submit a scientific issue concerning public health for further advice to the competent scientific committee, notably the Committee for Veterinary Medicinal Products. For previous situations in which the ECJ had to deal with scientific uncertainty, see case C-227/82 *Van Bennekom* [1983] ECR 3883. For a comment on this early case law on the 'precautionary principle', see A. Aresu, 'Derniers Developments Jurisprudentiels en Matière de Libre Circulation des Produits Alimentaires', *Revue du Droit de l'Union Européenne,* 4/1992, pp 251 ss.

[130] Case C-157/96, *National Farmers' Union,* [1998] ECR I-2211, and case C-180/96, *United Kingdom v Commission,* [1996] ECR 3903.

[131] SEAC is an independent scientific body which advises the United Kingdom Government. See Case 180/96 *UK v Commission* [1998] ECR 3903, para 9.

and derived products from the territory of the United Kingdom to the other Member States and to third countries.[132]

According to the Commission, despite the fact that BSE previously existed, the SEAC's opinion had 'significantly altered the *perception of risk* which that disease represented for human health':[133] BSE was no longer regarded merely as affecting cattle, but as a hazard to human health, thus justifying the adoption of safeguard measures in accordance with Directives 90/425 and 89/662.

The ban was challenged not only by the United Kingdom under Article 230 EC, but also by a lobby of farmers, the National Farmers' Union, before national courts, who referred the matter to the ECJ.[134]

In its analysis, the ECJ, after recalling the scope of judicial review in matters concerning the common agricultural policy, where the Community has a discretionary power corresponding to its political responsibilities,[135] developed the line of reasoning as follows.

The ECJ's analysis started off by noting that, at the time of the adoption of the ban, there was great uncertainty as to the risks stemming from BSE-infected bovine animals, bovine meat and derived products.[136] The publication of new scientific information (SEAC's opinion) had established a probable link between a disease affecting cattle in the United Kingdom and a fatal disease affecting humans for which no known cure yet exists.[137]

---

[132] The decision was adopted by the Commission and was based on the following legal sources: Council Directive 90/425/EEC (notably on its Article 10(4), concerning veterinary and zootechnical checks applicable in intra-Community trade in certain live animals and products with a view to the completion of the internal market (OJ 1990 L 224/29), as amended by Council Directive 92/118/EEC of 17 December 1992 laying down animal health requirements governing trade imports into the Community of products not subject to the said requirements laid down in specific Community rules referred to in Annex A (I) to Directive 89/662/EEC and, as regards pathogens, to Directive 90/425/EEC (OJ 1993 L 62/49); Council Directive 89/662/EEC (notably on its Article 9) concerning veterinary checks in intra-Community trade with a view to the completion of the internal market (OJ 1989 L 395/49), as amended by Directive 92/118; and also on EC Treaty rules (but with no mention of specific articles).

[133] Case C-180/96, *United Kingdom v Commission*, [1996] ECR 3903, at 53.

[134] Case C-157/96, *National Farmers' Union*, [1998] ECR I-2211, at 179.

[135] In Case C-157/96 the Court stated at para 61 that 'With regard to judicial review of compliance with the above-mentioned conditions, in matters concerning the common agricultural policy the Community legislature has a discretionary power which corresponds to the political responsibilities given to it by Articles 40 to 43 of the Treaty. Consequently, the legality of a measure adopted in that sphere can be affected only if the measure is manifestly inappropriate having regard to the objective which the competent institution is seeking to pursue'. See also Cases 160/88 *Fedesa v Council* [1988] ECR 6399, at 14 and Case 368/89 *Crispoltoni I* (1991) ECR 3715, at 42.

[136] Case 157/96, *The Queen v Ministry of Agriculture, Fisheries and Food, ex parte National Farmers' Union et al* [1998] ECR I-2211, at 62.

[137] Case 180/96 *UK v Commission* [1996] ECR 3903, at 61.

Against this backdrop, the ECJ developed what has become the general definition of the precautionary principle within the EC by stating that:

> where there is uncertainty as to the existence or extent of risks to human health, the institutions may take protective measures without having to wait until the reality and seriousness of those risks become fully apparent.[138]

The ECJ found that this approach is borne out by Article 130R(1) of the EC Treaty (current Article 174), according to which Community policy on the environment is to pursue the objective of, inter alia, protecting human health. Although not expressly referring to the precautionary principle as enshrined in the EC Treaty since the Maastricht Treaty, the ECJ stated that environmental protection requirements must be integrated into the definition and implementation of other Community policies.[139] Thus, the precautionary principle was for the first time extended beyond the environmental protection arena becoming, long before being codified by the General food law regulation, a food safety general principle.

The ECJ continued its analysis by stressing that the contested decision was adopted as an 'emergency measure' temporarily banning exports (fifth recital in the preamble of the attacked decision). It also upheld the concerns expressed by the Commission, the SCAN committee and one of its members about the scientific uncertainties concerning the risks of transmissibility of BSE.[140]

According to the court, in the light of the above, the ban on export of live bovine animals could not be regarded as a 'manifestly inappropriate measure'. Furthermore, as regards the claims that alternative measures were possible, the ECJ concluded that 'in view of the seriousness of the risk and the urgency of the situation', the Commission did not react in a manifestly inappropriate manner by imposing, on a temporary basis and pending the production of more detailed scientific information, a general ban on exports of bovine animals, bovine meats and derived products. Consequently, the Commission was not found to be in breach of the proportionality principle.

---

[138] Ibid, at 99.

[139] Case 180/96, *UK v Commission*, [1996] ECR 3903, at 100. This principle has been recently confirmed in Case 41/02 *Commission v Netherlands* [2004] at 45, where the court has held that 'it follows from case law of the Court that the precautionary principle may also apply in policy on the protection of human health which, according to Article 152 of the EC Treaty likewise aims at a high level of protection'.

[140] Case 180/96, *UK v Commission* [1996] ECR 3903, at 105.

Although giving shape to the precautionary principle, the *BSE* judgments did not refer to the principle as such. The first explicit reference to the principle in a court ruling was made by the CFI in 2000 in *Bergaderm*, where the court affirmed that:

> [...] the appellants dispute the references to the precautionary principle in paragraph 66 of the contested judgment.[141]

A previous reference to the principle was originally made by AG Cosmas in his opinion in *Diego Cali*, where he limited himself to quoting the new Article 130R(2) EC and the Rio Declaration.[142] In further cases, Advocates General, without developing a comprehensive analysis of the principle, contributed nonetheless to the evolution of its understanding.[143]

Other explicit references to the principle may be found in the *Lirussi and Bizzaro* judgment,[144] wherein the ECJ mentioned it together with the principle of preventive action, in relation to Article 4 of Directive 75/442/EEC on waste, in conjunction with Article 130r of the Treaty. The principle was then invoked by *Greenpeace France* to contest the functioning of Council Directive 90/220/EEC on the deliberate release into the environment of genetically modified organisms.[145]

Yet, although the number of cases expressly dealing with the principle was growing, one could not say that its invocation by either EC institutions (*BSE* cases), Member States (*Eyssen, Sandoz, Hijn*, etc) or private parties against the EC institutions (*Greenpeace*) had been systematised.

---

[141] Case C-353/98 P *Laboratoires pharmaceutiques Bergaderm a.o. v Commission* [2000] ECR 5291, at 52.

[142] Opinion of AG G Cosmas in Case C-343/95, *Diego Cali & Figli* [1997] ECR 1549, at 59.

[143] See, for instance, Opinions of AG Mischo (Case C-184/97 *Commission v Germany* [1999] ECR I-7837), La Pergola (Case C-94/98 *Rhône Poulenc Rore a. O. v Licensing Authority* [1999] ECR I-8789), Cosmas (Case C-318/98 *Criminal proceedings against Giancarlo Fornasar a. O.* [2000] ECR I-4785) and Fenelly (Case C-352/98 P [2000] I-5291).

[144] Joined cases C-175/98 and C-177/98, *Paolo Lirussi and Francesco Bizzaro* [1999] ECR 5291, at 51–52.

[145] The ECJ came to the conclusion that observance of the precautionary principle was reflected, within the Directive, in the notifier's obligation to notify the competent authority of new information concerning the risks of the product to human health and also in the right of any Member State provisionally to restrict or prohibit the use and/or sale on its territory of a product which has been marketed, every time there is a justifiable reason to consider that it constitutes a risk to human health or the environment. See at 44.

(c)   The 2000 Communication on the PP

Against this backdrop, the Commission decided to issue a Communication on the use of the precautionary principle,[146] mainly aimed at:

– outlining its approach to using the principle;
– establishing Commission guidelines for applying it;
– building a common understanding of how to assess, appraise, manage and communicate risks that science is not yet been able to evaluate fully, and
– avoiding unwarranted recourse to the principle, as a disguised form of protectionism.

Among the reasons that spurred the Commission to adopt such a Communication, there was not only the internal pressure applied by the other EC institutions,[147] but also some external factors such as the comments of the Appellate Body on the precautionary principle in its report in the *Hormones* case[148] and the recurring complaint by WTO members that the principle was not adequately defined.

After having described the precautionary principle itself, by pinpointing the factors that trigger recourse to it and the kind of measures that may result from its application, the Commission provides some procedural safeguards to be adhered to when relying on this principle in order 'to avoid unwarranted recourse to the principle, as a disguised form of protectionism'.

In applying the principle, decision-makers are called to balance 'the freedom and rights of individuals, industry and organisations with the need to reduce the risk of adverse effects to the environment, human, animal or plant health'. In order to achieve the correct balance, they are required to adopt a 'structured decision-making process' relying on 'detailed scientific' and 'other objective' information. More pragmatically, the implementation of the principle should start with a scientific evaluation 'as complete as possible' and 'where possible, identifying at each stage the degree of scientific uncertainty'. Judging what is an 'acceptable' level of risk for society is 'an eminently political responsibility'.

---

[146] Commission Communication on the precautionary principle, supra note 30.
[147] For instance, in a resolution of 28 June 1999 on Community Consumer Policy 1999–2001, the Council called on the Commission 'to be in the future even more determined to be guided by the precautionary principle in preparing proposals for legislation and in its other consumer-related activities and develop as a priority a clear and effective guidelines for the application of this principle'.
[148] *EC–Hormones*, AB Report, at 120–125.

Where action is deemed necessary, precautionary-based measures should be: *proportionate* to the chosen level of protection, *non-discriminatory* in their application, *consistent* with similar measures already taken, *based on an examination* of the potential benefits and costs of action or lack of action, *subject to review*, in the light of new scientific data, and *capable of assigning responsibility for producing the scientific evidence* necessary for a more comprehensive risk assessment.

Notwithstanding this set of procedural safeguards surrounding the invocation of the principle, it has been argued that, contrary to its declared goals, this communication did not place meaningful and effective constraints on the application of the precautionary principle.[149] While imposing a 'balancing' prerequisite on decisions of whether or not to have recourse to the principle, the communication clearly tipped in favour of adopting preventive measures by failing to set a risk threshold triggering its invocation. Similarly, it can reasonably be argued that the Communication's approach to the principle completely overlooked the costs entailed in the adoption of a protective measure, by emphasizing solely the expected benefits to health.[150]

Notwithstanding these clear limitations, the Communication was endorsed by the Nice European Council in December of the same year.[151]

d)   The EFTA Kellog's Case

Following the adoption of the Commission Communication, the EFTA Court has delivered a major judgment which has significantly contributed to the shaping of the precautionary principle, particularly when it is invoked by a Member State.[152]

At the origin of this judgment lies infringement proceedings brought by the EFTA Surveillance Authority against the Kingdom of Norway

---

[149] See, eg, N. McNelis, 'EU communications on the precautionary principle', in *J Int Economic Law* 2000 3, pp 545–551. For similar critics of the principle, see also E. Fisher, 'Precaution, Precaution Everywhere: Developing a "Common Understanding" of the Precautionary Principle in the European Community', 9 *Maastricht Journal of Comparative Law*, 2002, p 7 and G. Majone, 'What Price Safety? The Precautionary Principle and its Policy Implications', *Journal of Common Market Studies* 2002, Volume 40, p 89.

[150] This critique to the principle seems to be shared by A.G. M. Maduro in Opinion C-41/02 *Comission v the Netherlands*, at 31.

[151] Council Resolution on the Precautionary Principle, Annex III to the Presidency Conclusions, Nice European Council Meeting, 7–9 December 2000.

[152] EFTA Court of 5 April 2001, Case E-3/00 *Efta Surveillance Authority v Norway* [2001] EFTA Court Report 2000/2001, 73, at 30. For a comment of this case, see Alemanno, 'Le Principe de Precaution ...', supra note 71, pp 947–50. Among the judgments of the EFTA Court dealing with the precautionary principle, see also the more recent E-4/04 *Pedicel AS v Directorate for Health and Social Affairs* [2006], not yet reported.

because of its legislative prohibition on the import and marketing of fortified corn flakes which had been lawfully manufactured and marketed in other EEA states.

On the one hand, the Norwegian authorities oppose the import and marketing of these cereals on the grounds that there is no nutritional need in the Norwegian population for the fortification and that, in the absence of scientific data on this point, its 'approach is in accordance with the precautionary principle, as developed and applied internationally and within the Community'. On the other hand, the EFTA Surveillance Authority argues that the ban on imports of fortified products cannot be justified under Article 13 EEC (corresponding to Article 30 EC),[153] because Norway has not substantiated its claim that the fortification in question would constitute a danger to public health.

Facing these opposing claims, the EFTA Court had, for the first time, to take a position on the emerging precautionary principle within the EEA. By relying heavily on the ECJ's *Sandoz* case,[154] the court held that:

> In the absence of harmonization of rules, when there is uncertainty as to the current state of scientific research, it is for the Contracting Parties to decide what degree of protection of human health they intend to assure, having regard to the fundamental requirements of EEA law, notably, the free movement of goods within the European Economic Area.[155]

In laying down the basis for the invocation of the precautionary principle within the EEA, the court showed itself to be rather familiar with the traditional structured risk analysis model, although it had not yet been codified within the EC/EEA context, by stating:

> This means that a *risk management* decision rests with each Contracting party. It is within the discretion of the Contracting Party to make a policy decision as to what level of risk it considers appropriate.[156]

Against this backdrop, the court has set the conditions under which EEA contracting parties may validly invoke the precautionary principle

---

[153] Article 13 EEA, similarly to Article 30 EC, states that Article 11 EEA (corresponding to Article 28 EC) does not preclude prohibitions justified on grounds of inter alia protection of human health, as long as a given prohibition does not constitute a means of arbitrary discrimination or a disguised restriction of trade.

[154] Case 174/82, *Sandoz BV* [1983] ECR 2445, at 16–18.

[155] Case E-3/00 *Efta Surveillance Authority v Norway* [2001] EFTA Court Report 2000/2001, 73, at 25.

[156] Case E-3/00 *Efta Surveillance Authority v Norway* [2001] EFTA Court Report 2000/2001, 73, at 25.

> [...] measures taken [...] must be based on scientific evidence; they must be proportionate; non-discriminatory, transparent and consistent with similar measures already taken.[157]

In particular, concerning the scientific requirement, it added that while '[a] purely hypothetical or academic consideration will not suffice',[158] there is a requirement for 'a comprehensive evaluation of the risk to health based on the most recent scientific information'.[159]

By applying these criteria to the case at hand, the court concluded that the Norwegian ban did not fulfil the requirement of EEA law to the extent:

> Firstly, it was inconsistent in that, on the one hand, authorization to market fortified cornflakes had been refused because of a lack of need, while on the other hand, Norway maintained as a matter of policy fortification of brown whey cheese [...].[160]

Secondly, it had not been demonstrated that a comprehensive risk assessment had been carried out by the Norwegian authorities in response to Kellogg's submission of its application for authorization'.[161]

2.   Definitions

Article 7 of the general food regulation provides the first legally binding definition of the precautionary principle in Community law.[162] This definition relies heavily on the 2000 Commission Communication on the precautionary principle[163] and builds upon the ECJ's case law developed on the matter. According to the adopted formulation:

---

[157] Case E-3/00 *Efta Surveillance Authority v Norway* [2001] EFTA Court Report 2000/2001, 73, at 26.
[158] Idem, at 29.
[159] Idem, at 30.
[160] Idem, at 41.
[161] Idem, at 42.
[162] At the same time, it is the first time that the precautionary principle finds an explicit reference in a specific policy field.
[163] Commission Communication on the precautionary principle, supra note 30. It must be observed that, in the meanwhile, as mentioned above, this communication had been endorsed by the Resolution of the 2000 Nice European Council calling on the Commission systematically to apply its guidelines and to rely on the precautionary principle wherever necessary in the drawing up of its proposals. See Annex III to the Presidency Conclusions, Nice European Council Meeting, 7–9 December 2000.

[i]n specific circumstances where, following an assessment of available information, the possibility of harmful effects on health is identified but scientific uncertainty persists, provisional risk management measures necessary to ensure the high level of health protection chosen in the Community may be adopted, pending further scientific information for a more comprehensive risk assessment.[164]

Therefore, whenever a risk assessment concludes that 'the possibility of harmful effects on health is identified but scientific uncertainty persists', *provisional* risk management measures *necessary* to ensure the high level of health protection chosen in the Community may be adopted, while other scientific information to complement the assessment is awaited.

Such an open-ended characterisation of the principle is relevant to the extent that it enables, although always within the limits of the proportionality principle, not only the Community but also the Member States to rely upon it. According to established case law, that means that, in exercising their discretion relating to the protection of public health, the Member States must choose measures that:

must [...] be confined to what is actually necessary to ensure the safeguarding of public health; they must be proportional to the objective thus pursued, which could not have been attained by measures which are less restrictive of intra-Community trade.[165]

2.1   The Role of the Precautionary Principle in Risk Analysis

As has been noted, the definition contained in the general food regulation draws inspiration from the European Court of Justice's original formulation of the principle in the *BSE* line of cases, where it was held that:

[w]here there is uncertainty as to the existence or extent of risks to human health, the institutions may take protective measures without having to wait until the reality and seriousness of those risks become fully apparent.[166]

However, when compared with such an embryonic formulation of the principle, the version provided by the general food regulation looks much more comprehensive. That is because this definition places the principle for the first time within the broader context of risk analysis. In

---

[164] Article 7.1 of the regulation.
[165] See, eg, Case 174/82 *Sandoz* [1983] ECR 2445, at 18; Case C-192/01 *Commission v Denmark* [2003] ECR 9693; Case C-24/00 *Commission v France* [2004] not yet reported, paragraph 52 and C-41/02 *Commission v Denmark* [2004] ECR not yet reported, at 46.
[166] Case 180/96 *UK v Commission* [1996] ECR 3903, at 99.

particular, by espousing the 'other legitimate factors' philosophy' underpinning the food risk analysis scheme,[167] the general food regulation's definition contextualises the invocation of the precautionary principle within the risk management stage.[168] This emerges clearly from the wording employed in Article 7 which allows the adoption of 'provisional risk management measures' only after 'an assessment of available information'.

In a risk analysis model where risk management decisions cannot depend solely on the outcome of scientific expertise but must also take into account 'other legitimate factors', such as 'societal, economic, traditional, ethical and environmental factors as well as the feasibility of controls',[169] the precautionary principle finds fertile ground in which to lay roots. Conversely, the precautionary principle would find no room in a risk analysis model where only the scientific element dictates the permitted regulatory action.

As a result, within the EC food safety risk analysis scheme, the precautionary principle, which does not feature in the risk assessment stage, is called to play a role exclusively as a risk management tool.

However, notwithstanding the crystal clear identification, in Article 6(3) of the regulation, of the precautionary principle as a risk management tool, it remains controversial as to whether a precautionary approach may already enter into play within the risk assessment stage, thereby influencing the conduct of such a delicate stage of risk analysis[170].

In fact, there seems to be nothing to preclude the risk assessment step being conducted in accordance with the precautionary principle's requirements. In particular, the 2000 Commission Communication on the precautionary principle recognised, although within the WTO context, that the precautionary principle may also play a role in risk assessment by stating that:

---

[167] See Article 7.2, which requires that precautionary measure 'shall be proportionate and no more restrictive of trade than is required to achieve the high level of health protection chosen in the Community, regard being had to technical and economic feasibility and other factors regarded as legitimate in the matter under consideration'.

[168] Articles 6(3) and 7 of the regulation.

[169] See recital (19) of the preamble, Article 3(12) and Article 6, paragraph 3 of Regulation 178/2002. See also Article 6(6) of Regulation 1829/2003 on GM food and feed which provides that as risk assessment cannot provide all the information on which a risk management decision should be based 'other legitimate factors' relevant to the matter under consideration may be taken into account.

[170] See on this point de Sadeleer, supra note 100, p 186, who argues that 'the precautionary principle may influence both assessment methodology and the proper role of scientific expertise'.

The concept of risk assessment in the SPS leaves leeway for interpretation of what could be used as a basis for a precautionary approach. The risk assessment on which a measure is based may include *non-quantifiable data of a factual or qualitative nature and is not uniquely confined to purely quantitative scientific data*. This interpretation has been confirmed by the WTO's Appellate body in the case of growth hormones, which rejected the panel's initial interpretation that the risk assessment had to be quantitative and had to establish a minimum degree of risk.[171]

The case law does not offer any definitive answer on this point. Indeed, while, on the one hand, it seems to relegate the invocation of the principle to the risk management stage, on the other, it has never expressly ruled out that the principle may also play a role in risk assessment.

An example of such a vague approach to defining the role occupied by the principle within risk analysis emerges clearly from *Artegodan*, wherein it has been stated that:

[...] where scientific evaluation does not make it possible to determine the existence of a risk with sufficient certainty, whether to have recourse to the precautionary principle depends as a general rule on the level of protection chosen by the competent authority in the exercise of its discretion.[172]

2.2 Precaution: Facultative or Obligatory?

By stating that 'provisional risk management measures ... *may* be adopted', the definition contained in the general food regulation seems to put an end to the debate over whether reliance on the precautionary principle would be an obligation for the competent risk managers.

In reality, the question whether recourse to the precautionary principle is obligatory or facultative is too complex to be solved by a mere textual argument. While it is truly tempting to conclude, by relying on the wording employed in Article 7(1) of the regulation, that the precautionary principle does not require, but merely enables, the competent authorities to take anticipatory preventive action in response to uncertainty, it is difficult to reconcile that conclusion with some statements made by European courts in the recent case law.

At the outset of its case law on the precautionary principle, notably in the *BSE* line of cases, the ECJ has held that:

---

[171] Commission Communication on the precautionary principle, supra note 30, at 11.
[172] Joined Cases T-144/00, T-76/00, T-83/00, T-84/00, T-85/00, T-132/00 and T-141/00 *Artegodan a.o. v Commission* [2002] ECR 4945, at 199.

> Where there is uncertainty as to the existence or extent of risks to human health, the institutions *may* take protective measures without having to wait until the reality and seriousness of those risks become fully apparent.[173]

Yet, only a few years later, the CFI would seem to have turned the principle into an autonomous source of legal obligations by stating in *Artegodan* that:

> [...] the precautionary principle can be defined as a general principle of Community law *requiring* the competent authorities to take appropriate measures to prevent specific potential risks to public health, safety and the environment, by giving precedence to the requirements related to the protection of those interests over economic interests. Since the Community institutions are responsible, in all their spheres of activity, for the protection of public health, safety and the environment, the precautionary principle can be regarded as an autonomous principle stemming from the abovementioned Treaty provisions.[174]

On this basis, the CFI concluded that the principle 'requires', in the framework of the rules applicable to the re-authorisation of a medicinal product, 'the suspension or the withdrawal of marketing authorisation where new data give rise to serious doubts as to either the safety or the efficacy of the medicinal product in question and those doubts lead to an unfavourable assessment of the benefit/risk balance of that medicinal product'.[175]

This approach seems to have been confirmed and further strengthened in *Pfizer* where the CFI has held:

> The institutions cannot be criticised for having chosen to withdraw provisionally the authorisation of virginiamycin as an additive in feedingstuffs, in order to prevent the risk from becoming a reality, and, at the same time, to continue with the research that was already under way. Such an approach, moreover, was consonant with the precautionary principle, by reason of which a public authority *can be required* to act even before any adverse effects have become apparent.[176]

Against this backdrop, one may seriously wonder whether the application of the principle has become mandatory, at least for the EC institutions.

---

[173] Case 180/96 *UK v Commission,* [1996] ECR 3903, at 99.
[174] Joined Cases T-144/00, T-76/00, T-83/00, T-84/00, T-85/00, T-132/00 and T-141/00 *Artegodan a.o. v Commission* [2002] ECR 4945, at 184.
[175] Ibid, at 192.
[176] Ibid, at 444.

As to Member States, it is submitted that the precautionary principle cannot be interpreted as a source of legal obligation for them. This position relies on the following arguments.

According to established case law,[177] in the absence of harmonisation and insofar as uncertainties continue to exist in the current state of scientific research, Member States are free to decide on their intended level of protection of human health and life and, accordingly, to adopt the measures apt to reach such a result. In particular, unlike Community measures - which have to attain a high level of protection,[178] national measures are not subject to the respect of any safety threshold.

In particular:

> [t]hat discretion relating to the protection of public health is particularly wide where it is shown that uncertainties continue to exist in the current state of scientific research as to certain substances [...].[179]

By virtue of their discretion, Member States are free to decide not only whether or not to invoke the precautionary principle, but also – once they have called upon that principle – to adopt a precautionary principle that may vary very much in intensity and scope. Thus, for instance, it may happen that, faced with the same source of risk, one country may decide to enact soft measures, such as those consisting in merely informing the public about the risk that may stem from a product, and another may take a stricter stance, by prohibiting *tout court* the marketing of that product.

In the light of the above, it is argued that any interpretation of the precautionary principle transforming it into a binding source of legal obligation would run against Member States' sovereign right to regulate. Going back to the question of whether the principle may be considered compulsory for Community action, it must be observed that such recognition would constitute not only a chronological but also a conceptual *prius* within international law. Indeed, no international law text explicitly recognising the existence of the principle is interpreted as a binding principle, but rather as merely enabling the competent authorities to act despite the fact that their action may enter into conflict with several international trade rules.[180]

---

[177] Case C-174/82 *Sandoz* [1983] ECR 2445, at 16: Case C-42/90 *Bellon* [1990] ECR 4863, at 11; Case C-400/96 *Harpegnies* [1998] ECR 5121, at 33 and Case 192/01 *Commission v Denmark* [2003] ECR 9693, at 42.

[178] Articles 95(3), 152(1), 152(3) and Article 174(2) EC impose on the EC institutions to ensure an increased level of protection of human health, consumer protection and protection of the environment.

[179] Case 192/01 *Commission v Denmark* [2003] ECR 9693, at 43.

[180] See, eg, Article 5.7 of the SPS Agreement; Articles 10.6 e 11.8 of the Cartagena Protocol on Biosafety, also the Codex Alimentarius Working Principles for Risk Analysis.

Moreover, it must be observed that in the same *Artegodan* judgment the scope of the above-mentioned critical statement would seem to be mitigated by the subsequent explicit recognition of the wide margin of discretion that the EC institutions enjoy when deciding whether to act or not. Thus, the CFI held that:

> [w]here scientific evaluation does not make it possible to determine the existence of a risk with sufficient certainty, whether to have recourse to the precautionary principle depends as a general rule on the level of protection chosen by the competent authority in the exercise of its discretion.[181]

According to da Cruz Vilaça, some elements surrounding the adoption of the *Artegodan* judgments by the CFI would explain its more 'maximilist' approach when compared with Pfizer[182].

In particular, he argued that not only were these judgments rendered by two different chambers of the CFI, but the reason why *Pfizer* is not even mentioned in *Artegodan* is because that latter judgment was already deliberated when *Pfizer* was made public. Although the *Artegodan* judgments were appealed, the appeal did not examine the conditions of application of the precautionary principle.

Finally, another disturbing element stemming from the definition provided by this regulation is that it does not establish who will determine that scientific uncertainty exists: should it be a national or a Community authority? As will be shown in the next Chapter analysing the functioning of EFSA, it is extremely difficult to answer that question as there is no hierarchy between research bodies and it is therefore difficult to see how, in the event of conflicting scientific studies, following one set of scientific opinions rather than another can be justified. Hence, disputes and divergences between national and community bodies are likely to arise.

3.   *Framing of the Principle and its Conditions of Application*

After acknowledging the potential spill-over effects stemming from its improper invocation, the regulation tries to define the scope of the principle and to lay down the necessary limits on its use by both the EC

---

[181] Joined Cases T-144/00, T-76/00, T-83/00, T-84/00, T-85/00, T-132/00 and T-141/00 *Artegodan a.o. v Commission* [2002] ECR 4945, para 186. On the distinction between scientific advice, on the one hand, and the discretionary assessment of the competent authority, on the other, the judgment refers to Case C-405/92 *Mondiet* [1993] ECR I-6133, paragraph 31, and the Opinion of Advocate General Gulmann in that case, point 28.

[182] J.L. da Cruz Vilaça, 'The Precautionary Principle in EC Law', 10 *European Public Law* 2, p 402.

institutions and the Member States 'in order to adopt a uniform basis throughout the Community'.[183] Similar to what was previously established in the above-mentioned Communication, the measures adopted on the basis of the precautionary principle presuppose the existence of a situation of scientific uncertainty and must be proportionate and no more restrictive of trade than is necessary to achieve the high level of health protection chosen in the Community, having regard to 'technical and economic feasibility and other factors regarded as legitimate in the matter under consideration'.[184] These measures are to be reviewed within a reasonable period of time, depending on the nature of the risk to life and health identified and the type of scientific information needed to clarify the scientific uncertainty and to conduct a more comprehensive assessment.

This formulation of the principle, by building upon the jurisprudence developed by the Community courts during the last years, does not seem to add any additional requirements. In particular, it does not seem to solve, at least prima facie, the most controversial issue surrounding the application of the principle, which consists in determining how much scientific certainty about uncertain risks must be provided, ie the scientific threshold triggering its invocation. However, as will be shown below, it is exactly on this point that the new definition carries the potential to improve the application of the principle by clarifying the type of scientific uncertainty relevant for its invocation. It is submitted that once the kind of scientific uncertainty surrounding the functioning of the principle is identified, it will be easier to tackle the even more difficult question of identifying and determining the exact risk threshold triggering its application.

3.1 Risk Threshold or the 'Uncertainty Paradox'

The level of proof needed to prompt the application of the precautionary principle has been called 'knowledge condition' in order to show the 'uncertainty paradox' underlining its functioning: on the one hand, the principle assumes that science cannot provide decisive evidence on uncertain risks, on the other, decision-makers (and consequently, judges) appeal to science for some kind of certainty.[185]

---

[183] Recital (20) of the preamble of the regulation.

[184] Article 7.2 reads as follow: '[m]easures adopted on the basis of paragraph 1 shall be proportionate and no more restrictive of trade than is required to achieve the high level of health protection chosen in the Community, regard being had to technical and economic feasibility and other factors regarded as legitimate in the matter under consideration. The measures shall be reviewed within a reasonable period of time, depending on the nature of the risk to life or health identified and the type of scientific information needed to clarify the scientific uncertainty and to conduct a more comprehensive risk assessment'.

[185] M. Van Asselt and E. Vos, 'The Paradox of the Precautionary Principle', *Risk Analysis*, 2004.

A crystal clear expression of the precautionary paradox may be found in *Pfizer*:

> [...] a preventive measure cannot properly be based on a purely hypothetical approach to the risk, founded on mere conjecture which has not been scientifically verified [...] Rather, it follows from the Community Courts' interpretation of the precautionary principle that a preventive measure may be taken only if the risk, although the reality and extent thereof have not been 'fully' demonstrated by conclusive scientific evidence, appears nevertheless to be *adequately backed up by the scientific data available* at the time when the measure was taken.[186]

In other words, although scientific uncertainty is recognised, science is still expected, under the current approach, to reveal as much truth as possible about uncertain risks. Science is still the tool both Member States and EC institutions must rely upon when they want to adopt measures in situations of scientific uncertainty. We will see, in examining the *Pfizer* judgment, how this 'knowledge condition' represents the most difficult requirement for the judiciary to assess: to what extent may a judge, who is by definition a non-scientist, verify whether a preventive measure is 'adequately backed up by the scientific data available at the time when the measure was taken'? This test, by aiming to establish the amount of scientific evidence necessary to trigger the application of the principle, seems to require from the judge the ability to discuss the scientific plausibility of the scientific arguments advanced by the parties.

The CFI in the same *Pfizer* judgment showed itself to be aware of the precautionary paradox which surrounds the required knowledge condition when it declared that:

> [...] unless the precautionary principle is to be rendered nugatory, the fact that it is impossible to carry out a full scientific risk assessment does not prevent the competent public authority from taking preventive measures, at very short notice if necessary, when such measures appear essential given the level of risk which the authority has deemed unacceptable for society.[187]

---

[186] Case T-13/99 *Pfizer Animal Health v Council*, 2002 E.C.R. II-3305, at 143-144. For a brief review of the judgment, A. Alemanno, 'Protection des consommateurs: Arrêts Alpharma/Pfizer', 4 *Revue du droit de l'Union Europénne*, pp 842–845 (2002) and Walker, 'The Myth of Science as a Neutral Arbiter for Triggering Precautions', supra note 71, pp 221–225; for a critical assessment of the judgment, see also Ladeur, 'The Introduction of the Precautionary Principle into EU law: A Phyrric Victory for Environmental and Public Health Law?' supra note 44 and the reaction to this article by S. Wolf, 'Risk Regulation, Higher Rationality, and The Death of Judicial Self-Restraint: A Comment on Ladeur', 41 *Common Market Law Review* 1175–1180 (2004).

[187] Case T-13/99 *Pfizer Animal Health v Council*, 2002 E.C.R. II-3305, at 160.

In particular, the formulation used by the CFI according to which a preventive measure must be '*adequately* backed up by the scientific data available at the time when the measure was taken' gives rise to an even more paradoxical situation, notably in cases of scientific uncertainty, to the extent that it seems to require that the higher the expected risk, the greater the scientific justification needed.

3.2   Scientific Uncertainty: What's That?

To understand fully the elements of novelty introduced by the new definition of the precautionary principle, it is essential to examine the notion of scientific uncertainty. In particular, as scientific uncertainty is the essence of the precautionary principle, it is necessary to identify the possible scenarios which hide behind the term 'uncertainty'.

The problem of understanding, conceiving and defining uncertainty within the framework of risk assessment is extremely difficult, but it is undisputable that it represents the logical precondition to a viable use of the principle.

Therefore, as there is much debate in relation to different forms of uncertainty, it is imperative when discussing the application of the precautionary principle within a defined legal system, to distinguish and identify the kind of scientific uncertainty which is relevant for the invocation of the principle.

It is possible to distinguish between several types of situations giving rise to scientific uncertainty by looking in particular at how uncertainty manifests itself in the risk assessment process. In light of the above, it is submitted that one should first distinguish scientific uncertainty deriving from conflicting scientific results, from that stemming from situations of ignorance. It is suggested that the former situation can be labelled as 'genuine uncertainty', as opposed to all other categories of scientific uncertainty attributable to ignorance. 'Genuine uncertainty' regroups all those scenarios where, although there exists available scientific studies, the resulting science may not establish a direct causal link between an activity, process or substance and an identified adverse effect.[188]

---

[188] This definition belongs to Christoforou, 'The Precautionary Principle and Democratizing Expertise: a European Legal Perspective', supra note 48, p 207. According to the Commission, such a situation corresponds to 'absence of proof of the existence of a cause-effect relationship, a quantifiable dose/response relationship or a quantitative evaluation of the probability of the emergence of adverse effects following exposure'. See Commission Communication on the precautionary principle, supra note 30, at 6.2.

Within the broad category of scientific uncertainty attributable to ignorance, it is crucial to differentiate between situations where the impossibility of achieving certainty is merely material, inasmuch as the costs involved in conducting scientific research arc too high, and those where such an impossibility is due to the unavailability of definitive scientific data, which in turn can be ascribed to the novelty of the product concerned and to the consequent lack of sufficiently developed assessment techniques. It is proposed that, while the former be regrouped together under the label of 'unjustifiable uncertainty', the latter be qualified as 'justifiable uncertainty'.

In the light of the proposed tassonomy,[189] one may wonder which, among the three categories of scientific uncertainty identified above, validly justifies the application of the precautionary principle.

The newly introduced definition of precaution contained in the general food regulation allows recourse to the principle when 'following an assessment of available information, the possibility of harmful effects on health is identified but scientific uncertainty persists'. As a result, the idea being that there must be an *identification* of the persisting risk, it seems that the only category of scientific uncertainty capable of triggering the application of the principle would be that of 'genuine uncertainty'. In other words, the wording employed by the legislator focusing on the *identification* 'of the possibility of harmful effects on health' would rule out from the scope of the precautionary principle all situations of scientific uncertainty attributable to ignorance, regardless of whether these may be qualified as 'justifiable' or 'unjustifiable'. The risk stemming from such an interpretation of the kind (or degree) of scientific uncertainty triggering the invocation of the principle in European food law is that the competent authorities would be prevented from taking precautionary action in situations of 'justifiable uncertainty', that is, where the insufficient scientific evidence collected is due to the novelty of a product rather than being the product of financial choices aimed at capping risk assessment expenses.

This result is not entirely unexpected as it has somehow been anticipated by the most recent case law developed on the application of the precautionary principle. As will be shown below, this case law has gradually given shape to the first reference made to the notion of

---

[189] Nevertheless, it should always be remembered that, notwithstanding the importance of the proposed distinctions in the context of risk assessment, 'although distinguishable, uncertainty and ignorance very frequently coexist in a risk assessment and this can further increase the potential for error in the degree of confidence regarding the existence of harm to health, the environment or in the work place'. See Christoforou, 'The Precautionary Principle and Democratising Expertise ...', supra note 48, p 51.

scientific uncertainty, in the landmark BSE case *National Farmers' Union* as a prerequisite for precautionary action. According to this judgment, EC institutions may take protective measures:

> [...] where there is uncertainty as to the existence or extent of risks to human health.[190]

No further indication was given as to the kind of scientific uncertainty required for legitimising precautionary action.

Therefore, this definition of scientific uncertainty being rather vague, in subsequent cases, the courts attempted to substantiate it in order to turn it into a more workable concept. Thus, since the above-mentioned *Kellogg's* case, the EC courts have begun to qualify the kind of scientific uncertainty that is relevant for the invocation of the principle, by restricting it to situations 'where it proves to be impossible to determine with certainty the existence or extent of the alleged risk because of the *insufficiency, inconclusiveness, or imprecision* of the results of studies conducted'.[191]

Although the courts offered no guidance on how to interpret the notions of insufficiency, inconclusiveness and imprecision, it will be illustrated how, from that moment on, they began requiring a rather demanding and detailed assessment of the risk by the competent authorities, thus giving rise to the above-mentioned 'precautionary paradox'. Hence, the courts have required that risk management decisions inspired by the precautionary principle be based not only 'on the most reliable scientific data available'[192] and 'on cogent information',[193] but also 'on solid and convincing evidence'.[194]

In particular, in *Commission v. Denmark*[195], the ECJ has clearly required from the Danish authorities invoking the principle:

> [...] in the first place, the *identification* of the potentially negative consequences for health of the proposed addition of nutrients, and, secondly, a comprehensive assessment of the risk to health

---

[190] Case C-157/96, *National Farmers' Union* [1998] ECR I-2211, at 63.

[191] See, eg, Case E-3/00 *EFTA Surveillance Authority v Norway*, at 31; Case 192/01 *Commission v Denmark* [2003] ECR 9693, at 52 and Case T-13/99 *Pfizer Animal Health v Council*, 2002 E.C.R. II-3305, at 393.

[192] Case C-236/01 *Monsanto Agricoltura Italia and Others* [2003] ECR I-8105; Case 192/01 *Commission v Denmark* [2003] ECR 9693, at 51 and T-13/99, Case T-13/99 *Pfizer Animal Health v Council*, 2002 E.C.R. II-3305, at 196.

[193] T-13/99 *Pfizer Animal Health v Council*, 2002 E.C.R. II-3305, at 162.

[194] Joined Cases T-144/00, T-76/00, T-83/00, T-84/00, T-85/00, T-132/00 and T-141/00 *Artegodan a.o. v Commission* [2002] ECR 4945, at 192.

[195] Case 192/01 *Commission v Denmark* [2003] ECR 9693.

based on the most reliable scientific data available and the most recent results of international research.[196]

It is submitted that this trend of requiring more and more detailed risk assessment cannot but have influenced the legislator's choice explicitly to introduce, within the first legally binding definition of the precautionary principle, as enshrined in the general food regulation, a risk assessment obligation requiring the competent authorities to literally 'identify' the possibility of harmful effects on health.

4. Recent Case Law

4.1. The *Pfizer/Alpharma* Judgments

In September 2002, the CFI delivered two important judgments dealing with the role of the precautionary principle. Two pharmaceutical companies, Pfizer and Alpharma, brought an action seeking the annulment of a precautionary measure, Regulation 2821/98, by which the authorisation for use of certain antibiotics, including Virginiamycin and Bacitracin zinc as growth promoters in animal feedstuff was withdrawn.[197]

This regulation has been adopted as a result of the attempts made by Sweden and Denmark to introduce safeguard measures. Indeed, by relying on the safeguard clause provided for in Article 11 of Directive 70/524, Denmark adopted a ban on the use in its territory of virgiamycin in feedstuffs. In so doing, the Danish authority relied on a report from the National Veterinary Laboratory. For its part, the Commission asked the Scientific Committee for Animal Nutrition (SCAN) for its opinion on the risks to be expected from the use of these antibiotics as growth promoters.[198] Despite the fact that SCAN concluded that the use of virgiamycin did not constitute an immediate risk to public health in

---

[196] Ibid, at 51.

[197] The use of additives in feedstuffs has been regulated at the Community level since 1970 (Council Directive 70/524/ECC concerning additives in feedstuffs, OJ L270/1). In 1996 a Community authorisation system was introduced according to which only additives that obtained prior Community authorization could be used in feedstuffs (Council Directive 96/51/EEC, amending Council Directive 70/524/ECC concerning additives in feedstuffs, OJ L235/9).This regulatory regime allows Member States temporarily to suspend or restrict the use of an authorized additive. In this case, the relevant Member State has a duty immediately to inform the other Member States and the Commission and share the grounds on which it considers the additive dangerous. It is up to the Commission or the Council to confirm the national safeguard decision or to decide that the Member State must lift the measure.

[198] More precisely, it asked SCAN to give an opinion on whether the conclusions in the Danish report 'are scientifically justified' and on the question 'whether or not' the use of virgiamycin as a growth promoter constitutes a public health risk in the future.

Denmark,[199] both the Commission and the Council, relying on the precautionary principle, referred to the remaining uncertainty,[200] which had, albeit to a different degree, been confirmed by the scientists consulted, and, consequently, decided to revoke the authorisation. Therefore, notwithstanding SCAN's opinion, the Commission proposed issuing a ban. Both the Commission and the Council reached this conclusion after having evaluated and having interpreted the same uncertainty information differently than SCAN.

As stated, although SCAN tried to provide a proof showing the plausibility of its evidence, as requested by the Commission, 'because of the impossibility to provide certainty about uncertain risks, uncertainty information unsystematically crept into its advice'.[201]

Pfizer invoked several grounds supporting its challenge to the Council regulation, the most important of which relate to manifest errors in risk assessment and management and a misapplication of the precautionary principle.

As the court did not detect any manifest errors, it eventually upheld the Council's decision.

However, the European Court of First Instance, after endorsing the philosophy behind this principle, has defined the terms under which the principle can be invoked. Thus, the court has stated:

> [...] a preventive measure cannot properly be based on a purely hypothetical approach to the risk, founded on mere conjecture which has not been scientifically verified ... Rather, it follows from the Community Courts' interpretation of the precautionary principle that a preventive measure may be taken only if the risk, although the reality and extent thereof have not been 'fully' demonstrated by conclusive scientific evidence, appears nevertheless to be adequately backed up by the scientific data available at the time when the measure was taken.[202]

---

[199] Opinion of the SCAN on the immediate and longer-term risk to the value of Streptogramins in Human Medicine posed by the use of Virgiamycin as an animal growth promoter of 10 July 1998.

[200] Indeed, the SCAN report, though concluding that 'the use of virginiamycin as a growth promoter does not constitute an immediate risk to public health in Denmark', also recognised that 'the nature of resistance to the streptogramins is not fully understood and mechanisms other that those descript above may operate'.

[201] van Asselt and Vos, supra note 185, at 11.

[202] Case T-13/99 *Pfizer Animal Health v Council*, 2002 E.C.R. II-3305, at 143–144. For a brief review of the judgment, Alemanno, 'Protection des consommateurs: Arrêts Alpharma/Pfizer', 4 *Revue du Droit de l'Union Europénne*, pp 842-845 (2002) and Walker, 'The Myth of Science as a Neutral Arbiter for Triggering Precautions', supra note 71, pp 221–225; for a critical assessment of the judgment, see also van Asselt and Vos, supra note 185; Ladeur,

(continued...)

It follows that the precautionary principle's invocation always requires a prior objective evaluation of the relevant existing scientific data as 'it is not a joker or wild card that can be played at any moment as a pretext for unjustified measures'.[203] This principle can therefore be validly applied only in situations in which there is a risk, notably to human health, which, although it is not founded on mere hypotheses that have not been scientifically confirmed, has not yet been fully proven. However, although recognising the CFI's efforts in defining the risk threshold triggering the application of the principle, one cannot but notice that the language of the court remains tentative: if uncertainty cannot be 'purely hypothetical', the use of the word 'purely' seems to admit the acceptance of a certain level of theoretical uncertainty.[204]

Moreover, although not entirely successfully, the CFI had then for the first time made an attempt at defining the nature of the risk assessment that may validly justify reliance on the principle by stating:

> [...] if it is not to adopt arbitrary measures, which cannot in any circumstances be rendered legitimate by the precautionary principle, the competent public authority must ensure that any measures that it takes, even preventive measures, are based on as thorough a scientific risk assessment as possible, account being taken of the particular circumstances of the case at issue. Notwithstanding the existing scientific uncertainty, the scientific risk assessment *must enable the competent public authority to ascertain, on the basis of the best available scientific data and the most recent results of international research, whether matters have gone beyond the level of risk that it deems acceptable for society* [....]. That is the basis on which the authority must decide whether preventive measures are called for.[205]

It must be observed how the CFI has made this determination in qualitative rather than in quantitative terms, by stating that if a complete risk assessment may be impossible in cases of uncertainty, it must allow the competent authorities to determine whether the situation has exceeded the level of risk deemed acceptable for society. This is the required risk assessment justifying the adoption of a precautionary measure.

'The Introduction of the Precautionary Principle into EU law: A Pyrrhic Victory for Environmental and Public Health Law? Decision-making Under Conditions of Complexity in Multi-Level Political Systems', supra note 44 and the reaction to this article by Wolf, 'Risk Regulation, Higher Rationality, and The Death of Judicial Self-Restraint: A Comment on Ladeur', supra note 186, pp 1175–1180.

[203] See Speech D. Byrne, available at http:// europa.eu.int/comm/dgs/health_consumer/library/speeches/speech168_en.pdf.

[204] E. Ni Chaoimh, 'Trading in Precaution – A Comparative Study of the Precautionary jurisprudence of the European Court and the WTO's Adjudicating Body', 33(2) *Legal Issues of Economic Integration*, p 150 (2006).

[205] Case T-13/99 *Pfizer Animal Health v Council* [2002] ECR II-3305, at 162.

At the same time, the risk assessment must also:

> enable the competent authority to decide, in relation to risk management, which measures appear to it to be appropriate and necessary to prevent the risk from materialising.[206]

This is the risk assessment required to prove the proportionality of the precautionary action.

It follows that, to review the legality of a precautionary measure the EC courts must first know which is the level of protection sought by the competent authorities who adopted that measure and only afterwards may proceed to verifying whether the outcome of the required risk assessment has reasonably led them to believe that matters would have gone beyond the level of risk that it deems acceptable for society.

On this point, it must be remembered that EC courts have indicated that when adopting Community measures:

> the Community institutions enjoyed a broad discretion, in particular when determining the level of risk deemed unacceptable for society.[207]

The result is that after *Pfizer*, while the exact threshold of risk which must be established in order to validly take precautionary action would seem to remain largely undefined, it is clear what kind of risk assessment must be conducted by the invoking authorities.

The required risk assessment no longer has to satisfy a mere negative condition (not to rely on hypothetical considerations to establish scientific uncertainty),[208] but it also has to consist in 'sufficiently reliable and cogent information' allowing the authority to ascertain whether the feared situation has exceeded the level of risk deemed acceptable for society.[209] This means that in order to judicially review a precautionary measure, in particular its adequacy to its scientific basis, courts do need to know what level of protection the competent authorities are seeking to achieve. Without a determination of this element, it will prove impossible for them to verify whether a contested precautionary regulation is 'adequately backed up by the scientific data available at the time when the measure was taken'.[210]

---

[206] Ibid, at 163.

[207] Case T-13/99 *Pfizer Animal Health v Council*, 2002 E.C.R. II-3305, at 167.

[208] See on this point, the opinion by AG Poiares Maduro in Case C-41/02 [2004] not yet reported, para 28.

[209] Case T-13/99 *Pfizer Animal Health v Council*, 2002 E.C.R. II-3305, at 162.

[210] Case T-13/99 *Pfizer Animal Health v Council*, 2002 E.C.R. II-3305, at 144. For a review of the judgment, Alemanno, 'Protection des Consommateurs: Arrêts Alpharma/Pfizer', supra

(continued...)

4.2. The *Vitamins* Line of Cases

A recent line of judgments involving fortified food has provided a useful judicial opportunity for further defining the conditions triggering the application of the precautionary principle by the Member States. In these cases the court had been called upon to examine four infringement proceedings brought against Denmark,[211] France,[212] Italy[213] and the Netherlands.[214] In particular, the Commission contested, on the one hand, the Danish and Dutch practices entailing the systematic prohibition on marketing of foodstuffs fortified with certain nutrients which did not meet a nutritional need of the Danish and Dutch populations. On the other hand, the Commission challenged the French and Italian systems of prior approval for fortified foods lawfully produced and marketed in other Member States.[215] At the time of the infringement actions, no Community legislation had been adopted laying down the conditions regulating the addition of vitamins and minerals to foodstuffs.[216] While it proved rather easy for the court to come to the conclusion that the national practices and prior approval procedures qualified as obstacles to intra-Community trade under Article 28 EC, it proved much more difficult to establish whether and to what extent such restrictions on free movement could be justified under Article 30 EC.

As both the Danish and the Dutch Governments relied on the precautionary principle to justify their trade-restrictive administrative practices, the ECJ recalled, by drawing on the 2001 EFTA *Kellogg's* case, that:

note 186 and Walker, 'The Myth of Science as a Neutral Arbiter for Triggering Precautions', supra note 71, pp 221–225; for a critical assessment of the judgment, see also van Asselt and Vos, supra note 185; Ladeur, 'The Introduction of the Precautionary Principle into EU law: A Pyrrhic Victory for Environmental and Public Health Law? Decision-making Under Conditions of Complexity in Multi-Level Political Systems', supra note 44 and the reaction to this article by Wolf, 'Risk Regulation, Higher Rationality, and The Death of Judicial Self-Restraint: A Comment on Ladeur', 41 *Common Market Law Review* 1175-1180 (2004).

[211] Case 192/01 *Commission v Denmark* [2003] ECR 9693.

[212] Case C-24/00 *Commission v France* [2004] not yet reported.

[213] Case C-270/02 *Commission v Italy* [2004] not yet reported.

[214] Case C-41/02 *Commission v Netherlands* [2004] not yet reported.

[215] For a comment on the Italian and French judgments, see F. Erlbacher, 'Restrictions to the Free Movement of Goods on Grounds of the Protection of Human Health: Some Remarks on Recent ECJ Judgments', *European Law Reporter*, 2004, p 118.

[216] Since legislation on fortified foods was announced in the White Paper on Food Safety in 2000, supra note 145, the European Commission has proposed a Regulation (COM(2003) 671 final) setting out common rules for the voluntary addition of vitamins and minerals and of certain other substances to foods. This proposal has been voted by the EP in May 2006 and it has been finally adopted by the European Parliament and the Council on December 20, 2006. See Regulation (EC) No 1925/2006 of the European Parliament and of the Council of 20 December 2006 on the addition of vitamins and minerals and of certain other substances to foods, OJ L 404, 30 December 2006.

a proper application of the precautionary principle presupposes, in the first place, the identification of the potentially negative consequences for health of the proposed addition of nutrients, and, secondly, a comprehensive assessment of the risk to health based on the most reliable scientific data available and the most recent results of international research.[217]

Having recalled these procedural requirements for a valid application of the principle, it made an attempt at defining the threshold triggering its invocation, by holding that:

when it proves to be impossible to determine with certainty [after having undertaken the prescribed comprehensive risk assessment] the existence or extent of the alleged risk because of the insufficiency, inconclusiveness or imprecision of the results of studies conducted, but the *likelihood of real harm to public health persists should the risk materialise*, the precautionary principle justifies the adoption of restrictive measures.[218]

That means that under EC law Member States may take precautionary action whenever their comprehensive assessment shows that the likelihood of real harm still persists where the negative eventuality occurred.

Although it is doubtful whether this rather vague threshold might translate into a useful benchmark for the judge called upon to verify the legality of a precautionary-based measure, the court's efforts better to define the 'knowledge condition' prompting its invocation must be applauded. Indeed, the court has, similarly to what the CFI has done in *Pfizer*, gone beyond the mere negative condition ruling out all the alleged hypothetical risks as a basis for precautionary action and has established a positive threshold for the invocation of the principle by a Member State. Once a Member State's precautionary measure is preceded by a comprehensive risk assessment showing that the likelihood of real harm may persist should the negative eventuality occur, that measure will be allowed to stand. It remains, however, to be seen what exactly the ECJ meant when it referred to such a rather hermetic risk threshold. Does this requirement imply that the likelihood that the negative event will occur has to be proven by the invoking party? If this is the case, one may wonder how that could be done in a context of scientific uncertainty, ie a situation where it lacks evidence establishing a direct link between an activity or substance and an identified adverse effect.

Yet, what is striking in these judgments is the lack of any reference to the provisional nature of all precautionary-based measures. As is clearly

[217] *Commission v Denmark*, para 51; *Commission v The Netherlands*, para 53.
[218] *Commission v Denmark*, para 52; *Commission v The Netherlands*, para 54.

stated in the 2000 Communication and in the general food law regulation, precautionary measures are, by their very nature, provisional and may only be maintained for so long as the scientific data remain inadequate, imprecise and inconclusive. The ECJ's lack of reference to the limited duration of precautionary measures remains particularly controversial if examined within the WTO/SPS context. In fact, all measures adopted under Article 5.7 SPS are subject to a strict time limit, under which a precautionary measure may be authorised only insofar as scientific research has not yet proven the existence of a risk or the extent of that risk to public health.

4.3. The *GMO* Austrian Judgments

One of the latest attempts to invoke the precautionary principle has occurred in the recent *GMO* Austrian cases, where the Austrian authorities, claiming to be entitled to create a GMO-free zone, challenged the Commission decision rejecting the ban on the use of genetically modified organisms in Upper Austria (Land Oberösterreich).[219]

In order to obtain a derogation, on the basis of Article 95(5), from Directive 2001/18 on the deliberate release into the environment of GMOs, on 13 March 2003 the Republic of Austria notified to the Commission a draft law of the province of Upper Austria intended to prohibit the cultivation of seed and planting material composed of or containing GMOs. As seen above, under Article 95(5) EC, the introduction of new national provisions must be based on new scientific evidence relating to the protection of the environment or the working environment on grounds of a problem specific to that Member State arising after the adoption of the harmonisation measure. In light of the above, the Commission requested EFSA to issue an opinion, in accordance with Article 29(1) and Article 22(5)(c) of the general food regulation, on the probative value of the scientific study set forth and relied upon by the Austrian authorities. In its scientific opinion of 4 July 2003, EFSA found that that scientific information did not contain any new scientific evidence which could justify banning GMOs in the Land Oberösterreich. In particular, it concluded that the Republic of Austria failed to establish that the territory of the Land Oberösterreich contained unusual or unique ecosystems that required separate risk assessments from those conducted for Austria as a whole or in other similar areas of Europe.[220] In light of the

---

[219] Joined Cases T-366/03 and T-235/04, *Land Oberösterreich and Republic of Austria v Commission*, not yet reported.

[220] According to the conclusions of EFSA: first, 'the scientific evidence presented contained no new or uniquely local scientific information on the environmental or human health impacts of existing or future GM crops or animals' and, secondly, 'no scientific evidence was presented which showed that this area of Austria had unusual or unique ecosystems that required separate risk assessments from those conducted for Austria as a whole or for other similar areas of Europe'. See recitals 70 and 71 of the Commission Decision

(continued...)

above, the Commission adopted Decision 2003/653/EC rejecting the Austrian safeguard measure. It is against this decision that both the Land Oberösterreich and the Republic of Austria brought the actions registered under case numbers T-366/03 and T-235/04, respectively. Having recalled that Article 95(5) allows Member States to derogate from EU harmonised legislation only to the extent that they show new scientific evidence and the existence of specific problems justifying such a departure, the CFI found that neither of these conditions of application had been met in the present case.

As a result, the CFI unfortunately did not examine the plea relating to the alleged breach of the precautionary principle. The court dismissed this plea as 'irrelevant' insofar as:

> [...] a request had been submitted to the Commission under Article 95(5) EC. It decided that the conditions for application of that article were not met. This Court has found, following examination of the third plea, that the contested decision was not incorrect. The Commission therefore had no option in any event but to reject the application which was submitted to it.[221]

An appeal against this judgment having been lodged by Austria on 5 October 2005, this case is currently pending before the ECJ.[222] It remains to be seen whether the ECJ will be driven, by the pleas of the appellant, to take a position on whether the Commission's rejection of the safeguard measure may amount to a violation of the precautionary principle as invoked by the Austrian authorities. This outcome looks rather unlikely.

5. *Conclusions: the Courts and the Challenge of Reviewing Precautionary Measures*

Although the introduction of a precautionary approach in the health field dates back to the 1970s, it is only since 1992 that this principle, although limited to the environmental protection field, has been codified by Article 130r(2) of the Treaty. Its scope has been subsequently widened by the interpretative activity of the ECJ so as also to apply to other domains of EC law, such as public health.[223]

2003/653/EC of 2 September 2003 relating to national provisions on banning the use of genetically modified organisms in the region of Upper Austria notified by the Republic of Austria pursuant to Article 95(5) of the EC Treaty (OJ 2003 L 230/34).

[221] Joined Cases T-366/03 and T-235/04, *Land Oberösterreich and Republic of Austria v Commission*, not yet reported, at 71.

[222] Appeal brought on 22 December 2005 by the Republic of Austria against the judgment delivered on 5 October 2005 by the Court of First Instance of the European Communities (Fourth Chamber) in Joined Cases T-366/03 and T-035/04 (Case C-454/05P). See OJ C 60/20, 2006.

[223] One of the latest references to the horizontal nature of the precautionary principle may be found in Case C-41/02 [2004] not yet reported, at 45, where it is said that: 'It is

(continued...)

In particular, it was in the *BSE* line of cases that this principle was upheld by the EC courts. However, it was only in the *Pfizer/Alpharma* judgments that the CFI sketched out a rationalisation of the principle by defining its conditions of application when it is invoked by Member States.

To understand fully the philosophy underpinning the precautionary principle it must be borne in mind that neither its meaning nor its significance end with scientific analysis. The principle invites a more overtly political decision about the balance of risks involved. As we have seen, deciding on the appropriate balance between burden and risk involves social choices transcending mere scientific data. Thus, the same general food regulation recognises that scientific risk assessment alone cannot, in some cases, provide all the information on which a risk management decision should be based, and that other factors relevant to the matter under consideration may be legitimately taken into account, including societal, economic, traditional, ethical and environmental factors and the feasibility of controls.

According to the court, in cases of scientific uncertainty as to the existence of a risk to human health, the EC institutions as well as the Member States may invoke the precautionary principle in order to adopt protective measures, in spite of the fact that a proper risk assessment showing conclusive scientific evidence cannot be conducted. Such measures cannot, however, be based on a purely hypothetical approach founded on mere hypotheses and may be adopted only if the risk, although the reality and the extent thereof have not been fully demonstrated by conclusive scientific evidence, appears to be properly backed up by the scientific studies available at the time when the measure is taken. Once a competent authority has enacted a precautionary-based measure, the principle of proportionality is called upon to verify the legality of the measures intended to pursue the declared public policy objectives.[224] The measure will be considered disproportionate if it is

clear from Article 130r of the EC Treaty (now, after amendment, Article 174 EC) that the protection of human health is one of the objectives of the Community policy on the environment, that that policy aims at a high level of protection and is to be based inter alia on the precautionary principle, and *that the requirements of that policy must be integrated into the definition and implementation of other Community policies.* In addition, it follows from the case-law of the Court that the precautionary principle may also apply in policy on the protection of human health which, according to Article 129 of the EC Treaty (now, after amendment, Article 152 EC) likewise aims at a high level of protection'.

[224] It is important to remember that '[p]rior to the enshrinement in case-law of the precautionary principle, on the basis of the Treaty provisions, that principle was implicitly applied in the review of proportionality'. See Joined Cases T-144/00, T-76/00, T-83/00, T-84/00, T-85/00, T-132/00 and T-141/00 *Artegodan a.o. v Commission* [2002] ECR 4945, at 185 referring to Case C-180/96 R *United Kingdom v Commission*, [1996] ECR 3903, at 73–78, and the order of the President of the Court of First Instance in Case T-76/96 R *National Farmers' Union and Others v Commission* [1996] ECR II-815, at 82–93, in particular at 89.

manifestly inappropriate or when it can be shown that other, less onerous, measures exist that would allow the objective pursued by such a measure to be achieved.

After *Pfizer*, indication has been provided as to what kind of risk assessment must be conducted by the invoking authorities. The required risk assessment no longer has to satisfy a mere negative condition (not to rely on hypothetical considerations to establish scientific uncertainty),[225] but it has to consist in 'sufficiently reliable and cogent information' allowing the authority to ascertain whether the feared situation has exceeded the level of risk deemed acceptable for society.[226] This means that in order judicially to review a precautionary measure, in particular the adequacy of its scientific basis, courts do need to know what level of protection is sought to be achieved by the competent authorities. Without a determination of this element, it will prove impossible for them to verify whether a contested precautionary regulation is 'adequately backed up by the scientific data available at the time when the measure was taken'.[227]

However, the threshold of risk which must be established by a Member State in order validly to take precautionary action remains largely undefined. The only indication provided in the case law is that, under EC law, Member States may take precautionary action whenever their comprehensive assessment shows that the likelihood of real harm still persists where the negative eventuality occurred.

Although it is doubtful whether this rather vague threshold might translate into a useful benchmark for the judge called upon to verify the legality of a precautionary-based measure, the court's efforts better to define the 'knowledge condition' prompting its invocation must be applauded. Indeed, the ECJ has, similarly to what the CFI has done in *Pfizer*, moved beyond the mere negative condition ruling out all the alleged hypothetical risks as a basis for precautionary action and it has established a positive threshold for the invocation of the principle by a Member State.[228] Once a Member State's precautionary measure is preceded by a comprehensive risk assessment showing that the likelihood of real harm may persist should the negative eventuality occur, that measure will be allowed to stand. It remains, however, to be seen what exactly the ECJ meant when it referred to this rather ambiguous risk threshold.

---

[225] See on this point, the Opinion by AG M Poiares Maduro in Case C-41/02 [2004] not yet reported, para 28.

[226] Case T-13/99 *Pfizer Animal Health v Council*, 2002 E.C.R. II-3305, at 162.

[227] Case T-13/99 *Pfizer Animal Health v Council*, 2002 E.C.R. II-3305, at 144.

[228] *Commission v Denmark*, para 52; *Commission v The Netherlands*, para 54.

Therefore, while the definition of the precautionary principle provided by the general food regulation has clarified certain points, such as the type of scientific uncertainty surrounding the invocation of the principle, the exact balance between science and political discretion still remains contentious.

As a result, notwithstanding the efforts undertaken by the framers of the new food safety regime, the scope of the precautionary principle remains vague and still responds to the idea contained in the 2000 Communication according to which:

> like other general notions contained in the legislation, such as subsidiarity or proportionality, it is for the decision-makers and ultimately the courts to flesh out the principle.[229]

In other words, while remaining textually vague, it is likely that the EC courts will define the scope of the principle by further detailing the factors prompting its application.

This outcome is certainly unfortunate as it is likely to exacerbate even further the debate over the scope of the precautionary principle. This discussion is currently on going not only within the European Union, but also between the two sides of the Atlantic. During recent years the EC has relied heavily upon this principle in the area of food policy and has triggered trade disputes with the United States. Although the US has traditionally followed a precautionary approach in adopting risk regulations, it has opposed the recognition of it as a principle of risk assessment.[230]

The main argument against the invocation of this principle is that, by providing a basis for action in the face of scientific uncertainty, it may

---

[229] See Commission Communication on the precautionary principle, supra note 30, at 10.
[230] Although the 'conventional wisdom' is that the EU endorses the precautionary principle and seeks proactively to regulate risks, while the US opposes its invocation, basing risk assessment on scientific evidence, 'neither actor can claim to be more precautionary than the other' and 'sometimes one actor is more precautionary than the other and sometimes it is the other way around'. See Speech by T. van der Haegen, *EU View of Precautionary Principle in Food Safety*, American Branch of the International Law Association, New York, 23–25 October 2003 available at http://www.eurunion.org/News/speeches/2003/031023tvdh.htm. See also on this point Christoforou, 'The Precautionary Principle, Risk Assessment, and the Comparative Role of Science in the European Community and the US Legal Systems', supra note 98, pp 18 and 41 and de Sadeleer, *Environmental Principles: From Political Slogans to Legal Rules*, Oxford University Press, 2002, pp 139–146. This conclusion subverting the conventional wisdom on the major use of precaution by the EU compared to the USA has recently been confirmed by a study which relied for the first time on quantitative methods in order to compare reliance on precautionary action between the two sides of the Atlantic. See J.K. Hammit, J.B. Wiener, B. Swedlow, D. Kall and Z. Zhou, 'Precautionary Regulation in Europe and the United States: A Quantitative Comparison', 25 *Risk Analysis* 1215 (2005).

easily be invoked to adopt protectionist measures. The same former EC Commissioner Byrne has conceded:

> [p]recaution can be a thinly disguised trade protection measure, not to mention a badge of political cowardice if not adequately framed.[231]

Moreover, it is interesting to observe that the language employed by the CFI, and today codified within the general food law regulation, to frame the invocation of the precautionary principle is largely resonant of that of the Appellate Body in the *Hormones* case. As has been noted, although WTO law has been denied direct effect within the EC legal order to preserve the autonomy of the political and legislative branches, these judgments prove how this margin of manoeuvre may be easily bypassed by way of judicial interpretation.[232] As will be apparent below, a dialogue between EC and WTO courts seems to exist on how to interpret the precautionary principle.[233]

It is in these circumstances that the difficult tasks of evaluating the scientific uncertainty triggering the invocation of the principle and the assessment of the proportionality of the precautionary measure adopted is entrusted to the judicial bodies. Indeed, the courts are called upon to resolve the ambiguities which remain in relation to the application of the precautionary principle by reaching a definitive answer any time a precautionary measure is contested before them.

The question is therefore the following: what is the standard of review applicable to the decisions taken on the basis of the precautionary principle? In other terms:

> [...] must the Community judicature's review be restricted to addressing the various stages of the decision-making process, or should it assess the quality of the scientific analysis conducted or even review the latitude attributed to policy as opposed to science?[234]

---

[231] See Speech D. Byrne, *The Regulation of Food Safety and the Use of Traceability/Tracing in the EU and USA: Convergence or Divergence?*, Food Safety Conference, Washington D.C., 19 March 2004, 4, available at http:// europa.eu.int/comm/dgs/health_consumer/library/speeches/speech168_en.pdf.

[232] On this point, see J. Scott, 'European Regulation of GMOs: Thinking about 'Judicial Review' in the WTO', in *Jean Monnet Working Paper*, 04/04, 5.

[233] In particular, the Commission Communication having been built upon the analysis developed by the AB in *Hormones*, much of the WTO terminology and attitude towards the principle has entered into the EC legal jargon.

[234] See, on this point, the Opinion by AG Poiares Maduro in Case C-41/02 [2004] not yet reported, at 32.

It is submitted that the applicable standard of review should in principle not depart from that applied to any other public health measures ('manifest error'), but it requires from the judges some particular sensitivity to the peculiar context in which the contested decision to act has been adopted.

Thus, for instance, in *Pfizer*, the CFI, while admitting that under the precautionary principle the Community institutions are entitled 'to adopt, on the basis of as yet incomplete scientific knowledge, protective measures which may seriously harm legally protected positions' it added that:

> [...] in such circumstances, the guarantees conferred by the Community legal order in administrative proceedings are of even more fundamental importance. Those guarantees include, in particular, the duty of the competent institution to examine carefully and impartially all the relevant aspects of the individual case.[235]

Besides this heightened procedural duty, which has been imposed by the CFI, it is submitted that to facilitate a proper review of precautionary measures, these decisions must respect three further procedural conditions. This is because, as has been convincingly argued, 'the problem of understanding and defining uncertainty in the context of a risk assessment can be large, complex and nearly intractable, unless the risk analysis is structured into small and simpler concepts for each stage and component of risk assessment'.[236]

The first step to be taken in order to achieve this result consists in proceduralising the risk assessment stage by first making the science policies which permeate risk analysis more transparent. As seen above, these policies need to be elaborated whenever normal science does not specify which data, models or assumptions may lead to an acceptable risk assessment outcome. Indeed, unless the assumptions and policies that have been employed to overcome scientific uncertainties in risk assessment are made explicit, courts may struggle in reviewing the legality of a precautionary-based measure. In these circumstances, courts will not be able to analyse a measure and to determine to what extent it is science-based and whether 'other factors' have already been included within the risk assessment stage. On the contrary, as has been argued, it is necessary that:

> the reasoning underlying the decisions [...] clearly indicate the policy choices adopted, setting them apart from the scientific

---

[235] Case T-13/99 *Pfizer Animal Health v Council*, 2002 ECR II-3305, at 171.
[236] T. Christoforou, 'The Precautionary Principle and Democratizing Expertise: a European Legal Perspective', supra note 48, p 207.

results on which they are based, so that every citizen can identify them.[237]

The second condition that precautionary measures must respect in order to facilitate the task of the judge reviewing their legality is represented by the need to disclose the level of protection sought to be achieved by the competent authorities when adopting those measures ('risk response'). Without a clear determination of this element, it will prove to be impossible for the courts to verify whether a contested measure inspired by the precautionary principle is 'adequately backed up by the scientific data', that is when scientific evidence enables 'the competent public authority to ascertain whether matters have gone beyond the level of risk that it deems acceptable for society [....]'.[238]

The third condition, which stems directly from the previous one, requires that the findings of scientific studies must be presented in the decision-making process before the adoption of the precautionary measure.

It is submitted that such a proposed procedural approach, being structured into small and simpler concepts for each stage and component of risk analysis, may facilitate the judicial review task entrusted to the judge when called upon to review precautionary measures. In particular, by enabling him to distinguish the various stages of the decision-making process, in particular the scientific element from the policy element, this model would enable the judicial bodies to scrutinise the legality of the contested precautionary measure. In fact, the introduction of such a proceduralised model of risk analysis carries the potential of separating not only risk assessment from value judgments but also risk management from its policy goals for the purposes of the court's review. Finally, it is submitted that once the contested decision has been x-rayed through this three-pronged test, it should be easier for the judge to apply the manifest error standard of review and to verify the proportionality of the contested measure.

D.   General Obligation to Ensure that Food is Safe

Article 14 introduces an EC-wide general obligation to ensure that only foodstuffs which are safe, wholesome and fit for consumption be placed on the market for consumers.[239] As has been recently stated:

> The universalistic and abstract language of the provision condenses local difference and provides a single, objective

---

[237] See the Opinion by AG Poiares Maduro in Case C-41/02 [2004] not yet reported, para 34.
[238] Case T-13/99 *Pfizer Animal Health v Council*, 2002 ECR II-3305, at 162.
[239] In line with the language of the Codex Alimentarius, the food safety requirement imposed by Article 14 comprises two elements: a) food should not be injurious to health; or b) unfit for human consumption. Only one of these two elements has to be in place for the food to be considered unsafe.

standard for safety enabling economies of scale and trade liberalization across the Union.[240]

The introduction of this general obligation was originally envisaged in the 1997 Green Paper on Food Law to 'reinforce the overall level of consumer protection within the Community, by encouraging all businesses to introduce their own internal safety and supervision procedures'[241]. In this document the Commission noted that although Community food legislation sets out a series of specific obligations on food manufacturers and traders[242], it does not contain a 'general legal obligation that only food which is safe, wholesome and fit for human consumption should be placed on the market.

Along the same lines, recital 26 of the regulation declares that although some Member States have adopted horizontal legislation on food safety imposing, notably, a general obligation on economic operators to market only food that is safe, 'these Member States apply different basic criteria for establishing whether a food is safe'. As a result, 'given these different approaches, and in the absence of horizontal legislation in other Member States, barriers to trade in foods are liable to arise'. It is therefore necessary – according to the following recital – to establish general requirements for only safe food and feed to be placed on the market, to ensure that the internal market in such products functions effectively.

This obligation of safety is an obligation owed directly by foodstuff businesses to the competent authorities under the criminal or administrative law of the Member States concerned. Being applicable to the whole food chain, from primary production to the final sale of the foodstuff to the consumer, it introduces a greater joint responsibility throughout the food chain, rather than dispersing individual responsibilities. It is indeed likely that at each level of the food chain economic operators will take the measures necessary to ensure food safety within the context of their specific activities.

In sum, introducing a general food safety obligation at the European level contributes to reinforcing the overall effect of consumer protection within the EC by inducing all food businesses to establish their own internal food safety and supervision measures.

---

[240] Chalmers, '"Food for thought": Reconciling European risks and Traditional Ways of Life', 66 *The Modern Law Review* 532, p 545.

[241] Green Paper, available available at http://europa.eu.int/scadplus/leg/en/lvb/l21220.htm, at 45.

[242] Thus, for instance, the general hygiene directive (Council Directive 93/43/EC (OJ 1993 L175/1)) imposes, in its Article 3(1), a precise obligation on manufactures by stating that 'in the preparation process in manufacturing, packaging, storage, transportation, handling and offering for sale or supply of foodstuffs, shall be carried out in a hygienic way'.

Food is considered to be unsafe when it is either injurious to health or unfit for human consumption.[243] In particular, in order to determine whether a food is injurious to health, one has to consider not only the probable immediate and/or short-term and/or long-term effects of that food on the health of a person consuming it, but also on subsequent generations; the probable cumulative toxic effects and, finally, the particular health sensitivies of a specific category of consumers where the food is intended for that category of consumers. Under the regulation, a particular food is unfit for human consumption when it is unacceptable for human consumption according to its intended use, for reasons of contamination, whether by extraneous matter or otherwise, or through putrefaction, deterioration or decay. It seems therefore that food unfit for human consumption tends also to be potentially injurious to health. In fact, Article 3 of the regulation defines risk as 'a function of the probability of an adverse health effect and the severity of that effect, consequential to a hazard', which in turn is represented by 'a biological, chemical or physical agent in, or condition of, food or feed with the potential to cause an adverse health effect'.

The introduction of a general obligation of safety is then coordinated with the more specific food disciplines in such a way that '[f]ood that complies with specific Community provisions governing food safety shall be deemed to be safe insofar as the aspects covered by the specific Community provisions are concerned'.[244] However, such a presumption of conformity is limited to the extent 'conformity of a food with specific provisions applicable to that food shall not bar the competent authorities from taking appropriate measures to impose restrictions on it being placed on the market or to require its withdrawal from the market where there are reasons to suspect that, despite such conformity, the food is unsafe'.[245] Finally, where there are no specific Community provisions, the regulation introduces a presumption of safety for any food conforming 'to the specific provisions of national food law of the Member State in whose territory the food is marketed, such provisions being drawn up and applied without prejudice to the Treaty, in particular Articles 28 and 30 thereof'.[246]

---

[243] Article 14(2) of the regulation.

[244] Article 14.7 of the regulation.

[245] Article 14.8 of the regulation.

[246] Article 14.9 of the regulation. These principles have recently been confirmed by the ECJ in Joined Cases C-211/03, C-299/03 and C-316/03 to C-319/03 *HLH Warenvertriebs Gmbh and Orthica* [2005] ECR 5141, at 37, where it has declared that: '[u]nder Article 14(1) of Regulation No 178/2002, food is not to be placed on the market if it is unsafe and, in accordance with Article 14(2), food is to be deemed to be unsafe if it is considered to be injurious to health or unfit for human consumption. Under Article 14(7), food that complies with specific Community provisions governing food safety is to be deemed to be safe in so far as the aspects covered by the specific Community provisions are concerned. However, Article 14(8) provides that conformity of a food with specific provisions

(continued...)

Moreover, by virtue of Article 21, the insertion of this general safety obligation does not prejudice the application of the Product Liability Directive 85/374/EEC[247] setting out the principle that '[T]he producer shall be liable for damage caused by a defect in his product'.[248] It follows that, to the extent the latter directive currently also applies to foodstuffs, the marketing of an unsafe product could possibly give rise to two separate violations of EC law: breach of the general obligation to ensure that food is safe, established by Article 14 of the regulation, on the one hand, and violation of the Product Liability Directive on the other.[249] However, clarification has been provided by the 2004 guidance document on the implementation of the General Food law:[250] '[al]though the requirement laid down in Article 17(1) is directly applicable from 1 January 2005, the liability of food business operators should flow in practice from the breach of a specific food law requirement (and from the rules for civil or criminal liability which can be found in the national legal order of each Member State)'.[251] As a result '[t]he liability proceedings will not be based on Article 17 but on a legal basis to be found in the national legal order and in the specific infringed legislation'.

As to the relationship between this regulation and Directive 2001/95/EC on General Product Safety, which imposes on manufacturers the obligation to place only safe products on the market,[252] the latter clearly states that it 'shall be without prejudice to the application of Directive 85/374/EEC'.[253]

Similarly, Article 21, although concise, has contributed to the creation of a macro system of food safety liability on which final consumers may rely in order to recover damages suffered as a result of business operators' violations.

---

applicable to that food is not to bar the competent authorities from taking appropriate measures to impose restrictions on it being placed on the market or to require its withdrawal from the market where there are reasons to suspect that, despite such conformity, the food is unsafe.'

[247] Council Directive 85/374/EEC of 25 July 1985 on the approximation of the laws, regulations and administrative provisions of the Member States concerning liability for defective products, OJ L 210/29, as amended by Directive 1999/34/EC OJ 1999 14/20.

[248] Article 1 of this directive provides for an absolute liability for damage caused by any defective (subject to a number of exceptions that are not relevant here). For a detailed analysis of the European regime on the liability for defective products, see M. Cannarsa, *La Responsabilité du Fait des Produits Défectueux: Etude Comparative*, Giuffré, Milano (2005).

[249] See Chalmers, supra note 240, p 542.

[250] Guidance on the implementation of Articles 11, 12, 16, 17, 18, 19 and 20 of Regulation 178/2002 on general food law – Conclusions of the Standing Committee on the Food Chain and Animal Health.

[251] Article 17(1) provides that '[f]ood and feed business operators at all stages of production, processing and distribution within the businesses under their control shall ensure that foods or feeds satisfy the requirements of food law which are relevant to their activities and shall verify that such requirements are met'.

[252] This directive repealed and replaced Directive 92/59/EEC on general product safety, OJ L 228.

[253] Article 17 of Directive 2001/95.

However, we know that in practice it is particularly difficult for the person injured by a defective product to prove the damage, the defect and the causal relationship between the two. This is because of the difficulty in pinpointing precisely the source of outbreaks such as *BSE*. These factors contribute inter alia to explaining the very few applications and overall modest success of this directive, which tends to be put aside to the advantage of the national law provisions regulating product liability, as they provide the applicant with more defined procedural mechanisms.[254] However, as will be argued below, it is believed that, armed with an EFSA opinion suggesting that a product is not safe, it would be easier for a plaintiff to prove his case before national courts. Finally, of particular significance is the last paragraph of Article 14 codifying the principle of mutual recognition within the food safety arena: where there are no specific Community provisions, 'food shall be deemed to be safe when it conforms to the specific provisions of national food law of the Member State in whose territory the food is marketed'. This provision establishes a presumption of safety in favour of Community-wide free trade in foodstuffs that are lawfully available in a Member State.

Apart from the question of defining the exact scope of application of the liability regime established by this regulation, which has been tackled here, the next section will be devoted to one of the most pressing issues that has to be addressed by those seeking to interpret the general food regulation, i.e the allocation of food safety liability among food actors.

E.   Allocation of Responsibilities among Food Actors

Article 17 allocates responsibilities between food business operators and Member States in the implementation of the food regulation.

It first imposes a general duty on business operators to ensure that foods and feeds satisfy the requirements of food law which are relevant to their activities. It then entrusts public authorities with the mission of enforcing food law and of monitoring compliance with it by food and feed business operators at all stages of production, processing and distribution. Member States are also asked to lay down rules on measures and penalties applicable to infringements of food and feed law.[255]

It follows that the primary responsibility for monitoring and verifying that the relevant requirements of food law are fulfilled lies on the businesses, which are entrusted with the following duties: a duty to be

---

[254] Cannarsa, supra note 248, pp 422 ss, 429 and 510.
[255] See Article 17 of the regulation.

informed and to inform (traceability) and a duty to act (withdrawal and recall). Both duties are analysed in the next paragraphs.

However, while this provision defines the responsibilities of food business operators by differentiating them from those of Member States, it does not have the effect of introducing a Community regime regulating the allocation of liability among the different links in the food chain. This is due to the fact that, as explained by the 2004 guidance document on the implementation of the General Food law (hereinafter '2004 Guidance Document'),[256] '[d]etermining the facts and circumstances which may render an operator liable to criminal penalties and/or civil liability is a complex matter which depends very much on the structure of the different national legal systems'. In particular, it should be noted that 'any discussion related to matters of responsibility should take into account the fact that interactions between producers, manufacturers and distributors are becoming increasingly complex. Thus, for example, in many cases primary producers have contractual obligations to manufacturers or distributors to meet specifications which cover quality and/or safety. Distributors increasingly have products produced under their own brand-name and play a key role in product conception and design'.

The question as to how this responsibility should be allocated among the food actors would seem to have recently drawn the attention of Advocate General Stix-Hackl, who declared in her Opinion in *Lidl Italia:*

> [u]nder Article 17(1) of Regulation No 178/2002, food and feed business operators at all stages of production, processing and distribution within the business under their control are to ensure that foods or feeds satisfy the requirements of food law which are relevant to their activities and are to verify that such requirements are met.
>
> Accordingly, in view of the ever closer and increasingly complex relationship between manufacturers, producers and distributors, responsibility ought in principle to be joint rather than individual.[257]

The AG announced this principle in the context of a preliminary ruling where a national judge asked the court to determine who is liable under EC law for the fact that the particulars on the label of a prepackaged food, notably the percentage of alcohol content of a herbal liqueur, are not consistent with the actual value determined. Should it be the manufacturer of the product or the distributor of the foodstuffs, or both?

---

[256] Guidance on the implementation of Articles 11, 12, 16, 17, 18, 19 and 20 of Regulation 178/2002 on general food law – Conclusions of the Standing Committee on the Food Chain and Animal Health.

[257] Opinion in Case C-315/05 *Lidl Italia Srl/Comune di Arcole*, delivered on 12 September 2005, not yet reported, at 58–59.

As the relevant directive on labelling of foodstuffs does not contain any express rules on liability for inaccurate particulars, the AG has turned her attention to other legislation setting forth a liability regime, such as Directive 98/37/EC on the approximation of the laws of the Member States relating to machinery,[258] Directive 85/374/EC on the approximation of the laws of the Member States concerning liability for defective products,[259] Directive 2001/95 on general product safety[260] and the General Food Regulation.

By relying on these texts, the AG came to the conclusion that the food safety obligations arising from the labelling directive are not to be interpreted as meaning that they are imposed only on the manufacturer of a prepackaged foodstuff, but rather also on 'all persons involved in the production and distribution process'.[261]

1.   Traceability

The introduction of a general obligation to ensure that food is safe requires the establishment of a mechanism providing a continuous flow of information, allowing for the retrieval of the history and the origin of a product at any point in the food chain.

Although traceability does not itself make food safe, it is a risk management tool to be used in order to assist in containing a food safety problem.

Its primary aim is therefore to ensure food safety and to assist in enabling unsafe food/feed to be removed from the market, notably by making the recall of a product easier. This goal is translated into an operational duty by Article 18 of the regulation which requires food operators to be able to identify any person who has supplied them with a food and other businesses to which their products have been supplied.

There is also another important aim pursued by a traceability system, which is related to consumer information. A traceability system, by making products identifiable, not only facilitates recall but also allows for the verification of the authenticity of labelling claims, thus guaranteeing to consumers that the information stated on the label is truthful. In other words, traceability enables consumers to be provided with targeted and accurate information concerning a certain product.

---

[258] OJ 1998 L 207/1.

[259] OJ 1985 L 210/29.

[260] OJ 2002 L 11/4.

[261] Opinion in Case C-315/05 *Lidl Italia Srl/Comune di Arcole (VR)* delivered on 12 September 2005, not yet reported, at 60.

Aside from this function, traceability is also intended to avoid the potential for unnecessary wider disruption in the event of food safety problems.

Traceability is defined by Article 3(15) of the regulation as 'the ability to trace and follow a food, feed, food-producing animal or substance intended to be or expected to be incorporated into a food or feed in all stages of production, processing or distribution'.

The current system of traceability has been defined as a 'one step back'– 'one step forward' approach, requiring each operator to know the step before him in the food chain and the step after.[262] Everyone involved in the food chain has to be put in the position of identifying any person responsible for the supply of an unsafe food. Thus, Article 18(1) establishes the principle of traceability in the following terms:

> [t]he traceability of food, feed, food-producing animals and any other substance intended to be, or expected to be, incorporated into a food or feed shall be established at all stages of production, processing and distribution.

According to the 2004 Guidance Document on the implementation of the General Food law, the reference to *'any substance intended to be, or expected to be, incorporated into a food or feed'* should not be interpreted in the sense that veterinary medicinal products, plant protection products or fertilisers may fall within the scope of the requirement. The substances covered are rather those intended or expected to be *'incorporated'*, as part of a food or feed during its manufacture, preparation or treatment. Thus, for instance, this reference, by covering all types of food and feed ingredients, would include grain when incorporated in a feed or food, but would exclude it when used as seed for cultivation.

To facilitate the implementation of this principle, it is provided that food or feed which is placed on the market, or is likely to be placed on the market in the Community, be adequately labelled or identified through relevant documentation and information in accordance with the relevant legislation.[263] Such a system has also been conceived to facilitate the

[262] Speech by D. Byrne, supra note 56.
[263] Although Article 18 does not specify what types of information should be kept by the food and feed business operators, according to the 2004 Guidance document the registration of the following information is considered necessary. This information can be classified in two categories according to its level of priority:
– The first category of information includes any information which shall be made available to the competent authorities in all cases:
    – name, address of supplier, nature of products which were supplied from him.
    – name, address of customer, nature of products that were delivered to that customer.
(continued...)

withdrawal of goods that can be potentially traded through 25 Member States.

In particular, the 'one step back'–'one step forward' requirement implies for food business operators that:

–   they shall have in place a system enabling them to identify the immediate supplier(s) of and immediate customer(s) for their products;
–   a link 'supplier-product' shall be established (which products supplied from which suppliers);[264] and
–   a link 'customer-product' shall be established (which products supplied to which customers).

However, according to the 2004 Guidance Document, food business operators do not have to identify the immediate customers when they are final consumers[265].

As has been observed,[266] Article 18 is worded in terms of its goal and intended result, rather than in terms of prescribing how that result is to

– date of transaction / delivery.
The registration of date of transaction/delivery flows directly from the registration of the two other items. When the same type of product is provided several times to a food business operator, the sole registration of name of supplier and nature of products would not ensure the traceability requirement.
– the second category of information includes additional information which is highly recommended to be kept:
    – volume or quantity
    – batch number, if any.
    – more detailed description of the product (pre-packed or bulk product, variety of fruit/vegetable, raw or processed product).
The information to be registered has to be chosen in light of the food business activity (nature and size of business) and the characteristics of the traceability system. Food crises in the past have shown that tracing the commercial flow of a product (by invoices at the level of a company) was not sufficient to follow the physical flow of the products.
Therefore, it is essential that the traceability system of each food / feed business operator is designed to follow the physical flow of the products: the use of delivery notes (or registration of the address of producing units) would ensure more efficient traceability.
[264] This person can be an individual (for example a hunter or a mushroom collector) or a legal person. Recital 29 stipulates that a food business must identify at least the business from which the food/feed or substance that may be incorporated into a food/feed has been supplied. It has been clarified by the 2004 Guidance Document that the term 'supply' should not be interpreted as the mere physical delivery of the food/feed or food producing animal (eg truck driver who is an employer for a certain operator). Identifying the name of the person physically delivering is not the objective pursued by this rule and it would not be sufficient to guarantee the traceability along the food chain.
[265] This document indicates that: 'A food business operator must identify only the other businesses (legal entity) to whom it provides its products (excluding final consumers). In case of trade between retailers, such as a distributor and a restaurant, the traceability requirement is also applicable'.
[266] Ibid.

be achieved. As a result, without prejudice to specific requirements, this more general approach would seem to leave industry with greater flexibility in the implementation of the requirement and is thus likely to reduce compliance costs. Conversely, it tends to require both food businesses and the control authorities to be proactive in ensuring effective implementation. This may present some difficulties, although the elaboration of industry codes of practice could alleviate the problem. To tackle part of these difficulties, the Commission's Health and Consumer Protection Directorate General has set up a working group with experts from Member States in order to examine and reach consensus on a series of issues concerning the implementation and interpretation of the regulation, notably those relating to the traceability requirement. The conclusions reached by this group have been approved by the Standing Committee on the Food Chain and Animal Health at its meeting of 20 December 2004 under the above-mentioned guidance document.[267]

Although traceability is not entirely a new notion in the food chain, it is the first time that the obligation for all food business operators to identify the suppliers and direct recipients of their food/feed is stipulated explicitly in a horizontal community legal text. Prior to this regulation, the EC adopted specific traceability regimes in the beef and genetically modified organisms sectors. In the beef sector, the EC adopted Regulation 1825/2000 with the express aim of avoiding the spread of diseases such as BSE and to protect the health and safety of consumers. Under this regulation, operators must keep a complex identification and registration system for beef at each of the various stages of production and sales. Such system must be able to record the quantity of the cattle and provide a link between the cattle and the meat consumed. As to the GMOs, they are subject to a similar set of rules, in accordance with a common position adopted by the Council on 17 March 2003.[268] The goal pursued by the GMO regime is to facilitate the labelling of products consisting of, or containing, GMOs, in order to monitor their effects on the environment and to implement appropriate risk management measures. Business operators must set up systems and procedures to allow the identification of the parties to each transaction.

---

[267] Guidance on the implementation of Articles 11, 12, 16, 17, 18, 19 and 20 of Regulation 178/2002 on general food law – Conclusions of the Standing Committee on the Food Chain and Animal Health.

[268] Common Position (EC) No 21/2003 of 17 March 2003 adopted by the Council, acting in accordance with the procedure referred to in Article 251 of the Treaty establishing the European Community, with a view to adopting a regulation of the European Parliament and of the Council concerning the traceability and labelling of genetically modified organisms and the traceability of food and feed products produced from genetically modified organisms and amending Directive 2001/18/EC, OJ C113 E/21.

Although in the US there is still a tendency to stick to voluntary recall and trace-back approaches, after the 'Starlink' GM contamination of foodstuffs and the findings of the first *BSE* case, there has been a growing demand for trace-back and for mandatory animal identification systems.[269]

Some degree of convergence with Europe on the issue of traceability is therefore likely to happen notwithstanding the past disagreements within the Codex. In that context, although it has been impossible to reach an agreement on a common definition of traceability, a consensus was reached as to the need to develop a definition.[270] A 'Preliminary Set of Principles on Traceability/Product Tracing' is currently circulating amongst Codex members for comments.[271]

2. *Withdrawal and Recall*

To ensure compliance with food law regulations, business operators also have the duty to act by withdrawing their products every time they consider that a food which they have imported, produced, processed, manufactured or marketed does not fulfil all the relevant requirements of food law. In particular, according to the 2004 Guidance Document, the obligation to withdraw from the market applies when the following two cumulative criteria are met:

– the food in question is considered by the operator as not being in compliance with the food safety requirements;[272]
– a food is on the market and has left the immediate control of the initial food business[273].

---

[269] Ibid.

[270] Report of the 18th Meeting of the Codex Commission on General Principles, April 2003, at 97.

[271] Preliminary Set of Principles on Traceability/Product Tracing (CL 2005/23-FICS). See also the EC Comments to Circular Letter 2005/23-FICS, Request for comments on a Preliminary Set of Principles on Traceability/Product Tracing, where the EC states that: 'The EC is fully convinced that the two main objectives of Codex, protecting the health of the consumers and ensuring fair practices in the food trade, cannot be dissociated when dealing with the question of traceability. Traceability/product tracing is indeed a tool that may be applied within a broader food inspection and certification system for different purposes: food safety, protection of consumers against deceptive marketing practices and facilitation of trade on the basis of accurate product description'.

[272] Article 14 of Regulation 178/2002 provides for the approach to follow in making this type of consideration, as its paragraphs 2, 3, 4 and 5 provide for general criteria that have to be taken into account to consider a food unsafe.

[273] This criterion derives from the wording used in Article 19(1) 'withdrawal from the market', which implies that the food was placed on the market. Moreover, Article 19(1) provides that a withdrawal shall be undertaken only when the food in question has left the immediate control of the initial operator. As a result, the scope of the withdrawal foreseen in the framework of Article 19(1) does not concern actions of withdrawal undertaken before the placing on the market of a product.

Moreover, should their product have reached the consumer, the operators shall 'effectively and accurately' inform the consumers of the reasons for its withdrawal, and if necessary, recall from consumers products already supplied to them 'when other measures are not sufficient to achieve a high level of health protection'.[274] Having an adequate traceability system may favour the withdrawal activity.

In the absence of a definition of 'withdrawal' within the general food regulation, it is suggested that reference be made to the definition laid down in Directive 2001/95/EC on General Product Safety which states that 'withdrawal means any measure aimed at preventing the distribution, display or offer of a product dangerous to the consumer'.

Food business operators also have a duty to inform the competent authorities if they consider or have reason to believe that a food which has been placed on the market may be injurious to human health.[275] This provision is likely to become controversial to the extent that it does not establish whether the information which business operators are supposed to provide could be used by the authorities when imposing sanctions stemming from the contested behaviour. The German Act on food and equipment,[276] which imposes an equivalent duty of disclosure, explicitly states that the information provided by the food business operator may not be used against him in criminal proceedings. It is submitted that a similar provision, by undoubtedly providing an incentive to food business operators to come forward with problems they may encounter in their activity, should also be inserted into the EC legislative framework.

Finally, food business operators are required to collaborate with the authorities on subsequent action taken to avoid or reduce risks posed by a food which they have supplied.[277]

Similar obligations are also imposed on feed business operators by Article 20 of the regulation.

It can be observed that these provisions, by imposing a burden on business operators in a phase subsequent to the production and marketing of the product, do give rise to a different and autonomous liability hypothesis than the one contemplated by the product safety directive which refers solely to 'place to the market'.

---

[274] Article 19 of the regulation.
[275] Article 19.3 of the regulation.
[276] Article 40a of the Lebensmittel und Bedarfsgegenständegesetz.
[277] Article 19.4 of the regulation.

The food operator cannot disregard the product once it has been marketed, rather it is liable for monitoring the whole of the market in which it operates.

F.   External Dimension of the EC Food Legislation

The effects of the Community's food legislation are not confined to the Community alone. In accordance with the EEA Agreement, Community food legislation is applied in Norway and Iceland, and will shortly be applied in Liechtenstein. The new accession countries of Bulgaria and Romania are in the process of adjusting their legislation to apply Community rules in preparation for their accession to the Community. The customs union agreement between the Community and Turkey provides for the harmonisation of legislation. Legislation and negotiations with Switzerland are also at an advanced stage. A number of other third countries are also using Community legislation, which often closely reflects the relevant international standards established by Codex Alimentarius, as a model for their own legislation.

The principles of the internal market also apply to goods from non-Member countries which have been put into free circulation within the Community. According to Article 24 EC, those products which have been cleared through all custom formalities and have not benefited from total or partial drawback of such duties or charges should be considered to be products in free circulation.[278] Such products must meet all the requirements which are laid down in Community legislation for products manufactured within the Community. For foodstuffs of animal or plant origin, there are specific veterinary and phytosanitary inspection and certification procedures which are undertaken at the point of entry into the Community, and specific controls relating to quality standards for unprocessed fruits and vegetables for export and import. The Community also carries out inspections in non-Community countries. In other cases, there are no special procedures for the inspection or certification of imports and exports. Controls on products are undertaken on a random basis, at the point of entry, or at the point of destination, and the activities of importers may also be subject to control. Consideration may need to be given to better coordination of controls on imports. It is also worth recalling that foodstuffs are part of the list of products which are more specifically covered by controls performed under Council Regulation (EEC) 339/93 on checks for conformity with the rules on product safety in the case of products imported from third countries.[279]

---

[278] See Article 24 EC.
[279] OJ L 40/1.

As to the origin of products, there are no special rules for foodstuffs. Therefore, as for the other categories of goods, the country of origin of a foodstuff is obviously the one in which it has been produced. When the production of a foodstuff has involved more than one country ' ... [it] shall be deemed to originate in the country where they underwent their last, substantial, economically justified processing or working in an undertaking equipped for that purpose and resulting in the manufacture of a new product or representing an important stage of manufacture'.[280] Therefore, the criterion chosen to determine the country of origin of these products is where the most substantial transformation of the product has taken place.

In addition to being a major food importer, the Community is also a major food exporter. In these circumstances, it is important to ensure that the Community's own internal legislation provides adequate reassurances for our major trading partners, and that our exports do not encounter unjustified restrictions in gaining access to markets outside of the Community.

Recent years have seen important changes in the multilateral trading system applicable to foodstuffs, and in the bilateral relationships between the Community and its major trading partners. This will be the subject of Part II, which focuses on the regulation of food within the WTO.

---

[280] See Article 24 of Council Regulation (EEC) 2913/92 of 12 October 1992 establishing the Community Customs Code, OJ L 302/1.

CHAPTER III
THE EUROPEAN FOOD SAFETY AUTHORITY:
THE CORNERSTONE OF THE NEW FOOD SAFETY POLICY

Undoubtedly, the establishment of the much-awaited European Food Safety Authority is the most prominent innovation introduced by the new Community food regime.[1] However, it must be borne in mind that the authority merely represents one of the components of an entirely new strategy adopted by the European Union in relation to food safety. Although pivotal to the functioning of the new food safety regime, the EFSA has not been vested with any regulatory power in the matter, which remains with the Commission and the Member States. However, as food law is heavily based on science, the delegation for scientific assessment of risk to the authority could also be said to provide EFSA with a quasi-regulatory power. As will be shown below, this seems to be especially true insofar as the authority has been entrusted with scientific self-tasking powers, allowing it to begin conducting a scientific assessment without being asked by the Commission or a Member State.

The primary responsibility of the authority is to provide scientific opinions in the food arena, an activity which was previously carried out by eight sectoral committees. Thus, this body is to replace and absorb the Community's scientific committees.

In the following pages, we will provide a detailed description of the EFSA origins, of its institutional structure and powers by emphasising, where necessary, the main points of difference between it and the US Food and Drug Administration ('FDA').

1. The Origins

There had been recurrent calls for the creation of a Community food regulatory agency long before the outbreak of the food scares which have outraged Europe.[2] At least until the mid-1990s, such suggestions

---

[1] On the European Food Safety authority, see I.S. Roda, 'La Autoridad Alimentaria Europea: la Problematica Eficacia de Una Nueva Agencia Comunitaria para la Protección de los Consumidores', in *Comunidad Europea Aranzadi*, 11, 2001, p 29; S. Romero Melchor, 'La Futura Agencia Europea para los Alimentos: ¿ un Organismo sin Autoridad?', in *Gaceta iuridica de la UE*, 212, Marzo/Abril 2001, p 113.

[2] See M. D. Matthee, 'Regulating Scientic Expertise with regard to Risks Deriving from Genetically Modified Organisms: Procedural Rules on Risk Assessment Committees under European Community and International Law', in V. Kronenberg, *The European Union and*

(continued...)

were taken into serious consideration by the EC Commission[3]. They were subsequently abandoned[4] before being revamped by the President of the EC Commission, Jacques Santer, when, appearing before the European Parliament Temporary committee of Enquiry into *BSE*, he declared:

> Our job is and will no doubt remain, in a spirit of subsidiarity, to monitor the monitoring mechanisms set up by our Member States and their operation, even if, personally I think that in the long term the *creation of an agency modeled on the American Food and Drug Administration should not be ruled out.*[5]

Only a month later, facing a motion of censure from the European Parliament for alleged mismanagement of the *BSE* crisis,[6] the same Commission President Santer seemed to be more determined about the need to establish an independent European Food Agency modeled on the US Food and Drug Administration :

> I also think that *an independent agency*, to meet the specific needs of the Community but *based on the positive aspects of the United States Food and Drug Administration*, should be considered.

the International Legal Order : Discord or Harmony ?, T.M.C. Asser Press, Amsterdam; J.L. Valverde, A.J. Piqueras Garcia, M.D. Cabezas Lopez, 'La Nouvelle Approche en Matière de Santé des Consommateurs et de Sécurité Alimentaire : la Nécessité d'une Agence Européenne de Sécurité des Aliments', *Revue du Marché Unique Européenne*, 1997, n. 4, pp 31 ss.

[3] See, eg, Lister, *Regulation of Food Products by the European Community*, 285, Butterworths, 1992, pp 295-6. See the discussions in Snyder, *A Regulatory Framework for Foodstuffs in the Internal Market*, Report on the Conference 6-7 May 1993, European University Institute, Department of Law, Florence, EUI Working Papers in Law No 94/4. For instance, following the BSE crises, the creation of a European Agency for Veterinary and Phytosanitary Inspection was launched (Commission's proposal for a Council Regulations, [1996] OJ C239/9), but subsequently withdrawn in the Commission communication to the European Parliament and the Council on Food, Veterinary and Plant Health Control and Inspection, COM (98) 32 final.

[4] Finally, the Council adopted a system of scientific assistance and cooperation in the scientific examination of food issues. See Council directive 93/5/EEC on assistance to the Commission and co-operation by the Member States in the scientific examination of questions relating to food [1993] OJ L52/18. See also Written Question 904/91, OJ (C 311), 18; *Financial Times*, 15 March 1991. Several reasons justifying the deferral of a new agency were put forward by the EC Commission ranging from bureaucratic concerns linked to the establishment of a new entity to the belief that the agency might distract the Commission's specialists from the primary objective of completing the 1985 programme for the internal market. See also the interview with Caroline Jackson, MEP, in 1 *World Food Regulation Review* 22–23 (1991).

[5] EP Temporary Committee on BSE – President Santer Statement of 15 January 1997.

[6] In the European Parliament's debate on the report by the Temporary Committee of Inquiry into BSE on the 18 February 1997, the Parliament called on the Commission to bring together all the activities spread out among the various directorates general within a single DG, to set up a framework directive on food law, to ensure the safety of the foodstuffs which circulate freely within the Community, to change the way in which scientific committees work, etc. See Debate in plenary session of the EP, 18 Feb. 1997, *EU Bulletin*, 1–2, 1997, at 163–6.

> Compliance with the principle of subsidiarity, to which we are
> all attached, must not be used as a pretext for obstructing the
> emergence of a credible European health protection system, as a
> necessary follow-on from the single market.[7]

From this moment on, most of the advocates of a European food agency
crafted their proposals taking as a model the US FDA, a very large and
centralised agency in charge of risk assessment, risk management
controls and inspections throughout the US, as well as risk
communication.[8] By relying on the great confidence that both US
consumers and the food industry have in its activities, they played, not
without some ambiguity, on the FDA analogy in order to gain consensus
around their proposals for the creation of a not well-defined European-
style FDA. While Health Commissioner Emma Bonino, after visiting
the States in 1997, declared that the FDA was not a good model for
Europe, mainly because of its lack of political independence,[9] the EC
Commission President Romano Prodi in his first speech to the EC
Parliament advocated the establishment of a 'European FDA'.[10]

The conflict embedded within these proposals lay in the question
whether to invest the agency not only with risk assessment and
communication powers, but also with management tasks.

The conundrum facing the Community in shaping the administrative
powers of the agency has been effectively summed up by the following

---

[7] Speech by Jacques Santer, President of the European Commission, to Parliament on 18
February 1997 available at http://europa.eu.int/abc/doc/off/bull/en/9701/p203001.htm.
[8] For a detailed examination of the FDA's power and administrative organisation, see
Barton Hutt & Merril, *Food & Drug Law*, Cases and Materials, 2nd ed, New York,
Foundation Press, 1991, pp 4–6; for an historical overview, see P. Barton Hutt, 'A Historical
Introduction', 45 *FDC L.J.* 17, (1990). For the purpose of our analysis, it is sufficient to
know that the FDA is an institution under the responsibility of the Secretary of Health
within the US Department of Health; it has 9,000 employees and monitors the manufacture,
import, transport, storage and sale of a broad range of products throughout the U.S. It
relies on about 2,100 scientists working in 40 laboratories throughout the country. It goes
without saying that it is one of the most powerful administrative agencies in the world.
[9] Among the other reasons she provided: FDA did not cover the primary products of
meat, poultry and fish and it would be unrealistic at EU level to have an organisation
with a staff of 9,000. It is worth noting that the European Commission currently employs
approximately 20,000 individuals.
[10] Address delivered to Parliament by Romano Prodi, President-designate of the
Commission, on 21 July 1999, in Bulletin EU 7/8-1999, available at http://europa.eu.int/
abc/doc/off/bull/en/9907/p202001.htm. See also *International Herald Tribune*, 'Prodi Urges
EU to Set Up a U.S.-Style Food Overseer' ('The European public has lost confidence in
both national and European food and drug regulators. They no longer trust their
governments or the scientists. In my view, we have to take the initiative and look toward
the idea of an independent European food and drug agency to help win back consumer
confidence') available at http://www.iht.com/IHT/BJ/99/bj072299.html. See also Speech
of Romano Prodi to European Parliament, Plenary Session, 5 October 1999 (SPEECH/99/
121).

question: 'to what degree should, could, or does 'expertise' replace legal, political and ethical criteria?'[11] In other words, should the agency be invested with regulatory and enforcement powers similar to those of the US FDA?

This question was central to the mandate given by the Commission to three leading European Scientists – James, Kemper and Pascal[12] – who had 'to consider the most effective system for providing scientific advice which was independent, transparent, excellent and readily understood by non-experts' and to assess 'whether an independent agency type structure could lead to further improvements in scientific advice at the EC level'.[13] The 'Future of Scientific Advice' report, presented by these three scientists, represented the first serious attempt to analyse the opportunity and desirability of establishing an independent agency by setting out the benefits and the drawbacks relating to the development of a system analogous to the US FDA.[14]

Starting from the premise that it would be 'unwise to continue to deal with issues of such immense public concern simply by devising an improved system within DG SANCO', James, Kemper and Pascal expressed the need for 'structural changes' in the way these issues are handled within the Community in order to recapture public confidence[15]. They proposed the institution of a Brussels-based organisation, to be called the European Food and Public Health Authority (EFPHA), with the combined scope of the US Centers for Disease and Control (CDC)[16] and the Food and Drug Administration. Although the proposed agency would have shared some features with the US FDA, it was conceived as being more 'independent of political and industrial interests'.[17] Stressing the importance of not artificially compartmentalising the analysis of risk between risk assessment and risk management, they decided not to confine the new organisation to providing scientific advice. Rather, they

[11] C. Joerges, 'Law, Science and the Management of Risks to Health at the National, European and International Level – Stories on Baby Dummies, Mad Cows and Hormones in Beef', in 7 *Columb. Journal of European Law* 1 (2001).
[12] This informal working group, composed of the three Professors and the four Secretaries, was referred to as 'Future of Scientific Advice' (FSA) and the final report as 'A European Food and Public Health authority: The Future of Scientific Advice' (Brussels: Commission, 1999).
[13] The full text of the mandate given to them has been made public at http://europa.eu.int/comm /food/fs/sc/future _mandate _en.html.
[14] Philippe James, Francois Kemper, Gérard Pascal, *A European Food and Public Health authority: The Future of Scientific Advice in the EU*, Report commissioned by the Director General of DG XXIV (now DG SANCO), Dec. 1999, 6.
[15] Ibid, at 15.
[16] According to the report, the CDC 'has a crucial influence in ensuring that activities of industrially sensitive issues such as those handled by the FDA are geared to public concerns', 6. To know more about this institution see http://www.cdc.gov/.
[17] Report, supra note 14, at 7.

promoted interaction between risk assessors (EFSA's scientists) and risk managers (Commission services in charge of drafting legislation) from the beginning of the process when the questions are defined, to the final stage when the advice is translated into management proposals. According to the report:

> Confining a new organisation to providing advice which is divorced from the realities of what consumers have to confront will lead to further disenchantment with the European system for assuring public health and is therefore unwise.[18]

In other words, under their proposal 'in one bold brush' the Commission, the Council, and Parliament would have lost legislative and executive power to a regulatory authority.[19] Finally, since 'the current scientific advice relates to many areas in addition to those of food safety', the Report underlined the importance of also including environmental and public health concerns within their proposed authority as 'public health issues are in health terms a greater burden on society than the effects of poor food safety which has dominated thinking so far'[20] (see diagram 3).

---

[18] Report, supra note 14, at 8.
[19] See L. Buonanno, in Ansell C. and Vogel D. (eds), *What' the Beef? The Contested Governance of European Food Safety*, pp 259 ss.
[20] Report, supra note 14, at 6.

Diagram 3. The proposed structure of the new EC institution (EFPHA) by James, Kemper and Pascal[21] (Source: James, Kemper and Pascal, 1999)

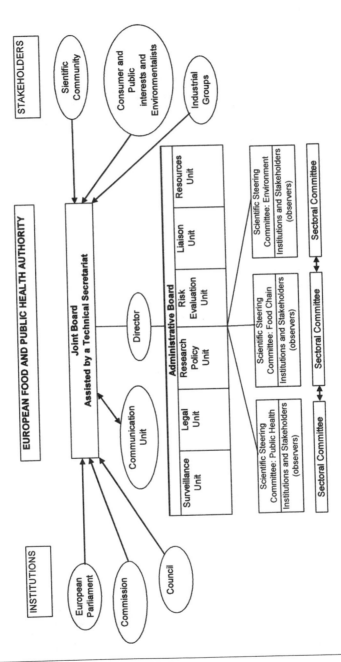

[21] Report, supra note 14, at 46.

However, three months after the release of this report, the Commission published its White Paper on Food Safety,[22] calling for the establishment of an independent agency, the European Food Authority (EFA), entrusted with a number of key tasks embracing:

- independent scientific advice on all aspects relating to food safety (risk assessment)
- communication and dialogue with consumers on food safety and health issues (risk communication)

Thus, the Commission, under the pressure of the Member States, who were reluctant to give up their involvement in the risk management stage by devolving food control powers to an independent food agency, clearly rejected the transfer of risk management powers from the Commission (*rectius*, from the Food and Veterinary Office (FVO)) to the EFA as suggested by the James, Kemper and Pascal report. To justify this decision the White Paper raised 'three very serious issues':[23]

- The transfer of regulatory powers to an independent authority could lead to an 'unwarranted dilution of democratic accountability';
- The Commission must retain both regulation and control if it is to discharge the responsibilities placed upon it under the Treaties;
- An authority with regulatory power could not be created under the current institutional arrangements of the EC, and would require modification of the existing provisions of the EC Treaty.[24]

Although debatable,[25] these arguments led to the definitive abandonment of the FDA analogy in the European food policy's discourse: the FDA

---

[22] White Paper on Food Safety COM (99) 719, 12 January 2000 available at http://europa.eu.int/comm/dgs/health/ consumer /library/pub/pub06_en.pdf.

[23] Ibid, at 15.

[24] Ibid, at 17, para 33.

[25] The last assumption is especially controversial among scholars since it relies heavily on the so-called 'Meroni doctrine', establishing the principle of the institutional balance of powers. According to this doctrine, the delegation of power to Agencies would be subject to the following conditions: the Commission cannot delegate broader powers than it enjoys itself; it can delegate only 'clearly defined executive powers'; no discretionary power may be delegated; the exercise of delegated powers remains subject to the conditions to which they would have been subject if they had been directly exercised by the Commission; the institutional balance between the EC institutions may not be distorted. The EU Parliament Committee on Legal Affairs and the Internal Market, in its opinion on the White Paper, clearly adopted a narrow interpretation of the doctrine by stating: 'If the authority is to act autonomously, then official authority must be transferred to it. However, limits have been placed on the transfer of official authority by the Court of Justice case law. The transfer must relate to precisely defined implementing powers, the exercise of which is fully supervised by the transferring bodies, without the authority to which the powers are transferred being given any margin of discretion. A transfer of

(continued...)

was no longer to be considered to be a valid model. Presenting the White Paper to the European Parliament majority party group, the EC Commissioner David Byrne said:

> Looking across the Atlantic, I saw the American public placed great confidence in the work of the US Food and Drug Administration. An institution that was science-based. But also an institution that was involved in management and legislation. I concluded that *such a model, while attractive in itself and clearly working for the US, would not be appropriate for the European scene.* I wanted to ensure that risk assessment and risk management would be separated. Such an approach would be in line with the provisions of the Treaty, which entrusted management, and legislation, to the Commission, Parliament and Council.[26]

Although the White Paper did not settle all aspects of the EFA's activities,[27] it sketched out the main features of the new agency, thereby paving the way to the publication of the first regulation's proposal.[28] The amended proposal,[29] after completion of first reading by the EC Parliament and Council, was finally adopted on 28 January 2002.[30]

---

power does, however, entail a shift of competencies, which are thus removed from the sphere of influence of the bodies legitimised by the Treaties [...] Legal provisions on food safety exist at both national and European level. It is, however, extremely doubtful whether a Food authority could carry out local checks or impose sanctions, even in order to enforce the rules, or whether this would be desirable'. For a reconstruction of the debate about the scope of the Meroni doctrine, see K. Lenaerts, 'Regulating the Regulatory Process: Delegation of Power' in the European Community' 18 *European Law Review* 23–49 (1993) and J.H.H. Weiler, 'Epilogue: "Comitology" as Revolution—Infranationalism, Constitutionalism and Democracy' in C. Joerges and E. Vos (eds), *EU Committees: Social Regulation, Law and Politics*, pp 339–350.

[26] Speech by David Byrne, European Commissioner for Health and Consumer Protection to the Group of the European People Party and European Democrats in the European Parliament (EPP/ED), Brussels, Sept. 27 2003 available at http://europa.eu.int/comm/dgs/health_consumer/library/speeches/speech57_en.html.

[27] A significant number of questions remained open, such as the exact relationship between the EFA and the Commission, the functioning of the network with national agencies, the composition of the internal bodies and the management of the early warning system. For a report of the reactions triggered by the presentation of the White Paper EFA's idea, see *Libération*, 13 January 2000; *Financial Times*, 12 January 2000 and Donald G. McNeil, 'At birth, EU's Food Watchdog is on Defence', *International Herald Tribune*, 13 January 2000. For a reaction of the Scientific Steering Committee, see Integrated Comments and Remarks of the SSC on the White Paper on Food Safety, 14 April 2000.

[28] Proposal for a regulation of the European Parliament and of the Council laying down the general principles and requirements of food law, establishing the European Food authority, and laying down procedures in matters of food safety. COM (2000)716, Brussels, Nov. 8, 2000.

[29] Amended Proposal for a regulation of the European Parliament and of the Council laying down the general principles and requirements of food law, establishing the European Food authority, and laying down procedures in the matter of food safety. COM (2001) 475 final, Brussels. Jul. 8, 2001.

[30] The regulation came into force on 21 February 2002. See Article 65 of the regulation.

Finally, from a political science perspective, the establishment of EFSA may be explained in light of 'credibility theory' according to which governments delegate powers to independent agencies in order to increase the credibility of their policies.[31]

2. Mission and Tasks of the Authority: the 'Scientific Point of reference' for the Whole Union

The primary responsibility of the authority is to provide scientific opinions in the areas falling within its broad jurisdiction by relying on its eight scientific panels. Risk assessment is EFSA's core activity.

2.1 Mission

Article 22 of the regulation establishing the EFSA defines its mission as providing 'scientific advice and scientific technical support for the Community's legislation and policies in all fields which have a direct or indirect impact on food safety and feed safety. It shall provide independent information on all matters within these fields and communicate on risks'. Thus, in accordance with the White Paper, the EFSA is supposed to 'become the scientific point of reference for the whole Union'[32], by providing scientific opinions which will serve as the scientific basis for the drafting and adoption of Community measures in the fields falling within its mission[33]. As stated in recital 32 of the regulation, the scientific and technical basis of Community legislation relating to the safety of food and feed should contribute to the achievement of a high level of health protection within the Community. In other words, this regulation reflects the strong belief of the EC legislator according to which there is a tight connection between science based food safety legislation and the assurance of consumer confidence in the decision-making process underpinning food law.

Its mission also includes the provision of scientific advice on matters related to human nutrition, animal health and welfare and plant health. In the exercise of these activities, the authority shall act 'in close cooperation with the competent bodies in the Member States carrying out similar tasks to those of the Authority'[34]. This provision is crucial in

---

[31] F. Gilardi, 'Policy Credibility and Delegation to Independent Regulatory Agencies: a Comparative Empirical Analysis', 9:9 *Journal of European Public Policy*, 2002, 873.

[32] White Paper on Food Safety COM (99) 719, 12 Jan. 2000 available at http://europa.eu.int/comm/dgs/health/ consumer /library/pub/pub06_en.pdf, , at 2.

[33] In particular, Article 22 (7) states that '[t]he authority shall carry out its tasks in conditions which enable it to serve as a point of reference by virtue of its independence, the scientific and technical quality of the opinions it issues and the information it disseminates, the transparency of its procedures and methods of operation, and its diligence in performing the tasks assigned to it'.

[34] Article 22 (7) of the regulation.

understanding the *raison d'être* underpinning the creation of the authority: EFSA has not been conceived as a pan-European scientific body aimed at imposing its scientific voice over national opinions in food matters, rather it aims at providing an independent European view which ideally complements Member States' studies. Similarly, the authority, the Commission and the Member States must cooperate to promote effective coherence between risk assessment, risk management and risk communication functions. In the absence of clear indications within the regulation, it still remains to be seen how this cooperation will be realised in practice.

2.2   Tasks

More precisely, EFSA is given responsibility for the following tasks:

a)   to provide the Community institutions and the Member States with the best possible scientific opinions in all cases provided for by Community legislation and on any question within its mission (Articles 23(a) and 29);

b)   to promote and coordinate the development of uniform risk assessment methodologies in the fields falling within its mission (Article 22(b));

c)   to provide scientific and technical support to the Commission in the areas within its mission and, when so requested, in the interpretation and consideration of risk assessment opinions (Articles 22(c) and 31);[35]

d)   to commission scientific studies necessary for the accomplishment of its mission (Articles 22(d) and 32);

e)   to search for, collect, collate, analyze and summarise scientific and technical data in the fields within its mission, notably in order to identify emerging risks (Articles 22, 24 and 34);

f)   to undertake action to identify and characterize emerging risks, in the fields within its mission (Articles 22(f) and 34);[36]

g)   to establish a system of networks of organisations operating in the fields within its mission and be responsible for their operation (Articles 22(g) and 36);

h)   to provide scientific and technical assistance, when requested to do so by the Commission, *in the crisis management procedures* implemented by the Commission with regard to the safety of food and feed (Articles 22(h) and 55);

---

[35] This work does not involve 'scientific evaluation' but rather the application of 'well-established scientific or technical principles'. These tasks may include the establishment or evaluation of technical criteria or assisting the Commission in the development of technical guidelines. See Article 31 of the regulation.

[36] The EFSA is to establish monitoring procedures with a view to 'systematically searching' for and collecting information about emerging risks.

i)   to provide scientific and technical assistance, when requested to do so by the Commission, with a view to improving cooperation between the Community, applicant countries, international organisations and third countries, in the fields within its mission (Article 22(i));

j)   to ensure that the public and interested parties receive rapid, reliable, objective and comprehensible information in the fields within its mission (Articles 22(j) and 40);

k)   to express independently its own conclusions and orientations on matters within its mission (Articles 22(k) and 37);

l)   to undertake any other task assigned to it by the Commission within its mission (Article 22(l)).

These tasks should be undertaken in conditions that respect the virtues of 'independence', 'scientific and technical quality', 'transparency' and 'diligence'.[37]

It is noteworthy that under Regulation 178/2002, the EFSA has received less functions than those originally provided for by the regulation as originally proposed.[38] In particular, the authority is not responsible for the operation of the Rapid Alert System for food and feed established by this regulation (which is under the Commission's responsibility) and it has also lost its role in the communication on health-policy-related nutritional issues.[39]

From a reading of the list of tasks given to EFSA it seems to be clear that EFSA's scientific activity cannot be reduced to the delivery of scientific opinions in response to questions posed by its (institutional) customers. Rather, EFSA's scientific involvement breaks down into four main activities:

---

[37] Article 22.7 Regulation 178/2002.

[38] Proposal for a regulation of the European Parliament and of the Council laying down the general principles and requirements of food law, establishing the European Food authority, and laying down procedures in matters of food safety. COM (2000)716, Brussels, 8 November 2000.

[39] See Article 22(h) and (k) of the amended proposal, supra note 152. However, EFSA remained invested with an important role in nutritional issues. In particular, EFSA's involvement with health-policy-related nutritional issues began practically following the entry into force and the practical implementation of the first EC regulation on the use of nutrition and health claims for foods. On 16 July 2003 the Commission adopted a proposal for a regulation on the use of nutrition and health claims made on foods with reference Proposal No COM(2003) 424. After the first reading vote by the European Parliament on the Commission's proposal (26 May 2005), on 3 June 2005, EU health ministers unanimously endorsed the Commission's proposal, including the provision for nutrient profiles and the authorisation procedure, during a first reading vote at the Health Council. The European Parliament second reading vote took place on 16 May 2006, paving the way for final adoption of the new health and nutrition claims Regulation. Formal adoption of the Regulation by the Council has occured on December 20, 2006. See Regulation (EC) No 1925/2006 of the European Parliament and of the Council of 20 Decebme 2006 on the addition of vitamins and minerals and of certain other substances to foods, OJ L 404, 30.12.2006, pp 26–38.

- providing scientific opinions, guidance and advice in response to questions submitted by the European Commission, the European Parliament or the Member States;
- assessing the risk of regulated substances, such as GMOs, pesticides and food/feed additives, following notification procedures and time schedules established by EC vertical legislation;
- monitoring of specific risk factors and diseases as well as identifying and characterising emerging risks;
- developing, promoting and applying new and harmonised scientific approaches for hazard and risk assessment of food and feed.

In accomplishing the first two tasks, the EFSA fulfils its main mission: to prepare and present scientific opinions. While in the former case the authority acts in response to food safety questions addressed on a voluntary basis by the competent institutions, in the latter, EFSA's intervention is requested by European vertical legislation. Thus, for instance, the legislative framework for the marketing of food additives[40] and feed additives,[41] being based on a positive list system, relies on EFSA's assessment. Similarly, the new GMOs legislative regime provides for the risk assessment of GMO and derived food and feed to be carried out by EFSA.[42] Given their character of *lex specialis*, this set of vertical legislation dealing with regulated substances determines the modalities of EFSA's scientific intervention. In particular, these pieces of vertical legislation entrust the Commission (sometimes together with EFSA) with laying down the guidelines to be followed by risk assessors in conducting their assessment.

Where the vertical legislation does not require the Commission and/or the authority to establish these guidelines, these should be established by the Commission after consulting the Authority.[43] In particular, the Commission should elaborate the guidelines governing the scientific evaluation of substances, products or processes which are subject, under Community legislation, to a system of prior authorisation or entry on a positive list, in particular where Community legislation makes provision for, or authorises, a dossier to be presented for this purpose by the applicant.

---

[40] Council Directive 89/107/EEC of 21 December 1988 on the approximation of the laws of the Member States concerning food additives authorised for use in foodstuffs intended for human consumption, as amended.

[41] Since 18 October 2004, applications for authorising the placing and use of feed additives in the market are regulated in the European Union under Regulation (EC) No 1831/2003. EFSA is responsible for the scientific assessment of the feed additives.

[42] Regulation 1829/2003 of the European Parliament and of the Council of 22 September 2003 on genetically modified food and feed, OJ L268, p 1–23.

[43] Article 30 (6) lett. b of the regulation.

Moreover, under Article 32 of the regulation, the authority is entitled to commission scientific studies necessary for the performance of its mission. In doing so, it should seek to avoid duplication with Member State or Community research programmes and shall foster cooperation through appropriate coordination. Finally, the authority shall inform the European Parliament, the Commission and the Member States of the results of its scientific studies.

3.   Institutional framework

The authority consists of the following:

3.1   Management Board

The management board is responsible for guiding EFSA's activities and ensuring that the authority carries out its mission and performs its tasks. Unlike other EC agencies[44], it is not composed of representatives of all Member States, since management board members are chosen for their independence, not for their connection to Member States: they are experts in their own right and collectively have a blend of expertise in the management of key organisations involved in food safety and in the most current issues within the area.

It chooses 14 members appointed by the Council in consultation with the European Parliament from a list (a 'roster') provided by the Commission,[45] plus a representative of the Commission. Although the Council would have preferred to have the board formed solely by national representatives,[46] four of its Members 'shall have a background in organisations representing consumers and other interests in the food chain'.[47] These Members inevitably represent a particular interest in the food sector since they retain their previous posts while sitting on the board. Given the 'free movement bias' affecting EFSA's foundations, it would appear to be advisable to increase the number of consumer representatives, who do not dispose of the same resources as the food

---

[44] Within the other EC agencies, members of the board are appointed either by the Member States independently or by the Council on the basis of one member per Member State. See E. Chiti, 'The Emergency of a Community Administration: the Case of European Agencies', in *Common Market Law Review* 37, pp 309-342 (2000); see also K. Kanska, 'Wolves in the clothing of sheep? The case of the European Food Safety authority', 24 *European Law Review* 2004, p 715.

[45] The Commission, by preparing 30 candidates for 14 places, did not give the Council much margin of manoeuvre in the exercise of its appointment power.

[46] E. Vos, 'Mondialisation et régulation-cadre des marches – Le principe de précaution et le droit alimentaire de l'Union européenne', in 2–3 *Revue international de Droit Economique* (2002), 219 p 244.

[47] Article 25(1) of the regulation.

industry to lobby the Commission or to carry out their own risk assessment in order to give greater balance to EFSA's opinions.

The composition represents a significant and innovative institutional aspect aimed at ensuring 'its independence, high scientific quality, transparency and efficiency'.[48]

After the enlargement to 25 Member States, the number of the members of the board turned out to be much smaller than the number of the Member States. However, in order partly to mitigate such under-representation, the regulation provides that 'the broadest possible geographic distribution within the Union' should be guaranteed within the board.[49] Furthermore, Recital 41 of the preamble dictates a 'rotation of the different countries of origin of the Members of the management board without any post being reserved for nationals of any specific Member State'. To fully understand the meaning of such a provision, reference must be made to the BSE crisis when 'the influence of 'British thinking' on the Commission was increased by the presence of many persons of British nationality on the two committees operating in this field: the scientific veterinary committee and the standing veterinary committee'.[50]

This crisis clearly showed the need for a geographic rotation of members, as different Member States not only have different interests as regards the food sector but also different perceptions as regards risk assessment. As the term of office of the board Members is four and six years (only for half of its members), nationals of the new Members States of the May 2004 enlargement may not be appointed before 2007.[51]

The Commission, after a widely publicised call for interested candidates, published a short list of suitable candidates on 8 April 2002. Those candidates who had a background in organisations representing consumers and other interests in the food supply chain were specifically identified on the short list from which five, not four as provided in the text, were selected by the Council and they met for the first time on 18–19 September 2002.[52]

---

[48] See recitals (40) and (41) of the regulation.

[49] Article 25(1) of the regulation.

[50] E. Vos, *Institutional Frameworks of the Community Health and Safety Regulation. Committees, Agencies and Private Bodies* (1999), p 144. See also the Temporary Committee of Inquiry into BSE available at http://www.bseinquiry. gov.uk/evidence/ibd/idb.htm.

[51] As of today, only one Member of a scientific committee comes from a new Member State.

[52] See Council decision appointing the members of the management board of the European Food Safety authority [2002] OJ C179/2. See also EFSA, Annual Report for the year 2002, pp 5–6, available at http://www.efsa.eu.int.

3.2 Executive Director

Together with the management board, the regulation provides for the appointment of an executive director, who is the legal representative of the authority and is responsible for:

a) the day-to-day administration of the authority;
b) drawing up a proposal for the Authority's work programmes in consultation with the Commission;
c) implementing the work programmes and the decisions adopted by the management board;
d) ensuring the provision of appropriate scientific, technical and administrative support for the scientific committee and the scientific panels;
e) ensuring that the authority carries out its tasks in accordance with the requirements of its users, in particular with regard to the adequacy of the services provided and the time taken;
f) the preparation of the statement of revenue and expenditure and the execution of the budget of the authority;
g) all staff matters;
h) developing and maintaining contact with the European Parliament, and for ensuring a regular dialogue with its relevant committees.

Among these tasks, the most important is the design of the work programme of EFSA because, due to its limited capacity, the agency cannot deal with all possible issues within its mission. The executive director is therefore responsible for priority setting, as confirmed by Article 27(3) stating that the 'Director may also ask the advisory forum for advice on the prioritisation of requests for scientific opinions'. Contrary to what was required by the original proposal, in designing the work program of EFSA, the director is not required to obtain the agreement of the Commission, but simply to consult it. This undoubtedly reinforces his independence (as well EFSA's independence) vis-à-vis the Commission.

As regards the term of office, the director is appointed for five years by the management board on the basis of a list of candidates proposed by the Commission after an open competition. The authority being a separate legal entity, independent of the other EC institutions, the executive director is not answerable to the Commission or other Community or national institutions, but to the management board. The entire responsibility for risk management decisions remains with the competent EC institutions (Commission, Council and Parliament) as established in the Treaty. However, he can be dismissed by the board by a simple majority of votes.

Since 1 February 2003, Geoffrey Podger, former chief executive of the UK Food Standards Agency,[53] is the EFSA's executive director. His appointment was certainly motivated by the role he played in UK food policy in the aftermath of the BSE crisis. After a *pro tempore* direction by the Dutch Koëter, on 10 February 2006 the EFSA management board officially nominated Catherine Geslain-Lanéelle as future EFSA executive director.[54]

3.3 Advisory Forum

The advisory forum is the link between EFSA and the Member States[55]. It is composed of representatives from competent bodies (eg, national food agencies[56]) in the Member States which undertake tasks similar to those of the authority, these representatives being designated by each Member State.

Members of the advisory forum may not be members of the management board. The executive director convenes and chairs the Forum, but a third of its members may also initiate a meeting. The Forum has to meet at least four times per year and its meetings are open to the participation of Commission officials. Representatives from the European Parliament and other relevant bodies may also be invited to participate.

The advisory forum gives the executive director advice on all aspects of his tasks, and notably on making proposals for the EFSA's work programme. The director may also ask the Forum for advice on the prioritising of requests for scientific opinions.

Being an organ totally unknown within the Community agency structure, it is the most original organ within the EFSA. In the words of the regulation, it constitutes a 'mechanism for an exchange of information on potential risks and the pooling of knowledge'.[57]

---

[53] Midday-express, October 2, 2002, Executive Director of the European Food Safety authority nominated.
[54] Before joining EFSA Catherine Geslaine-Lanélle used to be the Regional Director of Agriculture and Forestry for the Ile-de-France region and one of the Vice Presidents of the EFSA management board.
[55] Article 27 of the regulation.
[56] Unlike in the area of drugs, not all Member States have a national food agency. Thus, for instance, Luxembourg and Italy do not have one as yet.
[57] Article 27.4 of the regulation.

The creation of this mechanism may be seen as responding to two different goals: one of reinforcing Member States' participation in EFSA's activities and the other to facilitate co-operation between the agency and the Member States.

In fact, being a forum, it aims at fostering co-operation between the national food bodies represented and the EFSA, thus avoiding conflicts arising amongst these entities in relation to specific scientific opinions. In particular, the advisory body also ensures close cooperation between the authority and the competent bodies in the Member States to avoid duplication of EFSA's scientific studies with Member States, to promote the European network of organisations operating within the fields of the Authority's mission and where EFSA or a Member State identifies emerging risk.[58]

The newly appointed executive director, being particularly aware of the key role that the advisory forum might play within EFSA's mission, is showing great willingness to enhance the exchange of scientific information amongst the advisory forum Members and EFSA.[59] In particular, she envisions that advisory forum members might become 'the focal point for EFSA's activities' in each Member State, thereby acting as 'ambassadors for EFSA with the key players in the food chain at national level.'[60]

3.4 Scientific Committee and Scientific Panels: the Very Heart of EFSA

The scientific committee and the eight permanent scientific panels, being responsible for providing the scientific opinions, constitute the core of the authority. As seen above, these committees used to be attached to the EC Commission and they emerged from the EC Commission reorganisation of its scientific advice which took place in 1997. Now they form part of EFSA.

The scientific committee, replacing the former scientific steering committee,[61] is responsible for the general coordination necessary to ensure the consistency in the scientific opinions of the different panels.[62]

---

[58] Article 27.4 a), b), c) and d).
[59] See the text of the speech of C. Geslain-Lanéelle delivered on the occasion of the 18th Meeting of the EFSA Advisory Forum, Berne, 29 September 2006.
[60] Ibid, at 4.
[61] This Committee (Commission Decision 97/404/CE of June 1997 setting up a Scientific Steering Committee, OJ L 169, p 85) coordinated the work of eight other scientific committees (Commission Decision 97/579/EC of 23 July 1997 setting up Scientific Committees in the field of consumer health and food safety, OJ L237/18.
[62] Article 28(2) of the regulation.

In order to do so, it is entrusted with the critical task of developing 'working procedures and harmonisation of working methods'. The realisation of this objective is crucial to the extent that, since EFSA advice represents the main basis for decision making in the food sector, risk managers and the public need to have access to the procedures through which the risks have been evaluated. Indeed, as will be argued below, the elaboration of harmonised transparent approaches to risk assessment is not only a prerequisite for a proper functioning of the authority but will also be a decisive factor for EFSA's success. Showing great awareness of this issue, EFSA has recently asked the scientific committee to provide guidance that would ensure transparency in the risk assessments carried out by EFSA's scientific committees and panels. One of the most relevant issues in relation to the objective of ensuring transparency in risk assessment is that of the terms of reference of scientific opinions, ie the information required to be included in EFSA's scientific opinions.

Besides this horizontal competence, the scientific committee is also entrusted with a purely scientific activity: the provision of scientific advice on multi-sectorial issues falling within the competence of more than one panel. Here the scientific committee's intervention pursues again the goal of ensuring consistency in scientific advice. For those issues which do not fall within the scope *ratione materiae* of any of the panels, the scientific committee must set up a working group.[63]

It is composed of the Chairs of the scientific panels and six independent scientific experts who do not belong to any of the scientific panels. The six independent experts are appointed by the management board.

As for the scientific panels, they are composed of independent experts who are not employees of the authority. The following are the scientific panels, replacing five of the former DG SANCO scientific committees, which dealt with issues falling within the competence of EFSA, following the 1997 reform:

a)   panel on Food Additives, flavourings, processing aids and materials in contact with food (ACF);[64]

---

[63] According to Article 28(2): 'Where necessary, and particularly in the case of subjects which do not fall within the competence of any of the Scientific Panels, the Scientific Committee shall set up working groups. In such cases, it shall draw on the expertise of those working groups when establishing scientific opinions'.

[64] The Panel on food additives, flavourings, processing aids and materials in contact with food deals with questions of safety in the use of food additives, flavourings, processing aids and materials in contact with food; with associated subjects concerning the safety of other deliberately added substances to food and with questions related to the safety of processes.

b) panel on additives and products or substances used in animal feed (FEEDAP);[65]

c) panel on plant health, plant protection products and their residues (PPR);[66]

d) panel in genetically modified organisms (GMO);[67]

e) panel on Dietetic products, nutrition and allergies (NDA);[68]

f) panel on biological hazards (BIOHAZ);[69]

g) panel on contaminants in the food chain (CONTAM);[70]

h) panel on animal health and welfare (AHAW).[71,72]

The eight panels are responsible for providing the scientific opinions of EFSA.[73] Their tasks are stated in similar terms to those of the former scientific committees. Thus, the ACF panel delivers 'scientific opinions' on questions relating to 'safety in use of food additives, flavourings, processing aids and materials in contact with food; associated subjects concerning the safety of other deliberately added substances to food and questions related to the safety of the processes'. The scientific committee and the panels can form working groups of additional experts on specialised subjects so as to draw on the best scientific advice available in the EC and, when necessary, beyond.

---

[65] The Panel on additives and products or substances used in animal feed deals with questions of safety for the animal, the user/worker, the consumer of products of animal origin, the environment and with the efficacy of biological and chemical products/substances intended for deliberate addition/use in animal feed.

[66] Plant protection products are active substances and preparations (substances or microorganisms including viruses, having general or specific action through chemical or biological means) that protect plants or plant products against harmful organisms or prevent the action of such organisms. They can also influence the life processes of plants (eg growth regulators) as well as destroy undesired parts of plants or control or prevent undesired growth of plants.

[67] The Panel on additives and products or substances used in animal feed deals with questions on safety for the animal, the user/worker, the consumer of products of animal origin, the environment and with the efficacy of biological and chemical products/substances intended for deliberate addition/use in animal feed.

[68] The Panel on dietetic products, nutrition and allergies deals with questions on dietetic products, human nutrition and food allergy, and other associated subjects such as novel foods.

[69] The Panel on biological hazards deals with questions on biological hazards relating to food safety and food-borne disease, including food-borne zoonoses and transmissible spongiform encephalopathies, microbiology, food hygiene and associated waste management.

[70] The Panel on contaminants in the food chain deals with questions on contaminants in food and feed, associated areas and undesirable substances such as natural toxicants, mycotoxins and residues on non-authorised substances not covered by another Panel.

[71] The Panel on animal health and welfare deals with questions on all aspects of animal health and animal welfare, primarily relating to food producing animals including fish.

[72] Other (non-food related) scientific committees have been established by Decision 2004/210/EC of 3 March 2004, OJ L 66/45.

[73] The full list of EFSA panels is available at www.efsa.eu.int/science/catindex_en.html.

Following the entry into force of Regulation (EC) No 575/2006,[74] an additional panel was created, the Panel on Plant Health (PLH), to tackle an increasing number of requests for scientific assessment of plant health risks. Numerous plant pests arrive in the European Union each year. These organisms can cause harm to plants, plant products or biodiversity and the risks need to be evaluated. The objective pursued by the new panel is to peer review and assess those risks in order to help secure the safety of the food chain. The panel brings together a wide range of expertise in the various fields relevant to plant health. The first meeting was held in Parma on 13 and 14 June 2006.

All scientists sitting in the committee and in the panels are appointed by the management board on the proposal of the executive director on the basis of an open competition.[75] Neither the Commission nor the Member States play a formal role in the selection process. Their term of office is for three years and is renewable.

EFSA's own scientific staff supports the scientific committee and Expert panels. In addition, the authority has reinforced its science department by creating a series of expert service 'teams', each dedicated to a specific area of risk assessment (eg data collection, epidemiology and exposure...). EFSA has created scientific expert groups composed of some of its own scientists and experts from Member States. This applies to: the peer review of existing pesticides; geographical BSE risk assessment; the evaluation of TSEs (Transmissible Spongiform Encephalopaties), and the coordination and scientific assessment of the monitoring of zoonoses and zoonotic agents. In total, EFSA's team of highly qualified scientists, experts in their respective fields, and support staff used to represent 29% of total headcount in 2003, whereas it represented approximately 50% of total headcount by the end of 2005. The initial procedures for operation and cooperation of the scientific committee and the scientific panels have been laid down, in conformity with the regulation,[76] by the Decision concerning the establishment and operations of the scientific committees and panels.[77] Furthermore, rules on the procedure applied by the European Food Safety Authority to requests for scientific opinions referred to it have been set up by Commission Regulation 1304/2003 of July 2003.[78]

---

[74] Commission Regulation (EC) No 575/2006 of 7 April 2006 amending Regulation (EC) No 178/2002 of the European Parliament and of the Council as regards the number and names of the permanent Scientific Panels of the European Food Safety authority OJ L100/3.

[75] Membership of each scientific panel is published on the website of EFSA.

[76] Article 28, paragraph 9, of the regulation.

[77] Adopted by the management board on 17 October 2002. Available at http://www.efsa.europa.eu/etc/medialib/ efsa/mboard/mb_meetings/86.Par.0007.File.dat/decision_panels_mb_04_en1.pdf.

[78] Commission Regulation 1304/2003 of July 2003 on the procedure applied by the European Food Safety authority to requests for scientific opinions referred to it, OJ L185/6.

Decisions are made by a simple majority vote, minority opinions are recorded with the name of the author and the main arguments supporting it.

Members of the scientific committee, the scientific panels, and the working groups have to sign a commitment of independence, and have to report each year on their direct or indirect interests that are relevant to EFSA.[79] Scientific committee and permanent scientific panels may, when necessary, organise public hearings.

During 2002 this component of the authority was not operational. Instead, the Commission continued to provide management and support to its own scientific committees. The call for the recruitment of scientists to the committee and panels was launched in 2003.

EFSA's scientific committee and panels were reconstituted as of June 2006 in accordance with the procedure in place for renewing the scientific committee and panels every three years. As a result, especially after the creation of an additional scientific panel on plant health, the PPR panel's name and mandate has changed. The new name 'panel on Plant Protection Products and their Residues' replaces the 'Panel on Plant Health and Plant Protection Products and their Residues'. This reflects its main work related to pesticide risk assessment issues. Questions on plant health will now be dealt with by the new Panel on Plant Health (PLH).

As of June 2006, 191 scientists started working for the EFSA scientific committee and panels for a new three-year mandate.[80] Their selection resulted from an EFSA call for expressions of interest launched in November 2005 which, after closing in February 2006, had attracted a total of 874 applicants.

3.5   Resources: Personnel and Budget

The authority's activities are funded from the Community budget based on a proposal from the Commission and approved by the budgetary authority of the Council and the Parliament. The Community's subvention is used in a number of areas covering science, communications, institutional relations and administration. Much of the

[79] See Article 37(2) of the regulation and the Decision adopted by management board on 10 March 2004 (MB Doc.10.03.2004-5), 'EFSA Code of Conduct on Declaration of Interests', amended by Guidance on Declarations of Interests, endorsed by the management board on 16 December 2004.

[80] The full list of the chosen scientific experts who accepted their nomination, together with the report outlining the procedure followed for evaluation of the candidates, is available at www.efsa.eu.int/science/catindex_en. html.

focus is currently on recruitment – especially of the scientific staff required to carry out the important increase in risk assessments entrusted to the authority.[81] Although in principle it is up to EFSA to determine how to use the available resources, some limits exist to this freedom. Thus, for instance, a recent amendment to the regulation has introduced a provision according to which EFSA is to seek an opinion of the budgetary authority if it intends to implement a project which 'may have significant financial implications for the funding of the budget'[82].

The authority employs up to 300 people by the end of 2006, with a budget of approximately €47 million.[83] It may be interesting to observe that, by comparison, the Food Standards Agency in the UK has a staff of 570 for food safety functions only, and its annual budget is approximately €140 million.

Once it is operational, EFSA, like the US FDA, will try to rely on its substantial in-house scientific expertise.[84]

Unlike the FDA, EFSA does not currently collect user fees from industry to fund its activities. However, the regulation requires the Commission to publish a report within three years after the effective date of the legislation 'on the feasibility and advisability of presenting a legislative proposal under the co-decision procedure and in accordance with the Treaty and for other services provided by the Authority'[85]. Collecting these fees may contribute to the EFSA's financial independence, since Article 16 of the Framework Financial Regulation provides that if the balance of accounts of the agency is positive, the EFSA has to repay to the Commission only the amount up to the subsidy granted, but all the amounts exceeding the subsidy may be kept as revenue in its budget for the next financial year.[86]

---

[81] The recruitment goal pursued by the end of 2006 is to recruit 80 people so as to reach a total number of EFSA employees of approximately 300 persons.

[82] Regulation 1642/2003 amending Regulation 178/2002 [2003] OJ L 245/4.

[83] These figures have to be reviewed within the three initial years of operations. The authority is expected to employ at least 370 people, with a budget in excess of €70 million at the end of the next financial perspectives period ending in 2013. See also EFSA, Information Note Budget 2003-2004, available at http://www.efsa.eu.int/mboard/ statutory_texts/business_documents/408/mboard_meeting _012_doc5 _en11.pdf

[84] The US FDA obtains more than 90% of its scientific opinions and studies from its own services. Information collected from an FDA official (on file with the author).

[85] Article 45, Fees received by the authority. The Health and Consumer Protection Directorate General (DG SANCO) of the European Commission launched on 15 November, a consultation to gather the views of interested parties on the possibility of enabling the European Food Safety authority (EFSA) to receive fees for processing authorisation files. The consultation paper can be found on http://ec.europa.eu/ food/ consultations/index_en.htm.

[86] Council Regulation 2343/2002 on the financial regulation applicable to the general budget of the European Communities [2002] OJ 357/72.

Finally, as a European public body, EFSA must respect EC regulations on procurement and budgetary matters in the conclusion of contracts for the purchase of goods and services. In compliance with these regulations, EFSA is required to publish an annual list of contracts awarded with a value below the application threshold of the EC public procurement directives as well as of the annual list of awarded building contracts. EFSA annual financial reports are available on the EFSA website[87].

3.6   Location

The regulation establishing the authority does not specify a location for its seat. Although both the James, Kemper and Pascal report and White Paper underlined the need to locate the EFSA in an 'easily accessible place close to the risk managers' (Brussels?), Member States finally agreed to establish the Authority's permanent headquarters in Parma, Italy.[88] This decision by the European Council has arrived after Helsinki and Parma have spent more than 18 months fighting their corners. With a strong food culture – Parma is home to some 8,000 food-related businesses and farms producing an annual turnover of around • 5.5 billion – this Italian city believed in its validity as the location for Europe's first food agency.

4.   Operation

4.1   Risk Assessment: Scientific Opinions

As previously seen, EFSA's primary responsibility is to provide scientific advice in the areas falling under its broad competence. To understand fully EFSA's operation it is therefore important to analyse who is entitled to ask the authority for a scientific opinion, when the authority may or should refuse such a request, which is the procedure applied by the authority to requests for scientific opinions referred to it and, finally, what is the legal status of EFSA's scientific opinions. Some special attention has also to be devoted to EFSA's role within the Rapid Alert System.

Whilst the basic rules governing the operation of the authority are contained in Regulation 178/2002, some have been introduced by Commission Regulation 1304/2003 of July 2003 laying down the procedure applied by the European Food Safety Authority to requests for scientific opinions referred to it.[89]

---

[87] See http://www.efsa.europa.eu/en/about_efsa/efsa_funding/accounts.html

[88] See http://www.efsa.eu.int/press_room/press_release/32/15-12-2003_en1.pdf.

[89] Commission Regulation 1304/2003 of July 2003 on the procedure applied by the European Food Safety authority to requests for scientific opinions referred to it, OJ L 185/6.

We start this analysis by turning to the question of referral to the authority.

A.   Referral to the EFSA

Unlike the previous system where only the Commission could request advice from the scientific committees, the EFSA may respond to requests for scientific advice from a variety of entities. Besides the Commission, Member States, national food authorities and the EC Parliament are entitled to address EFSA to obtain a scientific opinion in relation to food ....ᵈ feed safety issues.[90] This is vital to the EFSA in establishing itself at the centre of the networks as originally envisaged by the White Paper. Where consultation is mandatory under Community law[91], the Commission continues to have exclusive authority to obtain scientific advice from EFSA. In these circumstances, the Commission is legally obliged to consult the authority.

Furthermore, the authority may refuse the request for an opinion if the background information explaining the scientific issue is not given, the Community interest is lacking[92] or there are no new scientific elements justifying the re-examination.[93]

Furthermore, the EFSA, acting *ex officio*, may carry out scientific assessment on any matter that may have a direct or indirect effect on the safety of the food supply, including matters relating to animal health, animal welfare and plant health.[94] This authority's self-tasking activity contributes not only to strengthening EFSA's scientific respectability but also EFSA's independence.[95]

The authority is also entitled to give scientific advice on non-food and feed GMOs, and on nutrition, particularly in relation to Community legislation.

---

[90] Article 29 of the regulation.

[91] See, for instance, Directive 2001/18 on the deliberate release of genetically modified organisms, OJ [2001} L106/1 and food supplements and Directive 89/107/EEC on the approximation of the laws of the Member States concerning food additives authorised for use in foodstuffs intended for human consumption, as amended.

[92] Article 29, paragraph 4 of the regulation.

[93] Article 29, paragraph 5 of the regulation.

[94] Article 29, paragraph 1, (b) of the regulation.

[95] Recital (10) of Commission Regulation 1304/2003 on the procedure applied by the European Food Safety authority to requests for scientific opinions referred to it provides that '[t]he authority's right to issue own-initiative opinions is an essential aspect of its independence' and also that 'in the context of its internal organisation, the authority must ensure that this right is exercised in line with the provisions of Article 29 of Regulation (EC) No 178/2002 and of the present regulation'.

The authority is also authorised to modify a request for an opinion, or refuse it, when it is unclear, different requests are made on the same issues or when it has already delivered a scientific opinion on the specific topic.[96] In these circumstances, the finalised request, as agreed to by the applicant, must be forwarded to the scientific committee or a permanent scientific panel of the authority for preparation of an opinion.

Against this backdrop, it may be noted that the authority exercises broader tasks than those entrusted to the previous scientific committees, notably in the area of data collection. In that regard, Article 33, paragraph 4, allows the authority to transmit:

> to the Member States and the Commission appropriate recommendations which might improve the technical comparability of the data it receives and analyses, in order to facilitate consolidation at Community level.

Opinions issued by the scientific committee and scientific panels are subject to mandatory public disclosure as soon as possible after adoption,[97] provided that their publication does not violate the prohibitions against disclosure of proprietary information and of personal data.[98] However, EFSA's scientific opinions relating to foreseeable health effects can never be kept confidential[99].

If we look at the register of requested opinions listing all scientific opinions asked of EFSA during the first years of its existence (from 2003 to 2006)[100] we discover that from a total of almost 800 requests, more than 600 have been introduced by the Commission, around 100 by Member States and with some (around 60) commenced by the agency *sua sponte*.[101] However, it is well known that the Commission views EFSA self-tasking disfavourably.

---

[96] Article 29(4) and (5) of the regulation.

[97] Article 38 1(b). Also the agendas and minutes, the annual declarations of interest, the results of its scientific studies and research and the annual report of its activities have to be made public. See Article 38, paragraph 1, of the regulation.

[98] Article 39 of the regulation.

[99] Article 39(3) of the regulation.

[100] The register for requested opinions and own-initiative opinions has been established by Commission Regulation 1304/2003 of July 2003 (on the procedure applied by the European Food Safety authority to requests for scientific opinions referred to it) 'to ensure sound management' (see preamble (3)). It must be accessible to the public and allow the progress of requests for opinions to be followed with effect from the date on which they are received. See its article 2. It is available at http://www3.efsa.europa.eu /register/qr_dateofreceipt_1_en.html.

[101] Around 35 by the end of July 2005.

There are also some requests introduced by the European Parliament: on 'the safety of wild and farmed fish marketed in the EC'; on the BSE Risk and contaminant risk in fish meal; etc.[102]

The high number of requests coming from the Commission, which represents 80 per cent of the overall requests, reflects the growing number of applications introduced by food operators to obtain authorisations before entering the European market.

The question has recently arisen as to whether a national court may refer questions to the EFSA. In *HLH Warenvertriebs*,[103] a German court has notably asked the ECJ to establish whether a national judge may refer questions on the classification of a product to EFSA.

The court has denied such a possibility mainly by relying on textual arguments. Neither Regulation 178/2002, where EFSA's tasks are listed, nor Regulation 1304/2003, on EFSA's procedure in relation to requests for scientific opinions, include national courts among the applicants authorised to ask the authority for a scientific opinion.[104] In particular, the latter regulation, by referring to 'government authorities or authorities authorised to request scientific opinions' would seem to definitely rule out national courts from those bodies which may refer to EFSA.[105]

Therefore, as the Community rules stand, national courts may not refer questions to EFSA. Similarly, neither consumers nor food businesses and their associations may request the issuance of scientific opinions from EFSA.

Finally, the Authority may be requested by the Commission not solely to issue scientific opinions but also to provide scientific and technical assistance, consisting in scientific or technical work involving the application of well-established principles which do not require scientific evaluation by the scientific committee or a scientific panel.

1.   Refusal of Requests for Opinions

The authority may refuse to issue a scientific opinion in the following circumstances:

---

[102] See the register of requested opinions available at www.efsa.eu.int/register/qr_applicants_1_en.html.
[103] Cases C-211/03, C-299/03 and C-316/03 to C-318/03, *HLH Warenvertriebs GmbH* [2005] not yet published, at 89-94.
[104] Ibid, at 90–91.
[105] Ibid, at 91.

- when different requests are made on the same issues;[106]
- when the request is not accompanied by background information explaining the scientific issue to be addressed and the Community interest;[107]
- when the request is unclear.[108]

In all these circumstances, justification for the refusal shall be given to the institution or the Member State that made the request. However, whenever the requesting institution falling into one of these categories is the Commission, EFSA may ask it for additional information or propose an amendment to the request, thus rendering less likely the refusal of its request for a scientific opinion.

Regulation 1304/2003 on the procedure applied by EFSA to requests for scientific opinions referred to it has recognised some new hypotheses for refusal.[109] Thus, the authority shall not issue a scientific opinion in the event of requests from applicants not authorised to ask EFSA for a scientific opinion under Community legislation or requests for opinions on matters which are not part of the Authority's mission.[110] Unlike the cases referred to in Regulation 178/2002, those introduced by this regulation do not allow the authority to decide whether or not to provide a scientific opinion, but actually prevent it from doing so. To implement fully the duty of refusal imposed on EFSA in the first case, Member States are supposed to inform the authority of the 'government authority or authorities authorised to request scientific opinions from the Authority'.[111]

Finally, under the transparency requirement imposed on EFSA's activities, the authority is supposed to make public all requests from the European Parliament, the Commission or a Member State for scientific opinions which have been refused or modified and the justifications for the refusal or modification.[112]

2.   Time Limits and Emergencies

Community vertical legislation, such as, for instance, Regulation 2065/ 2003 on smoke flavourings used or intended for use in or on foods[113]

---

[106] Article 29, paragraph 4, of the regulation.
[107] Article 29, paragraph 2 and 4, of the regulation.
[108] Article 29, paragraph 4, of the regulation.
[109] Commission Regulation 1304/2003 of July 2003 on the procedure applied by the European Food Safety authority to requests for scientific opinions referred to it, OJ L185/6.
[110] Article 3, paragraph 1 of the regulation.
[111] Ibid, Article 9 of the regulation.
[112] See Article 38, paragraph 1, lett. g) of the regulation.
[113] See Article 8(1) of Regulation (EC) No 2065/2003 of the European Parliament and of the Council of 10 November 2003 on smoke flavourings used or intended for use in or on foods, OJ L309/1.

and Directive 1829/2003 on genetically modified food and feed,[114] generally provides that, in giving its opinion, the authority must respect a time limit of six months as from the receipt of a valid application.

Where Community legislation does not already specify a time limit for the delivery of a scientific opinion, the authority shall issue scientific opinions within the time limit specified in the requests for opinions, except in duly justified circumstances.[115]

In particular, Regulation 1304/2003 establishes that, in as far as Community (vertical) legislation does specify a time limit for such a delivery, the applicant may stipulate a deadline by when the opinion is required, giving the reasons. Where the authority cannot meet this deadline, it should inform the applicant, explain the reasons and propose a new deadline. Should the applicant not stipulate a deadline, the authority should inform the applicant of the anticipated time needed to deliver the opinion.

There are special rules governing the time limits in case of emergencies. In particular, EFSA is supposed to take the measures necessary to ensure that a request or an own-initiative opinion is delivered as soon as possible where the information accompanying the request testifies to an urgent need for a scientific opinion. Urgent need exists either when there is an emerging risk likely to constitute a serious risk to human or animal health or the environment and likely to have a Community dimension or when the Commission looks for a more detailed scientific basis for managing a serious risk to human or animal health or the environment.

3. Transparency Requirements for Scientific Advice

The regulation provides for several provisions establishing transparency requirements for the scientific opinions. Transparency is a must for EFSA, especially in the light of its objective of restoring consumer confidence in food safety.

All its activities, according to Article 38, have to be carried out with a high level of transparency, meaning that not only the agendas and minutes of the meetings of its scientific bodies shall be made public but also the opinions, including minority opinions.

Moreover, the information on which EFSA opinions are based must also, in principle, be made public without delay.[116]

---

[114] See Article 6(1) of Regulation 1829/2003 on genetically modified food and feed [2003] OJ L268/1.
[115] Article 29(3) of the regulation.
[116] Article 38(1) lett. c) of the regulation.

Nevertheless, confidential information for which a confidential treatment has been requested shall not be divulged by EFSA,[117] with the exception that conclusions of the scientific opinions delivered by the authority relating to foreseeable health effects shall on no account be kept confidential.[118]

Any other non confidential information concerning the mission of the authority shall rapidly be made public. Wide access to documents in its possession shall equally be ensured.

Finally, the Authority's right to issue own-initiative opinions is also subject to the procedure applied by the European Food Safety Authority to requests for scientific opinions referred to it which has been laid down by Regulation 1304/2003.

B.   The Legal Status of the EFSA's Scientific Opinions

Although the EC institutions are expressly required to take EFSA's opinions into account when drafting a Community measure,[119] the Agency lacks formal authority to reach binding resolutions on potentially contentious scientific issues.[120] In other words, similar to the old scientific committees,[121] it does not have the final word in case of diverging scientific opinions between its own decisions and those issued by other bodies. This may be inferred from Article 30 of the regulation which, while establishing a procedure aimed at solving problems arising from 'diverging scientific opinions', attributes neither an authoritative nor a

---

[117] Article 39, paragraph 3 of the regulation provides that '[by] way of derogation from Article 38, the authority shall not divulge to third parties confidential information that it receives for which confidential treatment has been requested and justified, except for information which must be made public if circumstances so require, in order to protect public health'.

[118] Article 39(3) of the regulation.

[119] Article 22 (6) of the regulation.

[120] This conclusion deserves to be further elaborated by looking at those situations where EFSA risk assessment is required by EC vertical legislation. In these circumstances, EFSA opinions enjoy the express status recognised by the legislation. Thus, for instance, under the GMO pre-market approval system, where the Commission decision is not in accordance with the EFSA opinion, the Commission must provide an explanation for the differences. See Article 7 of Regulation 1829/2003 (which reads: '[...] where the draft decision is not in accordance with the opinion of the authority, the Commission shall provide an explanation for the differences'). See on this point S Krapohl, 'Credible Commitment in Non-Independent Regulatory Agencies: A Comparative Analysis of the European Agencies for Pharmaceuticals and Foodstuffs', in *European Law Journal* 10 (5), p 532.

[121] Case 247/84 *Motte* [1985] ECR 3887, para 20, where the court said that Member States must 'take into account the results of international scientific research', but it also stated that 'it must be emphasised that the Opinions of the Committee do not have binding force'.

mediating role to EFSA, but simply duties of 'vigilance' and 'cooperation'. This outcome is, at least on its first appearance, surprising if analysed in light of the EFSA's ambition to become 'the point of reference in risk assessment' for the whole Community.[122]

More precisely, under the regulation, the authority has to exercise vigilance in order to identify at an early stage any potential source of divergence between its scientific opinions and the opinions issued by national food agencies or other bodies carrying out similar tasks.[123] Where there is a conflict between its opinion and those of bodies carrying out similar tasks, the EFSA must contact the body in question to ensure that all relevant scientific information is shared and to identify potentially contentious scientific issues.[124] Where accommodation is not possible despite EFSA's effort and the body is either a Community agency, a Commission scientific body or a Member State body, the authority is 'obliged to cooperate'[125] with the aim of resolving the differences or present a joint document, which will be made public, identifying the uncertainties and the 'contentious scientific issues'.[126] This system recalls the compulsory notification system of draft technical regulations to the extent that it functions as a preventive mechanism (sort of 'early-warning') aimed at solving *ex ante* any conflict arising between the national and European views of risk.[127]

A prima facie reading of these provisions clearly shows that EFSA has not been entrusted with the power to act as the ultimate body of scientific advice in the European Union. To understand the practical consequences stemming from this decision, it is sufficient to remember the crisis involving France and the United Kingdom regarding the Commission's decision to lift the embargo on beef exports in July 1999, two years after the BSE outbreak.[128] The French Food Safety Authority (AFFSA) and the EC Commission scientific steering committee strongly differed on the scientific interpretations of the risks associated with beef. France, relying on its scientific opinion, refused to lift the embargo on British beef in

---

[122] Preamble (34) and (47), Article 22(7).

[123] Article 30(1) of the regulation.

[124] Article 30(2) of the regulation.

[125] Although it is not expressly provided within the regulation, this duty of cooperation must be read in light of Article 10 of the Treaty.

[126] Article 30(3–4) of the regulation.

[127] J. Scott and E. Vos, 'The Juridification of Uncertainty: Observations of the Ambivalence of the Precautionary Principle within the EU and the WTO' in Joerges C. and Dehousse, *Good Governance in Europe's Integrated Market* 43, p 283.

[128] For background information and a detailed description of the situation leading to the case, see Shears, Zollers and Hurd, 'The European Food Safety authority. Towards coherence in food safety policy and practice', 106 British Food Journal 336-352 (2004); T. Harmoniaux, 'Principe de Précaution et Refus de la France de lever l'Embargo sur la Viande de Bovin Britannique', *L'Actualité Jurisprudentielle, Droit Administrative*, pp 164–169 (February 2002).

contravention of the EU scientific data and the EC Commission brought France before the European Court of Justice, claiming a violation of EC law.[129] This case clearly exemplifies the likelihood that, in spite of the high degree of integration within the EU food safety arena, conflicts may arise in the future between national authorities and the EFSA on contentious scientific issues.

The introduction of a mere duty of co-operation does seem to fall short in providing an effective answer to the fundamental question as to the relationships between the EFSA and the national authorities responsible for food safety issues. The institution of an advisory body, as a mechanism of exchange of information between the national authorities and the EFSA, is unlikely to prove decisive in overcoming the difficulties arising from diverging scientific opinions. In light of the above, the current regulatory framework and the institution of the EFSA cannot realistically be expected to put an end to the competition in scientific matters pertaining to food among national authorities in the Member States. This is notwithstanding the committed declaration by the EFSA deputy executive director that EFSA should not 'compete with the excellent science in the Member States'.[130]

Finally, the above-mentioned provisions certainly cast some doubts on the possibility that EFSA will become 'the scientific point of reference for the whole Union', as announced by the regulation.

Most of these considerations found confirmation in the recent *GMO Austrian* cases where the Austrian authorities, claiming to be entitled to create a GMO-free zone, tried to obtain a derogation, on the basis of Article 95(5), from the marketing in its territory of an authorised GMO under Directive 2001/18[131]. Not being successful, the Austrian authorities challenged the Commission decision rejecting the ban on the use of genetically modified organisms in Upper Austria (Land Oberösterreich) by relying on their own scientific assessment.[132] As illustrated above, the CFI has rejected the Austrian action to the extent that it did not provide new scientific evidence justifying the creation of a GMO-free zone in Upper Austria.

---

[129] For a review of this judgment, see A. Alemanno, 'Contentieux, Arrêt "Commission/ France"', *Revue du droit de l'Union Européenne*, 1/2002, pp 159–162, 2002; C. Szawloska, 'Risk Assessment in the European Food Safety Regulation: Who is to decide Whose Science is Better? Commission v France and Beyond ...', 5 *German Law Journal* No. 10, European & International Law (2004) and Harmoniaux, supra note 128.

[130] EFSA news, 2, 2004, at 1.

[131] Directive 2001/18/EC of the European Parliament and of the Council of 12 March 2001 on the deliberate release into the environment of genetically modified organisms and repealing Council Directive 90/220/EEC, OJ L 106, 17.4.2001, p 1.

[132] Joined Cases T-366/03 and T-235/04, *Land Oberösterreich and Republic of Austria v Commission*, not yet reported.

By not endowing EFSA opinions with scientific supremacy over national scientific studies, the regulation promotes an alternative method of tackling the issue of diverging scientific opinions between the EFSA and the national scientific bodies. In order to prevent the emergence of scientific controversies, EFSA is required to promote European networking of organisations operating in food safety risk assessment[133]. More specifically, the official aim of such networking is 'to facilitate a scientific cooperation framework by the coordination of activities, the exchange of information, the development and implementation of joint projects, the exchange of expertise and best practices'.[134] To this end, the management board, acting on a proposal from the executive director, is required to draw up a list to be made public of competent organisations designated by the Member States which may assist the authority, either individually or in networks, with its mission.[135] Member States are not free in designating their competent organisations, but have to abide by the criteria set out by Regulation 2230/2004 laying down detailed rules for the implementation of the general food regulation with regard to the network of organisations operating in the fields within the European Food Safety Authority's mission.[136] Such an external control of the national bodies which are potential members of the network is justified insofar as EFSA may entrust certain tasks to these organisations.[137] In particular, the authority may require them to provide some preparatory

---

[133] Article 36 of the regulation titled 'Networking of organisations operating in the fields within the authority's mission'.

[134] Article 38 of the regulation.

[135] Article 2(2) of Regulation 2230/2004 of 23 December 2004 laying down detailed rules for the implementation of European Parliament and Council Regulation 178/2002 with regard to the network of organisations operating in the fields within the European Food Safety authority's mission, OJ L 379/64.

[136] Commission Regulation 2230/2004 of 23 December 2004 laying down detailed rules for the implementation of European Parliament and Council Regulation 178/2002 with regard to the network of organisations operating in the fields within the European Food Safety authority's mission, OJ L379/64.

[137] Under Article 1(1) of Regulation 2230/2004, the criteria that the national authorities must satisfy in order to become full members of the network are the following: (a) they must carry out scientific and technical support tasks in the fields within the mission of the [...] the authority, especially those with a direct or indirect impact on food or feed safety; in particular, these tasks must include the collection and analysis of data connected with risk identification, exposure to risks, risk assessment, food or feed safety assessment, scientific or technical studies, or scientific or technical assistance for risk managers; (b) they must be legal entities pursuing public interest objectives, and their organisational arrangements must include specific procedures and rules ensuring that any tasks entrusted to them by the authority will be performed with independence and integrity; (c) they must possess a high level of scientific or technical expertise in one or several fields within the authority's mission, especially those with a direct or indirect impact on food or feed safety; (d) they must have the capacity to operate in a network on scientific actions as referred to in Article 3 of this regulation and/or the capacity to perform efficiently the types of task referred to in Article 4 of this regulation which may be entrusted to them by the authority.

work for scientific opinions, scientific and technical assistance, collection of data and identification of emerging risks.[138]

Member States are required to forward to the authority, with a copy to the Commission, the names and details of the designated organisations, evidence that they comply with the criteria set out by Regulation 2230/2004 and details of their specific fields of competence. In particular, for the purposes of application of Regulation 1829/2003, Member States must communicate the names and details of the competent organisations in the field of safety assessment of genetically modified foods and feeds. After consulting the Commission, the authority is also required to lay down harmonised quality criteria for the performance of tasks which it entrusts to the organisations on the list, in particular (a) the criteria to ensure that tasks are performed to high scientific and technical standards; (b) the criteria relating to the resources which may be allocated to the performance of tasks; and (c) the criteria relating to the existence of rules and procedures for ensuring that specific categories of tasks are carried out with independence, integrity and respect for confidentiality.[139]

This sort of network activity is not without precedent[140] and it plays a vital role within EFSA's operation. In fact, the establishment of this network is necessary in order to support EFSA's scientific activities, in particular in conducting scientific opinions.

1. Indirect legal Effect

Notwithstanding the fact that they are not legally binding, the Authority's opinions are likely to produce some significant indirect normative effects. In particular, EFSA's opinions have the potential to become a source of constraint not only for the EC institutions, but also for Member States and private parties.

EFSA, being at the centre of the collection and communication of scientific information, has the potential to create a new information network through which it may become the leading competent source for all EC actors.

As for the EC institutions, the recent *Pfizer Animal Health* judgment has clearly established a general duty to consult the available scientific reports prepared by experts on behalf of the EC.[141] The EC institutions

---

[138] Article 4 of Regulation 2230/2004.

[139] Article 6 of Regulation 2230/2004.

[140] T.A. Borzel, 'Organizing Babylon – On the different Conceptions of Policy Networks' (1998) 76 *Public Administration* 253.

[141] Case T-13/99 *Pfizer Animal Health v Council*, [2002] ECR II-3305. See also the parallel case T-70/99 *Alpharma v Council*, [2002] ECR II-3495. For a review of these judgments see, eg, Alemanno, 'Protection des Consommateurs: Arrêts Alpharma/Pfizer', 4 *Revue du Droit de l'Union Europénne*, p 259.

would be allowed to depart from this duty only in those exceptional circumstances where equivalent scientific evidence can be found and a justification for relying on it is provided. There are therefore good reasons to believe that these constraints on the possibility of departing from scientific evidence will be maintained by the EC courts with regard to EFSA's opinions by transforming them into de facto authoritative measures. In other words, it is likely that within the new food safety regime it will be more and more difficult for the EC institutions to exercise their discretion beyond the boundaries drawn by a scientific administrative network led by an independent and authoritative authority such as EFSA. This is proven by Directive 1829/2003 governing the marketing of GMO foods within the EC, where it provides that, should the Commission decision not be in accordance with an EFSA opinion, the Commission must 'provide an explanation for the differences'.[142]

It is submitted then that the EFSA's opinions are likely to acquire some authoritative value vis-à-vis national decision-makers as well. Although the regulation introduces the presumption that, in the absence of specific Community provisions, all food is deemed to be safe where it complies with the specific national provisions of the country where it is marketed,[143] the same regulation imposes on Member States the duty to take account of the results of risk assessment, particularly the opinions of the authority, when regulating the food sector. In sum, while domestic authorities are not procedurally required to consult the EFSA, they are still required to abide by its scientific opinions in passing new legislation.[144] It would therefore seem impossible for the national authorities to derogate from the EFSA's opinions without giving some reasons justifying their rejection.

The authority's position also has the potential to acquire some legal significance for private parties. As seen above, the regulation also imposes a general obligation on private business operators engaged in production, processing and distribution to ensure that food placed on the market is safe.[145] Any breach of this duty gives rise, at least in principle, to two separate violations of EC law: breach of the general obligation to ensure that food is safe, established by Article 14 of the regulation, on the one hand, and violation of the Product Liability Directive on the other.[146] Although national courts are not required to consult the authority when investigating such violations, they are likely

---

[142] See Article 7 of Regulation 1829/2003.

[143] Article 14 (9) of the regulation.

[144] Article 6 (3) of the regulation.

[145] Article 14 (1) of the regulation.

[146] D. Chalmers, '"Food for thought": Reconciling European Risks and Traditional Ways of Life', 66 *The Modern Law Review* 532, 534 (2003).

to rely on its scientific opinions. In other words, if the EFSA has issued an opinion suggesting that a product is unsafe, it would be extremely difficult for a private individual to prove the opposite.

Finally, EFSA's opinions can also produce some legal effects vis-à-vis national courts. In *HLH Warenvertiebs*, where the ECJ had expressly been asked to determine whether the scientific opinions of that authority may have binding force on the national courts, it has been held that:

> [a]n opinion delivered by that authority, possibly in a matter forming the subject-matter of a dispute pending before a national court, may constitute evidence that that court should take into consideration in the context of that dispute.[147]

Notably, the court has stated that national courts should ascribe to such an opinion the same value as that accorded to an 'expert report'.[148] Thus, EFSA's scientific opinion may be susceptible to acquiring a legal status similar to that of scientific expertise requested by the same national courts of third parties. Although not binding per se, the scientific report 'should be taken into consideration in the context of the dispute'.[149]

In conclusion, while the EFSA's opinions have not been expressly granted a direct regulatory authority, they are likely to acquire a de facto legally binding value for both the EC and the Member State authorities when passing legislation and amount to a strong probative authority against private business operators placing unsafe food on the market. More generally, it can reasonably be expected that EFSA's opinions will structure the terms of debate on several issues by influencing enforcement within the Member States and public opinion.

C.   Judicial Review of EFSA's Scientific Opinions

1.   *European Courts and Scientific Opinions*

Although the issue as to whether Community courts may review the legality of an EFSA scientific opinion is an open question to the extent that it has not yet been resolved, it is possible to make some reflections. A comparative analysis of the 'judicial accountability' of the different European agencies does not seem to offer any help in finding an answer to that question insofar as their constituent regulations provide for very different solutions. Thus, for instance, while some of these regulations explicitly provide that the acts adopted by the agency are challengeable

---

[147] Cases C-211/03, C-299/03 and C-316/03 to C-318/03, *HLH Warenvertriebs GmbH* [2005] not yet published, at 94.
[148] Ibid, at 93.
[149] Ibid, at 94.

under Article 230 EC,[150] some others entrust a specific chamber of the agency[151] or the same Commission[152] with the task of reviewing the legality of the agency's decisions. In the case of EFSA, the general food regulation which establishes EFSA does not even contemplate the possibility of submitting its acts to legal review. A role for EC courts is envisaged exclusively in the area of contractual and non-contractual liability of the authority.[153]

As a result, the question as to whether EFSA acts, in particular its scientific opinions, may be challenged before the European courts is governed by Article 230 EC. Under such a provision, judicial persons can bring a nullity claim against decisions by the European institutions before EC courts, notably the CFI, if those decisions are *addressed to that person*. They may also bring an action against a decision which, although in the form of a regulation or a decision addressed to another person, is of *direct and individual concern* to the former.

The application of this provision to EFSA acts, in particular, to its scientific opinions, raises several problems. First, Article 230 EC does not contain any reference, neither explicit nor implicit, to acts of European agencies.[154] It merely refers to the 'acts adopted jointly by the European Parliament and the Council, [...] acts of the Council, [...] the Commission and [...] the ECB, other than recommendations and opinions, and [...] acts of the European Parliament intended to produce

---

[150] Article 17 of Council Regulation (EEC) No 302/93 of February 1993 on the establishment of a European Monitoring Centre for Drugs and Drug Addition, OJ L36/1. This provision clearly states that 'the Court of Justice shall have jurisdiction in actions brought against the Centre under the conditions provided for under Article 173 [now 230] of the Treaty'. See also Article 15(3) of Council Regulation (EC) No 1035/97 of 2 June 1997 establishing a European Monitoring Centre on Racism and Xenophobia, OJ L 151/1.

[151] Articles 57 and 63 of Council Regulation (EC) No 40/94 of 20 December 1993 on the Community trade mark OJ L 11/1.

[152] This is the case, for instance, of the Community Plant Variety Office (CPVO) as established by Council Regulation (EC) No 2100/94 of 27 July 1994 on Community plant variety rights OJ L 227/1.

[153] According to Article 47 of the regulation: '1. [t]he contractual liability of the authority shall be governed by the law applicable to the contract in question. The Court of Justice of the European Communities shall have jurisdiction to give judgment pursuant to any arbitration clause contained in a contract concluded by the authority. 2. In the case of non-contractual liability, the authority shall, in accordance with the general principles common to the laws of the Member States, make good any damage caused by it or its servants in the performance of their duties. The Court of Justice shall have jurisdiction in any dispute relating to compensation for such damage. 3. The personal liability of its servants towards the authority shall be governed by the relevant provisions applying to the staff of the authority'.

[154] Article 230, paragraph 1, reads: '[t]he Court of Justice shall review the legality of acts adopted jointly by the European Parliament and the Council, of acts of the Council, of the Commission and of the ECB, other than recommendations and opinions, and of acts of the European Parliament intended to produce legal effects vis-à-vis third parties'.

legal effects vis-à-vis third parties'. However, this obstacle per se would not appear insurmountable to the extent that the ECJ, in the past, has shown itself to be ready to interpret broadly the category of acts reviewable under Article 230 EC.[155] Secondly, EFSA, being an independent agency, cannot be described as one of the institutions or bodies listed therein. Put differently, EFSA decisions do not strictly speaking come from one of those EC institutions listed in Article 230, paragraph 1, EC.

It must be noted that it is by relying exactly on these arguments that the CFI, in *Associazione delle Cantine Sociali Venete*, has declared inadmissible an action for failure to act directed against the European Ombudsman.[156] Third, being merely preparatory acts, EFSA scientific opinions would not seem to fall within the category of acts which can be subject to an action for annulment, ie which covers solely those acts 'intended to produce legal effects vis-à-vis third parties'.

In any case, even in the case in which it might be proven that some of the acts adopted by EFSA may fall within the scope of reviewable acts under Article 230 EC, it would be difficult to satisfy the locus standi requirements, as interpreted by the EC courts. In fact, not being addressed to a specific subject, EFSA scientific opinions would be challengeable only when the applicant can prove direct and individual concern. In particular, having been interpreted in a particularly restrictive way by Community courts, it is the notion of 'individual concern' which may raise some difficulty. In fact, in order to allow individuals to attack a decision not addressed to the plaintiff, EC courts require that this act affect the plaintiff:

> [...] by reason of certain attributes, which are particular to them or by reason of circumstances in which they are differentiated from all other persons and by virtue of these factors distinguished individually.[157]

However, notwithstanding their non-binding legal nature, it has been established, with reference to the scientific opinions given by the EMEA Committee for Proprietary Medicinal Products (CPMB), that they are:

---

[155] Case 294/83, *Les Verts v Parliament*, ECR 1986, p 1339 and Case 193-4/87, *Maurissen v Court of Auditors*, ECR 1989, p 1045. In these judgments the ECJ considered that insofar as the Community is based on the rule of law all acts adopted by its organs may be reviewed.

[156] Case T-103/99 *Associazione delle Cantine Sociali Venete v Médiateur européen and Parliament* [2000] ECR II-4165, paras 44-48. For a detailed analysis and comment of this judgment, see L. Raimondi, 'Mediatore Europeo e Mezzi di Ricorso Giurisdizionale', *Il Diritto dell'Unione Europea*, 2004, pp 547 ss.

[157] See Case 25/62 *Plaumann v Commission* [1963] ECR 1963, para 95.

> [n]onetheless extremely important so that any unlawfulness of
> that opinion must be regarded as a breach of essential procedural
> requirement rendering the Commission's decision unlawful.[158]

In other words, although these scientific opinions do not bind the
Commission, they provide it with the evidence of scientific assessment
which is necessary to determine, 'in full knowledge of fact', the
appropriate measure to ensure a high level of health protection.
Therefore, whenever the scientific opinions are vitiated, their illegality
will reflect on the subsequent decision.

In light of the above, in the *Artegodan* judgments, subsequently confirmed
by the ECJ, the CFI held that EC courts may be called upon to review
the formal legality of an agency scientific committee's opinion as well
as the Commission's exercise of its discretion.

Although the CFI has stated that it cannot 'substitute its own assessment
for that of the scientific committee', it has held that it may nonetheless
review the proper functioning of the committee, the internal consistency
of the opinion and the statement of reasons contained therein.

In so doing, EC courts might rely on the growing number of guidance
documents which are prepared by the EFSA's scientific panels in order
to define their own way of conducting risk assessment.[159] In fact, only
these documents may potentially provide a useful legality benchmark
in reviewing the proper conduct of the panel when carrying out the risk
assessment.

It remains to be seen whether the EC courts will extend this reasoning,
developed within the EMEA context, to the review of EFSA scientific
opinions.[160] There seems to be no reason why EFSA's opinions may not
be subject to an analogous standard of review should the courts be called
upon to review the legality of a Commission decision based on an EFSA's
scientific opinion delivered by one of its panels, such as, for instance,
the panel on genetically modified organisms.

---

[158] Joined Cases T-144/00, T-76/00, T-83/00, T-84/00, T-85/00, T-132/00 and T-141/00 *Artegodan
a.o. v Commission* [2002] ECR 4945, at 197.
[159] Thus, for instance, the Scientific Panel on Genetically Modified Organisms has adopted
a Guidance document for the risk assessment of genetically modified microorganisms
and their derived products intended for food and feed use (The EFSA Journal (2006) 374,
1-115 Summary) and also a Guidance document for the risk assessment of genetically
modified plants and derived food and feed (the *EFSA Journal* (2004) 99, pp 1–94).
[160] This conclusion will certainly also depend on the outcome of the two following cases,
which are currently pending before the CFI: T-19/02 *Albert Albrecht GmbH and 17 others v
Commission and EMEA* and T-133/03 *Shering-Plough Ltd. v Commission and EMEA*.

This position seems to find support in the communication from the Commission entitled 'The operating framework for the European Regulatory Agencies', where it is stated that:

> [g]uarantees are needed ensuring that the regulatory agencies respect the principles of the institutional system of which they form a part, and the specific regulations applicable to them.[161]

Moreover, according to this Communication:

> [...] the regulatory agencies must assume legal responsibility for acts attributable to them. Consequently, provision must be made for compensating by them of any damages caused by such acts, where appropriate after judicial confirmation of their liability.[162]

This approach seems to have been impliedly endorsed by the CFI in the *GMO* Austrian judgments. As illustrated above, in these cases, the Austrian authorities challenged the Commission decision rejecting the ban on the use of genetically modified organisms in Upper Austria in reliance on an EFSA opinion.[163] The Commission requested EFSA to issue an opinion, in accordance with Article 29(1) and Article 22(5)(c) of the general food regulation, on the probative value of the scientific study set forth by the Austrian authorities in order to satisfy the 'new scientific evidence' requirement imposed by Article 95(5).

However, as EFSA's scientific opinion found that that scientific information did not contain any new scientific evidence which could justify banning GMOs in the Land Oberösterreich, the Commission rejected the Austrian safeguard measure by adopting Decision 2003/653/EC. It is against this decision that both the Land Oberösterreich and the Republic of Austria brought the actions registered under case numbers T-366/03 and T-235/04, respectively.

Both plaintiffs attacked the Commission decision by invoking inter alia a breach of Article 95(5).[164] In particular, they submitted that the Commission should have granted the Republic of Austria's request, since the requirements of Article 95(5) EC were satisfied. They claimed that the notified measure was intended to protect the environment, that it was based on new scientific evidence, that it was justified by a problem specific to Austria and that it complied with the principle of proportionality. In so

---

[161] Communication from the Commission, *The operating framework for the European Regulatory Agencies*, COM(2002) 718 final, at 13.
[162] Ibid.
[163] Joined Cases T-366/03 and T-235/04, *Land Oberösterreich and Republic of Austria v Commission*, not yet reported.
[164] Joined Cases T-366/03 and T-235/04, *Land Oberösterreich and Republic of Austria v Commission*, not yet reported, at 59–69.

doing, they made an attempt at rebutting the conclusions of EFSA's scientific opinion, in particular those according to which, first, 'the scientific evidence presented contained no new or uniquely local scientific information on the environmental or human health impacts of existing or future GM crops or animals' and, secondly, 'no scientific evidence was presented which showed that this area of Austria had unusual or unique ecosystems that required separate risk assessments from those conducted for Austria as a whole or for other similar areas of Europe'.[165]

Nonetheless, the CFI did not accept these arguments, by stating:

> [...] the applicants have failed to provide convincing evidence such as to cast doubt on the merits of those assessments as to the existence of a specific problem, but have confined themselves to drawing attention to the small size of farms and the importance of organic production in the Land Oberösterreich.[166]

Although the plaintiffs in the *GMO* Austrian judgments did not expressly seek review of EFSA's scientific opinion, such a review was, in effect, sought by means of a challenge to the Commission decision based on that scientific opinion. Even though the CFI did not review the procedural validity of EFSA's contribution to the Commission decision, the court not only avoided ruling out the possibility of exercising that review, but it left that option open when it assessed the plausibility of the plaintiff's arguments.

With these judgments currently pending on appeal before the ECJ,[167] it remains to be seen whether the ECJ will confirm, develop further or limit such an approach to the above described 'indirect review' of EFSA's scientific opinions.

Besides the issue of the judicial review of scientific opinions, another open question relates more generally to EFSA's locus standi before EC courts. To what extent may one bring an action against EFSA's decisions relating to its growing procurement activity? This question is expected to be answered in the pending case *European Dynamics*, wherein the applicant claims that the CFI should annul EFSA's decision which has rejected its bid for the software and services establishing an 'Extranet'

---

[165] Recitals 70 and 71 of Decision 2003/653/EC OJ L 230/34.

[166] Joined Cases T-366/03 and T-235/04, *Land Oberösterreich and Republic of Austria v Commission*, not yet reported, at 66.

[167] Appeal brought on 22 December 2005 by the Republic of Austria against the judgment delivered on 5 October 2005 by the Court of First Instance of the European Communities (Fourth Chamber) in Joined Cases T-366/03 and T-035/04 (Case C-454/05P). See OJ [2006] C 60/20.

between the Member States' national agencies, EFSA and the Commission.[168]

Judicial review of this kind of agency act may not be immediately excluded insofar as these decisions are, unlike scientific opinions, not mere preparatory acts, but rather are definitive and legally binding decisions producing effects vis-à-vis third parties. However, as illustrated above, the general food regulation does not foresee the applicability of Article 230 EC and provides that only disputes relating to contractual and non-contractual liability of EFSA can be brought before EC courts.[169]

From this line of thought, it seems that the conclusions reached in the recent *Eurojust* judgment may be extended to the admissibility of the present action relating to EFSA's decision on the award of its contract. In this recent judgment, the ECJ has held that:

> [...] it is for the applicant to choose the legal basis of its action and not for the Community judicature itself to choose the most appropriate legal basis (see, to that effect, Case 175/73 *Union syndicale and Others v Council* [1974] ECR 917, and the order of the Court of First Instance in Case T-148/97 *Keeling v OHIM* [1998] ECR II 2217). It is clear from the examination of the action that the applicant brought it under Article 230 EC. The admissibility of that action must therefore be examined in the light of that provision.

As is clear from Article 230 EC, the court 'shall review the legality of acts adopted jointly by the European Parliament and the Council, of acts of the Council, of the Commission and of the ECB, other than recommendations and opinions, and of acts of the European Parliament intended to produce legal effects vis-à-vis third parties'.

Clearly, the acts contested in the present action are not included in the list of acts the legality of which the court may review under that article'.[170]

Yet, while it is indisputable that the plaintiff is the *dominus litis* of the procedure, this outcome would be difficult to reconcile with the principle established in the recently proposed Draft Interinstitutional Agreement on the operating framework for the European regulatory agencies under which '[a]ctions may be brought before the Court of Justice for the annulment of acts carried out by an agency which are legally binding

---

[168] Case T-69/05 *European Dynamics S.A. v EFSA*, pending. Notice for the OJ C 106, 30.04.2005, p 34.
[169] See Article 47 of the regulation.
[170] Case C-160/03 *Kingdom of Spain v Eurojust*, not yet reported, at 35–37.

on third parties, for failure to act and for damages caused by any agency in the course of its activities'.[171] Finally, this outcome would be even more difficult to reconcile with the principle of effective judicial protection in the Community legal order. As our analysis has show, there is a clear scope for improvement of the rules governing judicial review of EFSA's acts.

2. National Courts and Scientific Opinions

Although in *HLH Warenvertriebs* the question has arisen as to whether national courts may review the legality of EFSA's scientific opinions,[172] neither the opinion of the AG nor the judgment itself have tackled this issue. The Court has confined itself to holding that such opinions, although not binding, 'may constitute evidence that the court would have to take into consideration as such',[173] notably by ascribing to them 'the same value as that recognised to an expert report'.[174] However, the possibility for a national court to review the legality of a scientific opinion delivered by EFSA may be rendered controversial not because of their mere preparatory nature, but rather because of the ECJ's monopoly on the legality review of EC acts under the *Foto-Frost* jurisprudence.[175] According to this case law, national jurisdictions do not have the power to declare acts of the Community institutions invalid and, accordingly, when they consider the arguments put forward by the parties to be well founded, they are supposed to refer questions of validity to the ECJ by means of a preliminary preference.[176]

4.2 The Rapid Alert System for Food and Feed (RASFF)

The Rapid Alert System for food emergencies (RASFF), originally established by Decision 84/133/CEE,[177] then integrated into the general product safety Directive 92/59/EC,[178] was revamped by its inclusion in the general food regulation, thus taking a huge leap forward. It is

---

[171] Draft Interinstitutional Agreement on the operating framework for the European regulatory agencies, presented by the EC Commission, 25/02/05, COM(2005) 59 final.
[172] See Opinion of AG Geelhoed, Case C-211/03, *HLH Warenvertriebs*, not yet published, at 98.
[173] Cases C-211/03, C-299/03 and C-316/03 to C-318/03, *HLH Warenvertriebs GmbH* [2005] not yet published, at 94.
[174] Ibid, at 93.
[175] Case 314/85, *Foto-Frost* [1986] ECR 2333.
[176] The duty of referral to the ECJ has recently been confirmed in Case C-461/03 *Gaston Schul Douane-expediteur BV v Minister van Landbouw, Natuur en Voedselkwaliteit* [2005] not yet reported, and that 'even where the Court has already declared invalid analogous provisions of another comparable regulation'.
[177] OJEC 1984 L70.
[178] OJEC 1992 L228/24.

activated when the health of EC consumers may be under threat from a food safety problem in more than one Member State.[179]

Although both the White Paper and the original regulation proposal entrusted EFSA with the management of the RASFF,[180] the current regulation designates the Commission as being 'responsible for managing' the system.[181]

The system relies on a network involving Member States, the Commission and the EFSA, each of which designate a contact point as a member of the network. When a member of the network has any information relating to the existence of a serious direct or indirect risk to human health deriving from food or feed, this information has to be notified to the Commission, who will transmit it to the other members of the network.

In particular, Member States are supposed to notify the Commission of any measures they adopt to restrict the placing of a product on the market (recall) or to demand its withdrawal. The RASFF notifications must be accompanied by a detailed explanation of the reasons for the action taken by the competent authorities of the Member State in which the notification was issued. It should then be followed, 'in good time', by supplementary information, in particular where the measures on which the notification is based are modified or withdrawn.

In order to assist the members of the network, RASFF notifications are classified as an 'alert notification' or an 'information notification' depending on whether the food or feed for which a risk has been identified has already reached the market of other Member States. Unlike the former, the latter category of notification mostly concerns food and feed consignments that have been tested and rejected at the external borders of the EU and, accordingly, aims at preventing attempts to import them through another point of entry. Moreover, any type of information related to the safety of food or feed which has not been communicated by a Member State as an 'alert' or an 'information' notification, but which is judged to be of interest to the food/feed control authorities in the Member States, is classified and made available as a 'news notification'.

Within the alert and information notifications it is appropriate to distinguish between 'original notifications', representing a new case

---

[179] For an introduction to the origin of the system, see N. De Grove-Valdeyron, 'La Protection de la Santé et de la Sécurité du Consommateur à l'Epreuve de l'Affaire de la Dioxine', *Revue du Marché Commun*, 1999, pp 700 ss.

[180] See Article 22 (h) of the amended proposal, COM/2001/0475 final, OJ 2001 C 304.

[181] Article 35 of the regulation.

reported on a health risk detected in one or more consignments of a food or feed and the 'additional information notifications' which are reactions from RASFF members reporting follow-up of an original notification.

According to the 2005 RASFF Annual Report, if, after evaluation by the Commission, the criteria for notification are not met or the information transmitted is insufficient, an original notification sent by a member of the RASFF system can be rejected and refused transmission through the RASFF system. In this circumstance, the notifying country is informed of the decision not to transmit the information through the RASFF system and is invited to provide additional information allowing the rejection to be reconsidered by the Commission.

Moreover, according to the 2005 RASFF Annual Report, an alert or information notification that was transmitted through the RASFF system can also be withdrawn by the Commission at the request of the notifying country if the information, upon which the measures sought to be taken are based, reveals unproven accusations or if the transmission of the notification was made erroneously.

This interpretation of the Commission's role under the RASFF mechanism is rather controversial to the extent that it lacks a clear textual basis. Indeed, contrary to what may seem to emerge from the reading of the 2005 RASFF Annual Report, Article 50 of the general food regulation does not entrust the Commission with a right of approval over Member States' notifications. Rather, under this provision, the Commission is merely required to 'transmit this information immediately to the members of the network'. Being an obligation expressed in such absolute terms, it would seem to rule out the conferral of any power to filter Member States' notifications on the Commission. It is submitted that the interpretation set forth by the RASFF Annual Report not only lacks a textual basis, but would deny the *effet utile* of Member States' notifications within the RASFF system.

The question of the role of the Commission within the RASFF, and the corollary issues of whether the Commission has been conferred with the power to reject or withdraw a notification, is not of mere academic interest as it is currently at the centre of a case pending before the Court of First Instance.[182]

Following a brief inspection of the premises of a food business operator by the Commission's Food and Veterinary Office, the UK Food Standards Agency issued a Rapid Alert Notification under RASFF, for inter alia

---

[182] Case T-212/06, *Bowland Dairy Products Ltd v Commission*, pending.

'improper production of dairy products'. However, after conducting a new inspection, the UK authorities concluded that the cheese produced by the food business operator could be marketed. In the light of the above, they submitted an additional notification to the Commission aimed at making the result of their audit known. The Commission refused to circulate under RASFF the additional notification of the UK Food Standards Agency as it did not share its conclusion. It is against this refusal that the food business operator has brought an action before the Court of First Instance seeking damages allegedly suffered as a result of the Commission's behaviour.

Under the RASFF, the Commission may be obliged, in specific circumstances, to transmit the information not only to the members of the network but also to third countries. This may occur every time it is known that a product subject to an alert notification has been exported to that third country or when a product originating from that country has been the subject of a notification, so as to allow it to take corrective measures and thus avoid repetition of the problems.[183]

Moreover, participation in the RASFF may be open to EU applicant countries, third countries or international organisations on the basis of agreements which, in turn, must be based on reciprocity and confidentiality measures equivalent to those applicable within the Community.

As is clear from this overview, the RASFF is primarily a tool for exchange of information between food and feed central competent authorities in the Member States in cases where a risk to human health has been identified and measures have been taken, such as withholding, recalling, seizure or rejection of the products concerned. The logic behind this system is therefore to set up a quick information-exchange mechanism allowing Member States to immediately identify whether they are also affected by a problem and to take the appropriate measures, thereby ensuring coherent and simultaneous actions and consumer safety.

However, under the RASFF, neither the Commission not the EFSA is entitled to determine whether a product presents a risk to human health. The system, which merely aims at disseminating risk information in response to notifications from Member States, does not provide for a procedure for assessing whether the risks warrant a European reaction. The only way to influence the risk management action in some way following the notification is the possibility for EFSA 'to supplement the notification with any scientific and technical information'.[184]

---

[183] Article 40(3) and (4) of the regulation.
[184] Article 50(2) second subparagraph of the regulation.

It is submitted that the RAS could have become more effective if the regulation had expressly entrusted EFSA with the authority to use its scientific expertise to assess the urgency of the notifications and analyse the information notified by the Member States to formulate scientific advice, rather than simply using the authority as a mere conduit for information supplied to the system by Member States. Such an *ex ante* involvement of EFSA, as opposed to the current *ex post* role, could have been pivotal in assuring the effectiveness of the RASFF.

Apart from this structural limitation, the RASFF is currently performing well. According to the 2005 Annual Report,[185] the number of notifications transmitted through the RASFF rose from 698 in 1999 to 6 897 in 2005.[186] In particular, in 2005, a total of 3158 original notifications, classified as 956 alert and 2202 information notifications, were received through the RASFF, giving rise to 3739 additional information notifications, representing on average about 1.2 follow-ups per original notification. When notifications are classified according to the type of control carried out, it becomes clear that the largest category of notifications relate to controls at the border posts of the outer EU (and EEA) borders when the consignment was not accepted for import ('import rejected').

Finally, much of the fortune of the RASFF will depend on the outcome of the above-mentioned *Bowland* case. This case, which is currently pending before the CFI, is likely to clarify the role of the Commission within the information network represented by RASFF.

4.3   Risk Communication

Communicating on risks associated with the food chain is a key part of the EFSA's mandate. This is because, by communicating on risks in an open and transparent way based on the independent scientific advice of its scientific expert panels, EFSA may contribute to regaining public confidence in the way food risks are assessed.

In the light of the above, the regulation entrusts the authority with the duty to communicate, on its own initiative, the 'results of its work' by acting in close collaboration with the Commission and the Member States 'to promote the necessary coherence in the risk communication process'.[187]

---

[185] The 2005 RASFF Annual Report provides information on the functioning of the RASFF in 2005 and, in particular, on the number of notifications, the origin of the notifications, the countries involved, the products and the identified risks. It is available at http://ec.europa.eu/food/food/rapidalert/report2005_en.pdf.

[186] As the following data shows, this trend in the annual number of notifications has been gradual: 823 in 2000, 1 567 in 2001, 3 024 in 2002, 4 414 in 2003 and 5 562 in 2004. From 2003 on, these figures include all notifications (alert, information, news and additional information) but not the rejected notifications.

[187] Article 40 of the regulation.

However, the Commission, being extremely concerned about losing this power, remains entrusted with the communication of risk management decisions, even though they are based on scientific opinions of the authority.

As a result, while EFSA's mission includes communication of scientific information on risks, the Commission is responsible for communicating risk management measures. This shared responsibility in relation to risk communication makes EFSA's attempts to issue communications about its scientific outcomes particularly difficult. This is especially due to the fact that, in developing public communication, EFSA will seek to translate scientific evidence into accessible and meaningful communications, addressing the needs of key audiences. In so doing, it is almost inevitable for EFSA to go beyond the mere reporting of its scientific opinions and, thus, to make reference to some possible risk management options.

The seriousness of the flaws stemming from the existing shared competence in relation to risk communication powers has recently been proven by the former EFSA Acting Director Herman Koëter. Following the publication of a scientific opinion conducted by EFSA[188], he declared that:

> We don't have any evidence that the virus can be transmitted through food. But we can't exclude it, either. *If you don't eat raw eggs and always cook poultry thoroughly, there should be no problems.*[189]

In so doing, Mr Koëter did not merely communicate to the public the outcome of EFSA scientific opinion, but he unequivocally suggested well-defined consumer risk management options, such as not eating raw eggs and cooking poultry thoroughly. By doing this, EFSA clearly went well beyond its mandate in risk communication, thereby encroaching on the Commission's powers. In fact, it clearly appeared from the media that the Commission did not really appreciate EFSA's move.

As a result, the newly-appointed executive director has dramatically modified the EFSA structure by putting, for the first time, its scientific

[188] The Scientific Panel on Animal Health and Welfare (AHAW) of the European Food Safety authority (EFSA) has carried out a scientific evaluation on the animal health and welfare aspects of Avian Influenza (AI). This opinion has been considered at the Panel's meeting on 13–14 September 2005 with a view to providing additional scientific support to the European Commission and Member States in addressing this issue.

[189] As reported by several newspapers and other media, such as the Daily Mail (available at http://www.dailymail.co.uk/pages/live/articles/health/healthmain.html?in_article_id=366607&in_page_id=1774&ito=1490), FOX News (available at http://www.foxnews.com/story/0,2933,173450,00.html) and News Scotsman (available at http://news.scotsman.com/international.cfm?id=2146272005).

activities on a equal footing with risk communication tasks (see Diagram 4).

Diagram 4. EFSA structure as emerging from the 2006 reformed organigramme (Source: EFSA website):[190]

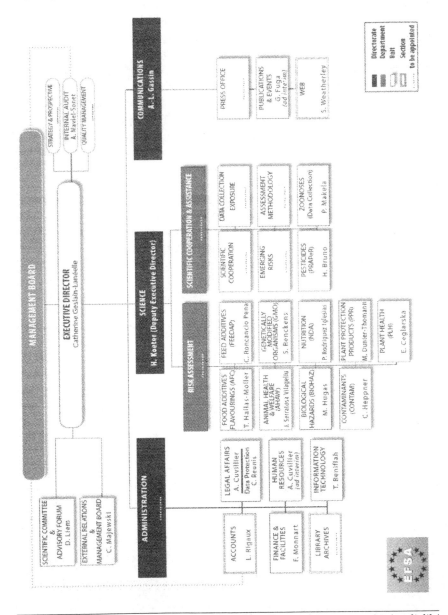

Although prima facie surprising, the decision to devote to risk communication the same amount of attention that is given to risk assessment is perfectly in line with the rationale underpinning the creation of the authority. EFSA has been established not only to ensure food safety, but especially to promote consumer confidence.

In the light of the above, the challenge for EFSA when exercising its risk communication competence is to disseminate complex scientific information in a consumer-friendly way in order to become the indispensable port-of-call for the most up-to-the-minute data on risk. To this end, under the umbrella of the advisory forum, EFSA has set up a Communication Working Group to facilitate message development and co-ordination with Member States as well as the sharing of best practices in the area of risk communications.[191] The communications working group works with the communications departments of the national food safety agencies to build a more collaborative and informed approach to communicating risks in the food chain and to promote coherence of food safety messages across the Community. To this end it regroups the heads of the communication units from all the national food safety authorities in Europe and is chaired by the Communications Director of EFSA. Meeting four times annually, the group seeks to share best practice and facilitate consistent risk communications messages in Europe. Moreover, since 2005, EFSA's Advisory Group on Risk Communication (AGRC) has been established, which is comprised of seven risk communication experts and provides advice to the EFSA executive director on risk communications and issues specific to the work of EFSA.[192]

Besides the above described difficult cooperation with the Commission, EFSA also acts in close collaboration with the national authorities and the Member States to promote the necessary coherence in the risk communication process, especially with regard to public information campaigns.[193]

The main objective pursued by the EFSA's risk communication policy is to ensure that the public and any interested parties are rapidly given objective, reliable and easily accessible information, in particular with regard to the results of its work.

---

[191] See http://www.efsa.eu.int/advisory_forum/working_groups/165_en.html.

[192] The terms of reference of this body are available at http://www.efsa.europa.eu /etc/ medialib/efsa/about _efsa /communicating_risk/adv_group_risk_comm/ 1160.Par.0027.File.dat/tor_agrc_010205_en1.pdf. Its members rank among the most famous experts in risk communication and are Jesus Contreras, University of Barcelona; Claude Fischler, CNRS, CETSAH, EHESS, Paris; Baruch Fischoff, Carnegie Mellon University; George Gaskell, London School of Economics; Ragnar Löfstedt, King's College, London and Professor Ortwin Renn, University of Stuttgart.

[193] Article 40(3) and (4) of the regulation.

Notwithstanding these laudable efforts, the modest communication budget (2.5 per cent of the overall budget of the authority) seems to cast some doubts on the attainment of this goal.[194]

Although prima facie surprising, the recent decision to devote to risk communication the same amount of attention that is given to risk assessment is perfectly in line with the rationale underpinning the creation of the authority. EFSA has been established not only to ensure food safety, but especially for promoting consumer confidence. It may be predicted that it is also against the latter objective that EFSA's legitimacy will ultimately be tested.

5. Organisational Independence and Accountability

It should not be surprising that the mission pursued by EFSA is not purely consumer protection-oriented. This is because the Authority's raison d'être can be found, similarly to the *ratio legis* underpinning Regulation 178/2002, in the free movement imperative. Indeed, although the regulation mentions that EFSA should contribute to 'a high level of protection of human life and health', that mission must be done 'in the context of the operation of the internal market'.

The result is that the authority finds itself caught in the same legislative tension underlying the functioning of Regulation 178/2002: on the one hand, it aims at offering a high level of health protection and, on the other, at ensuring the effective functioning of the internal market. It is therefore no accident that the regulation talks about 'consumer confidence' in the internal market rather that consumer protection. Thus, from a prima facie reading of EFSA's mission statement it seems clear that the internal market objective may, somehow, overshadow consumer protection.

Against this backdrop, one may legitimately wonder to what extent such a constant tension between the free trade imperative and the consumer protection goal may have been reflected in the institutional framework within which the authority is called to operate. In other words, to what extent will EFSA's activities be biased as a result of this tension? Is EFSA an 'independent scientific source of advice'?[195]

In order to ascertain to what extent the EFSA may be regarded as an autonomous and independent body, notwithstanding the tension underlying its functioning, various factors may be taken into account, such as the composition of its organs, the relationship of the authority with the Commission, its financial status, organisational autonomy, etc.

[194] EFSA Annual Report 2003.
[195] See recital (35) of the preamble of the regulation.

In the following pages, in order to assess EFSA's autonomy, focus will be mainly kept on the composition of the managing board and the mode of appointment of the scientists sitting on the scientific committees. We will then turn to assess the organisational independence of EFSA vis-à-vis the Commission.

5.1. The Questionable Independence of the Management Board

Given its relevance to the functioning of the EFSA, it is important to start by examining the management board's composition and its mode of appointment. Unlike other Community agencies, the board is not composed of representatives of all the Member States. Rather it consists of 15 members, of which one is a representative of the Commission and four should have their background in organisations representing different interests related to the food chain. To compensate partially for this situation of Member States' under-representation, the regulation expressly provides that 'the broadest possible geographic distribution' should be secured within the board.[196] Along the same lines, Recital 41 of the Preamble provides that there should be 'a rotation of the different countries of origin of the members of the management board, without any post being reserved for nationals of any specific Member State'.

This institutional framework seems to be guided mainly by the idea that the board should not represent national interests but should rather operate as an independent organ. However, as Member States may have different interests as regards the food-chain and, particularly, different perceptions of risk, it might be important to ensure the geographical rotation of its members.

While this institutional design, and notably its composition, may seem to be effective in ensuring the independence of the organ, the mode of appointment of its members seems to raise some doubts[197]. The regulation provides that the management board members be appointed by the Council, in consultation with the European Parliament, from a list drawn up by the Commission. However, as the regulation does not provide for an open competition for candidates to be appointed to the management board, it is not clear on what basis the Commission is to draw the list of candidates for the post. The only guideline concerning

---

[196] Article 25(1) of the regulation.
[197] Contra, Krapohl, 'Credible Commitment in Non-Independent Regulatory Agencies: A Comparative Analysis of the European Agencies for Pharmaceuticals and Foodstuffs', *European Law Journal* 10 (5), p 531, who argues that, contrary to what happened with the EMEA, since the Council, the European Parliament and Commission 'have control over the recruitment of the management board of the agency', the EFSA's personnel would be recruited independently from the Member States.

their selection is that they should be appointed 'in such a way as to secure the highest standards of competence and a broad range of relevant expertise'.[198] However, it is submitted that mere professionalism and competence are not sufficient guarantees of independence. This is because they do not ensure that the person concerned acts in the public interest, but simply indicate the level of knowledge and expertise possessed by the individual.

Furthermore, it must be noted that four members of the board, having their background in organisations representing consumers and other interests in the food chain, de facto represent a particular interest in the food sector. One may wonder whether it is at all appropriate to have members of the board who, while retaining their previous posts, may have a say on the functioning of the authority in charge of conducting scientific assessment within the sector of their main activity. If it is true that their presence may be useful to the extent that they possess an in-depth understanding of the different parts of the food supply chain, the danger exists that their particular interest in the sector may offset this potential benefit. This may reveal itself to be particularly true for those members of the board 'having a background' in the industry. How can it be that the main addressee of EFSA's activities, the food industry, is represented on the board?

If it is true that the 'background members' of the board have been called upon to be part of it because of their expertise in food safety matters, it is argued that it would have been possible to draw upon people with an equivalent level of knowledge from other environments, such as research institutes, national authorities and controlling bodies. In cases of doubt as to the functioning of the food chain, the board could always have sought the assistance of industry.

5.2   The Scientists' Autonomy

As EFSA is in charge of scientific advice, the mode of appointment of its scientists is crucial to determining its level of independence[199]. Contrary to what happens for the appointment of the board members, neither the Commission nor the Member States have a formal say in the selection process for scientists. All scientists sitting on the committee and in the panels are appointed by the management board upon the proposal of the executive director on the basis of an open competition.

---

[198] Article 25(1) of the regulation.
[199] On the recruitment of the expert or scientific committee of the agency, see Krapohl, 'Credible Commitment in Non-Independent Regulatory Agencies: A Comparative Analysis of the European Agencies for Pharmaceuticals and Foodstuffs', supra note 197, pp 531–532.

However, one may wonder whether this mode of selection is capable of eliminating any risk of political (by the Commission) or economic (by industry) influence over the scientists.

Some authors suggest that the short term of office (three years) and the possibility for renewal of their appointment may allow their selection and reselection to be guided by political factors.[200] It is indisputable that, by having the opportunity to assist in two selections of scientists during its five-year term of office, the Commission may be tempted to influence the selection process. However, the most serious way in which the Commission could actually exercise some political influence on the selection of scientists may be represented by the attendance of Commission officials at the deliberations of the panels. This is expressly authorised by the regulation, which states that 'the representatives of the Commission's departments shall be entitled to be present at the meetings of the scientific panels and their working groups'.[201] In EFSA's 2003 annual report, we read that Commission officials have actually attended all scientific panel meetings to 'ensure a seamless interface between the scientific adviser and the decision-makers'.[202] Although the participation of officials is subject to the condition according to which they 'shall not seek to influence discussions', it is likely that their mere presence at the meetings may in some cases influence the delivery of scientific opinions. Thus, the scientists, depending on the circumstances, may be induced to deliver opinions which are expected of them or they may fail to take due account of some scientific information available to them. According to Greenpeace, the latter is exactly what has already happened in the assessment made by EFSA of the first two genetically engineered crops submitted to its examination.[203] This NGO severely criticised European scientists for having ignored two critical scientific factors.[204]

Apart from this risk of political pressure over the scientists, the other source of influence may come from industry. Given the growing trend among multinationals to devote private resources to the financing of

---

[200] K. Kanska, 'Wolves in the Clothing of Sheep? The Case of the European Food Safety Authority', 24 *European Law Review* 2004, p 720.

[201] Article 28(8) of the regulation.

[202] 2003 EFSA annual report, at 17.

[203] See the critique made by Greenpeace to the EFSA's scientific assessment of NK603 maize available at http://eu.greenpeace.org/issues/gmo.html.

[204] Thus, for example, in its analysis of the risk assessment conducted by EFSA on Monsanto's Roundup Ready Maize, NK603, Greenpeace concluded that: 'Unintended fragments in NK603 appear to be functional. By itself, this should render this GE product unsafe. The EFSA have not evaluated the full significance of these fragments, including the ineffectiveness of the 'stop' codon. Significant differences have been noted between NK603 and its conventional counterpart. The significant differences have not been further investigated, but regarded simply as 'not of biological significance'.

scientific education and academic research, scientists employed in the panels may still retain close ties with industry.

In light of the above, the system for ensuring the independence of EFSA's members set up by the management, being based solely on 'declarations of interests',[205] does not seem to be adequate to overcome the flaws inherent in the composition of EFSA's organs.

5.3   EFSA and the European Commission

According to the functional separation between risk assessment and risk management laid down in Regulation 178/2002, EFSA is functionally (it enjoys legal personality) and organisationally (it has its own budget) separated from the Commission.

While the former is in charge of scientific advice, the latter is responsible for taking risk-management decisions. However, notwithstanding this clear-cut separation of roles, there exist some 'grey areas' where the EFSA's and the Commission's activities may enter dangerously close into contact, thus blurring the distinction between risk assessment and risk management. Thus, for instance, the power given to the Commission to assign the authority 'any other task [...] within its mission'[206] may lead the Commission to shape EFSA's scientific agenda, by imposing its own priorities. Thus, for instance, EFSA is also required to provide scientific and technical support to the Commission in the areas within its mission and, when so requested, in the interpretation and consideration of risk assessment opinions (Articles 22 (c) and 31).[207] This work does not involve 'scientific evaluation' but rather the application of 'well-established scientific or technical principles'. These tasks may, for instance, include the establishment or evaluation of technical criteria or assisting the Commission in the development of technical guidelines.

The Commission's influence over EFSA's activities may be even further strengthened by the lack of formal rules governing the requests addressed to the authority. Notably, lacking a clear indication as to how the terms of reference of a scientific request may be formulated, the Commission may be tempted to frame its request according to the particular result it may expect to obtain. This seems to have already happened on the request for a scientific opinion introduced by the Commission and in relation to the Austrian notification of national

---

[205] This system has originally been set up by the EFSA management board as the Code of Conduct on Declaration of Interests (Decision adopted on 10 March 2004 (MB Doc.10.03.2004-5), then amended by Guidance on Declarations of Interests on 16 December 2004.
[206] Article 23 (l) of the regulation.
[207] Article 31 of the regulation.

legislation governing GMOs under Article 95(5) EC. In the related opinion EFSA stated that it:

> [...] was not asked by the Commission to comment on the management of coexistence of GM and non-GM crops, but the panel recognized that this is an important agricultural issue.[208]

However, this danger is partly mitigated by Article 23(k) of the regulation allowing EFSA 'to express independently its own conclusions and orientations on matters within its mission'.

A further 'grey area' in the relationship existing between the authority and the Commission may be found in the GMO food and feed regulation[209] where the so called 'administrative review' clause has been inserted.[210] According to this clause, any EFSA decision, or failure to act, may be reviewed by the Commission on its own initiative or in response to a request from a Member State or concerned individual.[211] Such an open-textured provision inevitably vests broad powers of review in the Commission, who may thus be tempted to interfere with EFSA's scientific activities. It follows that such an administrative review clause not only has the potential to endanger EFSA's reputation, but also to put into question the functional separation between risk assessment and risk management underpinning the new food regime. Moreover, this provision deserves some special attention in relation to its possible impact on the issue of judicial review of scientific opinions. To what extent can (or should) the Commission's review of EFSA's opinions be subject to judicial review by Community courts?

Besides the administrative review clause, another possible situation where the functional separation between the Commission and EFSA may be put at risk is represented by the possibility allowed to the former to ask for scientific and technical support from the latter 'in the interpretation and consideration of risk assessment opinions'.[212] In fact, in providing a sort of 'authentic interpretation' of its scientific opinions or by merely interpreting the evidence of others, EFSA may considerably influence the Commission in its scientific understanding. In so doing, the authority would leave the scientific assessment field to enter into the political arena of risk management, without, however, bearing any related responsibility.

---

[208] See *EFSA Journal* 1, 2003, p 3.
[209] Regulation 1829/2003 on genetically modified food and feed [2003] OJ L 268/1.
[210] A similar clause has also been inserted in Regulation 1831/2003 on additives for use in animal nutrition.
[211] Article 36 of Regulation 1829/2003.
[212] Article 23(c).

6. The EFSA v FDA: Why the EFSA is not a European-style Food and Drug Administration. Some Elements for a Comparison

6.1. Different Missions

If compared with both the imposing institutional design and substantive framework of the US FDA, the newly-established EFSA comes across as a weak authority.[213] Both its resources and its powers are far from those which make the FDA one of the most authoritative administrative agencies in the world. However, it must be noted from the outset that these agencies pursue different missions: while the FDA protects the public health of Americans citizens, by monitoring the safety and effectiveness of products entering the market (or already in use) and by enforcing the Food and Drug Act against those who are in breach of its provisions,[214] the EFSA is a scientific advisory body charged with providing independent and objective advice on food safety issues associated with the food chain. In particular, the duality of EFSA's mandate (protecting consumers and ensuring free movement) contrasts sharply with the FDA's overarching mandate to protect public health.

6.2 Different Regulatory Universes

As shown above, by assuming a linear relationship between science and political decision-making, the EC legislator has shaped the new EC food institutional framework in accordance with a functional distinction between risk assessment and risk management. Accordingly, while the

---

[213] That is how the authority has been welcomed by many newspapers. See, eg, *Financial Times*, 'Comment and Analysis: EU Food Safety', 12 January 2000.

[214] FDA's public health protection role and mission were incorporated into the Federal Food, Drug, and Cosmetic Act by the FDA Modernisation Act of 1997 (PL 105-115). The Act outlined bold and innovative approaches to meet the increasingly complex public health challenges of the 21st century. More precisely, the FDA's statutory mission is:
– To promote the public health by promptly and efficiently reviewing clinical research and taking appropriate action on the marketing of regulated products in a timely manner.
– With respect to such products, to protect the public health by ensuring that:
  – foods are safe, wholesome, sanitary, and properly labelled;
  – human and veterinary drugs are safe and effective;
  – there is reasonable assurance of the safety and effectiveness of devices intended for human use;
  – Cosmetics are safe and properly labelled, and; public health and safety are protected from electronic product radiation.
– To participate through appropriate processes with representatives of other countries to reduce the burden of regulation, harmonize regulatory requirements, and achieve appropriate reciprocal arrangements; and,
– As determined to be appropriate by the Secretary of the Department of Health and Human Services, to carry out these activities in consultation with experts in science, medicine, and public health and in cooperation with consumers, users, manufacturers, importers, packers, distributors, and retailers of regulated products.
See http://www.fda.gov/oc/oms/ofm/budget/2001/fdamission.htm.

EFSA has been conceived as the risk assessor, the body in charge of doing risk assessment on behalf of the EC institutions, the EC Commission, has remained the risk manager, the entity in charge of adopting the decisions. Both entities exercise their functions in conformity with the risk analysis framework (the *Grundnorm*) sketched out by the regulation, which, as we have seen, allows the Commission, apart from the scientific opinions, to also take into account 'other factors legitimate to the matter under consideration' and the precautionary principle.[215]

The FDA's universe differs greatly from the EFSA's in the following respects:

1)   its substantive powers overcome the rigid distinction between risk assessment and risk management functions, since the FDA is in charge of both;

2)   its decisions are more science-based than those adopted within the Community, as the FDA risk managers are supposed to rely exclusively on scientific factors and not on 'social factors';[216]

3)   as shown above, its institutional organisation comprises approximately 9,000 employees in charge of monitoring the manufacture, import, transport, storage and sale of a broad range of products throughout the US and relies on about 2,100 scientists working in 40 laboratories throughout the country;

4)   the FDA obtains more than 90% of its scientific opinions and studies from its own services, while EFSA relies heavily on a plethora of Member State organisations and external scientific bodies;[217]

5)   unlike the EFSA, the FDA does not derive its powers from a regulation merely laying down general principles and requirements of food law, but rather from powerful texts such as the Food, Drug and Cosmetic Act (private enforcement).[218]

Moreover, the EFSA has not only been denied both regulatory and enforcement powers, but, it also seems to play a limited role even within its own area of competence, risk assessment. Although providing a common standard for conducting risk analysis throughout the

---

[215] Article 6 (3) of the regulation.

[216] *Briefing paper: US Experience*, available at http://www.ra-rm.com.

[217] See Article 36 of the regulation and the EFSA Guidance Document for the Risk Assessment of Genetically Modified Plants and Derived Food and Feed (April 2004).

[218] For a comment on the evolution of the Federal Food and Drug Legislation, see Barton Hutt & Merrill, *Food & Drug Law*, Cases and Materials, II[ed.], New York, Foundation Press, 1991, pp 6–15. The text of the Act is reproduced in P. Barton Hutt & R.A. Merrill, *1996 Statutory Supplement*, pp 1–269 and is also available at http://www.fda.gov/opacom/ laws/ fdcact/fdctoc.htm.

Community to be followed by both the EC and the Member States,[219] the current regime does not empower the EFSA to impose its own scientific vision on the Member States' competent authorities in case of diverging opinions.

As shown above, notwithstanding their relevant indirect effect not only on the EC institutions, but also on the Member States and the individuals, the authority's scientific opinions do not prevail in case of conflict with those elaborated by the competent national agencies. It follows that the lack of authoritative power is likely to produce conflicts analogous to those already seen in the past between the EC scientific authorities and the competent national bodies.

Does this outcome weaken or strengthen the EFSA's functioning and the overall EC food policy?

Unlike the US where arguably all local food differences have been obliterated,[220] Europe still shows long-rooted culinary traditions symbolising strong identity values. Thus, a claim by a domestic food authority that a certain good is safe or unsafe is likely to involve not only an assertion about science, but also the willingness of this country to bear or not to bear the level of risk considered acceptable in order to continue or reject a certain local tradition. In contrast, the assertion made at the EC level about the safety of a product to be marketed throughout the Community is both a claim about its risk component and a political claim aimed at favouring economic integration and free trade within Europe. Along the same lines, conflicts about food safety within the European context inevitably involve a tension between a European (universal) and a national (local) vision of both safety and of the socio-cultural perception of a particular food.[221]

Against this backdrop, giving the authority the last word in all contentious scientific matters would have amounted to forcing the establishment of a pan-European food safety standard, inevitably leading to the obliteration of local traditions.[222] Thus, although the lack of

---

[219] Article 6 of the regulation.

[220] E. Schlosser, *Fast Food Nation, The dark side of the All-American Meal*, Perennial ed., 2002, p 5.

[221] D. Chalmers, '"Food for thought": reconciling European risks and traditional ways of life', 66 *The Modern Law Review* 532–534.

[222] This was recently confirmed by the EFSA Executive Director, Geoffrey Podger, who stated that since 'Member States have important, valid and strongly held views of their own [in scientific matters] that are necessary in assessing and understanding risk […] we do not want to centralize food science; we want to distribute the work, the research and the expertise which is already present in Europe'. See the European Policy Centre, Communication to Member (59/03), *The role of the European Food Safety authority*, EPC-KBF Policy Briefing, 9 October 2003. Available at http://www.kbsfrb.be/files/db/EN/EPC_DocumentsPBP_ Role_of_the_ European_Food_Safety_authority_09.10.2003.pdf.

authoritative power in scientific matters may prima facie be seen as weakening the EFSA, it expresses the Community dislike for the mounting trend towards a standardisation of the food supply by revealing at the same time the strong Member State willingness to defend their national perception of risk.[223]

Therefore, under the current regulatory framework, it is us up to the European courts, and not to the EFSA, to solve the conflicts arising between the national and the Community's scientific opinions. More precisely, the EC courts are called upon to conduct a delicate balancing exercise between the local and the universal visions of risk.

The case presented above involving the French refusal to lift the embargo against British beef two years after the BSE outbreak symbolises the logic followed by the current approach. Although the ECJ condemned France for not having lifted the embargo, as requested by EC law,[224] it also recognised that traceability of UK Beef, essential up to the point of sale in order to enable a consignment not fulfilling the conditions of EC law to be recalled, was not guaranteed at the time of the Commission decision of 23 July 1999 lifting the ban, in particular as regards meat and products which had been cut, processed or rewrapped.

It follows that, in case of divergent scientific opinions between the Community and the local risk assessors, the EC courts are called upon to carry out the difficult task of reconciling the conflicting visions by examining the value of domestic measures to the local population as against the damage to the Community (free trade) interest.

As has been said, this approach 'condenses' local difference without providing a single, objective standard for 'safety enabling economies of scale and trade liberalisation across the Union'.[225]

This seems to be confirmed by Article 1.1 of the regulation which states that, in assuring a high level of protection of human health and consumers' interest in relation to food, account must be taken of:

> [...] the diversity of the supply of food including traditional products, while ensuring the effective functioning of the internal market.

---

[223] P. Testori Coggi, Conference on Risk Perception: Science, Public Debate and Policy Making, Speaking Notes, Brussels, Dec. 2003 available at http://europa.eu.int/comm/food/risk_perception/sp/testori_coggi.pdf.
[224] Commission decision 98/256/EC OJ L 113/32–43.
[225] Chalmers, supra note 221.

In sum, the new Community food regime constitutes an attempt to extend the mutual recognition model, originally developed to avoid a standardisation of food identity throughout Europe, in the field of analysis of risk between the Community and the Member States. Although the regulation provides for the first time ever a common model of analysis of risk applicable to both the Community and the Member States, it does not give the last word in scientific matters to the EFSA, but rather introduces a presumption of safety for all those products found in compliance with EC law, or in the absence of Community provisions, for those foods conforming to the national food laws of the Member States. Should the Community or a Member State doubt the presumed safety of a particular food, the question is decided by the EC courts and the burden of proof lies on the party claiming the product to be unsafe. Similar to what happens in situations when the mutual recognition principle does not work because of the lack of trust between Member States, it is up to the courts, not to the EFSA, to weigh the conflicting interests, thus striking a balance between the local and the universal interests involved.

6.3   Different Cultures

This study ventures to suggest that the main institutional and substantive differences between the EFSA and the FDA may be ultimately understood not only as a result of different systems of governance and regulatory environments, but also as a reflection of entirely different societal contexts. In recent years, Europeans and Americans have developed conflicting perceptions of risks and, inevitably, different cultural norms regarding food safety. This seems to be due to the complex interplay of inherent cultural models that we, as humans, use to interpret the environment and the world around us. In other words, the public perceives the risk within its own cultural model.

EC risk regulation is said to have become more risk averse in recent years.[226]

Conflicting perceptions of risks may significantly influence how these authorities respond to given risks by elaborating divergent risk analysis methods. It is becoming increasingly clear that risk perception plays a crucial role in the mechanics of risk management. Thus, scientists and citizens look at risks from different perspectives. While the scientific approach is rational, dealing with probabilities and science-based

---

[226] D. Vogel, 'The Politics of Risk Regulation in Europe and the United States', 3 *Yearbook of European Environmental Law* 1. See, also, Christoforou, 'Science, Law and Precaution in Dispute Resolution on Health and Environmental Protection: What Role for Scientific Experts?', in J. Bourrinet et S. Maljean-Dubois (eds), *Le Commerce International des Organismes Génétiquement Modifiés* (2003), p 238.

studies, people, being more value driven, behave according to perceptions rather that relying on facts.[227]

By also taking into account within its risk analysis the 'social factor', the EC seems to be more willing than the FDA to address the dichotomy existing between the perceptions of scientists and citizens. This may be seen by many as an irrational position, potentially hiding protectionist intent. But for many others, experience has shown that one day's scientific 'truth'[228] may turn out to be based on a partial understanding.[229]

A comparison of the perceptions of the riskiness of some foods and their production processes shows the impact of tradition on food regulation in Europe and of science in the US Whilst Europeans tend to favour traditional foods and express scepticism for new technologies, Americans have always been more in favour of new technologies than traditional food processing. This is best reflected in the European reluctance to consume GMOs and the US resistance to the consumption of unpasteurised raw milk cheeses.[230]

In sum, the comparison between the EFSA and the FDA clearly shows that culture and tradition play a silent, though crucial, role in the regulatory process and the resulting rules.[231]

It remains to be seen whether the EC Commission/EFSA approach will prove more satisfactory in protecting citizens' public health than the longstanding and more scientific-based attitude symbolized by the FDA. The ambition nurtured by the Europeans is that EFSA, though following a different path, could one day be described, similarly to the FDA, as 'one of the most venerable institution, whose employees have long memories and a tradition of dedicated, sometimes single-minded public service – in sum a strong commitment to the job of regulation'.[232]

---

[227] R. J. Coleman, Address concerning 'Communicating Risk to Consumers', at the Interim Scientific Advisory Forum, Brussels 30th October 2001, available at http://europa.eu.int/comm/dgs/health_consumer /library/speeches/ speech133_en.pdf.
[228] D. Vogel, 'The Hare and the Tortoise Revisited: The New Politics of Consumer and Environmental Regulation in Europe', *British Journal of Political Science*, 33, 4, pp 557-580.
[229] Thus, for instance, the unquestionably benign nature of nuclear was put into question by successive studies. See Late Lessons from Early Warnings: the Precautionary Principle 1996-2000, EEA, No 22.
[230] Echols, 'Food Safety Regulation in the European Union and the United States: different cultures, different laws', *Columb. J. Eur. L.* 525, pp 531–3.
[231] Ibid, p 543.
[232] Barton Hutt, *Food & Drug Law*, Cases and Materials, II[ed.], New York, Foundation Press, 1991, p 5.

Conclusions: Reconciling Science, Traditions, Consumer Concerns and Free Movement

In order to assess the success of EFSA within the context of the new European Food Safety regime, one has to verify whether this authority has provided a credible answer to the most pressing questions among policy-makers and lawyers: who's science to use?

The creation of the EFSA and the enactment of the new food policy regime stem directly from the food scares that slapped Europe at the end of the 1990s. It would certainly have taken longer for the Community to conceive this reform if several food scandals had not rendered its system of governance 'contested',[233] by showing the absence of a centralised European scientific assessment and a unifying text setting out the fundamental principles of EC food law. By producing a collapse of public trust in the European institutions, the contested governance of European food safety has not only accelerated this reform, but it has considerably helped EC food law to get rid of its original sin, its pro-market-bias, by illustrating the importance of assuring the safety of the products in free circulation throughout the Community. Under the new policy, only foodstuffs that are safe, wholesome and fit for consumption can be placed on the market for consumers.

By ceasing to be a fragmented area of Community law, European food law is based for the first time on comprehensive legislation covering the entire 'farm to fork' distribution chain and directly enforceable in all the EC Member States.

The role of EFSA in the implementation of the new food regime is far removed from that of the FDA within the US context. This is due not only to the authorities' different missions and diverging regulatory universes, but also to the conflicting perceptions of risk developed by their respective citizen-consumers. Risk analysis being the *Grundnorm* of the new regime, one could have expected the EFSA to become the scientific authoritative body for the whole Union and having the final word in all contentious scientific matters. But Member States did not want to make the authority an oracle of Delphi spelling out the 'truth' in all scientific matters. Rather they wanted to preserve the right of their national food agencies to carry out scientific studies, thus expressing their specific perception of a certain risk. In the words of EFSA:

---

[233] By 'contested governance', Ansell and Vogel mean a 'pervasive conflict in policy arenas that goes beyond politics-as-usual to challenge who should make decisions and where, how and on what basis they should be made'. In other words, '[c]ontested governance entails a significant challenge to the legitimacy of existing institutional arrangements'. See C. Ansell and D. Vogel, *What's the Beef? The Contested Governance of European Food Safety* (MIT Press, 2006), pp 283–285.

EFSA does not want to compete with the excellent science conducted in the Member States. On the contrary, it is eager to work with scientists from all Member States to share data and results from scientific studies and to harmonize national approaches to risk assessment, as appropriate. EFSA's scientific opinions do not supersede any national opinion; they provide an independent European view which ideally complements national opinions. EFSA's scientific opinions provide an authoritative reference for European risk assessment, and where EFSA risk assessments are required by EC legislation, it is EFSA's opinions which prevail.'[234]

While this approach is likely to bring about conflicts among Member States, it expresses the European attempt to defend its cultural patrimony and culinary richness against the mounting trend towards the obliteration of local traditions led by the multinational producers of processed food.[235] Accordingly, in case of diverging opinions between the EFSA and national food authorities, it is up to the EC courts, and not to the EFSA, to solve these conflicts by striking a balance between the universal and the local values. However, this judicial involvement could be reduced if EFSA is able to establish an effective network with the national food agencies aimed at solving scientific conflicts before they reach the EC courts.[236] Therefore, EFSA's success will mainly depend on its willingness to imbed itself into an effective dialogue with the Commission, the national competent authorities and the European scientific community so as to give all European consumers good grounds for a high level of confidence in the food that they eat.[237] For instance, EFSA's current involvement with GMOs rests on a network[238] in which EFSA carries the duty to address diverging scientific opinions under the General food law regulation.[239]

---

[234] Front cover article by H. Koëter, EFSA Deputy Executive Director and Director of Science, in EFSA news, 2/2004.

[235] Contra, D. Chalmers, '"Food for thought": Reconciling European Risks and Traditional Ways of Life', supra note 146, p 533 who argues that the new legal regime will 'probably reterritorialise conflicts so that these endemic and irresolvable disputes become reconfigured along European versus particularistic fault lines, with local groups either arguing a right to consume a food that is considered dangerous under EU law or to be protected from exposure to a product that is considered safe under EU law'.

[236] Alemanno, 'Food Safety and the Single European Market', in C. Ansel and D. Vogel, eds., 'What's the Beef? The Contested Governance of European Food Safety and Vincent, Mad Cows and Eurocrats – Community Responses to the BSE Crisis', 10 *European Law Journal* 517, 2004.

[237] Article 36 of the regulation and Commission Regulation 2230/2004 of 23 December 2004 laying down detailed rules for the implementation of European Parliament and Council Regulation 178/2002 with regard to the network of organisations operating in the fields within the European Food Safety authority's mission, OJ L379/64.

[238] Regulation 1829/2003.

[239] Article 30 of the regulation.

PART II: THE WTO REGULATION OF FOOD

INTRODUCTION

Among the several international organisations dealing with food-safety related activities, the WTO is the only one providing for a set of legally binding obligations for WTO members when they adopt food regulations. As has been stated, the GATT/WTO agreements today provide for a 'Multilateral governance framework for food safety'.[1]

Although public health and food safety issues are dealt with in several WTO Agreements,[2] the WTO regulation of food is mainly contained within the Sanitary and Phytosanitary Agreement (SPS) adopted during the 1994 Uruguay Round.[3]

Before providing an overview of the main features of this regime, it is important to stress that the core competency of the WTO is trade and that its members have never shown any interest in turning it into some kind of food safety organisation[4].

The preamble of the SPS Agreement notes the desire of the members to establish 'a multilateral framework of rules and disciplines to guide the development, adoption and enforcement of sanitary and phytosanitary (SPS) measures in order to minimise their negative effects on trade'.

Therefore, unlike the European regulation of food, the focus of the WTO discipline is on the trade impact that sanitary and phytosanitary measures may have on international trade, rather than on the safety concerns that may support these regulations. In fact, the WTO regime governing food is exclusively aimed at reducing the negative effects that members' food safety and quality regulations may have on

[1] T. Jostling, D. Roberts and D. Orden, *Food Regulation and Trade, Toward a Safe and Open Global System*, p 35.

[2] See GATT, the Agreement on Technical Barriers to Trade (TBT), the Agreement on Sanitary and Phytosanitary Measures (SPS), the General Agreement on Trade in Services (GATS), the Agreement on Agriculture (in the preamble, as well as in Article 20 of this agreement non-trade concerns in the Agricultural sector are mentioned), the Agreement on Trade-related Aspects of Intellectual Property Rights (TRIPs). In particular, this last agreement facilitates the international recognition of denominations of origin and certificates of specificity which have been granted in accordance with the relevant Community regulations.

[3] Key terms such as sanitary (to protect human life and health) and phytosanitary measures (to protect animal and plant life and health) are defined in the SPS Agreement, Annex A.

[4] V.R. Walker, 'Keeping the WTO from Becoming the "World Trans-Science organization": Scientific Uncertainty, Science Policy, and Factfinding in the Growth Hormones Dispute' 31 *Cornell international Law Journal* 1998, 251, pp 261–263.

international food trade by setting forth criteria which are useful to distinguish between legitimate food safety measures and illegitimate (protectionist) food regulations.

In other words, the WTO food framework aims at minimising the negative trade effects stemming from the adoption of food regulations, rather than at laying down a minimum benchmark for protection of public health. Thus, the WTO discipline is intended to circumscribe the exercise of members' regulatory autonomy 'in negative' – by imposing on them to reduce the trade effects – and not 'in positive' by requiring them to ensure a minimum level of safety for consumers. By stressing these regulatory differences, one may even contest the choice of qualifying the negative set of WTO provisions relating to food as 'WTO regulation of food'. However, as will be shown in this part of the book, the complex constraints imposed by the SPS Agreement, combined with the international standards to which it refers, turn the WTO set of negative provisions into a real multilateral regulatory framework for food, which deserves such a qualification.

In short, while the WTO regime follows an exclusively market-opening agenda, the EC discipline answers to a more complex public demand for health protection within an increasingly integrated Union, by requiring not only member State food measures but also EC-wide food regulations to attain a high level of protection. As will be shown, similar to what happened in the EC, the GATT/WTO's involvement in food safety policies came as a result of the growing expansion of the organisation to cover 'beyond the border' policies that may affect trade. In particular, it lies in the belief that while technical food regulations, rules and procedures can facilitate and enhance trade, by reducing the risk for consumers that they might purchase unsafe food, they can also become barriers to trade, in particular if they place a heavier regulatory burden on importers than the one applied to domestic producers. Therefore, its main challenge is to design measures in a way so that they meet science-based food safety objectives while minimising adverse impacts on trade and the risk that regulations may be employed for protectionist goals.

The non-discrimination principle not being adequate to address this policy challenge, the Uruguay Round developed a multilateral governance framework for food safety regulations, establishing a set of rules that member States must respect in the exercise of their legislative powers in food matters. According to Article 2(4) of the SPS Agreement, sanitary and phytosanitary measures which conform to this framework are presumed to be in accordance with the members' GATT obligations and, in particular, with Article XX(b). The best example showing why non-discrimination obligations are not capable by themselves of addressing technical barriers to trade, such as food safety regulations, is given by the *Hormones* case. Although the Community public health-grounded regime prohibiting the use of certain growth hormones in cattle was non-discriminatory, to the extend that it also applied domestically,[5] it had – and still has – a costly impact on foreign trade by having reduced US exports from about $100 million annually to zero.[6] The WTO's main concern in a *Hormones*-type dispute is to eliminate the disadvantages stemming from the adoption of the controversial regulation rather than determining whether that regulation is genuinely necessary to protect human health. In fact, the *Hormones* dispute did not revolve around the question of determining whether the use of growth hormones for cattle was safe or not but it boiled down to the issue of establishing whether their prohibition rested on an acceptable scientific ground, and, in particular, whether it was 'based on' a risk assessment as imposed by Article 5.1 SPS. That means that food safety concerns may qualify as deserving protection under WTO law, but only provided they are solidly supported by scientific evidence.

Under the WTO discipline a clear hierarchical relationship exists between the trade imperatives and the public health values. As a result, the latter are taken into account only residually and even if ultimately they are found to be genuinely supporting the adoption of the measure at stake it remains that that regulation has to justify its raison d'être because of the existence of a protectionist suspicion surrounding all public health-declared measures. This approach of stressing the peculiar trade-oriented philosophy underlying the WTO food (trade) regime allows it to be distinguished from the EC food (safety) discipline and, ultimately, it sits rather uneasily with Member States' paramount right to establish the level of protection they deem appropriate.

The EC being a full member of the WTO, and therefore bound by its agreements, it may be useful to analyse the WTO food safety regime (part II) in order to determine to what extent the current EC food safety regime, as established by Regulation 187/2001, may be held to be compatible with the WTO discipline (part IV). In particular, this study will emphasise some points of tension currently existing between the two regulatory regimes.

---

[5] In that sense, as all facially neutral regulations, the EC prohibition on the use of growth hormones in cattle was beyond the reach of the basic non-discrimination principle underlying the whole GATT construction.

[6] A.O. Sykes, 'Regulatory Protectionism and the Law of International Trade', 66 *University of Chicago Law Review* 1, p 17 (1999).

CHAPTER I
HISTORICAL BACKGROUND OF THE GATT/WTO
REGULATION OF FOOD

GATT's primary purpose was to promote trade in goods by reducing tariffs and eliminating quantitative restrictions. Its main focus has thus for a long-time been on the so-called border measures (as opposed to the 'within the border measures'[1] or domestic measures). Its main organising principle, aimed at tackling these obstacles to trade, was non-discrimination, prohibiting discrimination among GATT Members (the 'most-favoured-nation' obligation of Article I) and between foreign suppliers and domestic suppliers (the 'national treatment' obligation of Article III). This agreement already recognised the need to subject domestic regulations to international scrutiny so that the discriminatory and protectionist uses of technical regulations would not offset the trade benefits stemming from the gradual lowering of tariffs. GATT 1947 therefore set forth various rules aimed at preventing such abuses, amongst which were Article XI, prohibiting quantitative restrictions and Article III requiring Member States to respect 'national treatment' for 'like products' when adopting their internal taxes and regulations for imports.

As tariffs and quotas fell worldwide due to the success of the first six successive GATT Rounds,[2] countries appeared to be increasingly relying on the adoption of national regulations as a way of protecting their own industries.[3] Notably, Member States have gradually increased the adoption of food safety requirements and controls. While the adoption of these national measures may be legitimate to protect human health and the environment in an increasingly integrated food market, their adoption may also be motivated by a desire to shield domestic industries from imports coming from foreign countries.[4]

[1] J. N. Bhagwati and R. E. Hudec (eds), 'Fair Trade and Harmonization: Prerequisites for Free Trade?' *Volume 2: Legal Analysis* (Cambridge, MA: MIT Press, 1996).

[2] The main result from each of the first six rounds of negotiations to strengthen the GATT framework was to revise and update the list of tariff bindings, thus reducing the tariff impact on trade. Non-tariff measures (or 'beyond the borders' barriers) did not fall within the object of the negotiations.

[3] For the negotiating history of the SPS Agreement, see G. Marceau and J. Trachtman, 'The Technical Barriers to Trade Agreement, the Sanitary and Phytosanitary Measures Agreement, and the General Agreement on Tariff and Trade, A Map of the World Trade Organization Law of Domestic Regulation of Goods', 35 *Journal of World Trade* 5 (2002) pp 811–81 and S. Zarrilli, 'WTO Sanitary and Phytosanitary Agreement: Issues for Developing Countries', *TRADE Working Paper*, South Centre, 1999, p 3.

[4] For a detailed history of the evolution of GATT rules on domestic regulations, see A.O.

(continued...)

After the 1964–67 Kennedy Round, which resulted from the seventh round of negotiations, Member States' concerns about the increasing adoption of divergent national standards contributed to the launching of a debate on how to tackle the problem of the so-called non-tariffs barriers. On that occasion, most of the countries agreed to negotiate a code which, without interfering 'with the responsibility of governments for safety, health and welfare of their people', may seek 'to minimise the effects of such actions on international trade'.[5] Against this backdrop, during the negotiations that followed, the 1979 Tokyo Round, the 'Standards Code', which covered mandatory and voluntary technical specifications, mandatory technical regulations and voluntary standards for industrial and agricultural products, was signed by 43 countries. It prohibited discrimination and the protection of domestic production through specifications, technical regulations and standards, but it also urged its members to base their national measures on international standards and to cooperate in order to harmonise their norms. In particular, regulations governing product characteristics were subject to a 'least-trade restrictive' requirement regardless of whether they were discriminatory or not.

However, Member States failed to adequately comply with the code. In 1980, a GATT working group was established to measure the impact of Non-Tariff Barriers (NTBs) to trade and found product requirements to be among the most significant. This shift of attention from tariffs to NTBs to trade brought health, food safety and environmental polices under the scrutiny of the GATT and, subsequently, the WTO, thus paving the way for a greater GATT/WTO involvement in these areas of regulation. As the Standards Code showed itself not to be adequate in addressing the issue of the regulatory barriers to trade, notably in the area of sanitary and phytosanitary measures, the Uruguay Round negotiations attempted to remedy this weakness. Also, the GATT framework, being based on Articles I, III, XI and XX, was perceived as being incapable of addressing disputes over sanitary and phytosanitary measures.

By 1986, when the Uruguay Round was launched, nearly 90 per cent of US food imports were affected by non-tariff barriers to trade, up from only 57 per cent in 1996.[6] To tackle this increasingly abusive use of technical regulations, multilateral disciplines governing the use of technical measures had to be revised, expanded and strengthened. Thus, in the Punta del Este's Ministerial Declaration launching the Uruguay

Sykes, *Products Standards for Internationally Integrated Goods Markets*, Washington, DC: Brookings, 1995, pp 63–8.

[5] COM.IND/W/13, 20, 23 and Spec (71) 143, Idem.

[6] M.A. Tutwiler, 'Food Safety, the Environment and Agricultural Trade: The Links', 2 International Policy Council on Agriculture, Food & Trade cited in D. Vogel, *Trading Up: Consumer and Environmental Regulation in a Global Economy* 150 (1995).

Round negotiations, it was stated that the goal was to set up disciplines that would minimise the 'adverse effects that sanitary and phytosanitary regulations and barriers can have on trade in agriculture'.[7] It is in light of the above that, during the Uruguay Round, not only was the Standards Code amended so as to reappear as the Agreement on Technical Barriers to Trade (TBT), but a new agreement was also negotiated: the Agreement on Sanitary and Phytosanitary Measures (SPS).

The two agreements are designed to prevent technical legislation, which is intended for the protection of human health or safety, the protection of the health or life of humans animals or plants, consumer protection against deceptive practices and environmental protection, being used to create or resulting in unjustified barriers to international trade. Since sanitary and phytosanitary measures introduce specific concerns for trade in goods, a separate agreement, the SPS, was 'carved out' of the TBT.[8] As a result the two agreements differ in scope. While the TBT covers all technical regulations and voluntary standards, and the procedures to ensure that these are met,[9] the SPS Agreement applies to all measures to protect human, animal and plant life and health.[10] While both the SPS and the TBT apply to food, the TBT is more relevant to labelling requirements than to safety.

As will be illustrated below, the purpose of this new agreement is to minimise the negative effects on trade stemming from SPS measures, such as food safety regulations, by encouraging harmonisation of SPS measures through the adoption of international standards, guidelines and recommendations where they exist. As it has been aptly said, the SPS is a 'refined system of applied subsidiarity, subtly allowing national autonomy subject to certain constraints'.[11] The complex constraints imposed by the SPS Agreement, combined with the international

---

[7] GATT Punta del Este Ministerial Declaration of 20 September 1986. Point (iii) under the Agriculture title. Available at http://www.sice.oas.org/trade/Punta_e.asp.

[8] This separation between technical barriers and sanitary and phytosanitary measures has been inspired by the NAFTA Agreement. See NAFTA Chapters 7B and 9. Available at http://www.nafta-sec-alena.org.

[9] Most of the regulations falling under the TBT Agreement aim at protecting consumers through information, mainly in the form of labelling requirements, and at promoting fair trade practices. Other regulations include classification and definition, essential composition and quality factors, packaging requirements and measurements (size, weight, etc) so as to avoid deceptive practices.

[10] It follows that while it is the type of measure which determines whether it is subject to the TBT, it is the purpose of the measure which is relevant in determining whether a measure is covered by the SPS Agreement.

[11] J. Trachtman, 'FDI and the Right to Regulate', p 200, in *The Development Dimension of FDI: Policy and Rule-Making Perspectives*, UNCTAD, Proceedings of the Experts meeting held in Geneva from 6 to 8 November 2002. See also J. Trachtman, 'The World Trading System, the International Legal System and Multilevel Choice', in 12 *European Law Journal* 469, p 480 (2006).

standards to which it refers, established a system for reviewing certain types of state action at international level, notably food safety regulations.

The Community[12] is a full party to both agreements, which therefore apply to both Community legislation and legislation adopted by the Member States.

Finally, the negotiations also led to the conclusion of an Agreement on Trade-related Aspects of Intellectual Property Rights (TRIPs Agreements) imposing obligations to provide minimum protection to a set of intellectual property rights, including geographical indications (GIs) of commercial identity for both agricultural products and food.

Thus, the Uruguay Round, by strengthening the previous regime, improved the legal architecture for food safety technical regulations and standards.

1. SPS Measures under the GATT

The original GATT Agreement of 1947 – like the 1994 GATT agreement – left countries free to establish whatever food safety regulations they wished. The only constraints on the exercise of their legislative autonomy were set by Article III:4,[13] which required that these regulations had to be applied in a non-discriminatory way on imported and domestic goods, and Article XI,[14] prohibiting all restrictions 'instituted or maintained on the importation or exportation of any product'. Thus, the GATT implied that a country's regulation may take whatever form it chooses but must apply equally to domestic and imported products and not amount to an import or an export prohibition. Similarly to Articles 28 and 29 of the EC Treaty, it may appear that these GATT

---

[12] As competence for trade policy rests within the 'first pillar' of the EU (the second and the third pillars deal with foreign and security policy and with judicial cooperation in criminal matters, respectively), it is more appropriate to talk about the EC when dealing with the EU's involvement within the WTO.

[13] According to this provisions: 'The products of the territory of any contracting party imported into the territory of any other contracting party shall be accorded treatment no less favourable than that accorded to like products of national origin in respect of all laws, regulations and requirements affecting their internal sale, offering for sale, purchase, transportation, distribution or use. The provisions of this paragraph shall not prevent the application of differential internal transportation charges which are based exclusively on the economic operation of the means of transport and not on the nationality of the product'.

[14] This provision establishes that: 'No prohibitions or restrictions other than duties, taxes or other charges, whether made effective through quotas, import or export licences or other measures, shall be instituted or maintained by any contracting party on the importation of any product of the territory of any other contracting party or on the exportation or sale for export of any product destined for the territory of any other contracting party'.

provisions mandate the prohibition of quantitative restrictions on importation and exportation of goods as well as those measures having an equivalent effect. However, the non-discrimination obligation looks rather weak if compared with the *Dassonville* interpretative formula of Article 28 EC. While the GATT states that members' food measures may take whatever form it likes provided they apply equally to domestic and imported good, the EC – according to the catch-all *Dassonville* formula – prohibits all national measures capable of acting as obstacles to trade, regardless of whether they are discriminatory, unless they are justified on a legitimate ground.

However, notwithstanding this clear prohibition against quantitative restrictions, for many years GATT members failed to abide by this rule (notably Article XI) by tolerating quantitative restrictions in the fields of agricultural products, textiles and clothing.

Like the EC,[15] the WTO maintains general exceptions which enable a member to justify a violation of the general prohibition of quantitative restrictions. Similarly to Article 30 EC, Article XX GATT[16] allows any contracting party to depart from GATT obligations by adopting restrictions on imports and exports justified inter alia for the protection of health and life of humans, animals and plants (let. b).[17] Apart from having been invoked in relation to Articles III and XI, WTO's adjudicating practice shows that Article XX has also been invoked to justify alleged violations of Article I (MFN principle), Article II (tariff concessions), Article IV (anti-dumping and countervailing duties), Article X (publication and administration of trade regulations), Article XIII (non-discriminatory administration of quantitative restrictions) and Article XVII (State trading enterprises).

Notwithstanding the existence of this general exception, it may not be very common to find a discriminatory measure that is justified on this public policy ground. As has been stated, Article XX recognises:

---

[15] As has been stated, Article 30 EC has clearly been formulated with Article XX in mind. See J. Scott, 'Mandatory or Imperative Requirements in the EU and the WTO', in C. Barnard and J. Scott, *The Law of the Single European Market: Unpacking the Premises*, Oxford, (Hart Publishing, 2002) p 286.

[16] Article XX states: '[s]ubject to the requirement that such measures are not applied in a manner which would constitute a means of arbitrary or unjustifiable discrimination between countries where the same conditions prevail, or a disguised restriction on international trade, nothing in this Agreement shall be construed to prevent the adoption or enforcement by any contracting party of measures: [...] (*b*) necessary to protect human, animal or plant life or health'.

[17] Already in 1969 John Jackson noted that in theory all GATT obligations may be rendered subject to the exceptions of Article XX, because of the wording 'nothing in this Agreement shall [...] prevent'. See J.H. Jackson, *World Trade and the law of GATT: A Legal Analysis of the General Agreement on Tariffs and Trade* (Bobbs-Merrill Company, Indianapolis, 1969).

the importance of a sovereign national being able to promote health interests, even if contrary to its general obligations under the WTO Agreements.[18]

According to the WTO case law[19], a party invoking this exception must prove that:

-   the policy in respect of the measures for which Article XX(b) is invoked falls within the range of policies aimed at protecting public health, and that
-   the measures for which the exception is invoked are necessary to fulfil the policy objective.

In particular, to satisfy the necessity test it must be proven that there are no alternative measures consistent with the GATT, which the Member State could reasonably be expected to adopt in order to achieve its health policy objective.[20] Accordingly, to apply properly this test, it is necessary to establish the scope of the health policy objective pursued by the invoking Member State and consider the existence of measures consistent with GATT which may have been reasonably available to the same Member State.

Finally, according to the so-called *Chapeau* of Article XX, it is necessary to assess whether the adopted public health measure is not applied in a discriminatory manner (this applies solely to Article XI, not III:4) and whether it did not constitute a disguised restriction on international trade.

While the core regulatory discipline of the GATT is contained in Articles III:4, XI and XX(b), the rules governing food safety measures and standards are specifically expressed in the SPS and TBT Agreements, which were adopted during the Uruguay Round. In particular, the SPS Agreement, which is engaged in balancing health concerns against the goal of free trade, may be seen as an extension of Article XX GATT. In fact, it expands the scientific and procedural requirements that Member States have to abide by when adopting an SPS measure, by, in particular, urging them to develop and to adopt international standards. Yet, while the GATT did not specifically require the use of international standards, both the good faith and least-trade restrictive requirements imposed by Article XX already subtly expressed a preference for the adoption of an international standard over a unilateral one. This interpretation of the

---

[18] J. Jackson, *The World Trading System: Law and Policy of International Economic Relations* (The MIT Press, Cambridge, 1999) p 233.

[19] *EC–Measures Affecting Asbestos and Asbestos-Containing Products* WT/DS135/R adopted on 12 March 2001 paras 8.170 and 8.177 (*EC–Asbestos*), para 8.169.

[20] *Thai-Cigarettes*, Panel Report WT/DS10/R, adopted on 7 November 1990, para 75.

rationale underpinning these requirements of the *Chapeau* of Article XX seems to have been confirmed by the AB in the *US–Shrimp* case where, in applying this provision, it held:

> Clearly, and 'as far as possible', a multilateral approach is strongly preferred. Yet it is one thing to prefer a multilateral approach in the application of a measure that is provisionally justified under one of the subparagraphs of Article XX of the GATT 1994; it is another to require the conclusion of a multilateral agreement as a condition of avoiding 'arbitrary or unjustifiable discrimination' under the chapeau of Article XX. We see, in this case, no such requirement.[21]

Therefore, although Article XX does not impose their adoption, reliance on international standards may provide a de facto presumption of good faith within the meaning of that provision[22].

Although building upon Article XX GATT, the SPS scientific and procedural obligations are independent from GATT, so that members are obliged to comply with the SPS Agreement regardless of whether their SPS measure is otherwise consistent with a provision of GATT.[23] Should, then, an SPS measure be in conformity with the SPS Agreement, that measure is presumed to be consistent with GATT.[24]

This relationship of autonomy from GATT has been confirmed by the WTO judicial bodies' case law. While under the GATT, under established case law,[25] it is the defending member who bears the entire burden of proof of showing that its measure falls within Article XX(b), under the SPS it is the complaining party who bears the initial burden of proof of showing a prima facie case of inconsistency with the SPS.

This agreement provides new rules for WTO members such that, in the event of a trade dispute relating to food safety, the WTO judicial bodies would apply the rules contained within the SPS Agreement to determine whether the complaining party was justified in its complaint and, hence, whether the contested measure is allowed under WTO law. Therefore, the SPS Agreement forms the basis upon which members operate so as to ensure compliance with their WTO obligations.

---

[21] Article 21.5 Report - Malaysia, *United States–Import Prohibition of Certain Shrimp and Shrimp Products*, (hereinafter '*US–Shrimps*'), at para 124.

[22] J.P. Trachtman, 'The World Trading System, the International Legal System and Multilevel Choice', 12 *European Law Journal* 469 (2006), p 483. See, also, for a similar intuition, G. Marceau, 'A Call for Coherence in International Law', 33 *Journal of World Trade* (1999) 128-134.

[23] See *EC–Measures Concerning Meat and Meat Products (Hormones)* Panel Report WT/DS26/R 1997, para 8.36.

[24] Article 2.4 SPS.

[25] *EC–Hormones* Panel Report, para 8.42; *Australia – Salmon Measures Affecting the Importation of Salmon* WT/DS18/R modified Panel Report (hereinafter: *Australia-Salmon*) para 8.39.

CHAPTER II
THE SPS AGREEMENTS AND ITS MAIN OBLIGATIONS

The SPS Agreement, which forms part of the 1994 World Trade Agreement,[1] applies to all measures adopted by WTO members to protect human, animal or plant life or health 'which, directly or indirectly, may affect international trade'[2]. Notably, SPS measures – as defined in Annex A of the agreement – are those aimed at protecting animal or plant life or health arising from food-borne risks, pests, diseases, disease-carrying organisms, additives, contaminants, toxins or disease-causing organisms in foods.[3] More precisely, SPS measures can take the form of inspection of products, permission to use only certain additives in food, designation of disease-free areas, determination of maximum levels of pesticide residues, quarantine requirements, import bans, etc.

The basic aim of the SPS Agreement is to maintain the sovereign right of any member to provide the level of health protection it deems appropriate[4], but to ensure that these sovereign rights are not misused for protectionist purposes and do not result in unnecessary barriers to international trade. To achieve its goals, the scope of the agreement must receive a broad interpretation. Thus, the panel in *Japan – Agricultural Products* has stated, in a language resonant of the *Dassonville* formula, that:

---

[1] According to the 'single package' philosophy, being a mandatory portion of the WTO Agreement, the SPS Agreement binds all WTO Members.

[2] The agreement covers all relevant laws, decrees, regulations, testing, inspection, certification and approval procedures and packaging and labelling requirements directly related to food safety. See Article 1(1), which, being similar to Article III GATT, is likely to be interpreted in conformity with its jurisprudence. Case law on this provision suggests that what is being sought is equality of competitive conditions between domestic and imported goods. See Reports of the Panels in Italian discrimination against imported agricultural machinery (1959) BISD 7S/60, para 12 and in *US–Standards for reformulated and conventional gasoline*, WT/DS2/R, para 6.25.

[3] Following an *a contrario* reasoning, measures for environmental protection, to protect consumers or for the welfare of animals are not covered by the SPS Agreement. The SPS Agreement being *lex specialis* vis-à-vis the GATT and the TBT, these measures are subject to other WTO Agreements, such as the TBT and Article XX GATT.

[4] Annex A, paragraph 5, to the SPS Agreement defines 'Appropriate level of sanitary or phytosanitary protection' as '[t]he level of protection deemed appropriate by the [WTO] Member establishing a sanitary or phytosanitary measure to protect human, animal or plant life or health within its territory.' The note attached to this definition states that many WTO Members refer to this concept as the 'acceptable level of risk'. See also the preamble of the SPS Agreement which stipulates that 'no Member should be prevented from adopting or reinforcing measures necessary to protect human, animal or plant life or health'.

'this context indicates that a non-mandatory government measure is also subject to WTO provisions in the event compliance with this measure is necessary to obtain an advantage from the government or, in other words, if sufficient incentives or disincentives exist for the measure to be abided by'[5].

Article 2 of this agreement gives members the right 'to take sanitary and phytosanitary measures necessary for the protection of human, animal or plant life or health', as long as such measures are not inconsistent with the provisions of the SPS Agreement. Thus, this agreement, by supplementing the original Article XX GATT, provides members with a (multilateral) framework to develop their domestic public health policies, such as food safety. We will see that this regime being particularly intrusive into the members' regulatory autonomy, all of the major SPS cases to date – the *Hormones*, *Salmon*, *Agricultural products* and *Apples* cases – have been lost by the defending member.

The following key provisions give shape to the WTO regulation of food:

- Non Discrimination (Articles 2.3 and 5.5 SPS)
- Necessity and Proportionality Test (Articles 2.2 and 5.6 SPS)
- Scientific Basis (Articles 2.2, 3.3, 5.1-5.3 SPS)
- Harmonisation (Article 3.1, 3.5 SPS)
- Mutual Recognition and Equivalence (Article 4.1 SPS)
- Internal Consistency (5.5 SPS)
- Permission for Precautionary Action (5.7 SPS)
- Notification and Transparency Requirements (Article 7 and Annex B)

As is apparent from this list, while some of these provisions reiterate the original GATT commitments, others represent additional principles directed at reducing the number of technical regulations giving rise to obstacles to trade. The following sections will illustrate the scope of these provisions by referring to the case law developed by the WTO judicial bodies.

To sum up, WTO members are free to adopt all measures they deem necessary to protect food safety and they are also given considerable discretion in determining the appropriate level of protection they seek to achieve through their measures.[6] Thus, two countries addressing the

---

[5] *Japan–Measure Affecting Agricultural Products* WT/DS76/R, para 8.111 (hereinafter: Japan–Agricultural Products) upheld by the AB in WT/DS76/AB/R AB Report adopted 19 March 1999, paras 102–107.

[6] Article 2 SPS provides that: '[m]embers have the right to take sanitary and phytosanitary measures necessary for the protection of human, animal or plant life or health, provided that such measures are not inconsistent with the provisions of this Agreement'.

same risk may pursue broadly divergent levels of protection in taking action against that threat. In that sense, it may be argued that under the GATT/SPS framework members are allowed to trade off public health values against other societal and economic values.

However, members' regulatory freedom can be exercised only to the extent that:

–   there is a demonstrable scientific basis for their measures;
–   a risk assessment be conducted where these measures depart from international standards;
–   their measures are applied only to the extent necessary to protect human, animal or plant life or health.

Under the agreement, members also agree to base their standards on international standards, guidelines or recommendations where they exist. Members may introduce or maintain standards which result in a higher level of protection than would be achieved by measures based on such international standards, if there is scientific justification for such increased protection or where the member has engaged in a process of risk assessment as laid down in Article 5 of the agreement. That section explains that the SPS regime simply encourages, but does not impose, the adoption of international standards.

As will be shown below, the effect of the agreement is to mandate a particular approach to decision-making about issues concerning food safety, consumer protection and animal welfare which amount to a risk analysis model where the production of authorised knowledge and management of risk is mainly based on 'science'. This emerging risk analysis model, by cryptically ascribing a pivotal role to science, is extremely difficult to apply and, accordingly, it is generating growing disagreement among members and commentators.

1.   Non-Discrimination

SPS measures should not be applied in a way which arbitrarily or unjustifiably discriminates between countries where identical or similar conditions prevail, including between conditions within a country and other countries.

This obligation of non-discrimination contained in Articles 2.3 SPS and Article 5.5 SPS builds upon the operative language of the non-discrimination clause of the *Chapeau* of Article XX GATT discussed above.

However, as interpreted in the *Salmon* case, this obligation prohibits discrimination not only between similar products but also between different products.[7] Its scope, by focusing on the justification for discrimination between situations under SPS prohibition itself, is therefore broader than that contained in the *Chapeau* of Article XX.

While Article 2.3 relates to differences between the situations of the regulating member and other members and between the situations of the various other members, Article 5.5 focuses on differences in the level of protection chosen by a member in different situations. The scope of the latter provision is the focus of paragraph 5, on the consistency test.

2.   Necessity and Proportionality Test

The necessity test, also called the least trade-restrictive (LTR) discipline, is one of the most important general disciplining factors governing domestic regulations in WTO law. It has traditionally been interpreted as requiring domestic regulations to be the least restrictive means of achieving their declared goals.

This requirement originally developed from Article XX(b) GATT, which requires that measures derogating from Article III and XI be 'necessary' to protect human, animal or plant life or health.

However, the necessity test as enshrined in the SPS Agreement differs from that contained in Article XX(b) on several issues. Thus, while Article XX refers to the necessity test as a 'negative requirement' to be satisfied in order to benefit from an exception, the SPS Agreement, as well as the TBT, has turned this discipline into a 'positive' requirement for all SPS measures. This difference plays a role in allocating the burden of proof. Moreover, unlike the SPS, GATT Article XX(b) does not require any specific procedural requirement to be followed when adopting a public health measure, such as, for instance, the need for a risk assessment.

After reminding members to take into account the objective of minimising negative trade effects when determining the appropriate level of SPS protection (paragraph 4), Article 5 provides that, in establishing or maintaining SPS measures to achieve the appropriate level of protection, members must ensure that such measures are not

---

[7] Article 21.5 Panel Report, *Australia–Salmon*, WT/DS18/RW, adopted on 20 March 2000, para 7.112: 'we are of the view that discrimination in the sense of Article 2.3, first sentence, may also include discrimination between different products, eg not only discrimination between Canadian salmon and New Zealand salmon, or Canadian salmon and Australian salmon; but also discrimination between Canadian salmon and Australian fish including non-salmonoids'. On the *Salmon* case, see infra footnote 9.

more trade-restrictive than required, taking into account technical and economic feasibility (paragraph 6).

A textual interpretation of these two provisions, highlighting their different wording ('take into account' v 'must ensure'), would seem to suggest a proper 'necessity test' is imposed solely on the risk response component of risk management, ie the choice of a measure designed to attain the chosen level of protection.

This has been suggested by the panel in the *Hormones* case, where in a finding not reviewed by the Appellate Body, it held that Article 5.4 was of an hortatory nature:

> Guided by the wording of Article 5.4, in particular the words 'should' (not 'shall') and 'objective', we consider that this provision of the SPS Agreement does not impose an obligation. However, this objective of minimising negative trade effects has nonetheless to be taken into account in the interpretation of other provisions of the SPS Agreement.[8]

A related footnote (number 3) to Article 5 further qualifies the SPS LTR discipline by setting forth the test for breach of Article 5.6 SPS. The least trade-restrictive alternative must:

a)   be reasonably available;
b)   achieve the appropriate level of protection, and
c)   be *significantly* less restrictive to trade.

It is this last requirement which seems to differentiate the understanding of the necessity test within the SPS Agreement from the GATT.

This three-pronged test has been confirmed by the Appellate Body in the *Australia–Salmon* case. In this dispute, Canada challenged an import ban enacted by Australia on fresh, chilled or frozen salmon.[9] The AB held that:

> These three elements are cumulative in the sense that, to establish inconsistency with Article 5.6, all of them have to be met. If any of the elements is not fulfilled, the measure in dispute would be consistent with Article 5.6. Thus, if there is no alternative measure

---

[8] *EC–Hormones* (Canada), Panel Report, at para 8.169; *EC– Hormones* (US), Panel Report, at para. 8.166.
[9] The Australian Government, fearing the introduction of diseases not yet present in its waters which might have damaged its growing domestic production of salmon, unsuccessfully sought to justify its ban on its need to prevent the spreading of such 'exotic' diseases.

available, taking into account technical and economic feasibility, or if the alternative measure does not achieve the member's appropriate level of sanitary or phytosanitary protection, or if it is not significantly less-trade restrictive, the measure in dispute would be consistent with Article 5.6.[10]

In this case, the AB found that, although there existed available alternative measures, there was not sufficient evidence to determine whether they would have achieved Australia's appropriate level of protection. Similarly, in the *Agricultural Products* case, the AB refused to consider the contested measure to be in breach of Article 5.6 because, although alternatives existed, there was a lack of evidence to that effect.

In particular, the AB held that it is for the complaining party to suggest alternatives and to make out a prima facie case of violation of Article 5.6 SPS. That means that WTO judicial bodies, in assessing whether the contested measure complies with the necessity test, cannot rely on information provided to them by their experts, but solely on that advanced by the parties.

This rather deferential interpretation of the necessity test must be applauded to the extent that WTO judicial bodies cannot realistically assess the degree of necessity of an SPS measure taken out of its particular regulatory, societal and economical contexts. A more intrusive reading of these norms would inevitably lead the WTO to engage in complex questions of allocation of domestic resources and political choices, thus intruding into sensitive areas of members' sovereignty.

3. Scientific Basis

For a WTO member SPS measure to survive review under the SPS Agreement it must not only be non-discriminatory and necessary, but also based on scientific evidence.

SPS measures need to be 'based on scientific principles' and may not be 'maintained without sufficient scientific evidence' under Article 2.2 of the SPS Agreement.

This provision is the central pillar of the agreement as it shows its willingness to go beyond the discrimination principle by laying down a new organisational principle enabling the WTO to distinguish between legitimate and illegitimate regulations: 'sound science'.

---

[10] *Australia–Measures Affecting the Importation of Salmon* WT/DS18/AB/R AB Report adopted 6 November 1998, at para 199.

At the same time, scientific justification does not aim exclusively at eliminating sham health measures, but also at identifying scientifically unsupported regulations that, though not protectionist per se, may unnecessarily restrict trade.

In other words, the introduction of the scientific requirement, by allowing the survival of solely those health measures which are science-based, brought the GATT trade-liberalisation agenda a step further towards the goal of integration. The next sections will illustrate in detail the scientific justification discipline, as enshrined within the SPS Agreement.

3.1 Article 2.2 SPS: Scientific Principles and Sufficient Scientific Evidence

The primary SPS scientific justification discipline may be found in Article 2.2 SPS. That provision requires that any member's sanitary and phytosanitary measure be 'based on scientific principles and [...] not [be] maintained without sufficient scientific evidence'. A textual interpretation of this provision seems to suggest that, due to the use of the conjunction 'and', both scientific requirements have to be satisfied concurrently.

Although the WTO case law has so far devoted more attention to the notion of 'sufficient scientific evidence' than to that of 'scientific principles', the latter, by employing the word 'principle', seems to impose, unlike the former, the attainment of a certain scientific quality from the risk assessment. To give meaning to the notion of 'sufficient scientific evidence', the AB began interpreting the words 'scientific' and 'science' by relying on dictionary definitions.[11] Thus, while 'scientific' may be defined as 'having or appearing to have an exact, objective, factual, systematic or methodological basis' or 'pertaining to, using or based on the methodology of science',[12] 'sufficiency' is a 'relational concept' which 'requires the existence of a sufficient or adequate relationship between two elements, *in casu*, between the SPS measure and the scientific evidence'.[13]

In particular, to be 'adequate' the required relationship between the SPS measure and the scientific evidence must satisfy a set of requirements provided by the case law. First, it must be 'objective and rational' and, second, it must be determined 'on a case-by-case basis'.[14] Moreover, this determination depends not only 'upon the particular circumstances of

---

[11] See the AB Report in *Hormones*.
[12] See the AB Report in *Hormones*.
[13] Article 21.5 Report *Japan–Agricultural Products*, para 73.
[14] Article 21.5 Report *Japan–Agricultural Products*, para 84.

the case',[15] but also on 'the characteristics of the measure at issue and [by] the quality and quantity of the scientific evidence'.[16] This interpretation of the required 'adequate relationship' between the SPS measure and the scientific evidence has been confirmed by the AB in the *Apples* case where it stated:

> [...] the approach followed by the Panel in this case — disassembling the sequence of events to identify the risk and comparing it with the measure — does not exhaust the range of methodologies available to determine whether a measure is maintained 'without sufficient scientific evidence' within the meaning of Article 2.2. Approaches different from that followed by the Panel in this case could also prove appropriate to evaluate whether a measure is maintained without sufficient scientific evidence within the meaning of Article 2.2. Whether or not a particular approach is appropriate will depend on the 'particular circumstances of the case'. The methodology adopted by the Panel was appropriate to the particular circumstances of the case before it and, therefore, we see no error in the Panel's reliance on it.[17]

Furthermore, in the same case, the AB has elaborated further guidance on how to conduct the evaluation of the scientific justification requirements, notably the 'adequate relationship' test. By upholding the panel's finding according to which the disproportion between the risk identified by the scientific assessment and the SPS measure implies the lack of 'rational and objective relationship', the AB opened the door to the introduction of a sort of proportionality principle in the examination of the scientific justification discipline. If the SPS measure at issue is 'clearly disproportionate to the risk identified on the basis of the scientific evidence available', a 'rational and objective relationship' does not exist between that measure and the relevant scientific evidence, and, therefore, a panel may conclude that the measure is maintained 'without sufficient scientific evidence' within the meaning of Article 2.2 SPS.

To avoid any possible misunderstanding, the AB has pointed out that:

> [...] the 'clear disproportion' to which the Panel refers, relates to the application in this case of the requirement of a 'rational or objective relationship between an SPS measure and the scientific evidence.

Finally, the requirement of 'sufficient scientific evidence' may seem to require, like the notion of 'scientific principles', not only a certain

---

[15] Article 21.5 Report *Japan–Agricultural Products*, para 84.
[16] Article 21.5 Report *Japan–Agricultural Products*, para 84.
[17] *Japan–Apples* AB Report, para 164.

scientific quality but also a certain scientific quantity, both to be achieved through a predetermined set of methodologies.[18]

3.2   Article 5.1 SPS: Risk Assessment

In order fully to satisfy the scientific justification discipline provided by the SPS Agreement, members must also comply with Article 5 SPS. This provision provides that members should ensure that their measures be 'based on an *assessment*, as appropriate to the circumstances, of the risks to human, animal or plant life or health'. This requirement translates in operational terms the scientific duty imposed on members by Article 2.2, thereby completing the SPS scientific discipline. In particular, by laying down some common structure on the way in which WTO members enact SPS measures, it constitutes an attempt by the SPS framers to provide some guidance to the members when adopting such measures.[19]

The concept of 'assessment of the risks', as enshrined in Article 5.1, has originally been interpreted as 'a scientific examination of data and factual studies' as opposed to 'a political exercise involving social value judgements made by political bodies'.[20] This interpretation finds its origin in the panel's efforts, in the *Hormones* case, to distinguish from the requirements of risk assessment, as enshrined in Article 5.1, the notion of 'risk management', which is typically the second step in a decision by a WTO member to enact an SPS measure. As is well-known, after a risk assessment has been successfully conducted, WTO members are entitled to establish their appropriate level of sanitary and phytosanitary protection by then choosing the best measure aimed at achieving that result.

However, the AB refused to endorse this distinction, by stressing that:

> Article 5 and Annex A of the *SPS Agreement* speak of 'risk assessment' only and that the term 'risk management' is not to be found either in Article 5 or in any other provision of the *SPS Agreement*. Thus, the Panel's distinction, which it apparently employs to achieve or support what appears to be a restrictive notion of risk assessment, has no textual basis.[21]

---

[18] J. Peel, 'Risk Regulation Under the WTO SPS Agreement: Science as an International Normative Yardstick?', in *Jean Monnet Working Paper*, 02/04, NYU School of Law.
[19] Whether SPS scientific requirements establish a real risk analysis scheme remains an open question and is discussed further within Part IV when comparing the EC and the WTO Food Safety Risk Analysis schemes, notably in chapter II.
[20] *EC–Hormones* Panel Report, para 8.94.
[21] *EC–Hormones* AB Report, para 181.

By upholding in these terms the panel's finding, the AB 'virtually ignored risk management' merely because 'this phrase is not mentioned in the SPS Agreement'.[22] It is likely that the AB did so as it saw in the risk assessment/risk management dichotomy an attempt by the panel to narrow down the scope of the risk assessment requirements. It is submitted that, by adopting such an attitude, the panel has missed an important opportunity to shed some light on the way in which members should conduct risk management under the SPS/WTO.

Instead, by giving preference to a textual interpretation of the SPS Agreement, the AB seems to be willing to support the SPS negotiators' resolution not to be too prescriptive about risk management, but to focus on the structuring of the risk assessment stage. This approach clashes with reality where panels face situations where determinations of 'safety' do not derive exclusively from scientific evaluations, but may also be based on assumptions made pursuant to science policies and 'other factors', such as consumer anxiety and concerns.

While the exclusion of the concept of risk management from the SPS is not surprising in light of the AB's traditional willingness not to overstep the textual basis of WTO Agreements, this choice is very unfortunate insofar as it ruled out a potentially useful tool which would have contributed to clarifying the incomplete WTO risk analysis model.

The consequences of this unbalanced and incomplete risk analysis framework, not only in the modelling of risk analysis within the WTO but also in the elaboration of the standard of review applicable to SPS measures will be demonstrated later. In particular, analysis will be provided as to how this scientific justification discipline not being counterbalanced by adequate risk management guidelines is leading towards the elaboration of an intrusive standard of review that turns on an assessment of the available scientific evidence.[23]

Annex A to the SPS defines two types of assessment of risks to the life and health of humans and animals depending on the origin of the risks at stake, particularly food-borne risks and quarantine risks (or pest and disease risks).

While for the risks arising from the presence of certain substances in food, beverages and feedstuffs the required assessment consists in an 'evaluation of the *potential* for adverse effects on human or animal health arising from the presence of additives, contaminants, toxins or disease-

---

[22] V.R. Walker, 'Keeping the WTO from Becoming the "World Trans-Science organization": Scientific Uncertainty, Science Policy, and Factfinding in the Growth Hormones dispute', 31 *Cornell international Law Journal* 1998, 251, p 578.
[23] See infra Part IV, Chapter III.

causing organisms in food beverages or feedstuffs', with respect to quarantine risks the required assessment is defined as 'the evaluation of the *likelihood* of entry, establishment or spread of a pest or disease within the territory of an importing member according to the sanitary and phytosanitary measures which might be applied'.

Both types of risk assessment have been interpreted and developed further by the WTO judicial bodies. In particular, the food-borne risk assessment is a two-step process, whereas the quarantine risk assessment is a three-step analysis. In the former, the first step consists in the identification of adverse effects to human or animal health and life arising from the presence of certain substances, such as toxins or additives, in food, beverages and feedstuffs. When such adverse effects exist, the second step requires an evaluation of the potential or probability of occurrence of these effects[24]. This two-step analysis seems to be settled case law, even though the AB has initially expressed some doubts by defining it 'debatable' in the *Hormones* case.[25]

In the latter risk assessment type (quarantine, pest and disease), the first step consists in identifying 'the diseases (or pests) whose entry, establishment or spread a member wants to prevent within its own territory, as well as the potential biological and economic consequences associated with the entry, establishment or spread of these diseases'.[26] Once the quarantine risks are identified it must assess 'the likelihood of entry, establishment or spread of these diseases, as well as the associated potential biological and economic consequences'.[27] Finally, a risk assessment must 'evaluate the likelihood of entry, establishment or spread of these diseases according to the SPS measures which might be applied'.[28]

In *Japan–Apples* the panel, as subsequently confirmed by the AB, further clarified this last step of quarantine risk assessment, by requiring consideration of not only 'the particular measures that are already in place to the exclusion of other possible alternatives', but also consideration of the measures which 'might be applied', ie the measures which may potentially be applied[29].

It follows that each type of risk assessment calls for its own level of 'likelihood'. In particular, while quarantine risk assessment requires an 'evaluation of the *likelihood* of entry, establishment or spread of a pest or

---

[24] *EC–Hormones* Panel Report, para 8.98.
[25] *EC–Hormones* AB Report, para 184.
[26] *Australia–Salmon* AB Report, para 120.
[27] *Australia–Salmon* AB Report, para 120.
[28] *Australia–Salmon* AB Report, para 120.
[29] *Japan–Apples* Panel Report, para 8.283.

a disease', in the case of food-borne risk, Annex A only refers to an 'evaluation of the *potential* for adverse effects on human or animal health'. Although it is doubtful whether the SPS draftsmen had been aware of introducing such a semantic differentiation, the AB, being traditionally attentive to textualism in the exercise of its interpretative task, has given full meaning to it, by equating likelihood with probability and potential with mere possibility.[30]

It results from this that, according to the WTO judicial bodies, the quarantine risk assessment requires a higher level of probability than the food-borne type, by introducing a 'quantitative dimension to the notion of risk'.[31] This has been confirmed by the AB in *Australia–Salmon* where it held that:

> [...] for a risk assessment to fall within the meaning of Article 5.1 and the first definition in paragraph 4 of Annex A, it is not sufficient that a risk assessment conclude that there is a *possibility* of entry, establishment or spread of diseases and associated biological and economic consequences. A proper risk assessment of this type must evaluate the 'likelihood', ie, the 'probability', of entry, establishment or spread of diseases and associated biological and economic consequences as well as the 'likelihood', ie, 'probability', of entry, establishment or spread of diseases *according to the SPS measures which might be applied.*[32]

If the differentiation proposed by the AB between the different levels of 'likelihood' required under the two types of risk assessment finds a solid textual basis within the SPS Agreement, one may doubt whether the introduction of such a distinction is either scientifically or politically justified. As both types of risk assessment deal with risks that, though originating from different sources, endanger the same essential values, such as the life and health of humans and animals, it is hard to find persuasive reasons legitimising this differentiation.

Moreover, it remains to be seen how to reconcile the demand for quantitative evaluation imposed by the higher level of probability required by quarantine risk assessment with the AB position, according to which 'there is no requirement for risk assessment to establish a certain margin or threshold level of degree of risk'.[33] In fact, one may wonder what the rationale is for the required higher standard of 'likelihood' for quarantine risk assessment when, at the same time, there is no requirement, at least in principle, for a minimum threshold of risk. A

---

[30] *EC–Hormones* AB Report, para 184.
[31] *EC–Hormones* AB Report, para 184.
[32] *Australia–Salmon* AB Report, para 123.
[33] *EC–Hormones* AB Report, para 186; confirmed in *Australia–Salmon* AB Report, para 124.

way out from this apparently irreconcilable tension may be found in *Australia–Salmon*, where the AB, agreeing with the panel taking position on the requirement that the evaluation of the 'likelihood' be done quantitatively, declared that:

> [...] the likelihood may be expressed either qualitatively or quantitatively.[34]

This statement would seem to suggest a new trend aimed at overcoming the distinction introduced by the AB between 'potential' and 'likelihood' in order to harmonise the two types of risk assessment, by downgrading the degree of 'likelihood' required by the quarantine-type risk assessment to that imposed by the food-borne type risk assessment, ie mere possibility.

Article 5.2 lists some of the factors that should be taken into account when conducting a risk assessment. It mentions: 'available scientific evidence; relevant processes and production methods; relevant inspection, sampling and testing methods; prevalence of specific diseases or pests; existence of pest – or disease – free areas; relevant ecological and environmental conditions; and quarantine or other treatment' (5.2–5.4). In *EC–Hormones*, the AB interpreted this list as non-exhaustive[35] and as including non-scientific factors as well.

However, this last point is quite controversial among commentators not only because of the blurred nature of the factors listed in Article 5.2[36] but also because of the ambiguous character of the famous sentence employed by the AB to describe the kind of risk ascertainable under Article 5.1,[37] notably where it stated that:

> [...] the risk that is to be evaluated in a risk assessment under Article 5.1 is not only risk ascertainable in a science laboratory operating under strictly controlled conditions, but *also risks in*

---

[34] *Australia–Salmon* AB Report, para 124.

[35] AB Report in *EC–Hormones*, para 187 (' [...] there is nothing to indicate that the listing factors that may be taken into account in a risk assessment of Article 5.2 was intended to be a closed list').

[36] AB Report in *EC–Hormones*, para 187 (' [...] [s]ome of the kinds of factors listed in Article 5.2 such as 'relevant processes and production methods' and 'relevant inspection, sampling and testing methods' are not necessarily or wholly susceptible of investigation according to laboratory methods of, for example, biochemistry or pharmacology [...] ').

[37] For a criticism of this statement see, eg, R. Quick and A. Bluthner, 'Has the Appellate Body Erred? An Appraisal and Criticism of the Ruling in the WTO Hormones Case', 3 *Journal of International Economic Law* (1999) 603, pp 618–9. For a positive comment on the same statement, see R. Howse, 'Adjudicating Legitimacy and Treaty Interpretation in International Trade Law: The Early Years of WTO Jurisprudence', in J.H.H. Weiler, (ed.), *The EU, the WTO and the NAFTA: Towards a Common Law of International Trade?*, Oxford, 2000, pp 64 ss.

> *human societies as they actually exist,* in other words, the actual
> potential for adverse effects on human health in the real world
> where people live and work and die.[38]

Indeed, while it is objectively true that the factors listed in Article 5.2
are not 'wholly susceptible of investigation according to laboratory
methods',[39] the AB's allusion to 'the risks in human societies as they
actually exist'[40] did not necessarily 'open the door to the inclusion of
such factors as cultural preferences and societal values in the risk
assessment for SPS measures'.[41] It is indeed arguable whether these
elements may offer sufficient foundation for the conclusion that it is
possible to take into account non-scientific factors within risk assessment.
In fact, the language employed by the SPS when sketching out its
scientific discipline is rigorously and exclusively science-based and does
not leave any room for non-scientific considerations. Thus, for instance,
Annex A, defining risk assessment, does not recognise, either in the
identification phase or in the evaluation of likelihood of adverse effect,
any role to non-scientific considerations.

Always in relation to the factors susceptible to be validly integrated
into 'risk assessment', the AB considered in *EC–Hormones* that risks also
arising from difficulties of control of compliance with certain
requirements could be taken into account in the context of a risk
assessment:

> [i]t should be recalled that Article 5.2 states that in the assessment
> of risks, members shall take into account, in addition to 'available
> scientific evidence', 'relevant processes and production methods;
> [and] relevant inspection, sampling and testing methods'. We note
> also that Article 8 requires members to 'observe the provisions
> of Annex C in the operation of control, inspection and approval
> procedures ...'. The footnote in Annex C states that 'control,
> inspection and approval procedures include, inter alia, procedures
> for sampling, testing and certification'. We consider that this
> language is amply sufficient to authorise the taking into account
> of risks arising from failure to comply with the requirements of
> good veterinary practice in the administration of hormones for
> growth promotion purposes, as well as risks arising from
> difficulties of control, inspection and enforcement of the
> requirements of good veterinary practice.[42]

---

[38] *EC–Hormones* Appellate Body Report WT/DS26/AB/R, WT/DS48/AB/R adopted on 13 February 1998, para 187.

[39] AB Report on *EC–Hormones*, para 187.

[40] AB Report on *EC–Hormones*, para 187.

[41] R. Neugebauer, 'Fine-Tuning WTO Jurisprudence and the SPS Agreement: Lessons from the Beef Hormones Case', 31 *Law & Policy International Business* 1255, p 1267 (2000).

[42] AB Report on EC–Hormones, para 204.

However, the AB also added a limitation to its finding by stating that:

> [w]e do not mean to suggest that risks arising from potential abuse in the administration of controlled substances and from control problems need to be, or should be, evaluated by risk assessors in each and every case. When and if risks of these types do in fact arise, risk assessors may examine and evaluate them. Clearly, the necessity or propriety of examination and evaluation of such risks would have to be addressed on a case-by-case basis. What, in our view is a fundamental legal error is to exclude, on an *a priori* basis, any such risks from the scope of application of Articles 5.1 and 5.2.[43]

Whilst the definition of risk assessment has been elaborated through time, the meaning of 'based on' risk assessment, as employed in Article 5.1, soon revealed itself to be difficult to interpret.[44] Is this a substantive and/or a procedural requirement? In other words, to what extent does it impose on members a duty to conduct a risk assessment before acting? Moreover, should an SPS measure conform to an international standard or might it be sufficient for it to be inspired by that standard?

Although the panel in the *Hormones* case has interpreted this requirement as a 'minimum procedural requirement',[45] the AB in the same dispute

---

[43] AB Report on EC–Hormones, para 206.

[44] This question arose in the first SPS case that reached the DSB: the *Hormones* case. For an overview of this longstanding case, see, eg, M.M. Slotboom, 'The Hormones Case: An Increased Risk of Illegality of Sanitary and Phytosanitary Measures', *Common Market Law Review* (1999) 486; D. Wüger, 'The Implementation Phase in the Dispute Between the EC and the United States on Hormone-Treated Beef', 33 *Law & Pol'y Int'l Bus.*, pp 777 ss. (2002) and for a follow-up of the case, see A. Alemanno, 'Judicial Enforcement of the WTO Hormones ruling within the European Community: Toward an EC Liability for the non-implementation of WTO Dispute Settlement Decisions', 45 *Harvard International Law Journal* 547 (2004). In February 2005, at the request of the European Communities (EC), a panel has been established to determine the WTO-consistency of the continued retaliation by the United States and Canada, despite EC claims of compliance with the findings in the *European Communities–Hormones* dispute. See *United States/Canada: Continued Suspension of Obligations in the EC Hormones Dispute*, WT/DS320 and WT/DS321. Due to the complexity of the dispute and the matters involved, on 20 January 2006, the Chairman of the Panel informed the DSB that due to the complexity of the dispute, and the administrative and procedural matters involved, the panel would not be able to complete its work in six months. The panel has not circulated yet its final report.

[45] The panel, after having found that '[...] there is a minimum procedural requirement contained in Article 5.1', went on by stating that '[i]n our view, the Member imposing a sanitary measure needs to submit evidence that at least it actually took into account a risk assessment when it enacted or maintained its sanitary measure in order for that measure to be considered as based on risk assessment'. Concluding that the EC had not met its burden of proving that it had satisfied such a 'minimum procedural requirement' stemming from Article 5.1, the panel found that the EC measures inconsistent with the requirements of Article 5.1. See *EC–Hormones* Panel Report, para 8.113.

rejected this interpretation, by emphasising the 'substantive requirements' that regulate the adoption of SPS measures, in particular that an SPS measure must be justified by science. Accordingly, the Appellate Body held that, absent national procedural requirements, a member may rely on a risk assessment conducted 'by another member, or by an international organisation', and should therefore not necessarily carry out its 'own risk assessment'.[46] In contrast to a procedural interpretation, this approach promotes greater convergence of members' regulatory measures by requiring them to be rationally linked to the results of a risk assessment. At the same time, under a substantive standard, unless a member adopts the same regulatory measures as those recommended by international bodies, members always need to have sufficient technical capability to verify that there is an objective and rational relationship between the scientific data available and the measures they wish to adopt.[47]

In the same case, the Appellate Body also rejected the panel's narrow view that the measures must *conform* to the scientific conclusions reached in the risk assessment,[48] by stating that this requirement means that 'the results of the risk assessment must sufficiently warrant – that is to say, *reasonably support* – the SPS measure at stake'.[49] As to the degree of rational relationship between the measure and the risk assessment, the AB made the following statement:

> We do not believe that a risk assessment has to come to a monolithic conclusion that coincides with the scientific conclusion or view implicit in the SPS measure. The risk assessment could set out both the prevailing view representing the 'mainstream' of scientific opinion, as well as the opinions of scientists taking a divergent view. Article 5.1 does not require that the risk assessment must necessarily embody only the view of a majority of the relevant scientific community. In some cases, the very existence of divergent views presented by qualified scientists who have investigated the particular issue at hand may indicate a state of scientific uncertainty. Sometimes the divergence may indicate a roughly equal balance of scientific opinion, which may itself be a form of scientific uncertainty. In most cases, responsible and representative governments tend to base their legislative and

---

[46] *EC–Hormones*, AB Report, para 190. See also *EC–Biotech*, Panel Report, para 7.3015, where it is said: '[t]hus, an SPS measure may be based on risk assessment conducted by another Member or by an international organisation'.

[47] However, as will be illustrated below, the increasing demand for specific risk assessment puts a limit on the extent to which WTO Members may rely on risk assessment conducted by other countries or international bodies. See Button, *The Power to Protect* (Oxford and Portland, Oregon, 2004) p 67.

[48] *EC–Hormones*, Panel Report, para 8.117.

[49] *EC–Hormones*, AB Report, para 193–94 confirmed in *Japan–Agricultural Products* AB Report, para 76.

administrative measures on 'mainstream' scientific opinion. In other cases, equally responsible and representative governments may act in good faith on the basis of what, at a given time, may be a divergent opinion coming from qualified and respected sources. By itself, this does not necessarily signal the absence of a reasonable relationship between the SPS measure and the risk assessment, especially where the risk involved is life-threatening in character and is perceived to constitute a clear and imminent threat to public health and safety. Determination of the presence or absence of that relationship *can only be done on a case-to-case basis*, after account is taken of *all considerations rationally bearing upon the issue of potential adverse health effects.*[50]

Therefore, according to this AB's judicial interpretation, risk assessment, as enshrined in Article 5.1 would not be confined to the sole majority scientific opinions but may also include minority views, ie the opinions of scientists departing from mainstream scientific thought. The abovementioned statement remains, however, quite controversial. This is because, although minority opinions have been recognised as valid elements to be taken into account in risk assessment, their contemplation has been subject to a 'reliability/quality' condition (ie that they are 'coming from qualified and respected sources'). Thus, by relying on this ground, the 'single divergent opinion' of Dr Lucier has been rejected as being 'not reasonably sufficient to overturn the contrary conclusions reached in the scientific studies', and, in particular, these 'other studies' also being more specific. While this interpretation seems to reasonably impose that minority opinions also be adequately supported by sufficient evidence, it also suggests that, when a measure is based on minority scientific opinion, the required relationship between that measure and its scientific basis is susceptible to a particularly strict scrutiny.

It is believed that this approach is likely to render illusory the integration of minority opinions within risk assessment to the extent that those opinions, unlike mainstream science, tend to be based 'in the kind of suggestive but not definitive scientific evidence that qualifies as 'general' (or 'indirect') scientific evidence in the scheme of WTO decision-makers'.[51] However, given the question as to the legal status of minority scientific opinions within risk assessment is still open, it remains to be seen whether future cases will clarify it by giving full meaning to the vague notion of 'qualified and respected sources'.

To sum up, to verify whether an SPS measure satisfies the need for sufficient scientific evidence and the substantive standard required for risk assessment, respectively imposed by Articles 2.2 and 5.1 SPS, panels

---

[50] *EC–Hormones*, AB Report, para 194.
[51] Peel, supra note 18, p 66.

and the Appellate Body must examine whether there is 'a rational relationship' between the SPS measure and the scientific evidence. The relationship is to be assessed on a case-by-case basis and 'will depend upon the particular circumstances of the case, including the characteristics of the measure at issue and the quality and quantity of the scientific evidence'.[52] In particular:

> [...] a measure as a whole should be considered to be maintained 'without sufficient scientific evidence' if one or more of its elements are not justified by the relevant scientific evidence addressing the risk at issue.[53]

This clearly highlights the fact that the scientific discipline has become a new and autonomous principle of WTO law.

3.3   The Relationship between Articles 2.2 and 5.1 SPS

Although there is no doubt that Articles 2.2 and 5.1 are closely related, there exists some uncertainty as to the exact relationship between the two requirements imposed by these provisions. Unfortunately, the AB in the *Hormones* case, after expressing surprise that the Panel did not start its analysis on Article 2 but on Article 5, declared that 'further analysis of their relationship should await another case'.[54]

Defining the exact relationship between these provisions does not amount to a mere academic question, for the following reason: should these provisions be interpreted as two separate sources of legal obligations, they would amount to a scientific justification test which would open the door to a much more stringent scrutiny than that exercised so far. Up until that point the WTO judicial bodies had systematically begun, with the notable exception of the *Apples* case, their analysis of the scientific justification requirements from Article 5, then concluding that Article 2.2 should also be considered to be have been violated if the former had been breached.

However, there are signs in the WTO case law indicating a shift of attention away from consistency with Article 5.1 (procedural risk assessment) towards consistency with Article 2.2 (substantive scientific justification). It remains to be seen, however, whether this is enough to argue that these provisions, by giving rise to two separate sets of obligations, may lead to a (not yet seen) scenario where an SPS measure,

---

[52] *Japan–Agricultural Products*, AB Report, para 84.
[53] *Japan–Measures Affecting the Importation of Apples* Panel Report WT/DS245/R adopted on 10 December 2003, para 8.180 (hereinafter *Japan–Apples*).
[54] *EC–Hormones* Appellate Body Report, para 250.

although found to satisfy Article 5.1, may ultimately be found to be in breach of Article 2.2. To date this situation has not been tested in a WTO controversy but it is relevant to the extent that it is contentious whether 'a document that appears on its face to 'tick the boxes' under the Annex A definition of a risk assessment [...] might nevertheless still fail the scientific justification test under Article 5.1'.[55] In other words, to what extent can a 'proper risk assessment' under Article 5.1 guarantee that a measure is based on 'sufficient scientific evidence' within the meaning of Article 2.2?

In the *EC–Hormones* case, the AB, by upholding the panel's finding, has stated that Articles 2.2 and 5.1 SPS 'should constantly be read together'.[56] Indeed, '[t]he requirements of a risk assessment under Article 5.1, as well as of 'sufficient scientific evidence' under Article 2.2, are essential for the maintenance of the delicate and carefully negotiated balance in the *SPS Agreement* between the shared, but sometimes competing, interests of promoting international trade and of protecting the life and health of human beings [...]'.[57]

In particular, it was stated that 'Article 2.2 informs Article 5.1: the elements that define the basic obligation set out in Article 2.2 impart meaning to Article 5.1'.[58]

This interpretation has been confirmed by the AB in the *Japan– Agricultural products* case, where it has been held that:

> Article 5.1 may be viewed as a specific application of the basic obligations contained in Article 2.2.[59]

However, because of the differences existing between the requirements listed respectively in Articles 2.2 and in Article 5.1, it may reasonably be argued that although these provisions are closely related they give rise to two separate sources of legal obligations. Thus, while Article 2.2 requires an identification of the risk and an evaluation of the identified risk with the SPS measure, under Article 5.1 a much deeper analysis is required, notably, an evaluation of the likelihood of entry, establishment or spread of disease or the evaluation of the potential for adverse effects

---

[55] G. Goh, 'Tipping the Apple Cart: The Limits of Science and Law in the SPS Agreement after Japan – Apples', *Journal of World Trade* 40(4), p 664.

[56] *EC–Hormones* Appellate Body Report, para 250.

[57] *EC–Hormones* Appellate Body Report, para. 177.

[58] *EC–Hormones* Appellate Body Report, para 180; then, confirmed by *Japan – Agricultural Products*, AB Report, para 76 where the Appellate Body stated that 'the context of the word 'sufficient' or, more generally, the phrase 'maintained without sufficient scientific evidence' in Article 2.2, includes Article 5.1, as well as Articles 3.3 and 5.7 of the SPS Agreement. See, in particular, para 82.

[59] *Japan–Agricultural Products* Appellate Body Report, para 82.

on human or animal health from the presence of food-borne diseases depending on the SPS measure that might be adopted. As we have seen above, the degree of 'likelihood' required by Article 5.1 and Annex A depends on the type of risk assessment to be conducted. The quarantine-type risk assessment has been interpreted as requiring a higher level of 'likelihood' than the food-borne-risk-type.

The scientific justification discipline is also contained in Article 3.3, which allows members to introduce or maintain SPS measures which result in a higher level of protection than that provided for by measures based on international standards, but only if they are grounded on a 'scientific justification'. In this provision, the satisfaction of the scientific justification test is a clear precondition to the validity of the enacted measure derogating from international standards. According to the AB, the philosophy underpinning this provision shows and proves the existence of the integration of a precautionary approach within the SPS Agreement.[60] Finally, the Agreements also deal with situations of scientific uncertainty by stating that:

> [i]n cases where relevant scientific evidence is insufficient, a member may provisionally adopt sanitary or phytosanitary measures on the basis of available pertinent information, including that from the relevant international organisations as well as from sanitary or phytosanitary measures applied by other members. In such circumstances, members shall seek to obtain the additional information necessary for a more objective assessment of risk and review the sanitary or phytosanitary measure accordingly within a reasonable period of time.[61]

This provision symbolically contains all the difficult challenges raised by the WTO system including the complex interface between scientific evidence requirements and scientific uncertainty. The question is how to reconcile scientific uncertainty with the rigorously interpreted scientific discipline provided for by the SPS Agreement. It will be shown further how this provision has been interpreted thus far by the WTO judicial bodies by focusing in particular on the conditions triggering its invocation.

4.   Harmonisation

While each WTO member is allowed to adopt its food safety measure, provided it is based on science, the SPS Agreement negotiators clearly hoped that harmonised international standards would evolve. In fact, at the beginning of the Uruguay Round, there was general consensus

---

[60] *EC–Hormones* AB Report, para 124.
[61] Article 5.7 SPS Agreement. See infra Section 7, Permission for Precautionary Action.

that harmonisation could have significantly contributed to the fight against those trade obstacles stemming from diverging regulatory regimes. For this reason, the SPS Agreement, besides the recognition of members' right to set their own level of food safety protection, encourages the adoption of international standards, guidelines and recommendations. Harmonisation is defined by Annex A to the SPS Agreement as 'the establishment, recognition and application of common sanitary and phytosanitary measures by different members'.

More precisely, harmonisation is governed by Article 3 SPS, whose three paragraphs provide for an invitation, an encouragement and a derogation, respectively.

Article 3.1 provides that members must base their sanitary and phytosanitary measures on international standards, guidelines or recommendations, where they exist. Article 3.2 introduces a presumption: if the measure conforms to international standards, guidelines and recommendations, it is presumed to be consistent with both the SPS and the GATT 1994. Therefore, in an SPS dispute adjudicated before the WTO, if a member adopts a measure which is 'based on' an international standard, the member's measures will be presumed to be consistent with its obligations under the SPS Agreement. This provision, by representing a 'safe harbour', provides great incentives for members to comply with international standards.

However, under Article 3.3 and seemingly by way of derogation from Article 3.1, members may introduce or maintain SPS measures which result in a higher level of sanitary and phytosanitary protection than would be achieved by measures based on the relevant international standards, if scientific justification exists.[62] In other words, members remain free to 'introduce or maintain' measures more protective than those 'based on' international standards. As has been stated, 'this is a refined system of applied subsidiarity, subtly allowing national autonomy subject to certain constraints'.[63] Indeed, according to the AB, the right of a member State to establish its own level of protection must be seen as 'an autonomous right and not an exception from a 'general obligation' under Article 3.1'.[64] A footnote to this last paragraph (footnote

---

[62] This is one of the main points of divergence between the SPS and the TBT Agreements. While under the SPS Agreement the only justification for not using such standards for food safety and animal/plant health protection is scientific argument resulting from an assessment of the potential health risks, in contrast, under the TBT Agreement Members may decide that international standards are not appropriate for other reasons, including fundamental technological problems or geographical factors.

[63] J.P. Trachtman, 'The World Trading System, the International Legal System and Multilevel Choice', 12 *European Law Journal* 469, p 480 (2006).

[64] *EC–Hormones*, AB Report, para 172.

2) specifies that, for the purposes of this provision, there is scientific justification if, on the basis of an examination and evaluation of available scientific information in conformity with the relevant provisions of this agreement, a member determines that the relevant international standards, guidelines or recommendations are not sufficient to achieve its appropriate level of sanitary and phytosanitary protection.

Article 3.4 then states that WTO members must participate 'within the limits of their resources' in the relevant international bodies, and 'in particular' the Codex, IPPC and OIE. In other words, member States are expected to contribute to the development of standards within these international organisations. As SPS negotiators considered it inappropriate for the WTO to be more prescriptive about risk management, they considered these standard-setting organisations as the better forum for the elaboration of guidelines for regulatory action. These provisions, being rather obscure, have given rise to the following interpretative issues:

- As to paragraph 1, what is the scope of members' duty to base a measure on international standards? Should a member 'base' its measure on the standards or rather 'comply' with it? (a)
- As to paragraph 3:
  - in which circumstances may a member depart from an international standard? (b)
  - on whom does it lay the burden of proof? (c)

(a) While the panel in the *Hormones* case held that in order to be 'based on international standards' a measure should conform to that standard,[65] the AB rejected this strict interpretation by stating that to satisfy this obligation not all, but only some, elements of the standards have to be incorporated into the measure.[66] Therefore, 'based on' means simply derived from, thus providing greater flexibility to members than a 'conform to' requirement. It remains to be seen which is the minimum degree of conformity that must be attained by an SPS measure to satisfy this requirement and, accordingly, to benefit from the presumption of consistency set out by Article 3.2. On this point, the AB in the *Hormones* case has merely held that the panel erred in presuming that measures that did not conform to international standards were incompatible with the SPS Agreement and it has not clarified the meaning of the term 'in conformity with' as enshrined within Article 3.2.

---

[65] *EC–Hormones*, Panel Report, para 8.72.
[66] *EC–Hormones*, AB Report, paras 163–66.

(b) As to the circumstances triggering the invocation of Article 3.3 the AB has found that, contrary to what might appear from a textual reading of the provision, there is only one situation in which a member can pursue a higher level of protection: when it has complied with all the SPS discipline, notably the risk assessment requirements.[67] The complex constraints imposed by the SPS Agreement, combined with the international standards to which it refers, established a system for reviewing certain types of State actions at international level.

(c) As to the burden of proof within Article 3.3, the AB overturned the panel's finding in *Hormones*. It held that, this being a norm and not an exception, but laying down 'an autonomous right' to set a higher level of protection, it is the complainant party that bears the burden.[68]

It remains to be seen to which standards member States will choose to conform.

4.1 The SPS Agreement and the Relevant International Standards Organisations

As to the international standards upon which members should rely, Annex A to the SPS Agreement refers to three different standard-setting organisations, depending on their respective area of competence.[69] Thus, members should look at the following:

(a)   for food safety: the standards, guidelines and recommendations established by the Codex Alimentarius Commission (CAC);

(b)   for animal health and zoonoses: the standards, guidelines and recommendations developed under the auspices of the International Office of Epizootics (OIE);[70]

(c)   for plant health: the international standards, guidelines and recommendations under the auspices of the Secretariat of the International Plant Protection Convention in cooperation with regional organisations operating within the framework of the International Plant Protection Convention (IPPC).

---

[67] *EC–Hormones*, AB Report, paras 175–76.

[68] *EC–Hormones*, AB Report, para 104.

[69] For an overview of these three organisations, see T. Stewart and D.S. Johanson, 'The SPS Agreement of the World Trade Organization and International Organizations: the Roles of the Codex Alimentarius Commission, the International Plant Protection Convention, and the International Office of Epizootics', in 26:27 *Syracuse J. Int'l L. & C.*, (1998), pp 27 ss.

[70] As this international organisation is based in France, notably in Paris, it is most often referred to by the French-based acronym OIE, which stands for 'Office International des Epizooties'.

As seen above, the standards elaborated by these organisations are referred to by the SPS Agreement as a basis for presumed compliance with the agreement. Prior to the Uruguay Round, these organisations' standards had no binding force unless voluntarily accepted for application by national legislation.[71]

The obligation on WTO members to base their SPS measures on the international standards elaborated by these organisations justifies not only a description of their composition but also an analysis of the modalities according to which they adopt these standards.[72] In fact, the proper functioning of the SPS Agreement depends in part upon the standard-setting activities of the CAC, the OIE and the IPPC.

In general, the standards they set are voted upon by the delegates of each member of these organisations. These delegations are traditionally composed of scientists employed by their respective countries. Despite these common traits, the Codex, OIE, and IPPC diverge considerably, both in their roles and organisation. Since among the standards established by these three international organisations those of the Codex show the greatest potential to lead to disputes over food safety issues, our analysis will focus mainly on the Codex Commission's operation. Moreover, it must be stressed that, as they relate to human health, Codex' standards tend to give rise to more concerns amongst the population than those adopted by the IPPC and OIE, which deal respectively with plant and animal health.

Although the operation of these organisations has never been immune from politics, the work undertaken by its scientific bodies has never attracted great political attention. This lack of visibility is mainly due to the fact that the standards they elaborate are not legally binding, but merely advisory, so that they rarely draw the attention of non-scientists. However, as one might have expected, express reliance on these three organisations within the SPS has inevitably had an impact not only on their functioning but also on their nature. To become aware of the relevance of the standards elaborated by these organisations within the international trade arena one may look at the SPS cases brought before the WTO judicial bodies to date. In fact, now that international standards may play, directly or indirectly, a role in the outcome of highly-contested international trade disputes, WTO members have incentives to make

---

[71] M. Herdegen, 'Biotechnology and Regulatory Risk Assessment', in G.A. Bermann, M. Herdegen and P.L. Lindseth (eds.), *Transatlantic Regulatory Cooperation: Legal Problems and Political Prospects*, Oxford: Oxford University Press, 2001.

[72] For a summary of procedures for adoption of certain type standards, see D. Victor, 'The Sanitary and Phytosanitary Agreement of the World Trade Organization: An Assessment After Five Years', 32 *N.Y.U. J. Int'l L. & P.* 4 (2000), 865, pp 884–895.

sure that the new standards of the Codex, IPPC and OIE find inspiration in their current or future national SPS measures.

Although these three bodies are the only international organisations expressly mentioned in the SPS Agreement, other international entities concerned with SPS issues are affiliated with the WTO. Thus, for instance, the WHO, the FAO, UNCTAD and the ISO have regular observer status at the WTO.

Besides their standard-setting involvement, these international organisations also play a role within the risk assessment framework provided by Article 5 of the SPS Agreement. In fact, Article 5.1 states that, in conducting risk assessment for SPS measures, members must take into consideration the risk assessment processes developed by the 'relevant international organisations', which presumably include the Codex, IPPC and OIE. Furthermore, under Article 5.8 SPS, when a member believes that a measure of another member does not conform with the 'relevant international standards, guidelines, or recommendations' and the measure either interferes with or has the potential to interfere with that country's exports, that member can request that the other member provide it with explanations for the measure and the other member will be obliged to respond.

A.   Codex Alimentarius Commission (CAC)[73]

The Codex Alimentarius Commission was originally founded in 1962 by FAO and the WHO as an intergovernmental body in charge of implementing their Joint Food Standards Programme[74] and setting up the Codex Alimentarius.[75] This Codex, drawing on the previous experience of the *Codex Alimentarius Europeus*, may be defined as a set of general and commodity-specific standards, guidelines, and recommended codes of practice aimed at protecting the health of consumers and ensuring fair trade practices.

---

[73] For an overview of the Codex Alimentarius's activities, see T. Stewart and D.S. Johanson, *The SPS Agreement of the World Trade Organization and International Organizations ...*, supra note 69, p 27 ss.; J. Bizet, 'Sécurité Alimentaire: Le Codex Alimentarius', *Les Rapports du Sénat*, n. 450, 1999–2000; C. Riemenschneider, 'A Meeting of the Codex Alimentarius Commission', 5 *FDLI Update*, 3, (1999); D. Jukes, 'Codex Alimentarius – Current Status', in *Food Science and Technology Today*, December 1998, p 10; I. Meyers, 'The New International Trade Architecture and Food Regulation', *Third year paper* (Harvard Law School, 2000 - on file with the author).

[74] The purpose of this programme was to protect the health of the consumers and ensure fair practices in the food trade; to promote co-ordination of all food standards work undertaken by international governmental and non-governmental organisations,

[75] More precisely, the Codex was established since the adoption of two resolutions to set up the organisation in the Eleventh session of the FAO Conference in 1961 and the Sixteen World Health Assembly in 1963.

The CAC elaborates international standards, codes of practice, guidelines and related texts addressing the safety and quality of foods moving in the international food trade.[76] To date, it has developed more than 240 standards ranging from processed foods to raw foods and from maximum levels for pesticides to guidelines for contaminants. Although advisory in nature, as we have seen above, these standards become reference standards through the SPS Agreement.

The Codex's membership is open to FAO and WHO members interested in developing food standards. More than 165 countries are represented in it today.

The Codex, which is led by a 10-member executive committee, also comprises 6 regional coordinating committees, 8 general subject committees, 12 commodity committees and 3 ad-hoc inter-governmental task forces. Among these subsidiary bodies, there are at least eight whose main focus is related to food safety, namely: the Codex Committee on Food and Hygiene, Food Additives and Contaminants, Pesticide Residues, Residues of Veterinary Drugs in Food, and Meat Hygiene and Intergovernmental Task Forces on Food Derived from Biotechnology and Animal Feed. Moreover, all the activities related to the elaboration of general principles for food safety, such as the risk analysis working principles, have been considered by the Codex Committee on General Principles.

Most of these committees meet annually or biannually. The Codex allows the establishment of new subsidiary bodies to address new or emerging issues.

Needless to say, the Codex Commission acquired greater visibility only in 1995 when the SPS and TBT Agreements were adopted. Indeed, the SPS Agreement identifies standards, guidelines and recommendations adopted by the Codex Alimentarius Commission as the international benchmark for food safety. For the purposes of the SPS Agreement, the WTO does not differentiate between standards, guidelines and recommendations elaborated by Codex. They all benefit from the same status under WTO law. For food safety, the SPS Agreement refers to standards developed by the Codex in the following sectors: codes and guidelines on hygienic practices, contaminants, food additives, methods of analysis and sampling, veterinary drug and pesticide residues.

---

[76] Its stated goal is 'to guide and promote the elaboration and establishment of definitions and requirements for foods, to assist in the harmonisation and, in doing so, to facilitate international trade'. See Codex Alimentarius Commission, *This is Codex Alimentarius*, 1995.

With the new role given by the SPS Agreement to the Codex, the main centre of gravity of Codex activities has shifted from a focus on the (vertical) work of the commodity committees to the (horizontal) work of the general subject committees.

It is worth underlining that not all Codex members are members of the WTO. Although Codex standards are referred to by the WTO/SPS framework, the Codex does not establish food standards for the WTO. It mainly establishes food standards for the use of its members. As has been stated during the Forty-fifth Session of the Codex Executive Committee:

> [...] the work of Codex should move forward without concern arising from misunderstandings or misinterpretations as to how Codex standards and related texts might be used.[77]

1.   Operation

To understand the functioning and operation of the Codex it is necessary to look at the Codex Alimentarius Commission Procedural Manual.

When a Codex committee proposes to elaborate a new or revised standard, it should verify whether it fits within the priorities set up by the commission in the medium-term plan of work, before contacting the Codex or its executive committee for approval. Subsequently, the elaboration of standards, as provided for by the Codex elaboration procedure contained in the Manual, may follow two types of procedures:

- Uniform Normal Procedure
- Uniform Accelerated Procedure.

The normal procedure consists of eight steps. It starts with the decision to elaborate a standard and the appointment of the subsidiary body in charge of it (step 1). It follows with the preparation of a proposed draft standard, after having heard either the JMPR or the JECFA, depending on the matter at issue (step 2). The proposed draft is then distributed among CAC members for their comments (step 3). After receipt, the comments are considered by the subsidiary body (step 4) and a draft standard is to be submitted to the CAC for adoption, which has to take into due account the comments received (step 5). Once the standard is adopted, it is sent around members for their comments (step 6), which have to be considered by the member and the CAC (step 7). The procedure terminates with the adoption of the final standard by CAC

---

[77] Executive Committee of the Codex Alimentarius Commission, 45th Session, FAO Headquarters, Rome 3–5 June 1998.

after having considered both the amended draft standard and members' proposals (step 8).[78]

Following the adoption of standards, members have the chance to accept them. The CAC provides for specified forms of acceptance:

–   full acceptance: the country will apply the standard to all products and will not restrict distribution of products complying with the standard;
–   acceptance with specified deviations: the country will apply the standard to all products except those specific aspects which are not accepted;
–   free distribution: the country will not restrict distribution of products complying with the standards. This allows the accepting country to retain a separate national standard without blocking imports complying with the food standard.

All discussions at commission level are made through discussions with the member delegations. In principle, decisions are adopted by consensus. The Codex's history shows that this has been the case until quite recently.[79] This was possible since a national delegate, on returning to her country, could easily ignore the consensus decision taken at the Codex meeting.[80] However, given the heightened status accorded to Codex standards, this is no longer the case. Under the code manual of procedure, where every effort to reach an agreement fails, decisions may be taken by vote. In the event of a vote, decision is by majority of members present at the particular session. Compliance with the adopted standard is then voluntary under Codex principles.

Under the statements of principle concerning the role of science in the code decision-making process, 'when the situation arises that members of the Codex agree on the necessary level of protection of public health but hold different views about other considerations, members may abstain from acceptance of the relevant standard without necessarily preventing the decision by Codex'.[81]

The presumption of conformity introduced by the SPS Agreement makes the Codex and the other international standard-setting organisations

---

[78] See Procedural Manual of the Codex Alimentarius Commission, 14th edition, 2005.
[79] Jukes, 'Codex Alimentarius – Current Status, in Food Science and Technology Today', *Food Science and Technology Today*, December 1998, p 10.
[80] Ibid.
[81] CAC statements of principle concerning the role of science in the Codex decision-Making process and the extent to which other factors are taken into account (Decision of the 21st Session of the Commission 1995 ALINORM 95/37).

'quasi-legislators'.[82] This phenomenon today renders it more and more difficult to agree on the setting up of new standards. Given the incentives stemming from the presumption of conformity provided by Article 3.2 SPS, it is not surprising that the Codex's members tend to vote in a manner that would advance their trade interests. In fact, if a member can have its standard adopted in the Codex, it will not have to defend its measures under the SPS Agreement. This inevitably induces members to rely more frequently on the use of majority voting within the organisation, with the effect of rendering pretty slim the consensus behind the adoption of standards. Moreover, the Codex's works are increasingly influenced by the participation of commercially interested NGOs and, at the same time, by the absence of developing countries' involvement.

This increasing politicisation of the Codex's work inevitably leads to the adoption of standards by majority voting, thereby weakening their scientific authority. Having the support of a smaller number of members, the newly adopted standards do not enjoy international scientific consensus.

Finally, the length of the approval processes for new standards, combined with the diverging trade interests pursued by members, are likely to prevent the adoption of scientifically controversial standards.

2.   *The EC Involvement in Codex: from Observer Status to Full Membership*

The EC and its Member States take CAC's standards into account, but only as long as they are compatible with underlying EC food safety principles. Thus, for instance, the EC, in adopting Commission Directive 2002/82, laying down specific purity criteria on food additives other than colours and sweeteners,[83] has referred to and incorporated within the directive the relevant Codex standard. Another example is represented by Directive 2001/110 relating to honey where it is clearly stated that '[i]t is desirable to take account of the work achieved on a new Codex standard for honey, adjusted, as appropriate, to the specific requirements of the Community'.

The EC's reliance on these standards justifies an increasing European participation within the Codex, especially since measures relying on

---

[82] J. P. Trachtman and G. Marceau, 'The Technical Barriers to Trade Agreement, the Sanitary and Phytosanitary Measures Agreement, and the General Agreement on Tariff and Trade, A Map of the World Trade Organization Law of Domestic Regulation of Goods', 35 *Journal of World Trade* 5 (2002) pp 811–81 . See also J.P., Trachtman, 'The World Trading System, the International Legal System and Multilevel Choice', supra note 63, p 480.
[83] OJ L292/1 28 October 1998.

them benefit from a presumption of conformity with WTO/SPS rules.[84] This is particularly true after the WTO judicial bodies have held that not only standards adopted by consensus may qualify as 'relevant international standards', but also those adopted by a majority vote within the Codex. Indeed, it is in the EC interest to effectively contribute to the works of this body so as to make sure that new standards reflect as much as possible their food policy objectives.

In that light, the EC has recently become a full member of the Codex.[85] The EC's accession to Codex resulted from an intensive lobbying activity undertaken by the EC Commission to modify the Codex's provisions excluding regional organisations from its membership. In the past, the EC could only benefit from observer status. Today – thanks to the European involvement – all regional organisations can obtain full membership.[86] It is worth noting that, while the Council had authorised the Commission to begin negotiations with Codex as far back as 1993, it was only in 2003, after having lost two SPS/TBT disputes involving international standards (*Hormones* and *Sardines*[87]), that the Commission acted to obtain the desired status. The EC Commission wrote to the Director-General of the UN/FAO in November 2003 formally to complete the accession process. This means that the European Commission has relinquished its observer status in the Codex and now represents all EC countries on matters of EC competence.

In particular, the Commission speaks and votes in the Codex on behalf of the Community on all issues of exclusive Community competence. It also speaks and votes on behalf of the Community on all issues of mixed competence where the preponderance of the competence lays with the Community. However, EC Member States are still able to contribute to the debate in Codex matters of Community and mixed competence to support and develop the Community line, by voting on issues within areas of exclusive Member State competence and also on those issues of mixed competence when the preponderance of the competence lies with the Member States. In order to inject some clarity into the Commission's participation, the CAC Rules of Procedure (Article 11.5) require that 'before any meeting of the Commission or a subsidiary body of the

---

[84] See Enhancing Participation in Codex Activities, An FAO/WHO training package, 2005, at 74. See also on this point, A. Battaglia, 'Food Safety: Between European and Global Administration', *Global Jurist Advances*, Vol. 6, No. 3, Article 8 (2006), pp 4 ss.

[85] Council Decision of 17 November 2003 on the accession of the European Community to the Codex Alimentarius Commission, OJ L 309 of 26 November 2003.

[86] Rule VII of the Codex Statute. See Report of the 26th session of the CAC of 30 June–7 July 2003, para 78.

[87] *EC–Description of Sardines*, Report of the Panel, WT/DS231/R decided May 29, 2002 (adopted as modified by the Appellate Body 23 October 2002) and Report of the Appellate Body, WT/DS231/AB/R (decided 26 September 2002) adopted 23 October 2002 (hereinafter 'EC–Sardines'). Appellant: Peru; appellee: Canada, Chile, Ecuador, United States and Venezuela.

Commission in which a member organisation is entitled to participate, the member organisation or its members shall indicate in writing which, as between the member organisation and its Member States, shall exercise the right to vote in respect of each particular agenda item'.

The advantages stemming from a European membership to the Codex are self-evident. Although the EC does not accrue more votes (the principle being 'one nation, one vote') as a result of its full membership, it certainly acquires stronger 'bargaining power' within Codex negotiation activities. This means that not only will EC draft proposals be more able to achieve consensus (being already supported by 25 countries),[88] but also that the EC will be more easily able to block the adoption of a standard proposed by non-European members.

The European Community and its Members regularly present joint comments on issues discussed in Codex committees, which are within the competence of Community legislation. The procedure is described in the Council Decision of 17 November 2003 on the accession of the European Community to the Codex Alimentarius Commission. These comments are presented in the EC position papers. The Directorate General for Consumer and Health Protection acts as the contact point and coordinates this work.

3.   *The Role of Codex within the SPS Agreement*

At least until adoption of the WTO Agreements, the Codex has been regarded as a technical organisation that operates at an epistemic level, 'largely unaffected by national political interests as well as national and international law'.[89] The acceptance of standards has been very limited and mainly confined to those developing countries who were setting up new food legislation and have found it to be very practical to adopt the Codex, ready-made standards. Most of these countries were also expecting that reliance on Codex standards would have ensured them access into the markets of Europe and North America. This has not been the case since industrialised countries, such as the European Community Members and the USA, already disposing of evolved food laws, proved unwilling to modify their legislation to adapt them to the standards.

Now, however, because of the heightened legal status of its standards under the SPS Agreement, the Codex activities are becoming more

---

[88] It is worth noting that during the last session of the CAC, the delegation of the European Community was also acting on behalf of Bulgaria and Romania, for which the accession Treaty to the EC has already been signed and officially published. See Joint FAO/WHO Food Standards Programme, Report of the Codex Alimentarius Commission, 28th Session, Rome, 4–9 July 2005, at 1.

[89] F. Veggeland and S.O. Borgen, *Changing the Codex: The Role of International Institutions* (Norwegian Agricultural Economics Research Institute, Oslo , January 2002).

relevant and, accordingly, more sensitive, thereby inevitably coming more under the political spotlight.[90] Amongst the three organisations mentioned within the SPS Agreement, Codex is without doubt the one that has been more politicised as a result of the Uruguay Round. To support this statement one may refer to the long and controversial debates surrounding the vote on Codex beef hormone standards[91] in 1995, which subsequently led to the well-known *Hormones* disputes between the US and the EC.

More recently, the increasing politicisation of Codex has been demonstrated by its failure to adopt a recommended standard for recombinant bovine somatotropin (rbST), a synthetically produced version of a naturally occurring hormone intended to increase milk production. To prevent the adoption of this standard the EC invoked, for the first time ever, 'other legitimate factors relevant for the health protection of consumers and for the promotion of fair practices in food trade', as recognised in the 'Statements of Principles on the Role of Science in the Codex Decision-making Process and the Extent to Which Others Factors Are Taken into Account' as they had been incorporated within the Codex Procedural Manual in 1997.[92] During the negotiations leading to the drafting of this document, the US and the EC confronted each other on the setting up of guidelines defining the precise role of science in risk management, in order to give a more operative meaning to the Codex Statement of Principles.[93] While the US argued that food standards should rely solely on scientific evidence, the EC sought to introduce a 'need' criterion, aimed at preserving farmers against the productivity-enhancing food technologies.[94]

As shown above, the Codex Alimentarius Commission's mandate includes two competing goals: ensuring free movement of goods in international trade and protecting the health of consumers. This dichotomy inherent within the Codex's mandate makes it ill suited to be an effective safeguard for consumer health.

In particular, the Codex's voting rules tend to favour self-interested members voting for those standards promoting their own economic interests, at the expense of public health protection. Thus, in the past, several European countries have blocked the adoption of standards that

---

[90] For an analysis of the SPS impact on the Codex's activities, see Jukes, *The Codex Alimentarius Commission – Current Status*, supra note 73.

[91] On these issues, see infra Part IV, Chapter II.

[92] As amended in 1998, see Second Statement of Principle included in an Appendix to the Procedural Manual entitled 'General Decisions of the Commission'. For an overview of this discussion, see D. Jukes, 'The Role of Science in Internal Food Standards', *Food Control*, Volume 11(3), June 2000. See infra Part IV.

[93] See infra Part IV, Chapter II.

[94] See D. Jukes, supra note 92.

would mandate pasteurisation, whereas pottery-producing countries, such as Portugal and Spain have objected to high lead standards.[95]

Against this backdrop one can easily foresee that those standards that will be adopted in the future will be approved by slim majorities, rather than by consensus.[96] This, as the *Hormones* case clearly shows, means that all those controversial standards upon which agreement will be reached by a slim majority will be likely to trigger a move to the WTO's dispute settlement body.

In these circumstances, it seems that the question today facing the Codex is whether, when dealing with difficult and controversial issues, such as those discussed above, it would not be wiser to avoid the adoption of the standard and recognise that the parties could not reach an agreement. While it is true that the Codex is increasingly acting as a sort of Food Safety World Parliament, the adoption of standards by majority vote seems to weaken rather that to strengthen its legitimacy by inevitably giving rise to further tensions which may lead to trade disputes.

In the light of the above, one may wonder to what extent the Codex's inability to reach consensus on specific contentious issues will call into question its newly-entrusted harmonising role for food regulatory measures. At the moment, the Codex's efforts to develop meta-standards, such as a risk analysis framework for food safety risks, clearly illustrates how the new status acquired by the SPS is contributing to shifting its attention from standard-setting to other, more ambitious, agendas. However, not having been originally conceived to carry out these recently attributed tasks, the Codex is proving badly suited and unfit to realistically exercise its harmonisation mission. The Codex seems condemned to increasingly struggle with its 'de facto' universal food legislator role.

B.   International Office of Epizootics (OIE)

The French-based OIE, now known as the World Organisation for Animal Health, was created in 1924 as a member states-led organisation to improve hygiene and public health by preventing the spread of diseases in animals and animal products in international trade. It is the oldest veterinary organisation in the world and, similarly to the Codex, has a significant record of establishing international standards. Its structures comprise an international committee, composed of delegates from its member states meeting annually, a central office acting as an executive

---

[95] L. Sikes, 'FDA's Consideration of Codex Alimentarius Standards in Light of International Trade Agreements', 53 *Food & Drug L.J.* 327, p 328 (1998).
[96] This has been amply demonstrated by the recourse to votes since the 21st and 22nd sessions to the last one (the 29th held in 2006).

and several commissions serving as deliberative organs. Amongst its missions, OIE develops international standards, guidelines and recommendations relating to animals and animal products. More precisely, its main commissions deal with epizootic diseases, fish diseases and standards and have developed an International Animal Health Code and an International Aquatic Animal Health Code, which are periodically updated. The OIE's standards may be found in the OIE's Code, which lists standards for international trade, and manual, which sets forth standard diagnostic procedures for animal diseases as well as vaccine standards related to international trade.

Although this 155 member organisation is not part of the UN system, it regularly cooperates with FAO and WHO in global food safety issues. Unlike the Codex and the IPPC, the OIE has not experienced major reforms in its standards-setting process and structure since the entry into force of the SPS Agreement.

As the establishment of international standards for animal and animal products does not raise the same concerns as do the Codex's standards relating to human health, the OIE has not experienced any significant controversies when setting standards.

Although the OIE's role within the international trading system may seem to be minor when compared with the Codex and IPPC, the *Australia–Salmon* case has shown the contrary. The proposed EC ban on the use of 'specified risk materials' (SRMs), which may pose risks regarding transmissible spongiform encephalopaties, had been based on an OIE standard prohibiting the international trade of bovine brains and spinal cords originating from countries affected by BSE.

C.   International Plant Protection Convention (IPPC)

The IPPC is a treaty signed in 1952 and administered by the FAO through the IPPC Secretariat. It aims at securing common and effective action to prevent the spread and introduction of pests of plants and plant products, and at promoting appropriate measures for their control.[97] The Convention deals with the protection of plant life and therefore has no direct relevance to food safety.

A secretariat was established for the IPPC in 1989 by the FAO, but it began operations only in 1993. Its main task consists in coordinating international efforts concerning plant quarantine issues, compiling information concerning plant pest outbreaks, and providing technical

---

[97] See Article I of the IPPC.

assistance to the members on phytosanitary issues. Another of the Secretariat's functions is to coordinate the implementation of the IPPC through its nine regional organisations. The secretariat operates under the aegis of the FAO and is located in Rome.

One of the IPPC's most relevant tasks is its work with the FAO's pest management activities, but it is also in charge of developing international standards for phytosanitary measures, centralising and disseminating information on plant parasites that could be present in imports and providing technical assistance to developing countries.

Although the IPPC was amended in 1979 (the amended text became operative in 1991), this organisation revealed itself to be the least prepared among the three international organisations mentioned in the SPS Agreement. On this basis, the FAO Conference decided, in 1997, to amend it so as to adapt it to the new responsibilities provided for by the SPS Agreement. Amongst the most relevant changes introduced by this reform is the creation of a standard-setting procedure. In fact, originally, the IPPC did not contain any provision relating to the establishment of standards.

As to the voting rules, under the revised IPPC, if consensus cannot be reached on a matter that comes before the IPPC's Commission on Phytosanitary Measures, decisions have to be adopted by a two-thirds majority, not by a simple majority.

4.2. The Standard-setting Organisations' Role within the SPS Agreement

This brief analysis of the three standard-setting organisations shows how the SPS Agreement has brought changes not only in their functioning but especially in the role they play within the international trade arena. In particular, the presumption of conformity introduced by the SPS Agreement makes these standard-setting organisations 'satellites organisations' of the WTO[98] or 'quasi-legislators'.[99] While they do not legislate in the full sense of the term, the norms they produce have some legal effects when such standards are adopted and respected. However, their lengthy approval systems for international standards, the increasing number of scientific controversies surrounding new technologies and also the diverging economic interests of its members are rendering increasingly difficult the adoption of standards, notably in areas

[98] S. Poli, 'The Adoption of International Food Safety Standards', *European Law Journal*, Vol. 10, no. 5, September 2004, p 615.
[99] Marceau and Trachtman, supra note 82. See also J.P. Trachtman, 'The World Trading System, the International Legal System and Multilevel Choice', 12 *European Law Journal* 469, p 480.

characterised by scientific uncertainty. In other words, the SPS negotiators' decision to invest these organisations with the task of adopting international standards, in order to keep their elaboration far from political tensions, did not prove to be successful.

Although the possible increased politicisation of the standard-setting process of these organisations is regrettable, it seems to be inevitable today.

As the *EC – Hormones, Australia – Salmon* and *Japan – Agricultural Products* cases have shown, the outcome of many international trade disputes may revolve around the conformity by a WTO member's SPS measure with international standards. This explains the increasing involvement of WTO members in these standard-setting international organisations. Countries try to protect their current or possible future SPS measures by promoting their approaches to risk analysis through the work of the organisation. This trend is likely to lead to less consensus within the Codex, IPPC and OIE, thus inevitably harming the final objective of harmonisation.

5.   Mutual Recognition and Equivalence

Article 4.1 requires members to accept the SPS measures of another member as equivalent if the exporting member 'objectively demonstrates [...] that its measure achieves the importing member's appropriate level of sanitary and phytosanitary protection'. Moreover, Article 4.2 encourages members to enter into consultations with the aim of achieving bilateral and multilateral agreement on recognition of the equivalence of specified SPS measures.[100]

In order to make operational these provisions, the SPS Committee has given a decision, effective from 24 October 2001, on the implementation of this article. The decision, by detailing all the steps that members should undertake in applying this provision, aims at encouraging all WTO members to make use of the 'equivalence' provisions of the SPS Agreement, ie Article 4.

In particular, this decision imposes an obligation on importing members, upon the request of the exporting country, to explain the objective and rationale of the SPS measure, to identify clearly the risks that the relevant

---

[100] For an overview on the Mutual Recognition Agreements concluded by the EC and on their evolution, see, respectively, A. Alemanno, 'Gli Accordi di Mutuo Riconoscimento tra Esperienza Europea e Regole' *OMC*, 2–3 *Diritto del Commercio Internazionale* pp 379 ss. and A. Alemanno, 'Le Principe de la Reconnaissance Mutuelle au delà du Marché Intérieur. Phénomene d'Exportation Normative ou Stratégie de "Colonialisme" Règlementaire?', *Revue du Droit de l'Union Européenne*, 2/2006, pp 273 ss.
.

measure intends to address, and to indicate the appropriate level of protection sought[101]. Accordingly, exporting members must also provide reasonable access, upon request, to the importing member for inspection, testing and other relevant procedures.

6.   Internal Consistency

Article 5.5 SPS seeks to achieve consistency in the application of the appropriate level of SPS protection against health risks. It provides that WTO members should avoid arbitrary or unjustifiable distinctions in the levels they consider to be appropriate in different situations, if such distinctions in the level of risk result in discrimination or a disguised restriction on international trade. In other words, when conducting a risk assessment, members should adopt similar levels of risk for similar products.

By illustration, a member cannot impose a higher maximum acceptable level of pesticide residue for imported fruits than that required for domestic consumed fruits. The application of such an inconsistent determination of levels of protection cannot but suggest that protectionism, not a genuine public health concern, is the underlying goal of the adopted measure. As aptly stated, the presence of an arbitrary or unjustifiable character of differences in the level of protection chosen by a member as 'appropriate' in differing situations:

> may [...] operate as a 'warning' signal that the implementing measure in its application might be a discriminatory measure or might be a restriction on international trade disguised as an SPS measure for the protection of human life or health.[102]

This provision constitutes a corollary of the general principle of non-discrimination posed by Article 2.3 SPS. As stated by the AB in the *Hormones* case:

> [...] Article 5.5 may be seen to be marking out and elaborating a particular route leading to the same destination set out in Article 2.3.[103]

It aims at avoiding situations where a member could adopt a strict level of acceptable risk for one (imported) product and a more lenient approach for another comparable (domestic) product even though the potential risk of harm is very similar for the two products.

---

[101] See document G/SPS/19.
[102] *EC–Hormones*, AB Report, para 215.
[103] *EC–Hormones*, AB Report, para 212.

It is worth noting that, even if a challenged measure is based on a valid risk assessment, it may still be violating the SPS Agreement if all comparable products are not subject to similar regulatory measures based on equally detailed scientifically-based risk assessments. Put differently, a breach of Article 5.5 may override compliance with Article 5.1.

Although the greater part of the *Hormones* case focuses on the alleged violation of Article 5.1 (risk assessment), both the panel and the AB had also to address claims that the EC's ban on meat treated with growth hormones was in breach of Article 5.5.[104] This offered the AB the opportunity to clarify the scope of this provision by first determining the level of inconsistency that a measure should reach in order to be struck down by this provision:

> [...] the goal set [by Article 5.5] is not absolute or perfect consistency, since governments establish their own levels of protection frequently on an *ad hoc* basis and over time, as different risks present themselves at different times. It is only *arbitrary or unjustifiable inconsistencies* that are to be avoided.[105]

Since the consistency requirement applies to appropriate levels of protection established in 'different situations', this latter concept remained to be defined. Therefore, the AB, in the same report, has sought to determine what 'different situations' are in the sense of Article 5.5, by stating that:

> [...] The situations exhibiting differing levels of protection cannot, of course, be compared unless they are comparable, that is, unless they present some common element or elements sufficient to render them comparable. If the situations proposed to be examined are *totally* different from one another, they would not be rationally comparable and the differences in levels of protection cannot be examined for arbitrariness.[106]

Therefore, in spite of the language employed by such a provision, this expression refers to situations that, though revealing differing levels of protection, are 'comparable' within the meaning of Article 5.5.

---

[104] Both complainant, Canada and the USA, argued that the level of protection pursued by the EC ban was inconsistent with the level of protection underlying regulations governing foods containing the same or similar hormones. Thus, for instance, the Community allowed the administration of certain hormones, notably carbadox and olaquindox, to piglets for veterinary purposes.

[105] *EC–Hormones*, AB Report, para 213.

[106] *EC–Hormones*, AB Report, para 217.

Thus, for instance, in the *Hormones* case, the regulation of hormone-treated beef has been compared with the regulation of hormone-treated pork, allowing the administration of two other hormones for veterinary purposes. Although the regulations tackled different substances, the expected negative adverse effect stemming from them was absolutely the same. Therefore, such adverse effect has been qualified as a 'common element' permitting these different situations to be compared.

The required presence of 'some common elements' to render different situations comparable has then been further clarified by the AB in *Australia–Salmon*:

> [...] we believe that for situations to be comparable under Article 5.5, it is sufficient for these situations to have in common a risk of entry, establishment or spread of *one* disease of concern. There is no need for these situations to have in common a risk of entry, establishment or spread of all diseases of concern [...].[107]

This approach has been ultimately confirmed by the 'Guidelines to Further the Practical Implementation of Article 5.5', which have been adopted to facilitate the practical application of the requirements of such a provision.[108] There, it may be read that in order to test consistency '[...] situations involving the same type of substance or pathogen, and/or the same type of adverse health effect, could be compared to one another'.[109]

As to the test to be applied to establish a violation of Article 5.5, the AB has held that there is a violation of such a provision only when the following three elements are demonstrated:

–   'the first element is that the member imposing the measure complained of has adopted its own appropriate levels of sanitary protection against risks to human life or health in several *different* situations' (ie comparable situations);
–   'the second element to be shown is that those *levels of protection* exhibit arbitrary or unjustifiable differences ('distinctions' in the language of Article 5.5) in their treatment of different situations';
–   'the last element requires that the arbitrary or unjustifiable differences result in discrimination or a disguised restriction of international trade'.[110]

---

[107] *Australia–Salmon*, AB Report, para 152.
[108] See Doc. G/SPS//M/19 Section VII adopted on 18 July 2000. The text of the adopted Guidelines can be found at www.wto.org. The guidelines are periodically reviewed and revised as necessary by the SPS Committee in the light of experience gained through the implementation of the SPS Agreement, the use of the guidelines themselves and any pertinent work done by the relevant international standard-setting organisations.
[109] See Doc. G/SPS//M/19, at A2.
[110] *EC–Hormones*, AB Report, para 214.

The above three elements of Article 5.5 are 'cumulative in nature': all of them must be demonstrated to be present if a violation of such a provision must be found.

This interpretation has been confirmed by the AB in *Australia–Salmon* where the AB found that Australia's ban on salmon imports not only breached Article 5.1, not being 'based on' risk assessment, but also Article 5.5 SPS. By upholding the panel's finding, it held that because Australia prohibited importation of salmon and salmon products, while simultaneously allowing the importation of live herring for bait and live ornamental fish (both of which posed similar risks of disease introduction), it was contrary to Article 5.5 SPS[111] and, 'by implication', Article 2.3 SPS. In fact, the evidence clearly showed that, although the risks posed by these fish species were at least as great, if not greater, than those stemming from the importation of uncooked salmon from Canada, they had not been regulated at all by the Australian authorities.[112] As a result, due to the total absence of import controls, both live fish species could enter the Australian territory (*rectius*, waters).[113]

Such a distinction in the levels of protection assured to the Australian salmon population could not but amount to 'an arbitrary or unjustifiable distinction' and a disguised restriction.[114]

As a result, to bring an end to its breaches of the SPS Agreement, Australia had to adopt not only a revised set of quarantine measures, but also to increase controls on the import of other fish. This approach has subsequently been upheld by an Article 21.5 implementation panel, thus making *Australia–Salmon* the first case where a member's controversial SPS measure had been found to meet the rigorous scientific discipline of the SPS Agreement.

The consistency requirement seems to be, at least prima facie, much more respectful of regulatory sovereignty than the narrowly-interpreted scientific justification discipline imposed by Articles 2.2 and 5.1. Instead of preventing members from controlling risks which cannot be adequately 'based on' risk assessment, this requirement enables them

---

[111] *Australia–Salmon*, AB Report, para 236 and 239–240.

[112] The word 'risk' as employed by the Panel and AB was aimed at designing the probabilities of the introduction of the diseases of concern.

[113] However, although a visible inconsistency in the treatment of the different species would already seem to appear, it remained to be established how baitfish and ornamental fishes would have been able to enter into contact with salmon prepared for human consumption, thus transmitting the disease. It seemed to the panel that the most likely pathway by which these fishes could transmit their diseases to salmon would be by ingestion.

[114] *Australia–Salmon*, AB Report, para 240.

to freely regulate all perceived risks, provided that they do so consistently, ie by ensuring that consistent levels of protection will be maintained in comparable situations.

However, contrary to how it might appear, by inducing panels to enquire into the validity of a member's decision on the level of risk it is prepared to accept in comparable situations, the consistency requirement tends to open the door to a highly intrusive review.[115] Notably, by checking the regulatory consistency, panels may increasingly assess the members' choices about the level of protection they would like to offer their own citizens, thereby inevitably lessening their sovereign 'right to take SPS measures necessary for the protection of human, animal or plant life or health' expressly recognised by Article 2.1 SPS.

This outcome might, in principle, be contained should the AB maintain its original position, adopted in the *Hormones* case, according to which the consistency test should catch only 'arbitrary or unjustifiable inconsistencies'.[116] However, notwithstanding this initial deferential approach, there are some signs showing the incoming AB's willingness to follow a stricter reading of the consistency requirement.[117]

In particular, the *Australia–Salmon* case is quite revealing in that sense. When assessing Australia's quarantine measure prohibiting the import of fresh, chilled and frozen salmon in light of Article 5.5 SPS, the AB held that 'warning signals' and 'additional factors' may be relied upon to identify inconsistencies under this provision. Thus, for instance, the AB considered the violation of Article 5.1 risk assessment requirements to be a 'strong indication' that the contested measure was not really aimed at protecting health, but rather amounted to a protectionist measure adopted 'in the guise of' an SPS measure.

Only future cases will shown whether the AB will live up to its commitment to respect Member States' freedom in pursuing the level of protection they might consider the most appropriate vis-à-vis a certain risk. Signs show, however, that it will more likely adopt a stricter attitude vis-à-vis regulatory distinctions.

---

[115] See, eg, V. R. Walker, 'Consistent Levels of Protection in International Trade Disputes: Using Risk Perception Research to Justify Different Levels of Acceptable Risk' (2001) 31 *Environmental Law Reporter* 11317 and J. Atik, 'The Weakest Link: Demonstrating the Inconsistency of "Appropriate Levels of Protection" in *Australia–Salmon*', 24 *Risk Analysis: an International Journal* 483 (2004).

[116] *EC–Hormones*, AB Report, para 213.

[117] *Australia–Salmon*, AB Report, para 166. For a critical analysis of the way in which the consistency test has been applied to date, see W.J. Davey, 'Has the WTO Dispute Settlement System Exceeded Its Authority?', in T. Cottier and P. Mavroidis, *The Role of the Judge in International Trade Regulation: Experiences and Lessons for the WTO* (University of Michigan Publishing, Ann Arbor, 2003) p 43.

7. Permission for Precautionary Action

The idea of precautionary action is stated in a very limited form within the GATT/SPS framework.[118] Under Article 5.7, a precautionary approach to food safety risks is available to allow 'provisional measures' where scientific evidence is 'insufficient', where the member acts on the basis of 'available pertinent information', and where the member seeks to obtain the additional information needed for 'a more objective risk assessment' within a 'reasonable period of time'.

Reliance on precaution has been rigorously framed by these conditions as it constitutes the only way in which SPS measures, although failing to meet the scientific justification discipline as enshrined in Articles 2.2 and 5, may survive review under the WTO discipline.

Similarly to the European version, the rationale underlying a precautionary approach consists in recognising members' ability to address perceived risk to public health without waiting for definitive scientific answers.

The first appearance of the precautionary principle within the WTO context may be found in the *Hormones* case where the EC, although explicitly stating that it was not invoking Article 5.7,[119] tried to argue that this principle was:

> a general customary rule of international law or at least a general principle of law.[120]

Although the Appellate Body abstained from taking a position on the status of the precautionary principle in international law,[121] it then

---

[118] On the genesis of the principle in international and Community law, see supra Part I, Chapter I, section C. The Precautionary Principle.

[119] *EC–Hormones*, AB Report, para 207. The EC did so because it was aware that its legislation did not stand a chance of passing off as a provisional measure. This had been in force for several years already and had not originally been adopted in an emergency context. See on this point, T. Christoforou, 'Science, Law and Precaution in Dispute Resolution on Health and Environmental Protection: What Role for Scientific Experts', in J. Bourrinet et S. Maljean-Dubois (eds.), *Le Commerce International des Organismes Génétiquement Modifiés* (2003), pp 271–72; W. T. Douma, 'How Safe it Safe? The EU and the WTO Codex Alimentarius Debate on Food Safety Issues', in V. Kronenberg, *The European Union and the International Legal Order : Discord or Harmony ?* (T.M.C. Asser Press) p 185.

[120] *EC–Hormones*, Appellate Body Report, para 121.

[121] *EC–Hormones*, Appellate Body Report, para 123, where the AB merely stated that '[t]he status of the precautionary principle in international law continues to be the subject of academics, law practitioners, regulators and judges. [...] Whether it has been widely accepted by Members as a principle of general or customary international law appears less than clear. We consider, however, that it is unnecessary, and probably imprudent, for the Appellate Body in this appeal to take a position on this important, but abstract, question'.

recognised that several of its elements are reflected in some provisions of the SPS Agreement.[122] In particular, it found that:

> [...] First, the principle has not been written into the SPS Agreement as a ground for justifying SPS measures that are otherwise inconsistent with the obligations of the member set out in particular provisions of that Agreement. Secondly, the precautionary principle, indeed, finds reflections in Article 5.7 of the SPS Agreement. We agree, at the same time, with the European Communities that there is no need to assume that Article 5.7 exhausts the relevance of the precautionary principle. It is reflected also in the sixth paragraph of the preamble and in Article 3.3. These explicitly recognise the right of members to establish their own appropriate level of sanitary protection, which level may be higher (ie more cautious) than that implied in existing international standards, guidelines and recommendations. Thirdly, a panel charged with determining, for instance, whether 'sufficient scientific evidence' exists to warrant the maintenance by a member of a particular SPS measure may, of course, and should, bear in mind that responsible, representative government commonly act from perspective of prudence and precaution where risks of irreversible, e.g. life-terminating, damage to human health are concerned.[123]

Therefore, according to the Appellate Body, although the precautionary principle finds reflection not only in the preamble, but also in Article 3.3 and Article 5.7 of the SPS Agreement, such a principle would not override the need for members to prove that they have based their measure on a proper risk assessment, as provided in Article 5.1 and 5.2 SPS.[124] In other words, in the AB's view, those SPS measures which are validly adopted on the basis of Article 5.7 would also be required to comply with the SPS/WTO scientific discipline.

Along these lines, the Appellate Body concluded that theoretical risk, arising by virtue of the impossibility of ever providing a product or substance completely safe for all time, is not the kind of risk to be assumed under Article 5.1, and that, accordingly, food safety measures adopted pursuant to this kind of (non-ascertainable) risk cannot be considered as being 'based on' a risk assessment within the meaning of the SPS Agreement.[125]

---

[122] *EC–Hormones*, AB Report, at para 124.

[123] Ibid, para 124.

[124] Ibid, para 125.

[125] *EC–Hormones*, AB Report, at paras 123–125. The EC had until 13 May 1999 to bring its measure into conformity with its obligations under the SPS Agreement. For an account of the current status of the dispute see D. Wüger, 'The Implementation Phase in the Dispute Between the EC and the United States on Hormone-Treated Beef', 33 *Law & Pol'y Int'l Bus.* 777 (2002), and for the most recent developments within the Community see Alemanno, 'Judicial Enforcement of the WTO Hormones ruling within the European Community: Toward an EC Liability for the non-implementation of WTO Dispute Settlement Decisions', supra note 44, p 547.

Following this decision, it was unclear how the SPS Agreement, notably its Article 5.7, could effectively accommodate the precautionary principle within the WTO legal system insofar as its invocation would seem to require the same risk assessment prescribed for situations of scientific certainty. This uncertainty was even strengthened by the circumstance that neither the panel not the Appellate Body had the chance to interpret Article 5.7 of the SPS Agreement directly and this to the extent that the EC had not invoked it to justify the measures in dispute.[126] In particular, the AB did not address what constituted 'insufficient scientific evidence' and 'pertinent available information'.

In strict legal terms, the question left open after *Hormones* was whether the relationship between Article 5.1 (risk assessment) and Article 5.7 (precautionary action) is one of exclusion or of general rule-exception. This issue may be aptly summed up by the following question: to what extent should the risk assessment duty imposed by Article 5.1 also apply to measures falling within the scope of Article 5.7?

As has been pointed out, for this provision to be meaningful the threshold for the triggering of the invocation of the principle ('pertinent available information') would have to be lower than those thresholds prevailing elsewhere in the agreement.[127] In particular, 'pertinent available information' had to consist in information which was less authoritative and established under a less methodologically stringent manner than 'scientific evidence', as required by Article 5 SPS.[128] In other words, the 'knowledge' requirement for the triggering of the principle should not have coincided with that prescribed for the adoption of any other SPS measure. This argument could find support in the second sentence of Article 5.7, which, by referring to a *'more objective* assessment of risk', seemed to imply that the risk assessment required by Article 5.1 would have necessarily been different in nature from the kind of risk assessment envisaged in Annex A(4). Finally, it would be unreasonable to require SPS measures adopted on Article 5.7 to satisfy the same scientific discipline applicable to measures which are not enacted 'in cases where relevant scientific evidence is insufficient'.

---

[126] The EC simply stated that the precautionary principle is already ' [...] a general customary rule of international law or at least a general principle of law' and that it applies not solely in the management of risk, but also in the assessment of it. In the light of the above, it claimed that the Panel erred in law in holding that the precautionary principle was only relevant for 'provisional measures' under Article 5.7 SPS. See EC–Hormones AB Report, paras 120–125.

[127] Scott and Vos, 'The Juridification of Uncertainty: Observations of the Ambivalence of the Precautionary Principle within the EU and the WTO', in C. Joerges and R. Dehousse, *Good Governance in Europe's Integrated Market*, 2002, p 279.

[128] J.Bohanes, 'Risk Regulation in WTO Law: A procedure-Based Approach', 40 *Columbia Journal of Transnational Law*, pp 328–29.

It is in the successive *Japan–Agricultural Products* and *Japan–Apples* cases that the exact scope of Article 5.7 has been thoroughly considered and further elaborated. Thus, the principle has been recognised, neither as right per se nor as an exception from a general obligation, but as 'a *qualified* exemption' from the obligation under Article 2.2 SPS not to maintain SPS measures 'without sufficient scientific evidence'. This outcome has been reached to the extent that 'an overly broad and flexible interpretation of that obligation would render Article 5.7 meaningless'[129]. In the first case, Japan claimed that the challenged varietal test – requiring that the efficacy of a quarantine treatment be determined on each variety of fruit – was provisional and therefore compatible with Article 5.7 SPS. The panel found that the contested measure was not only in breach of Article 2.2 but also that it could not fall within the scope of Article 5.7 to the extent Japan had not met the four cumulative requirements imposed by this provision.[130] The four requirements, as defined by the panel, are the following:

a)   the measure has to be imposed in a situation where 'relevant scientific information is insufficient';
b)   the measure has to be adopted 'on the basis of 'available pertinent information';
c)   the member which adopted the measure must 'seek to obtain the additional information necessary for a more objective assessment of risk'; and
d)   the member which adopted the measure must review it within a reasonable period of time.

In particular, in the instant case, there was no evidence that Japan had taken the initiative to seek to obtain the necessary additional information. Moreover, the 11-year interval between the introduction of the Japanese program and the WTO claim exceeded the notion of reasonable delay for reconsidering a temporary measure.[131]

This finding was later upheld by the Appellate Body, which confirmed that these four cumulative requirements have to be met in order to validly invoke the precautionary principle under Article 5.7 SPS.[132] To support this finding, the Appellate Body argued that, as an exception, Article 5.7 SPS should be given a narrow meaning and that, consequently, if one of the requirements is not met, then the measure must be found to be inconsistent with the SPS Agreement.

---

[129] *Japan–Agricultural Products*, AB Report, para 80.
[130] *Japan–Agricultural Products*, AB Report, para 89 and *Japan–Apples*, Appellate Body Report, para 176.
[131] *Japan–Agricultural Products*, AB Report, para 143(b).
[132] Ibid, para 89.

By applying an *a contrario* reasoning to the panel's interpretative approach, one may legitimately come to the conclusion that if Japan had not failed to carry out the affirmative duty to review its varietal testing requirement within a reasonable period of time, the AB would have upheld the Japanese precautionary measure. However, this outcome depends once again on the question of the relationship between Article 5.1 and 5.7. If Article 5.7 may be qualified as a right per se, a precautionary measure which satisfies the four requirements won't be subject to Articles 2.2 and 5.1, whereas if it is an exception to Article 5.1, every time a precautionary measure departs from one of these requirements this will fall under the scope of Articles 2.2 and 5.1.

By qualifying Article 5.7 as a 'qualified exemption' from the scientific discipline, the WTO dispute settlement bodies had not entirely answered this question yet. It is submitted that, provided they comply with the requirements set out by Article 5.7, precautionary measures should be adopted and maintained, though on a provisional basis, even if they do not satisfy the risk assessment requirement imposed by Article 5.1 and defined in Annex A(4). If this approach is not going to be accepted by the WTO courts, the normative value of Article 5.7 would be put at stake. This provision must be read as allowing members to adopt SPS measures which they would normally not be permitted to under Article 5.1.

Among the requirements imposed by the Appellate Body for adopting precautionary action, the first (insufficient scientific evidence), which triggers the invocation of the principle, is without doubt the most controversial. After confirming the need for those four cumulative requirements validly to invoke Article 5.7, the Appellate Body in the *Apples* case mainly addressed the 'insufficiency' requirement.

In *Apples*, it was argued by Japan that its quarantine measures on US apples to protect against risk associated with fire blight,[133] being provisional, were consistent with Article 5.7 because, despite accumulated scientific evidence, 'unresolved uncertainty' remained which science could not solve.[134] The Panel held that Japan could not validly invoke Article 5.7 to justify its measures because, as regards the risk of transmission of fire blight through apple fruit, one could not say that there was insufficient scientific information.[135] It observed that

---

[133] Fire blight is a bacterial disease caused by the bacterium *Erwinia amylovora* and affects plants such as apples, pears, and loquats. See Japan Apples Panel Report, para 2.5.

[134] In reality, Japan relied on Article 5.7 only in the event that the panel rejected Japan's view that 'sufficient scientific evidence' exists to maintain the measure within the meaning of Article 2.2. This explains why the panel assigned the burden of proof to Japan to make a prima facie case in support of its position under Article 5.7. This particular aspect has not been challenged on appeal.

[135] *Japan–Apples* Panel Report, paras 8.221–8.222.

'scientific studies as well as practical experience have accumulated for the past 200 years'[136] on this question and that, in analysing whether Article 2.2 SPS had been respected or not, it had come across an 'important amount of relevant evidence'.[137] Stating that Article 5.7 was 'designed to be invoked in situations where little, or no, evidence was available on the subject matter at issue', the Panel concluded that the measure was not imposed in respect of a situation where relevant scientific evidence is insufficient within the meaning of Article 5.7.[138]

The Appellate Body endorsed this reading of Article 5.7 by confirming that the standard of sufficiency under the first requirement of the test mentioned above refers to the measure of information necessary to perform an adequate assessment of risks as provided for by Article 5.1.[139] In particular, the panel found that, with regard to fire blight 'not only a large quantity but a high quality of scientific evidence has been produced over the years'.[140] Against this backdrop, the AB concluded that this body of available scientific evidence 'permitted, in quantitative and qualitative terms, the performance of an assessment of risk, as required under Article 5.1 and as defined in Annex A to the SPS Agreement, with respect to the risk of transmission of fire blight through apple fruit exported from the United States to Japan'[141] and therefore the 'relevant scientific evidence' is not 'insufficient' within the meaning of Article 5.7 SPS.

The reasoning followed by the Appellate Body in this case carries the potential of diluting the scope of the precautionary principle as it has been conceived, interpreted and applied within the EC, by dramatically obliterating its main precondition: scientific uncertainty.

In rejecting Japan's contentions, according to which Article 5.7 is intended to also address 'unresolved uncertainty', ie uncertainty that the scientific evidence is not able to resolve, despite accumulated scientific evidence',[142] the Appellate Body reduced the scope for precautionary action to 'situations where little, or no, reliable evidence was available on the subject matter at issue'. In particular, the Appellate Body clearly indicated on this point that:

---

[136] Ibid, para 8.219. This is because fire blight was first reported in the USA in 1873, and by the 1890s spread to Canada and Mexico. On the spreading of the disease throughout the world, see *Japan–Apples* AB Report, at para 9.

[137] Ibid, paras 8.216.

[138] Ibid, paras 8.219.

[139] *Japan–Measures Affecting the Importation of Apples* WT/DS245/AB/R AB Report adopted 10 December 2003, para 179.

[140] *Japan–Apples* Panel Report, paras 8.219.

[141] *Japan–Apples*, AB Report, para 182.

[142] Ibid, para 183.

> [...] the application of Article 5.7 is triggered not by the existence of scientific uncertainty, but rather by the *insufficiency of scientific evidence*. The text of Article 5.7 is clear: it refers to 'cases where relevant scientific evidence in insufficient', not to 'scientific uncertainty'. The two concepts are not interchangeable.[143]

This narrow reading of Article 5.7 seems to heavily constrain the margin for precautionary action within the WTO/SPS food safety framework. In fact, this interpretation would rule out from the scope of Article 5.7 all those situations in which, notwithstanding the existence of a 'more than little' quantity of scientific evidence, scientific uncertainty persists. Thus, for instance, the present considerable amount of scientific studies regarding the actual or potential effects of GMOs on human health and on the environment might not be regarded as justifying precautionary action under Article 5.7 of the SPS Agreement.[144]

By shifting the focus of precautionary action from the 'knowledge' requirement ('pertinent available information') to the 'insufficiency', or 'unreliability', condition ('relevant scientific evidence is insufficient'), the AB seems to have considerably altered the scenarios which may justify precautionary action within the WTO.

Following the AB's interpretation of Article 5.7 in the *Apples* case, it has been argued that 'contrary to popular perception, it is not Article 5.7 of the SPS Agreement that allows for a precautionary approach, but the provisions of the Agreement on risk assessment'.[145] According to this view, risk assessment, being a tool for the evaluation of risks, creates by itself tremendous scope for precaution so that Article 5.7 could only have been intended to deal with 'emergency' situations, situations in which there has not yet been the time for scientific research.[146] This interpretation coincides with that proposed by the Community in *EC–Hormones* when it argued that the precautionary principle should be relevant not only for provisional measures under Article 5.7, but should also apply to the risk assessment requirement under Article 5.1.

---

[143] Ibid, para 184.

[144] This issue is touched upon in *EC–Biotech* where the EC has maintained that Member States 'product–specific moratoriums' (safeguards measures authorized by Article 16(1) of Directive 90/220/EC and Article 12(1) of Regulation 258/97) are provisional measures pending a full assessment at EC level and therefore should be assessed under Article 5.7, available at http://www.wto.org/english/news_e/news06_e/ 291r_e.htm. As the EC has exclusive competence on trade in goods, the action has been taken against the EC even if the alleged wrong-doings (national safeguard measures) are perpetrated by the EC Member States. See Article 133 EC.

[145] D.A. Motaal, 'Is the World Trade Organization Anti-Precaution?', *Journal of World Trade*, 39(3), p 496.

[146] Ibid, p 496.

Although this interpretation of Article 5.7 may find some support in the negotiating history of the SPS Agreement,[147] there are some doubts about whether it will be confirmed by the upcoming WTO judicial bodies' decisions. This is so because the AB's reasoning is so decidedly non-definitive that it is not, accordingly, possible to say whether it represents a veritable, and definitive, dismissal of scientific uncertainty from the WTO/SPS legal system.

This narrow interpretation of Article 5.7 would also seem to conflict with the definition of precautionary action contained in the Cartagena Protocol on Biosafety to the Convention on Biological Diversity.[148] In particular, Article 10.6 of this protocol refers to 'lack of scientific certainty due to insufficient relevant scientific information and knowledge' as the basis for taking precautionary action. According to this view, precautionary action would be justified every time 'the insufficient scientific information' would give rise to 'scientific uncertainty'. This may, in turn, be due to two different circumstances: either *after* having conducted a risk assessment there is still a lack of scientific certainty about the potential effect stemming from living modified organisms (LMOs) or *before* conducting a risk assessment there is not enough information to conduct a risk assessment. According to the AB's interpretation of Article 5.7, precautionary action would be allowed solely in the latter situation.[149]

Although the Biosafety Protocol rules out *expressis verbis* its supremacy over the WTO Agreements, by denying its status of *lex specialis* among international trade sources of law,[150] it is not excluded that WTO judicial bodies may refer to the protocol in order to draw inspiration for the interpretation of Article 5.7 SPS.[151] In fact, this outcome is not excluded insofar as the same Appellate Body stated, in the first case that came before it, that:

[147] Marceau and Trachtman, supra note 3, p 848, footnote 143 reporting a discussion with G. Stanton, Secretary of the SPS Committee.
[148] Cartagena protocol on Biosafety to the Convention on Biological Diversity, supra note 263. For an overview on the relationship between the Protocol and the WTO, see O. Rivera-Torres, 'The Biosafety Protocol and the WTO', in 26 *Boston College International & Comparative Law Review*.
[149] S. Zarrilli, 'International Trade in GMOs and GM Products: National and Multilateral Legal Frameworks', *Policy Issues in International Trade and Commodities, Study Series* No. 29, UNCTAD, p 33.
[150] See preamble of the Biosafety Protocol where it is stated: '[...] this Protocol should not be interpreted as implying a change in the rights and obligations of a Party under any existing international agreements'.
[151] For a more elaborated version of this argument as applicable to the *EC–Biotech* dispute, WT/DS293/1, see L. Boisson de Chazournes and M.M. Mbengue, 'GMOs and Trade: Issues at Stake in the EC Biotech Dispute', in *RECIEL*, 13(3), 2004, pp 298–99; see, also, S. Zarrilli, 'International Trade in GMOs and GM Products: National and Multilateral Legal Frameworks', supra note 149, p 38.

> [...] the General Agreement is not to be read in clinical isolation
> from public international law.[152]

Therefore, to the extent the disputing WTO Parties have ratified the existing Biosafety Protocol they may rely on it as a useful tool for interpreting WTO members' obligations, for instance, their right to take action in the face of scientific uncertainty under Article 5.7 SPS.[153]

In conclusion, the review of allegedly precaution-based measures has witnessed some reticence on the part of the WTO judicial bodies in recognising the application of the precautionary principle within the WTO/SPS legal system. Precautionary action is not solely perceived as 'a qualified exemption' to the scientific evidence regime imposed by Article 2.2 and 5.5 but it is also rigorously constrained by a set of demanding criteria.[154] In other words, both the panels and the Appellate Body seem to privilege measures addressing 'scientifically identifiable risks' rather than those facing 'uncertain risks'.

The reasons explaining the WTO courts' reluctance in expressly endorsing the precautionary principle may be found in the following excerpt:

> [...] the requirements of a risk assessment under Article 5(1), as well as of 'sufficient scientific evidence' under Article 2(2), are essential for the maintenance of the delicate and carefully negotiated balance in the SPS Agreement between the shared, but sometimes competing, interests of promoting international trade and protecting the life and health of human beings.[155]

To reconcile this statement with the inherently uncertain circumstances underlying the invocation of the precautionary principle does not seem an easy task for any WTO expert.

The challenge behind the acceptance of the precautionary principle within the WTO/SPS system is to prove that risk assessment (Article 5.1) and precaution (Article 5.7) are entirely compatible and that they may play complementary roles in the process of decision-making. It will be shown in part IV that the identification of a minimum scientific threshold that each scientific study must satisfy under Article 5.1 may somehow reconcile the scientific uncertainty inherent to precautionary action with the legal certainty required by a legal system.

---

[152] *United States–Standards for Reformulated and Conventional Gasoline*, AB Report, WT/DS2/AB/R, para 19.

[153] S. Zarrilli, 'International Trade in GMOs and GM Products: National and Multilateral Legal Frameworks, Policy Issues in International Trade and Commodities', supra note 149, p 38.

[154] *Japan–Agricultural Products*, Appellate Body Report, para 80.

[155] *EC–Hormones*, Appellate Body Report, para 177.

8. Notification and Transparency Requirements

Article 7 and Annex B to the SPS Agreement deal with transparency of SPS measures. The objective of these provisions is to enable interested members to become acquainted with all newly adopted SPS measures. Under Article 7 WTO members have a duty to notify to the SPS Committee all new SPS measures, and all modifications to existing measures that do not conform to international standards and that produce a significant effect on international trade. Notifications aim to make traders or the regulatory authorities in their countries aware of new legislation that may have a significant effect on trade so that they can have access and, if appropriate, submit comments.[156] Between 1995 and 2001, members submitted more than 2,400 SPS notifications to the WTO, far more than those submitted under the GATT obligations.[157]

Annex B provides that WTO members promptly publish all SPS measures that they adopt and provide an explanation of the reasons for these measures upon request. members are then directed, except in urgent circumstances, to allow a reasonable period of time between the publication of the SPS measure and its implementation.

Paragraph 3 of Annex B specifically imposes on WTO members the requirement to ensure that one 'enquiry point' exists that provides answers to all reasonable questions from interested WTO members as well as supplying all relevant documents.[158]

A footnote to Annex B, paragraph 1, specifies that the publication requirement extends to include 'SPS measures such as laws, decrees or ordinances which are applicable generally'. This provision has been interpreted extensively by the *Japan–Agricultural Products* panel which stated that: '[...] nowhere does the wording of this paragraph require such measures to be mandatory or legally enforceable [...]. This context indicates that a non-mandatory government measure is also subject to WTO provisions in the event compliance with its measure is necessary to obtain an advantage from a government or, in other words, if sufficient incentives or disincentives exist for that measure to be abided by'.[159] This finding was upheld by the Appellate Body in the same case, where it also said that this publishing requirement goes beyond '[...] laws,

---

[156] The number of notifications continues to increase. The incorporation to the SPS Agreement of China and other regional trading blocs has also led to an increase in notifications.

[157] T. Jostling, D. Roberts and D. Orden, *Food Regulation and Trade, Toward a Safe and Open Global System* (Institute for International Economics, Washington DC, 2004) pp 63–68.

[158] Unit SANCO/E03 (International Food, Veterinary and Phytosanitary Questions) is responsible for running the obligations of both the EC SPS Notification Authority (NA) and Enquiry Point (EP).

[159] *Japan–Agricultural Products*, Panel Report, para 8.111.

decrees or ordinances, but also includes [...] other instruments which are applicable generally and similar in character'.[160]

9. The SPS Committee

The SPS Agreement establishes a committee, the so-called SPS Committee, to monitor and review food safety measures, notably international harmonisation activities, by coordinating this effort with the 'relevant international organisations', which presumably include the Codex, IPPC and OIE.[161]

The committee not only ensures a correct implementation of the agreement by examining compliance issues, but it also provides a forum for information exchange and discussion on issues affecting trade in food. This committee, open to all WTO members, normally meets three times a year, with informal or special meetings.

In conformity with Article 12.4 SPS the committee has adopted, through time, procedures to monitor the use of international standards.

The role of this committee relies heavily upon the Codex, IPPC and OIE's activities. The committee is expected to work with the 'relevant international organisations' to develop a list of international standards, guidelines and recommendations that affect international trade.[162]

---

[160] *Japan–Agricultural Products*, Appellate Body Report, para 105.
[161] Article 3.5 SPS.
[162] Article 12, paragraph 4, provides that: '[t]he Committee shall develop a procedure to monitor the process of international harmonization and the use of international standards, guidelines or recommendations. For this purpose, the Committee should, in conjunction with the relevant international organisations, establish a list of international standards, guidelines or recommendations relating to sanitary or phytosanitary measures which the Committee determines to have a major trade impact. The list should include an indication by Members of those international standards, guidelines or recommendations which they apply as conditions for import or on the basis of which imported products conforming to these standards can enjoy access to their markets. For those cases in which a Member does not apply an international standard, guideline or recommendation as a condition for import, the Member should provide an indication of the reason therefore, and, in particular, whether it considers that the standard is not stringent enough to provide the appropriate level of sanitary or phytosanitary protection. If a Member revises its position, following its indication of the use of a standard, guideline or recommendation as a condition for import, it should provide an explanation for its change and so inform the Secretariat as well as the relevant international organisations, unless such notification and explanation is given according to the procedures of Annex B'.

PART III: JUDICIAL REVIEW OF FOOD SAFETY MEASURES WITHIN THE EC AND THE WTO

INTRODUCTION

Whereas the first two parts of this book provide an in-depth analysis of the food safety regulatory disciplines existing within the EC and in the WTO, Part III completes this analysis by examining how these frameworks have been judicially reviewed by their respective courts. In particular, while chapter I looks at the role played by science in the EC and WTO food disciplines, by focusing on the evolution of the so-called risk regulations, chapter II focuses on the issue of judicial review of science-based measures in both legal orders. After having analysed the WTO expert consultation practice, it lastly formulates some proposals aimed at reorienting the role of the WTO and EU judicial bodies in order to make them less involved with science when reviewing science-based measures.

As seen above, at the time of the negotiation of the SPS Agreement, rather than relying solely on discrimination to identify illegitimate health regulations, members decided to choose a neutral-value criterion such as scientific evidence. Similarly, the EC courts, followed by the EC legislator, quite soon began to refer to science as the main organising criterion allowing distinction to be drawn between legitimate and illegitimate health measures. The logic of the scientific requirement is easy to understand. If a regulation aimed at protecting public health is not supported by scientific evidence proving the danger to be avoided by means of that regulation, then the suspicion may legitimately arise that the regulation disguises protectionist intent. At the same time, however, the introduction of a scientific discipline may also cause difficulties for regulators who genuinely have legitimate non-protectionist intentions.

In the light of the above, the challenge is, when interpreting the scientific discipline, to reconcile its primary goal of spotting sham health regulations with Member States' recognised right to pursue the level of protection they deem appropriate for their society.

In doing so, it is crucial to bear in mind that, while the goal of the judicial process is the 'particularised resolution of legal disputes' the goal of science is epistemic, ie to achieve 'cosmic understanding'.[1] Hence, unlike law, science by its nature tends to be highly tentative and, accordingly, somewhat inconclusive. As a result, persuasive evidence of certain types

---

[1] *Daubert v Merrell Dow Pharmaceuticals, Inc,* 509 US 579 (1993).

of risk, especially those surrounded by scientific uncertainty, may be difficult to generate. As a result, 'in the face of such scientific uncertainty, scientific evidence requirements may stand in the way of honest regulatory efforts to manage risk'.[2]

Yet, since both the WTO and the EC require the presence of detailed scientific justification to determine the legitimacy of national (and supranational) food safety regulations to avoid disguised forms of protectionism,[3] their courts are increasingly called upon to review the scientific soundness (whether a scientific justification exists) of these measures, when assessing their legality.

But how may a judge, generally a non-scientist, assess whether a given measure has a sound scientific basis? What degree of scrutiny does a judge exercise, lawfully and practically, over the food regulations he is called upon to review? These are but some of the questions addressed in this part of the book.

These questions are currently sources of endless controversy in the international legal arena[4] and are at the centre of some international trade disputes.[5]

Answers to these questions are relevant to the extent that they determine not only the immediate outcome of some legal disputes, but also how much regulatory autonomy WTO and EC members enjoy in regulating to protect the health of their people, notably by adopting food safety regulations. This final question is obviously more sensitive within the WTO framework than within the EC, where not only EC courts have more adjudicatory power, but also Member States have transferred regulatory competences to the EC.

Chapter I provides an overview of the scientific justification disciplines existing within the EC and the WTO by summing up the main obligations imposed by their food safety risk regulation regimes. After a brief

---

[2] A.O. Sykes, 'Domestic Regulation, Sovereignty and Scientific Evidence Requirements: A Pessimistic View', G. Bermann and P.C. Mavroidis (eds), *Trade and Human Health and Safety* (Cambridge University Press, 2006) p 258.

[3] The broad area of public health measures is unique for the moment in its explicit invocation of scientific and quasi-scientific notions, such as the elements identifying their correctness.

[4] See C.D. Ehlermann, 'Six Years on the Bench of the "World Trade Court"', in 36 J. *World Trade* (2002) 605, pp. 612-13, who, when leaving the organ, noted that 'during the last months, the question of standard of review has thus become one of the most controversial aspects of the Appellate Body's jurisprudence'.

[5] See, for instance, the *Biotech* dispute between the US, Canada, Argentina and the EC regarding the European alleged general moratoria (the product specific moratoria and the national bans) on the importation of genetically modified organisms.

introduction to the issue of judicial review in both legal systems, the following chapter focuses notably on the standards of review applied by the EC and WTO courts to science-based measures. It then sketches out the level of scientific involvement required from the respective courts.

CHAPTER I
RISK REGULATIONS IN EC AND WTO LAW

1.   The EC and Scientific Justification

As the analysis of the current food safety regime has shown, scientific evidence is becoming crucial at all stages of the drawing up of new legislation and for the execution and management of existing European and national legislation, especially for national regulations derogating from European disciplines. The use of science as one of the sources of evidence to support decision-making is not limited to the food safety field, but it is relevant in a wide range of other policy areas, such as emission limits,[1] chemicals,[2] biocides,[3] GMOs,[4] pesticides,[5] food additives,[6] water protection,[7] consumer protection and worker safety and health.[8]

---

[1] See, eg, Council Directive 1999/30/EC of 22 April 1999 relating to limit values for sulphur dioxide, nitrogen dioxide and oxides of nitrogen, particulate matter and lead in ambient air and Directive 2001/80/EC of the European Parliament and of the Council of 23 October 2001 on the limitation of emissions of certain pollutants into the air from large combustion plants, OJ L 309 of 27 November 2001.

[2] Risk assessment of existing chemicals is provided by Council Regulation 793/93 and Commission Regulation 1488/94. As for new chemicals, risk assessment procedures are imposed by Commission Directive 93/67/EEC laying down the principles for assessment of risks to man and the environment of substances notified in accordance with Directive 67/548/EEC. See also Proposal for a Regulation of the European Parliament and of the Council concerning the Registration, Evaluation, Authorisation and Restriction of Chemicals (Reach), establishing a European Chemicals Agency and amending Directive 1999/45/EC and Regulation (EC) COM/2003/0644 final.

[3] Directive 98/08/EC concerning the placing of biocides on the market.

[4] See Articles 4(1) and (2) of Directive 2001/18/EC on the deliberate release of GMOs. Moreover, under Article 8 of the Regulation 258/97, a novel food or food ingredient is considered to be 'equivalent' to its conventional counterpart unless established risk assessment techniques can prove that this is not the case.

[5] Directive 91/414/EEC concerning the placing of plant protection products on the market. See also the 1998 Rotterdam PIC Convention which requires a 'risk evaluation' as a precondition for regulatory action.

[6] Directive 89/107/EEC concerning food additives authorized for use in foodstuffs intended for human consumption according to which the food additive must be subjected to appropriate testing and evaluation.

[7] See Article 16(2) of Directive 2000/60/EC establishing a framework for Community action in the field of water policy.

[8] Directive 80/1107/EEC on the protection of workers from the risks related to exposure to chemicals, physical and biological agents; Directive 89/391/EEC on the introduction of measures to encourage the improvements in the safety and health of workers at work; Directive 90/391/EEC on the protection of workers from the risks related to exposure to carcinogens at work.

1.1   The Origins

Originally, the 1957 Treaty of Rome did not impose, either on the EC institutions or on Member States, a duty to justify their health, safety and environmental protection measures scientifically. Indeed, its text did not contain any reference to scientific justification.

However, as Member States began invoking Article 36 (current Article 30) of the Treaty of the European Community, allowing them to adopt restrictions on trade justified inter alia on grounds of protection of health,[9] they often submitted scientific evidence to the European Court of Justice in order to demonstrate that their measures were covered under this exception. Thus, in the *Beer Purity* case[10], Germany, after having banned the marketing of beer containing *all* additives (not just some additives for which there was evidence of risks),[11] tried to justify its measure by arguing not only that Germans drank a lot of beer (sic) but also that the long-term effects of additives were unknown. To support its scientific claim, Germany also cited experts' reports referring to the risk inherent in the ingestion of additives in general[12]. In the same case, not only the parties but also the court hinted at the scientific element. The ECJ, referring to the previously decided *Sandoz*,[13] *Motte*[14] and *Muller*[15] judgments, held that the possibility for a Member State to restrict the free movement of a foodstuff legally marketed in another Member States is subject to 'the *findings of international research*, and, in particular, the work of the Community's scientific committee for food, the Codex alimentarius committee of the FAO and the World Health Organization'.[16] After having deferentially referred to the scientific findings of these entities, the court found that not only did the additives not present a risk to public health but also that the German policy was inconsistent

[9] See supra Part I, Chapter 1, Section 1. The exceptions: Article 30 EC. While Article 28 prohibits Member States adopting quantitative restrictions on imports and all measures having an equivalent effect to a quantitative restriction, Article 30 'shall not preclude prohibitions or restrictions on imports, exports or goods in transit justified on grounds of public morality, public policy or public security; the protection of health and life of humans, animals or plants; the protection of national treasures possessing artistic, historic or archaeological value; or the protection of industrial and commercial property'.
[10] Case 178/84, *Commission v Germany* [1987] ECR 1227.
[11] According to the Reinheitsgebot (the German beer purity law), originally enacted in 1516 by the Bavarian duke Wilhelm IV, only beer containing the following ingredients could be marketed on the German territory: water, hops, barley and yeast.
[12] Case 178/84, *Commission v Germany* [1987] ECR 1227, para 48.
[13] Case 174/82, *Sandoz BV* [1983], ECR 2445, para 214. In this case, the court had to face a Dutch refusal to grant authorisation for the importation of muesli bars with added vitamins from Germany (where they were lawfully sold). For a comment of this case, see M.M. Slotboom, 'Do Public Health Measures Receive Similar Treatment in European Community and World Trade Organization Law?', *Journal of World Trade* (2003) 553, p 557.
[14] Case 247/84 *Motte* [1985] ECR 3887. This case concerned the import of lumpfish roe prepared with colorants banned in Belgium but allowed in the country of export.
[15] Case 304/84 *Ministère Public v Muller and Others* [1986] ECR 1511.
[16] Case 178/84, *Commission v Germany* [1987] ECR 1227, para 44.

insofar as it allowed the use of these same additives in other drinks. References to 'the findings of international scientific research, and in particular of the work of the Community's Scientific Committee for Food, the Codex Alimentarius Committee of the Food and Agriculture Organization of the United Nations (FAO) and the World Health Organization' may also be found in subsequent judgments, such as *Bellon*[17] and *Debus*,[18] both involving national measures restricting the use of additives. In *KYDEP*, involving the Community rules governing the maximum levels of radioactive contamination permissible in foodstuffs following the Chernobyl nuclear accident, the ECJ has even referred not only to 'the opinions of national experts on radioactivity and foodstuffs, the recommendations of the International Commission on Radiological Protection (ICRP)' but even to 'the instructions of the US Food and Drug Administration'.[19]

Yet, whilst Member States must respect the findings of these international scientific organisations, the court allows departure from them insofar as there is some scientific uncertainty.[20] As more and more judgments show, the EC courts' reliance on scientific assessment when reviewing secondary law is current practice today.

Thus, without being formally introduced within the Rome Treaty, a de facto scientific requirement imposed itself in the regulatory practice developed around Articles 28–30 EC as applied to food regulations. While the court recognised that the ' health and the life of humans rank foremost among the property interests protected by Article 30',[21] it was suspicious of Member States' attempts to invoke health reasons as a means of affording a disguised restriction on trade. In particular, it established that, although not binding, the scientific opinions prepared by the Scientific Committee on Foodstuffs had to be taken into account by Member States while considering the approval or refusal of the circulation of a product on their markets.

It was only in 1999 that scientific justification was expressly inserted into Article 95, paragraph 5, as one of the requirements Member States must satisfy in order to *introduce* a measure derogating from European harmonisation legislation.[22] In particular, a Member State that deems it

---

[17] Case C-42/90 *Bellon* [1990] ECR 4863, at 14.

[18] Case C-13/91 and C-113/91, *Debus* [1992] ECR 3617, at 17.

[19] Case C-146/91 *Koinopraxia Enóséon Georgikon Synetairismon Diacheiríséos Enchorion Proïonton Syn. PE (KYDEP) v Council and Commission*, [1994] ECR 4199, at 42.

[20] Case 247/84 *Motte* [1985] ECR 3887; Case 174/82, *Sandoz BV* [1983] ECR 2445.

[21] Case 104/75 *De Peijper* [1976] ECR 613, para 15, and Case C-320/93 *Ortscheit* [1994] ECR 5243, at 16.

[22] According to Article 95, paragraph 5, 'if, after the adoption by the Council or by the Commission of a harmonisation measure, a Member State deems it necessary to introduce

(continued...)

necessary to introduce a national measure aimed at the protection of the environment after the adoption of a Community measure on the matter, must provide 'new scientific evidence'. It is controversial as to whether this evidence must have necessarily been elaborated after the adoption of the Community measure or could have merely been unknown to the Community legislator at the time of the adoption.[23]

Although a similar scientific requirement is not expressly provided with reference to the situation where a Member State does *maintain* a measure derogating from a harmonised measure (Article 95, par. 4),[24] it has recently been stated that a:

> Member State may, in order to justify maintaining such derogating national provisions, put forward the fact that its assessment of the risk to public health is different from that made by the Union legislature in the harmonisation measure.[25]

Therefore, although the risk assessment provided by the interested party does not have to be 'necessarily [...] based on new or different scientific evidence', the reference made to 'its assessment of the risk' would also seem to introduce a scientific justification test in this specific scenario.[26] In particular, this is the conclusion one may reasonably reach after having read the court's statement according to which, to comply with Article 95, para. 4:

> [...] it falls to the applicant Member State to prove that those national provisions ensure a level of health protection which is higher than the EC harmonisation measure and that they do not go beyond what is necessary to attain that objective.[27]

Thus, as it would be particularly difficult, if not impossible, to satisfy such a heightened burden by not relying on scientific evidence, a scientific requirement is also de facto imposed within the context of the application of paragraph 4 of Article 95.

---

national provisions based on new scientific evidence relating to the protection of the environment or the working environment on grounds of a problem specific to that Member State arising after the adoption of the harmonisation measure, it shall notify the Commission of the envisaged provisions as well as the grounds for introducing them'.

[23] See, on this point, Commission Decision 1999/830/EC on the Danish request for derogation on the use of of sulphites, nitrites and nitrates in foodstuffs, OJ 1999 L392/1.

[24] The ECJ in Case 3/00, *Denmark v Commission*, [2003] ECR 2643, has stated that 'the requirement for new scientific evidence [...] is not one of the conditions imposed for maintaining such provisions' (Article 95, para. 4 EC).

[25] Ibid, at 63.

[26] Contra, N. De Sadeleer, 'The Precautionary Principle in EC Health and Environmental Law', 12 *European Law Journal*, p 106.

[27] Ibid, p 64.

In conclusion, Member States must today scientifically justify their measures not only when they act outside of a harmonised area, relying on Article 30 ECT, but also when, after the adoption of a harmonisation measure, they deem it necessary to maintain or introduce a national provision derogating from the European one. However, to discourage Member States from adopting diverging national standards susceptible to the restriction of free movement within the internal market, the EC legislation has been setting very high standards of health and environmental protection.[28] Accordingly, as seen above, should a Member State seek to introduce, or maintain, a national provision setting up a stricter or a higher level of protection than that attained by the EC legislation, its measure should be 'based on new scientific evidence'.[29] It follows that an embryonic and 'de facto' scientific discipline has evolved through time to resist national protectionism, thereby permitting the establishment of the internal market.

In the meanwhile, the scientific justification discipline originally developed in relation to Member State measures based on public health had been extended to the acts adopted by the European institutions. In 1997, when the aim of achieving a 'high level' of health and environmental protection was given the status of a general objective in the EC Treaty (Article 3(1) (p)), Article 100a (current 95 EC) was amended in order to specify that this objective should be pursued and based on 'scientific facts'.[30] It must be observed that, already in the late 1970s, the ECJ's case law established that the Treaty prohibitions on restriction on free trade within the Union not only applied to Member States but also to the EC itself.[31] In other words, a Community measure enacted on the basis of one of the Treaty articles concerning the realisation of the internal market, such as Article 95 EC, must be in conformity with the prohibitions concerning free movement. However, insofar as the EC health measures are non-discriminatory, these should not be prohibited and thus fall outside the scope of Article 28–30 ECT regardless of whether they have a negative effect on trade between Member States[32]. It is

---

[28] Christoforou, 'Science, Law and Precaution in Dispute Resolution on Health and Environmental Protection: What Role for Scientific Experts?', in J. Bourrinet et S. Maljean-Dubois (eds), *Le Commerce International des Organismes Génétiquement Modifiés* (2003), p 239.
[29] Article 95, paragraph 5, EC.
[30] Article 100a(3) of EC, current Article 95, paragraph 3.
[31] Case 80-81/77 *Ramel* [1978] ECR 927 followed by Case 179/78 Rivoira [1979] ECR 1147; Case 218/82, *Commission v Council* (rum quotas) [1983] ECR 4063;Case 15/83 Denkavit [1984] ECR 2171 and Case 216/84, *Commision v France* [1988] ECR 793; Case C-47/90, *Delhaize* [1992] ECR I-3669; Case C-388/95, *Belgium v Spain* 2000 ECR I-3123. For a systematic approach to the relationship between primary and secondary law in the context of the internal market, see K. Mortelmans, 'The Relationship Between the Treaty Rules and Community Measures for the Establishment and Functioning of the Internal Market – Towards a Concordance Rule', 39 *Common Market Law Review*, pp 1303-1346 (2002).
[32] This is a controversial point since the court has not as yet explicitly dealt with the question whether the prohibitions are more limited vis-à-vis the EC legislature as compared with the

(continued...)

submitted that, nowadays, with the scientific requirement being expressly imposed on the Community institutions, the privileged status of EC legislation in relation to the scientific element has disappeared.[33]

1.2 The Codification of the Scientific Justification Requirements: from Scientific Evidence to Risk Assessment

Thus, since 1999, when the Amsterdam Treaty entered into force, all Community legislation concerning health, safety and environmental protection and consumer protection (including food regulations) should aim at achieving a high level of protection by 'taking account in particular of any development based in scientific facts'.[34] Notably, EC policy on the environment aiming at a high level of protection should 'take account of available scientific and technical data'.[35] This is because the Commission intends 'to use this advice for the benefit of the consumer in order to ensure a high level of protection of health'.[36] As the Commission has pointed out in its 1997 Communication on Consumer Health and Food Safety:

> [...] scientific evidence is of the utmost importance at all stages of the drawing up of new legislation and for the execution and management of existing legislation.[37]

Recently, scientific justification has been expressly defined as 'an essential requirement for Commission proposals, decisions and policy' relating to consumer safety, public health and the environment.[38] To fulfil its function, scientific advice on matters relating to consumer health must be based on the principles of excellence, independence and transparency.[39]

These are the only references contained in the Treaty laying down a general duty for the EC and the national decision-makers to provide for

Member States. For an apparently limited interpretation see, for instance, Case C-180/96 *UK v Commission* [1996] ECR 3903. On this point see also R. Barents, *The Agricultural Law of the EC*, 1994, pp 20-21. Contra, Mortelmans, supra note 31, p 1322.

[33] This would seem to be especially true after joined cases C-154/04 and 155/04 *National Alliance for Health* [2005] not yet reported.

[34] Article 95, paragraph 3, EC. See also, Articles 152 (1) and (4), 153, 174 (2).

[35] Article 174, paragraph 3, EC.

[36] Communication from the Commission on Consumer Health and Food Safety, COM(97) 183 final.

[37] Ibid.

[38] See Commission Decision of 3 March 2004 setting up Scientific Committees in the field of consumer safety, public health and the environment, recital 6 of the Preamble.

[39] Communication from the Commission on Consumer Health and Food Safety, supra note 36, and Commission Communication on the precautionary principle, COM (2000) 1, 2 February 2000.

scientific justification when adopting legislation concerning consumer safety, public health and the environment.[40] However, as seen in the food sector, this mandatory requirement to base regulations on science has been extended to all secondary legislation regulating risk.[41] More precisely, the scientific justification requirement has developed in greater detail not only in the food safety regulations but in all risk-related secondary legislation, thus evolving into a better defined risk assessment requirement. As seen above, risk assessment represents the first step of the traditional structured approach to risk analysis and consists of a scientifically based process, which in turn, is based on four stages: hazard identification, hazard characterisation, exposure assessment and risk characterisation.[42]

Nowadays, risk assessment procedures can be found not only in food safety but also in areas such as worker health and safety,[43] chemicals,[44] medicinal products, GMOs,[45] biocides,[46] contaminants, pesticides,[47] food additives,[48] water protection,[49] etc.

As noted above, the European Union being a WTO member together with its Member States, it is also subject to those further scientific constraints set by the WTO/SPS Agreement. Under this legal framework,

---

[40] It has also to be noted that the Treaty, although establishing a risk assessment duty, does not define the subjects who must be in charge of such an assessment, by thus leaving open the question on whether the risk assessors must be distinguished from those who have to decide if and how to act. In other words, the Treaty does not set forth a complete risk analysis model aimed at defining the role of those involved in such an analysis.

[41] Christoforou, supra note 28, p 240.

[42] See, eg, Article 3 of the general food regulation.

[43] Directive 80/1107/EEC on the protection of workers from the risks related to exposure to chemicals, physical and biological agents; Directive 89/391/EEC on the introduction of measures to encourage the improvements in the safety and health of workers at work; Directive 90/391/EEC on the protection of workers from the risks related to exposure to carcinogens at work.

[44] Risk assessment of existing chemicals is provided by Council Regulation 793/93 and Commission Regulation 1488/94. As for new chemicals, risk assessment procedures are imposed by Commission Directive 93/67/EEC laying down the principles for assessment of risks to man and the environment of substances notified in accordance with Directive 67/548/EEC. See also Proposal for a Regulation of the European Parliament and of the Council concerning the Registration, Evaluation, Authorisation and Restriction of Chemicals (Reach), establishing a European Chemicals Agency and amending Directive 1999/45/EC and Regulation (EC) COM/2003/0644 final.

[45] See Articles 4(1) and (2) of Directive 2001/18/EC on the deliberate release of GMOs.

[46] Directive 98/08/EC concerning the placing of biocides on the market.

[47] The 1998 Rotterdam PIC Convention refers to 'risk evaluation' as a precondition for regulatory action.

[48] Directive 89/107/EEC concerning food additives authorized for use in foodstuffs intended for human consumption according to which the food additive must be subjected to appropriate testing and evaluation.

[49] See Article 16(2) of Directive 2000/60/EC establishing a framework for Community action in the field of water policy.

measures to protect the health and life of humans, animals and plants must be based on a scientific risk assessment and not maintained without sufficient scientific evidence. Moreover, international standards must be followed unless there is a scientific justification for a more stringent measure.

1.3   The Use of Scientific Evidence within the EC

EC institutions' efforts to improve the quality and the credibility of the scientific data they rely upon in the decision-making process have not been limited to the food safety area. Thus, besides EFSA, a risk assessment agency for medicines (EMEA) has also been established.[50] Furthermore, the whole Scientific Advisory Committee structure has been reorganised and new committees have been established.[51] Finally, policies and guidelines for the use of scientific advisors have been developed by the EC Commission. Notably, this growing scientific advice policy is contained in three main documents: the Science and Society Action Plan (2002), the Commission Communication on the Collection and Use of Expertise (2002),[52] and the Commission Decision to set up Scientific Committees in the Fields of Consumer Safety, Public Health and the Environment (2004).[53] These documents impose 'sound and timely science' as an essential requirement for risk management in the areas of consumer safety, public health and the environment and they recommend a set of guiding 'core principles' for the collection and use of scientific expertise by the Commission departments: quality, openness, effectiveness, independence, pluralism, excellence, impartiality, proportionality and transparency.

Notwithstanding these institutional and normative efforts, there is currently no common system providing scientific advice to the EC policy-makers. Rather, scientific support is ensured through a range of different mechanisms, depending on the relevant policy area.

The most common sources of advice used to support EC policies, legislation and regulatory decisions are the following: formal scientific committees under the control of the Commission Health and Consumer Protection Directorate General (DG SANCO), scientific committees

---

[50] Council Regulation (EEC) No 2309/93 of 22 July 1993 laying down Community procedures for the authorisation and supervision of medicinal products for human and veterinary use and establishing a European Agency for the Evaluation of Medicinal Products, OJ L 214 of 24 August 1993.
[51] The Scientific Committee on Consumer Products (SCCP); the Scientific Committee on Health and Environmental Risks (SCHER) and the Scientific Committee on Emerging and Newly Identified Health Risks (SCENIHR).
[52] European Commission, COM(2002) 713 final of 11 December 2002.
[53] European Commission, Decision 2004/210/EC of 3 March 2004, OJ L 66/45.

within EFSA and EMEA; reports by advisory agencies, such as the European Environmental Agency (EEA); reports provided by external consultants (individuals, groups or companies, possibly using study contracts); national reports provided by Member States' advisory bodies; reports by ad hoc expert groups; in-house analysis conducted by Commission officials; reports and opinions by the Joint Research Centre (JRC) and the Scientific and Technical Options Assessment group in the European Parliament (STOA).

It is in light of the above that, since 2000, some efforts have been aimed at setting up a harmonised approach to risk assessment procedures among the Scientific Committees advising the European Commission in the area of human, animal and plant health and on the environment.[54] The risk analysis sketched out by Regulation 178/2002 constitutes without doubt the main source of inspiration for the drawing up of these general guidelines. Moreover, in order to promote some consistency in the delivery of advice from so many different sources of expertise, the abovementioned Commission Communication on the Collection and Use of Expertise established a set of core principles and guidelines applicable to all expertise intervening at all stages of Commission policy-making. Thus, whenever the Commission departments collect and use advice of experts coming from outside the responsible department they should ensure quality, by seeking advice from an appropriately high quality source (ie excellence, independent and pluralism), by showing flexibility when looking for advice, and effectiveness, by making sure that its methods for collecting and use of expert advice are effective.[55] However, these principles and guidelines are not legally binding. Nor do they apply to the formal stages of decision-making as provided by the Treaty and in other EC legislation. Therefore, not only the formal legislative procedures but also the formal exercise of the Commission's implementing powers through the 'comitology' committees are excluded.

1.4 Conclusions

While the EC case law has made it clear since the 1970s that, in the absence of Community harmonisation, any national measure purporting to regulate risk should be based on scientific evidence and respect proportionality,[56] it is only since 1999 that European harmonised risk

[54] According to the Updated Opinion of the Scientific Steering Committee on Harmonisation of Risk Assessment Procedures, adopted on 10-11 April 2003, a full Second Report on the Harmonisation of Risk Assessment Procedures is currently under editing and will be published shortly.
[55] European Commission, COM(2002) 713 final of 11 December 2002, at 8–10.
[56] T. Christoforou, 'The Precautionary Principle, Risk Assessment, and the Comparative Role of Science in the European Community and the US Legal Systems', in N. J. Vig and M.G. Faure (eds), *Green Giants? Environmental Policies of the United States and the European Union* (MIT Press, 2004) pp 31 ss.

regulations have explicitly been subject to similar constraints. According to Article 95, para. 3 ECT, EC health and environmental protection regulations must take 'as a base a high level of protection, taking account in particular of any new development based on scientific facts'. In particular, the 'elaboration of polices and measures with an impact on health must from the outset take account of, and be coherent with, public health policies'.[57] By making health requirements a constituent part of the Community's other policies, this provision plays a crucial role in extending the scientific discipline beyond the public health domain.

As to the harmonised areas, similarly to what happen within the WTO context with reference to international standards, when a Member State wants to achieve (by maintaining or by introducing a national measure) a level of protection which is higher than that ensured by the EC harmonisation measure, it has to base its provision on scientific evidence. Furthermore, this mandatory requirement to base regulation on science has been extended not only to food safety regulations but also to all secondary legislation regulating risk, which contain detailed provisions on how to conduct a risk assessment in the different policy areas, such as dangerous substances, medicinal products, contaminants, pesticides, GMOs, food additives etc. As has been argued, 'in the EC legal system, regulatory action is nearly always based on a risk assessment of the highest possible quality'.[58] This is crucial, not only to satisfy consumer protection interests and to bolster the EC's legitimacy vis-à-vis its citizens, but also to prevent Member States from systematically relying on Article 95 safeguard clauses, thus disrupting the functioning of the internal market. In fact, where a Member with stringent standards is not satisfied with a less strict common agreed rule, it might rely on Article 95 in order to enact a standard more stringent than that commonly agreed. Although this measure will immediately be subject to a strict set of requirements and, subsequently, will be likely to be rejected, it will produce a disruptive effect on the functioning of the internal market. This explains why the Community, notably the Commission by virtue of its agenda-setting role in putting forward proposals, has an incentive to support stricter rather than looser regulatory standards.

As to the creation of a common risk assessment for the whole Community, the EC Commission has elaborated a communication on the collection and use of expertise in order to promote some consistency in the delivery of advice from so many different sources of expertise. However, not being subject to judicial review, this Communication merely represents a moral commitment by the Commission departments when relying on expertise.

---

[57] Commission Communication on the framework for action in the field of public health, COM(93) final, at point 32.
[58] See, on this point, Christoforou, supra note 28, p 222.

Finally, if the requirement that a risk analysis be conducted to show the potential danger of a certain substance has been introduced by the court's case law in order to primarily ensure a proper functioning of the internal market, the same requirement has subsequently been codified and incorporated within both EC primary and secondary law in order to also ensure another legitimate objective: a high level of protection of health within the Community.

2. The WTO and Scientific Justification

2.1 The Origins

As the WTO's involvement with health and environmental risk regulation is of even more recent origin and far less relevant than in the EC, its scientific justification discipline is, at least from a normative perspective, less developed. There are only two WTO agreements that make an explicit reference to 'science', the Agreement on Technical Barriers to Trade (TBT) and the Agreement on the Application of Sanitary and Phytosanitary Measures (SPS). As for the GATT, although Article XX GATT – similarly to Article 30 EC – allows Member States to adopt measures restricting the free flow of goods when it is necessary to protect human, animal and plant health (Article XX (b)) or to conserve natural exhaustible resources (XX (g)), it does not make any reference to science. Therefore, at least in principle, under this Article, Member States may adopt health or environment related measures without being asked to justify them scientifically, but simply by complying with the requirements listed in the *Chapeau* of Article XX. Nonetheless, in practice, it would be difficult for the defendant to satisfy its burden of proof that its measure is 'necessary' for the protection of health without resorting to scientific evidence. In fact, states in the past have often turned in scientific evidence to the WTO in order to demonstrate that their measures were covered under the exceptions provided by Article XX (ie not discriminatory, but truly health or environment related). Thus, for instance, in *US–Gasoline*, involving a US measure applying stricter rules on the chemical characteristics of imported gasoline than it did for domestically refined gasoline, it had already been established that 'inasmuch as they include the notion of 'protection', the words 'policies designed to protect human life or health' imply the existence of a *health risk*' and that, accordingly, the plaintiff must determine whether the prohibited product poses a risk to human life or health.[59] In the subsequent *Shrimp–turtle* case,[60] after the US prohibited the import of

---

[59] *United States - Standards for Reformulated and Conventional Gasoline* Appellate Body report WT/DS2/AB/R and *United States - Standards for Reformulated and Conventional Gasoline* WT/DS2/R Panel report as modified by the Appellate Body report.

[60] *United States - Import Prohibition of Certain Shrimp and Shrimp Products* WT/DS58/R, paras 73-119, available at http://www.wto.org/english/tratop_e/dispu_e/distab_e.htm#r58.

shrimps harvested with technology that may adversely affect certain sea turtles,[61] it tried to justify its ban by referring to a multitude of national (mainly by the National Research Council) and internationally led studies proving that all species of turtles face the danger of extinction.

In *EC–Asbsestos*, the panel has clearly established that the health risk invoked under Article XX must be proven.[62] Notably, in determining how 'the existence of a health risk' should be assessed,[63] it has stated that while 'it is not its function to settle a scientific debate, not being composed of experts in the field', 'it should base its conclusions with respect to the existence of a public health risk on the scientific evidence put forward by the parties and the comments of the experts consulted'.[64] Against this backdrop, the panel has undertaken a meticulous scientific examination to establish whether the French ban on chrysotile-cement products was necessary to protect human life or health under Article XX(b) GATT. By assessing 'the nature and the character of the risk' posed by these products, it found that 'no minimum threshold of level of exposure or duration of exposure has been identified with regard to the risk of pathologies associated with chrysotile, except from asbestosis'.[65] Therefore, the panel concluded that there was no alternative measure, other than a ban against these products that would have met the level of protection chosen by France.

2.2 The SPS Discipline

As seen above, since 1995, when the WTO came into being, two additional agreements also apply to health regulations: the TBT and SPS. While the SPS Agreement expressly identifies itself as an elaboration of GATT Article XX (b), the TBT does not. Nevertheless, both agreements have been designed to deal with the same kind of measures: those inspired by the protection of human, animal or plant life or health. Notably, these agreements have been established to prevent technical legislation which is intended for the protection of human health or safety, the protection of the health or life of humans animals or plants, consumer protection against deceptive practices and environmental protection being used to create or resulting in unjustified barriers to international trade.[66]

---

[61] This is unless the harvesting nation was certified to have a regulatory programme and an incidental take-rate comparable to that of the US, or that the particular fishing environment of the harvesting nation did not pose a threat to sea turtles.

[62] *EC–Asbestos*, Panel Report, paras 8.170 and 8.177.

[63] Ibid, para 8.180.

[64] Ibid, para 8.182.

[65] Ibid, para 8.202.

[66] Since the 1979 Tokyo Round some countries feared that the lowering of border measures would be circumvented by disguised protectionist measures in the form of technical

(continued...)

In order to attain this goal, the agreements lay down a number of principles: the measures of the contracting countries should have a legitimate objective;[67] the measures adopted should be appropriate or proportionate to those objectives,[68] there should be no alternatives which cause less disruption to international trade and there should be no discrimination.[69] Measures that conform to international standards are presumed to be consistent with WTO obligations.[70]

In particular, Article 2.2 TBT stipulates that: 'technical regulations shall not be more trade restrictive than necessary to fulfil a legitimate objective', which can include 'the protection of human health or safety, animal or plant life or health, or the environment', 'taking account of the risks non-fulfilment would create'. In other words, this agreement asks countries to only adopt product regulations that are 'proportionate' ('take into account') to the risks that they are trying to address. The same provision states that:

> in assessing such risks, relevant elements of consideration are, *inter alia*: *available scientific and technical information*, related processing technology or intended end-uses of products.

While the TBT refers to science exclusively as one of the elements to be 'considered' in assessing the 'proportionality' of a contested measure, the SPS requires Member States to base their measures on science, by going into what that science should entail. So, what are the requirements of the SPS Agreement with respect to science?

In particular, the primary scientific justification requirement may be found in Article 2.2 SPS. That article requires that any Member State's sanitary and phytosanitary measure be 'based on scientific principles and [that] it not [be] maintained without sufficient scientific evidence'.

---

regulations, notably sanitary and phytosanitary regulations. For this reason, already on that occasion, a plurilateral agreement was adopted on Technical Barriers to Trade, also called 'Standards Code'. See M. Trebilcock and R. Howse, *The Regulation of International Trade* (London-New York, Routdlege, 1999) p 145. See also G. Marceau and J. Trachtman, 'The Technical Barriers to Trade Agreement, the Sanitary and Phytosanitary Measures Agreement, and the General Agreement on Tariff and Trade, A Map of the World Trade Organization Law of Domestic Regulation of Goods', 35 *Journal of World Trade* 5 (2002), pp 811–881.

[67] While Article 2.2 TBT affirms that: '[…] [s]uch legitimate objectives are, *inter alia*: national security requirements; the prevention of deceptive practices; protection of human health or safety, animal or plant life or health, or the environment', Article 2.2 SPS refers solely to the legitimate objective 'to protect human, animal or plant life or health'.

[68] Articles 2.2 TBT ; 2.2 SPS ('only to the extent necessary').

[69] Articles. 2.1 TBT; 2.3 SPS.

[70] Articles 3.1 TBT; 3.2 SPS.

Furthermore, Article 5 SPS translates this duty into operational terms by providing that countries should ensure that their measures be 'based on an *assessment*, as appropriate to the circumstances, *of the risks* to human, animal or plant life or health'. This requirement constitutes an attempt by the SPS framers to set up some common structure on the way in which WTO Members enact SPS measures. This emerges in particular from Article 5.1 which imposes on Member States, when conducting their risk assessment, to take into account the 'risk assessment techniques' developed by the 'relevant international organisations', notably Codex, OIE and IPPC.

The panels and AB have elaborated on these requirements, by interpreting them cumulatively[71] as requiring that there must be an 'objective or rational relationship' between the SPS measure and the scientific evidence.[72] Therefore, these two SPS obligations focus on the capability of the measure to tackle the health concern. The WTO judicial bodies are called upon to determine to what extent the measure at issue is reasonably related to the public policy goal it pursues.

Furthermore, the AB offered some further clarification on how to apply this test by stating that:

> whether there is a rational relationship between an SPS measure and the scientific evidence is to be determined on a case-by-case basis and will depend upon the particular circumstances of the case, including the characteristics of the measure at issue and the quality and quantity of the scientific evidence.[73]

The country adopting an SPS measure, therefore, is entitled to determine the appropriate level of protection[74], subject to this rational relationship constraint.

Annex A to the SPS Agreement defines risk assessment as: 'The *evaluation of the likelihood* of entry, establishment or spread of a pest or disease within the territory of an importing Member according to the sanitary or phytosanitary measures which might be applied, and of the associated

---

[71] *EC–Measures Concerning Meat Products* Appellate Body Report WT/DS26/AB/R, WT/DS48/AB/R adopted on 13 February 1998, para 160–168; confirmed by *Japan –Agricultural Products*, para 76, where the Appellate Body has stated that 'the context of the word 'sufficient' or, more generally, the phrase 'maintained without sufficient scientific evidence' in Article 2.2, includes Article 5.1, as well as Articles 3.3 and 5.7 of the SPS Agreement. See, notably, para 82.

[72] *EC–Hormones* AB Report, para 189; then confirmed in *Japan–Agricultural Products* Panel Report WT/DS76 para 8.29, 8.42; *Japan–Agricultural Products* AB Report, para 82.

[73] *Japan–Agricultural Products*, para 84.

[74] This freedom has been recognised not only by Article 2.1 SPS but also by the AB in *Australia–Salmon*. In its report, the AB has stated that the panel or AB should not substitute

(continued..)

potential biological and economic consequences; or the *evaluation of the potential* for adverse effects on human or animal health arising from the presence of additives, contaminants, toxins or disease-causing organisms in food, beverages or feedstuffs'.

The same article lists some of the factors that should be taken into account: 'available scientific evidence; relevant processes and production methods; relevant inspection, sampling and testing methods; prevalence of specific diseases or pests; existence of pest – or disease – free areas; relevant ecological and environmental conditions; and quarantine or other treatment'.[75] In *EC–Hormones*, the AB interpreted this list as non-exhaustive[76] and as including non-scientific factors as well.[77]

The scientific justification discipline is also contained in Article 3.3 SPS, which, by presumption, consider in conformity with the requirements of the agreement those measures which result in a higher level of protection than that provided for by measures based on international standards, but only if they are grounded on a 'scientific justification'. This mechanism has effectively been defined as a 'refined system of applied subsidiarity, subtly allowing national autonomy subject to certain constraints'.[78]

As both the SPS and the TBT Agreements introduced significant new obligations for WTO Members, with the effect of inevitably constraining Members' sovereign right to regulate to avoid unwanted risk for their citizens, both agreements provide at their outset that no Member should be prevented from taking measures necessary for the protection of human, animal or plant life or health, or the environment.[79]

---

its own reasoning about the implied level of protection for that expressed consistently by Australia. See para 199.

[75] See, notably Article 5.2 and 5.4 SPS.

[76] AB Report on *EC–Hormones*, para 187 ('there is nothing to indicate that the listing factors that may be taken into account in a risk assessment of Article 5.2 was intended to be a closed list').

[77] AB Report on *EC–Hormones*, para 187 ('[...] the risk that is to be evaluated in a risk assessment under Article 5.1 is not only risk ascertainable in a science laboratory operating under strictly controlled conditions, but also risk in human societies as they actually exist, in other words, the actual potential for adverse effects on human health in the real world where people live and work and die'). The interpretation of this statement remains particularly controversial today. For a criticism see, *ex multis*, R. Quick and A. Bluthner, 'Has the Appellate Body Erred? An Appraisal and Criticism of the Ruling in the WTO Hormones Case', 3 *Journal of International Economic Law* (1999) 603, pp 618–9. For a positive comment see R. Howse, 'Adjudicating Legitimacy and Treaty Interpretation in International Trade Law: The Early Years of WTO Jurisprudence', in J.H.H. Weiler, (ed.), *The EU, the WTO and the NAFTA: Towards a Common Law of International Trade?*, pp 64 ss.

[78] J.P. Trachtman, 'The World Trading System, the International Legal System and Multilevel Choice', 12 *European Law Journal* 469, p 480.

[79] See the Preambles of these Agreements.

The clear purpose of these statements of principle is to reassure the governments that the WTO does not want to take over from their task of deciding which risks are acceptable for society. In contrast, the goal pursued by the WTO is to seek to minimise the negative effects stemming from the existence of divergent regulations by making sure that such regulations are not more detrimental to trade in goods than necessary.

2.3   Conclusions

This overview of the WTO requirements for scientific justification clearly shows that the SPS Agreement is the only WTO instrument that expressly imposes on its Members the requirement to base their measures on scientific evidence, and this regardless of whether the measures are discriminatory.[80] It is this agreement that has provided some of the vocabulary and basic normative foundations of the WTO risk analysis.

In an effort to eliminate protectionist and unnecessary non-tariff barriers, the SPS Agreement imposes strict scientific justification requirements. By doing so, the agreement not only imposes a higher justificatory burden on WTO members wishing to adopt measures aimed at protecting themselves from health risks but, conversely, it also makes it easier for potential complainants to challenge them.[81] In line with the SPS Preamble, no member is prevented from adopting or enforcing measures necessary to protect human, animal or plant life and health, but is entitled to take sanitary and phytosanitary measures necessary for the protection of these values, 'provided that such measures are not inconsistent with the provision of this Agreement', notably with the scientific justification discipline. However, these requirements being particularly cumbersome, all of the major SPS cases to date – the *Hormones*, *Salmon*, *Agricultural Products* and *Apples* cases – have been lost by the defending member. In particular, the risk assessment discipline sketched out by Article 5 has been pivotal in the functioning of the agreement during its first years of operation. In all SPS cases to date, the contested national measures have been found to be inconsistent with the risk assessment requirements, ie, not sufficiently specific or not rationally or objectively related to the relevant scientific evidence to

---

[80] This has been expressly recognised by the same panel in the *Asbestos* case. See Panel Report, WT/DS135/R, para 8.180. The only difference between justification under Article XX (b) and the scientific evidence requirement in the SPS text is that while under Article XX the defendant bears the burden of proof for justifying its measure, under the SPS it is the plaintiff that has to raise at least a presumption that the contested measure is not based on scientific evidence.

[81] See R. Howse and P.C. Mavroidis, 'Europe's Evolving Regulatory Strategy for GMOs – The Issue of Consistency with WTO Law: of Kine and Brine', 24 *Fordham International Law Journal* 317, p 320 (who notes that the complainant has to at least raise a presumption that the Member's SPS measure is not based on scientific evidence).

satisfy Article 5.1. However, national authorities have never been found to have wrongly conducted a risk assessment, but they had rather failed to support their measures with either 'specific enough' evidence (*Hormones*,[82] *Apples*[83]) or with 'objective evidence' (*Agricultural products*;[84] *Salmon*[85]).

Before analysing how and to what extent these scientific justification disciplines have been implemented by the competent courts, the following section provides for a comparison between the WTO and EC disciplines, by looking at their respective goals.

3. Why do both the EC and the WTO Rely on Science?

As seen above, both the WTO and the EC embraced science as the organising principle when regulating public health measures. Rather than relying solely on non-discrimination as the main criterion enabling them to distinguish between legitimate and illegitimate barriers to trade inspired by public health protection, the WTO and the EC have introduced a new, more demanding element, with reference to those measures: scientific justification. Under this view, the scientific element would ensure that SPS measures address a real, objectively established health risk and are not protectionist measures disguised as health regulations or unnecessarily restrictive health regulations. In particular, according to this vision, scientific justification would be more effective than non-discrimination in spotting protectionist measures and in dismantling sham health measures framed as de facto trade barriers.

However, the current practices of scientific risk assessment do not seem to reflect, and thereby comfort, this vision. In fact, despite science's promise of value-neutrality, its mechanisms of scientific assessment often rely on science policies, such as assumptions, inferences and techniques, which enable it to overcome uncertainties and fill in gaps inherent to scientific methods.[86] Thus, for example, one of the most common science

[82] *EC–Hormones*, AB Report, paras 199-201 (where the panel rejected general studies of the carcinogenic risk of hormones and suggested that a proper risk assessment of these substances should have been undertaken on an individual basis).

[83] *Japan–Apples*, Panel Report, paras 8.127, 8.277–280 (where the Panel rejected Japan's risk assessment because it did not focus sufficiently on the risk of transmission of fire blight through apple fruit as opposed to other modes of transmission).

[84] *Japan–Agricultural products*, AB Report, para 113.

[85] *Australia–Salmon Measures Affecting the Importation of Salmon* WT/DS18/R modified Panel Report, para 8.99; *Australia*–Salmon, AB report, paras 128-135. However, it is worth mentioning that, following the adoption of a revised set of quarantine measures, this dispute has been successfully closed by an Article 21.5 implementation panel. It therefore represents the first case where a member's controversial SPS measure has been upheld as meeting the rigorous scientific discipline of the SPS Agreement.

[86] On the role of science policies in risk analysis, see V. Walker, 'Keeping the WTO from Becoming the "World Trans-Science organization": Scientific Uncertainty, Science Policy,

(continued...)

policies is the presumption that positive effects in animal cancer studies indicate that the agent under study can have carcinogenic potential in humans.[87] Other examples include the use of a linear dose-response model, the assumption that absorption in animals and humans is approximately the same or the use of body weight scaling for interspecies comparisons.[88]

Against this backdrop, one may legitimately wonder whether the use of these policies and assumptions may jeopardise the role of scientific justification as the organising principle in the trade-health interface. In particular, this blurred relationship existing between risk management components and scientific justification may render extremely difficult the task of the international adjudicator called to review the legality of these measures.

Apart from these inherent limits of science as a criterion chosen to distinguish between legitimate and illegitimate measures, the scientific justification disciplines in the EC and in the WTO do not entirely respond to the same logic. While scientific justification in the SPS/WTO system is conceived as an exclusively free-trade mechanism aimed at dismantling not only deliberately discriminating protectionist SPS measures, but also those genuine health regulations which are unnecessary because they are more trade-restrictive than they need to be,[89] the European scientific requirements found their raison d'être in the European attempt to also integrate into its market-oriented agenda other interests deserving equal protection, such as European citizens' consumer protection.

In short, if the WTO scientific regime, without establishing any minimum level of health protection, follows an exclusively market-opening agenda, the EC discipline, by imposing, not only on Member

---

and Factfinding in the Growth Hormones Dispute', 31 *Cornell International Law Journal* 1998, pp 261–3 and the more recent work from the same author, 'The Myth of Science as a "Neutral Arbiter" for triggering Precautions', 26 *Boston College International and Comparative Law Review* 197, pp 198 ss.

[87] See T.O. McGarity, 'On the Prospect of "Daubertizing" Judicial Review of Risk Assessment', 66 *Law & Contemp. Probs.* 155, p 163 and by the same Author, 'Substantive and Procedural Discretion in Administrative Resolution of Science Policy Questions: Regulating Carcinogens in EPA and OSHA', 67 *Geo. L. J.* 729 (1979).

[88] For an illustration of the most common risk assessment policies used by the Codex bodies in charge of conducting many of the risk assessments leading to the adoption of the Codex standards (JECFA and JMPR), see Joint FAO/WHO Consultation Risk Management and Food Safety, (FAO Food and Nutrition Paper 65, Rome 1997), pp 7–9. See also Breyer, *Breaking the Vicious Circle*, Harvard University Press ed., 1993, pp 43–4.

[89] In this sense, see Button, *The Power to Protect*, Oxford and Portland, Oregon, 2004, p 45, who argues that the SPS agreement aims at 'a broader objective': identifying and dismantling all instances in which markets are unnecessarily closed by scientifically unsupported health measures.

States' measures but also on EC-wide regulations, the requirement to attain a high level of protection, answers to a more complex public demand for health protection within an increasingly integrated Union.

As a result, as illustrated below, while in the EC risk analysis scheme science is necessary but not sufficient to authorise regulatory action,[90] in the WTO imprecise risk analysis model science seems to be both necessary and sufficient to validate a national health measure.

In the next chapter it will be shown how the different objectives underpinning the two scientific justification regimes will influence the standard of review to be applied by their respective courts.

Diagram 5. Scientific justification requirements in the WTO and the EC © A. Alemanno 2006

"Nothing in this agreement shall be construed to prevent the adoption or enforcement of measures": "to protect human, animal or plant life or health" (Article 2.2 SPS; Article XX (b) GATT)	"The provisions of Articles 28 and 29 [...] shall not preclude prohibitions or restrictions on imports, exports: "justified on grounds of [...] the protection of health and life of humans, animals or plants" (Article 30 EC)
"Applied only to the extent necessary"(Article 2.2 SPS)	Proportionality principle as enshrined in Article 5 EC and developed by the case law[91]
"Based on scientific principles and not maintained without sufficient scientific evidence (Article 2.2 SPS)"	Scientific evidence (according to the case law, Article 30 EC requires scientific justification)
"not applied in a manner which should constitute a means of arbitrary or unjustifiable discrimination" (Article XX) "Do not arbitrarily or unjustifiably discriminate between Members where identical or similar conditions prevail" (Article 2.3 SPS)	"not constitute a means of arbitrary discrimination" (Article 30 EC)

[90] In the *Pfizer* case, Case T-13/99 *Pfizer Animal Health v Council*, 2002 E.C.R. II-3305, at para 201 the CFI has clearly stated that '[s]cientific legitimacy is not a sufficient basis for the exercise of public authority'.
[91] On the genesis of the proportionality principle, see Cases 9/73, *Carl Schlüter* [1973] ECR 1156, para 22 and 5/73 *First Balkan* [1973] ECR 1112.

"not applied in a manner which would constitute a disguised restriction on international trade" (Article XX; Article 2.3 SPS)	"not constitute [...] a disguised restriction on trade between Member States" (Article 30 EC)
Members may "introduce or maintain measures which result in a higher level of protection than would be achieved by measures based on international standards, "if there is scientific justification" (Article 3 SPS)	Members may "maintain national provisions on grounds of major needs referred to Article 30 EC" (Article 94, par. 4, EC) or "introduce" new measures derogating harmonized legislation "based on new scientific evidence" (Article 95, par. 5)

Having seen the nature of the EC and WTO scientific justification disciplines, and how they are understood, it is appropriate to review the extent to which the respect of the relevant scientific requirements is assessed by their respective courts. In other words the question remains as to the standard of review applicable to food safety (science-based) measures.

CHAPTER II:
JUDICIAL REVIEW OF FOOD SAFETY (SCIENCE-BASED) MEASURES IN THE EC AND THE WTO

1.   An Introduction to Judicial Review

The standard of review is a key issue for any court or tribunal, domestic or international, called upon to review legislation or administrative decisions.

When the examination of a regulation falls within its jurisdiction, the question arises as to what extent a court should review determinations of the legislative or administrative authorities. Routinely, courts face the following questions: how intense should this review be? To what extent should it second-guess the determinations first made by decision-makers? Does a court have the tools, experience and knowledge to carry out a full-scale re-examination of both factual and legal issues?

While from a domestic law perspective the answers to these questions affect solely the balance of powers between the legislative, executive, and judicial branches of government, in an international context the answers touch upon an even more sensitive area: the division of powers between a State and a supranational and multilateral entity, such as the European Union or the WTO[1]. As has been stated, within non-state polities, the standard of judicial review is relevant not only to the extent that it has a procedural function (within a system of checks and balances), but also because it is a critical element of allocating power between an international tribunal and a national government'[2]. In addition, it is also one of the decisive elements that balance the rights and obligations under the WTO Agreements, 'namely the sovereignty of national governments in implementing and justifying measures versus the right of other WTO Members to benefits under the WTO Agreements'[3].

---

[1] On this point, see, eg, S.P Croley and J.H. Jackson, 'WTO Dispute Procedures, Standard of Review and Deference to National Governments', 90 *American Journal of International Law* 193 (1996) and G. Goh, 'Tipping the Apple Cart: The Limits of Science and Law in the SPS Agreement after Japan – Apples', *Journal of World Trade* 40(4), p 665.

[2] J. Jackson, 'The Great 1994 Sovereignty Debate: United States Acceptance and Implementation of the Uruguay Round Results', in J. Jackson, *The Jurisprudence of GATT and WTO: Insights on Treaty Law and Economic Relations*, 2002, pp 367–369.

[3] Goh, supra note 1, p 665.

Thus, as it is frequently argued not only in anti-global contexts, but also in legal writings, the courts should respect national governments' determinations up to some point. The determination of this point is 'the crucial issue that has sometimes been labelled the standard of review'[4]. Similarly, borrowing from the European Court of Human Rights jargon, the notion of standard of review defines the *margin of appreciation* which the courts grant to Members' authorities in enacting and enforcing their obligations under the relevant international agreement[5].

Besides marking the boundary of a Member State's discretion, the standard of review shapes the boundaries within which a court can scrutinise the acts of a Member State against its legal obligation. Therefore, its choice depends on the legal rights and obligations laid down in the relevant provisions[6].

It will be shown that, while the standard of review is traditionally a divisive topic in trade remedies cases, it is becoming an even more contentious issue in disputes concerning the protection of life and health, such as the SPS food safety cases.

1.1. Differing Levels of Intensity of Review

If the 'standard of review' refers to the nature and intensity of a court's scrutiny of the legal validity of a piece of legislation or an administrative decision, *de novo review* and 'total deference' are generally referred to as the two extreme standards of review[7]. While the former allows a judge to substitute his or her own findings for those of the national authority, the latter prevents a judge from reviewing in substance the investigations conducted by the decision-makers. Both being standards which are not in reality legally viable, the entire judicial review debate boils down to the challenge of finding a proper standard along the spectrum ranging between these two extreme standards of review[8]. There is, in fact, no

---

[4] S. Croley and J. Jackson, 'WTO Dispute Settlement Panel Deference to National Government Decision: The Misplaced Analogy to the US Chevron Standard-Of-Review Doctrine', E.U. Petersmann (ed.), *International Trade Law and the GATT/WTO Dispute Settlement System*, 1997, p 188.

[5] E. Brems, 'The Margin of Appreciation Doctrine in the Case Law of the European Court of Human Rights', in *Zeitschrift für Ausländisches Offentliches Recht und Völkerrecht*, 1996, pp 240–93.

[6] H. Spamann, 'Standard of Review for World Trade Organization Panels in Trade Remedy Cases: A Critical Analysis', 38 *Journal of World Trade* 2004, p 509.

[7] T.D. Rakoff, P.L. Strauss & C.R. Farina. *Gellhorn and Byse's Administrative Law: Cases and Comments* (Foundation Press 10th and rev. 10th ed. 2003), p 902.

[8] In the US, for instance, various standards of review are provided for by federal statutes, which include, among others, 'substantial evidence', the 'clearly erroneous', and the 'arbitrary and capricious' tests. For an overview of the scope of review of administrative action, see, eg, T.D. Rakoff, P.L. Strauss & C.R. Farina, *Gellhorn and Byse's Administrative Law: Cases and Comments* (Foundation Press 10th and rev. 10th ed. 2003) pp 902 ss.

single or proper standard of review: each legal system must develop the standard that satisfies its own needs. This is because judicial review is valuable as a mechanism to discourage authorities from engaging in conduct prohibited within a legal system, which, if effective, either deters the illegal conduct or removes it sooner than it otherwise would.

The elaboration of an appropriate standard of review requires a balance to be found between the need to strike at what is illegal and the concern to respect Member States' discretion, without the judicature substituting its assessment of the facts for the assessment made by the authority concerned. In particular, according to the Appellate Body

'[t]he standard of review appropriately applicable in proceedings [...] must reflect the balance established [...] between the jurisdictional competences conceded by the Members to the WTO and the jurisdictional competences retained by the Members for themselves'[9].

1.2. The Specificity of Reviewing Science-based Measures

In the specific context of reviewing science-based measures (like all food regulations), the determination of the applicable standard is particularly relevant to the extent that it determines not only how much regulatory autonomy WTO and EC Member States enjoy in regulating to protect the health of their people but also the power of a tribunal to investigate, evaluate and review Member States' acts. In particular, the choice of a particular standard of review decides the level of scientific involvement required from a court.

Depending on the applicable standard of review, a court may be called upon to determine one or more of the following issues: whether the scientific evidence has been duly taken into account in the decision-making process, whether the scientific evidence underpinning a certain measure is reliable or plausible, whether the scientific evidence underpinning a certain measure is valid, etc.

2. The standard of Review in the EC

2.1 Introduction to the General Standard of Review

As seen above, the European scientific justification discipline has emerged gradually and quite recently, having been first spontaneously introduced by the Member States in order to support their measures

---

[9] *EC–Hormones*, AB report, at 115.

derogating from EC law, and then subsequently codified and extended to EC action in the field of health and environmental protection, notably in the food safety area. As a result, there is a growing body of case law by the European courts dealing with measures adopted by EC Member States and by EC institutions to address risks to health and the environment.

In the absence of an express indication of the standard of review to be applied to those measures, it is necessary to look at this body of case law in order to determine the level of intensity of the scrutiny exercised by the EC courts.

More generally, unlike the ECSC Treaty,[10] the EC Treaty does not provide any indication as to the standard of review that courts should apply when scrutinising EC acts. Finding themselves in such a normative vacuum, the European courts filled it by drawing inspiration from the ECSC treaty, which set forth a rather deferential standard. Thus, in solving a specific legal dispute, EC courts tend, traditionally, to limit their review to questions as to whether the authorities have or have not used their regulatory discretion in an arbitrary or unjustifiable manner.[11]

2.2   Reviewing EC Food Safety Regulations

While in principle the review of EC action is limited to examining 'whether the exercise of its discretion is vitiated by a manifest error or a misuse of power',[12] this standard of review has, through time, been

---

[10] Article 33(1) of the European Coal and Steel Community reads: '[...] The Court of Justice may not, however, examine the evaluation of the situation, resulting from economic facts or circumstances, in the light of which the Commission took its decisions or made its recommendations, save where the Commission is alleged to have misused its powers or to have manifestly failed to observe the provisions of this Treaty or any rule of law relating to its application'.

[11] This is settled case law. See, in particular, in the competition law field, Joined Cases 56/64 and 58/64 *Consten and Grundig v Commission* [1966] ECR 299, at page 347; in the agricultural field, Case 55/75 *Balkan–Import Export v Hauptzollamt Berlin-Packhof* [1976] ECR 19, at 8 and Case 98/78 *Racke v Hauptzollamt Mainz* [1979] ECR 69, paragraph 5; Case 265/87 *Schräder* [1989] ECR 2237, paragraph 22; Joined Cases C-267/88 to C-286/88 *Wuidart and Others* [1990] ECR I-435, paragraph 14; Case C-331/88 *Fedesa and Others* [1990] ECR I-4023, at 14; Case C-157/96 *National Farmers' Union and Others* [1998] [1998] ECR I-2211, at 39; in the civil servants case law, Case 9/82 *Khrgaard and Delvaux v Commission* [1983] ECR 2379, at 14; in the state aid field, Case C-225/91 *Matra v Commission* [1993] ECR I-3203, at 24–25. However, it should be noted that in the field of competition law the CFI has recently shown that it was ready to perform in depth analysis of the Commission's decisions. See for instance, the Babyliss case, T-114/02 *Babyliss SA v Commission* [2003] ECR II-1279.

[12] Ibidem.

specifically adapted and shaped so as to apply to public health measures, notably to food safety measures.

Thus, for instance, when the ECJ was called upon to determine whether the Commission lacked the competence to adopt Decision 96/239 providing for a total ban on exports of bovine animals, bovine meat and derived products from the territory of the United Kingdom to the other Member States and to third countries in the aftermath of the BSE crisis, it declared that:

> [...] since the Commission enjoys a wide measure of discretion, particularly as to the nature and extent of the measures which it adopts, the EC judicature must, when reviewing such measures, restrict itself to examining whether the exercise of such discretion is *vitiated by a manifest error or a misuse of powers or whether the Commission did not clearly exceed the bounds of its discretion.*[13]

Furthermore, it is settled case law that:

> [...] where a Community authority is required to make complex assessments in the performance of its duties, its discretion also applies, to some extent, to the establishment of the factual basis of its action.[14]

This deferential approach to judicial review of Community measures has been further elaborated in the *Upjohn* judgment, dealing with medicinal products, where the ECJ has declared:

> [...] where a Community authority is called upon, in the performance of its duties, to make complex assessments, it enjoys a wide measure of discretion, the exercise of which is subject to a limited judicial review in the course of which *the EC judicature may not substitute its assessment of the facts for the assessment made by the authority concerned.* Thus, in such cases, the EC judicature must restrict itself *to examining the accuracy of the findings of fact and law* made by the authority concerned and to verifying, in particular, that the action taken by that authority is not vitiated

---

[13] Case C-157/96, *National Farmers' Union and Others* [1998] ECR I-2211, para 39; referring to Case 98/78 *Racke v Hauptzollamt Mainz* [1979] ECR 69, para 5.

[14] Case 138/79 *Roquette Frères v Council* [1980] ECR 3333, paragraph 25; Joined Cases 197/80 to 200/80, 243/80, 245/80 and 247/80 *Ludwigshafener Walzmühle v Council and Commission* [1981] ECR 3211, paragraph 37; Case C-27/95 *Bakers of Nailsea* [1997] ECR I-1847, paragraph 32; Case C-4/96 *Nifpo and Northern Ireland Fishermen's Federation* [1998] ECR I-681, paragraphs 41 and 42; Case C-120/97 *Upjohn* [1999] ECR I-223, paragraph 34; and *Spain v Council*, cited at paragraph 115 above, paragraph 29 and, lastly, T-13/99, *Pfizer*, at 168.

by a manifest error or a misuse of powers and that it did not clearly exceed the bounds of its discretion.[15]

Recently, this deferential standard of review has been specifically extended by the CFI to those situations where Community institutions are:

[...] required to undertake a scientific risk assessment and to evaluate highly complex scientific and technical facts.[16]

Accordingly, in the *Bellio* case,[17] the ECJ upheld the right of the EC to pursue a policy of 'zero tolerance' in regard to the contamination of animal feed with material possibly containing the agent that causes BSE, even in circumstances where the contamination was probably accidental and there was scientific uncertainty as to the minimum amount of infected material required to lead to disease in humans.[18] The court came to this conclusion after having considered that that policy had been adopted 'on the recommendation of experts having at their disposal the relevant scientific data' and formed 'part of a coherent body of legislation the purpose of which is to combat TSEs'.[19] By relying on the same deferential standard of review, the court has recently overturned, in *CEVA*, a CFI judgement in so far as it found that there had been an inaction on the part of the Commission in the establishment of a maximum residue level for progesterone under Regulation 2377/90.[20] While the CFI established that the political and scientific complexity of the progesterone file 'does not excuse the Commission's inaction', the ECJ confirmed that:

in delicate and controversial cases, the Commission must have a sufficiently broad discretion and enough time to submit for re-examination the scientific questions which determine its decision'.[21]

---

[15] See Case C-120/97, *Upjohn Ltd* [1999] ECR 223, para 34. See, also, Case C-405/92 *Mondiet* [1993] ECR 6133. See, for a similar statement, in the competition law field, Joined Cases 56/64 and 58/64 *Consten and Grundig v Commission* [1966] ECR 299, at page 347, See, in particular, the mbidost recent interpretation of this judgment in Case C-168/01 *GlaxoSmithKline Services Unlimited v Commission* [2006] not yet reported, at 241 where it is said that: 'the Court dealing with an application for annulment of a decision applying Article 81(3) EC carries out, in so far as it is faced with complex economic assessments, a review confined, as regards the merits, to verifying whether the facts have been accurately stated, whether there has been any manifest error of appraisal and whether the legal consequences deduced from those facts were accurate'.

[16] See Case T-13/99 *Pfizer Animal Health v Council*, 2002 ECR II, paras 168–69 and 323.

[17] Case C-286/02 *Bellio F.lli Srl v Prefettura di Treviso*, [2004] not yet reported.

[18] See A. Alemanno, 'Protection des consommateurs : Bellio', *Revue du Droit de l'Union Européenne*, 2/04, pp. 319–323.

[19] Case C-286/02 *Bellio F.lli Srl v Prefettura di Treviso*, para 61.

[20] Case C-198/03 P, *Commission v Ceva/Pfizer*, [2005], not reported yet.

[21] Ibid, at 75.

It must also be noted that the assessment made by the EC institutions can be contested only:

> if it appears incorrect in the light of the elements of fact and law which were available to them at the time when the contested regulation was adopted.[22]

The question relating to the admissibility of evidence to be taken into account in the process of legal review is particularly controversial in EC law. Unlike other legal systems, the European Community legal order does not provide for any specific rule governing the admissibility of evidence which may be qualified under the 'expertise' label and which is generally advanced by the parties to the dispute.

Besides the evidence that both parties may state in their briefs, under the rules of procedure of the CFI, 'the parties may supplement their arguments and offer further evidence in the course of the oral procedure'.[23] However, in this circumstance, 'they must [...] give reasons for the delay in offering such further evidence'.[24]

However, apart from this express recognition of the possibility for parties to keep bringing evidence into the procedure, these rules do not provide any specific rule governing the admissibility of this evidence.

In these circumstances, it is for the courts to elaborate appropriate criteria aimed at determining which evidence can be validly taken into account when they are called upon to review a contested EC act.

The general approach elaborated so far by EC courts is that:

> that review is carried out solely by reference to the elements of fact and of law existing on the date of adoption of the contested decision.[25]

The only exception being:

> [...] the possibility afforded to the parties, in the exercise of their rights of defence, of supplementing them by evidence established

---

[22] Pfizer, supra note 16, para 324 and Crispoltoni, Case 368/89 *Crispoltoni* I (1991) ECR 3715, at 43.
[23] Article 76a(3) of the Rules of Procedure of the CFI.
[24] Ibid.
[25] This approach has recently been confirmed in Case C-168/01 *GlaxoSmithKline Services Unlimited v Commission* [2006] not yet reported, which refers to Joined Cases 15/76 and 16/76 *France v Commission* [1979] ECR 321, para 7, and Case T-395/94 *Atlantic Container Line and Others v Commission* [2002] ECR II-875, para 252.

after that date, but for the specific purpose of contesting or defending that decision.[26]

It is submitted that this approach which has mainly be been developed in the area of competition law risks being inadequate if extended to the public health field. What if a scientific study proving that a feared risk to health is certain is produced after the adoption of the contested authorising measure?

It is believed that in these specific circumstances the CFI, by relying on the above-mentioned provisions recognising that the parties may supplement their arguments and offer further evidence in the course of both the written and oral procedure, must also take into account scientific evidence which did not exist at the moment of the adoption of the contested act.

Furthermore, after the *Artegodan* judgments, the court may also be called upon to review the respect of the procedural requirements prescribed for the adoption of a decision based upon the precautionary principle,[27] notably to review the formal legality of any scientific committee's opinion.

Lastly, the CFI in *Pfizer* has highlighted a set of elements peculiar to the judicial review of a precautionary measure. While admitting that under the precautionary principle the Community institutions are entitled 'to adopt, on the basis of as yet incomplete scientific knowledge, protective measures which may seriously harm legally protected positions, and they enjoy a broad discretion in that regard', it has immediately framed such discretion by adding that:

> [...] in such circumstances, the guarantees conferred by the Community legal order in administrative proceedings are of even more fundamental importance. Those guarantees include, in particular, the duty of the competent institution to examine carefully and impartially all the relevant aspects of the individual case.[28]

In general, in all these cases, the court, after having relentlessly recalled the limited scope of review applicable to science-based measures, has

---

[26] Case C-168/01 *GlaxoSmithKline Services Unlimited v Commission* [2006] not yet reported, as relying on Case T-87/05 *EDP v Commission* [2005] not yet reported, para 158 and Case 75/84 *Metro v Commission* [1986] ECR 3021, paras 75 and 78, and *Atlantic Container Lines and Others v Commission*, [2002] ECR II-875, para 254.

[27] Joined Cases T-144/00, T-76/00, T-83/00, T-84/00, T-85/00, T-132/00 and T-141/00 *Artegodan a.o. v Commission* [2002] ECR 4945. Upheld by Case C-39/03 P *Commission v Artegodan e.o.* [2003] ECR.

[28] Case C-13/99 *Pfizer*, supra note 16, para 171.

always refrained from addressing the merits of the scientific findings brought by the parties, thus showing great deference to the EC scientific bodies.

2.3   Reviewing National Food Safety Regulations

While the EC judiciary shows itself to be quite deferential in examining the EC's efforts to attain a high level of protection of health, through the adoption of food (and feed) safety regulations, when it comes to the Members States' use of science in pursuing health protection goals, it adopts a rather different approach.[29]

As seen above, Member State health regulations come under the scrutiny of the ECJ when they are challenged as being inconsistent with Article 28 EC, prohibiting all national measures which are capable of hindering intra-Community trade. In these circumstances, Member States traditionally tend to justify them on public health grounds by invoking Article 30 ECT. In so doing, States quite early began making reference to scientific studies proving the existence of a health threat. In the meanwhile, the ECJ has imposed on Member States relying on Article 30 the duty to prove harm by reference to credible evidence.

Thus, for instance, in the *Greek Butter* case, a Greek measure requiring imported butter to be accompanied by a health certificate was not only found to be inconsistent with Article 28 but also found not to be justifiable on public health grounds because Greece failed to substantiate its health claims.[30] Similarly, Italy was condemned by the court for not having substantiated alleged health threats posed by gelatine.[31] Here the court clearly stated that:

> the Italian Government has not produced, in support of its contention, any evidence or information showing that public health was actually threatened by the use of animal gelatine.[32]

In an infringement proceeding against Belgium,[33] the court, by building upon the *German Purity Beer* case,[34] affirmed that:

---

[29] See, eg, J. Peel, 'Risk Regulation Under the WTO SPS Agreement: Science as an International Normative Yardstick?', in *Jean Monnet Working Paper*, 02/04, NYU School of Law, p 45; C. Button, *The Power to protect*, Oxford and Portland, Oregon, 2004, pp 204–10; Slotboom, 'The Hormones Case: An Increased Risk of Illegality of Sanitary and Phytosanitary Measures', *Common Market Law Review* (1999) 486, p 486.

[30] Case 205/89 *Commission v Greece* [1991] ECR 1361, para 12.

[31] Case 51/83 *Commission v Italy* [1986].

[32] Case 51/83 *Commission v Italy* [1986], para 17.

[33] Case C-17/93 *Criminal Proceedings v J Van der Veldt* [1994] ECR 3537.

[34] Case 178/84 *Commission v Germany* [1987] ECR 1227.

the [claimed health] risk must be measured, not according to the yardstick of general conjecture, but on the basis of relevant scientific research.[35]

It therefore concluded that:

in neglecting to produce scientific data on the basis of which the Belgian law (limiting the maximum salt content in bread to 2 %) would have been justified in enacting and retaining the measures at issue, the Belgian authorities have failed to demonstrate the risk to public health of a salt content in excess of 2%.[36]

More recently, the ECJ has been called upon to examine the compatibility with EC law (notably, with Article 28) of a Danish regulatory practice under which enriched foodstuffs lawfully produced or marketed in other Member States could not be marketed in Denmark unless shown to meet a nutritional need in the Danish population. Although the court recognised that Member States enjoy the right to choose their own level of protection in the absence of harmonisation, it established that any claim that a risk to health existed had to be sufficiently established on the basis of:

a comprehensive assessment of the risk to health based on the most reliable scientific data available and the most recent results of international research.[37]

In sum, EC courts' scrutiny of science-based measures tends to be scientifically demanding. Although never engaging in the scientific debates underlying the contested measures, the court, usually by showing deference to the scientific findings adduced by the parties, is rather demanding in assessing whether the contested measure is adequately backed up by credible scientific evidence. Thus, for instance, a national measure prohibiting the use of a specific additive which is authorised in the Member State of destination violates Article 28 and cannot be justified under Article 30 to the extent that the additive in question, on the basis of the findings of international scientific research and, in particular, the work of the EC's competent scientific committees, does not present a risk to public health. Finally, as it has been correctly emphasised, not only science but also 'pragmatism and common-sense reasoning form a prominent part of the ECJ's approach to health claims.[38]

---

[35] Case C-17/93 *Criminal Proceedings against J Van der Veldt* [1994] ECR 3537, para 17.
[36] Ibid, para 18.
[37] Case 192/01 *Commission v Denmark* [2003] ECR 9693, at 52, referring to *EFTA Surveillance Authority v Norway*, para 30, and Case C-236/01 *Monsanto Agricoltura Italia and Others* [2003] ECR I-8105, at 113.
[38] Button, supra note 29, p 205.

2.4   Why Diverging Standards of Control?

This brief comparison between the EC courts' approach to EC health regulations and their approach when they review Member State health claims clearly shows that EC courts tend to be less deferential vis-à-vis the latter.

This distinction seems to be first due to the specific normative framework within which Member States must act when adopting national health regulations, such as a food safety measure. As illustrated above, either in the absence or in the presence of harmonisation, Member States, in order to take advantage of, respectively, Article 30 or Article 95, paragraphs 4 or 5, EC, must show that the measure in question is a genuine health measure.[39] This implies that the existence of a threat to health must be shown in both situations, thereby inevitably opening this issue to the scrutiny of the judiciary. In contrast, as shown above, EC action is not subject to such a detailed set of scientific constraints. Article 95, paragraph 3, merely requires the Commission, in its proposals concerning health, safety, environmental protection and consumer protection, to take:

> as a base a high level of protection, taking into account in particular of any new development based on scientific facts.

As to the duty imposed on both EC institutions and Member States to base food safety measures on the risk analysis framework provided by Article 6 of Regulation 178/2002, it is probably too early to foresee whether that duty will be interpreted as imposing a procedural obligation on them.

Secondly, the more intrusive approach into Member States' determinations relating to the adoption of those measures may be explained if contextualised within the internal market mechanisms, notably within the dialogue existing between the EC Treaty's positive and negative integration tools. Taken from this perspective, the reasons for this distinction in reviewing EC and national health measures become easier to guess at. In fact, the introduction by a Member State of a health measure inevitably carries the risk of balkanising the functioning of the internal market, and this regardless of whether it is guided by protectionist considerations or not. In fact, unlike an EC health regulation, a national measure does not usually take into account and therefore cannot reflect the views of other Member State interests in the

---

[39] For another example of Member States' failure to provide credible evidence demonstrating the alleged risk, see Case 123/00 *Criminal Proceedings against Christina Bellamy and English Shop Wholesale* [2001] ECR 2795, para 12.

matter. As the court has stated, the objective of a Community measure is different in that it is not:

> [...] prescribed by each Member State in order to protect some interest of its own but by the Community legislature in the general interest of the Community.[40]

Finally, the different approaches of the EC courts to the review of science-based measures fully reflect the objectives underlying the European construction. As the free circulation of goods lies at the heart of the EC integration model, all Member State measures potentially restricting that freedom are subject to a strict scrutiny by the court. In contrast, since any action by the EC institutions presumably contributes to the realisation of the internal market and to the achievement of other goals deserving equal protection, their measures deserve very light review. This idea finds expression in the case law of the court developed on the relationship between primary law and secondary law. Under this case law, the Community is bound by the Treaty rules on free movement but not in the same way as the Member States.[41]

In conclusion, though the EC courts have developed different standards of review depending on the EC or Member State origin of the health claim, they have generally tended, under both standards, not to get involved in the scientific issues underlying the contested measure, by refraining from examining the merits and the methodologies of the scientific findings advanced by the parties.

2.5 Towards a More Intrusive Scrutiny of Food Safety (Science-based) Measures within the EC?

The recent *Pfizer* judgment seems to cast some doubts not only on the EC courts' traditional deferential approach in reviewing EC science-based measures,[42] but also on its traditional reticence in addressing the scientific basis of the contested regulations. This judgment, which has already been examined above for its findings on the precautionary principle, has recently been followed by a line of cases where the ECJ would seem to have shown some willingness to get more involved in scientific matters when judicially reviewing science-based regulations.

---

[40] Case 46/76 *Bauhuis* [1977] ECR 5.
[41] For an illustration and systematisation of this case law, see K. Mortelmans, 'The Relationship Between the Treaty Rules and Community Measures for the Establishment and Functioning of the Internal Market – Towards a Concordance Rule', 39 *Common Market Law Review*, pp 1303 ss.
[42] Case T-13/99 *Pfizer Animal Health v Council*, 2002 ECR II-3305.

A.   The *Pfizer* Judgment

In this recent judgment,[43] the CFI seems to have shown some readiness to become more involved in the examination of the scientific evidence adduced by the parties to the dispute and this even if the contested measure had a Community origin.[44] Immediately after the adoption of an EC Regulation banning the use of four antibiotics as additives in animal feedstuffs,[45] Pfizer, producer of one of these antibiotics (virginiamycin), challenged this EC measure by alleging manifest errors of risk assessment and a misapplication of the precautionary principle. Although the CFI clearly stated from the outset that it was not for it 'to assess the merits of either of the scientific points of view argued before it and to substitute its assessment for that of the Community institutions', it could not prevent itself from discussing the scientific validity and merits of the scientific evidence advanced by the parties. This inevitably led the court to engage in a quasi-scientific debate on the main scientific controversy underlying the legal dispute, ie whether there is a link between the use of virgiamycin as an additive in feedstuffs and the development of streptogramin resistance in humans. In particular, the court expressly decided to consider whether, as maintained by Pfizer, the contested regulation was unlawful 'because of the inadequate nature of the scientific data' provided by the parties. In other words, the court went so far, in its judicial-scientific involvement, as to directly ask itself whether the scientific evidence available to the EC institutions was 'sufficiently reliable and cogent for them to conclude that there was a risk associated with the use of virgiamycin as a growth promoter'.[46]

---

[43] See also the parallel case that concerned the same decision, revoking the authorization of some antibiotics as growth promoters: T-70/99, *Alpharma Inc. v Council* [2002] ECR II-3495. For a comment on these two judgments, see *ex multis*, V. Walker, 'The Myth of Science as a 'Neutral Arbiter' for triggering Precautions', 26 *Boston College International and Comparative Law Review* 197, pp 207–8; E. Vos, 'The Precautionary Principle Reviewed: the Judgments of the Court of First Instance of 11 September 2002 Concerning the EU Ban of Two Antibiotics', *Journal of Risk Research* 7, 2004; F. Mariatte, *Commentaire n. 362 – Principe de precaution*, Europe, Novembre 2002, p 12; L. Gonzalez Vaqué, 'El Principio de Precaucion en la jurisprudencia comunitaria: la sentencia "virginiamicina"' *(asunto T-13/99), Revista de Derecho Comunitario Europeo*, 2002, n. 13, p 925 and A. Alemanno, 'Protection des consommateurs – Arrêts Alpharma/Pfizer', 4 *Revue du droit de l'Union Europénne*, p 842.

[44] Contra, see Peel, supra note 29, p. 43 who argues that 'Although the Court stressed that regulatory authorities must have at their disposal scientific information which is sufficiently reliable and cogent to allow them to understand the ramifications of the scientific questions raised and to make a decision on policy measures in full knowledge of the facts, the CFI displayed a 'strongly deferential attitude when reviewing the institutions' interpretation of the scientific material and their judgments as to the existence of genuine scientific uncertainty'.

[45] These antibiotics were used as growth promoters and they also had the useful side effect of preventing certain animal diseases.

[46] Case T-13/99 *Pfizer Animal Health v Council*, [2002] ECR II-3305, at 322.

For the first time, an EC court felt the need to make an express reference to the quality of the scientific evidence the EC institutions should rely upon. Such evidence must be 'sufficiently reliable and cogent'[47].

Before starting its analysis, the CFI recalled the purpose and scope of judicial review of a Community measure. It held that in a situation where the EC institutions are required to make complex assessments of a scientific and technical nature and the parties to the dispute have submitted for review by the court a large number of arguments of a scientific and technical nature, based on a large number of studies and scientific opinions from eminent scientists,

> [...] judicial review is restricted and does not imply that the Community judicature can substitute its assessment for that of the Community institutions.[48]

Notwithstanding this declared commitment, the CFI carried out a detailed review of the scientific findings brought by the parties to determine whether the EC institutions erred when they concluded, 'on the basis of the scientific knowledge available at the time of the adoption of the contested regulation', that the use of virginiamycin as an additive in feeding stuffs entailed a risk to human health. By engaging in a quasi-scientific analysis of the scientific studies advanced by the parties to the dispute, the court found that:

> [...] the Community institutions could *reasonably* take the view that they had a *proper scientific basis* for a possible link between the use of virginiamycin as an additive in feeding-stuffs and the development of streptogramin resistance in humans.[49]

In other words, the Community was right to take the view that

> [...] the various experiments and observations [...] were *not mere conjecture* but amounted to *sufficiently reliable and cogent scientific evidence* .

B.   The *Vitamins* Line of Cases

A trend towards more scientific involvement by the EC courts, inaugurated in the *Pfizer* case, may seem to have been followed up by a recent line of cases decided by the ECJ.

---

[47] Ibid, para 162.
[48] Ibid, para 323.
[49] Ibid, para 393.

In this line of cases involving fortified foods, the court had been called upon to examine four infringement proceedings brought against Denmark,[50] France,[51] Italy[52] and the Netherlands.[53] In particular, the Commission contested, on the one hand, the Danish and Dutch practices requiring that enriched foodstuffs lawfully produced and marketed in other Member States may be marketed in their territories only if it was shown that such enrichment with nutrients meets a need in the Danish and Dutch populations and, on the other hand, the French and Italian systems of prior approval for fortified foods lawfully produced and marketed in other Member States.

In these judgments, the court has established that in order to show that the national measures are necessary to give effective protection to public health the competent authorities must base their decisions:

> [...] on a *detailed assessment* of the risk alleged by the Member State invoking Article 30 EC.

This detailed scientific requirement had originally been sketched out by the EFTA court in the *Kellogg's* case, where it was established, although within the EEA context, that Member States must, when invoking the precautionary principle, conduct a 'comprehensive evaluation of the risk to health'.[54]

While in the Italian case the court directly found that the government failed to show 'any alleged risk to public health' and to 'explain on what scientific data or medical reports' it relied,[55] in the case brought against France, the court found that the scientific opinions cited by the government were not specific enough to prove the alleged risk since they refer

> *vaguely* to the possibility of a general risk of excessive intake, without specifying the vitamins concerned, the extent to which those limits would be exceeded or the risk incurred.[56]

Moreover, in the same French case, the court found that, contrary to the studies focusing on L-tarrate and L-carnitine, the studies it relied upon

---

[50] Case 192/01 *Commission v Denmark* [2003] ECR 9693.
[51] Case C-24/00 *Commission v France* [2004] not yet reported.
[52] Case C-270/02 *Commission v Italy* [2004] not yet reported.
[53] Case C-41/02 *Commission v Netherlands* [2004] not yet reported.
[54] EFTA Court of 5 April 2001, Case E-3/00 *Efta Surveillance Authority v Norway*, in EFTA Court Report 2000/2001, p. 73, para 30. For a comment of this case, see A. Alemanno, 'Le Principe de Précaution en Droit Communautaire: Stratégie de Gestion des Risques ou Risque d'Atteinte au Marché Intérieur?', in *Revue du Droit de l'Union Européenne*, pp 947–50.
[55] Case C-270/02 *Commission v Italy*, [2004] not yet reported, para 24.
[56] Case C-24/00 *Commission v France*, supra note 51, para 61.

concerning drinks such as *Redbull* fulfilled the requested scientific requirement ('detailed assessment') and proved that excessive caffeine content and the presence of taurine was harmful to human health. On this basis, it concluded that the Commission failed to explain or to adduce evidence to rebut those studies. But, who is going to decide whether the scientific opinion a state relies upon in the adoption of public health measures is a 'detailed assessment' within the meaning of the ECJ's case law?

This line of cases clearly shows that the court, by imposing a stricter scientific discipline (a 'detailed assessment'), seems to be willing to get increasingly involved in scientific matters. Not only the CFI (in *Alpharma/ Pfizer*), but also the ECJ (after the *Vitamins* line of cases) would seem eager to play with science by weighing the merits and assessing the validity of scientific opinions set forth by the parties to the dispute. Both the CFI and the ECJ have thus inaugurated a new approach to scientific issues allowing them to 'pick and choose' those scientific opinions they believe better fulfil the minimum scientific requirements they would require in order for a measure to be considered to be 'based on a detailed risk assessment'. The consequences stemming from the adoption of this intrusive approach to science-based measures will be further examined and, subsequently, it will be shown why this approach is not viable and therefore should not be applauded.

3. The Standard of Review in the WTO Dispute Settlement System

3.1 An Introduction to the General Standard of Review

As is often the case in international dispute resolution, the issue of the standard of review has not been explicitly settled by the WTO's negotiators.[57] This has left panels and the Appellate Body free to identify a proper standard of review. The only guide offered to the WTO judicial bodies is the vague and open-textured formulation of Article 11 DSU which provides that a panel must make:

> an *objective assessment* of the matter before it, including an objective assessment of the facts of the case and the applicability of and conformity with the relevant covered agreements, and make such other findings as will assist the DSB in making the recommendations or in giving the rulings provided for in the covered agreements.[58]

[57] M. Oesch, *Standards of Review in WTO Dispute Resolution* (Oxford University Press, 2003) p. 16. According to Christoforou this general lack of attention paid to procedural rules should be seen as a result of greater Members' efforts to improving the substantive rules on trade and health regulations. See T. Christoforou, 'Settlement of Science-Based Trade Disputes in the WTO: A Critical Review of the Developing Case Law in the Face of Scientific Uncertainty', 8 *N.Y.U. Environmental Law Journal*, pp 625–6.
[58] The DSU applies to virtually all disputes brought before the WTO.

Yet, the 'objective assessment', by itself, does not seem to disclose a meaningful standard of review, notably as it does not say how intense the scrutiny should be.[59] In fact, any assessment of the facts, whether inspired by 'total deference', by 'reasonable deference' or by de novo *review*, can be virtually 'objective'. The objective standard rather hints at the panel's obligation to exercise in good faith its responsibilities under the DSU.[60]

The only explicit standard of review which is provided within the SPS Agreement may be found in Article 17.6 of the Antidumping Agreement. This is because, at the time of the negotiation of this Agreement, SPS draftsmen expressed much more concern over the standard that panels would apply in anti-dumping cases than with the standards that panels may use in any other area susceptible to be covered *ratione materiae* by the WTO Agreements, such as food safety, environmental protection or intellectual property.[61]

Unlike Article 11 DSU, Article 17.6(i) of the Antidumping Agreement narrowly prescribes the function of a panel as establishing whether the importing authority had properly determined the facts in an investigation and whether its evaluation was objective. Therefore, under this standard:

> [...] if the [authorities'] establishment of the facts was proper and their evaluation was unbiased and objective, even though the panel may have reached a different conclusion, the evaluation should not be overturned.[62]

As a result, a panel in an antidumping dispute is not 'to perform a *de novo review* of the evidence that was before the investigating authority' in the case, but merely 'to assess whether its establishment of the facts

---

[59] Several commentators have expressed some suspicion about the possibility that this expression may disclose a meaningful standard of review. See, *ex multis*, C.D. Ehlermann, 'Standard of Review in WTO Law', in 7 *Journal of International Economic Law* 3, p 498 and Button, supra note 29, p 173, who after having stated that 'objective assessment' only provides a 'minimum standard for its review' defines it as 'a guarantee of due process or fairness in panel proceedings', rather than 'a particular standard of review'.

[60] See Article 11 of the Understanding on Rules and Procedures Governing the Settlement of Disputes (DSU), in Annex 2 to the Agreement Establishing the World Trade Organization, 15 April 1994, Final Act Embodying the Results of the Uruguay Round of Multilateral Trade Negotiations, Article 2(2), Apr. 15, 1994, Legal Instruments – Results of the Uruguay Round vol. 1 (1994), 33 *I.L.M.* 1125 (1994) reprinted in *World Trade Organization, The Legal Texts: The Results of the Uruguay Round of Multilateral Trade Negotiations* 161 (1994).

[61] One might notice that, unlike other WTO Agreements, such as the GATT or the GATS, the whole Anti-dumping Agreement is characterised by laying down rules that, by their own nature, are more procedural than substantive in nature.

[62] Article 17.6(i) of the Agreement on implementation of Article VI of the General Agreement on Tariffs and Trade 1994.

was proper and the evaluation of those facts was unbiased and objective'.[63]

A European attempt to regard the DSU's generalised 'objective standard' as tantamount to the 'deferential reasonable standard' expressed by Article 17.6(i) of the Anti-dumping Agreement was rejected by the Appellate Body in the first SPS case it had to face.[64] In the view of the EC, panels, in developing the 'proper standard of review', may either follow 'de novo review' or show 'deference'. Under the former, a panel 'would have to verify the determination by the national authority was 'correct', both factually and procedurally'. Under the latter, a panel 'should not seek to redo the investigation conducted by the national authority but instead examine whether the 'procedure' required by the relevant WTO rules had been followed'.[65] According to the Community, such a 'deferential 'reasonableness' standard' would be applicable in 'all highly complex factual situations, including the assessment of the risks to human health arising from toxins and contaminants' and should have been applied by the panel in such a case.

In rejecting this claim, the Appellate Body held that the standard set out in Article 17.6(i) had no relevance in controversies under the SPS Agreement. It also recalled that, under the decision on the review of Article 17.6 of the Agreement on Implementation of Article VI of the General Agreement on Tariffs and Trade 1994, the same standard had to be reviewed after a period of three years with a view to considering the question of whether it is capable of general application.

Subsequently, it held that, although:

> we find no indication in the SPS Agreement of an intent on the part of the Member to adopt or incorporate into that Agreement the standard set out in Article 17.6(i) [...] we do not mean, however, to suggest that there is at present no standard of review applicable to the determination and assessment of the facts in proceedings under the SPS Agreement.

In fact, in this particular case:

> [...] Article 11 of the DSU bears directly on this matter and, in effect, articulates with great succinctness but with sufficient clarity

---

[63] Guatemala – Definitive Anti-Dumping Measures on Grey Portland Cement from Mexico (hereinafter 'Guatemala-Cement'), WT/DS156/R, para 8.19.

[64] The European Community argued for the adoption of this standard by stressing the fact that it was already applicable in all highly complex factual situations, such as those characterising trade remedies cases. See *EC–Hormones* AB report, paras 112–13, citing paras 128–29 of the EC's appellant submission.

[65] *EC–Hormones* AB report, para 111.

the appropriate standard of review for panels in respect of both the ascertainment of facts and the legal characterisation of such facts under the relevant agreements [...] So far as fact-finding by panels is concerned, their activities are always constrained by the mandate of Article 11 of the DSU: the applicable standard is neither *de novo* review, nor 'total deference', but rather the 'objective assessment of the facts.[66]

By insisting on the wording employed in Article 11 DSU ('objective assessment of the facts'), the Appellate Body clearly refused to accept the extension of the anti-dumping standard of review, as enshrined in Article 17.6(i) ADA, to the review of SPS measures.

Moreover, in the same case, the AB has not solely ruled out the possibility of extending the procedurally-oriented anti-dumping standard of review to the SPS disputes, but it has completely missed the opportunity to define the standard of review applicable to SPS measures, by tautologically holding that the 'objective assessment' applicable standard is:

neither *de novo* review as such, nor 'total deference', but rather the 'objective assessment of the facts. Many panels have in the past refused to undertake *de novo* review, wisely, since under current practice and systems, they are in any case poorly suited to engage in such a review. On the other hand, 'total deference to the findings of the national authorities', it has been well said, 'could not ensure an 'objective assessment' as foreseen by Article 11 of the DSU.[67]

Therefore, while clearly refusing to interpret the objective assessment standard as *de novo review* (panels are 'poorly suited' to engage in it), the AB has not made clear to what extent panels are allowed to establish for themselves the facts underlying the national authority's assessment or the deductions that the national authority drew from those facts. By hinting at the fact that the proper standard of review should lie somewhere between de *novo review* and 'total deference' review, the AB has failed effectively to identify such a standard.

Nonetheless, by taking a negative approach in the description of the proper standard of review, it has clarified what a panel cannot do by defining what it envisages as *de novo review*: 'a situation where the panel redoes the investigation into the facts that has been done by a national authority'.[68]

---

[66] *EC–Hormones* AB report, paras 116–117.

[67] *EC–Hormones*, AB report, para 117. This would amount to a tautology according to D Palmenter, 'The WTO Standard of Review in Health and Safety Disputes', in G. Bermann and P.C. Mavroidis, *Trade and Human Health and Safety* (Cambridge University Press, 2006) p. 229.

[68] *EC–Hormones*, panel report, para 111.

In particular, according to the AB, instead of performing a *de novo review*, a panel:

> must put itself in the place of the [national authority] at the time it made its determinations.[69]

Although this statement may seem to indicate that panels should accord a considerable degree of discretion to national authorities, we will see further that it has not always been the case in the case law.

This uncertainty about the applicable standard of review means that in every case they face, panels and the Appellate Body must decide how intensively a measure should be reviewed and how much deference should be granted to national decision makers. As the same AB has implicitly recognised,[70] the requirement for an 'objective assessment' must operate with another, more precise, underlying standard of review. It follows that, although panels perform an 'objective assessment', the scope of and the intensity of their assessment is inevitably not the same for every issue, in every dispute. The final arbiter on the definition of the appropriate standard of review is the AB as it decides claims that panels have failed to make an 'objective assessment' of the matters before them.

The four SPS disputes decided to date (*Hormones, Australia–Salmon, Japan– Agricultural Products* and *Japan–Apples*) have involved quite different SPS measures. While the *Hormones* cases concerned the complaints submitted by the US and Canada against the EC ban on the importation of meat and meat products from cattle treated with six particular hormones for growth promotion purposes, the three latter disputes related to the challenges to quarantine regulations imposed by particular WTO members. To determine the standard of review adopted vis-à-vis (food safety) science-based measures we must therefore look at these cases.

It will be shown that panels have closely scrutinised the scientific evidence advanced by the parties.[71] However, although this trend towards an intrusive review was already visible in the *Hormones* and

---

[69] *United States–Transitional Safeguard Measure on Combed Cotton Yarn from Pakistan* (hereinafter 'US Cotton Yarn'), appellate body report, WT/DS192/AB/R, adopted on 5 November 2001, para 78.

[70] In the *US–Hot-Rolled Steel*, the AB held that 'it is inconceivable that Article 17.6(i) should require anything other than that panel make an objective 'assessment of the facts of the matter'. See, *United States–Anti-Dumping Measures on Certain Hot-Rolled Steel Products from Japan* Appellate Body Report WT/DS184/AB/R, adopted on 23 August 2001, para 55.

[71] For a description of the AB's tendency to get entangled in detailed analysis of the factual evidence, see A. Green, 'Climate Change, Regulatory Policy and the WTO' 8 *Journal of International Economic Law* (2005) 143, pp 170–173.

Salmon cases, it was in the *Apples* case that the panel went so far as to adopt a quasi-*de novo review* involving an assessment of the quality of the scientific information brought by the parties, thus totally ignoring the previous AB's veto on the adoption of this standard.

3.2. The Standard of Review under the SPS Agreement

A WTO member's health measure may not survive review under the SPS Agreement unless it is grounded on science. In other words, according to the SPS Agreement, a Member State measure, although not discriminatory, may be struck down for being scientifically flawed. Similarly, an EC Member national health measure, or a Community health measure, should it be lacking a solid scientific justification, may not survive an EC courts' review.

The scientific justification discipline prevailing in the WTO raises questions as to what 'sufficient scientific evidence' is, and as to when a measure is based on 'scientific principles' and in relation to 'on risk assessment', according to Articles 2.2 and 5.1 SPS, respectively. As seen above, these provisions have been interpreted together as requiring that there must be an 'objective or rational relationship' between the SPS measure and the available scientific evidence.[72] This interpretation of the scientific justification discipline, combined with the 'objective assessment' standard set forth in Article 11 DSU, does not seem to require a specific (more or less rigorous) standard of review for SPS measures. In particular, by focusing solely on the existence of a rational relationship between the evidence and the measure, this criterion per se does not seem to be excessively intrusive into Member States' regulatory autonomy.[73] In fact, by implying some deference, it provides for a less stringent approach than a strict necessity test insofar as it leaves great discretion to Member States and allows for inclusion of non-scientific factors.[74]

Therefore, following this interpretation of the WTO scientific discipline, members would remain free to adopt risk regulations based on what *they* consider to be 'sufficient evidence', provided that there is a rational relationship between the evidence and the measure.[75] Thus, for instance,

---

[72] For a synthesis of the case law on this point, see *Japan–Agricultural Products*, panel report, paras 8.28, 8.42.

[73] See, eg, R.D. Thomas, 'Where's the Beef? Mad Cows and the Blight of the SPS Agreement', 32 *Vanderbilt Journal of Transnational Law*, 487, p 507 (1999) and M.G. Bloche, 'WTO Deference to National Health Policy: Toward an Interpretative Principle', 5(4) *Journal of International Economic Law* 825, p 837 (2002).

[74] R.D. Thomas, 'Where's the Beef? Mad Cows and the Blight of the SPS Agreement', 32 *Vanderbilt Journal of Transnational Law*, 487, p 507 (1999).

[75] This freedom is recognised not only by the text of the SPS Agreement but also by the AB. See *Australia–Salmon*, para 199. Here, the AB has clearly stated that the panels should not substitute its own reasoning about the implied level of protection for that expressed consistently by Australia.

the panel in *Japan–Agricultural Products* has stated that in determining whether 'the varietal testing requirement (the contested measure) is maintained without sufficient scientific evidence (ie, whether there is a lack of an objective or rational relationship between the measure at issue and the scientific evidence before the panel)', the panel is neither 'empowered, nor are the experts advising the panel, to conduct [their] own risk assessment'.[76]

This approach seems to have been confirmed in the more recent SPS case report *Japan – Apples*. In this case, the WTO judicial bodies had to verify the SPS compatibility of the quarantine restrictions applied since 1994 by Japan on US apples to protect against the introduction of fire blight.

Dealing with the question of determining the standard of review applicable in the pending case, the panel has declared:

> [...] we are mindful that we are not supposed to conduct our own risk assessment or to impose any scientific opinion on Japan. Like the panels in *Australia - Salmon* and *Japan - Agricultural products II*, we will only examine and evaluate the evidence, including the information we have received from the experts advising the Panel, and the arguments put before us in light of the relevant WTO provisions.[77]

These repeated assertions seem to prove that the WTO judicial bodies' awareness that the process of scientific assessment undertaken by governments cannot be easily replicated by a WTO court or by its scientific experts.

Yet, one may legitimately wonder how panels are to make an 'objective assessment' of the facts without considering them afresh.

In fact, contrary to what may appear from these relentless statements of principle, panels, in applying the 'rational relationship' test to verify the conformity of SPS measures to the WTO scientific justification discipline, tend to adopt a rather intrusive approach.[78] By traditionally relying on advice from independent experts, panels tend to determine whether the scientific theory or risk assessment outcome put forward by a defending member is properly backed up by the available scientific

---

[76] Panel report, *Agricultural Products*, para 8.32.

[77] Article 21.5 panel report. *Japan–Measures Affecting the Importation of Apples*, WT/DS245/RW, para 8.137.

[78] See, eg, A. Guzman, 'Food Fears: Health and Safety at the WTO', in *Boalt Working Papers in Public Law*, 2004, who, after criticising such an intrusive approach, makes a claim for a more deferential WTO review of SPS measures.

evidence. In doing this, the panels have increasingly sparked scientific controversies, especially after the AB offered the following interpretation of the rational relationship test:

> [...] whether there is a rational relationship between an SPS measure and the scientific evidence is to be determined on a case-by case basis, and will depend upon the particular circumstances of the case, including the characteristics of the measure at issue and the *quality and quantity of the scientific evidence*'[79].

This AB's elaboration of the rational relationship test, by referring to 'the quality and quantity of the scientific evidence', inevitably opens up the Pandora's box of scientific discussion to the WTO judicial bodies, thereby legitimising their involvement in controversial scientific matters. Accordingly, in the same case, the panel has invested itself with the task:

> to *examine and weigh* all the evidence validly submitted to us, including the opinions we received from the experts advising the Panel in accordance with Article 13 of the DSU.[80]

The existence of such a non-deferential standard of review of science-based measures has been expressly endorsed by the AB in the *Apples* case. Called upon to clarify the issue of the standard of review that a panel must apply in the assessment of scientific evidence submitted in proceedings under the SPS Agreement, the AB has declared that:

> [...] total deference to the findings of the national authorities would not ensure an objective assessment as required by Article 11 of the DSU.[81]

On this basis, the AB rejected Japan's contention according to which, under Article 2.2, a panel would be obliged to give precedence to the importing member's approach to scientific evidence and risk when analysing and assessing scientific evidence.[82]

In determining whether the Japanese quarantine measures were supported by sufficient scientific evidence (rational relationship test), the panel had to face numerous specific scientific issues boiling down to the question as to whether imported mature and apparently symptomless apples could nevertheless be infected and thus capable of transmitting the fire blight disease.

---

[79] *Japan–Agricultural Products* AB report, para 84.

[80] *Japan–Agricultural Products*, panel report, para 7.10.

[81] *EC–Hormones*, AB report, para 117.

[82] *Japan–Apples* AB report, para 165, where it stated that 'Japan's submission that the panel was obliged to favour Japan's approach to risk and scientific evidence over the views of the experts conflicts with the Appellate Body's articulation of the standard of objective assessment of facts'.

In evaluating this question, by relying on its own experts' advice, the panel got enmeshed in a quasi-scientific debate on the merits of the data advanced by the parties before reaching its own conclusion, thus acting as a real arbiter of a scientific controversy. For instance, on the specific scientific issue as to whether a mature, symptomless apple could harbour endophytic bacteria,[83] the panel, since the scientific opinions brought by the US and Japan were divergent, turned to the opinion of its experts to reach its own conclusion. By endorsing its experts' opinions,[84] the panel dismissed the scientific validity of the study by Dr van der Zwet et al. cited by Japan, by criticising not only its methodology (this study 'did not specify the degree of maturity of the fruit') but also the results they reached ('this made its conclusions confused, difficult to interpret or even unconvincing').[85] After having fully engaged in such a scientific debate, the panel concluded by stating that:

> [...] on the basis of the elements before us, there was not sufficient scientific evidence to support the view that apples are likely to serve as a pathway for the entry, establishment or spread of fire blight within Japan.

This conclusion was reached notwithstanding the fact that 'some slight risk of contamination cannot be totally excluded'.[86] However, as 'the experts all categorised the risk *as negligible*', the panel denied the scientific evidence brought by Japan the qualification of 'sufficient' within the meaning of Article 2.2 SPS, thus condemning the Japanese measures at stake.

In light of the above, it is clear that, contrary to what was expressly stated by the panel in the *Asbestos* case, the panel, though relying heavily on its experts' opinions, undoubtedly acted as 'an arbiter of the opinions expressed by the scientific community'[87], by assessing not only the quality of the scientific studies brought before it but also setting up a 'minimal' level of risk (more than 'negligible') justifying the adoption of an SPS measure.

---

[83] In other words, whether a mature, symptomless apple could harbour bacteria inside the fruit without itself being infected.

[84] It is worth noting that, on that specific controversial scientific issue, only one of the panel experts (Dr. Smith) expressly criticised the study (as 'not convincing in several aspects'), cited by Japan, by van der Zwet. See paras 6.72–6.75.

[85] *Japan–Apples* panel report, para 8.127.

[86] *Japan–Apples* panel report, para 8.173.

[87] *EC–Asbestos*, panel report, para 8.181. In this case the panel, before analyzing whether the French ban on asbestos products could be justified under Article XX GATT, declared that 'its role [...] is to determine whether there is sufficient scientific evidence to conclude that there exists a risk for human life or health' and not to 'set itself up as an arbiter of the opinions expressed by the scientific community'.

One may observe that this deliberately intrusive approach has been adopted in a case where for the first time the panel has assessed the sufficiency of the scientific underpinnings of a member's risk regulatory measures directly, rather than coming to this question mainly through an analysis of its role as part of the process of risk assessment supporting the member's regulation.[88] In other words, the panel, instead of looking at scientific evidence as a part of the process of risk assessment under Article 5.1, focuses on what might count as science within the meaning of Article 2.2 SPS.[89] It is argued that the adoption of this way of proceeding intrinsically induces a panel to explore more deeply the scientific evidence gathered by the parties and, accordingly, to adopt a less deferential scrutiny.[90] This is because Article 2.2, unlike Article 5.1, provides for less specific disciplines by thus leaving the panel without any guidance on how to verify whether the SPS measure at stake is 'based on scientific principles'. In the light of the above, it is submitted that an examination of the scientific justification beginning with Article 5.1, instead of Article 2.2, is likely to favour the adoption of a more constrained approach in the exercise of judicial review.

Finally, the result is that today panels not only owe no deference to national authorities' interpretations of WTO provisions but they are not even expected to give precedence to the importing member's approach to scientific evidence and risk when analysing and assessing scientific evidence. This proves that, in the absence of clearly framed substantive rights and obligations, it ultimately remains to the WTO judicial bodies to determine the margins of members' power to identify risk and to act accordingly.

A. Towards a 'Minimum Specificity Threshold' of Science?

There are mainly two consequences stemming from the adoption of such an intrusive standard of review of SPS measures, both imposing significant limits on the scope of risk assessment undertaken by members to support their science-based measures. In particular, the rigorous approach taken by WTO courts vis-à-vis the scientific material that members have taken into account in assessing risks leads to the

---

[88] As panels may choose to commence their analysis with any of the breaches alleged by the complainant, they traditionally examine whether the studies supporting the contested measure amount to a 'risk assessment' under Article 5 SPS. In doing so, they verify whether 'available scientific evidence' has been taken into account in the risk assessment to integrate the 'sufficient evidence' requirement imposed by Article 2.2 SPS.

[89] *Japan–Apples*, panel report, para 8.92.

[90] Contra, see Peel, supra note 29, p. 20 who argues that 'in both cases where the parties to an SPS dispute disagree over the interpretation of the available science and its relevance in determining the significance of the risk at issue, WTO decision-makers are likely to encounter complex questions which lie at the interface between law and science'.

introduction of a sort of 'minimum specificity threshold' this material has to comply with in order to qualify as 'sufficiently scientific'. As seen above, by insisting that the scientific evidence advanced by the parties must meet a specificity-threshold, the WTO judicial bodies seem willing and ready to assess the scientific 'validity', or at least adequacy, of the scientific studies cited by the parties in a particular dispute.[91] This has clearly happened in the *Apples* case where the panel dismissed the risk assessment conducted by Japan to the extent that it did not focus sufficiently on the risk of transmission of fire blight through apple fruit, as opposed to other modes of transmission.[92] While this trend is particularly visible in this case, it is possible to interpret some findings of the Appellate Body in the *Hormones* case as similarly establishing a 'minimum specificity threshold' for evidence to be 'sufficiently specific' to satisfy Article 5.1. In this case, the AB dismissed not only the opinion by Dr Lucier for not being 'the result of scientific studies carried out by him or under his supervision focusing *specifically* on residues of hormones in meat from cattle fattened with such hormones'[93] but also the scientific studies relied upon by the EC because these, by relating to the carcinogenic potential of entire *categories* of hormones, or of the hormones at issue *in general*', '[...] are [...] in the nature of general studies of or statements on the carcinogenic potential of the named hormones'.[94] Against this backdrop, the AB went on to hold that these scientific studies not only failed to assess 'the carcinogenic potential of those hormones when used specifically *for growth promotion purposes*' but also did 'not evaluate the specific potential for carcinogenic effects arising from the presence *in 'food'*, more specifically, 'meat or meat products' of residues of the hormones in dispute'.[95]

As a result, these studies are 'relevant' but, by not focusing on and not addressing 'the particular kind of risk here at stake [...] do not appear to be *sufficiently specific* to the case at hand'.[96] The question whether this conclusion was correct or not implies an evaluation of the 'validity', or adequacy, of scientific evidence. Since Dr Lucier's opinion and the other

---

[91] See R. Howse and P.C. Mavroidis, 'Europe's Evolving Regulatory Strategy for GMOs – The Issue of Consistency with WTO Law: of Kine and Brine', 24 *Fordham International Law Journal* 317, p 326.

[92] *Japan–Apples*, panel report, paras 8.277–280. This finding was subsequently upheld by the AB report, para 206.

[93] *EC–Hormones*, AB report, para 198. This EC expert witness argued before the panel that the ingestion of growth hormone residues in meat would cause a small increase of cancers. In particular, he stated that if of every one million women 110,000 would contract breast cancer, one of those 110 000 would come from eating meat containing growth promoters such as oestrogen.

[94] *EC–Hormones*, AB report, para 199.

[95] *EC–Hormones*, AB report, para 199. In general, these studies only dealt with the general association between exposure to increased hormone levels and the development of cancer, rather than the specific situation of cancer posed by consuming hormone residues in beef.

[96] *EC–Hormones*, AB report, para 200.

EC scientific studies did not meet an (undetermined) specificity evidence threshold, they have been rejected by the Appellate Body.

Along the same lines, the panel in the *Apples* case, after having stated that 'direct' or 'indirect' evidence may equally be considered, clearly stated that, though scientifically equivalent, the latter is of greater probative value. Here again the panel did not hesitate in assigning a specific scientific value to a certain study in order to make it qualify as 'sufficient' within the meaning of Article 2.2 SPS.

What appears to be particularly difficult is to apply this specificity requirement to low-level risk situations, ie when, for instance, the presumed adverse effect may be estimated to be one in a million.[97] As WTO members are entitled to adopt any level of protection they deem appropriate to the circumstances, it might happen that they may decide to act in situations of low-risk or even of zero-risk. In both such situations, a member enacting an SPS measure will be likely to face enormous difficulties in proving that its regulation satisfies the specificity requirement as increasingly required, although lacking any textual basis, by the WTO judicial bodies.

One may wonder whether such a trend of evaluating the 'scientific specificity' of the evidence advanced by the parties may somehow find a raison d'être in the fact that WTO procedures do not set out restrictions on the admissibility of evidence. This lack of an admissibility check may possibly enable parties to put junk science on the panel record.[98] What is sure today is that the WTO dispute settlement bodies increasingly require a highly specialised risk assessment addressing the particular circumstances of the case.[99] It is argued that such interpretation not only lacks a textual basis within the SPS Agreement but also fails to ensure a proper balance between the WTO members' rights and obligations as stemming from the SPS Agreement. In particular, it is submitted that

---

[97] A.O. Sykes, 'Domestic Regulation, Sovereignty and Scientific Evidence Requirements: A Pessimistic View', 3 *Chicago J. Int'l L.* 353, pp 364–5 (2002). Also published under the same title in G. Bermann and P.C. Mavroidis, *Trade and Human Health and Safety* (Cambridge University Press, 2006) pp 257ss.

[98] To the contrary, in the United States, there exist strict rules on the admissibility of scientific evidence and most of the law and science debate revolves around this specific procedural issue. See K. Foster and P.W. Huber, *Judging Science. Scientific Knowledge and the Federal Courts*, MIT Press, 1999. This ex ante control may perhaps explain the traditional deference shown by US Federal Courts when reviewing agencies' science-based measures. Thus, for instance, the DC Circuit stated: 'It is not our function to resolve disagreement among the experts or to judge the merits of competing expert views. Our task is the limited one ascertaining that the choices made by the Administrator [notably, EPA] were reasonable and supported by the record'. See *Am. Trucking Associations v EPA*, 283 F.3D 355, 362 (D.C.Cir.2002).

[99] Button, supra note 29, p 66.

this approach puts into question members' right to establish the level of protection they deem appropriate, as enshrined in the preamble and in Article 5 SPS.

B.   Towards a 'Minimum Risk Threshold'?

The adoption of such an intrusive standard of review of science-based measures limits even further the scope of risk assessment undertaken by members to support their regulations. As egregiously illustrated by the *Apples* case, since the AB has turned the 'rational relationship test' into an assessment of the 'quality and quantity of the scientific evidence', this has immediately led to the introduction of a further requirement that the scientific evidence brought by the parties must comply with in order to justify the adoption of an SPS measure. Thus, to be 'sufficient' within the meaning of Article 2.2 SPS, the scientific evidence supporting a member measure not only has to satisfy a 'minimum specificity threshold', but it also has to reach a 'minimum risk threshold' justifying the adoption of an SPS measure.

In fact, if one looks at the way in which the panel analysed the scientific evidence in the *Apples* case, it appears that it came to the conclusion that the Japanese measures were not supported by scientific evidence (proving the risk of contamination) notwithstanding the fact that 'some slight risk of contamination cannot be totally excluded'. Through an assessment of the quality and quantity of the scientific evidence supporting the contested measure, the panel concluded that this evidence showed a risk that it was too low to qualify as 'sufficient scientific evidence' justifying the adoption of a member SPS measure. In other words, as 'the experts all categorised the risk as *negligible*', the panel denied the scientific evidence advanced by Japan the qualification of 'sufficient' within the meaning of Article 2.2 SPS, thus condemning the Japanese measures at issue.

The introduction of such a 'minimum risk threshold' that the scientific evidence brought by a party must satisfy to comply with the SPS requirements seems to contradict the accepted view according to which WTO member enjoy complete freedom in deciding the level of risk they can accept, provided that they are able to show that the claimed risk exists. Thus, for instance, relying on this line of thought, the AB, in the *Salmon* case, went so far as to admit that a member can choose 'zero risk' as its appropriate level of protection.[100] However, after the *Apples* case, it seems that a WTO panel, when reviewing a member's chosen level of protection, could strike down a measure simply because it

---

[100] *Australia–Salmon*, AB report, para 125.

considers the risk involved to be too low to justify the adoption of that measure.[101]

It remains to be seen how this new approach may be reconciled with Article 5.7 SPS which expressly recognised the possibility of adopting SPS measures on the basis of available pertinent information where 'relevant scientific evidence is insufficient', albeit on a provisional basis.

C. Conclusions

This analysis of the standard of review applicable to SPS measures within the WTO context shows a growing trend towards a narrowly-construed interpretation of the scientific requirements leading to an intrusive role for panels and the AB in reviewing (food safety) science-based risk regulations adopted by WTO members. As closer attention has been paid to the 'quality and quantity' of the scientific evidence underlying SPS measures, the panels and the AB have begun imposing not only a 'minimum specificity threshold' of science, which translates into a specific scientific requirement, but also into a minimum risk criterion (yet to be quantified) that the scientific evidence brought by the parties must satisfy. Lacking a clear textual basis within the SPS Agreement, both the specificity requirement for risk assessment and the minimum risk criterion clash with the right of the members to establish their chosen level of protection. By relying on the AB's language, it is submitted that 'compliance with Article 5.1' instead of being 'a countervailing factor in respect of the right of members to set their appropriate level of protection',[102] is gradually becoming the dominant factor upon which to establish the legitimacy of an SPS measure with WTO law.

The adoption of such an intrusive standard of review carries with it the clear implication that panels and the AB are increasingly called upon to engage in complex scientific debates by not only assessing the quality of the scientific studies brought before them but also by setting up a minimum level of risk justifying the adoption of science-based measures. Such growing engagement with scientific evidence raises the question of whether WTO panellists and AB members and, more generally, international courts are adequately equipped to make such scientific judgments.

While these questions will be tackled in the next sections of this part of the book, exploring the role of experts in judicial review of science-based acts, Chapter III of the next and last Part will make an attempt at

---

[101] Contra I. Cheyne, 'Risk and Precaution in World Trade organization Law', 40(5) *Journal of World Trade* 837 (2006), p 850.
[102] *EC–Hormones* AB report, para 177.

identifying an appropriate standard of review of these measures, by proposing to follow as closely as possible the structure of risk analysis underlying the contested science-based measures.

4. How to Improve the Role of the Judge in the Review of Science-based Measures?

The previous analysis of the WTO and EC risk regulation disciplines and of the standards of judicial review of science-based measures, as interpreted and applied by their respective courts, clearly show the struggle faced by WTO and EC judges when they are called upon to interact with science in their activity of *dicere legem*.

Though developed in a domestic law context, the most authoritative formulation of this struggle belongs to the US Supreme Court Chief Justice Rehnquist. In his dissenting opinion in the *Daubert* case, he noted that

> 'the various briefs filed in this case are markedly different from typical briefs ... they deal with definitions of scientific knowledge, scientific method, scientific validity, and peer review – in short, matters far afield from the expertise of judges ...'[103].

It is indeed true that, in international legal *fora*, most legal opinions and judgments do not ordinarily rest on this kind of intellectual foundation, but rather are based on other sources of knowledge which are closer to the educational background of the judges. However, given the specificity of certain subject matters, it may happen that most of the scientific sources cited in a legal decision could not be easily read and understood by the majority of the judges composing the court.

As seen above, not only the intrusive standard of review adopted by WTO panels, but also that followed by EC courts (a sort of 'reasonable deference standard') when reviewing science-based national measures may seem to implicitly require some scientific expertise from these judges. As previously illustrated, this seems particularly true after the adoption of the *Pfizer* and *Vitamins* line of cases.

Even if the EC courts and the WTO judicial bodies are not being directly asked to establish whether a certain risk exists or, more generally, to settle a scientific debate, they tend to evaluate the competing scientific claims made by the parties in order to determine whether the contested measures conform to the scientific discipline in force within their legal system.

---

[103] *Daubert v Merrell Dow Pharmaceuticals, Inc.*, 509 U.S. 579 (1993), paras 598–9.

However, one would not reasonably expect any AB member or panellist or any European court judge called upon to decide a science-based case to have any specific scientific knowledge in the scientific field in question. The members of these courts are typically staffed by individuals without scientific expertise and, moreover, operate under time constraints. Indeed, these judicial bodies lack the resources to carry out a more informed and independent evaluation of the risk assessment outcomes submitted by the parties. In that light, it is of no surprise that both EC and WTO courts, being poorly equipped to evaluate scientific evidence, struggle in accomplishing this task. Nevertheless, notwithstanding the lack of scientific knowledge and appropriate resources, under the applicable standards of review, both European and WTO courts tend to carry out their own examination of the quality of the scientific data advanced by the parties.

These factors raise the question as to how the judiciary, notably the WTO and EC courts, may deal with scientific evidence.

4.1 The Role of Experts in Judicial Review: the External Expert Consultation in the WTO

To somehow mitigate such difficulties the WTO panels, unlike the EC judiciary, tend to rely on external advisers[104]. According to the Dispute Settlement Understanding, a panel may consult 'experts', either individually, or by convening an 'expert review group', to obtain their opinion on scientific and technical matters in dispute settlement.[105] Similar provisions already existed under the GATT system.[106] Both the

[104] Such consultations have taken place in most of the health and environmental disputes that have been settled by the WTO DSB. See J. Pauwelyn, 'Expert Advice in WTO Dispute Settlement', in G. Bermann and P.C. Mavroidis, *Trade and Human Health and Safety* (Cambridge University Press, 2006) p 235.

[105] Article 13 DSU (*Right to Seek Information*) reads as follows: '1. Each panel shall have the right to seek information and technical advice from any individual or body which it deems appropriate. However, before a panel seeks such information or advice from any individual or body within the jurisdiction of a Member it shall inform the authorities of that Member. A Member should respond promptly and fully to any request by a panel for such information as the panel considers necessary and appropriate. Confidential information which is provided shall not be revealed without formal authorisation from the individual, body, or authorities of the Member providing the information. 2. Panels may seek information from any relevant source and may consult experts to obtain their opinion on certain aspects of the matter. With respect to a factual issue concerning a scientific or other technical matter raised by a party to a dispute, a panel *may* request an advisory report in writing from an expert review group. Rules for the establishment of such a group and its procedures are set forth in Appendix 4'. It seems that while panels may ask experts their views on the matter, they cannot dispose any new risk assessment. On the scope of WTO external expertise, see infra 4.1.2.

[106] Christoforou notices that the 1966 Conciliation-Procedures under Article XXIII (in Decisions and Conclusions of the Contracting Parties, 5 April 1966, GATT B.I.S.D, 14th Suppl., 1966, at 18) contained virtually the same provisions as those of Article 13.1 and

(continued...)

SPS and TBT Agreements contain some additional provisions relating to the expert assistance procedure and encourage the panels to rely on this opportunity for external help.[107]

Generally, the selection process of experts and the operation of an expert consultation procedure take places according to the steps indicated below.[108] However, it must be noted from the outset that no WTO Agreements provide for detailed rules and procedures for the appointment and the operation of experts acting on an individual basis, but that they only do so for expert review groups.[109]

the first sentence of paragraph 2 of the same article. See Christoforou, in J. Bourrinet et S. Maljean-Dubois (eds), *Le Commerce International des Organismes Génétiquement Modifiés* (2003), p 254.

[107] Article 11.2 SPS provides that a panel should seek advice from experts chosen by the panel in consultation with the parties. To this end, the panel may, when it deems appropriate, establish an advisory technical experts group, or consult the relevant international organisations, at the request of either party to the dispute or on its own initiative. Article 14.2 TBT states that, at the request of a party to a dispute or at its own initiative, the panel may establish a technical assistance expert group.

[108] The detailed description of the general expert consultation procedure which follows builds upon the previous cases in which the panels have selected and consulted scientific experts. For an analysis of these modalities see J. Pauwelyn, 'The use of Experts in WTO Dispute Settlement', in 51 *ICQL* (2002) 328.

339–340; D.A. Motaal, 'Is the World Trade Organization Anti-Precaution?', *Journal of World Trade*, 39(3), p. 499 and Christoforou, supra note 106, pp 258–9.

[109] Appendix 4 of the DSU, entitled Expert Review Groups, states: 'The following rules and procedures shall apply to expert review groups established in accordance with the provisions of paragraph 2 of Article 13. 1. Expert review groups are under the panel's authority. Their terms of reference and detailed working procedures shall be decided by the panel, and they shall report to the panel. 2. Participation in expert review groups shall be restricted to persons of professional standing and experience in the field in question. 3. Citizens of parties to the dispute shall not serve on an expert review group without the joint agreement of the parties to the dispute, except in exceptional circumstances when the panel considers that the need for specialised scientific expertise cannot be fulfilled otherwise. Government officials of parties to the dispute shall not serve on an expert review group. Members of expert review groups shall serve in their individual capacities and not as government representatives, nor as representatives of any organisation. Governments or organisations shall therefore not give them instructions with regard to matters before an expert review group. 4. Expert review groups may consult and seek information and technical advice from any source they deem appropriate. Before an expert review group seeks such information or advice from a source within the jurisdiction of a member, it shall inform the government of that member. Any member shall respond promptly and fully to any request by an expert review group for such information as the expert review group considers necessary and appropriate. 5. The parties to a dispute shall have access to all relevant information provided to an expert review group, unless it is of a confidential nature. Confidential information provided to the expert review group shall not be released without formal authorization from the government, organization or person providing the information. Where such information is requested from the expert review group but release of such information by the expert review group is not authorized, a non-confidential summary of the information will be provided by the government, organisation or person supplying the information. 6. The expert review group shall submit a draft report to the parties to the dispute with a view to obtaining their comments, and taking them into account, as appropriate, in the final report, which shall also be issued to the parties to the dispute when it is submitted to the panel. The final report of the expert review group shall be advisory only.

The panel requests relevant international bodies (such as the WHO, IOE or the IPPC) and the parties to indicate the names of suitably qualified scientific experts and asks for their CVs. After having circulated all CVs to the parties for comments, the panel then appoints the best experts, generally ranking them with numbers between three and five. In general, panels do not select experts that are nationals of the parties to the dispute, unless they are expressly authorised by the parties to do so.[110]

Before the appointment of the experts, the panel prepares specific questions to be addressed to them. To the extent possible, these questions are also provided to the parties. The parties then have the possibility not only of expressing their objections to any particular expert[111] but also to comment on the proposed questions before these are sent to the experts. At this stage, the panel appoints the experts by informing the parties of its selection.

The experts are required to provide answers in writing to the questions and their answers are provided to the parties. Moreover, should the panel feel it necessary, or on a party's request, a meeting with experts may take place in which the panel, parties and experts gather just before the second substantive meeting with the parties.

Finally, the panels' practice in expert consultation shows that panels may have recourse to scientific experts even if none of the parties to the dispute requests it or if a party objects to it.[112]

In all the health cases in which expert consultations have taken place to date – *EC-Hormones*,[113] *US-Shrimp/Turtle*,[114] *Australia-Salmon*,[115] *Japan-Agricultural products, EC–Asbestos, Japan–Apples* and, finally *EC–Biotech* – the panels have consulted more than one expert, but always on an individual basis. In other words, to date not a single panel has set up an expert review group.

---

[110] This exclusion rule is expressly provided by Appendix 4 of the DSU establishing rules and procedures applicable to expert review groups.

[111] The parties may raise 'compelling objections' by, for instance, pointing to the fact that the experts were employees of either party to the dispute or that they were involved in the procedures at issue. See *EC–Biotech* panel report, at 7.21.

[112] Thus, for instance, neither in the *Salmon* case nor in the *Agricultural Products* the parties to the dispute have requested expert advice.

[113] The same set of experts has been appointed for two panels.

[114] *United States–Import prohibition of certain shrimp and shrimp products*, DS58/R, DS58/AB/R, DS58/AB/RW, DS58/RW.

[115] Here, the implementation panel has appointed a different set of experts than that used in the original panel.

The issue as to whether the panels, in a dispute involving scientific or technical matters, are limited to seeking advice from an expert review group or whether they may consult experts on an individual basis is controversial. Unfortunately, neither the relevant DSU and SPS provisions nor the panels/AB case law contribute to resolving the matter. As will be shown below, though it might appear to be a mere procedural question, the choice of appointing an expert review group or individual scientists is pivotal in determining the level of scientific involvement requested from the WTO judicial bodies.

A.   Individual Experts vs. Expert Review Group

Each time a party expressly asked for the appointment of an expert review group (typically the EC), the panel appointed individual experts instead.[116] The Appellate Body has endorsed this preference by interpreting Article 13 DSU as referring to expert review groups as a mere option (a panel *may* request). This constant practice raises several procedural and substantive questions which deserve closer scrutiny.

Although rendered controversial by the wording of the WTO texts, this preference for the appointment of individual experts tends to be justified on practical grounds.[117] The main argument presented in favour of such an option is that expert individual consultation is not only less time-consuming than group review (not having to generate a common written report) but it would also ensure more flexibility in the consultation process. In an expert individual consultation – the argument goes – a panel, by asking specific questions of each expert and by adding questions during the process, would obtain the individual opinion of each expert rather than a common and monolithical consensus position. This would help the panel in better assessing the scientific evidence brought by the parties. However, contrary to conventional wisdom, the provision of expertise by individual experts within the judicial review context is not necessarily more efficient than the setting up of an expert review group.

While reliance on individual experts may appear to render the expertise consultation process more expeditious and flexible than the expert

---

[116] This has happened notwithstanding the expressed request of the complaining party to appoint an expert review group in the *Shrimps–Turtle* case and notwithstanding the complainant and defendant common request in the *Hormones* case. See for a criticism of this position, T. Christoforou, 'Settlement of Science-Based Trade Disputes in the WTO: A Critical Review of the Developing Case Law in the Face of Scientific Uncertainty', *N.Y.U. Environmental Law Journal*, pp 622, 630–1 and Christoforou, supra note 106, p 255.
[117] For a complete description of the practical arguments generally invoked to justify the panels' preference for individual expert consultation, see J. Pauwelyn, 'The Use of Experts in WTO Dispute Settlement', supra note 108, p 328.

advisory group scheme, past cases have clearly shown how these expectations cannot realistically be met. In fact, the provision of various opinions by individual experts inevitably produces the effect of providing the judge with further scientific material to consider and evaluate. This has been expressly recognised by the panel in *Japan – Agricultural Products*, which stated that:

> we are called to examine and to weigh all the evidence [...] including the opinions we received from the experts advising the panel.[118]

In particular, being opinions elaborated on an individual basis and according to different methodologies, they lead the panel to engage in a complex quasi-scientific analysis aimed at verifying whether there is a common ground among these opinions. This evaluation becomes even more complex when individual experts hold divergent views.

While the main objective of the expert consultation procedure should be to prevent the panellists from getting involved in scientific issues by providing them with an assessment of the plausibility of the scientific evidence advanced by the parties to the dispute, the individual consultation practice described is likely to achieve the exact opposite result. Indeed, by introducing into the review process additional (often conflicting) scientific materials to be assessed together with the competing scientific claims brought by the parties, reliance on individual experts renders, paradoxically, the task of the judges even more (scientifically) cumbersome. How can judges be expected to be epistemically capable of assessing the possibly conflicting individual scientific opinions expressed by the experts?

In the light of the above, it is argued here that the appointment of an expert review group, though apparently more time-consuming, may potentially simplify the scientific task that judges are increasingly called upon to accomplish. Being entrusted with the duty of coming up with a written report, the expert group would be forced to either find common grounds on the different specific scientific issues at stake or, at least, to genuinely represent the whole spectrum of scientific opinions (ie majority and minority) existing in the current scientific state-of-the-art research on that controversial issue. In fact, adherents to different schools of thought should be represented among the experts. By borrowing the AB's language, the expert review group may set out, according to this model:

---

[118] Panel report in *Japan–Agricultural Products*, para 7.408.

both the prevailing view representing the mainstream opinion, as well as the opinions of scientists taking a divergent view.[119]

Furthermore, besides these arguments of merit, there also exist some textual reasons for privileging reliance on expert review groups over that of individual experts. As has been observed, although the wording of the relevant WTO texts does not help in identifying the appropriate form of expert consultation in a scientific-based controversy, it is undisputed (and perhaps meaningful) that they do provide for detailed rules and procedures solely for an expert review group.[120] This has meant that the panels' current practice of appointing individual experts has taken place not only contrary to the customary rules of interpretation of international treaties, as codified by the relevant 1969 Vienna Convention,[121] but also in a sort of legal vacuum in which panels had to determine by themselves the rules to follow in the following matters: appointment of the experts, decision as to the terms of reference, nationality of the experts etc.

Thus, for instance, it should be observed that the current trend of WTO panels to request the assistance of competent international bodies (such as the WHO, IOE or the IPPC) in selecting the experts does not find any textual support in the WTO Agreements. Although the panels have limited their requests for assistance in the selection of experts to those international organisations mentioned in the SPS Agreement (in the quality of standard-setting bodies), this does not necessarily mean that the experts should come exclusively from those organisations. In particular, this practice looks controversial to the extent that the appointed experts are likely to come from the same organisations which have set the international standards the WTO members may have tried to depart from. Against this backdrop, it is unavoidable that these experts will tend to defend the existing international standards elaborated by their organisation, if not by themselves.[122]

The most forceful and most articulated *j'accuse* expressed against the current expert consultation practice has been formulated by Christoforou who foresees that:

[119] *EC–Hormones*, AB report, para 194.
[120] It is by relying on this systematic argument that the EU has contested the current expert consultation practice based on individual experts in the *Asbestos* case.
[121] According to Article 31 of the 1969 Vienna Convention on the Law of Treaties the interpretation must give meaning and effect to all the 'terms of a treaty'. See Christoforou, supra note 106, p 264 (footnote 115).
[122] As an example of this phenomenon, one may refer to the *Hormones* case where three experts out of the five appointed by the panel were scientists regularly participating in the Codex Alimentarius committees and one of them was even the *rapporteur* in the risk assessment on the hormones at issue in the dispute. This example is provided by Christoforou, supra note 106, p 256 (footnote 98).

the developing practice of panels seeking advice only from experts individually, if applied systematically, would render the provisions of the DSU and the SPS and TBT Agreements on expert review groups useless and obsolete.[123]

It is in the light of the above arguments that scientific advice from an expert review group should be preferred over individual expertise. It is not only more efficient, objective and clear, but is also the sole procedure capable of attaining the main purpose of external expertise: to avoid the judges having to face troubling scientific issues by providing a report reflecting the current scientific debate on a specific issue (ie mainstream and minority scientific opinions). Besides this, major reliance on expert review groups would be more respectful towards the WTO Agreements' *littera legis* and more in line with the current practice in relation to the use of science.

B.   The Scope of the Expert Consultation: What Role for Scientific Experts?

It is appropriate to leave aside the expertise consultation procedural issues and to move to the nature and scope of this procedure.

The expert consultation finds its rationale in the assumption that panel members, by consulting scientists specialised in the areas related to the dispute, may be better placed to understand and critically assess the scientific evidence advanced by the parties. In fact, as stated by the panel in the *Salmon* case, the:

> expert opinions are opinions on the evidence submitted by the parties.[124]

Accordingly:

> a panel is entitled to seek information and advice from experts and from any other relevant source it chooses [...] to help it to understand and evaluate the evidence submitted and the arguments made by the parties, but not to make the case for a complaining party.[125]

---

[123] Ibid, p 264.

[124] See also panel report on *Australia–Salmon*, paras 8.41, 8.126 and 8.172. In full conformity to this approach, in the *Agricultural Products* case, Dr Ducon simply stated: '[t]he arguments put forward by Japan for requiring varietals trials are not based on scientific data. They are supported by a few experimental data in which varietals difference exists, in terms of LD50, among a lot of other data in which it does not'. See panel report *Agricultural Products*, para 8.36.

[125] *Japan–Agricultural Products*, AB report, para 129.

However, panels have shown some confusion about the appropriate role for scientific expertise. Although it might seem that the expert advice should not cover more than the evidence submitted by the parties, panels tend to directly ask experts the very same disputed scientific question that the panel itself has to answer.[126] This clearly happened in the *Agricultural Products* case, where the experts advising the panel were asked whether:

> in their expert opinion, there is an objective or rational relationship between, on the one hand, the varietal testing requirement imposed by Japan and, on the other hand, any evidence submitted by the parties.[127]

This trend towards a 'delegation' of responsibility in deciding the outcome of a dispute has caused uneasiness with an expert appointed in the *Hormones* dispute. On the occasion of the joint meeting with experts, Dr Ritter vocally denounced the fact that the provision of an answer to the question of whether residual hormones in beef would produce a biological effect on consumers would 'really pre-empt the outcome of the dispute'.[128]

Although it might clearly seem to be abusive, this practice may find some support in the open-textured formulation of Article 13 DSU, which recognises the almost unfettered right of the panel to seek information and technical advice from any individual or body which it deems appropriate and to seek information from any relevant source. Therefore, to avoid the abovementioned risk of 'delegation', it might be necessary to somehow constrain the scope of the expertise consultation. In order to achieve that result, the main purpose of the expert consultation must be borne in mind, which is to avoid panels getting involved in scientific issues by them providing an assessment of the plausibility of the scientific arguments brought by the parties. In other words, if we want to reduce the role of the panel in addressing and deciding scientific issues without delegating the decision on the final outcome of the dispute there is a need to frame from the outset the scope of the external consultation.

Ideally, experts' review should therefore be limited to a determination of whether that scientific opinion represents a sufficiently sound application of scientific principles to justify its conclusions.

---

[126] See J.O. Mc Ginnis and ML Movsesian, 'The World Trade Constitution', 114 *Harvard Law Review* 511, p 594 (2000) and T.P. Stewart and A.A. Karpel, 'Review of the Dispute Settlement Understanding: Operation of Panels', 31 *Law & Pol'y Intl Bus* 593 (2000).

[127] *Japan–Agricultural Products*, panel report, para 8.35.

[128] *EC–Hormones*, panel report, Annex: Joint Meeting with Experts, para 64.

This analysis will help the judges in determining whether the measure conforms to the risk assessment requirements imposed by the SPS Agreement, thus freeing them from any scientific involvement.

Further confusion would seem to exist concerning the tasks with which experts might be entrusted. Thus, for instance, in the *Hormones* case, the panel asked the appointed experts to address questions that touched upon the cost effectiveness of different regulatory alternatives.[129] But, how can laboratory natural scientists give answers to questions dealing with regulatory politics and economics?

After the famous Appellate Body's statement according to which the risk that is to be evaluated in a risk assessment under Article 5.1 is 'not only risk ascertainable in a science laboratory, but *also risk in human societies as they actually exist*',[130] one may legitimately wonder whether the relevant expertise within the WTO system should be limited to natural scientists.[131] Should the focus of risk analysis remain on 'the real world in which people live and die', it might be reasonable to imagine that panels will also consult experts coming from other fields, capable, for example, of assessing the effectiveness and the consequences stemming from a particular regulatory decision.

Thus, for instance, in the EC Commission's practice of collection and use of expertise it is considered 'appropriate to mobilise experts beyond the scientific community'.[132] These experts may include lawyers, ethicists, or those with practical knowledge gained from day-to-day involvement in an activity.

C.   The Legal Status and Authority of the Experts' Opinions

A further drawback of the current expert consultation practice must be found in the panels' tendency towards attributing undue authority to the opinion of any one expert. In the *Hormones* case, for instance, the panel dismissed one of the EC arguments by relying solely on the opinion of one of the experts.[133] While the EC argued that an alternative to

---

[129] Ibid, at paras 24, 172, 236, 268, 828, 838–848.

[130] *EC–Hormones*, AB report, para 187.

[131] See, on this point, R. Howse and P.C. Mavroidis, 'Europe's Evolving Regulatory Strategy for GMOs – The Issue of Consistency with WTO Law: of Kine and Brine', supra note 91, p. 320 (who argue that '[...] expertise concerning the effectiveness and consequences – social and economic, or even cultural – of particular forms of risk management and regulatory intervention may be appropriate').

[132] EC Commission, Communication on the Collection and Use of Expertise by the Commission: Principles and Guidelines COM(2002) 713 final, at 16.

[133] This example is provided by Walker, 'Keeping the WTO from Becoming the 'World Trans-Science organization': *Cornell international Law Journal* Hormones Dispute', 31 *Cornell International Law Journal* 1998, vol. 27, p 311 (footnote 282).

carbadox existed with the same therapeutic action, the panel dismissed this argument by relying on the sole advice of one expert who argued that oxytetracycline was a readily available alternative.[134]

This 'pick and choose' approach from individual experts' opinions does seem to bring the panels back to the original problem of having judges playing with science. It shows how panellists may resort to scientific advice for the sole reason of imbuing a determined outcome with apparent 'scientific legitimacy'.

Although expert advice is not legally binding,[135] the panel must show deference to it to the extent that it comes from a source that has epistemically more authority.

Finally, the readiness of WTO panels to call on experts contrasts with the reluctance of the EC courts to rely on external advice. EC courts prefer to review the contested measures by relying solely on their (by definition, non-scientific) evaluation of the scientific evidence brought to the dispute by the parties. As will be illustrated below, although in principle both EC courts would have the expertise option open through their internal rules, they tend not to use it.

D.   Conclusions on the WTO Expert Consultation System

While recourse to expert advice undoubtedly increases the ability of WTO panels to understand and assess the scientific evidence brought by the parties, there seem to be some flaws in the current practice of external consultation as developed by WTO panels.

In primis, the current practice of appointing solely individual experts may be perceived as ineffective and not entirely in conformity with the letter of the WTO treaty. Past cases have shown how recourse to individual experts inevitably entrusts panel members with an extra scientific role. Instead of avoiding judges having to face the troubling scientific issues raised by the dispute, the current (individual) expert consultation practice entrusts them with an even more demanding scientific task: to assess the merits of the expert opinions formulated on the plausibility of the scientific evidence brought by the parties and to verify whether there exists common ground among the diverging opinions of individual experts, thus legitimising an even more complex involvement in scientific matters. Furthermore, the panels, when 'picking and choosing' among the various individual experts' opinions, may be

---

[134] *EC–Hormones*, panel report, para 8.234.
[135] This is expressly established by Appendix 4 of the DSU, paragraph 6, which states that 'the final report of the expert review group shall be advisory only'.

tempted to accord undue authority to the opinion of any one of these experts and this notwithstanding their own lack of scientific knowledge. As to the scope of the requested expertise, there is a growing risk that panels will ultimately delegate the responsibility of deciding on a dispute to the chosen individual experts it traditionally relies upon. This outcome is quite unfortunate to the extent that these experts, not being a WTO institution, do not enjoy the legitimacy necessary to accomplish this task.[136] More sensitively, there is no real control on their scientific activity within the current WTO framework.

Last but not least, following the Appellate Body's famous statement according to which the risk that is to be evaluated in a risk assessment under Article 5.1 is 'not only risk ascertainable in a science laboratory, but *also risk in human societies as they actually exist*',[137] one may legitimately wonder whether the relevant expertise within the WTO system should be limited to natural scientists. Should the focus of risk analysis remain on 'the real world in which people live and die', it might be reasonable to imagine that panels will also consult experts coming from other fields, capable, for example, of assessing the effectiveness and the consequences stemming from a particular regulatory decision.[138] This position would seem to find some textual support within the same SPS Agreement, where article 5.6 conditions the application of the least trade-restrictive test to the 'technical and economic feasibility'. Technical and economic feasibility are therefore factors that may play a role in assessing an SPS regulatory measure. Although these factors have not received particular attention within the WTO case law so far, they are believed to be supportive of the introduction of multidisciplinary expertise within the WTO dispute settlement system.

Some signs of an opening towards non-exclusively scientific oriented expertise may be found in the Article 21.5 implementation panel in *Japan–Apples*.[139] Here, the panel, when revisiting the previous finding of the experts in the original panel, according to which 'it would be appropriate not to export apples from (severely) blighted orchards',[140] asked its experts to further elaborate on the matter. In answering that request, Dr Geider said 'There may be no strict scientific basis to say that this is something that you should not do. On the other hand, there are practical

---

[136] However, it may be noted that neither the WTO judicial bodies nor the experts are politically accountable.

[137] *EC–Hormones*, AB report, at 187.

[138] For example, in the *EC–Hormones* case, some risk management issues such as cost effectiveness, relative efficacy of regulatory responses and compliance have been discussed during the meeting with the experts. See Annex to the panel report: Joint Meeting with Experts, paras 24, 172, 268, 828, 838–847.

[139] *Japan–Apples* Article 21.5 Panel Report WT/DS245/RW.

[140] *Japan–Apples*, panel report, para 8.226.

reasons. I think this is what we say is good practice so it's good orchard practice not doing that'.[141] From his side, Dr Hale stated that 'it would not be economic to even harvest [fruits from severely blighted orchards], never mind export them'.[142] Against this backdrop, the panel concluded that, to the extent that these concerns relate to 'good agricultural and commercial practice', they do not override the scientific conclusion that mature symptomless apples pose only a negligible risk of transmitting fire blight, even if harvested from several blighted orchards.[143]

It is submitted that multidisciplinary and multi-sectoral expert review groups may not only encourage a cross-fertilization of ideas but also stimulate debate and lead to 'better' opinions.

Despite the above-mentioned limits of the current expert consultation practice, the increasing use of expert advice within the WTO is a positive development that must be applauded.[144] Expert advice not only ensures quality, transparency and legitimacy to WTO decisions but, if adequately fine-tuned, it might potentially reduce the level of scientific involvement currently required by the standard of legal review of science-based measures. In particular, to make the expert consultation a useful tool to somehow lighten the panels' involvement with scientific matters, it is necessary to favour reliance on expert advisory groups (instead of on individual experts) and to determine the exact scope of the consultation expertise.

5.   Towards an EC Expert Consultation System?

Although in need of some adjustments, the WTO expert consultation system may potentially inspire the development of a similar mechanism within the EC judicial system. As the *Pfizer/Alpharma* judgments have recently clearly shown, the EC courts might also need to rely on external expertise to assess the scientific plausibility of the scientific claims of both Member States and EC institutions. There are good reasons to

---

[141] Dr Geider, Transcript, Annex 3, para 187.

[142] Dr Hale, Transcript, Annex 3, para 188.

[143] *Japan–Apples* Article 21.5 panel report, para 8.88.

[144] Similarly, also the International Court of Justice's experience with the use of experts may be seen as a positive development (Article 50 of the Statute of the Court states that: 'The Court may, at any time, entrust any individual, body, bureau, commission, or other organization that it may select, with the task of carrying out an enquiry or giving an expert opinion.' Article 51 of the statute continues by stating that: 'During the hearing any relevant questions are to be put to the witnesses and experts under the conditions laid down by the Court in the Rules of Procedure referred to in Article 30.'). See, notably, for an excellent survey of expert evidence in the first fifty years of the International Court of Justice, G. White, 'The Use of Experts by the International Court', in V. Lowe and M. Fitzmaurice eds, *Fifty years of the International Court of Justice, Essays in Honour of Sir Robert Jennings*, (Cambridge University Press, 2005).

believe that reliance on this external help tool might facilitate the role that EC courts are increasingly called upon to play with science when reviewing science-based measures.

Although under the current statute[145] and their respective Rules of procedure,[146] both the CFI and ECJ 'may at any time entrust any individual, body, authority, committee or other organisations it chooses with the task of giving expert opinion', they have so far been quite reluctant to rely on external advice. This seems to be especially true for scientific matters. While the courts, notably the CFI, have ordered expert reports to inter alia to assess the quality of a translator's work,[147] an official's mental state,[148] to examine the rates for and conditions of transport of mineral fuels,[149] price rises and the market in dyestuffs[150] and the economic consequences of certain gas tariffs,[151] in order to verify the conclusions drawn in the contested act, the evidence relied on and the characteristics of the market,[152] they have rarely done so in scientific matters. Occasionally, the parties have themselves submitted an expert's report or, at the hearing, an expert has addressed the court on behalf of one of the parties.[153]

The decision to obtain an expert's report is made by the court in the form of an order after the parties have been given an opportunity to be heard. The same order appoints the experts, defines the scope of the expertise and sets a time limit for the drafting of the report.

Despite this rather simple framework for having expertise at its disposal, EC courts have traditionally been unwilling to use it.

Therefore, before sketching out a possible expertise system within the EC judicial system, it might be crucial to look at the reasons that have so far discouraged the EC courts from relying on this possibility. An explanation for the European courts' reticence in asking external advice may be found within the EC institutional framework itself. As EC courts, especially when reviewing a Community measure, may be called upon to review scientific studies coming from the EC scientific committees, they might feel that submitting one of these studies to a third party

---

[145] EC Statute, Article 25.

[146] ECJ Rules, Article 49 and CFI Rules, Article 70.

[147] Case 10/55, *Mirossevich v High Authority* [1954–56] ECR 333.

[148] Case 12/68, *X v Audit Board* [1969] ECR 109

[149] Case 24 and 34/58 *Chambre Syndicale de la Sidérurugie de l'Est v High Authority* [1960] ECR 281.

[150] Case 48/69 *ICI Ltd v Commission* [1972] ECR 619.

[151] Case C-169/84, *Société CdF Chimie Azote et Fertilisants SA* [1990] ECR 3083.

[152] Cases C-89, 104, 114, 117, 125 to 129/85, *Ahlstrom v Commission* [1993] ECR 1307.

[153] Case 204/80 *Procureur de la République v Vedel* [1982] ECR 465.

review would amount to putting into question both the scientific and institutional legitimacy of these committees, which ultimately belong to the same system of governance. However, this argument, which boils down to the idea according to which the CFI/ECJ is an institution among other institutions, does not seem to be entirely persuasive if examined from a US perspective. In fact, US federal courts do not hesitate to review the risk assessments undertaken by federal regulatory agencies.[154] It is therefore controversial whether this legitimacy argument may justify by itself the EC courts' deferential attitude vis-à-vis the scientific reports prepared by the European scientific committees.

A more credible argument aimed at explaining this deferential approach to science marked by a Europe label refers to judicial tradition. Having hardly ever relied on scientific expertise, judges (notably the judge *rapporteur* in the EC judiciary jargon) might be somehow discouraged in proposing to other court members to have recourse to expertise under the courts' rules of procedure. Finally, if tradition continues to play a crucial role in explaining the courts' wariness, fears of ultimately delegating the task of solving a dispute may also exist.

In attempting to develop a credible and effective expert consultation system for EC courts when dealing with scientific matters, it is important to take due account of the institutional scientific framework upon which the Community relies when adopting legislation.

In fact, unlike the WTO judicial bodies, the European courts, when called upon to judicially review a science-based measure, are likely to already dispose of a scientific study supporting that measure or, at least, dealing with its scientific foundations. While this is certainly the case when the courts are called upon to examine the legality of an EC measure, it might not be the case when the contested regulation has been adopted by a Member State. In the latter case, the national measure is supported instead by a national scientific opinion coming from its own authorities.

Against this backdrop, one may wonder who might be consulted by the EC courts to examine the scientific adequacy of the evidence brought by the parties to the dispute. Should they ask the EC scientific committee members, perhaps those sitting within EFSA, to review the evidence they have themselves developed? Or should they rely on some third-party scientists? And *quid* in case of science-based national measures? Should the court submit the national scientific evidence to the scrutiny of the EC scientific committees?

---

[154] See on this point T. O. McGarity, 'On the Prospect of "Daubertizing" Judicial Review of Risk Assessment', 66 *Law & Contemp. Probs*, p 155.

It is extremely difficult to answer these questions as there is no hierarchy between research bodies and their scientific advice. It is therefore difficult to see how, in the event of conflicting scientific studies, it could be justified to follow one set of scientific opinions rather than another.

In the light of the above, an expertise consultation system might be imagined in which the courts may rely respectively on national experts to examine the European studies advanced by the EC institutions and on the EC scientific committees to review the national scientific opinions brought by the parties to the dispute. A similar consultation procedure may be more than adequate to assist the EC judges in verifying the existence of a minimum scientific level in the studies put forward by the parties. Furthermore, through its cross-consultation mechanism between Member States and EC experts, this procedure could effectively avoid a situation where the same scientist who has developed the scientific opinion supporting the contested measure may be called upon to review ex post the same study. Last but not least, this system would be in line with the European idea according to which scientific studies could not be ranked depending on their national or European origin. In fact, as shown above, EFSA's scientific opinions do not have precedence over diverging national opinions.[155]

6. The Role of Peer Review in Judicial Review

A valid alternative method to external expertise might be represented by reliance on peer review.[156] This is a formal science-based process that is traditionally used after a scientific work is nearly complete, and utilises independent experts who were not involved in the development of the scientific study.

Although it is used primarily by publishers, to select and to screen submitted manuscripts,[157] and by funding bodies, to decide the awarding of monies for research, peer review process is also utilised for risk assessment products. In these circumstances, it involves an in-depth assessment of the assumptions, calculations, alternate interpretations, methodology and conclusions. In particular, by taking the form of a deliberation, it involves an exchange of judgments about the appropriateness of methods and the strength of the author's inferences.[158]

---

[155] See A. Alemanno, 'Food Safety and the Single European Market', in C. Ansel and D. Vogel, (eds), *What's the Beef? The Contested Governance of European Food Safety* (MIT Press, 2006). See also Regulation 178/2002.

[156] For an introduction to peer-review, see, eg, Office of Management and Budget, Final Information Quality Bulletin for Peer Review, 15 December, 2004.

[157] As a result, publications and awards that have not undergone peer review are likely to be regarded with suspicion by scholars and professionals in many fields.

[158] See the Final Information Quality Bulletin for Peer Review by the Office of Management and Budget (OMB), December 2004, at 2.

Peer review panels tend to seek to reach consensus or common agreement regarding the adequacy of the product review. The final goal pursued by peer review is endorsement of the work product's conclusions.

In the United States, the Office of Management and Budget (OMB) has established since 2004 that 'important scientific information shall be peer reviewed by qualified specialists before it is disseminated by the federal government'.[159] Within this context, the purpose followed by peer review is 'to enhance the quality and credibility of the government's scientific information'.[160] The introduction of the peer review mechanism in the federal legislative mechanism is part of the Information Quality Act,[161] under which Congress has directed OMB to issue guidelines 'to provide policy and procedural guidance to Federal agencies for ensuring and maximising the quality, objectivity, utility and integrity of information' disseminated by Federal agencies.

The practice of peer review of risk assessment products is not entirely unknown in the Community or in the WTO. Thus, for instance, within the framework of the European directive on the placing of plant protection products on the market, EFSA has launched the peer review process of the assessments made by Member States aimed at creating a 'positive lists' of pesticides.[162] This process is managed by EFSA's Pesticide Risk Assessment Peer Review Unit (PRAPER).

---

[159] Ibid, p. 1.

[160] Ibid.

[161] The Information Quality Act was developed as a supplement to the Paperwork Reduction Act, 44 U.S.C. §3501 et seq, which requires OMB , inter alia, to 'develop and oversee the implementation of policies, principles, standards and guidelines to [...] apply to Federal agency dissemination of public information'. Besides this Act, Executive Order 12866 (58 Fed. Reg. 51,735 (4 October 1993)), establishes that the Office of Information and Regulatory Affairs (OIRA) is 'the repository of expertise concerning regulatory issues' and it directs OMB to provide guidance to the agencies on regulatory planning. The same Order also requires that 'each agency shall base its decisions on the best reasonably obtainable scientific, technical, economic, or other information' (§ 1(b)(7)).

[162] Council Directive 91/414/EEC of 15 July 1991 concerning the placing of plant protection products on the market (OJ L 230/1–32) was required to be implemented by Member States from 26 July 1993. The main elements of the directive are as follows: a) to harmonize the overall arrangements for the authorization of plant protection products within the European Union (EU). This to be achieved firstly by harmonising the process for considering the acceptability of active substances at a European Community level to environment and health and, secondly, even though individual product authorization remains the responsibility of individual Member States, by establishing harmonised risk assessment criteria for Member States to use when considering the safety of those products. b) The Directive provides for the establishment of a positive list (Annex I) of active substances which have been shown to be without unacceptable risk to people or the environment. c) Member States are only permitted to authorise marketing and use of plant protection products where the active substances are listed in Annex I, except where transitional arrangements apply. d) The directive provides for a series of transitional
(continued...)

Within the WTO, the Appellate Body has even shown some propensity towards the idea of relying on *peer review* in order to assess the quality of scientific expertise. In fact, in *Hormones*, the AB has recognised that Member States may also rely on minority opinions in order to satisfy the risk assessment requirement, but provided they come from 'qualified and respected sources'.[163]

The scope mandated in a peer review is generally called 'charge' and aims at providing instructions regarding the objective of the analysis and the specific advice sought. These tend to be determined in advance of the selection of the reviewers.

It is suggested that not only decision-makers but also courts may rely on peer review, by either asking some experts to peer review some of the scientific evidence advanced by the parties or by simply showing deference to that evidence whenever this has been subject to peer review. One of the main advantages stemming from judges' reliance on peer review is that via this tool they might determine the exact scope of experts' review, by, for instance, asking them to distinguish scientific facts from professional (science policies) judgments.

This might turn out to be especially useful in both the EC and WTO legal contexts, where neither risk analysis frameworks recognise that uncertainty is inherent in science and that in many cases scientific studies do not produce conclusive evidence.

In the light of the above, it is submitted that peer review mechanisms might either be used by courts or simply inspire the WTO and EC external expert consultation system, by providing guidance on how to define the scope of the expert advice.

Whatever the case may be, both EC and WTO courts should show deference to the scientific evidence which has been advanced by the parties to the dispute and which has been previously peer reviewed. In particular, it is suggested that proof of a prior peer review must give rise to a presumption of conformity of that evidence with the relevant scientific evidence. However, prior peer review is not by itself sufficient ground for triggering such a presumption. There is clearly a need for

arrangements and derogations until 25 July 2003 to allow for the progressive re-evaluation of those active substances already on the market in the EU on 25 July 1993. e) The directive also makes provision for a system of mutual recognition, such that following the listing of an active substance on Annex I of the directive, Member States are obliged to grant authorisations (on request) on the basis of those granted in other Member States; insofar as it can be shown that the agricultural, plant health and environmental conditions are comparable in the two Member States.

[163] *EC–Hormones*, AB report, para 194.

some evidence proving the adequacy of prior peer review. Thus, for instance, publication in an important scientific journal may mean that adequate peer review has been performed.

An example of such a deferential approach to peer reviewed scientific evidence may be seen in *Methanex*,[164] a recent case decided by NAFTA under the provisions in the North American Free Trade Agreement's (NAFTA) Chapter 11 on investment and the UNCITRAL arbitration rules.[165] At the heart of this case there is an investment dispute between Canada-based Methanex Corporation and the United States. Methanex is a major producer of methanol,[166] a gasoline additive which has been banned by California in 2002 on environmental and human health grounds. Methanex, after having submitted a claim before NAFTA, argued, inter alia, that the ban was not a genuine environmental measure but a disguised restriction of trade.[167] In replying to this argument the NAFTA Tribunal, 'having considered all the expert evidence adduced', accepted the scientific evidence underpinning the contested measure 'as reflecting a serious, objective and scientific approach to a complex problem in California'.[168] In particular, the Tribunal came to this conclusion by taking account of the fact that this scientific evidence 'was subject at the time to public hearings, testimony and peer-review'. In light of the above, it concluded that:

> its emergence as a serious scientific work from such an *open and informed debate* is the best evidence that it was not the product of a political shame engineered by California.[169]

It is believed that there is a great deal to be learned from this use of peer-review within judicial review of science-based measures and, as will be illustrated below, there is even more to be learned from the application of such a procedure-based standard of review in both the EC and WTO.

---

[164] *Methanex Corp v the United States of America*, Final Award of the Tribunal on Jurisdiction and Merits, in the matter of an international arbitration under chapter 11 of the north American free trade agreement and the uncitral arbitration rules. S. Sagarika (2006) 'Methanex Corporation and the USA: The Final NAFTA Tribunal Ruling', *Review of European Community & International Environmental Law* 15 (1), 110–4.

[165] The text of the NAFTA Agreement is available at http://www.nafta-sec-alena.org/.

[166] This substance is a key component in MTBE (methyl tertiary butyl ether), which is used to increase oxygen content and act as an octane enhancer in unleaded gasoline.

[167] In particular, the plaintiff argued that the California ban was tantamount to an expropriation of the company's investment; a violation of NAFTA's Article 1110, and was enacted in breach of the national treatment (Article 1102) and minimum international standards of treatment (Article 1105) provisions. By relying on these arguments, Methanex sought financial compensation from the United States in the amount of over US$900 million.

[168] Part III, Chapter A, 51, para 101 of the final award.

[169] Ibid.

7.   Some Proposals to Help the Judge when Reviewing Science

While the scientific process is engaged with scientific research and publication of formulation, corroboration, and advancement of scientific principles and theories, the legal process does not establish nor attempt to develop scientific theories, principles or 'truth' for the purposes of science, but only for the purposes of adjudication.

Accordingly, EC courts and WTO judicial bodies are not being directly asked to establish whether a certain risk exists or, more generally, to settle a scientific debate, they are, rather, increasingly required to evaluate the competing scientific claims made by the parties in order to determine whether the contested measures conform to the scientific discipline in force within their legal system. While this tendency is particularly significant with the WTO, EC courts would also seem to be increasingly playing a quasi-scientific role, by engaging in scientific controversies in order to adjudicate between diverging scientific claims. As these courts began referring to 'the quality and quantity' of the scientific evidence (WTO) and the requirement for a 'detailed assessment' (EC) they have invested themselves with a non-legal task which, as shown above, they cannot realistically carry out. Indeed, on the courts' benches do not sit scientists, but lawyers.

This interpretation of their respective scientific disciplines inevitably opens up the Pandora's box of scientific discussion to these judicial bodies, thereby somehow legitimising their involvement in controversial scientific matters.

The problem raised by this approach is that judges, being non-scientists, are not epistemically capable of discerning between good science and bad science. And this is exactly what EC and WTO courts (must) aim at doing when reviewing science-based measures. They want to make sure that the contested measure is adequately backed up not simply by a claim of science, but by a proper and adequate scientific study.

In fact, under the current interpretation adopted by the respective courts, both the EC and WTO scientific disciplines, by requiring the authorities to base their measure on science, not only establish a procedural requirement (necessity of scientific evidence or risk assessment), but also introduce a substantive test ('detailed risk assessment'; 'quality and quantity of scientific evidence') which finally boils down into a *minimum scientific threshold*. Indeed, the panel in the *Apples* case has clearly stated that the evidence to be considered under Article 2.2 SPS should be:

> [...] evidence gathered *through scientific methods*, excluding by the same token information not acquired through a scientific method.[170]

Similarly, the ECJ in the *Vitamins* line of cases has held that public authorities must justify their health regulations on 'a detailed assessment of the risk' alleged.[171]

By borrowing the language used by the Supreme Court in *Daubert*, it would seem that both the WTO and the EC courts have interpreted their scientific disciplines as requiring that the submitted evidence must be 'grounded in the methods and procedures of science'.[172]

However, to be 'good science' the scientific evidence supporting a measure does not merely have to be a scientifically-dressed study, but has to meet some minimum criteria assuring its scientific character.

It is by engaging in this exercise that judges, although not adequately equipped for the inevitable scientific evaluations required, attempt to adjudicate between diverging scientific claims, by 'picking and choosing' among different scientific opinions advanced by the parties. This happens because judges must, somehow, draw lines between scientific evidence that is 'detailed enough' or 'sufficient enough' and scientific evidence that is not 'detailed enough' or 'sufficient enough'. The result is that some scientific studies pass the legal test and are considered adequate in backing up a certain measure and others do not. Thus, the minimum scientific threshold reveals itself as a 'pass or fail' test.

Since it is *how* the conclusions have been reached, not *what* the conclusions are that make good science today, both WTO and EC courts have interpreted their respective scientific discipline as requiring the evidence submitted by the parties to satisfy some *minimum scientific requirements*. This trend seems to challenge the traditional uncritical view that the law has embraced vis-à-vis science's claims of universal truth[173]. While this approach to the review of science-based measures may seem reasonable to the extent that it simply allows the judge to verify *how* the scientific study supporting a contested measure has been conducted and *what* its conclusions are, this task cannot be done by the judge alone and it also presupposes the development of some general guidelines establishing which *minimum criteria* a scientific study must satisfy to be considered 'scientific'.

---

[170] *Japan–Apples*, panel report, para 8.92.

[171] Case 192/01 *Commission v Denmark* [2003] ECR 9693, at 47.

[172] *Daubert v Merrell Dow Pharmaceuticals, Inc*, 509 US 579 (1993).

[173] J. Atik, 'Science and International Regulatory Convergence', 17 *Northwestern J. Int'l L. & B.* 736, p 740.

7.1. How a Judge May Assess whether a Scientific Study is 'Scientifically Adequate'?

In answering this question it is crucial to take due account of the limited role that courts and tribunals may play in reviewing scientific information, notably in assessing the 'quality' of the scientific studies quoted by the parties to a dispute. In fact, judges can neither develop by themselves the criteria determining whether a study is 'scientific enough' nor judge whether these criteria are met by a scientific opinion brought by the parties to the dispute.

Therefore, since a court may not realistically assess whether the scientific evidence advanced by one party meets the *minimum scientific requirements* required to consider it 'good science', reliance on external advice, in the form of external experts or peer-review mechanisms, is increasingly needed.

As seen above, the WTO expert consultation system may reveal itself to be a useful experience upon which to build in order to develop an external scientific support for international courts called upon to review science-based measures.[174] In fact, this system of external help has been generally successful in facilitating the scientific tasks judges are increasingly called upon to perform when reviewing science-based measures. Although presenting some drawbacks, such as, for example, the continual preference of panels for the appointment of individual experts rather than expert review groups, the WTO dispute settlement body practice with external expert consultation has been positive. In the light of the above, it has been submitted that, although in need of some adjustments, the WTO external consultation system could also be extended and become current practice within the EC judicial architecture. Thus, it could be envisaged that, not only the WTO judicial bodies but also the EC courts, when reviewing either a Member State or an EC science-based measure, might rely on some external scientific advice in order to assess whether the scientific evidence brought by the parties is 'adequately scientific'. This use of experts would help the judge in ascertaining whether a minimum scientific threshold claimed by the contested measure has been met, thereby preventing the judge from engaging in scientific tasks.

---

[174] The use of experts by other international organisations is not the object of this book. For an excellent survey of expert evidence in the first 50 years of the International Court of Justice, see G. White, 'The Use of Experts by the International Court', in V. Lowe and M. Fitzmaurice eds, *Fifty years of the International Court of Justice, Essays in Honour of Sir Robert Jennings* (Cambridge University Press, 2005).

Alternatively, courts, as seen above, may also rely on peer review as an effective tool aimed at establishing whether the scientific study underpinning a contested measure is adequately grounded on science. They may do so by either asking some experts to peer review the scientific evidence advanced by the parties or by merely showing deference to that evidence whenever this has previously been subject to peer review. Of course, in the latter case, peer review should, in turn, satisfy certain minimum scientific soundness requirements, which may boil down to, for instance, a publication in an internationally renowned publication.

An excellent example of this use of peer-review within judicial review of science-based measures is represented by the abovementioned *Methanex* case. Here, the NAFTA Tribunal, 'having considered all the expert evidence adduced', accepted the scientific evidence underpinning the contested measure 'as reflecting a serious, objective and scientific approach to a complex problem in California' and this to the extent that this scientific evidence 'was subject at the time to public hearings, testimony and peer-review'.[175]

In light of the above, it concluded that:

> its emergence as a serious scientific work from such an *open and informed debate* is the best evidence that it was not the product of a political shame engineered by California.[176]

7.2   What is a Minimum Scientific Threshold?

As to the issue of determining what is the minimum scientific threshold that both WTO and EC courts seem to hint at when reviewing science-based measures, it is neither for the judge nor for the external experts to develop minimum standards of scientific adequacy to be met by scientific evidence advanced by the parties to a dispute.

There is currently a strong trend, internationally, to formalise procedures for dealing with risk analysis issues and to promote commonalities of approaches throughout the different sectors where risk assessment may be developed.[177] Thus, for instance, at EC level, some efforts have been

---

[175] Part III, Chapter A, 51, para 101.

[176] Ibid.

[177] This trend is also visible at national level. See, for example, in the US, the Envtl. Protection Agency, Proposed Guidelines for Carcinogenic Risk Assessment, 61 Fed. Reg. and, especially, the more general Office of Management and Budget (OMB) Proposed Bulletin on Risk Assessment, which aims at providing clear minimum standards for the scientific quality and presentation of federal risk assessments. The proposed text is available at http://www.whitehouse.gov/omb/inforeg/ proposed_risk_assessment _bulletin_010906.pdf.

deployed to develop a harmonised approach to risk assessment procedures among the Scientific Committees advising the European Commission in the area of human, animal and plant health and on the environment.[178] At international level, this trend towards formalising procedures for risk assessment is even more significant and is traditionally led by some of the international standardisation bodies mentioned within the SPS Agreement. In recent years, these standards organisations have contributed more to the trade system by setting out scientific approaches to regulation than by promulgating standards that are identical across countries.[179] Thus, as illustrated above, the Codex Alimentarius Commission is engaged, since 1995, in developing Working Principles for Risk Analysis aimed at determining the main steps and procedures that scientific assessors must follow when engaging in risk analysis applied to food safety issues.[180] Similarly, the UN Food and Agricultural Organization (FAO) has developed new guidelines that will help countries assessing the risks of living modified organisms (LMOs) to determine whether some should be considered to be weeds or other organisms that damage plants.[181]

The objective of these international efforts is to provide guidance to their respective Member States so that food safety and health related aspects of their decisions and recommendations are based on risk analysis.

From a conceptual point of view, it might be useful to underscore that the harmonisation activity brought forward by these bodies does not aim at setting up technical standards, but merely at developing a common approach to the risk analysis in a specific field.[182] These common approaches to risk analysis have been dubbed as 'meta-standards'.[183]

---

[178] To this end, it has been established a Working Party on 'Harmonisation of Risk Assessment Procedures' to address specifically the general principles of risk assessment and its application to broad consumer health issues, with a particular reference to measures that would enhance compatibility of approaches between the Scientific Advisory Committees. See the Updated Opinion of the Scientific Steering Committee on Harmonisation of Risk Assessment Procedures, adopted on 10–11 April 2003. A full second report on the Harmonization of Risk Assessment Procedures was expected by the end of the following year but it has not yet seen the light of the day.

[179] T. Jostling, D. Roberts and D. Orden, *Food Regulation and Trade, Toward a Safe and Open Global System* (Institute for International Economics, Washington DC, 2004) p 46.

[180] The Codex Alimentarius Commission has been discussing policies for risk analysis since its 20th Session (1995), when it adopted an Action Plan for Codex-wide Development and Application of Risk Analysis Principles and Guidelines. The Joint FAO/WHO Committee on General Principles, meeting in Paris in April 2005, is elaborating further guidance specific to the food safety field, see Proposed Draft Working Principles on Risk Analysis for Food Safety.

[181] These guidelines are available at http://www.fao.org/newsroom/en/news/2004/43684/ Similarly, FAO has established Guidelines for Pest Risk Analysis. These guidelines have been discussed in the *Japan–Agricultural Products* case. See, eg panel report, paras 2.25–2.33.

[182] See also the efforts deployed by WHO in harmonisation of risk analysis within its area

(continued...)

It is argued that this task, which may be called 'light harmonisation' or 'soft convergence' in risk analysis, carries the potential of not only guiding scientists in conducting risk assessment but also facilitating the task of the experts called to determine the scientific adequacy of the opinions and studies adduced by the parties. In other words, these guidelines may help the experts in evaluating not the validity of scientific studies, but instead their methodologies. Should these scientific studies satisfy the general guidelines on risk analysis developed on that particular scientific area, experts and, accordingly, panels should show deference to them.

This approach does not seem to be totally unknown to the WTO/SPS system. As seen above, under Article 5.1 SPS, if a national requirement is not based on a specific international standard, the WTO member adopting that requirement must justify its measure by a risk assessment that takes into account 'the risk assessment techniques' developed by Codex, the International Office of Epizootics (OIE) and the International Plant Protection Convention (IPPC). It is submitted that the insertion of this provision within the SPS Agreement legitimises the possibility for the interpreter to rely upon 'light harmonisation' tools in order to find guidance on how to apply risk analysis requirements.

This seems to be further confirmed by the *EC-Biotech* panel report, where the panel, after consulting the parties, has requested several international organisations (Codex, FAO, the IPPC Secretariat, WHO, OIE, the CBD Secretariat and UNEP):

> [...] to identify materials (reference works, glossaries, official documents of the relevant international organisations, *including conventions, standards and guidelines*, etc.) that might aid [the panel] in determining the ordinary meaning of certain terms used in the definitions provided in Annex A to the SPS Agreement.

In light of the above, '[t]he materials' the panel has obtained in this way 'have been taken into account [...], as appropriate'.[184]

---

of competence. WHO, jointly with FAO, are developing guidelines documents for undertaking each of the four components of a risk assessment namely hazard identification, hazard characterisation, exposure assessment and risk characterization. To date guidelines for hazard characterisation of pathogens in food and water have been finalized, and the draft guidelines for exposure assessment of pathogen in food have been prepared and are currently under review. FAO and WHO are now planning the development of practical guidelines for risk characterisation of microbiological hazards in foods. See http://www.who.int/foodsafety/micro/en/.

[183] Jostling, supra note 179.

[184] *EC–Biotech* panel report, at 7.96.

As has been argued above, such an interpretation by an AB proves that Article 5.1, by referring to the 'risk assessment techniques developed' by the international standard-setting organisations, may prove to be a useful legal basis for the WTO judicial bodies to rely upon in order to find some guidance when reviewing complex science-based measures.

8.   Conclusions

Given the increasingly strict scrutiny applied by EC and WTO courts to science-based measures, which has led their judges to become enmeshed in scientific debates, this chapter, by adopting a critical stance on the current trend, has attempted to reorient the role of the judge when reviewing science-based regulations. After having illustrated the struggle faced by both EC and WTO judicial bodies when reviewing strictly science-based measures, it has been found that their growing scientific involvement has to be redirected towards the effort to assess whether the scientific evidence advanced by the parties to the dispute constitutes 'good science'. This effort seems to be more justified within the WTO context than in the EC, since WTO judicial bodies, by not disposing of a complete risk analysis framework upon which to rely when reviewing a food safety measure, tend to be more demanding vis-à-vis the scientific basis of a contested measure.

Since it is *how* the conclusions have been reached, not *what* the conclusions are that makes 'good science' today, both WTO and EC courts have interpreted their respective scientific discipline as requiring that the evidence submitted by the parties satisfies some scientific quality requirements. This interpretation of their respective scientific disciplines inevitably opened up the Pandora's box of scientific discussion to these judicial bodies, thus somehow legitimising their involvement in controversial scientific matters. However, judges, being non-scientists, are not epistemically capable of discerning between 'good science' and 'bad science'.

Against this backdrop, it has been argued that this task cannot be done by the judge alone and that it presupposes the development of some general guidelines establishing which *minimum criteria* a scientific study must satisfy in order to be considered 'scientific enough'.

To solve the first problem it has been suggested to improve (within the WTO) and to develop (within the EC) the external experts' consultation practice, as this might facilitate the current attempt by judicial bodies to verify whether the scientific evidence advanced by the parties to the dispute is 'scientifically adequate'. This method, however, might become superfluous should the scientific study which has been advanced by the parties be subject to peer review.

As to the second, related problem of facilitating the task of the expert in accomplishing her task, it might be advisable to rely on those guidelines, currently elaborated by several international standardisation organisations and by the same EC scientific committees, aimed at promoting commonalities of approaches in risk analysis for different sectors. This solution not only finds a solid textual basis within the WTO but has also been endorsed by the *EC-Biotech* panel report.

In the light of the above, it is advisable that courts, notably when reviewing the scientific basis of a contested measure, rely, first, on peer review as a tool aimed at verifying – loosely speaking – the scientific plausibility of a contested measure and, second, when necessary, on external experts in order to attain the same goal.

Reliance on these external expertise tools will ensure that courts will not get involved in the scientific merits of the evidence, thereby allowing an objective and scientifically-restrained review.

It is believed that this approach, by reducing the level of scientific involvement of courts and by giving an operational meaning to what 'minimum science' is, might prove successful in finding a more appropriate role for the international judge in risk analysis.

PART IV: COMPARING THE EC AND WTO FOOD REGIMES

INTRODUCTION

Part IV, by building upon the previous parts, ventures a comparison between the EC and WTO food safety regimes in order to show the main points of tension existing between them.

In particular, Chapter I provides for a comparison between the EC and WTO food disciplines, by looking at their respective goals and at their instruments. Chapter II furthers this examination by notably comparing their food safety risk analysis models, thus identifying the main points of tension existing between the two regimes: the role of 'other legitimate factors' in risk analysis and the status of the 'precautionary principle'. Due to the lack of risk management policy within the WTO/SPS risk analysis model, the analysis expands, when appropriate, on the Codex's principles for risk analysis. Chapter III offers a comparison of the standards of review applied by the EC courts and the WTO judicial bodies, by focusing notably on the respective level of scientific involvement required from them. It finally proposes the development of a procedural, intensity-variable standard of review of science-based measures within the WTO as a viable solution for re-establishing the balance originally designed by the SPS Agreement between members' regulatory autonomy and free trade.

Chapter I
Comparing Food Safety Regulatory Frameworks

This chapter provides a comparison between the WTO and EC food disciplines, by looking at their respective goals and also at their instruments.

1. The Goals: Food Safety as an Exception (WTO) and as a Goal per se (EC)

As is clear from their historical evolution, the WTO and EC food regimes do not entirely respond to the same logic. Although both disciplines impose a number of significant constraints on the ability of their Member States to regulate the safety of food, they aim at very different objectives. While both the EC and WTO food safety disciplines have originally been conceived as exclusively free-trade mechanisms allowing public health regulations as an exception (Articles XX GATT and 30 EC, respectively) to their main prohibitions, the European regime acquired through time an additional and autonomous objective: the protection of human health and consumer interests. Accordingly, where under the WTO/SPS framework food safety regulations are tackled as potential obstacles to trade that may exceptionally (when all scientific requirements are met) be authorised – within the EC – food safety is an autonomous goal to be pursued together with the objective of ensuring an effective functioning of the internal market.

This is proven by Regulation 178/2002 which states that the overriding principles of the EC food safety policy are not only to ensure the free movement of foodstuffs within the internal market, but also 'to seek to achieve a high level of protection of human health and consumers' interest'.[1] This regulation, by focusing specifically on the food safety objective per se, may be seen as the founding act establishing food law as an autonomous branch of EC law for the first time. Food legislation has evolved from being no more than a spill-over effect of the internal market construction to become an independent and particularly relevant EC policy.

This increased EC focus on food safety has to be contextualised within a more general European attempt to also integrate into its market-oriented agenda other interests deserving equal protection, such as European citizens' public health protection.[2] Since 1992, EC health, safety,

[1] Article 1, Regulation 178/2002.
[2] For a wide-ranging analysis of this process, see P. Nebbia and T. Askham, *EU Consumer Law* (Richmond: Richmond Law, 2004).

environmental and consumer protection regulations must take 'as a base a high level of protection' (Article 95, para. 3 ECT)[3]. The introduction of such a minimum level of health protection clearly shows how the public health objective pursued by food safety regulations has become autonomous from their original focus on trade.[4]

In short, if the WTO scientific regime, without establishing any minimum level of health protection, exclusively follows a market-opening agenda, the EC discipline answers to a more complex public demand for health protection within an increasingly integrated Union by imposing, not only on Member States' measures but also on EC-wide regulations, the attainment of a high level of protection.

In the next chapter, it will be shown how the different objectives underpinning the two food regimes as well as the diverse institutional contexts surrounding them have influenced the standards of review to be applied by their respective courts. In the section that follows, it will be illustrated how the different logics underlying the two regimes are also reflected in their different instruments of integration.

1.1 The Instruments: Negative Integration and Positive Integration Tools

Both the EC and the GATT/WTO food regimes have originally developed by relying on the negative integration provisions existing in their respective legal systems.[5] Thus, similarly to what happened in the EC context with Article 28 EC, Articles III and XI GATT have been used to tackle all those regulations aimed at protecting public health. As a consequence of such a negative integration approach, their respective food regimes began developing in a rather piecemeal fashion, by exclusively addressing those measures giving rise to a dispute.[6] It is therefore not surprising that, when so doing, both the EC and the GATT

---

[3] It must be observed, however, that health, safety, environmental and consumer protection still have the status of mere 'interests' and objectives of consumer policy, without being recognised as 'rights'.

[4] Preamble (8) of Regulation 178/2002 states that: 'The Community has chosen a high level of protection as appropriate to the development of food law, which it applies in a non-discriminatory manner whether food or feed is traded on the internal market or internationally'.

[5] As seen above, for the purpose of this study we employ the terms negative and positive integration as conceived and elaborated by J. Tinbergen back in the 1950s. While 'negative integration' refers to those instruments prohibiting the use or requiring the phasing out of a particular type of trade-restrictive measure, such as quantitative restrictions or tariffs, 'positive integration' refers to those normative standards that Members must follow in exercising their regulatory prerogatives.

[6] However, it is worth noting that, in contrast with the EC, the WTO cannot initiate legal proceedings against a Member State for an alleged violation of its agreements.

focused on the free movement of foodstuffs throughout the internal market and international world trade, respectively, rather than on the food safety goal.

As a result, the ECJ handed down a number of landmark judgments relating to food products which laid the foundations of the case law on the free movement of goods. These judgments, by defining the scope of Article 28 EC, paved the way for the development of a food law and policy within the Union. In fact, in parallel to the ECJ's activity, the Commission began to rely on the positive integration instruments offered by the Treaty (Article 100; current Article 94 EC) in order to adopt a number of legislative initiatives specifically aimed at promoting the free movement of foodstuffs within the EC. Thus, for instance, the EC adopted its first food legislative act: the 1962 food colours directive; it then prepared two Communications, one in 1985 entitled 'The Completion of the Internal Market: Community Legislation on Foodstuffs'[7] and another in 1989, entitled 'The Free Movement of Foodstuffs within the Community',[8] preparing the ground for a more punctual legislative intervention in that area of law. As it emerges from this brief historical excursus, EC food law began developing on the two parallel paths of negative and positive integration, with the ECJ ensuring the application of the Treaty provisions and the Commission proposing the adoption of legislative and policy initiatives.

It is common place to argue that, unlike the EC, the WTO does not dispose of positive integration tools. While it is true that its members did not transfer any regulatory powers to the WTO, the signature of the Uruguay Round Agreements has partly changed this exclusive 'negative integration' vision of the GATT/WTO legal system. The following paragraph tries to explain how the conventional negative-integration vision of the GATT/WTO no longer depicts reality.

A.   Positive Integration in the WTO: International Standards as WTO 'de facto' Food Legislation

The adoption of the TBT and SPS Agreements represents one of the most innovative features of this Round. As seen above, these agreements, building upon the previous plurilateral 1979 Agreement on the Technical Barriers to Trade, deal with the growing problem of non-tariff barriers to trade consisting in health and safety regulatory measures.

---

[7] Communication from the Commission to the Council and the European Parliament. Completion of the Internal Market: Community Legislation on Foodstuffs. COM(85) 603 final, 8 November 1985.
[8] Communication from the Commission on the free movement of foodstuffs within the Community, OJ C271, 04 October 1989, p 3

In order to ensure that these regulations genuinely pursue their declared public policy objectives and do not constitute disguised restrictions on trade, the TBT and the SPS have adopted an approach which goes far beyond the basic principles of GATT 1947. These agreements provide for a set of rules addressed to WTO members that, instead of constraining their regulatory powers through prohibitions, requires them to adopt positive behaviour.[9] Among these positive obligations, the most significant are the harmonisation requirements.

As seen above within the SPS framework, WTO members must base their sanitary and phytosanitary measures on international standards, guidelines or recommendations, where they exist. Although not directly establishing these standards but referring to some specific standard-setting organisations, the SPS Agreement, by encouraging the adoption of harmonised food measures in order to minimise the negative effects on trade stemming from diverging national regulations, pursues a positive integration agenda.

In particular, by assuming the conformity of all food safety measures based on international standards with the WTO, the SPS Agreement has delegated to these standard-setting bodies some quasi-legislative powers they did not have for themselves. In fact, even though they do not legislate in the full sense of the term, these organisations lay down rules that, as long as they are adopted and respected, may have some binding force.

For this reason, WTO members are encouraged to play a full part in the relevant international organisations and their subsidiary bodies, in particular in the Codex Alimentarius Commission, the International Office of Epizootics, and the international and regional organisations operating within the framework of the International Plant Protection Convention. As illustrated above,[10] as soon as they became fully aware of the indirect 'quasi-legislative' power given to these organisations, WTO members invested an increasing amount of resources in order effectively to participate within the activities of these bodies.

---

[9] Although the TRIPs may also seem to impose similar 'positive' constraints on WTO members, it is worth noting the difference existing between these TRIPS' requirements and those contained in the TBT/SPS. In contrast to the latter, the former merely refers to pre-existing norms developed in WIPO Treaties, rather than turning a 'mass of normative material that never before had the status of international law into international legal obligation'.

[10] See supra Part II, Chapter II, Section 4.1, The SPS Agreement and the Relevant International Standards Organisations.

The choice of the SPS drafsmen to set up this 'quasi-legislative' system outside of the WTO offers several advantages. The 'outsourcing' of the harmonisation system to some external organisations not only facilitates the negotiations leading to the adoption of a standard by skipping the need for unanimity, but might also be capable of insulating the WTO from any criticism that may be formulated about a particular standard. In fact, the previous analysis of the operation of CAC, OIE and IPPC has shown the existence of increasingly politicised debates surrounding the adoption of international standards within these organisations. As a result, most of the standards tend to be adopted today by slim majority rather than by unanimity. Yet, this outcome does not change the normative values of the adopted standards. In fact, once a standard is adopted, the Dispute Settlement Body does not consider it to be of any importance to take into account the institutional context in which the standards arise. In particular, as the *Sardines* case clearly shows,[11] a WTO Member may be bound to apply an international standard that it voted against even if it is only a voluntary norm. Although the AB came to this conclusion in a case involving the application of an international standard under the TBT, there are good reasons to believe that this answer could be extended to the interpretation of the SPS Agreement. Therefore, as a result of the *Sardines* ruling, international standards are binding through the SPS and the TBT Agreements regardless of whether they are made by consensus.

Last but not least, it may be noted that the SPS indirect harmonisation structure presents the remarkable advantage that it ensures that the international standards be negotiated by scientists, experts in the relevant subject-matter, rather than by trade negotiators.

Finally, to support our finding according to which the SPS harmonisation requirements do represent an innovative, though peculiar, instrument of positive integration within the WTO framework, one should look at the consequences stemming from a national food safety measure which relies on an international standard.

Similarly to what happens when an EC Member State conforms to an EC regulation, when a WTO member relies on an international standard, it does not have to defend its food safety measure under the SPS Agreement. In particular, the soundness of the scientific evidence supporting that particular standard is unreviewable even though it may restrict the trading opportunities of other Member States. Furthermore, in that circumstance, the opportunity is not given for other members to challenge the regulation based on an international standard by alleging

---

[11] *EC–Sardines*, Appellate Body Report, WT/DS231/AB/R (decided 26 September 2002) adopted 23 October 2002.

that a less trade restrictive measure would have been available. Thus, following international standards could provide some protection for domestic regulatory autonomy against the growing judicial intrusion shown by the WTO judicial bodies.

In the light of the above, one may conclude that, contrary to conventional wisdom, the WTO/SPS food framework relies not solely on negative integration instruments but also, and especially, on some specific instruments of positive integration.

Although representing a legislative tool much less developed than those available within the EC, the SPS 'harmonisation' requirements allow the WTO food regime to also rely, though indirectly, on some form of harmonising power.

The choice of the SPS negotiators to refer to standard-setting international organisations outside the WTO framework has inevitably invested them with a quasi-legislative power. Although their standards remain not legally binding, but merely advisory in nature, the consequences stemming from their adoption by a member render them 'de facto' WTO food legislation.

However, in drawing a parallel between EC food legislation and this 'de facto' WTO food regulation, one should remain cautious and highlight their different normative nature.

While it is true that the SPS's outsourced 'harmonisation' system represents an emerging and innovative form of positive integration within the WTO legal system, it does not entirely fit into the traditional dichotomy existing between negative and positive integration. In fact, such a conceptual scheme of integration traditionally implies a further dimension which distinguishes between free trade and the pursuit of other non-trade public policy objectives. In view of that, while the reduction of tariff barriers and the elimination of quantitative restrictions might be perceived as instruments exclusively aimed at liberalising trade, the adoption of harmonising measures might be seen as a tool used to promote other non-trade objectives, such as other legitimate public policy goals.[12] If one applies this additional meaning of the positive/negative integration dichotomy to the SPS indirect harmonising power, it is discovered that, unlike the EC food regulations, the international standards do not pursue other legitimate public policy objectives, but rather act as trade facilitation mechanisms. In other words, while EC

---

[12] See F. Ortino, *Basic Legal Instruments for the Liberalization of Trade* (Oxford and Portland Oregon) p 21; J. Scott, *GATT and Community Law: Rethinking the 'Regulatory Gap'*, J. Shaw and G. More (eds), *New Legal Dynamics of EU*, 1995, p 147.

regulations and directives differ from the negative prohibitions contained in the Treaty to the extent that they are not only trade liberalisation instruments but also tools to safeguard and further other legitimate policies, the international standards cannot be seen as promoting any other values but trade.

This finding is confirmed by the stated goal of the Codex which is to be read:

> to guide and promote the elaboration and establishment of definitions and requirements for foods, to assist in their harmonisation and, in doing so, *to facilitate international trade*.[13]

The ultimate goal pursued by these standard-setting organisations is clearly related to trade rather than to other legitimate public policy goals, such as food safety.

Nevertheless, it has been argued that, although trade-oriented, the international regulatory processes led by these organisations, as long as they are open to a greater variety of stake-holders than many domestic processes, may actually enhance democracy.[14] This may seem to be true if one looks at, for instance, the NGOs' participation in the Codex, which, though imperfect, shows much greater openness than in the WTO itself.[15] The recent *Biotech* negotiations have clearly shown the impact that growing public interest participation may produce within the Codex.[16]

Notwithstanding these positive developments, it remains that, traditionally, the Codex standard-setting practice has shown a large pro-industry bias, by not making it easier for consumer associations to participate in the highly technical debates in the CAC working groups and committees.[17]

Lastly, when comparing the instruments of both the EC and the WTO, one cannot ignore their respective enforcement capacities. Although the

---

[13] See Codex Alimentarius Commission, *This is Codex Alimentarius*, 2nd edition.

[14] J. Braithwaite, *Prospects for Win-Win International Rapprochement of Regulation in Organization for Economic Corporation and Development, Regulatory Co-operation for an Interdependent World* (Paris: OECD, 1994).

[15] EC Member States strongly support the NGOs' participation, such as, for instance, the European Consumers' Organisation (BEUC), within the Codex. See Agenda item 14, ALINORM 05/28/9E.

[16] For an overview of the current debate on GMO food within the Codex, see EC comments to Circular Letter 2005/2-FBT, request for proposals for new work to be undertaken by the Codex Ad Hoc Intergovernmental Task Force on Foods Derived from Biotechnology, 9 June 2005.

[17] C. Joerges and J. Neyer, 'Politics, Risk Management, World Trade Organization Governance and the Limits of Legalisation', *Science and Public Policy*, June 2003, p 222.

DSU stresses that 'prompt compliance with the recommendations or rulings of the DSB is essential in order to ensure effective resolution of disputes to the benefit of all members', no mechanism of enforcement is available. As has been stated:

> [t]he WTO's enforcement mechanisms function neither as a deterrent nor as a punishment, but merely have an offsetting effect, which leaves the non-compliant party at liberty to choose between complying with WTO law or accepting the cancellation of proportionate concessions.[18]

Moreover, in contrast with the EC,[19] the WTO is not competent to introduce legal proceedings, nor does it have the option of imposing administrative fines against a non-compliant member.

B.   The Lack of a Risk Analysis Scheme within the WTO/SPS Food Regime

There is a further important consequence stemming from the WTO/SPS's choice to refer to the standards elaborated by other international organisations as the benchmark international standard for WTO members. Since neither the WTO nor the SPS Committee is in charge of developing these 'de facto' food regulations, it follows that the WTO/SPS framework is almost silent on the modalities through which SPS measures should be established and, more generally, on how food risks should be managed by WTO members' decision-makers.

In other words, the WTO food regulatory framework, by relying on this 'outsourced' harmonisation system, does not provide for a complete risk analysis framework that members should follow when adopting (trade-restricting) food safety measures.

It is submitted that for that reason, as long as WTO 'de facto' food safety measures are adopted by the Codex and not by the WTO itself, it is at

---

[18] Ibid, at 223. On the functioning of the DSU, see P. van den Bossche, *The Law and Policy of the World Trade Organization, Text, Cases and Materials* (Cambridge University Press, 2005). For an overview of the role of private parties within the WTO DSU, see A. Alemanno, 'Private parties and WTO Dispute Settlement System', *Cornell Law School L.L.M. Papers Series. Paper 1*. Available at http://lsr.nellco.org/cornell/lps/clacp/1.

[19] See Articles 226–228 EC. The EC Commission's role as a guardian of the Treaties has recently been strengthened by a judgment of the ECJ of 12 July 2005 (case C-304/02, *Commission v France* [2005] not yet reported) holding that, following non-compliance with a previous 226 judgment, a lump sum and a penalty payment may be imposed simultaneously against a Member State. This ruling is likely to put an end to the recurrent Member States' practice of delaying implementation of an Article 226 judgment until a few days before the ECJ's 228 judgment is delivered in order to escape sanctions. This finding has already been endorsed by the Commission's Communication of December 2005 on the application of Article 228 EC (SEC (2005) 1658).

Codex's approach to risk analysis that one must look in order to compare the EC risk analysis schemes with those of the WTO.

Against this backdrop, the next chapter will venture a comparison between the risk analysis schemes underlying the WTO and EC food regimes, respectively, by thoroughly analysing the Codex's emerging food safety risk analysis model.

CHAPTER II
COMPARING FOOD SAFETY RISK ANALYSIS SCHEMES

This chapter provides for a comparison between the WTO and the EC food safety risk analysis models, by looking at their respective structures. In particular, due to the lack of risk management policy within the WTO risk analysis model, the focus will shift, when appropriate, to the Codex's principles for risk analysis.

1. Comparing EC and WTO/SPS Food Safety Risk Analysis: What Risk Analysis Model for the WTO?

Similarly to the general food regulation, the SPS Agreement also makes an attempt to impose some common structure on the way in which WTO members arrive at and adopt food safety measures.

However, while the EC has established its risk analysis by heavily relying on the traditional scheme originally developed on the other side of the Atlantic by the US National Research Council,[1] and subsequently adopted by several international organisations dealing with risk analysis,[2] the WTO preferred not to endorse any particular form of risk analysis.

---

[1] The NRC has conducted a series of studies on how society can understand and cope with those risks. In particular, the distinction between risk assessment and risk management has been originally conceived in *Risk Assessment in the Federal Government – Managing the Process*, a study that sought 'institutional mechanisms that best foster a constructive partnership between science and government'. Subsequently, this distinction played a crucial role in the development of an organisational separation of risk assessment and risk management in many US regulatory agencies. However, as we will see further, later publications of the NRC recognised the difficulties of maintaining a sharp dividing line between the two processes and emphasised the importance of ensuring interaction and communication between risk assessors and risk managers. See P. Stern and H. Fineberg (eds), *Understanding Risk: Informing Decisions in a Democratic Society* (National Academy Press, 1996) and for a brief account of this development also Ingrid Suezenauer, M. Tamplin, B. Buchanan, S. Dennis, L. Tollefson, A. Hart, *Briefing Paper: US Experience* (European Workshop on the interface between Risk Assessment and Risk Management, 2003).

[2] See, within the US, *NRC Science and Judgment, National* Academy Press, 1994 Washington, DC 1994, at 4; see, in the OECD, Descriptions of selected key generic terms used in chemical hazard/risk assessment; OECD/IPCS, October 2003, available at http://www.oecd.org; see within FAO and WHO, Joint FAO/WHO Expert Consultation, Application of Risk Analysis to Food Standards Issues (WHO/FNU/FOS/95.3, 13–17 March, 1995, Geneva 1995), p 6; Joint FAO/WHO Expert Consultation, Risk Management and Food Safety, (27–31 January, 1997), FAO Food and Nutrition Paper 65, 1997; Joint FAO/WHO Expert Consultation, The Application of Risk Communication to Food Standards and Safety Matters, Rome, 2–6 February 1998, FAO Food and Nutrition Paper 70, 1999.

Accordingly, from a reading of the WTO/SPS text, no specific model of risk analysis that members should follow when adopting SPS measures within their own legal systems emerges. Nevertheless, some signs of the conventional approach to risk, incorporating the three distinct but closely linked components of risk analysis, become visible through a careful reading of the SPS text.

As seen above, both the WTO and the EC embraced science as the organising principle when regulating public health measures. Rather than relying solely on non-discrimination as the main criterion enabling them to distinguish between legitimate and illegitimate barriers to trade inspired by public health protection, they introduced a new, more demanding element, in relation to those measures: scientific justification. In particular, according to their vision, the scientific element would ensure that SPS measures address a real, objectively established, health risk, that are not protectionist measures disguised as health regulations. According to the traditional structured risk analysis framework, this scientific requirement is procedurally translated into the risk assessment stage as opposed to the risk management stage.

However, as mentioned above, the only requirements imposed by the SPS Agreement relating to risk analysis boil down to a detailed risk assessment obligation that members should satisfy when adopting SPS measures. In other words, risk assessment is the only formalised risk analysis step expressly recognised and defined by the SPS Agreement. In particular, Annex A to the SPS distinguishes two main categories of assessment of risks to the life and health of humans and animals depending on the origin of the risks at stake: food-borne risks and the quarantine risks (or pest and disease risks).

While for the risks arising from the presence of certain substances in food, beverages and feedstuffs the required assessment consists in an 'evaluation of the potential for adverse effects on human or animal health arising from the presence of additives, contaminants, toxins or disease-causing organisms in food beverages or feedstuffs', with respect to quarantine risks the required assessment is defined as 'the evaluation of the likelihood of entry, establishment or spread of a pest or disease within the territory of an importing member according to the sanitary and phytosanitary measures which might be applied'. Thus, it follows that while expressly recognising and regulating in great detail the risk assessment stage of risk analysis,[3] the SPS does not even mention the risk management stage, ie the process, distinct

---

[3] As to the risk assessment procedural obligations, Article 5 tells member states to rely on the risk assessment techniques developed by the 'relevant international organisations', which presumably include the Codex, IPPC and OIE, and also to take in due account the following factors: available scientific evidence, relevant process and production methods;

(continued...)

from risk assessment, of weighing policy alternatives and selecting appropriate measures and control options.[4]

As has been previously submitted, this approach was very unfortunate to the extent that it ruled out a potentially useful tool which would have contributed to clarifying the incomplete WTO risk analysis model.

As a result, WTO members are free, at least in principle, to adopt all measures they deem necessary to protect food safety, provided there is a demonstrable scientific basis for their measures. This clearly stems from the SPS Agreement which expressly recognises WTO members' right to determine the level of sanitary and phytosanitary protection they consider appropriate.[5] However, the acknowledgement of Member States' freedom in managing food safety risk is accompanied by some constraints and, in any case, 'it does not represent a carte blanche for legitimising SPS measures'.[6]

In determining the level of protection they consider appropriate[7] and in selecting the measures that are instrumental in achieving this chosen level of protection[8] (ie when conducting risk management), members must take into account the objective of minimising negative trade effects.

However, when doing the former, 'Article 5.4 does not impose an obligation'.[9] This is due to the fact that, according to the panel in *EC–Hormones*, the provision's wording employs the words 'should' (and not 'shall') and 'objective'.

Besides this rather weak risk management requirement, members also have to avoid arbitrary or unjustifiable distinctions in the levels of protection they consider to be appropriate in different situations, if such

---

relevant inspections, sampling and testing methods; prevalence of specific diseases or pests; existence of pest- or disease-free areas; relevant ecological and environmental conditions; and quarantine and other treatment.

[4] It may be recalled that in the *Hormones* case the AB explicitly rejected the panel's effort to distinguish between risk assessment and risk management within the SPS Agreement, by stating that 'Article 5 and Annex A of the SPS Agreement speak of 'risk assessment' only and that the term 'risk management' is not to be found either in Article 5 or in any other provision of the SPS Agreement'. See *EC–Hormones*, AB Report, at para 181.

[5] Article 2 SPS provides that: '[m]embers have the right to take sanitary and phytosanitary measures necessary for the protection of human, animal or plant life or health, provided that such measures are not inconsistent with the provisions of this Agreement'.

[6] A. Desmedt, 'Proportionality in WTO law', 5 *JIEL* (2001) 441 p 458.

[7] See Article 5.4 SPS (Members should […] take into account the objective of minimising negative trade effects').

[8] See Article 5.6 SPS ('Members shall ensure that such measures are not more trade-restrictive than required to achieve their appropriate level of sanitary or phytosanitary protection, taking into account technical and economic feasibility').

[9] *EC–Hormones*, Panel Report, at 8.166.

distinctions result in discrimination or disguised restrictions on international trade.[10] This requirement gives rise to a sort of consistency discipline which must be abided by in adopting a risk management measure. However, as illustrated above, the simple fact that the level of protection chosen shows arbitrary or unjustifiable differences only acts as a warning that the measure may be discriminatory.[11] Therefore, 'the desired consistency is defined as a goal to be achieved in the future' and is not a legal obligation.[12] In fact, as has been held by the AB in the *Hormones* case:

> [...] the statement of that goal does not establish a *legal obligation* of consistency of appropriate levels of protection. We think, too, that the goal set is not absolute or perfect consistency, since governments establish their appropriate levels of protection frequently on an *ad hoc* basis and over time, as different risks present themselves at different times. It is only arbitrary or unjustifiable inconsistencies that are to be avoided.[13]

In light of the above, it results that the only 'binding' risk management constraint on members is the 'least-trade restrictive' requirement.

These SPS provisions, by imposing only the respect of the 'proportionality' principle[14], sketch out a really basic risk management policy, whose sole objective is to prevent food safety measures from producing unnecessary negative effects on international trade and being misused for protectionist purposes. As a result, members' sovereign right to choose an appropriate level of protection may appear to be well protected.

However, the risk analysis promoted by the WTO/SPS in these terms produce the effect of requiring its members to respond to food safety failures by further centralising risk assessment. Although this supposedly contributes to the free movement of foodstuffs in international trade, it does not seem to leave any room for consideration for other non-economic interests which may be at stake.

By not fully shaping a risk management policy of food safety risks, the WTO regime diverges from the EC discipline which lays down strict procedural requirements for both the risk assessment and risk management phases of the food risk analysis scheme that both the EC and its members must follow.

---

[10] See Article 5.5 SPS.

[11] *EC–Hormones*, Appellate Body Report, at 214–215.

[12] Ibid, at 213. See also *Guidelines to Further Practical Implementation of Article 5.5*, G/SPS/15.

[13] *EC–Hormones*, Appellate Body Report, at 213.

[14] On the interpretation of this requirement in WTO law and in particular the SPS and TBT Agreements, see F. Ortino, *Basic Legal Instruments for the Liberalisation of Trade* (Oxford and Portland Oregon) pp 445 ss, notably p 464.

Accordingly, WTO members, although instructed on how to conduct a risk assessment of a food product for the purposes of the SPS Agreement, are left alone when it comes to deciding about how to regulate the entry of that particular food into the market.

In particular, this vacuum in the WTO/SPS risk regulatory discipline gives rise to the following questions:

a) How members, once they have conducted the risk assessment of a particular foodstuff, should manage the risk stemming from its consumption? Which factors should they take into account ? (Section 2)

b) What should members decide in case of scientific uncertainty about the safety of a certain product? (Section 3)

These questions, relating to the risk management stage of risk analysis, do not find a direct answer in the SPS text. In fact, as SPS negotiators considered it inappropriate for the WTO to be more prescriptive about risk management, they considered the Codex as a better forum for the elaboration of guidelines for regulatory action.

Therefore, given the status of the Codex standards as international reference points in the framework of the SPS, it is suggested to have regard to the Codex's risk analysis scheme in order to obtain an answer to these questions. As the Codex international standards represent 'de facto' WTO food regulations, likewise, the Codex risk analysis techniques contribute to shaping the WTO risk analysis model. The appropriateness of this approach seems to receive confirmation by the same SPS Agreement, whose Article 5, paragraph 1, tells members to take into account 'risk assessment techniques developed by the relevant international organisations'.

Before addressing the abovementioned risk management issues, it might be useful to briefly introduce the main features of the risk analysis scheme developed within the Codex.

1.1   Risk Analysis in the Framework of the Codex

Risk analysis evolved within the the Codex Alimentarius Commission during the 1990s as a result of the imminent entry into force of the WTO Agreements.

Although the SPS Agreement placed no obligations on the Codex itself, it was inevitable that the Codex would determine what changes were needed to adapt itself to the new tasks. The implications stemming from the newly acquired status were recognised well before the entry into force of the WTO Agreements. Thus, in 1991, an FAO/WHO Conference on Food Standards, Chemicals in Food and Food Trade was convened in Rome to discuss the likely implications of the proposed SPS Agreement on the operation of the Codex. This conference stressed the importance of scientific committees such as the Joint FAO/WHO Meeting on Pesticides Residues (JMPR) and the Joint FAO/WHO Expert Committee on Food Additives (JECFA) in providing evaluations based on sound science and risk assessment principles.

There was general consensus that the expected adoption of the WTO Agreements meant that the Codex needed to develop new practices and procedures, notably with respect to the use of science. In the light of the above, with respect to the role of science, the Conference recommended the importance of:

> [e]stablishing a review programme to examine all the Codex standards as to their current relevance and sound scientific basis, with a view to facilitating international trade. This should include prioritisation of standards to be examined' and 'Requesting all the Codex Committees, as well as JECFA and JMPR, to continue to base their evaluations on suitable scientific principles and to ensure necessary consistency in their risk assessment determinations'.[15]

In particular, the SPS obligation on WTO members to base their food safety measures on scientific evidence required the Codex to develop further the methods it relied upon to elaborate and adopt standards. Most the Codex techniques were vague and subject to diverging interpretation and application from meeting to meeting. Since most of the Codex members had an obligation, stemming from their WTO membership, to use scientific principles, it was incumbent upon the Codex members to make full use of science when adopting the Codex standards relating to food safety. In light of the above, the FAO and WHO promoted additional consultations to address the three components of risk analysis: risk assessment, risk management and risk communication.[16]

The matter was further discussed at the 10th Session of the CCGP in September 1992 which asked the Secretariat to draft a paper on the issue. The following year, during the 20th CAC meeting, the Commission, after

---

[15] Report of the FAO/WHO Conference on Food Standards, Chemicals in Food and Food Trade, Rome, 18–27 March 1991, FAO/WHO Programme (ALICOM 91/22).

[16] Thus, for instance, in 1999, the Codex Committee on Food Hygiene has also developed the Principles and Guidelines for the Conduct of Microbiological Risk Assessment and is currently developing Principles and Guidelines for the Conduct of Microbiological Risk Management.

having experienced a difficult debate on hormones for beef, asked the CCGP to develop some guidance on how science and other factors should be taken into account in its standard-setting procedures. A paper was subsequently presented at the 11th Session of the CCGP in April 1994 entitled: 'Consideration on the Role of Science in the Codex Decision-Making Process'.[17] The most controversial point was whether these Statements should have been incorporated into the rules of procedure or merely in the general principles of Codex Alimentarius, which, unlike the former, do not constitute binding rules for the CAC work. After some lengthy and difficult debate, the Committee established a working group that finally indicated which sections of the procedural manual might have needed some revision. On that basis, during the 41st Session of the executive committee in June 1994, the Committee elaborated four 'statements of principle', that eventually became, at the 21st CAC meeting in July 1995, the 'statements of principle concerning the role of science in the Codex decision-making process and the extent to which other legitimate factors are taken into Account'. After some discussions, these statements have been finally incorporated as an appendix into the procedural manual entitled 'General Decisions of the Commission'.[18]

Risk analysis is, since then, considered an integral part of the standard-setting process within the Codex. For that purpose, the Commission has established not only the 'working principles for risk analysis for application in the framework of the Codex Alimentarius'[19] but also the 'definitions for the purposes of the Codex Alimentarius' of risk analysis terms related to food safety.[20] These principles for risk analysis are intended for application in the framework of the Codex Alimentarius. They provide guidance to the Codex Alimentarius Commission and the joint FAO/WHO expert bodies so that food safety and health aspects of the Codex standards are based on risk analysis.

The model of risk analysis chosen by the Codex members reflects the main features of the structured approach comprising the three distinct but closely linked components of risk analysis originally elaborated on the other side of the Atlantic by the National Research Council.

According to the definition given by the Codex, risk analysis provides:

> a process to collect, analyse and evaluate, systematically and transparently, relevant scientific and non-scientific information

---

[17] CX/GP 94/4.

[18] See the 10th Edition of the procedural manual published in 1997.

[19] The 'Working Principles for Risk Analysis' are contained in Section III of the CAC Procedural Manual, 14th edition, 2005, at 101 ss.

[20] The 'Definitions' are listed in Section I of the CAC Procedural Manual, 14th edition, 2005, at 43 ss.

> about a chemical, biological or physical hasard possibly associated with food, in order to select the best option to manage that risk based on the various alternatives identified.[21]

A fundamental principle of all the Codex standards stems directly from this vision of risk analysis: the food standards must be based on science.

As WTO members are obliged to base their SPS measures on an assessment of the risk taking into account all available scientific information, the usefulness of the Codex standards to the WTO/SPS Agreement is evident.

In particular, the risk analysis used in the Codex, as provided for by the 'Working principles for risk analysis', must be 'conducted in accordance' with two important texts annexed to the the Codex procedural manual:[22]

> – the statements of principle concerning the role of science in the Codex decision-making process and the extent to which other factors are taken into account[23]; and
> – the statements of principle relating to the role of food safety risk assessment[24].

In particular, the first text states that:

> (1) The food standards, guidelines and other recommendations of the Codex Alimentarius shall be based on the principle of sound scientific analysis and evidence, involving a thorough review of all relevant information, in order that standards assure the quality and safety of the food supply.

The importance of science is then tempered by two further points which state:

> (2) When elaborating and deciding upon food standards the Codex Alimentarius will have regard, where appropriate, to other legitimate factors relevant for the health protection of consumers and for the promotion of fair practices in food trade,
> (3) In this regard it is noted that food labelling plays an important role in furthering both objectives.

As to the statements of principle relating to the role of food safety risk assessment, this document provides that:

---

[21] Section I of the CAC Procedural Manual, 14th edition, 2005, at 43 ss.
[22] See Article 4, point 3, of the Working Principles for Risk Analysis are contained in Section III of the CAC Procedural Manual, 14th edition, 2005, at 101 ss.
[23] Originally adopted during the CAC 21st session. See Report of the 21st Session, at 61.
[24] See Appendix of the CAC Procedural Manual, 14th edition, 2005, at 188 ss.

> Health and safety aspects of the Codex decisions and recommendations should be based on a risk assessment, as appropriate to the circumstances', and 'Food safety risk assessment should be soundly based in science, should incorporate the four steps of the risk assessment process, and should be documented in a transparent manner.

As will be shown in the following pages, these documents, combined with the Working Principles, have shaped the Codex risk analysis scheme. It will be illustrated how this model of risk analysis is gradually becoming, by virtue of the bridge offered by the SPS harmonisation requirements, a 'de facto' WTO risk analysis model.

2. The Integration of 'Other Legitimate Factors' into the EC and WTO/SPS Risk Analysis Models

In an effort to eliminate protectionist barriers to trade, both the EC and WTO regimes impose strict scientific justification requirements, notably a duty to conduct a risk assessment when adopting food safety measures. However, risk assessment does not provide the decision-makers with a definitive regulatory answer, rather it offers them some information upon which to take regulatory action.

While both food safety risk analysis schemes require this scientific requirement to be satisfied, it is only the EC risk analysis model which tells regulators how to take the subsequent risk management decision, by listing the 'other (non-scientific) factors' to be taken into account in the risk management stage of the regulatory process.

According to the EC food safety risk analysis model, besides scientific findings, 'other factors legitimate to the matter under consideration', such as societal, economic, traditional, ethical and environmental considerations may play a role in the decision to take protective action[25]. Although science plays the major role at the risk management stage, the general food regulation expressly reserves the right of risk assessors to take these 'other factors' into consideration when reaching a final decision[26]. This is because:

---

[25] See preamble (19) of Regulation 178/2002 and its Article 6, paragraph 3. See also the broader list of 'other factors' contained within the White Paper (COM(99) 719, 12 January 2000 available at http://europa.eu.int/comm/dgs/health/ consumer /library/pub/ pub06_en.pdf, para 4), which mentions 'environmental considerations, animal welfare, sustainable agriculture, consumers' expectation regarding product quality, fair information and definition of the essential characteristics of products and their process and production methods'. However, both lists containing mere examples, their differences do not carry any particular value and should not be overemphasised.

[26] The regulation states several times that risk management decisions may consider not only risk assessment but also 'other legitimate factors'. See Preamble (19), Article 3 (12) and Article 6 (3).

it is recognised that scientific risk assessment alone cannot, in some cases, provide all the information on which a risk management decision should be based.[27]

It is indeed settled case law that a decision taken at Community level within the context of risk management may depart from the findings of a scientific assessment.[28] The perceived need to also consider non-science based factors within the decision-making process characterises the European approach to risk analysis by differentiating it greatly from the one adopted within the WTO/SPS legal frameworks.

In fact, contrary to the EC risk analysis model, the WTO food safety risk analysis does not specify the extent to which 'other factors', such as social values and consumer preferences, may be taken into account in national regulatory decision-making processes. As shown above, by mainly focusing on the risk assessment stage of risk analysis, the WTO does not endorse any particular model of risk analysis. Yet, this exclusively scientific-oriented approach would seem to suggest that the risk management phase should focus solely on the rational, science-driven data stemming from risk assessment, by thus ruling out all 'other factors' from consideration. That basis for law-making would seem to exclude, or at least marginalise, other public concerns or other forms of knowledge from consideration as part of the process of regulating food safety risk. By exalting the role of science, the SPS Agreement tends to rule out all non-scientific factors from standard setting.[29] The only risk management requirements imposed by the SPS, the 'consistency' and 'proportionality' tests, contained as they are in open-textured provisions, fail to offer useful guidance to members when establishing the appropriate level of protection and choosing the measure designed to achieve that level.

This clear divergence between the food safety risk analysis schemes of the EC and the WTO deserves great attention as it carries the potential to bring the EC food regime into conflict with WTO law.

2.1 'Other Legitimate Factors' in the EC Food Safety Risk Analysis: a Potential Incompatibility Issue under WTO Law?

There are several interesting questions that may arise from the role of these 'other factors' in regulation-making. In particular, there is an emerging debate as to whether the EC risk analysis model, by explicitly

---

[27] See Regulation 178/2002, preamble (19).

[28] Case C-3/00 [2003] *Commission v Denmark*, para 144.

[29] J. Cameron, 'The Precautionary Principle', in G. P. Sampson and W. B. Chambers (eds), *Trade, Environment, and the Millennium* (Tokyo, New York and Paris: United Nations University Press, 1999) p 261.

acknowledging the importance of non-scientific factors, may be considered compatible with the SPS risk assessment requirements imposed by Article 5.1 SPS.

The issue is whether an EC food safety measure taking into account 'other factors' could still be considered as 'based on' risk assessment within the meaning of the SPS Agreement. According to the EC Commission, the concept of risk assessment as enshrined within that SPS provision 'leaves leeway for interpretation of what could be used as a basis for a precautionary approach' and, notably, it does not need to be confined to purely quantitative scientific data, but could include 'non-quantifiable data of a factual or quantitative nature'.[30]

But, before tackling that question, it must be asked whether WTO judicial bodies can review members' reliance on such factors and, also, to what extent the WTO should recognise such factors as having a legitimate role in decision-making.

Members' reliance on 'other factors' would not seem to be directly reviewable under Article 5.1 SPS to the extent that that provision does not empower the WTO judicial bodies to determine the legitimacy of any of the 'other factors' considered in the risk management stage, but merely the scientific basis of the adopted measure. However, in determining whether there is a rational relationship between the adopted food safety measure and the outcome of risk assessment, it is inevitable that panels will be influenced by their perception of the legitimacy of the 'other factors' taken into account by the national authorities when adopting the contested measure. Thus, on the one hand, should the panel share the consumer fears related to the consumption of a certain product, it is likely that it will be particularly willing to endorse the adoption of a conservative regulation. On the other hand, if a panel were not so favourably disposed towards a certain 'other factor', it would be more keen to look on the relevant measure as no longer enjoying that logical relationship.

By entrusting WTO judicial bodies with a great deal of subjectivity in their assessment, this situation gives rise to a significant amount of legal uncertainty in the international food trade arena.

Which 'other factors' may be accommodated into the SPS risk analysis scheme?

---

[30] Commission Communication on the precautionary principle, COM(2000) 1, 2 February 2000, at 11.

As shown above, the current SPS Agreement, by merely listing those factors that may be taken into account in the risk assessment stage, does not provide a definitive answer to that question.

For this reason, it is suggested that regard should be had to the food safety risk analysis scheme provided by the Codex Alimentarius Commission as the relevant benchmark for predicting which 'other factors' may, or may not, play a legitimate role in the risk analysis of food products within the WTO/SPS Agreement. Indeed, it is likely that the WTO judicial bodies, in establishing whether a national food safety measure is 'based on risk assessment', will also be influenced by the risk analysis model, notably by the risk management policy, developed by the Codex.

A.   The Role of 'Other Factors' in the Codex's Risk Analysis

In 1995, the Codex adopted the statements of principle concerning the role of science in the Codex decision-making process and the extent to which other factors are taken into account. These were adopted at the 21st session of the CAC meeting and subsequently incorporated into the the Codex procedural manual.[31]

While Principle 1 states that the Codex 'food standards, guidelines and other recommendations shall be based on the principle of sound scientific analysis and evidence', Principle 2 states that 'when elaborating and deciding upon food standards, the Codex Alimentarius will have regard, where appropriate, to other legitimate factors relevant for the health protection of consumers and for the promotion of fair practices in food trade'. This last statement remains quite obscure since it does not indicate which other factors may be taken into account and to what extent they can legitimately be invoked in the adoption of food standards. Furthermore, similarly to what happens in the application of the SPS Agreement, one may wonder to what extent a food safety standard justified by 'other legitimate factors' may still be considered to be 'based on the principle of sound scientific analysis and evidence' under Principle 1.

An opportunity to launch a debate on the revision of these statements of principle arose in 1998 during the negotiations that should have led to the adoption of Maximum Residues Levels (MRLs) for Bovine Somatropin (BST) within the Codex.[32] This was the first occasion ever

---

[31] CAC statements of principle concerning the role of science in the Codex decision-making process and the extent to which other factors are taken into account (Decision of the 21st Session of the Commission 1995 ALINORM 95/37).

[32] BST is a synthetically produced version of a naturally occurring hormone intended to increase milk production. The Codex Committee for the Residues of Veterinary Drugs in Food (CCRVDF) had discussed the definition of MRLs for this substance for many years, but without ever reaching an agreement.

on which a the Codex member, notably the EC, invoked 'other factors', as quoted in Principle 2, in order to prevent the adoption of the relevant standard.

While the US was in favor of adopting the MRLs for the BST, the EC Member States opposed it strongly by invoking the need to consider 'legitimate factors other than science' in determining the relevant standard. In fact, the adoption of a limit would have implied that scientific evidence could allow the setting of a safe level, contrary to the position in the EC where the use of the substance had been banned. In particular, the EC stressed the need to give consideration to the technological justification for using the hormone concerned, animal welfare and consumers' concerns for BST.

Lacking consensus on the use of 'other factors' in the standard-setting process, the EC enacted a moratorium on the use of BST within the European Community until 1999.

It is against this backdrop that the the Codex Alimentarius Commission gave mandate to the the Codex Committee of General Principles (CCGP)[33] to identify which 'other factors' may be considered in the risk management of food safety standards.[34]

Accordingly, in 1998, the CCGP began revising the statements of principle on the role of science and the extent to which others factors may be taken into account.[35] Some delegations noted the difficulties of determining the relevance and legitimacy of other factors, the need to base them on objective criteria, especially to prevent their use as a barrier to trade. The joint FAO/WHO Expert Consultation on Risk Management and Food Safety recommended that the Commission should clarify the application of the second statement of principle. In particular, the consultation indicated that:

> [...] this clarification should include explicit description of the factors which may be considered, the extent to which these factors

---

[33] The terms of reference of this committee within the Codex are: 'To deal with such procedural and general matters as are referred to it by the Codex Alimentarius Commission. Such matters have included the establishment of the General Principles which define the purpose and scope of the Codex Alimentarius, the nature of Codex standards and the forms of acceptance by countries of Codex standards; the development of Guidelines for Codex Committees; the development of a mechanism for examining any economic impact statements submitted by governments concerning possible implications for their economies of some of the individual standards or some of the provisions thereof; the establishment of a Code of Ethics for the International Trade in Food'.

[34] See the 22nd Report of the CAC, paras 67–68.

[35] Report of the 13th Meeting of the CCGP, 1998, paras 59–70.

should be taken into account and the procedures to be used in this regard'.[36]

For that purpose, the Codex Secretariat published a paper revealing that there were several categories of 'other factors' that had previously been used in the Codex standard-setting activities, mainly relating to technological, economic and safety factors.[37] While the EC argued that these categories of factors, combined with other specific factors, such as consumer concerns, environmental risks and ethical and cultural elements, were essential in assuring a general acceptance of the Codex international standards, other members stated that giving consideration to these factors 'could open a Pandora's box'.[38] In fact, the same the Codex paper clarified that:

> these recommendations should not be interpreted as allowing for the consideration of elements which are not related to health protection, such as consumer preference, because they differ significantly from one country or one region to another.[39]

This debate led to the launch of a general discussion on the role of 'other legitimate factors' in the the Codex risk analysis model within the 14th meeting of the Committee on General Principles held in 1999. After two years of fervid discussion, notably between the European countries and the US, the Codex Commission adopted a Statement entitled 'Criteria for consideration of the other factors referred to in the second statement of principle'.[40] These criteria have been incorporated as an appendix into the procedural manual and read as follows:

–   when health and safety matters are concerned, the statements of principle concerning the role of science and the statements of

---

[36] Risk Management and Food Safety – Report of a Joint Committee FAO/WHO Consultation, 1997.

[37] See review of the statements of principle on the role of science and the extent to which other factors should be taken into account (1) role of science and other factors in relation to risk analysis (CX/GP 99/9). These elements are: economic implications in trade; feasibility from the technological point of view; food security; good agricultural practice in relation to pesticide MRLs; good veterinary practice in relation to veterinary drugs MRLs; technological justification in the case of food additives; the nature of the production or processing methods and their particular constraints; the availability of methods and analysis and sampling plans and the feasibility of control and inspection measures. For a comment on this paper, see Jukes, *The Role of science*, Food Control, Volume 11(3), June 2000, p 29.

[38] See S. Poli, 'The Adoption of International Food Safety Standards', *European Law Journal*, Vol. 10, no. 5, September 2004, p 624 citing OECD, Food Safety and Quality: Trade Considerations (2000), at 34.

[39] Paper prepared for the Codex Committee on General Principles (14th session), CX/GP99/09, at para 9.

[40] Decision of the 24th CAC Session, 2001.

principle relating to the role of food safety risk assessment should be followed;

– *other legitimate factors* relevant for health protection and fair trade practices *may be identified in the risk management process*, and risk managers should indicate how these factors affect the selection of risk management options and the development of standards, guidelines and related texts;

– *consideration of other factors should not affect the scientific basis of risk analysis*; in this process, the separation between risk assessment and risk management should be respected, in order to ensure the scientific integrity of the risk assessment;

– it should be recognised that some legitimate concerns of governments when establishing their national legislation are not generally applicable or relevant worldwide; (*Confusion should be avoided between justification of national measures under the SPS and TBT Agreements and their validity at the international level*);

– only those other factors which can be accepted on a worldwide basis, or on a regional basis in the case of regional standards and related texts, should be taken into account in the framework of the Codex;

– the consideration of specific other factors in the development of risk management recommendations of the Codex Alimentarius Commission and its subsidiary bodies should be clearly documented, including the rationale for their integration, on a case-by-case basis;

– the feasibility of risk management options due to the nature and particular constraints of the production or processing methods, transport and storage, especially in developing countries, may be considered; concerns related to economic interests and trade issues in general should be substantiated by quantifiable data;

– the integration of other legitimate factors in risk management should not create unjustified barriers to trade (*according to the WTO principles, and taking into account the particular provisions of the SPS and TBT*); particular attention should be given to the impact on developing countries of the inclusion of such other factors.

Although not a model of clarity, the Criteria seem to make it possible to also invoke, on a case-by-case basis, non-scientific factors in the risk management phase of risk analysis.

This outcome has clearly represented a success for the EC and a defeat for the US, who had constantly argued that risk management be exclusively 'grounded on science-based risk assessment'.

However, the possibility that other legitimate factors relevant for the health protection and fair trade practices may be identified in the risk management process is severely constrained by the same Criteria. In fact, such a possibility is made subject to four conditions.

First:

> [c]onsideration of other factors should not affect the scientific basis of risk analysis.

This scientific constrain of reliance on other factors is likely to rule out the invocation of 'other factors' every time these factors may conflict with scientific evidence.

Second:

> only those factors which can be accepted on a world-wide basis, or on a regional basis in the case of regional standards and related texts, should be taken into account.

This means that factors recognised solely at national level may not be validly invoked by Codex countries. Thus, if the EC would like to invoke some 'other factors', it should be demonstrated that these factors are accepted in the whole Community. This positive approach vis-à-vis 'collective preference' seems to have received some endorsement in *EC–Hormones*. Here the AB could not share the panel's conclusion according to which there was a protectionist intent behind the import ban on growth-hormones beef because of the evidence showing 'the depth and extent of the anxieties experienced [...], the dangers of abuse of hormones [...] and the intense concern of consumers' within the European Communities.[41]

Thirdly, in taking into account 'other legitimate factors', the Codex members should also consider the impact that their measure may produce on developing countries.

Fourthly, the integration of other legitimate factors in risk management should not create unjustified barriers to trade. In evaluating the trade impact of the 'other factors'-based measures the Codex members must take into account 'the particular provisions of the SPS and TBT Agreements'.[42]

From all the above it results that, although the possibility of also relying on non-scientific factors has been explicitly recognised by the model of

---

[41] *EC–Hormones*, Appellate Body Report, at 245.
[42] Footnote 38 of the Codex Procedural Manual at 189.

risk analysis developed by the Codex, the constraints surrounding such a possibility render it almost impossible to validly invoke these factors. As a result, notwithstanding some countries' attempts to invoke them, no 'other legitimate factors' have ever been taken into account in the elaboration of a the Codex standard.

In particular, it must be noted that neither the general acknowledgement that 'other factors' may be taken into account contained in the 'Working Principles'[43] nor the Criteria enumerate which factors may be 'relevant for the health protection of consumers and for the promotion of fair practices in food trade'. The CCGP's proposal to consider only those 'other factors' that had been explicitly recognised in the recommendations of the relevant multilateral international organisations was rejected.

Although further debate on the need to identify 'other legitimate factors' has taken place within the the Codex Ad Hoc Intergovernmental Task Force on Food Derived from Biotechnology (IGTF), its work does not seem to have brought any progress on the matter. In fact, the 'Principles for the Risk of Food Derived from Modern Biotechnologies', after referring to the Codex Working Principles for Risk Analysis, merely rephrase the conventional risk management formula, by stating:

> [r]isk management measures for foods derived from modern biotechnology should be proportional to the risk, based on the outcome of the risk assessment, and, where relevant, taking into account other legitimate factors in accordance with the general decisions of the Codex Alimentarius Commission.[44]

Recently, the CAC has requested comments on proposals for new work to be undertaken by the IGTF.[45] The EC has proposed several subjects for the new work to be covered by the taskforce.[46]

B.   Conclusions on the Role of 'Other Factors' in the Codex

The heated discussions taking place within the Codex on the role of 'other legitimate factors' have led to a rather disappointing result. Although the possibility of invoking these factors has been explicitly recognised, no consensus has been reached on a list of factors relevant

[43] Working Principles, para 28.

[44] Principles for the Risk of Food Derived from Modern Biotechnologies (CAC/GL 44-2003). See also Fourth Report of the IGTF, 2003, para 82.

[45] Circular Letter 2005/2 – FBT.

[46] EC comments to Circular Letter 2005/02-FBT, Request for proposals for new work to be undertaken by the Codex Ad Hoc Intergovernmental Task Force on Foods Derived from Biotechnology.

for health protection and fair trade practices. At the same time, the use of 'other legitimate factors' in the Codex's standard-setting activities being severely constrained, a valid reliance on these factors is almost ruled out under the current the Codex food safety risk analysis frame. Accordingly, notwithstanding some countries' attempts to invoke 'other legitimate factors', such factors have, at least so far, never been taken into account in the elaboration of a the Codex standard.

Thus, although the the Codex statements of principle are now supposed to define the risk analysis adopted by the Codex, reliance on 'other legitimate factors' continues to cause uncertainty.

On one side, it is constantly argued that Codex, after having conducted a risk assessment, should set up a standard on the basis of that result without taking into account any other factors which may potentially disguise the scientific factor. On the other, it is stated that exclusive reliance on the scientific element may not suffice in managing the risk stemming from a certain product. Although the acceptable level of risk may be difficult to define, where the use of the product confers little benefit, even a low risk may be considered unacceptable by many consumers.

2.2   Conclusions: 'Other Factors' as an Open Question

The current discussion on the importance of non-scientific factors in determining the outcome of legislative and regulatory decisions is becoming increasingly complex. The issue is about how to ensure that science retains its central role in the decision-making process, whilst taking appropriate account of other legitimate factors that may play a role in the risk management phase of risk analysis. In fact, while science constitutes a valid constraint on protectionist non-tariff barriers, if left unchecked it may go too far in limiting countries' ability to regulate food safety in a way which is satisfactory for its own constituencies.

The EC model of risk analysis incorporating 'other legitimate factors' seems to start from the assumption according to which policy-makers must let citizens choose between different potential risks if they are to retain public trust in the event of a crisis. For this reason, the EC approach to risk is more open to non scientific factors than the one developed within the WTO/SPS framework. While science makes many future outcomes possible, whether these are acceptable or not should be a social, economic or ethical issue, and not a scientific one.

Scientific evidence, although crucial, is therefore only one of the elements to be taken into account in the European risk analysis. This means that the risk management stage must integrate into the scientific data other factors such as economic feasibility, the desired level of protection and other consumers' preferences. This model of risk analysis has recently been endorsed by the European Court of First Instance, which stated that science is necessary but not sufficient to authorise regulatory action.[47] By relying on this approach, it concluded that the decision to ban a product is not a matter for the scientists to decide, but rather is one for the public authority to whom political responsibility has been entrusted.

But why, contrary to the SPS/WTO model of risk analysis, does the European model reserve such a limited role to science?

As illustrated above, while scientific justification has been initially introduced to attain a similar anti-protectionist goal – as within the SPS/WTO system – by requiring members to base their derogating measures on science, it has subsequently acquired another objective: making sure that EC legislation would attain a high level of protection of health. Again, science is necessary, but not sufficient, to support the adoption of food safety measures.

The risk analysis model contained in the SPS/WTO is based on different premises. Contrary to the European model, the scientific evidence is exclusively required to make sure that Member States do not adopt protectionist measures. The role of science is therefore limited to an anti-protectionism mechanism and it is not motivated by consumer protection grounds. In fact, the SPS model does not set up a minimum standard of protection at world-wide level, rather it aims at making sure that the adopted SPS measure be the least trade-restrictive amongst the various management options available.

The choice made by SPS negotiators to delegate to Codex the 'other factors' issue, by declining to define a clear cut risk management policy within the WTO, has proved UN successful so far. Despite some progress on the definition of the role of 'other factors' having been made in the Codex, the extent to which consumer concerns, cultural and other social factors may be taken into account in food safety risk management policy remains unclear. Thus, the debate over the use of 'other factors' is still open within the Codex and does not seem to be ready to give rise to an agreement amongst its members. At the same time, from the cases decided so far by the WTO judicial bodies, it is not clear to what extent a measure also motivated by 'other (non-scientific) factors' may still be considered 'based on' risk assessment as provided by Article 5.1. Lacking

---

[47] In the *Pfizer* case (Case T-13/99 *Pfizer Animal Health v Council*, [2002] ECR II-3305, at para 201) the CFI has clearly stated that '[s]cientific legitimacy is not a sufficient basis for the exercise of public authority'.

a clear risk management policy within the SPS Agreement, the WTO judicial bodies tend to exalt the scientific element by applying a rather demanding standard of review, thus inevitably disfavouring Member States' reliance on non-scientific factors. At the same time, the consistency requirement, which together with the 'proportionality' condition exhausts the WTO risk management policy, does not provide a definitive answer to the 'other factors' conundrum. In particular, the case law developed so far on that requirement provides little guidance in establishing which are the permissible factors that would justify differences in the level of protection. Conversely, by inducing panels to enquire into the validity of a member's decision on the level of risk it is prepared to accept in comparable situations, it has the potential to open the door to a highly intrusive review.[48]

Until this debate is resolved, what must countries do to be allowed to rely on 'other factors' when developing their food safety policies?

This question remains particularly relevant within the European context where consumer concerns continue to be heightened by various real issues, such as the risk of contamination between bird flu-affected animals and humans[49] and the continuing uncertainty over the possible long-term effect of GMOs.[50]

The existing tensions within the Codex and between the EC and other WTO members on the 'other factors' issues show how urgent it is to develop a clearer conceptual framework. In particular, this framework should indicate which factors and at what point in the WTO/Codex risk analysis process such factors may be appropriately weighed. This issue has to be contextualised within the larger discussion, ongoing within the Codex, on the definition of the food safety risk analysis processes. The development of a clearer, transparent risk analysis scheme within the Codex is a prerequisite to the accomplishment of the Codex's dual

---

[48] See, eg, V. R. Walker, 'Consistent Levels of Protection in International Trade Disputes: Using Risk Perception Research to Justify Different Levels of Acceptable Risk' (2001) 31 *Environmental Law Reporter* 11317 and J. Atik, 'The Weakest Link: Demonstrating the Inconsistency of 'Appropriate Levels of Protection' in Australia–Salmon', 24 *Risk Analysis: an International Journal*, p 483 (2004).

[49] Avian Influenza , also called 'Bird Flu', is a highly contagious viral infection which can affect all species of birds and can manifest itself in different ways depending mainly on the ability of the virus involved to cause disease (pathogenicity) and on the species affected. See FAQs on Avian Influenza and Food, available at the EFSA website: http://www.efsa.europa.eu/en/press_room/questions_and_answers/1378.html and also Avian Influenza FAQs available at the WHO website: http://www.who.int/csr/disease/avian_influenza/ avian_faqs/en /#present.

[50] Although more and more genetically modified foods are being produced and marketed and as many different types of GMOs continue to be released into the environment, there is no long-term study showing that GMOs are safe.

missions: to promote harmonisation and to prevent trade disputes. In fact, failure to develop a clear and consistent 'other factors' policy within the Codex is likely to give rise to some trade disputes before the WTO DSB.

3.   What Role for the Precautionary Principle?

The analysis of EC and WTO food safety disciplines has shown that both regimes recognise the idea, whether it is called a principle or not, according to which authorities may adopt a precautionary approach to uncertain food risks. More generally, both regimes seem to allow regulatory authorities to take action to protect health before there is conclusive scientific evidence that harm is occurring.

However, in order to understand the exact scope of such a recognition it is necessary to compare the conditions upon which precaution may be invoked within the EC and WTO regimes.

While in the WTO the circumstances in which precaution may be used are listed within Article 5.7 of the SPS Agreement, in the EC, Article 174 of the Treaty merely mentions the precautionary principle as a basis for the Community environmental policy. The exact conditions upon which this principle may be validly invoked within the EC have been set forth by the 2000 European Commission's Communication on the Precautionary Principle,[51] which has also extended the principle outside the environment to make it applicable within the field of health protection and food safety.[52]

It may be recalled that, on the one hand, Article 5.7 states that:

> [i]n cases where relevant scientific evidence is insufficient, a member may provisionally adopt sanitary or phytosanitary measures on the basis of available pertinent information, including that from the relevant international organisations as well as from sanitary and phytosanitary measures applied by other members. In such circumstances, Members shall seek to obtain the additional information necessary for a more objective assessment of risk and review the sanitary and phytosanitary measure accordingly within a reasonable period of time.

On the other hand, according to the Commission Communication, the precautionary principle may be invoked where:

[51] European Commission, Communication from the Commission on the precautionary principle, COM (2000) 1, 2 February 2000, at 5.1.2 Scientific Evaluation.
[52] In reality, Article 174 already acknowledged that protection of public health is one of the objectives to which environmental policy contributes.

scientific information is insufficient, inconclusive or uncertain and where there are indications that the possible effects on the environment, or human, animal or plant health may be potentially dangerous and inconsistent with the chosen level of protection'.[53]

A similar description is provided in the general food law regulation which states that:

[i]n specific circumstances where, *following an assessment of available information,* the possibility of harmful effects on health is identified but *scientific uncertainty persists,* provisional risk management measures necessary to ensure the high level of health protection chosen in the Community may be adopted, pending further scientific information for a more comprehensive risk assessment'.[54]

As previously established in the above-mentioned Communication, the measures adopted on the basis of the precautionary principle 'must be proportionate' and 'no more restrictive of trade than is required to achieve the high level of health protection chosen in the Community', having regard to 'technical and economic feasibility and other factors regarded as legitimate in the matter under consideration'.[55] These measures are to be ('shall be') reviewed within a reasonable period of time, 'depending on the nature of the risk to life and health identified and the type of scientific information needed to clarify the scientific uncertainty and to conduct a more comprehensive assessment'.

From a prima facie reading of these provisions a common raison d'être of the precautionary principle emerges: a method which permits protective action in circumstances of uncertainty. Not surprisingly then the first requirement triggering the invocation of the principle is common to the two regimes: scientific uncertainty.

When comparing the conditions for its invocation, the EC version of the precautionary principle seems in many ways to be consistent with Article 5.7 SPS. Like Article 5.7, those precautionary measures adopted in the absence of a proper scientific basis are subject to review as scientific knowledge develops.

---

[53] European Commission, Communication from the Commission on the Precautionary principle, supra note 51.
[54] Article 7 of the general food regulation.
[55] Article 7.2 reads as follow: 'Measures adopted on the basis of paragraph 1 shall be proportionate and no more restrictive of trade than is required to achieve the high level of health protection chosen in the Community, regard being had to technical and economic feasibility and other factors regarded as legitimate in the matter under consideration. The measures shall be reviewed within a reasonable period of time, depending on the nature of the risk to life or health identified and the type of scientific information needed to clarify the scientific uncertainty and to conduct a more comprehensive risk assessment.'

However, while this duty of review under Article 5.7 does not enjoy any flexibility, the same duty imposed by the general food regulation is tempered by the particular nature of the risk to life or health identified and the type of scientific uncertainty involved.

Therefore, where Article 5.7 SPS takes the view that uncertainty may (and therefore could) always be solved by further scientific studies, the EC expressly recognises that invocation of the precautionary principle may also accommodate measures taken in situations of lasting uncertainty. Thus, for instance, the 2000 Communication on the precautionary principle has interpreted this requirement as follow: '[t]he measures, although provisional, shall be maintained as long as the scientific data remain incomplete, imprecise or inconclusive and *as long as the risk is considered too high to be imposed on society*'.

Despite this significant difference, the precautionary models elaborated within the two systems are in many ways similar, being notably structured upon the same conditions of application.

Both the EC and the WTO/SPS precautionary action models, by subjecting reliance on precaution to a set of cumulative and rather strict conditions, aim at avoiding unwarranted recourse to disguised protectionism. The idea is to make sure that reliance on precaution may not depart from the science-based risk analysis schemes supporting both food safety regimes. According to this shared view, precautionary action should not be perceived as an alternative model of regulation to the traditional structured approach of risk analysis, but rather as fitting within this model and providing a valid risk management tool where risk assessment cannot be completed because of uncertainty.[56]

Hence, the set of principles sketched out in both regimes give rise to very similar interpretative problems. In particular, the problem begins when we want to define more precisely the concepts of 'scientific insufficiency' (Article 5.7 SPS) or 'scientific uncertainty' (Article 7 General food law regulation). Neither the EC nor the WTO frameworks regulating precautionary action specify what scientific uncertainty is, nor, notably, *how* much science is needed to trigger the application of the precautionary principle.

However, both the EC and WTO courts have made an attempt at defining a minimum scientific threshold that should be met by decision-makers

---

[56] For a study proving the scientific soundness of the precautionary principle, see A. Arcuri, 'The Case for a Procedural Version of the Precautionary Principle Erring on the Side of Environmental Preservation', *Global Law Working Paper* 09/04, NYU School of Law.

before adopting a precautionary measure. What is becoming increasingly clear in both systems is that countries could not validly act under the precautionary approach by basing their measures solely on unscientific concerns about possible, merely hypothetical, negative health effects.

Thus, for instance, the AB in the *Hormones* case has stated that:

> the principle has not been written into the SPS Agreement as a ground for justifying SPS measures that are otherwise inconsistent with the obligations of the member set out in particular provisions of that Agreement'.[57]

The result is that, although Articles 5.7 and 3.3 incorporate a 'precautionary principle', such principle does not override the need for members to prove that they have based their measure on a proper risk assessment, as provided for in Articles 5.1 and 5.2 SPS. In particular, Article 5.1 must be construed as requiring that:

> the results of risk assessment must sufficiently warrant – that is to say reasonably support – the SPS measure at stake'.[58]

Similarly, the CFI has emphasised, according to a language clearly resonant of the WTO AB's, that a precautionary measure cannot properly be based on a purely hypothetical approach to the risk, funded on mere conjecture that has not been scientifically verified.[59] Rather, it follows from the Community courts' interpretation of the principle, that a precautionary measure may be taken only if the risk, although the reality and extent thereof have not been fully demonstrated by conclusive scientific evidence, appears nevertheless to be adequately backed up by the scientific data available at the time when the measure is taken. In other words, the precautionary principle may be validly invoked within the EC only in situations where there is a risk, notably to human health, that, although it has not yet been fully demonstrated, is not based on mere hypotheses that have not been scientifically confirmed.

Thus, for instance, the ECJ took the view that precautionary measures:

> presuppose, in particular, that the risk assessment available to the national authorities provides specific evidence which, without precluding scientific uncertainty, makes it possible reasonably to conclude on the basis of the most reliable scientific evidence available and the most recent results of international research

---

[57] *EC–Hormones*, AB Report, para 124.
[58] *EC–Hormones*, AB Report, para 193.
[59] Case T-13/99 *Pfizer Animal Health v Council*, [2002] ECR II-3305, at 143.

that the implementation of those measures is necessary in order to avoid novel foods which pose potential risks to human health being offered on the market.[60]

In particular, the court has held that:

those measures can be adopted only if the Member State has first carried out a risk assessment which is as complete as possible given the particular circumstances of the individual case.[61]

Although there seems to be some consensus on the fact that precautionary action must be based on some sort of empirical evidence of risk ('ascertainable risk'[62]), there does not seem to be a similar consensus as to how this (minor) scientific basis should look.

This conundrum lies at the centre of the current debate on how to reconcile the traditional, demanding risk assessment procedures, required by both the WTO/SPS Agreement and the EC, and the ability of Member States to act on the basis of the precautionary principle.

The primary condition upon which precautionary action may be taken ('available pertinent information') under the WTO seems to have become even more obscure following the *Apples* case.

Herein, after endorsing the panel's reading of Article 5.7 according to which this provision is 'designed to be invoked in situations where little, or no, evidence was available on the subject matter at issue',[63] the Appellate Body held that 'the application of Article 5.7 is triggered not by the existence of scientific uncertainty, but rather by the insufficiency of scientific evidence'.[64]. By rejecting Japan's contentions, according to which Article 5.7 is intended to also address 'unresolved uncertainty', uncertainty that the scientific evidence is not able to resolve, despite accumulated scientific evidence',[65] the Appellate Body reduced the scope of precautionary action to 'situations where little, or no, reliable evidence was available on the subject matter at issue'.

The reasoning followed by the Appellate Body in this case carries the potential of diluting the scope of the precautionary principle as it has been conceived, interpreted and applied within the EC, thus putting the European version of the precautionary principle at odds with the WTO legal system.

[60] Case C-236/01 *Monsanto Agricoltura Italia and Others* [2003] ECR I-8105, at 113.
[61] Ibid, at 114.
[62] *Australia–Salmon*, AB Report.
[63] *Japan–Apples*, Panel Report, paras 8.219.
[64] *Japan–Apples*, AB Report, para 184.
[65] Ibid, para 183.

This narrow reading of Article 5.7 seems to heavily constrain the margin for precautionary action within the WTO/SPS food safety framework. In particular, this interpretation seems to rule out from precautionary action all those situations in which, notwithstanding the existence of a 'more than little' quantity of scientific evidence, scientific uncertainty persists. Thus, for instance, the present considerable amount of scientific studies regarding the actual or potential effects of GMOs on human health and on the environment would not be regarded as justifying precautionary action under Article 5.7 of the SPS Agreement.

Although this interpretation of Article 5.7 may find some support in the negotiating history of the SPS Agreement,[66] there are some doubts as to whether it will be confirmed by the future WTO judicial bodies' decisions. This is so because the AB's reasoning is so decidedly non-definitive that, accordingly, it is not possible to say whether it represents a veritable paradigm shift in the application of the precautionary principle within the WTO legal system.

Another question that remains open after the interpretation given to Article 5.7 in the *Apples* case by the Appellate Body is whether a member may rely on this provision to support an import ban merely because, due to lack of resources, it has not yet conducted a risk assessment of that product. Would this situation fall within the notion of 'scientific insufficiency' held by the Appellate Body as triggering the invocation of precautionary action?[67] In other words, may a situation of 'little evidence' be determined by a 'lack of resources'?

Australia would be particularly interested in receiving an affirmative answer to this question as it is currently trying to justify its quarantine systems, which came under review by the WTO,[68] on the basis of Article 5.7. Australia is relying on this provision because, due to resource constraint and the ordering of domestic priorities, it has not yet conducted a proper risk assessment of the products covered by its quarantine measures.[69]

---

[66] Marceau and Trachtman, 'The Technical Barriers to Trade Agreement, the Sanitary and Phytosanitary Measures Agreement, and the General Agreement on Tariff and Trade, A Map of the World Trade Organization Law of Domestic Regulation of Goods', 35 *Journal of World Trade* 5 (2002), p 848, footnote 143 reporting a discussion with G. Stanton, former Secretary of the SPS Committee.

[67] *Japan–Apples*, AB Report, para 184.

[68] *Australia–Quarantine Regime for Imports*, WT/DS287 (brought by the EC) and *Australia–Certain Measures Affecting the Importations of Fresh Fruits and Vegetables* WT/DS270 (brought by the Philippines).

[69] A panel was established in August 2003 at the request of the Philippines but has not yet been composed.

As illustrated above in relation to the 'other factors' issue, it might be useful to look at the food safety risk analysis scheme provided by the Codex Alimentarius Commission as the relevant benchmark for predicting the role the precautionary principle may play in the risk analysis of food products within the WTO/SPS Agreement. Indeed, it is likely that the WTO judicial bodies, in establishing whether a national food safety measure is validly based upon Article 5.7 SPS, will also be influenced by the risk analysis model, notably by the precautionary action policy, developed by the Codex.

In the light of the above, the following section will illustrate the approach which has been developed vis-à-vis the precautionary principle within the framework of the Codex.

3.1   The Role of the Precautionary Principle within the Codex

The Codex's discussion on the role of the precautionary principle has developed alongside the negotiations that have led to the adoption of the working principles for risk analysis in 2003.

As seen above, in 1997 the Codex Committee on General Principles received the mandate to develop a set of principles offering guidance in the conduct of risk analysis not only to the Codex committees but also to member governments.

Within that broad discussion, the role of the precautionary principle as a legitimate basis for food safety decisions has been thoroughly debated. The discussion was primarily motivated by the need to determine how the Codex should have addressed uncertainty within its scientific evaluation activities. More precisely, the question facing the CCGP was whether the Codex, when it has insufficient information, should adopt standards or leave the matter to its members' competent authorities.

The whole debate began during the CCGP of 1999 and immediately showed the ideological rift between the USA and the EC on all the issues related to precautionary action.[70] While the European members promoted the recognition of the precautionary principle within the Codex risk management policy,[71] the US delegation strongly opposed

---

[70] See Report of the 14th Session of the CCGP, 1999, para 30.

[71] The EC position builds upon the following statement already contained in its communication on the precautionary principle (at 11): 'International guidelines are being considered in relation to the application of the Precautionary Principle in Codex Alimentarius. Such guidance in this, and other sectors, could pave the way to a harmonised approach by the WTO Members, to drawing up health or environment protection measures, while avoiding the misuse of the precautionary principle which could otherwise lead to unjustifiable barriers to trade'.

the inclusion of the principle within the Codex working principles by arguing that this not only lacked a reliable definition but also that 'a precautionary approach was already built into risk assessment' and that, in any event, Article 5.7 SPS already dealt with scientific uncertainty[72].

At the end of the meeting, the following working definition was proposed:

> Lack of full scientific certainty shall not be used as a reason to delay measures intended to prevent adverse effects on human health from a hazard present in food. When a preliminary risk assessment indicates a threat of adverse effects on human health from a hazard present in food, it is justifiable to take measures to prevent such effects without awaiting additional scientific data and a full risk assessment. Such measures should be proportionate to the potential health risk and should be kept under review.

Although the objective should be to base food safety measures on science, situations exist where there is a lack of scientific evidence. But, does this recognition make the precautionary principle an 'other legitimate factor'?

When discussing the 'other legitimate factors' issue, the Secretariat prepared a paper addressed to the 1999 CCGP meeting and took position on this point. It made it clear that, according to its view, the precautionary principle applies when the prescribed scientific foundation is still being developed and that, consequently, it fits within the first Statement of principle imposing the use of science rather than within the second addressing the 'other legitimate factors'.[73]

During the subsequent CCGP meeting in 2000, a new text describing the use of precaution in taking risk management measures was proposed:

> [w]hen relevant scientific evidence is insufficient to objectively and fully assess risk from a hazard in food, and there is reasonable evidence to suggest that adverse effects on human health may occur, but it is difficult to evaluate their nature and extent, it may be appropriate for risk managers to apply precaution through interim measures to protect the health of consumers without awaiting additional scientific data and a full risk assessment. However, additional information for a more objective risk assessment should be sought and the measures taken reviewed accordingly.[74]

---

[72] See Report of the 14th Session of the CCGP, 1999, para 30.
[73] Paper prepared for the 14th Session of the CCGP, CX/GP 99/09.
[74] Report of the 15th meeting of the CCGP, 2000.

After long discussion, no agreement was reached on this new text. In order to modify it, a working group was established.[75].

As the debate on the role of the precautionary principle became increasingly more contentious during the 16th CCGP meeting held in 2001, the Codex Commission decided to intervene in the matter by stating that 'precaution was and should remain an essential element of risk analysis in the formulation of national and international standards'.[76]

Following this statement in support of the principle, an agreement was reached on the following compromise text:

> Where there is evidence that a risk to human health exists but scientific data is insufficient or incomplete, the Commission should not proceed to elaborate a standard, but should consider elaborating a related text, such as a code of practice, provided that such a text would be supported by the available scientific evidence.[77]

Notwithstanding some attempts to put the agreed compromise up for discussion, the 2002 meeting of CCGP decided to retain the text in order to submit it to the following meeting of CAC.[78] However, this conclusion has been made possible by a decision to limit the application of the draft working principles for risk analysis for use within the Codex and to elaborate a separate standard for use by governments. The finalised text had to apply exclusively in the framework of the Codex Alimentarius and not to governments.

This compromise, resolving the deadlock over the role of precaution in risk analysis, has led some to suggest that Codex is becoming the latest battleground for trade negotiators, rather than health practitioners.[79]

Finally, during the 2003 CAC meeting, the draft working principles for risk analysis, containing recognition of precaution, were adopted for inclusion in the procedural manual. In particular, paragraphs 10 and 11 of the approved text read:

> 10. When there is evidence that a risk to human health exists but scientific data are insufficient or incomplete, the Codex Alimentarius Commission should not proceed to elaborate a standard but should consider elaborating a related text, such as a code of practice, provided that such a text would be supported by the available scientific evidence.

[75] Report of the 16th meeting of the CCGP, 2001.
[76] Report of the 24th meeting of CAC, 2001, para 77.
[77] Report of the 24th meeting of CAC, 2001.
[78] Report of the 17th meeting of CCGP, 2002.
[79] BRIDGES weekly, 1 May 2001, available at http://www.ictsd.org.

415

> 11. Precaution is an inherent element of risk analysis. Many sources of uncertainty exist in the process of risk assessment and risk management of food related hazards to human health. The degree of uncertainty and variability in the available scientific information should be explicitly considered in the risk analysis. Where there is sufficient scientific evidence to allow proceeding to elaborate a standard or related text, the assumptions used for the risk assessment and the risk management options selected should reflect the degree of uncertainty and the characteristics of the hazard.[80]

It is difficult to fully understand the meaning of these two paragraphs. Paragraph 10 reflects the US' vision of risk analysis favouring a risk management policy where only scientific evidence may be taken into account. In fact, it prevents the Codex standard-setting activities in the presence of scientific uncertainty, by allowing, at best, the adoption of a code of practice.

The following paragraph is characterised by the kind of deep vagueness which is often the hallmark of consensus-based drafting. Although recognising precaution as an important element of risk analysis, it does not offer any clear guidance on when and how to use it. As will be illustrated below, shortly after the 2002 decision to limit the scope *ratione personae* of the Working Principles to the Codex framework, the CCGP began new negotiations aimed at developing risk analysis standards for governments.

3.2   Conclusions on the Role of Precaution in the EC, WTO/ Codex Food Safety Risk Analysis Regimes

While the EC food safety risk analysis has evolved steadily towards the recognition of the precautionary principle at the same time as this principle has developed in the domestic laws of Member States, the incomplete WTO risk analysis model has been more reluctant in recognising this principle as a risk management tool allowing Member States to take action in situations of scientific uncertainty.

In particular, if the EC pioneered reliance on the precautionary principle through the Commission Communication and the European courts' case law, the WTO jurisprudence has shown great wariness in explicitly endorsing this principle. In particular, by narrowly reading the risk assessment requirements and by subverting the main condition triggering the invocation of Article 5.7 SPS, the WTO courts are currently limiting the ability of Member States' authorities to take precautionary measures.

---

[80] Report of the 26th meeting of CAC, 2003.

The Codex Alimentarius Committee, for its part, has made an attempt at developing some further guidance on how and when to use the principle by trying to reconcile very different positions amongst its members. However, it follows that, although it is true that 'few legal concepts have achieved the notoriety of the precautionary principle',[81] its scope is still far from being clear in the international trade arena.

4. Conclusions on the Comparison between the EC and the WTO Food Safety Risk Analysis Models: Towards a Common Food Safety Risk Analysis Regime within Codex?

A comparison between the EC and WTO food safety risk analysis regimes clearly shows that the two most significant points of tension between these disciplines relate to the 'other factors' that may be taken into account in risk management and to the role of the precautionary principle, respectively.

It is not surprising that both issues belong to the risk management phase of risk analysis. Indeed, as shown above, the risk analysis model developed within the WTO/SPS framework does not contain any meaningful provision dealing with risk management. The panel's genuine efforts in the *Hormones* case to introduce the traditional structured approach to risk analysis by establishing a distinction between risk assessment and risk management has expressly been rejected by the Appellate Body which noted that there was no textual basis in the SPS Agreement that would justify such an insertion.

Therefore, the SPS Agreement leaves, at least in principle, WTO members free to determine how to address and to regulate risks, provided they satisfy the risk assessment requirements imposed by the SPS Agreement. However, the resulting prioritisation of scientific and technical evidence makes the political decision-making especially problematic, notably when this is inspired by precautionary action or by other non-scientific factors. It will be illustrated below how such a reading of the WTO risk analysis framework also produces a similar effect on the process of judicial review, by rendering it extremely difficult to be accomplished. The lack of any risk management guidance to WTO members stems directly from the SPS negotiators' choice to 'delegate' to Codex all harmonisation activities. Since it was not the WTO, but a third entity which was entrusted with the 'positive integration' task of elaborating substantive rules and standards, it was not necessary to shape a complete risk analysis model for the WTO. Accordingly, the Codex has become not only a 'quasi-legislator' in charge of elaborating international

---

[81] Scott and Vos, 'The Juridification of Uncertainty: Observations of the Ambivalence of the Precautionary Principle within the EU and the WTO', in C. Joerges and R. Dehousse, *Good Governance in Europe's Integrated Market*, 2002, p 250.

standards but, gradually, also a unique forum for the elaboration of guidelines for regulatory action in the food safety sector, including not only risk assessment but also the risk management stage of risk analysis.

Thus, being invested with the regulatory task of developing international standards, the Codex, unlike any other WTO Committee, had no choice but to sketch out a risk analysis model guiding the work not only of the Joint FAO/WHO expert bodies and risk assessors but also that of the Commission and its subsidiary bodies (risk managers). Although this risk analysis model, notably represented by the 2003 'Working Principles for Risk Analysis', has been intended for application in the framework of the Codex Alimentarius,[82] and is not addressed to governments, it currently provides the most relevant commonly-agreed food safety risk analysis model in the world.

In the light of the above, the need has been expressed to explore the approach adopted by the Codex Alimentarius vis-à-vis these two controversial issues.

It has been argued that, given WTO's reliance on the Codex's international standards, the risk analysis model developed within the Codex to elaborate these standards is likely to produce a significant influence on international food safety trade disputes, notably on the interpretation of the key SPS provisions dealing with risk analysis.

In the absence of a full risk analysis scheme within the WTO/SPS framework, it is foreseeable that the WTO judicial bodies, when called upon to review the conformity with the SPS Agreement of food safety measures based not solely on risk assessment but also on 'other factors', will turn to the Codex activities in order to find some guidance. Similarly, WTO judicial bodies called to determine the legitimacy of national food safety measures based on a precautionary approach may be tempted to read Article 5.7 through the lenses of the Codex risk analysis' reference to the precautionary principle.

As seen above, this outcome would seem to find a solid textual basis within the same SPS Agreement, notably in its Article 5.1. Under this provision, if a national requirement is not based on a specific international standard, the WTO member adopting that requirement must justify its measure by a risk assessment that takes into account 'the risk assessment techniques' developed by the Codex, the

---

[82] Point 2) of Appendix IV of the Working Principles for Risk Analysis provides that: 'The objective of these Working Principles is to provide guidance to the Codex Alimentarius Commission and the joint FAO/WHO expert bodies and consultations, so that food safety and health aspects of Codex standards and related texts are based on risk analysis'.

International Office of Epizootics (OIE) and the International Plant Protection Convention (IPPC).

While it is true that reference to relevant international organisations' activities is limited to their 'risk assessment techniques', it has been submitted that such an indication may validly offer to the WTO judiciary a suitable legal basis upon which to rely in order to apply the abovementioned meta-standards elaborated by the Codex even if such principles also cover risk management issues.[83] Through such an express reference to the international standard-setting bodies' activities contained within the SPS Agreement, the risk analysis principles developed within the Codex may be relevant in the interpretation of the WTO Agreements without having to qualify as 'any relevant rules of international law applicable in the relations between the parties', as required by the Vienna Convention on the Law of the Treaties, which codifies the customary rules of interpretation of international law.[84]

This seems to be further confirmed by the *EC–Biotech* panel report, where the panel, after consulting the parties, has requested several international organisations (Codex, FAO, the IPPC Secretariat, WHO, OIE, the CBD Secretariat and UNEP):

> [...] to identify materials (reference works, glossaries, official documents of the relevant international organisations, *including conventions, standards and guidelines*, etc.) that might aid [the panel] in determining the ordinary meaning of certain terms used in the definitions provided in Annex A to the SPS Agreement.[85]

In light of the above, '[t]he materials' the panel has obtained in this way:

> have been taken into account [...], as appropriate.[86]

In particular, it has been observed that the panel has relied upon such texts enacted outside of the WTO Agreements without suggesting that it was required to do so pursuant to the provisions of Article 31(3)(c) of the Vienna Convention. Indeed, the panel did mention this provision. This would appear to prove that the WTO courts' reliance on the Codex principles for risk analysis in order to find some guidance on the risk management options available to the WTO members cannot be excluded

---

[83] The Risk Analysis Framework as sketched out by the latest proposed draft expressly provides principles dealing not only with risk assessment, but also with risk management, offering, for instance, a selection of risk management options. See Proposed Draft Working Principles for Risk Analysis for Food Safety, as enshrined in CX/GP 06/23/23/3, are available ftp://ftp.fao.org/codex/ccgp23/gp23_03e.pdf.

[84] Article 31(3)(c) of the Vienna Convention.

[85] *EC–Biotech*, panel report, at 7.96.

[86] Ibid.

under the current SPS Agreement. Conversely, Article 5.1, by referring to the 'risk assessment techniques developed' by the international standard-setting organisations may prove a useful legal basis for the WTO judicial bodies to rely upon in order to find some guidance when reviewing complex science-based measures.

Moreover, the WTO judiciary's reliance on the Codex meta-standards, when assessing the legality of food safety measure, may also find some further legitimacy if read in the light of the final part of Article 5.6 SPS. In fact, this provision, in order to offer some common structure on the way in which management decisions should be taken, provides that WTO members adopt the least trade-restrictive measure 'taking into account technical and economic feasibility'. In our view, by giving full meaning to this reference, WTO courts may rely on external sources, such as the working principles for the Codex and guidelines, in order to verify whether a contested regulatory measure represents the 'least restrictive means' to achieve the chosen level of protection.

The value of the Codex's risk analysis as a benchmark for WTO/SPS compatibility, or at least as an important complementary source of inspiration for WTO courts, will be further strengthened by the Codex's current efforts to draft specific 'Working Principles for Risk Analysis for Food Safety'. In fact, unlike the previous the Codex documents on risk analysis, these working principles expressly aim at providing guidance not only to its own bodies but also to 'governments' on food safety risk analysis. As illustrated above, the decision to prepare this separate set of risk analysis rules has been pivotal in the adoption of the draft working principles for risk analysis by overcoming deadlock over the status of the precautionary principle in risk analysis. In particular, according to the EC, the development of these principles will help the governments to develop a risk analysis policy aimed not solely at protecting consumer health but also at 'fulfil[ing] their obligations arising from Article 5(1) of the SPS Agreement'[87].

According to the first paragraph of the proposed draft working Principles for risk analysis for food safety for governments:

> [t]he purpose of these Principles is to provide a framework for the conduct of risk analysis applied to food safety issues, as guidance to governments, in light of the purpose of the Codex Alimentarius Commission.

---

[87] EC Comments on Proposed Draft Working Principles for Risk Analysis for Food Safety, Codex Circular Letter CL 2004/34-GP. These comments have been confirmed by the most recent contribution to the Draft Working Principles for Risk Analysis for Food Safety. See CX/GP 06/23/23/3, available at ftp://ftp.fao.org/codex/ccgp23/gp23_03e.pdf.

Furthermore, according to the second paragraph:

> [t]he objective of these principles is to provide guidance to Codex members so that food safety aspects of their decisions and recommendations are based on risk analysis.

In the light of the above, it is believed that agreement on this additional Codex meta-standard on how the principles of risk analysis for food safety should be applied by governments is critical for the future development of a harmonised food safety risk analysis model. In particular, the development of a common food safety risk analysis scheme within the Codex would be capable of filling the current gap existing within the WTO risk analysis, notably regarding its risk management policy. As a result, both points of tension existing between the EC and the WTO food regimes would be attenuated.

However, the whole issue, mainly because of the disagreement on both 'other factors' and the precautionary principle, is still under debate. A revised draft, discarding the previous one mainly inspired by the format of the previously adopted working principles for the Codex application, was circulated in July 2005 with a request for proposals on the objective and scope of the working principles from governments[88]. The draft consists of 37 paragraphs and the (electronic) Working Group, established in November 2004 to look at comments on the first draft, only considered the first 22 of these, thus leaving aside for the moment those dealing with the most controversial issues: the 'other legitimate factors' issue and also the precautionary principles (at paragraphs 32 and 33). At the 22nd Session of the CCGP, amid tensions among the members over the necessity and merits of such a document, it was agreed to return the proposed draft working principles to step 2/3 for redrafting and further comments.[89] While some countries, such as Argentina and Brazil, suggested that work on the document should be suspended since discussions showed little consensus, both the EC and the WTO representatives stressed the importance of resuming that work. According to them, the development of principles of risk analysis for food safety could be useful to WTO members insofar as they could help them in adopting national standards compliant with the provisions of the WTO/SPS Agreements. Moreover, as both the OIE and IPPC have developed guidance for risk analysis in their areas of competence *rationae materiae*, the WTO insisted that the Codex, by relying on its own Working principles and also the newly-adopted FAO/WHO risk analysis Manual,[90] should also provide similar guidance to governments.

[88] CL 2005/17-GP, 27 July 2005. Deadline for comments was 30 July 2005.
[89] Report of the 22nd Session of the CCGP, CL 2005/17-GP, April 2005.
[90] Food Safety Risk Analysis – An Overview and Framework Manual, available at http://www.fsc.go.jp /sonota/foodsafety_riskanalysis.pdf.

Finally, in 2006, during the 23rd Session, the committee decided to send the 'Proposed Draft Working Principles for Risk Analysis for Food Safety for Governments' to a newly established working group for examination before discussing them again at the next CCGP meeting.[91] Predicting whether an agreement on this text will be reached on that occasion is not an easy task, but the final outcome is likely to depend on whether a consensus will be reached over the inclusion of the controversial paragraph dealing with precaution in risk management. In the meanwhile, as proposed by Argentina, a working group meeting will be convened by the end of 2006 to discuss and articulate the rationale underpinning such a guidance document on risk analysis addressed to governments.

In conclusion, the Codex's present inability to solve at the regulatory level the long-standing issues of the role of the precautionary principle and that of 'other factors' in risk management does not facilitate the relationship between the EC food safety regime and WTO law. Rather, the actual negotiating *impasse* contributes to rendering such a relationship increasingly difficult today, by notably putting the EC regime at odds with WTO law.

As shown above, these controversial aspects are currently dealt with by the Codex because of the SPS negotiators' choice to 'delegate' to this body the elaboration of de facto WTO food legislations. However, despite some progress on the definition of the role of the precautionary principle and other factors in risk analysis having been made in the Codex, the extent to which members may rely on this principle and the other factors in food safety risk management policy is not yet clear. Thus, the debate over the use of 'other factors' is still open within the Codex and does not seem to be ready to give rise to an agreement among its members. Until this debate is resolved, the question arises as to what happens if countries invoke the precautionary principle or rely on 'other factors' when developing their food safety policies.

These questions have not found an answer in the recently released panel report in the *Biotech* dispute, between the US, Canada and Argentina and the EC and, consequently, are likely to give rise to further disputes in the near future.

This shows how the original decision not to delineate a well-defined management policy within the SPS Agreement is producing the effect of transferring the responsibility of shaping a WTO risk analysis model from the decision-making dimension to the dispute-settlement level; in

---

[91] Proposed Draft Working Principles for Risk Analysis for Food Safety, as enshrined in CX/GP 06/23/23/3, are available ftp://ftp.fao.org/codex/ccgp23/gp23_03e.pdf.

other words, from the 'executive-legislative' powers to the 'judiciary'. Consequently, by borrowing the words of the Appellate Body, it is up to the WTO judicial bodies to find an appropriate:

> [...] balance in the SPS Agreement between the shared, but sometimes competing, interests of promoting international trade and of protecting the life and health of human beings.[92]

It is submitted that, notwithstanding their well-known commitment to textual fidelity, the WTO judicial bodies will inevitably be obliged to develop answers that, rather than stemming directly from the texts of the WTO Agreements, will flow from their understanding of the risk management policies developed in national and international contexts, such as the Codex. This excess of discretion impliedly accorded to the WTO courts, if not appropriately offset, is likely to harm the WTO system by diminishing the level of legitimacy and social acceptability of its decisions. WTO courts' reliance on the emerging the Codex meta-standards guiding members when conducting risk analysis may provide an adequate answer to this problem as it finds a solid textual basis within the same SPS Agreement (Article 5.1 and 5.6).

In particular, the emerging working principles for risk analysis for food safety, by filling the current gap existing within the WTO risk analysis model, may provide valid guidance not only to the governments but also to the WTO courts when called upon to review their adopted measures.

---

[92] *EC–Hormones*, AB Report, para 177.

Chapter III
Comparing Standards of Review

1. Comparing the EC and WTO Courts' Standards of Judicial Review of Food Safety Measures

Although partly motivated by different goals, both the EC and WTO food safety scientific justification disciplines impose the respect of similar scientific requirements: all measures addressing food safety risks must be based on science.

It follows that, even though in different institutional settings, the EC and the WTO courts are called upon to perform a very similar legal task: examining whether the contested risk regulations pursue legitimate, as opposed to false, health concerns, in light of scientific risk assessments performed by agencies with superior technical expertise. As a result, they both centre their review on the need for objective scientific reasons to support the contested measures.

In particular, when dealing with harmonisation initiatives, the WTO judiciary is called upon to examine the legality of national measures departing from international standards and the EC courts to review Member States' measures derogating from Community regimes, in the absence of harmonisation initiatives, both judicial bodies are supposed to verify the legality of the contested national measure adopted against the basic rules governing the adoption of such a regulation within their respective food regimes.

There is, however, an important difference in their respective competence *ratione materiae*.

Unlike the EC courts, which are regularly called upon to scrutinise the legality of EC acts, the WTO judicial bodies cannot be called upon to examine the legality of the 'harmonised' regulation, notably the de facto WTO harmonised legislation, such as the Codex international standards. These rules, having been developed outside of the WTO context, are not amongst the rules which can be subject to the WTO judicial bodies' scrutiny.

Notwithstanding this difference, both courts encounter very similar questions when called upon to scrutinise the legitimacy of science-based measures supposedly aimed at protecting food safety. They both question how intense the scientific justification for a member's measure must be, and the extent to which members should be allowed to pursue their own level of protection by taking into account 'non-scientific factors' or the precautionary principle.

However, in spite of such an apparently similar epistemological context (neither the Luxembourg-based nor the Geneva-based judges are scientists), our previous analysis of the standards of review applied in the two systems has revealed that the WTO's scrutiny of science-based measures tends to be more intrusive than the one exercised by EC courts. Although the European courts' review of Member States' measures becomes less deferential when exercised over national measures than when scrutinising Community measures, it never attains the level of WTO's intrusiveness into the scientific basis of the measure in dispute.

While the approach taken by EC courts is generally one which defers to the judgment of the legislator about the existence of risk and the regulatory response, particularly in circumstances of scientific uncertainty, the WTO judicial approach is rather intrusive and scientifically demanding. Thus, for instance, the panel, in *Japan–Agricultural Products*, has stated that the DSU requires them to examine, weigh and resolve all the evidence validly submitted to them, including the opinions received from the experts advising the panel.[1] Furthermore, as has been highlighted above, the Appellate Body tends to prescribe some demanding criteria for risk assessment. Since the *Hormones* case[2] the risk assessment requirement is interpreted as requiring the defending party to carry out a *specific* risk assessment capable of addressing the particular circumstances of the case at issue. On this basis, in the recent *Apples* case, the panel dismissed the scientific studies cited by Japan because they did not focus sufficiently on the risk of transmission of fire blight apple fruit as opposed to other modes of transmission.[3]

In contrast, EC courts have always appeared more reluctant in addressing the scientific basis of the contested measures, by rather showing deference to both EC and Member State scientific bodies. Contrary to the WTO courts, the EC judiciary has generally managed not to get involved in the scientific validity of the arguments advanced by the parties, by refusing to become embroiled in the scientific controversies underlying the disputes. However, as illustrated above, such a traditional deferential attitude of the European courts vis-à-vis scientific evidence seems to be currently put into question not only by

---

[1] *Japan–Agricultural Products*, para 7.10. Then confirmed by the AB, para 127.
[2] *EC–Hormones*, AB report, para 199.
[3] *Japan–Apples*, panel report, paras 8.277-280.

the *Alpharma/Pfizer* judgments but also by the more recent *Vitamins* line of cases. This new trend is likely to expose the EC courts to challenges similar to those faced by the WTO courts. As has been stated:

> the language used by the CFI in *Pfizer* reminds one very much of the language the WTO dispute settlement organs used in EC-*Hormones* and Japan-*Agricultural Products*.[4]

Leaving aside this recent trend, which has been examined in the previous part, an attempt will be made to analyse the reasons that might be adduced to explain the WTO legal system's propensity to adopt a stricter approach than its European counterpart over SPS measures.

As has been argued,[5] a more intrusive scrutiny by the WTO over national measures than the review carried out by EC courts may appear to be a paradox to the extent that the WTO pursues a lesser integration goal. However, it is submitted that this finding ceases to be a paradox once thought is given to the different structural contexts in which these courts are called upon to exercise their duties. In particular, it is suggested that the different standards of review taken by WTO courts when compared with those followed by its EC counterparts may be explained by the following factors:

– different institutional (unlike the EC Courts, the WTO judiciary does not operate in a developed constitutional structure which also includes entities in charge of scientific advice) and normative contexts (WTO scientific discipline is more detailed than the EC regime) and; (1.1)

– different risk analysis frameworks (contrary to the EC, the WTO risk analysis model, lacking any reference to the management stage, is centred exclusively on the risk assessment stage). (1.2)

In the following paragraphs, it will be demonstrated how these factors may explain, on the one hand, the (scientifically demanding) strict

---

[4] M. Slotboom, 'Do Public Health Measures Receive Similar Treatment in European Community and World Trade Organization Law?', *Journal of World Trade* (2003) 553, p 594.

[5] See Slotboom, supra note 4, p. 553 and 594. This author, in an interesting series of articles, has shown that although 'in view of the different objects and purposes of the WTO Agreements and the EC Treaty' one may expect that where the WTO and the EU have rules on the same subjects, the EU law is stricter than WTO law, the 'legal reality does not always correspond to this expectation'. Thus, he has reached the following findings: EC law is not stricter to EU Member States that WTO law is to WTO members with regard to discriminatory internal taxes; WTO subsidy rules seem to be stricter to WTO members than EC rules on State Aid in EU law and, finally, that WTO law is stricter (or at least as strict as) to SPS measures than the EU legal system. For a more articulated version of his argument, see M. Slotboom, *A Comparison of WTO and EC Law*, (London, Cameron May, 2006).

scrutiny exercised by WTO courts on Member States' science-based regulations and, on the other, the Community's deferential approach to similar measures. As will be shown, notwithstanding some general statements allowing flexibility in domestic risk management procedures and recognising members' right to establish their own level of protection, the AB's interpretation of the SPS Agreement has always privileged the scientific element, and the views of scientists, in reviewing the legitimacy of food safety risk regulation.

1.1   Different Institutional and Normative Contexts

Although imposing similar scientific requirements, the WTO and EC operate in different institutional and normative contexts.[6] It is commonplace to argue that, while the EC integration agenda relies on both negative and positive integration tools, the WTO's agenda relies solely on negative integration provisions. In reality, as we have pointed out above, the WTO, by referring to the Codex and other standard-setting organisations' activities, also promotes positive integration amongst its members. However, its positive integration authority has not only been outsourced to external standard-setting bodies such as the Codex but, unlike in the EU, it does not operate in an highly developed constitutional framework where well-defined institutions share and assure the balance of power. In fact, notwithstanding its de facto positive integration role, the WTO has no general authority to directly set health and food safety policies for its members. Acting in such a context of lesser integration, the WTO courts tend to operate in an institutional vacuum. An integrated and institutionalised food safety dimension is simply lacking in the WTO.

As a consequence, when they are called upon to examine the legality of a science-based measure they do not dispose of and, accordingly, cannot be biased in favour of the scientific advice supporting the contested measure. This is because, contrary to what happened in the EC – which disposes of its own scientific committees – the panels and the AB cannot make reference to previous studies made within a sort of WTO legislative process. As a result, unless the contested measure draws on an international standard, the WTO adjudicators must somehow get involved with scientific data. It is by relying on external scientific experts that panels and the AB assess factual matters of a scientific nature. And these experts are not themselves a WTO institution. Therefore, in the absence of a relationship of trust and a common sense of belonging

---

[6] See F. Ortino, *Basic Legal Instruments for the Liberalization of Trade*, (Oxford and Portland Oregon) and M. Slotboom, *A Comparison of WTO and EC Law* (London, Cameron May Ltd, 2006).

between the judge and his source of expertise, the WTO courts feel less bound to it and, for that reason, they tend to be less deferential to the scientific source. Conversely, because the EC courts form part of a more developed and integrated legal structure they show more deference to the scientific-basis supporting the measure whose legality they are called to examine. Similarly, it has been said that the EC judiciary 'is aware that, as one player wishing to maximise its power in a project, unnecessary interference with politically sensitive and complex issues should be avoided'.[7]

While it is certainly true that this 'belonging-factor' may explain European courts' self-constraint when reviewing science-based Community measures, it must be observed that it tells only one part of the story as it does not satisfactorily apply to those measures adopted by Member States, which generally do not find scientific support in Community sources, but rather rely on national studies.

Besides their different institutional contexts, it is suggested that the different normative dimensions surrounding the regulation of food within the EC and the WTO may also provide a valid answer to their different approaches to judicial review of science-based measures.

On this point, one may notice that the WTO set of scientific requirements, notably those imposed by the SPS, are particularly detailed compared to those imposed by the EC regime. It may be recalled, for instance, that Article 5 SPS, after having required WTO members to conduct a risk assessment 'as appropriate to the circumstances', lists the scientific, technological and economical factors that should be taken into account, together with the risk assessment techniques developed by the relevant international organisations. It is suggested that the standard of review developed by WTO courts inevitably reflects this normative framework. This framework, in turn, contributes to legitimising this standard of review by thus strengthening the increasing scientific involvement of WTO judicial bodies.

1.2 Different Risk Analysis Schemes

The different standards of review adopted by the EC and the WTO courts may also be explained by reference to their respective approaches to risk analysis. While the EC has embraced the generally-accepted risk analysis scheme based on a clear-cut distinction between risk assessment and risk management, the WTO/SPS texts have never tied their scientific

---

[7] E. Ni Chaoimh, 'Trading in Precaution – A Comparative Study of the Precautionary jurisprudence of the European Court and the WTO's Adjudicating Body', 33(2) *Legal Issues of Economic Integration* 139–165, p 159 (2006).

discipline to any particular mode of risk analysis.[8] In particular, the SPS provides little in the way of elaboration of risk management principles to guide resolution of disputes, providing only a definition of risk assessment.[9] By emphasising the rational, science-based stage of risk assessment this ambiguous model of risk analysis inevitably leads the judge to focus mainly on the scientific element.

To sum up, one may say that while in the EC risk analysis model the scientific element is necessary but not sufficient to authorise regulatory action,[10] in the WTO imprecise risk analysis model, science seems to be both necessary and sufficient to validate a national health measure.

This approach to risk analysis, by focusing solely on the rational, scientific basis of risk regulation, legitimises a standard of review which is fully in line with the SPS scientific justification regime, where there is no room, at least formally, for non-scientific factors, such as the social dimension of risk. In particular, the adoption of a particularly intrusive standard of review, by allowing science to be placed in a privileged position, allows the panel to avoid the problem of giving recognition to policy concerns that are neither neutral-value as to the scientific element nor common among member States. Conversely, the adoption of a standard of review focusing solely on the rational relationship between science and the measure is more impermeable to non-scientific factors. Thus, despite the initial attempts made by the Appellate Body to leave the door open for 'other legitimate factors' within risk assessment in order to preserve the Member States' right to determine their own level of protection,[11] the adoption of such an intrusive standard of review allowing the judge to assess the quality of the scientific information supporting a measure tends to emphasise the role of science over other factors, thus rendering it more difficult for Member States to justify their measures on non-scientific grounds.

It is submitted, as this trend of entrusting the international judge – not only the panels and the AB but also, after the recent trend adopted in *Pfizer* and the *Vitamins* cases, the EC courts – with a scientific-based task

---

[8] See on this point Button who argues that the AB has been careful not to link the SPS system to any particular model of risk assessment and that it refused to draw a firm distinction between risk assessment and risk management under the SPS Agreement.

[9] On this point, see T. Jostling, D. Roberts and D. Orden, *Food Regulation and Trade, Toward a Safe and Open Global System* (Institute for International Economics, Washington DC, 2004) p. 48 who argues that SPS negotiators considered it inappropriate for the WTO to be more prescriptive about risk management, seeing the standard-setting organisations as the better forum for the elaboration of guidelines for regulatory action.

[10] In the *Pfizer* case (Case T-13/99 *Pfizer Animal Health v. Council*, [2002] ECR II-3305, at para 201) the CFI has clearly stated that '[s]cientific legitimacy is not a sufficient basis for the exercise of public authority'.

[11] *EC–Hormones*, AB Report, para. 187

increases, that the role of expertise may well become crucial. For this reason, several sections of Part III have been devoted to the role of experts and to the peer review mechanisms within both legal systems.

1.3 Conclusions

The comparison between the EC and the WTO courts' standards of review developed vis-à-vis food safety science-based measures shows the increasing intrusiveness of the WTO judicial approach, notably in relation to the scientific foundation of the contested measures.

Although a stricter scrutiny by the WTO courts than that conducted by the EC courts over national measures may appear paradoxical to the extent that the former organisation pursues a lesser integration goal, several reasons seem to render this paradox illusory.

Above all, the WTO judicial approach to science-based measures takes place in very different normative and institutional contexts than in the EC. Unlike European courts, WTO judicial bodies do not operate within a highly integrated constitutional structure where well-defined institutions interact in order to assure a balance of powers. As a consequence, they do not have any incentive to secure acceptance of their ruling and, by lacking institutional sources of scientific information, they are not biased vis-à-vis the scientific basis supporting the contested measure.

Moreover, aside from not disposing of their own sources of scientific information, WTO courts cannot count on clear risk management principles guiding the resolution of disputes. They rather rely exclusively on a set of extremely detailed risk assessment requirements. By emphasising the rational, science-based stage of risk assessment, this emerging ambiguous model of risk analysis inevitably leads WTO courts to focus mainly on the scientific element of the contested measure.

In other terms, while in the EC risk analysis model science is necessary but not sufficient to authorise regulatory action,[12] under the imprecise WTO risk analysis model science seems to be both necessary and sufficient to validate a national health measure.

This approach to risk analysis, when interpreted through the judicial review process, presents the advantage of alleviating the judge's task of also taking into account non-scientific factors, such as the social dimension of risk, which vary, by definition, from country to country.

---

[12] Case T-13/99 *Pfizer Animal Health v Council*, [2002] ECR II-3305, at 201 ('scientific legitimacy is not a sufficient basis for the exercise of public authority').

However, contrary to conventional wisdom, science is not as neutral-value as it might first appear and, as has been shown above, it may be extremely difficult for the judge to also review and consider an apparently neutral value such as science. Apart from this conceptual flaw, such an approach to risk analysis, by totally denying the non-scientific dimension of risk, clashes with the reality of risk management as it is today.

It will be illustrated below, that, notwithstanding these shortcomings in the WTO risk analysis scheme, a different standard of review of science-based measures could realistically be read within the SPS Agreement without necessarily departing from the 'objective' review requirement. In order to do so, there is no need to amend the Agreement but to merely reinterpret, thereby completing, its risk analysis requirements.

2.   A Procedural, Intensity-variable Standard of Review for Science-based Regulatory Measures?

In the absence of a clearly-defined standard of review, both EC and WTO courts have found themselves entrusted with the task of establishing the level of intensity of review they must exercise over contested measures. As highlighted above, however, the choice of the proper applicable standard is especially sensitive in relation to public health measures. This is because, unlike other regulations, the legality of these regulations depends on the satisfaction not only of normative obligations but also of scientific requirements. In particular, the adoption of science-based measures in both the EC and WTO contexts implies strict adherence to a specific risk analysis framework as provided for by their respective underlying agreements.

Similarly to what has been previously submitted when discussing the standard of review applicable to precautionary-based regulations,[13] it is argued that in order to be effective the judicial review of SPS measures should review the decision-making process leading to their adoption by taking into account that such a process is normatively framed with a risk analysis structure. In other words, the risk analysis framework existing in both regimes is (and should be) an inescapable dimension for the consideration of courts when called upon to review science-based regulatory measures.

However, as shown above, risk analysis, and particularly the relationship between its main components, cannot realistically be perceived as a linear

---

[13] See supra Part I, Chapter II, Section C. The Precautionary Principle (PP): from Scientific Uncertainty to Legal Certainty, notably paragraph 5. Conclusions: the courts and the challenge of reviewing precautionary measures.

process where risk assessment and risk management can be clearly partitioned. While risk assessment is not an entirely neutral value exercise, but rather a socially constructed process, likewise risk management implies not only the adoption of the most appropriate measure to tackle the underlying concern, but also, and prior to it, the value-oriented task of defining the appropriate level of protection that must be assured by that measure.

Under this view, it appears that the risk assessment and risk management stages tend to characterise risk analysis as an unpredictable process, whose boundaries are difficult to trace.

Therefore, judicial review of measures based on such an erratic and subjective process cannot but be extremely complicated, unless it is performed according to a properly-defined and transparent framework.

In the light of the above, for the purposes of effectively reviewing science-based measures within the WTO framework, it is suggested that the risk analysis frameworks be reconceptualised, by sketching out a procedural, intensity-variable standard of review.

While the term 'procedural' refers to the nature of the judicial review to be exercised upon SPS measures, and this insofar as it has to follow a structured and transparent risk analysis process, its qualification as 'intensity-variable' describes the level of scrutiny it might perform.

Why a procedural standard of review and of what kind?

As seen above when defining the standard of review applicable to precautionary actions, to facilitate the judicial review of science-based measures, it might be crucial to structure this review upon small and simpler concepts for each stage and component of risk. In fact, a procedural review, by distinguishing the various stages of the decision-making process, in particular the scientific element from the policy element, would enable the judicial bodies to scrutinise the legality of the contested measure.

The necessity to proceduralise the approach to judicial review is particularly felt within the WTO/SPS normative context where not only the same basic distinction between risk assessment and risk management has been judicially rejected, but also where the latter concept is normatively empty.[14] In particular, as highlighted above, there is a clear

---

[14] In contrast, in the EC context, Community courts, being constrained by a rather detailed risk analysis model, have shown themselves to be familiar and respectful, when called upon to review science-based measures, with the risk analysis' main components. See Case T-13/99 *Pfizer Animal Health v Council*, [2002] ECR II-3305.

need in the WTO somehow to counterbalance the detailed scientific justification discipline with adequate risk management guidelines in order to limit the application of an increasingly intrusive standard of review that turns on the scrutiny of the 'specificity' of the scientific evidence brought by the defending party and the assessment of the chosen 'level of risk'.

In particular, it is submitted that it might be especially useful not only to resort to the concept of risk management but also to further frame this specific stage of risk analysis, by clearly identifying within it two well-defined steps: the choice of the necessary level of protection (risk choice) and the choice of the measure ensuring that result (risk response). Notwithstanding its initial rejection of the notion of risk management, the AB's current approach to the interpretation of the WTO risk analysis model emerging from the SPS Agreement would not seem to reject this view.[15]

In this regard, it must be stressed from the outset that the introduction of the proposed proceduralisation of risk assessment does not require an amendment of the SPS provisions, which would be not only technically difficult but also politically unfeasible in the current context, rather it demands a mere reinterpretation activity of those SPS provisions which lay down a risk analysis model for the WTO.

Under this reconceptualised version of risk analysis, designed for the purpose of reviewing science-based acts within the WTO, the judicial review exercise of risk regulatory measures should respectively look at risk assessment, risk choice and risk response.

Why an intensity-variable standard of review?

The choice of an intensity-variable standard of review depends, in turn, on the proceduralised nature of risk analysis, which characterises the decision-making process leading to the adoption of a regulatory measure under the SPS Agreement. It is submitted that, each step of risk analysis being subject to the respect of a different set of rights and obligations, only the adoption of an intensity-variable standard might effectively reflect and preserve such a diverging level of normative constraints which exist within each stage of risk analysis. It will be shown that, as a result, by varying its intensity depending on the rights and obligations of the Member States within each step of risk analysis, such a standard of review would be capable of re-establishing and preserving the balance

---

[15] In *Australia–Salmon*, Appellate Body Report, at 200–203, the AB held that only after the determination of the appropriate level of protection is it possible for risk managers to select the preferred management option.

originally designed by the SPS Agreement between Member States' regulatory autonomy and free trade obligations.

2.1   Reviewing Risk Assessment

In the case of risk assessment, the challenge facing judicial reviewers should be to make sure that the scientific underpinning of the contested measure exists and is plausible and this without engaging with the scientific merits of the evidence advanced by the parties.

As stressed above, since it is *how* the conclusions have been reached, not *what* the conclusions are that make 'good science' today, the WTO judicial bodies, similarly to EC courts, should interpret the scientific discipline as requiring the evidence submitted by the parties to satisfy some minimal procedural requirements. This is the deferential approach that, in our view, should enlighten the WTO judicial bodies when interpreting the scientific requirements imposed by the SPS Agreement, notably by Articles 2.2 and 5.1 SPS. However, as illustrated above, the interpretation given to the scientific requirements, translating into the 'rational relationship test', has increasingly relied on the 'quality and quantity' of the scientific studies advanced by the parties in order to establish whether there exists a 'sufficient or adequate relationship between […] the SPS mesure and the scientific evidence'.[16]

As illustrated above, this interpretation of the scientific disciplines inevitably opened up the Pandora's box of scientific discussion to these judicial bodies with the result of getting them increasingly embroiled in controversial scientific matters. However, judges, being non-scientists, are not epistemically capable of discerning between 'good science' and 'bad science'.

In fact, as demonstrated above,[17] this task cannot be undertaken by the judge alone and it presupposes the development of some general guidelines establishing which minimal criteria a scientific study must satisfy to be considered 'scientific enough'.

To solve the first problem it has been suggested to improve the external experts' consultation practice as it might facilitate the current judicial bodies' attempt to verify whether the scientific evidence advanced by the parties to the dispute is 'scientifically adequate'. This method, however, might become superfluous should the scientific study which has been advanced by the parties have been subject to peer-review. As the *Methanex* case exemplifies, though in the NAFTA context, this tool

---

[16] See the AB Report in *EC–Hormones*.
[17] Sections 4–8 of Part III.

would enable the judge to verify in an effective and speedy way whether the evidence underpinning the contested measure is adequately scientific, thus fulfilling the risk assessment requirements. Reliance on these external expertise tools will ensure that courts will not get involved in the scientific merits of the evidence, thereby allowing an objective and scientifically-restrained review.

As to the second, related problem, to facilitate the task of WTO courts or of its experts in accomplishing their task it might be advisable to rely on those guidelines and meta-standards, currently elaborated by several international standardisation organisations, aimed at promoting commonalities of approaches in risk analysis for different sectors. This solution not only finds a solid textual basis within the WTO but has also been recently endorsed by the *EC–Biotech* panel report.[18]

In light of the above, to review effectively the compliance of an SPS measure with the risk assessment requirements, WTO courts, notably when applying the 'rational relationship' test, should rely, first, on peer review as a tool aimed at verifying the scientific plausibility of a contested measure and, second, should it be necessary, on external experts in order to attain the same goal.

It has been argued that this reasonably deferential approach, by reducing the level of scientific involvement of courts and by giving an operational meaning to what 'minimum science' is, might prove successful in assigning a more appropriate role for WTO judicial bodies when assessing the compliance of an SPS measure with the scientific discipline.

2.2 Reviewing Risk Choice

As to the review of the risk management stage, it is suggested that this should take place by looking separately at its two main sub-components of risk choice and risk response.

This is fundamental to the extent risk management, unlike risk assessment, is not an homogeneous stage of risk analysis which typically focuses exclusively on one factor, but is rather a phase involving different sets of considerations and values. In fact, by building upon the scientific evidence stemming from risk assessment, the risk management stage implies the determination by policy-makers not only of the level of protection they deem appropriate for their society (risk choice) but also of the best measure designed to achieve that objective (risk response). As these sub-components of risk management are subject to the respect of very different obligations, it is necessary, when reviewing the adopted

---

[18] *EC–Biotech* panel report, at 7.96.

management measure, to adjust the intensity of review in relation to the different underlying normative constraints.

Notwithstanding its initial rejection of the notion of risk management, the AB has subsequently interpreted the WTO risk analysis model emerging from the SPS Agreement as providing that only after the determination of the appropriate level of protection is it possible for risk managers to select the preferred management option.[19] This seems to prove that the notion of risk management is not totally unknown within the WTO/SPS context and that it is possible somehow to find an embryonic form of it behind the rather elliptic SPS provisions. Moreover, this finding of the AB would seem to confirm the above-mentioned need, within the WTO legal order, to dispose of a clearly structured and complete risk analysis scheme.

That said, it is important to define the level of intensity of the review that must be exercised upon the first subcomponent of risk management: risk choice.

It must be stressed from the outset that the goal pursued by the review of this element of risk management must be limited to identifying the level of protection sought to be achieved by the competent authorities when adopting the contested measure. This is because, without a clear determination of this element, it would prove impossible for the courts to establish whether a contested measure complies with the 'necessity test'.

Having said that, it must be observed that, unlike risk assessment, the risk choice element of risk management, consisting in the determination of how high a level of risk society is willing to tolerate, does not involve the exercise of an objective activity but rather the use of discretionary powers, which by definition, seem to exclude any form of external control. In other words, in view of Member States' right to set for themselves the level of protection they deem appropriate, the 'risk choice' component of the contested measure calls for a highly deferential scrutiny.

As has been suggested, the only way to legitimately subject to review this peculiar step of risk management would be by normatively restraining Member States' ability to determine the significance of risk. This could be done by subjecting the exercise of their sovereign risk choice to, for instance, the proof of the existence of relevant public concern or to the absence of protectionism.[20]

---

[19] *Australia–Salmon*, Appellate Body Report, at 200–3.

[20] See, eg, J. Bohanes who proposes to shift supranational oversight 'from substance to procedure'. Under his vision, a 'national trade-impeding health regulation unsupported by science could be purified by a *bona fide* public risk perception and pass muster under

(continued...)

However, in the absence of such normative constraints into members' discretionary power within the SPS Agreement, any external review of their chosen levels of protection would clash with members' sovereign right to establish the acceptable level of risk for their own society and constituencies.[21]

In the light of the above, it is argued that, in the absence of normative limitations to members' right to act in the face of perceived risks, it would be inappropriate to enable the courts to investigate into the merits of any given risk choice.

Nevertheless, though characterised by low intensity, the review of the risk choice component should not omit to verify the compliance of the contested measure with its main two normative limitations: Article 5.4 (trade-minimising objective) and Article 5.5 SPS (consistency requirement).

Although neither Article 5.4 nor 5.5, first part of the first sentence, impose a legal obligation on members,[22] they nevertheless introduce the duty to take into account, respectively, the objective of minimising trade and that of achieving consistency in the application of the concept of an appropriate level of sanitary or phytosanitary protection against risks to human life or health, or to animal and plant life or health. As to the binding part of Article 5.5 (consistency requirement), it has been highlighted above that even if the chosen level of protection might appear arbitrary, or as giving rise to an unjustifiable distinction, this fact will only act as a warning signal that the contested measure might be discriminatory or a disguised restriction on trade. The broad interpretation given to this provision would seem to confirm the need to protect members' sovereign right to choose their appropriate level of protection within the WTO/SPS context.

To conclude, it is submitted that the proposed low intensity review of the risk choice component of the contested measure, while effectively enabling the court to identify the chosen level of protection and its compliance with Articles 5.4 and 5.5, would potentially be capable of respecting, thus preserving, the legitimate public policy choice underlying the adoption of that measure. As seen above, this is crucial

WTO dispute settlement'. In his view, this approach, by re-interpreting the obligations of the Member States under the SPS Agreement, sidesteps the problem of adjusting the standard of review, by maintaining the current intensity of review. See Bohanes, 'Risk Regulation in WTO Law: A procedure-Based Approach', 40 *Columbia Journal of Transnational Law*, pp 360-69.

[21] This right is enshrined not only in the text of the SPS Agreement but it has also been expressly recognised by the AB. See *Australia–Salmon*, para 199.

[22] *EC–Hormones*, Panel Report, paras 8.166 and 8.169.

to the extent, notwithstanding countless Appellate Body statements recognising members' right to choose the level of protection they deem appropriate,[23] that this right finds itself being reduced under the current interpretation of the 'objective standard of review' which has been given by the WTO judicial bodies.

2.3 Reviewing Risk Response

Finally, it is submitted that the stage of risk response consisting in the choice of the best risk management option to attain a given level of protection is where the intensity of the review should be heightened. This is mainly because, the chosen measure being likely to obstruct international trade, it is imperative that courts could verify whether that measure be not only 'applied only to the extent necessary to protect human, animal or plant life or health',[24] but also be 'not more trade-restrictive than required to achieve their appropriate level of sanitary or phytosanitary protection'.[25] In other words, the potential disruptive effect on trade stemming from the adoption of a unilateral health measure calls for an intensive review on whether that measure may be considered to be in compliance with the main risk response requirements.

2.4 Conclusions on the Procedural, Intensity-variable Standard of Review

It must first be observed that the application of the proposed procedural, intensity-variable standard to the review of SPS measures implies neither a modification of members' rights and obligations under the SPS Agreement nor a departure from the objective standard of review, as enshrined in Article 11 DSU. Rather, as previously mentioned, the introduction of the proposed standard is made possible by a reinterpretation of the SPS Agreement which aims at giving full meaning to its risk analysis requirements. In particular, by completing the WTO risk analysis model, which is embryonically contained in the current provisions of the SPS Agreement, the proposed review would take place at different levels of intensity depending on the level of normative constraints present on each stage of risk analysis, and this always within the limits of the 'objective standard of review' recommended by the DSU.

There are several important results that may be achieved by adopting such an approach to the review of science-based measures.

---

[23] See, eg, *Australia–Salmon*, AB Report, para 199.
[24] Article 2.2 SPS.
[25] Article 5.6 SPS.

First, this standard carries the potential to adjust the current WTO incomplete risk analysis model by contributing to rebalancing the existing relationship between the detailed scientific obligations and the imprecise management constraints. As seen above, this is important to the extent that the particularly intrusive standard of review developed by the WTO judicial bodies finds its roots precisely in the normative imbalance underlying the SPS risk analysis model. In particular, the proposed standard, by relying on the notion of risk management, might correct the unfortunate AB's decision to deny any consideration for this relevant step of risk analysis. In this sense, it might contribute to breaking the current monopoly that scientific requirements enjoy in the review of a contested SPS measure and which is increasingly affecting members' recognised right to choose the level of protection they deem appropriate.

Secondly, varying its intensity depending on the rights and obligations of the members within each step of risk analysis, such a standard of review would produce the effect of focusing more on the risk response component of the contested measure, ie the risk management option, than on its risk assessment and risk choice elements. As a result, the legality of a science-based measure would mainly depend on its compliance with the risk management requirement of 'necessity', as enshrined in Article 5.6 SPS.

Thirdly, it is submitted that panels, by using this procedural, intensity-variable standard of review, will be in the position to respect the member's chosen level of protection, while disposing at the same time of the possibility of disagreeing with the way in which that level is pursued. Moreover, should they do so, they will not put into question the legitimate public choices surrounding the determination of the appropriate level of protection.

Therefore, it may reasonably be argued that the adoption of such an intensity-variable standard of review would ensure greater governmental discretion in the SPS areas, thus contributing to the acceptance of WTO DSB's decisions and favouring their compliance. This is because, by varying its intensity depending on the rights and obligations of the members within each step of risk analysis, such a standard of review would be apt to accommodate the legitimate democratic preferences of a given society.

In so doing, the proposed standard of review would re-establish the balance, originally designed by the SPS Agreement, between regulatory diversity and free trade.

In fact, one may say, by borrowing the language of the AB, that if the '[t]he requirements of a risk assessment under Article 5.1, as well as of 'sufficient scientific evidence' under Article 2.2, are essential for the maintenance of the delicate and carefully negotiated balance in the SPS Agreement between the shared, but sometimes competing, interests of promoting international trade and of protecting the life and health of human beings [...]',[26] it is even more essential, for the maintenance of this balance to ensure that the judicial review of these requirements is not too narrow and scientifically demanding.

Finally, it must be observed that this proposed standard of review would translate into operational terms the attitude, recommended by the AB in *Hormones*, that panels should adopt when embarking on the judicial review issue of a science-based measure. In this case, the AB has recommended that:

> [...] a panel charged with determining [...] whether "sufficient scientific evidence" exists to warrant the maintenance by a member of a particular SPS measure may, of course, and should, bear in mind that responsible, *representative governments commonly act from perspectives of prudence and precaution where risks of irreversible*, e.g. life-terminating, *damage to human health are concerned*.[27]

---

[26] *EC Hormones* Appellate Body Report, para 177.
[27] *EC-Hormones*, AB Report, para 124.

Conclusion

The recent high-profile food safety failures that have outraged Europe through the last years probably constituted the most serious challenge to the European integration process during its first 50 years of existence.[1] These food scandals dramatically showed the inadequacy of the way in which food laws are created and implemented by the EC institutions and the Member States, highlighting the complexity of the European system of governance and the limits of its functionalist approach to integration. Relying for too long on 'improvisational compromises',[2] the European governance of food safety became 'contested'.[3]

Unlike the legislation existing in most of the Member States, EC food policy has developed in a piecemeal fashion, being based on a variety of different legal bases provided in the European Community Treaty in order to serve different policy objectives. The Community began regulating the food sector, as in many other sectors, in conjunction with its effort to eliminate trade barriers arising from different domestic legislation in order to establish an internal market. However, various peculiarities of foodstuffs, such as their long-rooted tradition at national level and their risk component, have increasingly necessitated the involvement of the Community by requiring more and more supranational legislative intervention. In particular, the EC institutions have assumed new tasks that are largely related to what is generally

---

[1] See L. Azoulay, 'La Sécurité Alimentaire dans la Législation Communautaire, in J. Bourrinet and F. Snyder', *La Sécurité Alimentaire dans l'Union Européenne* (Bruxelles, Bruylant, 2003), comparing BSE to the other political crisis of the EU and also J. Bowis, Rapporteur of the EU Parliament Committee on the Environment, Public Health and Consumer Policy on the Draft Report on the Commission White Paper on Food Safety, who effectively summarised the dimension of the food safety crises: 'Poor practice and scandals have exercised the media, the public and their elected representatives in recent years. The list is long, ongoing and potentially endless given that absolute safety is not an attainable goal. Olive oil, contaminated wine, Perrier water, *E. coli, Listeria,* salmonella, polluted drinking water, BSE, dioxin sludge and slurry entering the human food chain, pesticides, animal feed, GMOs — all in their time and in their way have caused concern, fear, panic and public inquiry'.
[2] C. Lister, *Regulation of Food Products by the European Community,* 285, Butterworths, 1992.
[3] By 'contested governance', Ansell and Vogel mean a 'pervasive conflict in policy arenas that goes beyond politics-as-usual to challenge who should make decisions and where, how and on what basis they should be made'. In other words, 'contested governance entails a significant challenge to the legitimacy of existing institutional arrangements'. See C. Ansell and D. Vogel, *What's the Beef? The Contested Governance of European Food Safety* (MIT Press) pp 3–32.

referred to as 'risk regulation'.[4] Thus, under the pressure of public opinion induced by the recent food scandals, the Community became aware that to regulate the food sector only through the economic lens of the internal market could have been inadequate to address the new challenges brought about by the generally new perception of risks. In other words, its traditional functionalist approach to integration was proving unsuccessful in handling reality.[5]

While undermining the credibility of the EC's food safety regulatory system and balkanising the functioning of the internal market, the food crises of the 1990s brought their own impetus for reforming the EC food regime, leading to calls for an agency solution. Under the pressure of mounting political and public opinion, the Community had to rapidly design a new approach to consumer health and food safety moving away from its economic-oriented system towards an approach enlightened by consumer protection and food safety concerns.[6] Through the publication of several policy documents, such as the Green Paper on the general principles of food law[7] and the White Paper on food safety,[8] the Community launched an effective and exemplary policy-making process leading to the creation of a European Food Safety Authority, originally promoted as a 'European FDA'. For its effectiveness and speed, this process may be seen as a model for the conception and development of new EC policies. In less than five years, the Community managed to develop not only an institutional reform of its food policy, symbolised by the establishment of the EFSA, but also to combine this innovation with a profound regulatory reform of its food law: the 'Global Approach' to food Safety. In doing so, the Community involved virtually all interested parties: Member States, producers, manufacturers and consumers.[9]

The challenge facing Europe was to develop a food risk regulation model which would ensure ultimate political decision-making responsibility and, at the same time, appropriately take account of scientific and

---

[4] See, eg, S. Breyer, *Breaking the Vicious Circle*, (Harvard University Press ed., 1993); C. Hood, H. Rothstein and R. Baldwin, *The Government of Risk, Understanding Risk Regulation Regimes*, (Oxford Univeristy Press, 2004), and J.D. Graham and J.B. Wiener, *Risk v Risk: Tradeoffs in Protecting Health and the Environment* (Harvard University Press, 1995).

[5] For an overview of the functionalist theory, see, eg, B. Rosamond, *Theories of European Integration*, New York, 2000.

[6] Communication from the Commission on consumer health and food safety, COM(97) 183 final, 129.

[7] The General Principles of Food Law in the European Union – Commission Green Paper, supra note 119.

[8] White Paper on Food Safety COM(99) 719, 12 January 2000 available at http://europa.eu.int/comm/dgs/health/ consumer /library/pub/pub06_en.pdf.

[9] The 1997 Green Paper invited 'a public debate on our food legislation with a particular emphasis on how legislation was meeting the 'needs and expectations' of consumers, producers, manufacturers and traders'.

independent technical advice. To do this, the general food law regulation introduces an innovative institutional separation between the decision-making responsibility of risk managers (EC institutions) and the merely advisory role of experts (EFSA). This institutional separation finds a normative expression in the 'structured' risk analysis framework sketched out by the same regulation. This model of risk analysis, addressed not only to the EC institutions but also to the Member States, comprises the three distinct stages of risk assessment, risk management and risk communication. This approach to food risk has been in turn endorsed by subsequent legislation[10] and case law.[11]

However, risk assessment cannot be a wholly objective exercise. Not only is it influenced by the extensive use of 'science policies', but also by the values and beliefs of scientists and the judgments of the profession. This entirely legitimate process inevitably leads to stripping the 'functional separation' between risk assessment and risk management of its original goals: purity of scientific assessment and accountability of risk managers. These observations suggest that the EC's dichotomial model of risk regulation, which has found both institutional and normative expression in the general food law regulation, falls short of normatively recognising the value judgments implicit in the first stage of risk analysis. The risks stemming from this insistence on the need for a clear-cut separation is that the values and uncertainties inherent in risk assessment may go unexamined because they do not formally translate into 'science policies'. Notwithstanding the growing rhetoric over transparency in the EC scientific expertise,[12] the current reductionist Community approach to food safety risk analysis does not seem to ensure that the reasons underlying the decisions clearly indicate the policy choices adopted (judgments, uncertainties and biases in scientific assessment), thus setting them apart from the scientific results on which they rely, so that every citizen (and the courts) can identify them. To avoid this and to maintain the original goals pursued by the functional separation between risk assessment and risk management, it is absolutely imperative not only to render science policies explicit by furthering the current efforts aimed at elaborating guidance documents for each EFSA panel but also to clarify and frame the role played by EC Commission officials attending EFSA scientific panel meetings. In fact, although EFSA is institutionally independent, there are, however, some tensions arising

---

[10] See, for instance, Regulation 1829/2003 on Genetically Modified Food and Feed [2003] OJ L 268/1, which entrusts EFSA with the task to provide the initial assessment on the application.
[11] See, for instance, Case T-70/99 *Alpharma v. Council* [2002] ECR II-3495, paras 162–9 and Case T-13/99 *Pfizer Animal Health v. Council* [2002] ECR II-3305, paras 149-56.
[12] EC Commission, White Paper on European Governance, COM(2001) 428 final; EC Commission, Communication on the Collection and Use of Expertise by the Commission: Principles and Guidelines COM(2002) 713 final; EC Commission, The Operating Framework for the European Regulatory Agencies COM(2002) 718 final.

out of the 'grey areas' existing in its relationships with the Commission and from the current emphasis on the EFSA's contacts with stakeholders, including industry. While the need for industry's involvement in EFSA's scientific activities is questionable, greater consumer group representation is already an indisputable necessity in order to avoid consumer interests being overwhelmed by those of industry.

Despite these limitations, the EC food safety assessment policy, by denying any supremacy to EFSA scientific opinions over national opinions, preserves Member States' rights to carry out their own scientific studies and even strengthen their roles through the establishment of the European networking of food authorities. It is argued that this deliberate choice not to turn EFSA into an Oracle of Delphi, spelling out the 'truth' in all scientific matters, while likely to bring about conflicts among Member States, may be seen as an attempt to defend European culinary patrimony and cultural richness against the mounting trend towards the obliteration of local traditions led by the multinationals of processed food. Accordingly, in case of diverging opinions between the EFSA and national food authorities, it is up to the EC courts, and not to EFSA, to solve these conflicts by striking a balance between the European (universal) and a national (local) vision of both safety and of the socio-cultural perception of a particular food. Owing to the uncertainties surrounding EFSA locus standi before EC courts, it remains to be seen how these conflicts will take shape and will be resolved. Furthermore, the EC risk management policy, allowing risk managers to also take into account, apart from the scientific opinions, 'other factors legitimate to the matter under consideration' and the precautionary principle[13], must be applauded to the extent that it embraces the political nature of risk regulation. It is in the light of the above that it has been argued that the EC regulation of food carries the potential to emerge as an effective model to reconcile science, traditions, consumer concerns and free movement.

Since the EC food safety regime does not live in a normative vacuum, but is, rather, subject to the respect of a set of legally binding obligations, such as those of the WTO, the need has been felt to explore the scope of the WTO/SPS rules addressing food safety issues. Although the WTO food safety regime responds to an exclusively trade-oriented logic, by aiming at minimising the negative effects that members' food safety regulations may have on international trade, rather than at prescribing a minimum level of safety that these regulations should reach, it produces the effect of circumscribing the exercise of members' sovereign right to regulate food. The EC being a full member of the WTO together

---

[13] Article 6(3) of the regulation.

with its Members States, it is crucial to verify whether the EC food safety regime as illustrated above may be accommodated within the WTO/SPS legal system. There seems to exist several points of tension between these two food safety regimes, mainly arising out of their respective risk analysis schemes.

In particular, while the EC has held a line on risk regulation by asserting a dichotomy between the technical and the political, the WTO has refused to endorse any particular model of risk analysis by leaving its members free, at least in principle, to adopt the protective measures they consider the most appropriate to achieve their chosen level of protection, provided they comply with the prescribed risk assessment requirements. In the absence of a clear risk management policy, the WTO model totally declines to recognise the political nature of risk regulation as a whole and inevitably prioritises the scientific element over any other legitimate concerns. Accordingly, WTO courts have begun to interpret narrowly the scientific basis for SPS measures (ie Article 5.1), thus limiting members' ability to consider non-scientific factors within their management procedures and to take precautionary measures. The question has therefore arisen as to whether a food safety measure inspired by 'other legitimate factors' or by a 'precautionary approach' could validly be considered to be 'based on risk assessment' within the meaning of Article 5.1 SPS.

Although members' reliance on 'other factors' would not seem to be directly reviewable under that provision, which deals merely with the scientific basis of the adopted measure, panels could eventually consider the legitimacy of these factors when determining whether a rational relationship exists between the adopted food safety measure and the risk assessment. In doing so and in the absence of a well-defined risk management policy, it is inevitable that panels will be influenced by their own perception of the 'other factors' taken into account by the regulators when adopting the contested measure. At the same time the 'consistency' requirement, as enshrined in Article 5.5, which exhausts, together with the 'least-trade restrictive' condition, the incomplete WTO risk management policy, does not provide a definitive answer to the 'other factors' conundrum. In particular, the case law developed so far on that requirement provides little guidance in establishing what the permissible factors are that would justify differences in the level of protection. Conversely, by inducing panels to enquire into the validity of a member's decision on the level of risk it is prepared to accept in comparable situations, it has the potential to open the door to a highly intrusive review.

While the Appellate Body has not made clear its attitude to whether social and other non-economic factors may have a legitimate role in risk management, by rejecting the distinction between risk assessment and risk management, the most recent case law developed on the role of the precautionary principle seems to have diluted the scope of Article 5.7, by restricting its invocation to situations of 'scientific insufficiency' which are not well defined. The invocation of this provision would therefore seem, surprisingly in line with a teleological interpretation, to be limited to situations of urgency or natural disaster, requiring rapid risk management action without a full or adequate risk assessment. It remains to be seen whether, as pointed out by the Appellate Body in an obiter dictum of its report in the *Hormones* case, a precautionary approach may find support in some other provisions of the SPS Agreement.[14]

The lack of a complete and effective risk management guidance to WTO members stems directly from the SPS negotiators' choice to 'outsource' to the Codex Alimentarius its positive integration activities through the SPS harmonisation requirements. Hence, the Codex has become not only a 'quasi-legislator' in charge of elaborating international standards but, gradually, also a unique forum for the elaboration of guidelines for regulatory action in the food safety sector, including both the risk assessment and risk management stages of risk analysis.

In the light of the above, it is expected that, in settling present and future trade disputes centred on the compatibility of the EC, or other Member States', food regimes with WTO law, WTO judicial bodies will look at the emerging body of guidelines promoting commonalities of approaches in risk analysis which have developed within Codex, and notably at the draft working principles for risk analysis for food safety which are currently under consideration. This solution not only finds a solid textual basis within the WTO but has also been endorsed by the *EC–Biotech* panel report[15]. Against this backdrop, it is believed that agreement on this additional Codex meta-standard, which is intended for the first time for government use, is crucial for the future development of a worldwide harmonised food safety risk analysis model having the capacity to fill the current existing gap within the WTO risk analysis, particularly in relation to its risk management policy. Possibly, both points of tension existing between the EC and the WTO food regimes would thus be attenuated.

---

[14] *EC–Hormones*, AB Report, at para 124, where the AB indicated that ' [...] there is no need to assume that Article 5.7 exhausts the relevance of the precautionary principle. It is reflected also in the sixth paragraph of the preamble and in Article 3.3. These explicitly recognize the right of Members to establish their own appropriate level of sanitary protection, which level may be higher (i.e. more cautious) than that implied in existing international standards, guidelines and recommendations'.

[15] *EC–Biotech* panel report, at 7.96.

However, the problem is that, at present, no Codex risk analysis guidance seems to provide more useful answers than does the SPS Agreement itself. Hence, the Codex's present inability to solve, at the regulatory level, the long-standing issues of the role of the precautionary principle and that of 'other factors' in risk management makes the relationship between the EC food safety regime and WTO law increasingly difficult today, and keeps the EC regime at odds with WTO law.

This shows how the original decision not to agree on a well-defined management policy within the SPS Agreement is producing the effect of transferring the responsibility of shaping a WTO risk analysis model from the diplomatic level to the dispute-settlement level; in other words, from the 'executive-legislative' powers to the 'judiciary'. By borrowing the words of the Appellate Body, one may say that it is up to the WTO judicial bodies to find an appropriate 'balance in the SPS Agreement between the shared, but sometimes competing, interests of promoting international trade and of protecting the life and health of human beings'.[16]

One may legitimately wonder whether it should be the judges, by determining, when they are called upon to review science-based measures, which risk management policies could be compatible with the risk analysis model developed within SPS, who fulfil this function. In fact, notwithstanding their well-know commitment to textual fidelity, the WTO judicial bodies will inevitably be obliged to develop answers that, rather than stemming from the texts of the WTO Agreements, will flow from their own understanding of the risk management policies developed in national and international contexts, such as the Codex. This excess of discretion impliedly granted to the WTO courts, if not appropriately offset, is likely to harm the WTO system by diminishing the level of legitimacy and social acceptability of its decisions.

A comparison between the standards of review developed by the EC courts and the WTO judicial bodies has revealed that, because of the absence of clear risk management guidelines within the SPS Agreement, the WTO judicial approach to food safety measures tends to be much more intrusive than that adopted by the EC courts. This is because, by exalting the rational, science-based stage of risk assessment, the WTO ambiguous and fragmented model of risk analysis inevitably leads WTO courts, when reviewing the legality of a contested food safety measure, to prioritise the scientific and technical evidence over other legitimate interests.

---

[16] *EC–Hormones*, AB Report, para 177.

To mitigate partly this result, it has been proposed to develop a procedural, intensity-variable standard of review. This would, on the one hand, complete the WTO risk analysis framework, by structuring it in small and simpler concepts for each stage and component of risk, and, on the other, it would enable the courts to vary their intensity of review depending on the rights and obligations of the Member States within each of these risk analysis stages. Although apparently innovative, the application of the proposed standard would imply neither a modification of Member States' rights and obligations under the SPS Agreement nor a departure from the objective standard of review, as enshrined in Article 11 DSU. It would rather require a reinterpretation of the SPS Agreement aimed at giving full meaning to its risk analysis requirements. Hence, by completing the WTO risk analysis model, which is embryonically contained within the SPS Agreement itself, the proposed review would take place at different levels of intensity depending on the level of normative constraints present within each stage of risk analysis and this always within the limits of the objective standard of review recommended by the DSU. There are several consequences that might reasonably be expected to flow from the application of this standard.

By contributing to rebalancing the relationship between the detailed scientific discipline and the imprecise management constraints underlying the SPS Agreement, this standard might contribute, first, to breaking the current monopoly that the scientific requirements enjoy in the review of a contested measure. As a result, by varying its intensity depending on the rights and obligations of the Member States within each step of risk analysis, such a standard of review would lead the judges to focus more on the risk response component of the contested measure, ie the risk management option, than on its risk assessment and risk choice elements.

Therefore, courts, by using the proposed standard of review, would be in the position to respect the Member State chosen level of protection, while disposing at the same time of the possibility of disagreeing with the way in which that level is pursued. Moreover, should they do so, they will not put into question the legitimate public choices surrounding the determination of the appropriate level of protection.

In the light of the above, it has been argued that the adoption of such an intensity-variable standard of review would ensure greater governmental discretion in the SPS areas. In fact, by varying its intensity depending on the rights and obligations of the Member States within each step of risk analysis, such a standard of review would be apt to accommodate the legitimate democratic preferences of any given society.

In so doing, the proposed standard of review would ultimately carry the potential to re-establish the balance originally designed by the SPS Agreement between 'the shared, but sometimes competing, interests of promoting international trade and of protecting the life and health of human beings',[17] by incorporating the suggestion put forth by the AB in *Hormones* according to which:

> [...] a panel charged with determining [...] whether 'sufficient scientific evidence' exists to warrant the maintenance by a Member of a particular SPS measure may, of course, and should, bear in mind that responsible, *representative governments commonly act from perspectives of prudence and precaution where risks of irreversible,* e.g. life-terminating, *damage to human health are concerned.*[18]

It is predicted that it is only by integrating such a presumption of bona fide into their standard of review that the WTO judicial bodies will be able to produce not only legally valid but also socially acceptable rulings, by thus acquiring legitimacy vis-à-vis the public.

Finally, although it would be more constructive to resolve several of the most contentious issues relating to food regulation in negotiations rather than in controversial and highly technical disputes, such negotiations do not seem to be part of the Doha Round.

This is regrettable to the extent that, as our study has proven, a clarification of the current WTO/SPS risk analysis model, and in particular of its risk management policy, is an inescapable priority for the future of the world's increasingly integrated food system.

---

[17] *EC–Hormones*, Appellate Body Report, para 177.
[18] *EC–Hormones*, AB Report, para 124.

BIBLIOGRAPHY

Alemanno A., 'Le Principe de la Reconnaissance Mutuelle au delà du Marché Intérieur. Phénomène d'Exportation Normative ou Stratégie de 'Colonialisme' Règlementaire?', *Revue du Droit de l'Union Européenne*, 2/2006, pp 273–311.

Alemanno A., 'Food Safety and the Single European Market', in D. Vogel and C. Ansell (eds), *What's the Beef? The Contested Governance of Food Safety* (MIT Press, 2006) pp 237–258.

Alemanno, A., 'The Role of the Judge in Risk Analysis – Adjudicating science-based risk regulations in the European Union and the World Trade Organization', *Best Student Paper Award of the Society for Risk Analysis (SRA) Annual Meeting*, December 7, 2005, Orlando, Florida.

Alemanno A., 'Libre Circulation des Marchandises: "Arrêt Burmanjer"', *Revue du Droit de l'Union Européenne*, 02/05, 392 ss.

Alemanno A., 'Judicial Enforcement of the WTO Hormones Ruling within the European Community: Toward an EC Liability for the non-Implementation of WTO Dispute Settlement Decisions', 45 *Harvard International Law Journal* (2004) 547.

Alemanno A., 'Private parties and WTO Dispute Settlement System', in *Cornell Law School LL.M. Papers Series*, 1 (2004). Available at http://lsr.nellco.org/cornell/lps/clacp/1.

Alemanno A., 'Gli Accordi di Reciproco Riconoscimento di Conformità dei prodotti tra regole OMC ed Esperienza Europea', 2-3 *Diritto del Commercio Internazionale* (2003) 379 ss.

Alemanno A., 'Protection des Consommateurs: "Arrêts Alpharma/Pfizer"', *Revue du Droit de l'Union Europénne* 4/2002, 842 ss.

Alemanno A., 'Le principe de Précaution en Droit Communautaire: Stratégie de Gestion des Risques ou Risque d'Atteinte au Marché Intérieur?', *Revue du Droit de l'Union Européenne*, 4/2001.

Alemanno A., 'Contentieux : "Arrêt Commission/France"', *Revue du Droit de l'Union Européenne*, 1/2002, pp 159 ss.

Alemanno A., 'Protection des Consommateurs : "Arrêt Bellio"', *Revue du Droit de l'Union Européenne*, 2/04, pp 319-323.

Alemanno A., 'Marché intérieur : "Danemark/Commission"', *Revue du Droit de l'Union Européenne*, 02/03, pp 510-515.

Ansell C. and Vogel D. (eds), *What's the Beef? The Contested Governance of European Food Safety* (MIT Press, 2006).

Applegate J., *Environmental Risk*, 1-2, 2004.

Applegate J., 'Risk Assessment: Science, Law and Policy, Natural Resources and Environment', 14 *Yale Journal of Regulation* (2000), 219.

Applegate J., 'The Perils of Unreasonable Risk: Information, Regulatory Policy, and Toxic Substances Control', 91 *Columbia Law Journal* (1991) 261.

Arcuri A., 'The Case for a Procedural Version of the Precautionary Principle Erring on the Side of Environmental Preservation', *Global Law Working Paper* 09/04, NYU School of Law.

Aresu A., 'Derniers Développements Jurisprudentiels en Matière de Libre Circulation des Produits Alimentaires', in *Revue du Droit de l'Union Européenne*, 4/1992, pp 251ss.

Atik, J., 'Science and International Regulatory Convergence', *Northwestern Journal of International Law and Business*, Winter-Spring, 736.

Atik, J., 'The Weakest Link: Demonstrating the Inconsistency of appropriate levels of Protection in Australia Salmon' 24 *Risk Analysis: an International Journal* 483 (2004).

Aubry-Caillaud F., 'La Sécurité Alimentaire au Sein de l'Union Européenne: les Apports de l'Approche Globale', 4 *Europe* 4-7 (2003).

Azoulai L., 'La Sécurité alimentaire dans la législation communautaire, in J. Bourrinet and F. Snyder', *La sécurité Alimentaire dans l'Union Européenne* 95 (Bruxelles, Bruylant, 2003) pp 30 ss.

Babuscio T., *Alimenti Sicuri e Diritto. Analisi di Problemi Giuridici nei Sistemi Amministrativi delle Autorità per la Sicurezza Alimentare Europee e Statunitense* (Giuffré, 2005).

Barents R., 'The Internal Market Unlimited: Some observations on the Legal Basis of Community Legislation' (1993) 30 *CMLRev*, pp 85 ss

Barents R., *The Agricultural Law of the EC* (Kluver Academic International, 1994).

Barnard C. and Scott J., *The Law of the Single European Market: Unpacking the Premises Oxford* (Hart Publishing, 2002).

Barton Hutt P. and Merril R.A., *Food & Drug Law, Cases and Materials*, II[ed.] (New York, Foundation Press, 1991).

Barton Hutt P. and Merrill R.A., *Food and Drug Law, Cases and Materials*, II[ed], 1996 Statutory Supplement, 1996.

Battaglia A., 'Food Safety: Between European and Global Administration', *Global Jurist Advances*, Vol. 6, No. 3, Article 8 (2006).

Bermann, G.A., Goebel, R.J., Davey, William J., Fox, E.M., *Cases and Materials on European Union Law* (Thomson-West, 2002).

Bermann G. and Mavroidis P.C. (eds), *Trade and Human Health and Safety* (Cambridge: Cambridge University Press, 2006).

Bermann G.A., Herdegen M. and Lindseth P.L. (eds), *Transatlantic Regulatory Cooperation: Legal Problems and Political Prospects* (Oxford: Oxford University Press, 2001).

Bhagwati J. N. and. Hudec R. E (eds), *Fair Trade and Harmonization: Prerequisites for Free Trade?*, Volume 2: Legal Analysis (Cambridge, MA: MIT Press, 1996).

Biondi A., Eeckhout P. and Flynn J. (eds), *The Law of State Aid in the European Union* (Oxford University Press, 2004).

Bieber R., Dehousse R., Pinder J., Weiler J.H.H. (eds), 1992: *One European Market? A Critical Analysis of the Commission's Internal Market Strategy* (Nomos, Baden-Baden, 1988).

Bizet J., 'Sécurité Alimentaire: Le Codex Alimentarius', *Les Rapports du Sénat*, n. 450, 1999-2000.

Bloche M.G., 'WTO Deference to National Health Policy: Toward an Interpretative Principle', 5(4) *Journal of International Economic Law* 825 (2002).

Bloor D., *Knowledge and Social Imagery* (University Of Chicago Press; 2nd edition, 1991).

Boisson de Chazournes L. and Mbengue M.M., 'GMOs and Trade: Issues at Stake in the EC Biotech Dispute', in *RECIEL*, 13(3), 2004, pp 298-99.

Bohanes J., 'Risk Regulation in WTO Law: A procedure-Based Approach', 40 *Columbia Journal of Transnational Law* (2002), pp 323 ss.

Borzel T.A., 'Organizing Babylon – On the different Conceptions of Policy Networks' (1998) 76 *Public Administration* 253.

Bourrinet J. and Snyder F., *La Sécurité Alimentaire dans l'Union Européenne* (Bruxelles, Bruylant, 2003).

Braithwaite J., 'Prospects for Win-Win International Rapprochement of Regulation in Organization for Economic Corporation and Development', *Regulatory Co-operation for an Interdependent World* (Paris, OECD, 1994).

Brems E., 'The Margin of Appreciation Doctrine in the Case-Law of the European Court of Human Rights', in *Zeitschrift für ausländisches öffentliches Recht und Völkerrecht*, 1996, pp 240-93 ss.

Brickman R. et al., *Controlling Chemicals: The Politics of Regulation in Europe and in the United States* 112-15 (1985).

Brock, W.J., Rodricks, J.V., Rulis, A., Dellarco, V.L., Gray, G.M., and Lane R.W. (2003) 'Food Safety: Risk Assessment Methodology and Decision Making Criteria', *International Journal of Toxicology* 22, pp 435-451.

Brouwer O., 'Free Movement of Foodstuffs and Quality Requirements: Has the Commission Got it Wrong?', [1989] *CMLRev.*, pp 237-262.

Buonanno L. et al., 'Politics Versus Science in the Making of a New Regulatory Regime for Food in Europe', 5 *EIPoP* (2001).

Buonanno L., in Ansell C. and Vogel D. (eds), *What's the Beef? The Contested Governance of European Food Safety* (MIT Press, 2006).

Buschle D., 'Das "Precautionary Principle" im Lebensmittelrecht als universelles Rechtsprinzip', *European Law Reporter*, 11/2003, pp 414-421.

Buschle D., 'Neues vom "precautionary principle' Annotation to Case C-41/02' Commission v the Netherlands, *European Law Reporter* 2/2005, pp 58-62.

Button C., *The Power to protect* (Oxford and Portland, Oregon, 2004).

Byrne D., 'EFSA: Excellence, integrity and openness', Inaugural meeting of the Management Board of the European Food Safety Authority, Brussels, 18 December 2002.

Calman K. and Smith D., 'Works in Theory but not in Practice? The Role of the Precautionary Principle in Public Health Policy', 79 *Public Administration* (2001), 185.

Cameron J., 'The Precautionary Principle', in G. P. Sampson, and W. B. Chambers, (eds) *Trade, Environment, and the Millennium*, (Tokyo, New York and Paris: United Nations University Press, 1999) pp 239-269.

Cannarsa M., *La Responsabilité du Fait des Produits Défectueux: Etude Comparative* (Milano, Giuffrè, 2005).

Capelli F., Klaus B., Silano V., *Nuova Disciplina del Settore Alimentare e Autorità Europea per la Sicurezza Alimentare* (Milano, Giuffré, 2006).

Capelli F., 'Il Principio del Mutuo Riconoscimento non Garantisce Buoni Risultati nel Settore dei Prodotti Alimentary', in *Jus*, 1992, pp 141 ss.

Capelli F., 'Le Contrôle des Produits Alimentaires sur le Marche Unique Européen et la Responsabilité de Contrôleurs', *Revue du Marche Commun et de l'Union Européenne*, février 1996, pp 90 ss.

Cavicchi J., 'The Science Court: A Bibliography', 4 *Risk: Issues in Health & Safety* 171, 1993.

Chalmers D., '"Food for thought: reconciling European risks and traditional ways of life', 66 *The Modern Law Review* 532, 534 (2003).

Charlier C., Hormones, 'Risk Management Prevention and Protectionism' 14 *European Journal of Law & Economics* 83, (2002).

Cheyne I., 'Risk and Precaution in World Trade organisation Law', 40(5) *Journal of World Trade* 837 (2006).

Chiti E., 'The Emergency of a Community Administration: the Case of European Agencies', in *Common Market Law Review* 37, pp 309-342 (2000).

Chiva M., 'Les Risques Alimentaires: Approches Culturelles ou Dimensions Universelles?', in M. Apfelbaum (ed.), *Risques et Peur Alimentaires* (Paris, Odile Jacob, 1998) pp 131 ss.

Christoforou T., 'The Origins, Content and Role of the Precautionary Principle in European Community Law', C. Leben & J. Verhoeven (eds), *Le Principe de Précaution : Aspects de Droit International et Communautaire* (LGDJ : Éd. Panthéon-Assas, 2002).

Christoforou T., 'Settlement of Science-Based Trade Disputes in the WTO: A Critical Review of the Developing Case Law in the Face of Scientific Uncertainty', (2000) 8 *N.Y.U. Environmental Law Journal* 622.

Christoforou T., 'Science, Law and Precaution in Dispute Resolution on Health and Environmental Protection: What Role for Scientific Experts?', J. Bourrinet et S. Maljean-Dubois (eds), *Le Commerce International des Organismes Génétiquement Modifiés* (LGDJ : Éd. Panthéon-Assas, 2003) pp 239 ss.

Christoforou T., 'The Precautionary Principle and Democratizing Expertise: a European Legal Perspective', in *Science and Public Policy*, 30, pp 3 ss. (2003).

Christoforou T., 'The Precautionary Principle, Risk Assessment, and the Comparative Role of Science in the European Community and the US Legal Systems', in N. J. Vig and M.G. Faure (eds), *Green Giants? Environmental Policies of the United States and the European Union* (MIT Press, 2004) pp 31 ss.

Coleman R. J., Address concerning 'Communicating Risk to Consumers', at the Interim Scientific Advisory Forum, Brussels 30th October 2001, available at http://europa.eu.int/comm/dgs/health_consumer /library/ speeches/ speech133_en.pdf

Collingridge D. and Reeve C., *Science Speaks to Power: The Role of Experts in Policy Making*, 1986.

Costato L., *Compendio di diritto alimentare* (Padova, Cedam, 2002).

Costato L., 'Dal Mutuo Riconoscimento al Sistema Europeo di Diritto Alimentare: il Regolamento 178/2002 come Regola e come Programma', in *Rivista di Diritto Agrario*, 3/2003, pp 290 ss.

Cottier T. and Mavroidis P., *The Role of the Judge in International Trade Regulation: Experiences and Lessons for the WTO* (University of Michigan Publishing, Ann Arbor, 2003).

Craig P. and De Burca G. (eds), *The Evolution of EU Law* (OUP Oxford, 1999).

Cranor C.F., *Regulating Toxic Substances – A Philosophy of Science and the Law* (Oxford:Oxford University Press, 1993).

Cranor C.F., Science Courts, 'Evidentiary Procedures and Mixed Science-Policy Decisions', 4 *Risk: Issues in Health & Safety* 113 (1993).

Cranor C.F., 'Learning from the Law for Regulatory Science', 14 *Law and Philosophy*, 1995, pp 115 ss.

Crawford-Brown D., *Risk-based environmental decisions: methods and culture*, (Dordrecht: Kluwer Academic Publishers, 1999).

Croley S.P and J.H. Jackson, 'WTO Dispute Procedures, Standard of Review and Deference to National Governments', 90 *American Journal of International Law* 193 (1996).

Croley S. and Jackson J., 'WTO Dispute Settlement Panel Deference to National Government Decision: The Misplaced Analogy to the US Chevron Standard-Of.-Review Doctrine', in E.U. Petersmann (ed.), *International Trade Law and the GATT/WTO Dispute Settlement System*, Kluwer, 1997, pp 188 ss.

da Cruz Vilaça J.L., 'The Precautionary Principle in EC Law', 10 *European Public Law* 2, pp 369 ss.

Deboyser P., *Le Droit Communautaire Relative aux Denrées Alimentaires* (Louvain-La-Neuve, Story-Scientia, 1989).

Deboyser P., 'Le Marché Unique des Produits alimentaires', *Revue du Marché Unique Européen*, 1991, pp 65 ss.

Dehousse, R., 'Integration v. Regulation? On the dynamics of Regulation in the European Community', in 30 *Journal of Common Market Studies* 383, 1992.

De Burca G. and Scott J., 'The Impact of the WTO on EU Decision-making', *Harvard Jean Monnet Working Paper* 6/00.

De Burca G. and Scott J. (eds), *The EU and the WTO: Legal and Constitutional Aspects* (Oxford, Hart Publishing, 2001).

Dabrowska P., 'Risk, Precaution and the Internal Market: Did both Sides Win the day in the Recent Judgement of the ECJ?', 5 *German Law Journal* No 2 (1 February 2004), available at www.germanlawjournal.com

Defresne J. and Jeuffroy-Niehnes I., 'Tradition culturelle et expertise', in J. Thyes and B. Kalaora (eds), La Terre Octroyée, *Les experts sont formels !* (Ed. Autrement, Paris, 1992) pp 188 ss.

De Grove-Valdeyron N., 'La protection de la santé et de la sécurité du consommateur à l'épreuve de l'affaire de la dioxine', *Revue du Marché Commun*, 1999, pp 700 ss.

Demaret P., Bellis J.-F. and García Jiménez G. (eds), *Regionalism and multilateralism after the Uruguay Round : convergence, divergence and interaction* (Brussels, European Interuniversity Press, 1997).

de Sadeleer N., 'Les Principes du Pollueur-payeur, de Prevention et de Précaution', *Collection Universités Francophones* (Bruxelles, Bruylant/AUF, 1999).

de Sadeleer N., 'Le Statut Juridique du Principe de Précaution en Droit Communautaire: du Slogan à la Règle', *Cahiers de Droit Européen*, 2001, n. 1, pp 79-120.

de Sadeleer N., 'Les Clauses de Sauvegarde Prévues à l'article 95 du Traité CE – L'Efficacité du Marché Intérieur en Porte-à-faux avec les Intérets Nationaux Dignes de Protection', in *Revue Trimestrielle du Droit Européenne*, 38 (1), 2002.

de Sadeleer N. et Noiville C., 'La Directive Communautaire 2001/18/CE/CE sur la Dissémination Volontaire d'Organismes Génétiquement Modifiés dans l'Environnement : un Examen Critique', *Journal des Tribunaux, Droit Européen*, 2002, n°88, pp 81 ss.

de Sadeleer N., *Environmental Principles: From Political Slogans to Legal Rules* (Oxford, UK: Oxford University Press, 2002).

de Sadeleer N., 'Safeguard clauses under Article 95 of the EC Treaty', *Common Market Law Review*, 2003, n° 40, pp 889-915.

de Sadeleer N., 'The Precautionary Principle in EC Health and Environmental Law', *European Law Journal* 12 March, pp 139-172.

Dehousse, R., 'Regulation by Networks in the European Community: The Role of European Agencies', 4 *J. Eur. Pub. Pol'y* 246 (1996), pp 246 ss.

Demaret P., Bellis J.-F. and García Jiménez G. (eds), *Regionalism and multilateralism after the Uruguay Round : Convergence, Divergence and Interaction* (Brussels, European Interuniversity Press, 1997).

Desmedt A., Hormones, 'Objective Assessment, and (or as) Standard of review', 1 *Journal of International Economic Law* 695 (1998).

Desmedt A., 'Proportionality in WTO law', 5 *Journal of International Economic Law* 441 (2001).

Donahue A., 'Equivalence: Not Quite Close Enough for the International Harmonization of Environmental Standards', 30 *Envtl. L.* 363 Spring (2000).

Dordi C., La Discriminazione Commerciale nel Diritto Internazionale, (Milano Giuffré, 2002).

Douma W.T., 'The Beef Hormones Dispute and the Use of National Standards under WTO law', 8 *Environmental Law Review* 137, 1999.

Douma W.T., 'How Safe it Safe? The EU and the WTO Codex Alimentarius Debate on Food Safety Issues', in V. Kronenberg, *The European Union and the International Legal Order : Discord or Harmony ?* (T.M.C. Asser Press, Amsterdam) pp 185 ss.

Draft Final Act Embodying the Results of the Uruguay Round of Multilateral Trade Neogotiations (Dunkel Draft), GATT Doc. MTN.TNC/W/FA. Sec. L, pt. C, para 11. at L.37 (DEC.20, 1991), reprinted in "The Dunkel Draft" from the GATT Secretariat L. 35 (Institute for International Legal Information ed., 1992).

Echols M.A., 'Food Safety Regulation in the European Union and the United States : Different Cultures, Different Laws', in *Columb. J. Eur. L.* 525 (1998).

Eekhout P., 'Constitutional Concepts for Free Trade in Services', G. De Burca and J. Scott (eds), *The EU and the WTO: Legal and Constitutional Aspects* (Oxford, Hart Publishing, 2001).

Egan M., *Constructing a European Market: Standards, Regulation, and Governance* (Oxford, Oxford University Press, 2001).

Ehlermann C.D., 'Standard of Review in WTO Law', 7 *Journal of International Economic Law* 3, 498.

Ehlermann C.D., 'Six Years on the Bench of the "World Trade Court": Some Personal Experiences as Member of the Appellate Body of the World Trade Organization', 36 *J. World Trade* 605 (2002).

Emiliou N. and O'Keefe D. (eds), *The European Union and World Trade Law: After the Uruguay Round*, (London, John Wiley and Sons, 1996.)

Erlbacher F., 'Restrictions to the Free Movement of Goods on Grounds of the Protection of Human Health: Some Remarks on Recent ECJ Judgments', *European Law Reporter*, 118 (2004).

Esty D. and Geradin D., Market Access, 'Competitiveness, and Harmonization: Environmental Protection in Regional Trade Agreements', 21 *Harvard Environmental Law Review* 265 (1997).

Ferrari Bravo L., Moavero Milanesi E., *Lezioni di Diritto Comunitario* (Napoli, Editoriale Scientifica, 2002).

Fisher E., Precaution, 'Precaution Everywhere: Developing a "Common Understanding" of the Precautionary Principle in the European Community', 9 *Maastricht Journal of Comparative Law*, 2002.

Fischhoff B., *Acceptable Risk* (Cambridge Univ. Press, 1981).

Frison-Roche M.A., 'Le Besoin Conjoint d'une Réglementation Analogue des Relations Sociales et des Marches Globalisés', *Revue Internationale de Droit Economique*, 2002, 1, pp 67 ss.

Foster K.R., Vecchia P. and Repacholi M.H., 'Risk Management: Science and the Precautionary Principle', 288 *Science* 979 (2000).

Gaerner E., 'Le Controle des Denrees Alimentaires', M. Fallon and F. Maniet (eds), *Sécurité des Produits et Mécanismes de Contrôle dans la Communauté Européenne* (Story-Scientia, Louvain-La-Neuve, 1990) pp 119 ss.

Gaudillère, J.P., 'Echos d'une Crise Centenaire', *La Recherche*, n 339, février 2001, pp 14 ss.

Geradin D., and Petit N., 'The Development of Agencies at EU and National Levels: Conceptual Analysis and Proposals for Reform', *Jean Monnet Working Paper* 01/04.

Gilardi F., 'Policy Credibility and delegation to independent regulatory agencies: a comparative empirical analysis', 9:9 *Journal of European Public Policy*, 873, (2002).

Goh G., 'Tipping the Apple Cart: The Limits of Science and Law in the SPS Agreement after Japan – Apples', *Journal of World Trade* 40(4), 655-686 (2006).

Godard O., 'Social Decision-Making Under Conditions of Controversy – Expertise and the Precautionary Principle', in Joerges C., Ladeur C. and Vos E., *Integrating Scientific Expertise into Regulatory Decision-Making*, (1997)

Godard O., 'Le principe de precaution: Entre débats et gestion de crises', 274 *Regards sur l'Actualité* (2001), 33

Godard O., 'Embargo or not Embargo', *La Recherche*, février 2001, n 339, pp 50 ss.

Gollier C., Jullien P., Treich N., 'Scientific Progress and Irreversibility: An Economic Interpretation of the Precautionary Principle', 75 *Journal of Public Economics* (2000), 229

Gollier C. and Treich N., 'Decision-making under scientific uncertainty: The economics of the precautionary principle', *Journal of Risk and Uncertainty*, Vol. 27, n. 1, pp 77-103

Gonzalez Vaqué L., 'La législation communautaire relative aux additives alimentaires', *Revue du Droit de l'Union Européenne*, 3/1993, pp 119 ss.

Gonzalez Vaqué L., 'Objetivo: la seguridad alimentaria en la Unión Europea', 223 *Gaceta Jurídica de la UE* 59 (2003).

González Vaqué L., 'Novedades en la jurisprudencia del Tribunal de Justicia de las Comunidades Europeas relativa a las nociones de medicamento y alimento?: una primera valoración de la sentencia "HLH Warenvertriebs"', *Revista de Derecho Alimentario*, Julio 2005, pp 21 ss.

Gonzalez Vaqué L., Ehring L., Jacquet C., 'Le Principe de Précaution dans la Législation Communautaire et Nationale Relative a la Protection de la Santé', *Revue du Marché Unique Européenne* 1, 79 (1999).

Gonzalez Vaqué L., 'El Principio de Precaución en la Jurisprudencia Comunitaria: la Sentencia "Virginiamicina"' (asunto T-13/99), *Revista de Derecho Comunitario Europeo*, 2002, n. 13, pp 925 ss.

Gonzalez Vaqué L., 'La Definicion del Contenido y Ambito de Aplicación del Principio de Precaución en el derecho Comunitario', *Gaceta Juridica de la Union Europea y de la Competencia*, 4, 2002.

Gonzalez Vaqué L., 'El Principio de Precaución en la Jurisprudencia del TJCE: la Sentencia "Greenpeace France"', *Comunidad Europea Aranzadi*, 2001, n. 1, pp 33 ss.

Gonzalez Vaqué L., 'El Principio de Precaución en el Derecho de la UE : la Aplicación de un Principio General Basado en la Incertidumbre', *Derecho de los negocios*, 2005, 174.

Gonzalez Vaqué L., 'La Libre Circulación de los Productos Alimenticios en la Unión Europea : Tres Opciones para Asegurar la Protección de la Salud de los Consumidores', *Revista Española de Derecho Europeo*, 2004, 11, pp 393 ss.

Graham J.D. &. Wiener J.B, *Risk vs. Risk: Tradeoffs in Protecting Health and the Environment* (Cambridge, MA, Harvard University Press ed., 1995).

Gray P., 'Food Law and the Internal Market. Taking Stock', *Food Policy* (1990) 111.

Green A., 'Climate Change, Regulatory Policy and the WTO' 8 *Journal of International Economic Law* (2005) 143.

Guzman A., 'Food Fears: Health and Safety at the WTO', *Boalt Working Papers in Public Law*, 2004.

Hagenmeyer M., 'Modern food safety requirements – according to EC Regulation 178/2002', *Zeithscrift fur das gesamte Lebensmittelrecht* 443-459 (2002).

Hammit J.K., Wiener J.B., Swedlow B., Kall D. and Zhou Z., 'Precautionary Regulation in Europe and the United States: A Quantitative Comparison', 25 *Risk Analysis* 1215 (2005).

Hankin R., 'The Role of scientific advice in the Elaboration and Implementation of the Community's foodstuffs legislation', in C. Joerges,

K.H. Ladeur and E.Vos, *Integrating Scientific Expertise into Regulatory Decision-Making*, National Traditions and European Innovations, pp 158 ss.

Harmoniaux T., 'Principe de Précaution et Refus de la France de Lever l'embargo sur la Viande de Bovin Britannique', *L'actualité jurisprudentielle*, droit administratif pp 164-169 (Février 2002).

Hart A., *Final Report of EU Workshop on the interface between RA and RM*, 2003.

Herdegen M., 'Biotechnology and Regulatory Risk Assessment', in G.A. Bermann, M. Herdegen and P.L. Lindseth (eds), *Transatlantic Regulatory Cooperation: Legal Problems and Political Prospects* (Oxford, Oxford University Press, 2001).

Hermitte M.A. et Noiville Ch., 'Marrakech et Carthagène comme Figures Opposées du Commerce International', in J. Bourrinet et S. Maljean-Dubois (eds), *Le commerce international des organismes génétiquement modifiés* (La Documentation Française, 2002) pp 317 ss.

Heyvaert V., 'Guidance Without Constraint: Assessing the Impact of the Precautionary Principle on the European Community's Chemicals Policy' Vol 6. *Yearbook of European Environmental Law* (2006), pp 27-60.

Heyvaert V., 'Trade and the Environment: Proportionality Substituted?', Vol. 13 *Journal of Environmental Law* 2001, Issue 3, pp 392-407.

Heyvaert V., 'The Changing Role of Science in Environmental Regulatory Decision-Making in the European Union', *Revue des Affaires Européennes*, vol. 9, 3/4, 1999.

Heyvaert V., *Reconceptualizing Risk Assessment, in Review of European and Community International Law*, 1999/8, pp 135-143.

Hill R., Johnston S. and Sendashonga C., 'Risk Assessment and Precaution in the Biosafety Protocol', *RECIEL*, 13 (3), 2004.

Holland D. and Pope E., *EU Food Law and Policy*, *(Kluwer Law International*, 2004.

Holmes P. and Young A.R., 'Emerging Regulatory Challenges to the EU's External Economic Relations', *SEI Working Paper* 42 (Falmer: Sussex European Institute).

Hood C., 'Risk Regulation under Pressure: Problem Setting or Blame Shifting?', 33 *Administration and Society* (2001), pp 21 ss.

Hood C., Rothstein H. and Baldwin R., *The Government of Risk, Understanding Risk Regulation Regimes* (Oxford Univeristy Press, 2004).

Horn H. and Weiler J.H.H., 'European Communities – Trade Description of Sardines: Textualism and its Discontent', Discussion Paper prepared for the American Legal Institute project 'The Principles of World Trade Law: The World Trade Organisation', November 25 2003.

Horton L., 'Mutual recognition agreements and harmonization', 29 *Seton Hall L. Rev.* 692, 717-718 (1998).

Howse R. and Mavroidis P., 'Europe's Evolving Regulatory Strategy for GMO – the Issue of Consistency with WTO Law: of Kine and Brine', 24 *Fordham Int'l L.J.* 317 (2000).

Howse R., 'Democracy, Science and Free Trade: Risk Regulation on Trial at the WTO', 98 *Mich.L.R.* 2329 (2000).

Howse R., 'Adjudicating Legitimacy and Treaty Interpretation in International Trade Law: The Early Years of WTO Jurisprudence', in J.H.H. Weiler, (ed.), *The EU, the WTO and the NAFTA: Towards a Common Law of International Trade?* (Oxford University Press, 2000).

Howse R., *A New Evidence For Creating International Legal Normativity: the WTO Technical Barriers to Trade Agreement and "International Standards"* (on file with the Author).

Krapohl S., 'EU's Risk Regulation between Interests and Expertise: The Case of BSE' (2003), 10 *Journal of European Public Policy* 189-207.

Isaac, G., Banerji S. and Woolcock, S., 'International Trade Policy and Food Safety', *Consumer Policy Review*, 10/6, 223-33.

Jackson J.H., *World Trade and the law of GATT: A Legal Analysis of the General Agreement on Tariffs and Trade* (Indianapolis, Bobbs-Merrill Company, 1969).

Jackson J.H., 'The Great 1994 Sovereignty Debate: United States Acceptance and Implementation of the Uruguay Round Results', J.H. Jackson, *The Jurisprudence of GATT and WTO: Insights on Treaty Law and Economic Relations*, 2002, pp 367-369.

Jackson J.H., *The World Trading System: Law and Policy of International Economic Relations* (The MIT Press, Cambridge, 1999).

Jasanoff S., *The Fifth Branch: Science Advisors as Policy Makers* (Cambridge, MA, Harvard University Press, 1990).

Jasanoff S., 'Acceptable evidence in a pluralistic society', in Mayo D. and Hollander R. (eds), *Acceptable Evidence: Science and Values in Risk Management*, pp 31-47 ss.

Jasanoff S., 'Procedural Choices in Regulatory Science', 4 *Risk: Issues in Health & Safety* 143 (1993).

Jasanoff S., *Science at the Bar. Law, Science, and Technology in America* (Cambridge, MA, Harvard University Press, 1995).

Joerges C. and Micklitz H.W., 'Internal Market and Product Safety Policy', *EUI Working Papers in Law*, European University Institute, Florence, vol. 5.

Joerges C., Ladeur C. and Vos E., *Integrating Scientific Expertise into Regulatory Decision-Making* (Oxford, Hart, 1997).

Joerges C. and Vos, E., EU Committes: Social Regulation, Law and Politics (Oxford, Hart, 1999).

Joerges C. and Dehousse R., *Good Governance in Europe's Integrated Market*, (Oxford University Press, 2002).

Joerges C. and Neyer J., *Politics, Risk Management, World Trade Organisation Governance and the Limits of Legalisation*, (2003) 30 Science and Public Policy 219.

Joyce P., 'Governability and Setting Priorities in the new NHS', 23 *Sociology of Health and Illness* (2001), 594.

Jonson H., 'L'Union Européenne et la securité aliméntaire. Les leçons de la crise de l'ESB, Parlement Europeen', *Publications officielles des CE*, Luxembourg/Bruxelles.

Jostling T., Roberts D. and Orden D., *Food Regulation and Trade, Toward a Safe and Open Global System* (Institute for International Economics, Washington, D.C., 2004).

Jukes D., 'Codex Alimentarius – Current Status', in *Food Science and Technology Today*, December 1998.

Jukes D., 'The Role of Science in Internal Food Standards', in *Food Control*, Volume 11(3), June 2000.

Kanska K., 'Wolves in the clothing of sheep? The case of the European Food Safety Authority', 24 *E.L.Rev.* 720 (2004).

Krapohl S., 'Risk Regulation in the EU between interests and expertise – The case of BSE', 10 *Journal of European Public Policy* 189 (April 2003).

Kramer L., *Precaution, the protection of Health and the Environment and the Free Circulation of Goods within the European Community, The Role of Precaution in Chemicals Policy*, Diplomatische Academie Wien, 2002.

Krapohl, S., 'Credible Commitment in Non-Independent Regulatory Agencies: A Comparative Analysis of the European Agencies for Pharmaceuticals and Foodstuffs', *European Law Journal* 10 (5), pp 518-538.

Kronenberg V., *The European Union and the International Legal Order : Discord or Harmony ?* (T.M.C. Asser Press, Amsterdam, 2000).

Kunreuther H., 'Risk Management in an Uncertain World', 22 *Risk Analysis* (2002) 655.

Kuyper P.J., 'Booze and Fast Cars: Tax Discrimination Under GATT and the EC', 23 *Legal Issues of European Integration* 129 (1996).

Ladeur K.H., 'The Introduction of the Precautionary Principle into EU law: A Phyrric Victory for Environmental and Public Health Law? Decision-making Under Conditions of Complexity in Multi-Level Political Systems', in 40 *Common Market Law Review*, 1455-1479.

Lafond F.D., 'The Creation of the European Food Authority. Institutional Implications of Risk Regulation', 10 *European Issues* 4 (November 2001).

Lauwaars R.H., 'The Model Directive on Technical Harmonization and Standardisation', in R. Bieber, R. Dehousse, J. Pinder, J.H.H. Weiler (eds), *1992: One European Market? A Critical Analysis of the Commission's Internal Market Strategy* (Nomos, Baden-Baden, 1988) pp 155 ss.

Leben C. & Verhoeven J., *Le Principe de Précaution : Aspects de Droit International et Communautaire*, (LGDJ : Éd. Panthéon-Assas, 2002).

Lenaerts K., 'Regulating the Regulatory Process: "Delegation of Power" in the European Community' 18 *European Law Review* 23-49 (1993).

Lister C., *Regulation of Food Products by the European Community*, 285, Butterworths, 1992.

Loevinger, L., 'Standards of Proof in Science and Law', *Jurimetrics*, 32, 322-333 (1995).

Löfstedt, R. E., 'The Swing of the Regulatory Pendulum in Europe: from Precautionary Principle to (Regulatory) Impact Analysis', *Journal for Risk and Uncertainty* (2004).

Löfstedt, R. E. and Vogel D., 'The changing character of regulation: a Comparison of Europe and the United States', *Risk Analysis*, Vol. 23 (2001), n.2, pp 411-421.

Long A., 'Setting Priorities: A Formal Model', 20 *Risk Analysis* (2000) 339.

Lowe V. and Fitzmaurice M. (eds), 'Fifty years of the International Court of Justice', *Essays in Honour of Sir Robert Jennings* (Cambridge University Press, 2005).

Lugt M., *Enforcing European and National Food Law in the Netherlands and England* (Koninklijke Vermande, 1999).

MacMaolain C., 'Using the Precautionary Principle to Protect Human Health: Pfizer v. Council', 28 *ELRev.* (2003).

Majone G., 'State, Market, and Regulatory Competition in the European Union: Lessons for the Integrating World Economy', A. Moravscsik (ed.), *Centralizing or Fragmentation? Europe Facing the Challenges of Deepening, Diversity and Democracy* 94, 107-8 (1998).

Marceau G. and Trachtman J., 'The Technical Barriers to Trade Agreement, the Sanitary and Phytosanitary Measures Agreement, and the General Agreement on Tariff and Trade, A Map of the World Trade Organization Law of Domestic Regulation of Goods', 35 *Journal of World Trade* 5 811-881 (2002).

Marceau G., 'A Call for Coherence in International Law', 33 *Journal of World Trade* 128-143 (1999).

Marini L., *Il Principio di Precauzione nel Diritto Internazionale e Comunitario, Disciplina del Commercio di Organismi Geneticamente Modificati e Profili di Sicurezza Alimentare* (Padova, Cedam, 2004).

Maruyama W., 'A New Pillar of the WTO: Sound Science', *International Lawyer* (Fall, 1998), 651.

Mayo D. G. and Hollander Rachelle D., *Acceptable Evidence: Science and Values in Risk Assessment*, 1991.

Mattera A., *Le marché Unique Européen*, Paris, Jupiter, 1990.

Mattera A., 'Reconnaissance Réciproque dans le Cadre de l'article 30 du Traité', *La Qualité des Denrées Alimentaires dans le Grand Marché de 1993* (Commission des CE, Bruxelles-Luxembourg, 1994) pp 69 ss.

Mattera A., 'L'Article 30 du Traité CE, la Jurisprudence Cassis et le Principe de la Reconnaissance Mutuelle', *Revue du Marché Unique Européen*, fasc. 4, 1992, pp.35 ss.

Mattera A., 'L'Arrêt "Foie Gras" du 22 octobre 1998 : Porteur d'une Nouvelle Impulsion pour le Perfectionnement du Marché Unique Européen', *Revue du Marché Unique Européen*, fasc. 4, 1998.

Mattera A., 'Le Principe de la Reconnaissance Mutuelle et le Respect des Identités et des Traditions Nationales, Régionales et Locales', *Mélanges Jean-Victor Louis* (Bruxelles, Bruylant, 2004).

Matthee M. D., 'Regulating Scientific Expertise with regard to Risks Deriving from Genetically Modified Organisms : Procedural Rules on Risk Assessment Committees under European Community and International Law', in V. Kronenberg, *The European Union and the International Legal Order : Discord or Harmony ?* (T.M.C. Asser Press, Amsterdam 2001).

Mattix C., 'Scientific Uncertainty under NEPA', 54 *Administrative Law Review* (2002), 1125.

McGarity T.O., 'On the Prospect of "Daubertizing" Judicial Review of Risk Assessment', 66 *Law & Contemp. Probs.* 155.

McGarity T.O., 'Substantive and Procedural Discretion in Administrative Resolution of Science Policy Questions: Regulating Carcinogens in EPA and OSHA', 67 *Geo. L. J.* 729 (1979).

McGinnis J.O. and Movsesian M.L., 'Commentary: The World Trade Constitution', 114 *Harvard L. Rev.* 511, 544-52 (2000).

Mc Nelis N., 'The Role of the Judge in the EC and the WTO: Lessons from the BSE and Hormones Cases', 4 *Journal of International Economic Law* 1.

McNelis N., 'EU communications on the precautionary principle', in *Journal of International Economic Law* 2000 3: 545-551.

Mengozzi P., 'The jurisprudence of the Court of Justice and the Court of First Instance of the European Communities', in G. Sacerdoti, A. Yanovich and J. Bohanes, *The WTO at Ten: the contribution of the WTO Dispute Settlement System* (Cambridge: Cambridge University Press, 2006).

Merril R.A., 'Science in the Regulatory Process', (2003) 66 *Law and Contemporary Problems* 1.

Merril R.A. & Coller E.M., '"Like Mother used to Make": an Analysis of FDA Food Standards of Identity', 74 *Columbia L. Rev.* 561 (1974).

Mettke H., 'Uber die Notwendigkeit eines europaischen Rahmengesetzes fur das Lebensmittelrecht', *EFLR* 1/91, 5.

Meyers I., 'The New International Trade Architecture and Food Regulation', Third year paper, Harvard Law School, 2000 (on file with the Author).

Millstone E., 'Recent Developments in EU Food Policy: Institutional Adjustments or Fundamental Reforms?', 6 *ZLR* 815 (2000)

Montini M., *La Necessità Ambientale nel Diritto Internazionale* (Padova, Cedam, 2001).

Moravcsik A. (ed.), *Centralizing or Fragmentation? Europe Facing the Challenges of Deepening, Diversity and Democracy* (New York: Council on Foreign Relations Press, 1998).

Morris P., 'The Relationship between Risk Analysis and the Precautionary Principle', 181 *Toxicology* (2003), 127.

Mortelmans K., 'The Relationship Between the Treaty Rules and Community Measures for the Establishment and Functioning of the Internal Market – Towards a Concordance Rule', 39 *Common Market Law Review*, 1303-1346, 2002.

Motaal D.A., 'Is the World Trade Organization Anti-Precaution?', *Journal of World Trade* 39 (3) 499.

Myagishima K. and Kaferstei F., 'Food Safety in International Trade', 19 *World Health Food* 411 (1998).

National Academy of Sciences, Science and Judgment in Risk Assessment (Washington: National Academy Press, 1994).

Nebbia P. and Askham T., *EU Consumer Law*, Richmond: (Richmond Law, 2004).

Neugebauer R., 'Fine-Tuning WTO Jurisprudence and the SPS Agreement: Lessons from the Beef Hormones Case', 31 *Law & Policy International Business*, 1255 (2000).

Neumann, J. and Turk E., 'Necessity Revisited: Proportionality in World Trade Organisation Law after Korea-Beef, EC-Asbestos and EC-Sardines', *Journal of World Trade*, 37/1, 199-233.

Neumayer E., 'Greening the WTO Agreements – Can the Treaty Establishing the European Community be of Guidance?', 35 *Journal of World Trade* 145 (2001).

National Research Council (NRC), *Risk Assessment in the Federal Government: Managing the Process*, Washington, D.C.: National Academy Press, 1983.

Ni Chaoimh E., 'Trading in Precaution – A Comparative Study of the Precautionary jurisprudence of the European Court and the WTO's Adjudicating Body', 33(2) *Legal Issues of Economic Integration* 139-165 (2006).

Noiville C., 'EU Food Safety Pattern and the WTO', C. Ansell and D. Vogel (eds), *What's the Beef? The Contested Governance of European Food Safety* (MIT Press, 2006).

Noiville C. and De Sadeleer N., 'La Gestion des Risques Ecologiques et Sanitaires à l'Epreuve des Chiffres – Le Droit entre Enjeux Scientifiques et Politiques', *Revue du Droit de l'Union Européenne*, 2/2001.

Noiville C., 'Le Principe de Précaution, Quel Avenir ?', *Les Cahiers Français* (La Documentation Française, février 2002).

Noiville C., 'La Convention de Rio et ses Relations avec l'Accord de l'OMC sur les Aspects des Droits de Propriété Intellectuelle Touchant au Commerce. Une Analyse Juridique de l'Outil Economique', S. Maljean-Dubois (ed), *Outils Juridiques et Outils Economiques : Collaboration et Combinaison pour la Protection de l'Environnement* (La Documentation Française, février 2002).

Noiville C., 'Principe de Précaution et Organisation Mondiale du Commerce. Le Cas du Commerce Alimentaire', *Journal du Droit International*, 2000/2, pp 263 ss.

Noiville C., 'Le Principe de Précaution et la Gestion des Risques en Droit de l'Environnement et en Droit de la Santé', in *Le Principe de précaution*, Colloque Sénat, 10 décembre 1999, Les Petites Affiches, numéro spécial, 30 novembre 2000, pp 39 pp ss.

Notaro N., *Judicial Approaches to Trade and the Environment: The EC and the WTO* (London, Cameron May International Law Publishers, 2003).

Oesch M., *Standards of Review in WTO Dispute Resolution* (Oxford University Press, 2003).

O'Riordan T., Cameron J. and Jordan A., *Reinterpreting the Precautionary Principle* (London, Cameron May, 2001).

O'Rourke R., *EC Food Law*, 1st ed., 1998.

O'Rourke R., *EC Food Law*, 3rd ed., 2005.

Ortino F., *Basic Legal Instruments for the Liberalization of Trade* (Oxford and Portland Oregon, 2004).

Otsuki, T., Wilson J., and Sewadeh M., 'Saving Two in a Billion: Quantifying the Trade Effect of European Food Safety Standards on African Exports"', 26 *Food Policy* 5, (2002) pp 495-514.

Palmenter D., 'The WTO Standard of Review in Health and Safety Disputes', G. Bermann and P.C. Mavroidis, *Trade and Human Health and Safety* (Cambridge University Press, 2006).

Pardo Quintillán S., 'Free Trade, Public Health Protection and Consumer Information in the European and WTO Context', 33 *Journal of World Trade* 147 (1999).

Patterson E., 'International Efforts to Minimize the Adverse Effects of National Sanitary and Phytosanitary Regulation', 24 *Journal of World Trade L.* 91 (1990).

Pauwelyn J., 'Expert Advice in WTO Dispute Settlement', G. Bermann and P.C. Mavroidis, *Trade and Human Health and Safety* (Cambridge University Press, 2006).

Pauwelyn, J., 'The use of experts in WTO Dispute Settlement', *International and Comparative Law Quartely* 51, 325 (2002).

Pauwelyn J., 'Evidence, proof and persuasion in WTO Dispute Settlement, who bears the burden?', *Journal of International Economic Law*, 1, 227 (1998).

Peel J., 'Risk Regulation Under the WTO SPS Agreement: Science as an International Normative Yardstick?', *Jean Monnet Working Paper*, 02/04, NYU School of Law.

Pescatore P., 'Some Critical Remarks on the European Single Act', 9 *Common Market Law Review* (1987).

Pelkmans J., 'The New Approach to Technical Harmonisation and Standardization', *Journal of Common Market Studies*, 1987, pp 249 ss.

Petersmann E.U. (ed), *International Trade Law and the GATT/WTO Dispute Settlement System* (Kluwer, 1997).

Picone P. and Ligustro A., *Diritto dell'Organizzazione Mondiale del Commercio* (Padova, Cedam, 2004).

Picone P. and Sacerdoti G., *Diritto internazionale dell'economia*, (Milano, Franco Angeli, 1982).

Poiares Maduro M., *We the Court* (Hart Publishing, Portland, 1999).

Poli S., 'The Adoption of International Food Safety Standards', *European Law Journal*, Vol. 10, no. 5, September 2004, p. 615.

Pollack M. and Shaffer G., *Transatlantic Governance in the Global Economy*, (Lanham, MD, 2001).

Priess H.J. and Pitschas C., 'Protection of Public Health and the Role of the Precautionary Principle under WTO law', 24 *Fordham International Law Review*, 519 (2000).

Puoti P., 'Libera Circolazione delle Merci nei Sistemi CE e GATT/WTO e Sicurezza Alimentare: il Ruole dell'Armonizzazione', in *Scritti in memoria di Mario Buoncristiano*, (Napoli, Jovene, 2002), vol. II, pp 1105 ss.

Quick R. and Bluthner A., 'Has the Appellate Body erred? An Appraisal and Criticism of the Ruling in the WTO Hormones Case', 3 *Journal of International Economic Law* 603 (1999).

Radicati di Bronzolo L., 'Un Primo Confronto tra la Liberalizzazione delle Telecomunicazioni nel Sistema del WTO e della Comunità Europea', in *SIDI* (Società Italiana di Diritto Internazionale), Diritto ed Organizzazione del Commercio Internazionale dopo la Creazione della Organizzazione Mondiale del Commercio, (Milano, Editoriale Scientifica, 1998).

Raimondi L., 'Mediatore Europeo e Mezzi di Ricorso Giurisdizionale', *Il Diritto dell'Unione europea*, 2004, pp 547 ss.

Rakoff, T.D., Strauss P.L. and Farina C.R., *Gellhorn and Byse's Administrative Law: Cases and Comments*, (Foundation Press 10th and rev. 10th ed. 2003).

Randall E., 'Policy and Plans: Formulating a Food Safety and Public Policy Strategy for the Union', (2001), available at http://www.policylibrary.com/Essays/RandallEFARisk/ EFArisk2.htm

Rascoff S.J., 'The Biases of Risk Tradeoff Analysis: Towards Parity in Environmental and Health Safety Regulation', 69 *Chicago Law Review* (2002) 1763.

Reisman M., 'Designing Law Curricula for a Transnational Industrial and Science-Based Civilization', 46 *Journal of Legal Education* 322 (1996).

Riemenschneider C., 'A Meeting of the Codex Alimentarius Commission', 5 *FDLI Update*, 3, (1999).

Rivera-Torres O., 'The Biosafety Protocol and the WTO', 26 *Boston College International & Comparative Law Review* (1999).

Roberts D., 'Preliminary Assessment of the Effects of the WTO Agreement on Sanitary and Phytosanitary Trade Regulations', 1 *Journal of International Economic Law* 377 (1998).

Roda I.S., 'La Autoridad Alimentaria Europea: la Problematica Eficacia de una Nueva Agencia Comunitaria para la Protección de los Consumidores', *Comunidad Europea Aranzadi*, 11, 2001, pp 29 ss.

Romero Melchor S, 'La Futura Agencia Europea para los Alimentos: ¿ un Organismo sin Autoridad?', *Gaceta iuridica de la UE*, 212, Marzo/Abril 2001.

Rosamond B., *Theories of European Integration*, (New York, 2000).

Rossolini R., *Libera Circolazione degli Alimenti e Tutela della Salute nel Diritto Comunitario* (Padova, Cedam, 2004).

Ruckeshaus W. D., 'Risk, Science and Democracy', *Issues Sci. & Tech.*, Spring 1985.

Sacerdoti G., 'La Trasformazione del GATT nell'Organizzazione Mondiale del Commercio', *Diritto del Commercio Internazionale* 1995.

Sacerdoti G., 'The World Trade Organisation enlarged competence: from standard setting to implementation', *Contemporary international law issues: conflicts and convergence*, 1996, pp 227-229.

Sacerdoti G., 'Standards of Treatment, Harmonization and Mutual Recognition: a Comparison between Regional Areas and the Global trading system', in P. Demaret, J.-F. Bellis and G. García Jiménez (eds), *Regionalism and Multilateralism after the Uruguay Round : Convergence, Divergence and Interaction* (Brussels, European Interuniversity Press, 1997) pp 613-629.

Sacerdoti G., Profili Istituzionali dell'OMC e Principi Base degli Accordi di Settore, in Società Italiana di Diritto Internazionale, Diritto e organizzazione del Commercio Internazionale dopo la Creazione della Organizzazione mondiale del Commercio (Editoriale Scientifica, Napoli 1998).

Sacerdoti G., Yanovich A. and J. Bohanes, *The WTO at Ten: the contribution of the WTO Dispute Settlement System* (Cambridge: Cambridge University Press, 2006).

Sacerdoti G., 'The Dispute Settlement System of the WTO: structure and function in the perspective of the first 10 years', *The Law and Practice of International Courts and Tribunal*, Vol. 5, 2006, pp 49-76.

Sagarika S., 'Methanex Corporation and the USA: The Final NAFTA Tribunal Ruling', *Review of European Community & International Environmental Law* 15 (1), pp 110-114 (2006).

Salmon N., 'A European Perspective on the Precautionary principle, Food Safety and the Free Trade Imperative of the WTO' 27 *European Law Review* 138 (2002).

Schipper G.H., 'Herstel Consumentenvertrouwen en niet de Interne Markt Stond Centraal', *VMT* 18 Dec. 1997, No. 26-27.

Schlosser E., *Fast Food Nation, The dark side of the All-American Meal,* (Perennial ed., 2002).

Silbergeld E., 'The Uses and Abuses of Scientific Uncertainty in Risk Assessment', *Nat. Resources & Env't*, Fall 1986.

Scott J., 'Of Kith and Kine (and Crustaceans): Trade and Environment' in the EU and WTO, J.H.H. Weiler (ed.), *The EU, NAFTA and the WTO: Towards a Common Law of International Trade* (Oxford, OUP, 2000).

Scott J. and Vos E., 'The Juridification of Uncertainty: Observations of the Ambivalence of the Precautionary Principle within the EU and the WTO', in Joerges C. and Dehousse R., *Good Governance in Europe's Integrated Market* (Oxford University Press, 2002).

Scott J., 'European Regulation of GMOs: Thinking about Judicial Review in the WTO', *Jean Monnet Working Paper* 04/04.

Scott J., 'GATT and Community Law: Rethinking the 'Regulatory Gap', J. Shaw and G. More (eds), *New Legal Dynamics of EU*, 1995, pp 147 ss.

Scott J., 'Mandatory or Imperative Requirements in the EU and the WTO', C. Barnard and J. Scott, *The Law of the Single European Market: Unpacking the Premises* (Oxford, Hart Publishing, 2002).

Segnana O., 'The Precautionary Principle: New Developments in the Case Law of the Court of First Instance', 3 *German Law Journal* No. 10 (1 October 2002) available at germanlawjournal.com

Shaffer G.C. & Pollack M.A., 'Les Différentes Approches de la Sécurité Alimentaire', in J. Bourrinet & F. Snyder, *La Sécurité Aliméntaire dans l'Union Européenne*, pp 34 ss. (Bruxelles, Bruylant, 2003).

Shaffer G., 'Reconciling Trade and Regulatory Goals: the Prospects and Limits of New Approaches to Transatlantic Governance trough Mutual Recognition and Safe Harbor Agreements', *The Columbia Law Journal of European Law* 55 (2002).

Shapiro M., 'The Frontiers of Science Doctrine: American Experiences with the Judicial Control of Science-Based Decision-Making' in C. Joerges, H. Ladeur and E. Vos (eds), *Integrating Scientific Expertise into Regulatory Decision-Making* (Oxford, Hart, 1997).

Shaw J. and More G. (eds), *New Legal Dynamics of EU*, 1995.

Shears P., Zollers F.E. and Hurd S.N., 'The European Food Safety Authority. Towards coherence in food safety policy and practice', 106 *British Food Journal* 336-352 (2004).

Sikes L., 'FDA's Consideration of Codex Alimentarius Standards in Light of International Trade Agreements', 53 *Food & Drug L.J.* 327 (1998).

Simon D., *Le Système Juridique Communautaire* (PUF, 2001).

Skogstad G., 'The WTO and Food Safety Regulatory Policy Innovation in the European Union', 39 *Journal of Common Market Studies* 485, 490 (2001).

Slotboom M.M., 'The Hormones case: an Increased Risk of illegality of Sanitary and Phytosanitary Measures', *CMLR* 36, 471-491.

Slotboom M.M., 'Do Public Health Measures Receive Similar Treatment in European Community and World Trade Organisation Law?', *Journal of World Trade* (2003) 553.

Slotboom M.M., *A Comparison of WTO and EC Law* (London, Cameron May Ltd, 2006).

Snyder F., 'A Regulatory Framework for Foodstuffs in the Internal Market', *EUI Working Paper LAW* 94/4, Florence, 1994.

Spamann H., 'Standard of Review for World Trade Organisation Panels in Trade Remedy Cases: A Critical Analysis', 38 *Journal of World Trade* (2004).

Stephenson S.M., 'Mutual Recognition and its Role in Trade Facilitation', *Journal of World Trade*, 141 (1999).

Stern P. and Fineberg H. (eds), *Understanding Risk: Informing Decisions in a Democratic Society* (National Academy Press, Washington DC, 1996).

Stewart T.P. and Johanson D.S., 'The SPS Agreement of the World Trade Organization and International Organizations: The Roles of the Codex Alimentarius Commission, the International Plant Protection Convention, and the International Office of Epizootics', 26 *Syracuse J Int'l L & Com.* 27 (1998).

Stewart T.P. and Karpel A.A., 'Review of the Dispute Settlement Understanding: Operation of Panels', 31 *Law & Pol'y Intl Bus* 593 (2000).

Stumberg R., *WTO impact on State Law: California*, Center for Policy Alternatives, 2 (1994).

Suezenauer I., Tamplin M., Buchanan B., Dennis S., Tollefson L., Hart A., 'Briefing Paper: US Experience', *European Workshop on the interface between Risk Assessment and Risk Management*, 2003 available at http://www.ra-rm.com

Sunstein C.R., *Laws of Fear: Beyond the Precautionary Principle* (Cambridge University Press, 2005).

Sunstein C.R., *Risk and Reason* (Cambridge University Press, 2002).

Sykes A.O., 'Domestic Regulation, Sovereignty and Scientific Evidence Requirements: A Pessimistic View', 3 *Chicago J. Int'l L.* 353 (2002).

Sykes A.O., 'Regulatory Protectionism and the Law of International Trade', 66 *University of Chicago Law Review*, 1 (1999).

Sykes A.O., *Products Standards for Internationally Integrated Goods Markets* (Washington, DC: Brookings, 1995).

Szawloska C., 'Risk Assessment in the European Food Safety Regulation: Who is to decide Whose Science is Better? Commission v. France and Beyond ...', 5 *German Law Journal* No. 10 (1 October 2004) – European & International Law.

Tancredi A., 'EC Practice in the WTO: How Wide is the "Scope for Manoeuvre"', 15 *European Journal of International Law* 5 (2004).

Testori Coggi P., Conference on Risk Perception: Science, Public Debate and Policy Making, Speaking Notes, Brussels, Dec. 2003 available at http://europa.eu.int /comm/food/risk_ perception /sp/testori_coggi. pdf

Tinbergen J., *International Economic Integration*, 2ed, 1965.

Tizzano A., Il Codice dell'Unione Europea: con il Testo della Costituzione per l'Europa (Padova, Cedam, 2005).

Thomas R.D., 'Where's the Beef? Mad Cows and the Blight of the SPS Agreement', 32 *Vanderbilt Journal of Transnational Law* 487 (1999).

Trachtman J.P, FDI and the Right to Regulate, in The Development Dimension of FDI: Policy and Rule-Making Perspectives, UNCTAD, Proceedings of the Experts meeting held in Geneva from 6 to 8 November 2002, pp 200 ss.

Trachtman J.P., 'The World Trading System, the International Legal System and Multilevel Choice', 12 *European Law Journal* 469 (2006).

Trebilcock M. and Howse R., *The Regulation of International Trade* (London-New York, Routdlege, 1999).

Valverde J.L., Piqueras Garcia A.J., Cabezas Lopez M.D., 'La Nouvelle Approche en Matière de Santé des Consommateurs et de Sécurité Alimentaire : la Nécessité d'une Agence Européenne de Sécurité des Aliments', *Revue du Marché Unique Européenne*, 1997, n. 4, pp 31 ss.

van Asselt M. and Vos E., 'The Paradox of the Precautionary Principle', in *Risk Analysis*, 2004.

van den Bossche P., *The Law and Policy of the World Trade Organization, Text, Cases and Materials* (Cambridge University Press, 2005).

van den Daele W., 'Scientific Evidence and the Regulation of Technical Risks: Twenty Years of Demythologizing the Experts', in N. Stehr and V. Ericson (eds), *The Culture of Power Knowledge. Inquiries into Contemporary Society* (Walter de Gruyter, Berlin/New York, 1992).

van der Haegen T., *EU View of Precautionary Principle in Food Safety*, American Branch of the International Law Association, New York, Oct. 23-25, 2003.

van der Heijden, *The Scientific Committee for Food: Procedures and Program for European Food Safety*, 1992, Food Technology, 102-6.

Veggeland F. and Borgen S.O., *Changing the Codex: The Role of International Institutions*, Norwegian Agricultural Economics Research Institute, Oslo (January 2002).

Vellano M., *L'Organo d'Appello dell'OMC* (Jovene, Napoli, 2001).

Verheyen R., 'The Environmental Guarantee in European Law and the New Article 95 EC in practice – A Critique', *RECIEL*, 1/2000, 180.

Viale B., 'En Réponse à la Crise de la Vache Folle, Plaidoyer en Faveur d'une Politique Communautaire de l'Alimentation', *Revue du droit rural*, n 251, mars 1997, pp 158 ss.

Victor D.G., 'The Sanitary and Phytosanitary Agreement of the World Trade Organisation: An Assessment After Five Years', 32 *NYUJ Int' L. & P.* 865 (2000).

Vincent K., 'Mad Cows and Eurocrats – Community Responses to the BSE Crisis', 10 *European Law Journal* 517 (2004).

Viscusi, K., 'Risk – Safety at any price?', 25 *Regulation*, 54 (2002).

Vogel D., Trading Up, *Consumer and Environmental Regulation in a Global Economy* 156 (Harvard University Press 1995).

Vogel D., *Risk Regulation in Europe and in the United States, Yearbook of European Environmental Law*, Vol. III (Oxford University Press, 2003).

Vogel D., 'The Politics of Risk Regulation in Europe and the United States', 3 *Yearbook of European Environmental Law* 1.

Vogel D., 'The Hare and the Tortoise Revisited: The New Politics of Consumer and Environmental Regulation in Europe', *British Journal of Political Science*, 33, 4, pp 557-580.

Von Heydebrand H.C. and Lasa U.D., 'Free Movement of Foodstuffs, Consumer Protection and food standards in the EC: Has the Court got it wrong?', 16 *EL.Rev.* 391 (1991).

Vos E., 'Reforming the European Commission: What Role to Play for EU Agencies', 37 *CMLRev.* 1113 (2000).

Vos E., 'EU Food Safety Regulation in the Aftermath of the BSE Crisis', 23 *Journal of Consumer Policy* 233 (2000).

Vos E., *Institutional Frameworks of the Community Health and Safety Regulation. Committees, Agencies and Private Bodies* (Oxford Hart Publishing, 1999).

Vos E., 'Mondialisation et Régulation-Cadre des Marches – Le Principe de Précaution et le Droit Alimentaire de l'Union Européenne', 2-3 *Revue International de Droit Economique*, 219 (2002).

Vos E., 'The Precautionary Principle Reviewed: the Judgements of the Court of First Instance of 11 September 2002 Concerning the EU Ban of Two Antibiotics', *Journal of Risk Research* 7, 2004.

Zarrilli, S. 'International Trade in GMOs and GM Products: National and Multilateral Legal Frameworks, Policy Issues in International Trade and Commodities', *Study Series* No. 29, UNCTAD.

Zarrilli S., *WTO Agreement on Sanitary and Phytosanitary Measures: Issues for Developing Countries*, South Centre, Geneva, 1999.

Zarrilli S. and Kinnon C., (eds), *International Trade in Health Services: a Development Perspective* (United Nations and WHO, Geneva, 1998).

Wagner M.J., 'The WTO's Interpretation of the SPS Agreement has undermined the Right of Governments to Establish Appropriate Levels of Protection Against Risk', (2000) 31 *Law and Policy in International Business* 855.

Walker, V.R., 'Consistent Levels of protection in International Trade Disputes: Using Risk Perception Research to Justify Difference Levels of Acceptable Risk', 31 *Environmental Law Review* 11317 (2001).

Walker, V.R., 'The Myth of Science as a "Neutral Arbiter" for triggering Precautions,' 26 *Boston College International and Comparative Law Review* 197.

Walker V.R., 'Keeping the WTO from Becoming the "World Trans-Science organization": Scientific Uncertainty, Science Policy, and Factfinding in the Growth Hormones Dispute', 31 *Cornell international Law Journal* 251 (1998).

Walker V.R., 'Risk Regulation and the "Faces" of Uncertainty' 9 *Risk: Health, Safety & Environment* 27, Winter 1998.

Weatherill S. and Beaumont P., *EU Law* (Penguin Books, 3rd edition,1999).

Weiler J.H.H., *The Constitution of Europe* (Cambridge University Press, 1999).

Weiler J.H.H., 'The Transformation of Europe', 100 *Yale Law Journal* 2403.

Weiler J.H.H., 'The Constitution of the Common Market Place: Text and Context in the Evolution of Free Movement of Goods', in P. Craig and G. De Burca (eds), *The Evolution of EU Law* (OUP Oxford 1999) pp 349 ss.

Weiler J.H.H., 'Cain and Abel – Convergence and Divergence in International Trade Law', in J.H.H. Weiler (ed.), *The EU, the WTO, and the NAFTA, Towards a Common Law of International Trade?* (Oxford University Press, 2000).

Weiler J.H.H., 'Epilogue: "Comitology" as Revolution—Infranationalism, Constitutionalism and Democracy' in C. Joerges and E. Vos (eds), *EU Committees: Social Regulation, Law and Politics*, pp 339 ss.

Weinberg A., 'Science and Transcience', 10 *Minerva* 209, 222 (1972).

Welch D., 'From "Euro Beer" to "Newcastle Brown", A Review of European Community Action to Dismantle Divergent "Food Laws"' (1983-4) 22 *Journal of Common Market Studies* 57.

White G., 'The Use of Experts by the International Court', V. Lowe and M. Fitzmaurice (eds), *Fifty years of the International Court of Justice, Essays in Honour of Sir Robert Jennings* (Cambridge University Press, 2005).

Wiener J.B., 'Whose Precaution After All? A Comment on the Comparison and Evolution of Risk Regulatory Systems', 13 *Duke Journal of Comparative and International Law* 207 (2003).

Wiener J.B. and Rogers M.D., 'Comparing Precaution in the United States and Europe', *Journal of Risk Research* 5(4), 317-349 (2002).

Wiers J., *Trade and the Environment in the EC and in the WTO: A Legal Analysis*, (Groningen, Europa Law Publishing, 2002).

Wildavsky A., *Searching for Safety* 3rd ed., (Transaction, 1989).

Winter G. (ed), *Risk Assessment and Risk Management of Toxic Chemicals in the EC*, (Baden-Baden, Nomos, 2000).

Wirth, D.A., 'The Role of Science in the Uruguay Round and NAFTA Trade Disciplines' *Cornell International Law Journal*, Vol. 27, pp 817-859, (1994).

Wolf S., 'Risk Regulation, Higher Rationality, and The Death of Judicial Self-Restraint: A Comment on Ladeur', 41 *Common Market Law Review* 1175-1180 (2004).

Wynne B., 'Establishing the Rules of Laws: Constructing Expert Authority', R. Smith and B. Wynne (eds), *Expert Evidence: Interpreting Science in the Law* (London, Routledge, 1989).

Selected Articles from the Consolidated Version

of the Treaty Establishing the European Community

[...]

PRINCIPLES

Article 1

By this Treaty, the HIGH CONTRACTING PARTIES establish among themselves a EUROPEAN COMMUNITY.

Article 2

The Community shall have as its task, by establishing a common market and an economic and monetary union and by implementing common policies or activities referred to in Articles 3 and 4, to promote throughout the Community a harmonious, balanced and sustainable development of economic activities, a high level of employment and of social protection, equality between men and women, sustainable and non-inflationary growth, a high degree of competitiveness and convergence of economic performance, a high level of protection and improvement of the quality of the environment, the raising of the standard of living and quality of life, and economic and social cohesion and solidarity among Member States.

Article 3

1. For the purposes set out in Article 2, the activities of the Community shall include, as provided in this Treaty and in accordance with the timetable set out therein:

(a)   the prohibition, as between Member States, of customs duties and quantitative restrictions on the import and export of goods, and of all other measures having equivalent effect;

(b)   a common commercial policy;

(c)   an internal market characterised by the abolition, as between Member States, of obstacles to the free movement of goods, persons, services and capital;

(d)   measures concerning the entry and movement of persons as provided for in Title IV;

(e)   a common policy in the sphere of agriculture and fisheries;

(f)   a common policy in the sphere of transport;

(g)   a system ensuring that competition in the internal market is not distorted;

(h)   the approximation of the laws of Member States to the extent required for the functioning of the common market;

(i)   the promotion of coordination between employment policies of the Member States with a view to enhancing their effectiveness by developing a coordinated strategy for employment;

(j)   a policy in the social sphere comprising a European Social Fund;

(k)   the strengthening of economic and social cohesion;

(l)   a policy in the sphere of the environment;

(m)   the strengthening of the competitiveness of Community industry;

(n)   the promotion of research and technological development;

(o)   encouragement for the establishment and development of trans-European networks;

(p)   a contribution to the attainment of a high level of health protection;

(q)   a contribution to education and training of quality and to the flowering of the cultures of the Member States;

(r)   a policy in the sphere of development cooperation;

(s)   the association of the overseas countries and territories in order to increase trade and promote jointly economic and social development;

(t)   a contribution to the strengthening of consumer protection;

(u)   measures in the spheres of energy, civil protection and tourism.

2.   In all the activities referred to in this Article, the Community shall aim to eliminate inequalities, and to promote equality, between men and women.

[...]

Article 5

The Community shall act within the limits of the powers conferred upon it by this Treaty and of the objectives assigned to it therein.

In areas which do not fall within its exclusive competence, the Community shall take action, in accordance with the principle of subsidiarity, only if and in so far as the objectives of the proposed action cannot be sufficiently achieved by the Member States and can therefore, by reason of the scale or effects of the proposed action, be better achieved by the Community.

Any action by the Community shall not go beyond what is necessary to achieve the objectives of this Treaty.

Article 6

Environmental protection requirements must be integrated into the definition and implementation of the Community policies and activities referred to in Article 3, in particular with a view to promoting sustainable development.

Article 7

1. The tasks entrusted to the Community shall be carried out by the following institutions:

− a EUROPEAN PARLIAMENT,

− a COUNCIL,

− a COMMISSION,

− a COURT OF JUSTICE,

− a COURT OF AUDITORS.

Each institution shall act within the limits of the powers conferred upon it by this Treaty.

2. The Council and the Commission shall be assisted by an Economic and Social Committee and a Committee of the Regions acting in an advisory capacity.

[…]

Article 10

Member States shall take all appropriate measures, whether general or particular, to ensure fulfilment of the obligations arising out of this Treaty or resulting from action taken by the institutions of the Community. They shall facilitate the achievement of the Community's tasks.

They shall abstain from any measure which could jeopardise the attainment of the objectives of this Treaty.

[…]

Article 14

[…]

2. The internal market shall comprise an area without internal frontiers in which the free movement of goods, persons, services and capital is ensured in accordance with the provisions of this Treaty.

3. The Council, acting by a qualified majority on a proposal from the Commission, shall determine the guidelines and conditions necessary to ensure balanced progress in all the sectors concerned.

[…]

FREE MOVEMENT OF GOODS

Article 23

1. The Community shall be based upon a customs union which shall cover all trade in goods and which shall involve the prohibition between Member States of customs duties on imports and exports and of all charges having equivalent effect, and the adoption of a common customs tariff in their relations with third countries.

2. The provisions of Article 25 and of Chapter 2 of this title shall apply to products originating in Member States and to products coming from third countries which are in free circulation in Member States.

Article 24

Products coming from a third country shall be considered to be in free circulation in a Member State if the import formalities have been complied with and any customs duties or charges having equivalent effect which are payable have been levied in that Member State, and if they have not benefited from a total or partial drawback of such duties or charges.

THE CUSTOMS UNION

Article 25

Customs duties on imports and exports and charges having equivalent effect shall be prohibited between Member States. This prohibition shall also apply to customs duties of a fiscal nature.

Article 26

Common Customs Tariff duties shall be fixed by the Council acting by a qualified majority on a proposal from the Commission.

Article 27

In carrying out the tasks entrusted to it under this chapter the Commission shall be guided by:

(a)   the need to promote trade between Member States and third countries;

(b)   developments in conditions of competition within the Community in so far as they lead to an improvement in the competitive capacity of undertakings;

(c)   the requirements of the Community as regards the supply of raw materials and semi-finished goods; in this connection the Commission shall take care to avoid distorting conditions of competition between Member States in respect of finished goods;

(d)   the need to avoid serious disturbances in the economies of Member States and to ensure rational development of production and an expansion of consumption within the Community.

PROHIBITION OF QUANTITATIVE RESTRICTIONS BETWEEN MEMBER STATES

Article 28

Quantitative restrictions on imports and all measures having equivalent effect shall be prohibited between Member States.

Article 29

Quantitative restrictions on exports, and all measures having equivalent effect, shall be prohibited between Member States.

Article 30

The provisions of Articles 28 and 29 shall not preclude prohibitions or restrictions on imports, exports or goods in transit justified on grounds of public morality, public policy or public security; the protection of health and life of humans, animals or plants; the protection of national treasures possessing artistic, historic or archaeological value; or the protection of industrial and commercial property. Such prohibitions or restrictions shall not, however, constitute a means of arbitrary discrimination or a disguised restriction on trade between Member States.

[…]

AGRICULTURE

Article 32

1.   The common market shall extend to agriculture and trade in agricultural products. "Agricultural products" means the products of the soil, of stockfarming and of fisheries and products of first-stage processing directly related to these products.

2.   Save as otherwise provided in Articles 33 to 38, the rules laid down for the establishment of the common market shall apply to agricultural products.

3.   The products subject to the provisions of Articles 33 to 38 are listed in Annex I to this Treaty.

4.   The operation and development of the common market for agricultural products must be accompanied by the establishment of a common agricultural policy.

Article 33

1.   The objectives of the common agricultural policy shall be:

(a)   to increase agricultural productivity by promoting technical progress and by ensuring the rational development of agricultural production and the optimum utilisation of the factors of production, in particular labour;

(b)   thus to ensure a fair standard of living for the agricultural community, in particular by increasing the individual earnings of persons engaged in agriculture;

(c)   to stabilise markets;

(d)   to assure the availability of supplies;

(e)   to ensure that supplies reach consumers at reasonable prices.

2.   In working out the common agricultural policy and the special methods for its application, account shall be taken of:

(a)   the particular nature of agricultural activity, which results from the social structure of agriculture and from structural and natural disparities between the various agricultural regions;

(b)   the need to effect the appropriate adjustments by degrees;

(c)   the fact that in the Member States agriculture constitutes a sector closely linked with the economy as a whole.

Article 34

1.   In order to attain the objectives set out in Article 33, a common organisation of agricultural markets shall be established.

This organisation shall take one of the following forms, depending on the product concerned:

(a)   common rules on competition;

(b)   compulsory coordination of the various national market organisations;

(c)   a European market organisation.

2.   The common organisation established in accordance with paragraph 1 may include all measures required to attain the objectives set out in Article 33, in particular regulation of prices, aids for the production and marketing of the various products, storage and carryover arrangements and common machinery for stabilising imports or exports.

The common organisation shall be limited to pursuit of the objectives set out in Article 33 and shall exclude any discrimination between producers or consumers within the Community.

Any common price policy shall be based on common criteria and uniform methods of calculation.

3.   In order to enable the common organisation referred to in paragraph 1 to attain its objectives, one or more agricultural guidance and guarantee funds may be set up.

[....]

Article 37

1.   In order to evolve the broad lines of a common agricultural policy, the Commission shall, immediately this Treaty enters into force, convene a conference of the Member States with a view to making a comparison of their agricultural policies, in particular by producing a statement of their resources and needs.

2.   Having taken into account the work of the Conference provided for in paragraph 1, after consulting the Economic and Social Committee and within two years of the entry into force of this Treaty, the Commission shall submit proposals for working out and implementing the common

agricultural policy, including the replacement of the national organisations by one of the forms of common organisation provided for in Article 34(1), and for implementing the measures specified in this title.

These proposals shall take account of the interdependence of the agricultural matters mentioned in this title.

The Council shall, on a proposal from the Commission and after consulting the European Parliament, acting by a qualified majority, make regulations, issue directives, or take decisions, without prejudice to any recommendations it may also make.

3. The Council may, acting by a qualified majority and in accordance with paragraph 2, replace the national market organisations by the common organisation provided for in Article 34(1) if:

(a)   the common organisation offers Member States which are opposed to this measure and which have an organisation of their own for the production in question equivalent safeguards for the employment and standard of living of the producers concerned, account being taken of the adjustments that will be possible and the specialisation that will be needed with the passage of time;

(b)   such an organisation ensures conditions for trade within the Community similar to those existing in a national market.

4. If a common organisation for certain raw materials is established before a common organisation exists for the corresponding processed products, such raw materials as are used for processed products intended for export to third countries may be imported from outside the Community.

Article 38

Where in a Member State a product is subject to a national market organisation or to internal rules having equivalent effect which affect the competitive position of similar production in another Member State, a countervailing charge shall be applied by Member States to imports of this product coming from the Member State where such organisation or rules exist, unless that State applies a countervailing charge on export.

The Commission shall fix the amount of these charges at the level required to redress the balance; it may also authorise other measures, the conditions and details of which it shall determine.

[...]

APPROXIMATION OF LAWS

Article 94

The Council shall, acting unanimously on a proposal from the Commission and after consulting the European Parliament and the Economic and Social Committee, issue directives for the approximation of such laws, regulations or administrative provisions of the Member States as directly affect the establishment or functioning of the common market.

Article 95

1. By way of derogation from Article 94 and save where otherwise provided in this Treaty, the following provisions shall apply for the achievement of the objectives set out in Article 14. The Council shall, acting in accordance with the procedure referred to in Article 251 and after consulting the Economic and Social Committee, adopt the measures for the approximation of the provisions laid down by law, regulation or administrative action in Member States which have as their object the establishment and functioning of the internal market.

2. Paragraph 1 shall not apply to fiscal provisions, to those relating to the free movement of persons nor to those relating to the rights and interests of employed persons.

3. The Commission, in its proposals envisaged in paragraph 1 concerning health, safety, environmental protection and consumer protection, will take as a base a high level of protection, taking account in particular of any new development based on scientific facts. Within their respective powers, the European Parliament and the Council will also seek to achieve this objective.

4. If, after the adoption by the Council or by the Commission of a harmonisation measure, a Member State deems it necessary to maintain national provisions on grounds of major needs referred to in Article 30, or relating to the protection of the environment or the working environment, it shall notify the Commission of these provisions as well as the grounds for maintaining them.

5. Moreover, without prejudice to paragraph 4, if, after the adoption by the Council or by the Commission of a harmonisation measure, a Member State deems it necessary to introduce national provisions based on new scientific evidence relating to the protection of the environment or the working environment on grounds of a problem specific to that Member State arising after the adoption of the harmonisation measure, it shall notify the Commission of the envisaged provisions as well as the grounds for introducing them.

6.   The Commission shall, within six months of the notifications as referred to in paragraphs 4 and 5, approve or reject the national provisions involved after having verified whether or not they are a means of arbitrary discrimination or a disguised restriction on trade between Member States and whether or not they shall constitute an obstacle to the functioning of the internal market.

In the absence of a decision by the Commission within this period the national provisions referred to in paragraphs 4 and 5 shall be deemed to have been approved.

When justified by the complexity of the matter and in the absence of danger for human health, the Commission may notify the Member State concerned that the period referred to in this paragraph may be extended for a further period of up to six months.

7.   When, pursuant to paragraph 6, a Member State is authorised to maintain or introduce national provisions derogating from a harmonisation measure, the Commission shall immediately examine whether to propose an adaptation to that measure.

8.   When a Member State raises a specific problem on public health in a field which has been the subject of prior harmonisation measures, it shall bring it to the attention of the Commission which shall immediately examine whether to propose appropriate measures to the Council.

9.   By way of derogation from the procedure laid down in Articles 226 and 227, the Commission and any Member State may bring the matter directly before the Court of Justice if it considers that another Member State is making improper use of the powers provided for in this Article.

10.   The harmonisation measures referred to above shall, in appropriate cases, include a safeguard clause authorising the Member States to take, for one or more of the non-economic reasons referred to in Article 30, provisional measures subject to a Community control procedure.

[…]

COMMON COMMERCIAL POLICY

Article 131

By establishing a customs union between themselves Member States aim to contribute, in the common interest, to the harmonious development of world trade, the progressive abolition of restrictions on international trade and the lowering of customs barriers.

The common commercial policy shall take into account the favourable effect which the abolition of customs duties between Member States may have on the increase in the competitive strength of undertakings in those States.

Article 132

1.   Without prejudice to obligations undertaken by them within the framework of other international organisations, Member States shall progressively harmonise the systems whereby they grant aid for exports to third countries, to the extent necessary to ensure that competition between undertakings of the Community is not distorted.

On a proposal from the Commission, the Council shall, acting by a qualified majority, issue any directives needed for this purpose.

2.   The preceding provisions shall not apply to such a drawback of customs duties or charges having equivalent effect nor to such a repayment of indirect taxation including turnover taxes, excise duties and other indirect taxes as is allowed when goods are exported from a Member State to a third country, in so far as such a drawback or repayment does not exceed the amount imposed, directly or indirectly, on the products exported.

Article 133

1.   The common commercial policy shall be based on uniform principles, particularly in regard to changes in tariff rates, the conclusion of tariff and trade agreements, the achievement of uniformity in measures of liberalisation, export policy and measures to protect trade such as those to be taken in the event of dumping or subsidies.

2.   The Commission shall submit proposals to the Council for implementing the common commercial policy.

3.   Where agreements with one or more States or international organisations need to be negotiated, the Commission shall make recommendations to the Council, which shall authorise the Commission to open the necessary negotiations. The Council and the Commission shall be responsible for ensuring that the agreements negotiated are compatible with internal Community policies and rules.

The Commission shall conduct these negotiations in consultation with a special committee appointed by the Council to assist the Commission in this task and within the framework of such directives as the Council may issue to it. The Commission shall report regularly to the special committee on the progress of negotiations.

The relevant provisions of Article 300 shall apply.

4.   In exercising the powers conferred upon it by this Article, the Council shall act by a qualified majority.

5.   Paragraphs 1 to 4 shall also apply to the negotiation and conclusion of agreements in the fields of trade in services and the commercial aspects

of intellectual property, in so far as those agreements are not covered by the said paragraphs and without prejudice to paragraph 6.

By way of derogation from paragraph 4, the Council shall act unanimously when negotiating and concluding an agreement in one of the fields referred to in the first subparagraph, where that agreement includes provisions for which unanimity is required for the adoption of internal rules or where it relates to a field in which the Community has not yet exercised the powers conferred upon it by this Treaty by adopting internal rules.

The Council shall act unanimously with respect to the negotiation and conclusion of a horizontal agreement insofar as it also concerns the preceding subparagraph or the second subparagraph of paragraph 6.

This paragraph shall not affect the right of the Member States to maintain and conclude agreements with third countries or international organisations in so far as such agreements comply with Community law and other relevant international agreements.

6. An agreement may not be concluded by the Council if it includes provisions which would go beyond the Community's internal powers, in particular by leading to harmonisation of the laws or regulations of the Member States in an area for which this Treaty rules out such harmonisation.

In this regard, by way of derogation from the first subparagraph of paragraph 5, agreements relating to trade in cultural and audiovisual services, educational services, and social and human health services, shall fall within the shared competence of the Community and its Member States. Consequently, in addition to a Community decision taken in accordance with the relevant provisions of Article 300, the negotiation of such agreements shall require the common accord of the Member States. Agreements thus negotiated shall be concluded jointly by the Community and the Member States.

The negotiation and conclusion of international agreements in the field of transport shall continue to be governed by the provisions of Title V and Article 300.

7. Without prejudice to the first subparagraph of paragraph 6, the Council, acting unanimously on a proposal from the Commission and after consulting the European Parliament, may extend the application of paragraphs 1 to 4 to international negotiations and agreements on intellectual property in so far as they are not covered by paragraph 5.

Article 134

In order to ensure that the execution of measures of commercial policy taken in accordance with this Treaty by any Member State is not obstructed by deflection of trade, or where differences between such measures lead to economic difficulties in one or more Member States, the Commission shall recommend the methods for the requisite cooperation between Member States. Failing this, the Commission may authorise Member States to take the necessary protective measures, the conditions and details of which it shall determine.

In case of urgency, Member States shall request authorisation to take the necessary measures themselves from the Commission, which shall take a decision as soon as possible; the Member States concerned shall then notify the measures to the other Member States. The Commission may decide at any time that the Member States concerned shall amend or abolish the measures in question.

In the selection of such measures, priority shall be given to those which cause the least disturbance of the functioning of the common market.

[...]

PUBLIC HEALTH

Article 152

1. A high level of human health protection shall be ensured in the definition and implementation of all Community policies and activities.

Community action, which shall complement national policies, shall be directed towards improving public health, preventing human illness and diseases, and obviating sources of danger to human health. Such action shall cover the fight against the major health scourges, by promoting research into their causes, their transmission and their prevention, as well as health information and education.

The Community shall complement the Member States' action in reducing drugs-related health damage, including information and prevention.

2. The Community shall encourage cooperation between the Member States in the areas referred to in this Article and, if necessary, lend support to their action.

Member States shall, in liaison with the Commission, coordinate among themselves their policies and programmes in the areas referred to in paragraph 1. The Commission may, in close contact with the Member States, take any useful initiative to promote such coordination.

3. The Community and the Member States shall foster cooperation with third countries and the competent international organisations in the sphere of public health.

4. The Council, acting in accordance with the procedure referred to in Article 251 and after consulting the Economic and Social Committee and the Committee of the Regions, shall contribute to the achievement of the objectives referred to in this article through adopting:

(a)   measures setting high standards of quality and safety of organs and substances of human origin, blood and blood derivatives; these measures shall not prevent any Member State from maintaining or introducing more stringent protective measures;

(b)   by way of derogation from Article 37, measures in the veterinary and phytosanitary fields which have as their direct objective the protection of public health;

[...]

SELECTED ARTICLES FROM THE GENERAL AGREEMENT ON TARIFFS AND TRADE

[…]

Article I

General Most-Favoured-Nation Treatment

1.   With respect to customs duties and charges of any kind imposed on or in connection with importation or exportation or imposed on the international transfer of payments for imports or exports, and with respect to the method of levying such duties and charges, and with respect to all rules and formalities in connection with importation and exportation, and with respect to all matters referred to in paragraphs 2 and 4 of Article III, any advantage, favour, privilege or immunity granted by any contracting party to any product originating in or destined for any other country shall be accorded immediately and unconditionally to the like product originating in or destined for the territories of all other contracting parties.

2.   The provisions of paragraph 1 of this Article shall not require the elimination of any preferences in respect of import duties or charges which do not exceed the levels provided for in paragraph 4 of this Article and which fall within the following descriptions:

> (*a*)   Preferences in force exclusively between two or more of the territories listed in Annex A, subject to the conditions set forth therein;

> (*b*)   Preferences in force exclusively between two or more territories which on July 1, 1939, were connected by common sovereignty or relations of protection or suzerainty and which are listed in Annexes B, C and D, subject to the conditions set forth therein;

> (*c*)   Preferences in force exclusively between the United States of America and the Republic of Cuba;

> (*d*)   Preferences in force exclusively between neighbouring countries listed in Annexes E and F.

3.   The provisions of paragraph 1 shall not apply to preferences between the countries formerly a part of the Ottoman Empire and detached from it on July 24, 1923, provided such preferences are approved under paragraph 5[1], of Article XXV which shall be applied in this respect in the light of paragraph 1 of Article XXIX.

4.   The margin of preference* on any product in respect of which a preference is permitted under paragraph 2 of this Article but is not specifically set forth as a maximum margin of preference in the appropriate Schedule annexed to this Agreement shall not exceed:

>   (*a*)   in respect of duties or charges on any product described in such Schedule, the difference between the most-favoured-nation and preferential rates provided for therein; if no preferential rate is provided for, the preferential rate shall for the purposes of this paragraph be taken to be that in force on April 10, 1947, and, if no most-favoured-nation rate is provided for, the margin shall not exceed the difference between the most-favoured-nation and preferential rates existing on April 10, 1947;

>   (*b*)   in respect of duties or charges on any product not described in the appropriate Schedule, the difference between the most-favoured-nation and preferential rates existing on April 10, 1947.

In the case of the contracting parties named in Annex G, the date of April 10, 1947, referred to in subparagraph (*a*) and (*b*) of this paragraph shall be replaced by the respective dates set forth in that Annex.

Article II

Schedules of Concessions

1.   (*a*)   Each contracting party shall accord to the commerce of the other contracting parties treatment no less favourable than that provided for in the appropriate Part of the appropriate Schedule annexed to this Agreement.

>   (*b*)   The products described in Part I of the Schedule relating to any contracting party, which are the products of territories of other

---

[1] The authentic text erroneously reads "subparagraph 5 (a)".

contracting parties, shall, on their importation into the territory to which the Schedule relates, and subject to the terms, conditions or qualifications set forth in that Schedule, be exempt from ordinary customs duties in excess of those set forth and provided therein. Such products shall also be exempt from all other duties or charges of any kind imposed on or in connection with the importation in excess of those imposed on the date of this Agreement or those directly and mandatorily required to be imposed thereafter by legislation in force in the importing territory on that date.

(c) The products described in Part II of the Schedule relating to any contracting party which are the products of territories entitled under Article I to receive preferential treatment upon importation into the territory to which the Schedule relates shall, on their importation into such territory, and subject to the terms, conditions or qualifications set forth in that Schedule, be exempt from ordinary customs duties in excess of those set forth and provided for in Part II of that Schedule. Such products shall also be exempt from all other duties or charges of any kind imposed on or in connection with importation in excess of those imposed on the date of this Agreement or those directly or mandatorily required to be imposed thereafter by legislation in force in the importing territory on that date. Nothing in this Article shall prevent any contracting party from maintaining its requirements existing on the date of this Agreement as to the eligibility of goods for entry at preferential rates of duty.

2. Nothing in this Article shall prevent any contracting party from imposing at any time on the importation of any product:

(a) a charge equivalent to an internal tax imposed consistently with the provisions of paragraph 2 of Article III* in respect of the like domestic product or in respect of an article from which the imported product has been manufactured or produced in whole or in part;

(b) any anti-dumping or countervailing duty applied consistently with the provisions of Article VI;

(c) fees or other charges commensurate with the cost of services rendered.

3. No contracting party shall alter its method of determining dutiable value or of converting currencies so as to impair the value of any of the concessions provided for in the appropriate Schedule annexed to this Agreement.

4.   If any contracting party establishes, maintains or authorizes, formally or in effect, a monopoly of the importation of any product described in the appropriate Schedule annexed to this Agreement, such monopoly shall not, except as provided for in that Schedule or as otherwise agreed between the parties which initially negotiated the concession, operate so as to afford protection on the average in excess of the amount of protection provided for in that Schedule. The provisions of this paragraph shall not limit the use by contracting parties of any form of assistance to domestic producers permitted by other provisions of this Agreement.

5.   If any contracting party considers that a product is not receiving from another contracting party the treatment which the first contracting party believes to have been contemplated by a concession provided for in the appropriate Schedule annexed to this Agreement, it shall bring the matter directly to the attention of the other contracting party. If the latter agrees that the treatment contemplated was that claimed by the first contracting party, but declares that such treatment cannot be accorded because a court or other proper authority has ruled to the effect that the product involved cannot be classified under the tariff laws of such contracting party so as to permit the treatment contemplated in this Agreement, the two contracting parties, together with any other contracting parties substantially interested, shall enter promptly into further negotiations with a view to a compensatory adjustment of the matter.

6.   (*a*)   The specific duties and charges included in the Schedules relating to contracting parties members of the International Monetary Fund, and margins of preference in specific duties and charges maintained by such contracting parties, are expressed in the appropriate currency at the par value accepted or provisionally recognized by the Fund at the date of this Agreement. Accordingly, in case this par value is reduced consistently with the Articles of Agreement of the International Monetary Fund by more than twenty per centum, such specific duties and charges and margins of preference may be adjusted to take account of such reduction; *provided* that the CONTRACTING PARTIES (*i.e.*, the contracting parties acting jointly as provided for in Article XXV) concur that such adjustments will not impair the value of the concessions provided for in the appropriate Schedule or elsewhere in this Agreement, due account being taken of all factors which may influence the need for, or urgency of, such adjustments.

(*b*)   Similar provisions shall apply to any contracting party not a member of the Fund, as from the date on which such contracting party becomes a member of the Fund or enters into a special exchange agreement in pursuance of Article XV.

7.   The Schedules annexed to this Agreement are hereby made an integral part of Part I of this Agreement.

PART II

Article III*

National Treatment on Internal Taxation and Regulation

1.   The contracting parties recognize that internal taxes and other internal charges, and laws, regulations and requirements affecting the internal sale, offering for sale, purchase, transportation, distribution or use of products, and internal quantitative regulations requiring the mixture, processing or use of products in specified amounts or proportions, should not be applied to imported or domestic products so as to afford protection to domestic production.

2.   The products of the territory of any contracting party imported into the territory of any other contracting party shall not be subject, directly or indirectly, to internal taxes or other internal charges of any kind in excess of those applied, directly or indirectly, to like domestic products. Moreover, no contracting party shall otherwise apply internal taxes or other internal charges to imported or domestic products in a manner contrary to the principles set forth in paragraph 1.

3.   With respect to any existing internal tax which is inconsistent with the provisions of paragraph 2, but which is specifically authorized under a trade agreement, in force on April 10, 1947, in which the import duty on the taxed product is bound against increase, the contracting party imposing the tax shall be free to postpone the application of the provisions of paragraph 2 to such tax until such time as it can obtain release from the obligations of such trade agreement in order to permit the increase of such duty to the extent necessary to compensate for the elimination of the protective element of the tax.

4.   The products of the territory of any contracting party imported into the territory of any other contracting party shall be accorded treatment no less favourable than that accorded to like products of national origin in respect of all laws, regulations and requirements affecting their internal sale, offering for sale, purchase, transportation, distribution or use. The provisions of this paragraph shall not prevent

the application of differential internal transportation charges which are based exclusively on the economic operation of the means of transport and not on the nationality of the product.

5.   No contracting party shall establish or maintain any internal quantitative regulation relating to the mixture, processing or use of products in specified amounts or proportions which requires, directly or indirectly, that any specified amount or proportion of any product which is the subject of the regulation must be supplied from domestic sources. Moreover, no contracting party shall otherwise apply internal quantitative regulations in a manner contrary to the principles set forth in paragraph 1.

6.   The provisions of paragraph 5 shall not apply to any internal quantitative regulation in force in the territory of any contracting party on July 1, 1939, April 10, 1947, or March 24, 1948, at the option of that contracting party; *Provided* that any such regulation which is contrary to the provisions of paragraph 5 shall not be modified to the detriment of imports and shall be treated as a customs duty for the purpose of negotiation.

7.   No internal quantitative regulation relating to the mixture, processing or use of products in specified amounts or proportions shall be applied in such a manner as to allocate any such amount or proportion among external sources of supply.

8.   (*a*)   The provisions of this Article shall not apply to laws, regulations or requirements governing the procurement by governmental agencies of products purchased for governmental purposes and not with a view to commercial resale or with a view to use in the production of goods for commercial sale.

(*b*)   The provisions of this Article shall not prevent the payment of subsidies exclusively to domestic producers, including payments to domestic producers derived from the proceeds of internal taxes or charges applied consistently with the provisions of this Article and subsidies effected through governmental purchases of domestic products.

9.   The contracting parties recognize that internal maximum price control measures, even though conforming to the other provisions of this Article, can have effects prejudicial to the interests of contracting parties supplying imported products. Accordingly, contracting parties applying such measures shall take account of the interests of exporting

contracting parties with a view to avoiding to the fullest practicable extent such prejudicial effects.

10.　　The provisions of this Article shall not prevent any contracting party from establishing or maintaining internal quantitative regulations relating to exposed cinematograph films and meeting the requirements of Article IV.

[…]

Article XI*

General Elimination of Quantitative Restrictions

1.　　No prohibitions or restrictions other than duties, taxes or other charges, whether made effective through quotas, import or export licences or other measures, shall be instituted or maintained by any contracting party on the importation of any product of the territory of any other contracting party or on the exportation or sale for export of any product destined for the territory of any other contracting party.

2.　　The provisions of paragraph 1 of this Article shall not extend to the following:

> (*a*)　　Export prohibitions or restrictions temporarily applied to prevent or relieve critical shortages of foodstuffs or other products essential to the exporting contracting party;

> (*b*)　　Import and export prohibitions or restrictions necessary to the application of standards or regulations for the classification, grading or marketing of commodities in international trade;

> (*c*)　　Import restrictions on any agricultural or fisheries product, imported in any form, necessary to the enforcement of governmental measures which operate:

>> (i)　　to restrict the quantities of the like domestic product permitted to be marketed or produced, or, if there is no substantial domestic production of the like product, of a domestic product for which the imported product can be directly substituted; or

> (ii) to remove a temporary surplus of the like domestic product, or, if there is no substantial domestic production of the like product, of a domestic product for which the imported product can be directly substituted, by making the surplus available to certain groups of domestic consumers free of charge or at prices below the current market level; or

> (iii) to restrict the quantities permitted to be produced of any animal product the production of which is directly dependent, wholly or mainly, on the imported commodity, if the domestic production of that commodity is relatively negligible.

Any contracting party applying restrictions on the importation of any product pursuant to subparagraph (c) of this paragraph shall give public notice of the total quantity or value of the product permitted to be imported during a specified future period and of any change in such quantity or value. Moreover, any restrictions applied under (i) above shall not be such as will reduce the total of imports relative to the total of domestic production, as compared with the proportion which might reasonably be expected to rule between the two in the absence of restrictions. In determining this proportion, the contracting party shall pay due regard to the proportion prevailing during a previous representative period and to any special factors* which may have affected or may be affecting the trade in the product concerned.

[…]

Article XIV*

Exceptions to the Rule of Non-discrimination

1.   A contracting party which applies restrictions under Article XII or under Section B of Article XVIII may, in the application of such restrictions, deviate from the provisions of Article XIII in a manner having equivalent effect to restrictions on payments and transfers for current international transactions which that contracting party may at that time apply under Article VIII or XIV of the Articles of Agreement of the International Monetary Fund, or under analogous provisions of a special exchange agreement entered into pursuant to paragraph 6 of Article XV.

2.   A contracting party which is applying import restrictions under Article XII or under Section B of Article XVIII may, with the consent of the CONTRACTING PARTIES, temporarily deviate from the provisions of Article XIII in respect of a small part of its external trade where the benefits to the contracting party or contracting parties concerned substantially outweigh any injury which may result to the trade of other contracting parties.

3.   The provisions of Article XIII shall not preclude a group of territories having a common quota in the International Monetary Fund from applying against imports from other countries, but not among themselves, restrictions in accordance with the provisions of Article XII or of Section B of Article XVIII on condition that such restrictions are in all other respects consistent with the provisions of Article XIII.

4.   A contracting party applying import restrictions under Article XII or under Section B of Article XVIII shall not be precluded by Articles XI to XV or Section B of Article XVIII of this Agreement from applying measures to direct its exports in such a manner as to increase its earnings of currencies which it can use without deviation from the provisions of Article XIII.

5.   A contracting party shall not be precluded by Articles XI to XV, inclusive, or by Section B of Article XVIII, of this Agreement from applying quantitative restrictions:

> (*a*)   having equivalent effect to exchange restrictions authorized under Section 3 (*b*) of Article VII of the Articles of Agreement of the International Monetary Fund, or

> (*b*)   under the preferential arrangements provided for in Annex A of this Agreement, pending the outcome of the negotiations referred to therein.

[…]

Article XX

General Exceptions

Subject to the requirement that such measures are not applied in a manner which would constitute a means of arbitrary or unjustifiable discrimination between countries where the same conditions prevail, or a disguised restriction on international trade, nothing in this Agreement shall be construed to prevent the adoption or enforcement by any contracting party of measures:

(*a*)   necessary to protect public morals;

(*b*)   necessary to protect human, animal or plant life or health;

(*c*)   relating to the importations or exportations of gold or silver;

(*d*)   necessary to secure compliance with laws or regulations which are not inconsistent with the provisions of this Agreement, including those relating to customs enforcement, the enforcement of monopolies operated under paragraph 4 of Article II and Article XVII, the protection of patents, trade marks and copyrights, and the prevention of deceptive practices;

(*e*)   relating to the products of prison labour;

(*f*)   imposed for the protection of national treasures of artistic, historic or archaeological value;

(*g*)   relating to the conservation of exhaustible natural resources if such measures are made effective in conjunction with restrictions on domestic production or consumption;

(*h*)   undertaken in pursuance of obligations under any intergovernmental commodity agreement which conforms to criteria submitted to the CONTRACTING PARTIES and not disapproved by them or which is itself so submitted and not so disapproved;

(*i*)   involving restrictions on exports of domestic materials necessary to ensure essential quantities of such materials to a domestic processing industry during periods when the domestic price of such materials is held below the world price as part of a governmental stabilization plan; *Provided* that such restrictions shall not operate to increase the exports of or the protection afforded to such domestic industry, and shall not depart from the provisions of this Agreement relating to non-discrimination;

(j)   essential to the acquisition or distribution of products in general or local short supply; *Provided* that any such measures shall be consistent with the principle that all contracting parties are entitled to an equitable share of the international supply of such products, and that any such measures, which are inconsistent with the other provisions of the Agreement shall be discontinued as soon as the conditions giving rise to them have ceased to exist. The CONTRACTING PARTIES shall review the need for this sub-paragraph not later than 30 June 1960.

AGREEMENT ON THE APPLICATION OF
SANITARY AND PHYTOSANITARY MEASURES

Members,

Reaffirming that no Member should be prevented from adopting or enforcing measures necessary to protect human, animal or plant life or health, subject to the requirement that these measures are not applied in a manner which would constitute a means of arbitrary or unjustifiable discrimination between Members where the same conditions prevail or a disguised restriction on international trade;

Desiring to improve the human health, animal health and phytosanitary situation in all Members;

Noting that sanitary and phytosanitary measures are often applied on the basis of bilateral agreements or protocols;

Desiring the establishment of a multilateral framework of rules and disciplines to guide the development, adoption and enforcement of sanitary and phytosanitary measures in order to minimize their negative effects on trade;

Recognizing the important contribution that international standards, guidelines and recommendations can make in this regard;

Desiring to further the use of harmonized sanitary and phytosanitary measures between Members, on the basis of international standards, guidelines and recommendations developed by the relevant international organizations, including the Codex Alimentarius Commission, the International Office of Epizootics, and the relevant international and regional organizations operating within the framework of the International Plant Protection Convention, without requiring Members to change their appropriate level of protection of human, animal or plant life or health;

Recognizing that developing country Members may encounter special difficulties in complying with the sanitary or phytosanitary measures of importing Members, and as a consequence in access to markets, and also in the formulation and application of sanitary or phytosanitary measures in their own territories, and desiring to assist them in their endeavours in this regard;

Desiring therefore to elaborate rules for the application of the provisions of GATT 1994 which relate to the use of sanitary or phytosanitary measures, in particular the provisions of Article XX(b)[2];

Hereby agree as follows:

Article 1

General Provisions

1.   This Agreement applies to all sanitary and phytosanitary measures which may, directly or indirectly, affect international trade. Such measures shall be developed and applied in accordance with the provisions of this Agreement.

2.   For the purposes of this Agreement, the definitions provided in Annex A shall apply.

3.   The annexes are an integral part of this Agreement.

4.   Nothing in this Agreement shall affect the rights of Members under the Agreement on Technical Barriers to Trade with respect to measures not within the scope of this Agreement.

---

[2] In this Agreement, reference to Article XX(b) includes also the chapeau of that Article.

Article 2

Basic Rights and Obligations

1.   Members have the right to take sanitary and phytosanitary measures necessary for the protection of human, animal or plant life or health, provided that such measures are not inconsistent with the provisions of this Agreement.

2.   Members shall ensure that any sanitary or phytosanitary measure is applied only to the extent necessary to protect human, animal or plant life or health, is based on scientific principles and is not maintained without sufficient scientific evidence, except as provided for in paragraph 7 of Article 5.

3.   Members shall ensure that their sanitary and phytosanitary measures do not arbitrarily or unjustifiably discriminate between Members where identical or similar conditions prevail, including between their own territory and that of other Members. Sanitary and phytosanitary measures shall not be applied in a manner which would constitute a disguised restriction on international trade.

4.   Sanitary or phytosanitary measures which conform to the relevant provisions of this Agreement shall be presumed to be in accordance with the obligations of the Members under the provisions of GATT 1994 which relate to the use of sanitary or phytosanitary measures, in particular the provisions of Article XX(b).

Article 3

Harmonization

1.   To harmonize sanitary and phytosanitary measures on as wide a basis as possible, Members shall base their sanitary or phytosanitary measures on international standards, guidelines or recommendations, where they exist, except as otherwise provided for in this Agreement, and in particular in paragraph 3.

2.   Sanitary or phytosanitary measures which conform to international standards, guidelines or recommendations shall be deemed to be necessary to protect human, animal or plant life or health, and presumed to be consistent with the relevant provisions of this Agreement and of GATT 1994.

3.   Members may introduce or maintain sanitary or phytosanitary measures which result in a higher level of sanitary or phytosanitary protection than would be achieved by measures based on the relevant international standards, guidelines or recommendations, if there is a scientific justification, or as a consequence of the level of sanitary or phytosanitary protection a Member determines to be appropriate in accordance with the relevant provisions of paragraphs 1 through 8 of Article 5.[3] Notwithstanding the above, all measures which result in a level of sanitary or phytosanitary protection different from that which would be achieved by measures based on international standards, guidelines or recommendations shall not be inconsistent with any other provision of this Agreement.

4.   Members shall play a full part, within the limits of their resources, in the relevant international organizations and their subsidiary bodies, in particular the Codex Alimentarius Commission, the International Office of Epizootics, and the international and regional organizations operating within the framework of the International Plant Protection Convention, to promote within these organizations the development and periodic review of standards, guidelines and recommendations with respect to all aspects of sanitary and phytosanitary measures.

5.   The Committee on Sanitary and Phytosanitary Measures provided for in paragraphs 1 and 4 of Article 12 (referred to in this Agreement as the "Committee") shall develop a procedure to monitor the process of international harmonization and coordinate efforts in this regard with the relevant international organizations.

Article 4

Equivalence

1.   Members shall accept the sanitary or phytosanitary measures of other Members as equivalent, even if these measures differ from their own or from those used by other Members trading in the same product, if the exporting Member objectively demonstrates to the importing Member that its measures achieve the importing Member's appropriate level of sanitary or phytosanitary protection. For this purpose, reasonable access shall be given, upon request, to the importing Member for inspection, testing and other relevant procedures.

---

[3] For the purposes of paragraph 3 of Article 3, there is a scientific justification if, on the basis of an examination and evaluation of available scientific information in conformity with the relevant provisions of this Agreement, a Member determines that the relevant international standards, guidelines or recommendations are not sufficient to achieve its appropriate level of sanitary or phytosanitary protection.

2.   Members shall, upon request, enter into consultations with the aim of achieving bilateral and multilateral agreements on recognition of the equivalence of specified sanitary or phytosanitary measures.

Article 5

Assessment of Risk and Determination of the Appropriate Level of Sanitary or Phytosanitary Protection

1.   Members shall ensure that their sanitary or phytosanitary measures are based on an assessment, as appropriate to the circumstances, of the risks to human, animal or plant life or health, taking into account risk assessment techniques developed by the relevant international organizations.

2.   In the assessment of risks, Members shall take into account available scientific evidence; relevant processes and production methods; relevant inspection, sampling and testing methods; prevalence of specific diseases or pests; existence of pest- or disease-free areas; relevant ecological and environmental conditions; and quarantine or other treatment.

3.   In assessing the risk to animal or plant life or health and determining the measure to be applied for achieving the appropriate level of sanitary or phytosanitary protection from such risk, Members shall take into account as relevant economic factors: the potential damage in terms of loss of production or sales in the event of the entry, establishment or spread of a pest or disease; the costs of control or eradication in the territory of the importing Member; and the relative cost-effectiveness of alternative approaches to limiting risks.

4.   Members should, when determining the appropriate level of sanitary or phytosanitary protection, take into account the objective of minimizing negative trade effects.

5.   With the objective of achieving consistency in the application of the concept of appropriate level of sanitary or phytosanitary protection against risks to human life or health, or to animal and plant life or health, each Member shall avoid arbitrary or unjustifiable distinctions in the levels it considers to be appropriate in different situations, if such distinctions result in discrimination or a disguised restriction on international trade. Members shall cooperate in the Committee, in accordance with paragraphs 1, 2 and 3 of Article 12, to develop guidelines to further the practical implementation of this provision. In developing the guidelines, the Committee shall take into account all relevant factors,

including the exceptional character of human health risks to which people voluntarily expose themselves.

6.   Without prejudice to paragraph 2 of Article 3, when establishing or maintaining sanitary or phytosanitary measures to achieve the appropriate level of sanitary or phytosanitary protection, Members shall ensure that such measures are not more trade-restrictive than required to achieve their appropriate level of sanitary or phytosanitary protection, taking into account technical and economic feasibility.[4]

7.   In cases where relevant scientific evidence is insufficient, a Member may provisionally adopt sanitary or phytosanitary measures on the basis of available pertinent information, including that from the relevant international organizations as well as from sanitary or phytosanitary measures applied by other Members. In such circumstances, Members shall seek to obtain the additional information necessary for a more objective assessment of risk and review the sanitary or phytosanitary measure accordingly within a reasonable period of time.

8.   When a Member has reason to believe that a specific sanitary or phytosanitary measure introduced or maintained by another Member is constraining, or has the potential to constrain, its exports and the measure is not based on the relevant international standards, guidelines or recommendations, or such standards, guidelines or recommendations do not exist, an explanation of the reasons for such sanitary or phytosanitary measure may be requested and shall be provided by the Member maintaining the measure.

Article 6

Adaptation to Regional Conditions, Including Pest- or Disease-Free Areas and Areas of Low Pest or Disease Prevalence

1.   Members shall ensure that their sanitary or phytosanitary measures are adapted to the sanitary or phytosanitary characteristics of the area - whether all of a country, part of a country, or all or parts of several countries - from which the product originated and to which the product is destined. In assessing the sanitary or phytosanitary characteristics of a region, Members shall take into account, *inter alia*, the level of prevalence of specific diseases or pests, the existence of

---

[4] For purposes of paragraph 6 of Article 5, a measure is not more trade-restrictive than required unless there is another measure, reasonably available taking into account technical and economic feasibility, that achieves the appropriate level of sanitary or phytosanitary protection and is significantly less restrictive to trade.

eradication or control programmes, and appropriate criteria or guidelines which may be developed by the relevant international organizations.

2.		Members shall, in particular, recognize the concepts of pest- or disease-free areas and areas of low pest or disease prevalence. Determination of such areas shall be based on factors such as geography, ecosystems, epidemiological surveillance, and the effectiveness of sanitary or phytosanitary controls.

3.		Exporting Members claiming that areas within their territories are pest- or disease-free areas or areas of low pest or disease prevalence shall provide the necessary evidence thereof in order to objectively demonstrate to the importing Member that such areas are, and are likely to remain, pest- or disease-free areas or areas of low pest or disease prevalence, respectively. For this purpose, reasonable access shall be given, upon request, to the importing Member for inspection, testing and other relevant procedures.

Article 7

Transparency

Members shall notify changes in their sanitary or phytosanitary measures and shall provide information on their sanitary or phytosanitary measures in accordance with the provisions of Annex B.

Article 8

Control, Inspection and Approval Procedures

Members shall observe the provisions of Annex C in the operation of control, inspection and approval procedures, including national systems for approving the use of additives or for establishing tolerances for contaminants in foods, beverages or feedstuffs, and otherwise ensure that their procedures are not inconsistent with the provisions of this Agreement.

Article 9

Technical Assistance

1.		Members agree to facilitate the provision of technical assistance to other Members, especially developing country Members, either bilaterally or through the appropriate international organizations. Such assistance may be, *inter alia*, in the areas of processing technologies, research and infrastructure, including in the establishment of national regulatory bodies, and may take the form of advice, credits, donations and grants, including for the purpose of seeking technical expertise, training and equipment to allow such countries to adjust to, and comply with, sanitary or phytosanitary measures necessary to achieve the appropriate level of sanitary or phytosanitary protection in their export markets.

2.   Where substantial investments are required in order for an exporting developing country Member to fulfil the sanitary or phytosanitary requirements of an importing Member, the latter shall consider providing such technical assistance as will permit the developing country Member to maintain and expand its market access opportunities for the product involved.

Article 10

Special and Differential Treatment

1.   In the preparation and application of sanitary or phytosanitary measures, Members shall take account of the special needs of developing country Members, and in particular of the least-developed country Members.

2.   Where the appropriate level of sanitary or phytosanitary protection allows scope for the phased introduction of new sanitary or phytosanitary measures, longer time-frames for compliance should be accorded on products of interest to developing country Members so as to maintain opportunities for their exports.

3.   With a view to ensuring that developing country Members are able to comply with the provisions of this Agreement, the Committee is enabled to grant to such countries, upon request, specified, time-limited exceptions in whole or in part from obligations under this Agreement, taking into account their financial, trade and development needs.

4.   Members should encourage and facilitate the active participation of developing country Members in the relevant international organizations.

Article 11

Consultations and Dispute Settlement

1.   The provisions of Articles XXII and XXIII of GATT 1994 as elaborated and applied by the Dispute Settlement Understanding shall apply to consultations and the settlement of disputes under this Agreement, except as otherwise specifically provided herein.

2.   In a dispute under this Agreement involving scientific or technical issues, a panel should seek advice from experts chosen by the panel in consultation with the parties to the dispute. To this end, the panel may, when it deems it appropriate, establish an advisory technical experts group, or consult the relevant international organizations, at the request of either party to the dispute or on its own initiative.

3.   Nothing in this Agreement shall impair the rights of Members under other international agreements, including the right to resort to the good offices or dispute settlement mechanisms of other international organizations or established under any international agreement.

Article 12

Administration

1.   A Committee on Sanitary and Phytosanitary Measures is hereby established to provide a regular forum for consultations. It shall carry out the functions necessary to implement the provisions of this Agreement and the furtherance of its objectives, in particular with respect to harmonization. The Committee shall reach its decisions by consensus.

2.   The Committee shall encourage and facilitate ad hoc consultations or negotiations among Members on specific sanitary or phytosanitary issues. The Committee shall encourage the use of international standards, guidelines or recommendations by all Members and, in this regard, shall sponsor technical consultation and study with the objective of increasing coordination and integration between international and national systems and approaches for approving the use of food additives or for establishing tolerances for contaminants in foods, beverages or feedstuffs.

3.   The Committee shall maintain close contact with the relevant international organizations in the field of sanitary and phytosanitary protection, especially with the Codex Alimentarius Commission, the International Office of Epizootics, and the Secretariat of the International

Plant Protection Convention, with the objective of securing the best available scientific and technical advice for the administration of this Agreement and in order to ensure that unnecessary duplication of effort is avoided.

4.   The Committee shall develop a procedure to monitor the process of international harmonization and the use of international standards, guidelines or recommendations. For this purpose, the Committee should, in conjunction with the relevant international organizations, establish a list of international standards, guidelines or recommendations relating to sanitary or phytosanitary measures which the Committee determines to have a major trade impact. The list should include an indication by Members of those international standards, guidelines or recommendations which they apply as conditions for import or on the basis of which imported products conforming to these standards can enjoy access to their markets. For those cases in which a Member does not apply an international standard, guideline or recommendation as a condition for import, the Member should provide an indication of the reason therefore, and, in particular, whether it considers that the standard is not stringent enough to provide the appropriate level of sanitary or phytosanitary protection. If a Member revises its position, following its indication of the use of a standard, guideline or recommendation as a condition for import, it should provide an explanation for its change and so inform the Secretariat as well as the relevant international organizations, unless such notification and explanation is given according to the procedures of Annex B.

5.   In order to avoid unnecessary duplication, the Committee may decide, as appropriate, to use the information generated by the procedures, particularly for notification, which are in operation in the relevant international organizations.

6.   The Committee may, on the basis of an initiative from one of the Members, through appropriate channels invite the relevant international organizations or their subsidiary bodies to examine specific matters with respect to a particular standard, guideline or recommendation, including the basis of explanations for non-use given according to paragraph 4.

7.   The Committee shall review the operation and implementation of this Agreement three years after the date of entry into force of the WTO Agreement, and thereafter as the need arises. Where appropriate, the Committee may submit to the Council for Trade in Goods proposals to amend the text of this Agreement having regard, *inter alia*, to the experience gained in its implementation.

Article 13

Implementation

Members are fully responsible under this Agreement for the observance of all obligations set forth herein. Members shall formulate and implement positive measures and mechanisms in support of the observance of the provisions of this Agreement by other than central government bodies. Members shall take such reasonable measures as may be available to them to ensure that non-governmental entities within their territories, as well as regional bodies in which relevant entities within their territories are members, comply with the relevant provisions of this Agreement. In addition, Members shall not take measures which have the effect of, directly or indirectly, requiring or encouraging such regional or non-governmental entities, or local governmental bodies, to act in a manner inconsistent with the provisions of this Agreement. Members shall ensure that they rely on the services of non-governmental entities for implementing sanitary or phytosanitary measures only if these entities comply with the provisions of this Agreement.

Article 14

Final Provisions

The least-developed country Members may delay application of the provisions of this Agreement for a period of five years following the date of entry into force of the WTO Agreement with respect to their sanitary or phytosanitary measures affecting importation or imported products. Other developing country Members may delay application of the provisions of this Agreement, other than paragraph 8 of Article 5 and Article 7, for two years following the date of entry into force of the WTO Agreement with respect to their existing sanitary or phytosanitary measures affecting importation or imported products, where such application is prevented by a lack of technical expertise, technical infrastructure or resources.

ANNEX A

DEFINITIONS[5]

1.   *Sanitary or phytosanitary measure* - Any measure applied:

(a)   to protect animal or plant life or health within the territory of the Member from risks arising from the entry, establishment or spread of pests, diseases, disease-carrying organisms or disease-causing organisms;

(b)   to protect human or animal life or health within the territory of the Member from risks arising from additives, contaminants, toxins or disease-causing organisms in foods, beverages or feedstuffs;

(c)   to protect human life or health within the territory of the Member from risks arising from diseases carried by animals, plants or products thereof, or from the entry, establishment or spread of pests; or

(d)   to prevent or limit other damage within the territory of the Member from the entry, establishment or spread of pests.

Sanitary or phytosanitary measures include all relevant laws, decrees, regulations, requirements and procedures including, *inter alia*, end product criteria; processes and production methods; testing, inspection, certification and approval procedures; quarantine treatments including relevant requirements associated with the transport of animals or plants, or with the materials necessary for their survival during transport; provisions on relevant statistical methods, sampling procedures and methods of risk assessment; and packaging and labelling requirements directly related to food safety.

2.   *Harmonization* - The establishment, recognition and application of common sanitary and phytosanitary measures by different Members.

---

[5] For the purpose of these definitions, "animal" includes fish and wild fauna; "plant" includes forests and wild flora; "pests" include weeds; and "contaminants" include pesticide and veterinary drug residues and extraneous matter.

3.   *International standards, guidelines and recommendations*

   (a)   for food safety, the standards, guidelines and recommendations established by the Codex Alimentarius Commission relating to food additives, veterinary drug and pesticide residues, contaminants, methods of analysis and sampling, and codes and guidelines of hygienic practice;

   (b)   for animal health and zoonoses, the standards, guidelines and recommendations developed under the auspices of the International Office of Epizootics;

   (c)   for plant health, the international standards, guidelines and recommendations developed under the auspices of the Secretariat of the International Plant Protection Convention in cooperation with regional organizations operating within the framework of the International Plant Protection Convention; and

   (d)   for matters not covered by the above organizations, appropriate standards, guidelines and recommendations promulgated by other relevant international organizations open for membership to all Members, as identified by the Committee.

4.   *Risk assessment* - The evaluation of the likelihood of entry, establishment or spread of a pest or disease within the territory of an importing Member according to the sanitary or phytosanitary measures which might be applied, and of the associated potential biological and economic consequences; or the evaluation of the potential for adverse effects on human or animal health arising from the presence of additives, contaminants, toxins or disease-causing organisms in food, beverages or feedstuffs.

5.   *Appropriate level of sanitary or phytosanitary protection* - The level of protection deemed appropriate by the Member establishing a sanitary or phytosanitary measure to protect human, animal or plant life or health within its territory.

NOTE: Many Members otherwise refer to this concept as the "acceptable level of risk".

6.   *Pest- or disease-free area* - An area, whether all of a country, part of a country, or all or parts of several countries, as identified by the competent authorities, in which a specific pest or disease does not occur.

NOTE: A pest- or disease-free area may surround, be surrounded by, or be adjacent to an area - whether within part of a country or in a geographic region which includes parts of or all of several countries -in which a specific pest or disease is known to occur but is subject to regional control measures such as the establishment of protection, surveillance and buffer zones which will confine or eradicate the pest or disease in question.

7.   *Area of low pest or disease prevalence* - An area, whether all of a country, part of a country, or all or parts of several countries, as identified by the competent authorities, in which a specific pest or disease occurs at low levels and which is subject to effective surveillance, control or eradication measures.

ANNEX B

TRANSPARENCY OF SANITARY AND PHYTOSANITARY REGULATIONS

Publication of regulations

1.   Members shall ensure that all sanitary and phytosanitary regulations[6] which have been adopted are published promptly in such a manner as to enable interested Members to become acquainted with them.

2.   Except in urgent circumstances, Members shall allow a reasonable interval between the publication of a sanitary or phytosanitary regulation and its entry into force in order to allow time for producers in exporting Members, and particularly in developing country Members, to adapt their products and methods of production to the requirements of the importing Member.

Enquiry points

3.   Each Member shall ensure that one enquiry point exists which is responsible for the provision of answers to all reasonable questions from interested Members as well as for the provision of relevant documents regarding:

(a)   any sanitary or phytosanitary regulations adopted or proposed within its territory;

(b)   any control and inspection procedures, production and quarantine treatment, pesticide tolerance and food additive approval procedures, which are operated within its territory;

(c)   risk assessment procedures, factors taken into consideration, as well as the determination of the appropriate level of sanitary or phytosanitary protection;

(d)   the membership and participation of the Member, or of relevant bodies within its territory, in international and regional sanitary and phytosanitary organizations and

---

[6] Sanitary and phytosanitary measures such as laws, decrees or ordinances which are applicable generally.

systems, as well as in bilateral and multilateral agreements and arrangements within the scope of this Agreement, and the texts of such agreements and arrangements.

4.　　Members shall ensure that where copies of documents are requested by interested Members, they are supplied at the same price (if any), apart from the cost of delivery, as to the nationals[7] of the Member concerned.

Notification procedures

5.　　Whenever an international standard, guideline or recommendation does not exist or the content of a proposed sanitary or phytosanitary regulation is not substantially the same as the content of an international standard, guideline or recommendation, and if the regulation may have a significant effect on trade of other Members, Members shall:

(a)　　publish a notice at an early stage in such a manner as to enable interested Members to become acquainted with the proposal to introduce a particular regulation;

(b)　　notify other Members, through the Secretariat, of the products to be covered by the regulation together with a brief indication of the objective and rationale of the proposed regulation. Such notifications shall take place at an early stage, when amendments can still be introduced and comments taken into account;

(c)　　provide upon request to other Members copies of the proposed regulation and, whenever possible, identify the parts which in substance deviate from international standards, guidelines or recommendations;

(d)　　without discrimination, allow reasonable time for other Members to make comments in writing, discuss these comments upon request, and take the comments and the results of the discussions into account.

---

[7] When "nationals" are referred to in this Agreement, the term shall be deemed, in the case of a separate customs territory Member of the WTO, to mean persons, natural or legal, who are domiciled or who have a real and effective industrial or commercial establishment in that customs territory.

6.　　However, where urgent problems of health protection arise or threaten to arise for a Member, that Member may omit such of the steps enumerated in paragraph 5 of this Annex as it finds necessary, provided that the Member:

(a)　　immediately notifies other Members, through the Secretariat, of the particular regulation and the products covered, with a brief indication of the objective and the rationale of the regulation, including the nature of the urgent problem(s);

(b)　　provides, upon request, copies of the regulation to other Members;

(c)　　allows other Members to make comments in writing, discusses these comments upon request, and takes the comments and the results of the discussions into account.

7.　　Notifications to the Secretariat shall be in English, French or Spanish.

8.　　Developed country Members shall, if requested by other Members, provide copies of the documents or, in case of voluminous documents, summaries of the documents covered by a specific notification in English, French or Spanish.

9.　　The Secretariat shall promptly circulate copies of the notification to all Members and interested international organizations and draw the attention of developing country Members to any notifications relating to products of particular interest to them.

10.　　Members shall designate a single central government authority as responsible for the implementation, on the national level, of the provisions concerning notification procedures according to paragraphs 5, 6, 7 and 8 of this Annex.

General reservations

11.　　Nothing in this Agreement shall be construed as requiring:

(a)　　the provision of particulars or copies of drafts or the publication of texts other than in the language of the Member except as stated in paragraph 8 of this Annex; or

(b) Members to disclose confidential information which would impede enforcement of sanitary or phytosanitary legislation or which would prejudice the legitimate commercial interests of particular enterprises.

ANNEX C

CONTROL, INSPECTION AND APPROVAL PROCEDURES[8]

1. Members shall ensure, with respect to any procedure to check and ensure the fulfilment of sanitary or phytosanitary measures, that:

(a) such procedures are undertaken and completed without undue delay and in no less favourable manner for imported products than for like domestic products;

(b) the standard processing period of each procedure is published or that the anticipated processing period is communicated to the applicant upon request; when receiving an application, the competent body promptly examines the completeness of the documentation and informs the applicant in a precise and complete manner of all deficiencies; the competent body transmits as soon as possible the results of the procedure in a precise and complete manner to the applicant so that corrective action may be taken if necessary; even when the application has deficiencies, the competent body proceeds as far as practicable with the procedure if the applicant so requests; and that upon request, the applicant is informed of the stage of the procedure, with any delay being explained;

(c) information requirements are limited to what is necessary for appropriate control, inspection and approval procedures, including for approval of the use of additives or for the establishment of tolerances for contaminants in food, beverages or feedstuffs;

(d) the confidentiality of information about imported products arising from or supplied in connection with control, inspection and approval is respected in a way no less favourable than for domestic products and in such a manner that legitimate commercial interests are protected;

(e) any requirements for control, inspection and approval of individual specimens of a product are limited to what is reasonable and necessary;

[8] Control, inspection and approval procedures include, *inter alia*, procedures for sampling, testing and certification.

(f)   any fees imposed for the procedures on imported products are equitable in relation to any fees charged on like domestic products or products originating in any other Member and should be no higher than the actual cost of the service;

(g)   the same criteria should be used in the siting of facilities used in the procedures and the selection of samples of imported products as for domestic products so as to minimize the inconvenience to applicants, importers, exporters or their agents;

(h)   whenever specifications of a product are changed subsequent to its control and inspection in light of the applicable regulations, the procedure for the modified product is limited to what is necessary to determine whether adequate confidence exists that the product still meets the regulations concerned; and

(i)   a procedure exists to review complaints concerning the operation of such procedures and to take corrective action when a complaint is justified.

Where an importing Member operates a system for the approval of the use of food additives or for the establishment of tolerances for contaminants in food, beverages or feedstuffs which prohibits or restricts access to its domestic markets for products based on the absence of an approval, the importing Member shall consider the use of a relevant international standard as the basis for access until a final determination is made.

2.   Where a sanitary or phytosanitary measure specifies control at the level of production, the Member in whose territory the production takes place shall provide the necessary assistance to facilitate such control and the work of the controlling authorities.

3.   Nothing in this Agreement shall prevent Members from carrying out reasonable inspection within their own territories.

INDEX

ABOUT THE AUTHOR

Dr Alberto Alemanno is a *référendaire* at the European Court of Justice in Luxembourg. Before joining the European Courts, he has been teaching assistant at the College of Europe in Bruges. He is also a member of the New York Bar and sits in the Executive Committee of the Society for Risk Analysis Europe and in the Editorial Committee of the Revue du Droit de l'Union Européenne. He teaches and publishes in the areas of European Law and International Economic Law, and is a regular speaker at conferences in both domains.

He holds a *Laurea in Giurisprudenza* from the University of Torino, Italy as well as LLM degrees from the College of Europe and Harvard Law School. He has been awarded a PhD in International Economic Law from Bocconi University in 2005. He can be contacted at alemanno@post.harvard.edu.